T0330531

Monetary Macrodynamics

This book investigates the interaction of effective goods demand with the wage–price spiral, and the impact of monetary policy on financial and the real markets from a Keynesian perspective. Endogenous business fluctuations are studied in the context of long-run distributive cycles in an advanced, rigorously formulated and quantitative set-up. The material is developed by way of self-contained chapters on three levels of generality: an advanced textbook level, a research-oriented applied level and a third level that shows how the interaction of real with financial markets has to be modelled from a truly integrative Keynesian perspective.

Monetary Macrodynamics shows that the balanced growth path of a capitalist economy is unlikely to be attracting and that the cumulative forces that surround it are controlled in the large by changes in the behavioural factors that drive the wage–price spiral and the financial markets. Such behavioural changes can in fact be observed in actual economies in the interaction of demand-driven business fluctuations with supply-driven wage and price dynamics as they originate from the conflict over income distribution between capital and labour.

The book is a detailed critique of US mainstream macroeconomics and uses rigorous dynamic macro-models of a descriptive and applicable nature. It will be of particular relevance to postgraduate students and researchers interested in disequilibrium processes, real wage feedback channels, financial markets and portfolio choice, financial accelerator mechanisms and monetary policy.

Toichiro Asada is a Professor in the Faculty of Economics at Chuo University, Tokyo, Japan. **Carl Chiarella** is Professor of Quantitative Finance at the University of Technology, Sydney. **Peter Flaschel** is Professor Emeritus at Bielefeld University, Germany. **Reiner Franke** is a Lecturer in Economics at Kiel University, Germany.

Routledge Frontiers of Political Economy

Monetary Macrodynamics

**Toichiro Asada,
Carl Chiarella,
Peter Flaschel and
Reiner Franke**

with contributions by
Amitava Dutt/Peter Skott and Christian Proaño

 Routledge
Taylor & Francis Group

LONDON AND NEW YORK

First published 2010
by Routledge
2 Park Square, Milton Park, Abingdon, Oxon, OX14 4RN

Simultaneously published in the USA and Canada
by Routledge
711 Third Avenue, New York, NY 10017, USA

Routledge is an imprint of the Taylor & Francis Group, an informa business

Typeset in Times New Roman by Glyph International Ltd.

British Library Cataloguing in Publication Data
A catalogue record for this book is available from the British Library

Library of Congress Cataloguing in Publication Data
Monetary macrodynamics / Toichiro Asada ... [et al.].
    p. cm.
Includes bibliographical references and index.
1. Money–Mathematical models. 2. Macroeconomics–Mathematical models. I. Asada, Toichiro, 1954–
HG229.M7526 2010
339.5′3015195–dc22

                                                                    2009030563

ISBN10: 0-415-54837-3 (hbk)
ISBN10: 0-203-85996-0 (ebk)

ISBN13: 978-0-415-54837-3 (hbk)
ISBN13: 978-0-203-85996-4 (ebk)

Contents

General introduction

This chapter provides a brief introduction to the general aims, specific topics and methods that we wish to address and use in this book. The basic objective is to provide the reader with an alternative to the current mainstream approaches to monetary macrodynamics, on both a textbook level as well as on a more advanced research-oriented level. This alternative sometimes comes close in formal structure to the more orthodox approaches, but it nevertheless differs significantly in its conclusions compared to what is achieved by mainstream economic theory.

The AS–AD approach of the traditional Neoclassical Synthesis

This book grew out of a set of lectures of one of the authors (Peter Flaschel) over the last two to three decades in the area of monetary macrodynamics. Its initial point of departure was the A(ggregate)S(upply)–A(ggregate)D(emand) framework of the old Neoclassical Synthesis in the compact (but nevertheless very detailed) dynamic form in which it was presented in Sargent (1979, 1987), where the topics of inflation and growth were also treated in an integrated way.

As a rigorous introduction to the Keynesian AS–AD analysis of that time, Sargent's presentation was indeed a very valuable one; however, the current book will depart significantly from it, not only in the topics that are treated, but also in the substance of the analysis. Our approach is driven by the view that the dynamic analysis in Chapter 5 of Sargent (1987) does not portray a coherent and appropriate approach from a Keynesian perspective, if the latter's evolution after Keynes' General Theory is properly taken into account.

However, in view of Keynes' (1936) explicit acceptance of the marginal productivity or marginal costs relationship (where he only altered the direction of causation), Sargent's Chapter 5 is completely to the point in revealing that Keynes' revolution of the Classical Theory was still incompletely formulated, since the neoclassical assumption that prices are (under perfect competition) equal to marginal wage costs in fact destroys the Keynesian AD framework if a conventional type of money–wage Phillips curve is added to the AD model and if, in addition, perfect myopic foresight is assumed.

This is so since the money–wage Phillips curve implies, in this ideal case (which gives only a hint of a deeper inconsistency within this combination of Keynesian and Neoclassical building blocks), a real wage Phillips curve and therefore dichotomizes the conventional Keynesian AS–AD model into a model of Solovian underemployment growth (since there are real wage rigidities added to it) and an appended purely nominal AD theory of the rate of interest and the rate of price inflation.

Keynes' (1936) model of the GT therefore represented only a partial revolution of the Classical Theory that he was attempting to overcome:

> I have called this book *The General Theory of Employment, Interest and Money*, placing the emphasis on the prefix 'general'. The object of such a title is to contrast the character of my arguments and conclusions with those of the classical theory of the subject, upon which I was brought up and which dominates the economic thought, both practical and theoretical, of the governing and academic classes of this generation, as it has for a hundred years past. I shall argue that the postulates of the classical theory are applicable to a special case only and not to the general case, the situation which it assumes being a limiting point of the possible positions of equilibrium. Moreover, the characteristics of the special case assumed by the classical theory happen not to be those of the economic society in which we actually live, with the result that its teaching is misleading and disastrous if we attempt to apply it to the facts of experience.
>
> (Keynes, 1936, p.3)

The solution to the stated internal inconsistency of the original AS–AD growth model is, however, a simple and very plausible one. As Barro (1994), for example, observes, IS-LM is (or should be) based on imperfectly flexible wages *and* prices and thus on the consideration of wage as well as price Phillips curves (a feature that was typical of the Neokeynesian fix-price approaches of the 1970s and 1980s). This is precisely what we shall do in this book, following Malinvaud (1980) for example, but – as we have already argued in Chiarella, Flaschel, Groh and Semmler (2000) – not with the consequence that the Keynesian regime is only one of the three possible outcomes of the baseline fix-price rationing methodology (the other ones being capital shortage and repressed inflation).

We, thus, will assume gradual wage and price adjustment (in place of infinitely fast adjustment processes), and will extend this approach in later portions of the book also to quantity adjustment processes (including inventory adjustment), since here too it is not very plausible to have continuous goods market clearing at all points in time.

By and large, the book will therefore formulate and extend a Keynesian theory of aggregate demand (and money and interest) where there are gradual adjustment processes for the aggregate price and wage level, as well as the economy-wide output level and where, therefore, disequilibrium adjustment processes are driving the real markets of the economy. In such a setup, the resulting D(isequilibrium)

AS–D(isequilibrium)AD framework will no longer give rise to neoclassical anomalies of the type indicated earlier, since the marginal productivity relationship then only determines the (profit-maximizing) capacity output of firms that only in the steady state will be strictly positively correlated to the demand-driven actual output level of firms.

This is the basic scenario that underlies the modeling philosophy of the book and which will be extended into a variety of directions in the various chapters that follow. However, in Chapter 1, we first discuss the state of actual textbook presentations of the macroeconomics literature that is characterized by a collection of short-term, medium-term and long-term modeling approaches that lack internal consistency.

Beyond the Neoclassical Synthesis of perfect competition and effective demand

Consequently, in more technical terms, the main objective of this book is to demonstrate that there exists a matured type of the conventional Keynesian AD–AS theory of monetary macroeconomics that builds on traditional Keynesian models, but also goes beyond them in essential ways, which is primarily dynamic in nature, and which conceives temporary economic behavior as always adjusting to observed disequilibria by a variety of adaptive learning mechanisms. The reason for adopting such an approach is that time has to be treated on the macrolevel essentially by continuous methods, though there may exist pronounced delays in a certain range of activities.

However, the data-generating process of actual economies on the macro-level is definitely of a very high frequency in general, also on real markets, since, for example, the aggregate price level is subject to numerous changes even on a daily level. In a continuous time framework, however, it is not sensible to assume that markets clear every 'second' so that it is very natural then to assume the prevalence of disequilibrium adjustment processes – which at one extreme may be simple rules of thumb and, at the other extreme, sophisticated learning algorithms – coupled with certain desired levels or ratios that may be the objective of the rational choice of economic agents.

Behavior in the context of non-clearing markets is, therefore, the essential modeling strategy used in this book. Through it, we seek to understand the basic causal structure or market hierarchy that, according to Keynes (1936), characterizes the macroeconomy and, on this basis, the feedback channels (or repercussions as Keynes (1936) called them) which in addition are operating within the downward hierarchy of markets on the macrolevel. In our view, the market hierarchy of modern capitalist economies leads from financial markets and their relative autonomous behavior to the goods markets, since investment in particular is dependent on the outcomes on financial markets, and from there to labor markets, which have to adjust to the circuit of income that the interaction between output, income and sales creates on the market for goods.

This is the causal nexus that Keynes (1936) formulated for the working of the macroeconomy, which of course does not work in isolation, but is surrounded by a range of feedback channels of not-so-dominant, but nevertheless important, type working in the opposite direction compared to the asserted causal nexus of Keynesian macrodynamics. Such feedback channels, by and large, work through the impact they have on the expected excess rate of profit and thus can impact on various channels such as the dynamics of real wages, or on the real rate of interest.

The book approaches such topics at first, in Part I, on the textbook level. After taking stock of the progress that has been achieved there and in the literature in general, it then continues its analysis, in Part II, on a level that is comparable to the advanced New Keynesian baseline model with both staggered wages and prices as it is, for example, presented on an advanced textbook level in Galí (2008). As in the New Keynesian approach, a necessary next step thereafter is to confront the theoretical model with what is occurring in actual economies and to estimate its behavioral equations by more or less advanced econometric methods.

Such parameter estimates represent the important contribution of the later chapters of Part II. The concluding Part III provides a theoretical outlook on what needs to be done next, once the too simplistic representation of financial markets by just an interest rate policy rule, of the New Keynesian approach and also our matured DAD–DAS macrodynamics, is replaced by the consideration of a model with portfolio choice amongst financial assets as the representation of financial markets on the macrolevel.

These introductory characterizations of what we intend to do in this book may appear to be overly complex, but they are not really so once it is realized that they are just natural extensions of what even intermediate textbooks, such as Blanchard (2009), actually provide as building blocks for the understanding of modern capitalist economies. We have simply taken seriously and acted upon Blanchard's suggestion that these building blocks must sooner or later be treated in an integrated way.

Keynesian macrodynamics in the mainstream textbook literature

> As will quickly become clear, Keynesian models differ from real-business-cycle models not just in substance, but also in style. ... Keynesian models, in contrast, often begin by directly specifying relationships among aggregate variables. ... The idea behind this shortcut aggregate approach to model building is threefold. First, it is simple. ... Second, many features of the economy are likely to be robust to the details of the microeconomic environment. ... And third, by insisting on microeconomic foundations, we could in fact miss important elements. ... To give a more significant example, traditional Keynesian models give current income a particularly important role in consumption demand. ... Of course, there are also disadvantages. ...
>
> (Romer, 1996, 5.1)

In principle, we cannot but agree with these selective quotations from the second subsection of the first edition of Romer's introduction to his chapter on Keynesian macroeconomics.[1] However, the problem with the representation of the Keynesian model that follows these observations is that it is by and large only a static and very traditional representation of the Keynesian approach to macroeconomics, certainly much less advanced than, for example, what Sargent (1979) had already presented in his Macroeconomic Theory that we have briefly discussed earlier. Moreover, even when one restricts Keynesian analysis to the simple IS-LM-P(hillips)C(urve) framework – as it underlies for example Blanchard's (2009) intermediate textbook discussion – there follow conclusions, as we shall show in detail in Chapter 2, that have little in common with Romer's (2006) discussion of the Keynesian IS-LM analysis as a theory of business fluctuations and the nominal rigidities that may be their cause.

Traditional Keynesian IS-LM-PC analysis determines output and interest at each point in time as statically endogenous variables that then move in time through money–wage changes, transmitted in the simplest case through markup pricing into price level changes. These price level changes and the resulting rate of inflation are observed by the economic agents and lead to a revision of their expectation of future rates of price inflation. Again, in the simplest case of an adaptive learning rule, we can obtain, even then, four possible *dynamic* outcomes for the laws of motion that drive inflation and inflationary expectations, two of which are stable (monotonically or accompanied by business fluctuations). The other two possibilities are characterized by monotonic or cyclical divergence away from the steady state of the economy (where inflation is equal to the growth rate of money supply in the case that such a policy is pursued by the central bank).

These possibilities had already been discussed in Tobin (1975) and were later classified as Mundell(-Tobin) effects. These effects work through the real interest rate channel of the Keynesian IS-LM block via an assumed influence of the real rate of interest on investment (and durable consumption goods). Depending on the strength of the adjustment speed of inflationary expectations, we can then get instability in the IS-LM-PC framework when this parameter passes from below through a certain threshold level (which in fact need not be very large in magnitude).

This generation of at least local instability is, however, not discussed in the textbook literature as a *systemic* outcome of the traditional IS-LM-PC model, and thus as a possibility that is also of relevance during the normal (non-pathological) working of the economy. The exceptions are a few authors – see, for example, Scarth (1996), who have integrated Tobin's critical condition for instability of the real rate of interest channel into their macroeconomic thinking. However, the majority of macroeconomists do not like to see instability in their core reflections of the working of the macroeconomy, and thus put such observations, if they mention them at all, into considerations that are of marginal importance in their text.

---

1 These statements are no longer so definite in Romer (2006, 5.1).

Yet, Keynes himself had already stressed that situations may occur in which the economy becomes unstable and could even break down if one were to follow the orthodox advice of making money–wages as flexible as possible, and that workers are instinctively more reasonable than economists, to the extent that they are capable of making money–wages rigid at least in the downward direction. If instability is among the normal outcomes of the IS-LM-PC macro-model, the introduction of a downward rigidity of money–wages can indeed rescue the economy from economic breakdown. The resulting business fluctuations may not represent the best of all worlds, but such rigidities are at least able to generate persistent business fluctuations in place of processes of accelerating wage deflation or inflation, and thus definitely help to avoid the worst-case scenario.

Such are the results that one can already achieve from the most basic dynamic IS-LM analysis (discussed in detail in Chapter 2). It prepares the reader for a study of those situations where the macroeconomy does not work more or less perfectly, but is rather plagued by centrifugal forces for which certain behavioral changes are needed when these forces displace the economy too far away from its steady-state position. The real rate of interest channel (where the nominal rate component implies stability, but where the expected inflation component can generate an inflationary or deflationary spiral) is only one example from a set of the many feedback channels that may shape the movements of the macroeconomy over time. The discussion of such feedback channels is generally completely absent in the textbook literature, which instead uses IS-LM analysis only to discuss short-term restrictions on economic activity, while simpler monetarist constructions are generally used to discuss the theory of inflation, and where the entirely real model of Solow is then finally used to represent what will happen in the long run.

We will discuss such disintegrated views of the working of the macroeconomy in detail in the first chapter. After IS-LM-PC analysis proper (Chapter 2), we will then attempt in the third chapter to integrate the partial models of Chapter 1 into a coherent whole, also by including what has been achieved in Chapter 2 for the IS-LM-PC model, and will arrive then at our most basic AS–AD growth model, as it can be derived from a synthesis of the Keynesian theory of output and interest, the monetarist theory of money and inflation, and of the neoclassical theory of economic growth.

Yet, as already discussed above, if Solow's marginal productivity principle is used in this model type in its strict form (holding at each moment in time), we run into the difficulties of the AS–AD growth dynamics that we have described earlier and must therefore then at the least allow for gradual wage *and* price level adjustments in order to avoid (from a Keynesian perspective bizarre) the dichotomization into a core Solow underemployment model and an appended, purely nominal IS-LM theory of price inflation.

Part I of the book closes with a contribution (Chapter 4) of Amitava Dutt and Peter Skott, who reconsider Keynesian AD–AS analysis from a Post-Keynesian perspective and take stock of what has been achieved in this area so far.

This chapter also lays foundations, from a different perspective, for the contents of Part II of the book, which we discuss next.

Keynesian macrodynamics: new or matured?

For our purposes, the baseline New Keynesian model with both staggered wages and prices represents a combination of Keynesian as well as Walrasian structural equations (just as does the old Neoclassical Synthesis), with elements from the theory of monopolistic competition also interwoven. The Walrasian component is primarily given by the theory of consumer households, while the Keynesian element is harder to detect and may be related to the view that there are nominal rigidities present in this model type, since the model exhibits an IS curve that may be more Wicksellian than Keynesian in nature – see also Woodford (2003) in this regard. Nevertheless, we then have at our disposal a structural macromodel with only gradually adjusting prices and wages, an IS curve and, instead of an LM theory of the money market, a Taylor interest rate policy rule, which makes money supply endogenous at each moment of time.

The New Keynesian approach thus provides a baseline structure for macro-economic reasoning that is on the one hand very compact, but on the other hand already fairly advanced (concerning analytical tractability in particular). It is rigorously microfounded and basically of market clearing type (avoiding rationing procedures). It is, in this baseline formulation, purely forward looking, and makes use of the rational expectations methodology in its constructions of the actual trajectories of the dynamics that are generally convergent (by assumption). Instabilities, therefore, can only exist if rational bubbles are admitted as a possibility.

The rational expectations methodology has various appealing features, but it also exhibits a number of conundrums, if not even bizarre outcomes. These conundrums are considered in detail from a deterministic perspective in Chiarella, Flaschel, Franke and Semmler (2009) (in models with predetermined as well as non-predetermined variables) in detail, and so will not be reconsidered in the present book. In the baseline New Keynesian model under consideration here, there is one predetermined variable (given through the definition of real wages) and three non-predetermined ones. We refer the reader to Galí (2008) for a detailed presentation of the features of this model type.

We will consider this New Keynesian macrodynamic model briefly in the starting chapter of Part II. We show there that it provides reasonable determinacy properties from the New Keynesian rational expectations perspective. We then go on and confront this model type with a wage–price spiral representation of the interaction of wages and prices, and a conventional type of IS curve (exhibiting the Mundell-Tobin effect through its assumptions on investment behavior) and also an interest rate policy rule. This model is in its formal structure quite similar to the New Keynesian alternative, but radically different in its implications, in particular due to the fact that it makes use of predetermined variables throughout. Its implications in fact generalize the IS-LM-PC analysis of Chapter 2 and thus also the central implications of this model type, namely that its stability depends on a critical threshold condition separating convergence from divergence by way of a cyclical loss of stability.

The central message of this chapter is therefore that there is a matured alternative to the New Keynesian break with almost any Keynesian tradition that preserves insights of the old Neoclassical Synthesis, but avoids the inconsistencies stemming from the integration of Walrasian pricing procedures into an otherwise Keynesian framework. Part II therefore starts with the formulation of a model proposed as alternative to the New Neoclassical Synthesis of models of the RBC (Real Business Cycle) and NK (New Keynesian) type, an alternative that is designed in a way that makes it formally seem of the same type as the New Keynesian one.

This matured type of Keynesian AD–AS analysis is extended in the chapters of Part II in various directions, in particular towards a disequilibrium AD–AS (DAD–DAS) approach that is then also estimated and calibrated in various ways. One essential element in the wage–price spiral that the DAD–DAS dynamics exhibit is the inertia that is put into this spiral by way of the concept of an inflation climate. We use as a simplifying device, as in Sargent (1987, Ch.5), myopic perfect foresight as far as the evolution of nominal variables is concerned. However, this now secondary abstraction from short-term inflationary errors is embedded into a situation where agents are aware of the fact that a medium-term inflationary climate surrounds these contemporaneous changes in the rate of wage and price inflation.

Such a setup is comparable to a situation where people have perfect information on the next day's weather, but consider in addition the season into which this information is embedded and the averages that have characterized the current season so far (or some more complex concept of such averages; see Chapter 9 for details).

Thus, the contribution of Part II is basically a DAD–DAS theory of demand-driven business fluctuations where persistence is often implied by the joint occurrence of local instabilities and globally bounding mechanisms such as the kinked money–wage Phillips curve (that is horizontal for employment rates that are sufficiently low).

Part III relates this DAD–DAS theory to the more general K(eynes)M(etzler) G(oodwin) approach to goods–market dynamics; see Chiarella and Flaschel (2000) and Chiarella, Flaschel and Franke (2005) for the origins and quantitative applications of this model-building strategy. It provides, as a central extension of the KMG approach, an outlook on future work by adding a financial sector (with Tobinian portfolio choice) to the disequilibrium dynamics of the real sector and thus now shows how monetary policy has to work its way through the assumed asset market structure of the model before it can reach the real sector and influence its activity and the rate of inflation that the resulting business fluctuations generate. The model built by this stage can be considered as a fairly advanced disequilibrium approach to real markets, with gradual wage, price and quantity adjustment processes, with stress on Keynesian feedback structures and with focus on a balanced representation of both real and financial markets.

Methods, aims and readership

The focus of our modeling strategy is, as already stated, the disequilibrium adjustment processes that are assumed to characterize the real market – at least in a continuous time framework. With respect to the earlier quotation from Romer (1996), we do not insist on microeconomic foundations, since we would indeed then fail to capture some important elements that shape the evolution on the macroeconomic level. Our overall modeling approach is guided by our firm belief that the imposition of the 'straightjacket' of microfounded market-clearing procedures, coupled in addition with rational expectations in the extreme information-processing way they are formulated nowadays, removes too many aspects of real economic life from consideration.

Disequilibrium, non-market-clearing approaches or out-of-equilibrium perspectives are merely an admission, in more or less provocative terms, that the actual economy is a complex adaptive system that must be formulated in descriptive macro-terms in the first instance (in order to know what needs to be microfounded), before microfoundations should be attempted. As the discussion of rationing procedures as part of the non-Walrasian macro-theory in the 1970s has shown, the introduction of rationing schemes can be very arbitrary, so that not too much hope can be attached to the micro-foundations of the adjustment rules that economic agents actually use in response to the disequilibria that they are facing.

Moreover, the formulation of disequilibrium adjustment processes can reveal in very direct ways the presence of multiple interacting feedback channels of monetary macrodynamics, which can be studied in isolation to a certain degree in order to reveal how the economy, for example, reacts to wage deflation. However, the interaction of these feedback channels must eventually be studied. The resulting higher-dimensional dynamical systems then require a local stability analysis, and, if instability is obtained, call for behavioral assumptions that can guarantee the global boundedness of the business fluctuations that these types of models can generate. This modeling strategy of endogenously generated persistent fluctuations in output, employment and inflation can be called the Keynes paradigm (see Chapter 22, in the General Theory), as opposed to the Frisch paradigm (where the business cycle is primarily explained by stochastic shocks).

To study such endogenously driven business fluctuations, in an advanced, coherent, quantitative, and rigorous way, is the aim of the book. We do so by way of relatively self-contained chapters on three levels of generality: an advanced textbook level, a more advanced research-oriented level and, in the closing chapter, in a way that we believe the interaction of real with financial markets should eventually be modeled.

Since Part I of the book can be used for teaching purposes, we finally add a few words on this aspect. This part leads the reader in a systematic way towards an integrated Keynesian macromodel in the form of three lectures that build on each other, and are aimed at discussing and overcoming the weaknesses of the static and dynamic macro-models of traditional Keynesian AD–AS growth dynamics.

The fourth lecture provides on overview on mainstream and post-Keynesian approaches.

- Lecture 1 (Chapter 1) provides an introduction to the state of the art in disintegrated AD–AS growth theory, as it is usually presented on all levels of teaching about macrodynamics.
- Lecture 2 (Chapter 2) provides an introduction to the dynamics of aggregate demand. We here make use of a conventional money–wage Phillips curve (coupled with markup pricing), expectations- and NAIRU-augmented, and adaptive expectations formation, in order to investigate the dynamic implications of two fundamental macroeconomic feedback chains, the interaction of Keynes and Mundell effects that is unavoidable in IS-LM analysis, based on the real rate of interest channel in investment (and consumption) behavior. In place of the implications of the monetarist baseline model of Chapter 1, we here derive an IS-LM-PC analysis with a variety of stability and instability features, which can be used as an explanation of stable depressions or persistent business fluctuations if downward nominal wage rigidity is added. Here, we also study the potential for monetary policies to influence such dynamic outcomes, in particular the role of interest rate policy rules, for stabilizing a situation of unstable real rate of interest dynamics.
- Lecture 3 (Chapter 3) provides an introduction to the dynamics of aggregate supply. Starting from neoclassical Solovian unemployment growth dynamics, we show its relationship to Goodwin's (1967) classical growth cycle dynamics and even to conventional AS–AD growth dynamics when inflationary expectations are of the myopic perfect foresight variety. In such a case, a real wage Phillips curve finds application, with interesting implications on the real evolution of the economy, though there is not yet provided a convincing theory of nominal inflation dynamics, both on the level of the simple Goodwin-Solow synthesis as well as in the integrated AS–AD growth dynamics when subjected to myopic perfect foresight.
- Lecture 4 (Chapter 4) provides the stocktaking by Peter Skott and Amitava Dutt of what has been achieved in mainstream and Post-Keynesian AD–AS macroeconomics.

Altogether, the material of Part I can be used for advanced courses on monetary macrodynamics – courses that stress that today's macroeconomics must be dynamic in nature and thus is dependent on the demonstration of its result on the mathematical theory of dynamical systems (which in the macro-framework of continuous time are in fact much less demanding than are the equivalent tools for the treatment of the generally discrete time systems of mainstream macrodynamics).

Therefore, the lecture part of the book can be viewed as providing an alternative treatment of monetary macroeconomics, in comparison to the books by Blanchard and Fisher (1989), Carlin and Soskice (2006), Handa (2000) and Romer (2006). Carlin and Soskice also focus their textbook on the treatment of market imperfections and a graphical treatment of the adjustment dynamics that these imperfections imply. If Chapters 5 and 6, which extend our AD–AS approach towards a AD–D(isequilibrium)AS model, are also taken into account, the covered material can also be usefully compared with more advanced approaches like Galí's (2008) book, and also with Turnovsky (1995) and Walsh (2003). However, in spirit, the book is much more closely related with Taylor (2004) in the attempt to reconstruct macroeconomics from a non-mainstream perspective – see also Godley and Lavoie (2006) and Cencini (2001) in this respect.

It is hoped that the economists who have read through the advanced textbook treatment of Part I will be motivated to go on with this type of study of an advanced version of Keynesian monetary macrodynamics that is competing with the advanced New Keynesian alternative in rigor, results and applicability. The outcome of this competition must, of course, be left to the judgment of the reader.

January 11, 2010

Toichiro Asada, Tokyo
Carl Chiarella, Sydney
Peter Flaschel, Bielefeld
Reiner Franke, Kiel

Acknowledgement

Carl Chiarella wishes to acknowledge financial support from the Australian Research Council under grant DP0773776. Peter Flaschel acknowledges support through an Opus Magnum Research Grant from the Fritz Thyssen/Volkswagen Stiftungen, which allowed him to focus exclusively on research projects during the winter term 2007/8. Last, but not least, we have to thank anonymous referees for a variety of valuable suggestions that have helped to improve considerably the contents of this book. Of course, all remaining errors are our own.

References

Barro, R. (1994): The aggregate supply / aggregate demand model. *Eastern Economic Journal*, 20, 1–6.

Blanchard, O. (2009): *Macroeconomics*. London: Pearson Education International.

Blanchard, O. and S. Fisher (1989): *Lectures on Macroeconomics*. Cambridge, MA: The MIT Press.

Carlin, W. and D. Soskice (2006): *Macroeconomics: Imperfections, Institutions and Policies*. Oxford: Oxford University Press.

Cencini, A. (2001): *Monetary Macroeconomics: A New Approach*. London: Routledge.

Chiarella, C. and P. Flaschel (2000): *The Dynamics of Keynesian Monetary Growth: Macro Foundations*. Cambridge, UK: Cambridge University Press.

Chiarella, C., P. Flaschel and R. Franke (2005): *Foundations for a Disequilibrium Theory of the Business Cycle: Quantitative Analysis and Qualitative Assessment*. Cambridge, UK: Cambridge University Press.

Chiarella, C., P. Flaschel, G. Groh and W. Semmler (2000): *Disequilibrium, Growth and Labor Market Dynamics*. Heidelberg: Springer.

Chiarella, C., P. Flaschel, R. Franke and W. Semmler (2009): *Financial Markets and the Macroeconomy: A Keynesian Perspective*. London: Routledge.

Galí, J. (2008): *Monetary Policy, Inflation and the Business Cycle*. Princeton: Princeton University Press.

Godley, W. and M. Lavoie (2006): *Monetary Economics: An Integrated Approach to Credit, Money, Income, Production and Wealth*. New York: Palgrave Macmillan.

Goodwin, R.M. (1967): A growth cycle. In: C.H. Feinstein (ed.): *Socialism, Capitalism and Economic Growth*. Cambridge, UK: Cambridge University Press, 5458.

Handa, J. (2000): *Monetary Economics*. London: Routledge.

Keynes, J.M. (1936): *The General Theory of Employment, Interest and Money*. New York: Macmillan.

Malinvaud, E. (1980): *Profitability and Unemployment*. Cambridge: Cambridge University Press.

Romer, D. (1996): *Advanced Macroeconomics*. New York: McGraw-Hill (2006: 3rd edition).

Sargent, T. (1979): *Macroeconomic Theory*. New York: Academic Press (1987: 2nd edition).

Scarth, W.M. (1996): *Macroeconomics: An Integration of New Classical and New Keynesian Insights*. Toronto: Harcourt Brace.

Taylor, L. (2004): *Reconstructing Macroeconomics: Structuralist Proposals and Critique of the Mainstream*. Cambridge, MA: Harvard University Press.

Tobin, J. (1975): Keynesian models of recession and depression. *American Economic Review*, 65, 195–202.

Turnovsky, S. (1995): *Methods of Macroeconomic Dynamics*. Cambridge, MA: The MIT Press.

Walsh, C.E. (2003): *Monetary Theory and Policy*. Cambridge, MA: The MIT Press.

Woodford, M. (2003): *Interest and Prices: Foundations of a Theory of Monetary Policy*. Princeton: Princeton University Press.

Part I

Conventional AD–AS modeling

1 Models of growth, inflation and the real-financial market interaction

1.1 Disintegrated macro model building

The dominant tradition on the intermediate textbook level is to make use of the conventional IS-LM model of the real-financial market interaction to describe the short-run behavior of a closed economy on the macrolevel, while the medium run and inflation dynamics are modeled by a monetarist variant of this model type. For the long run, one, however, makes use of the real Solovian growth dynamics, the nonmonetary neoclassical growth model, in order to describe the basic forces of economic growth. The IS-LM equilibrium for output and interest is an attracting equilibrium if 'ultra-short-run' adjustment rules for output and the nominal rate of interest are added to this modeling framework; the steady state of the monetarist inflation dynamics of the medium run is attracting, since the interaction between the real rate of interest channel and the dynamics of inflationary expectations are modified in various ways in order to suppress the destabilizing Mundell effect; and the long-run balanced growth path of the Solow model is attracting, since one reduces everything here to the adjustment of the full-employment capital intensity state variable (by totally ignoring the unemployment models of the short- and the medium-run).

Thus, from the dominant traditional point of view, this foregoing sequence of models suggests that the dynamical processes shaping the macroeconomy are always convergent, that is, the deterministic core dynamics of employment, inflation and growth is of a shock absorber type. The basic message of this book, however, will be that such a conclusion is the result of a very particular sequence of models, and that this understanding of the working of the macroeconomy will not be confirmed if the three runs of this intermediate textbook literature are integrated into a consistent whole, relying strictly on the assumptions that are made in this literature. The first observation to be made here is that the neoclassical Solow growth model is not at all a model of IS-LM growth, since it neglects money and liquidity preference and since it does not consider the coordination of independent savings and investment decisions. The gap between this model type and Keynesian growth dynamics is therefore of a significant nature. Nevertheless, it is widely believed that the Solow model provides the essential explanation of the long-run growth dynamics of market economies, with short- and medium-run rigidities being of no importance for the understanding of this long-run process; this is, for example, the message of Mankiw's (1994) book. But the long run (not necessarily the steady state of an economy) is the result of its short- and medium-run evolution and thus cannot be separated from such an evolution by just reducing everything to the growth path of full-employment capital intensity driven by savings decisions and natural population growth.

Concerning the medium run, that is to say the theory of inflation, there have been various approaches that basically avoid discussion of the so-called Mundell(-Tobin) effects, which can destabilize the economy via accelerating inflation or deflationary spirals. Dornbusch and Fischer (1994) separate the real rate of interest effect in investment behavior into a stabilizing nominal effect (or Keynes-effect) which interacts with the real dynamics in the usual way as a shock-absorber, and a subsequent real interest rate dynamics which is also convergent. Blanchard (2006), by contrast, just assumes static inflationary expectations in order to avoid discussion of unstable expected real rate of interest adjustments in the normal working of his medium-run model (he does discuss, however, pathological processes of hyperinflation and of deflation in later chapters of his book). Nevertheless, in general, in the textbook literature on unemployment and inflation, there holds sway the view that this process is usually convergent to a steady state if not disturbed by monetary policy (or fiscal policy).

In this introductory chapter, we critically investigate these standard procedures of the textbook literature that divide the analysis into models of attracting balanced growth for the long-run, stable unemployment inflation dynamics for the medium-run, and finally output, employment and interest rate determination for the short-run. The modeling approaches chosen in each case are – as discussed earlier – too distinct from each other, with for example Say's Law applying in the first two cases, but not in the short run of the third. Due to this observation, they cannot therefore easily be integrated into a coherent whole, as is claimed in Blanchard (2006), to achieve dual objectives: first, the medium-run being obtained just as a continuation and extension (via wage–price dynamics) of the short run and growth dynamics being again just as an extension of the medium run, by adding the laws of motion for labor and capital; second, a confirmation of the conclusions drawn from the isolated dynamics of Keynesian IS-LM, the monetarist view on inflation and the neoclassical growth approach from such an integration perspective. We shall in fact see in the course of this book that the results of the disintegrated textbook treatments of steady growth, medium run inflation dynamics and short-run real-financial (output-interest rate) interaction are not at all supported by an integrated Keynesian treatment of IS-LM-P(hillips)C(urve) growth where wage–price dynamics and investment-driven growth interact with a real-financial view of goods and money market interdependence.

The extension of conventional Keynesian short-run real-financial interaction or simply IS-LM theory to topics concerning the medium- and the long-run evolution of the economy in a coherent way is the subject of Part I of the book, where we approach such questions, in Chapter 2, from a partial consideration of the dynamics of aggregate demand (representing dynamic AD or IS-LM-PC dynamics proper) and, in Chapter 3, from a partial consideration of the dynamics of aggregate supply (AS), later on, in combination with Keynesian AD. It is in Part II that we shall come to an integration of these two sides of traditional macrodynamic model building, in the form of a coherently formulated AD–AS growth dynamics. In Chapter 4, we shall in addition consider in detail alternative formulations of more or less Keynesian analysis of the short run and thus show there that the conventional IS-LM framework with given wages and prices (and thus a horizontal aggregate supply curve) need not be the only possibility as a starting point in the pursuit of fully integrated macrodynamics over the three runs considered. These alternative points of departure will, however, not be used in the present book to provide alternative formulations of fully integrated macrodynamics, but will be taken up again in future work where, in particular, Postkeynesian approaches to integrated macrodynamics will be presented and investigated.

We instead extend, in Part II, our AD–AS framework of Part I (which already overcomes a variety of weaknesses of conventional AS–AD growth dynamics) towards a fuller treatment of the dynamics of aggregate demand by also including in the framework adopted sluggish quantity adjustment processes, and thus full goods market disequilibrium (besides the already given sluggish wage and price adjustments based on disequilibrium in the use of the stock of capital and of labor, respectively). We thereby arrive at a model type that we consider to be the proper reformulation and extension of traditional Keynesian IS-LM short-, medium- and long-run analysis with full real market disequilibria on the one hand and full financial market equilibria on the other hand. This approach and some of its many extensions, here in the direction of endogenous average saving rates, endogenous natural growth, extended portfolio equilibria and more, will be the subject of Part III, the character of which is therefore more (but not exclusively) that of an advanced textbook or even research monograph, compared to the first two parts of the book.

In this current chapter, we discuss in compact form the conventional component models of textbook macrodynamics, the long-run (Solovian factor supply driven more or less steady growth), the short-run (IS-LM under- or overemployment equilibria with respect to both labor and capital) and the medium-run (AD–AS or wage–price dynamics of various types), on an elementary but to some extent also on an advanced level. We shall show that these components, often presented in splendid isolation from each other, are not easily linked together. We go on to show that, if such links between these three components of macrodynamic analysis are provided, the resulting dynamics do not at all confirm the conclusions obtained from the unlinked systems. Advanced textbooks that consider AD–AS growth dynamics through a complete set of behavioral and budget equations represent the exception, as for example Chapter 5 in Sargent's (1987) book, and in fact cannot really fulfill this task, as we shall demonstrate in Chapter 3.

The latter, still conventional, type of integration of Keynesian aggregate demand with supply-side dynamics of monetarist and Solovian type indeed creates more problems than it helps to solve, as we shall show in Part I. Our analysis, therefore, in fact, reveals that an integration along these lines may not be the final solution for the formulation of supply-side growth dynamics within Keynesian aggregate demand restrictions. Our strategy in Chapters 5 and 6 consequently will be to add further Keynesian elements to the traditional integrated AD–AS growth dynamics of the textbook literature such that these problems can be avoided completely. Our approach will be built on the analysis of growth, the interaction of output and interest on goods and financial markets, and wage–price dynamics augmented by inflationary expectations adjustments to be considered in the next three sections. These additions, basically of further delayed adjustment processes caused by disequilibria on the real side of the economy, will provide us finally, in Chapter 5, with a model type that indeed overcomes the problems that we have pointed out in the conventional type of AD–AS growth dynamics.

In the next section, we will present the Solovian real growth dynamics in basically the same terms as in the original approach of Solow (1956) and its numerous textbook representations. We will provide here two equivalent representations, in terms of labor intensity as well as capital intensity, augmented by the neoclassical theory of income distribution between labor and capital. There exist now many significant extensions and modifications of the Solow supply-side growth dynamics; see Romer (1996) and Barro and Sala-i-Martin (1995). Adding the insights of this new growth theory into the intended integrated framework of Keynesian growth dynamics is, however, not an easy task and will be left for future research, since the focus of this book is on the extension of this framework to a full disequilibrium treatment of the real markets (and a full equilibrium treatment of the financial markets), but not yet the inclusion into it of new growth theory.

With respect to the short run, in this chapter represented by traditional IS-LM analysis, we will provide in this introductory chapter only a brief characterization of Keynesian IS-LM model building, since this topic is taken up again in later parts of the book. We believe that the medium- and long-run behavior of the economy should be derived by a systematic extension of such short-run features, the topic of both Part I and Part II, and thus by the evolution of such alternative frameworks in place of their simple replacement through the neoclassical theory of economic growth and income distribution for discussion of long-run issues, and a quantity-theory-based analysis of inflation dynamics for the medium run. In Keynesian analysis, it will generally not be true that the economy is always on the transition to a steady state of Solovian type since its determination of steady-state positions can be different from the neoclassical one. More importantly, it will also be true that the forces that shape the dynamics of integrated Keynesian growth dynamics will often be such that persistent fluctuations are endogenously generated and thus characterize the long-run behavior of the economy, which moreover need not cycle around its steady-state position, and can thus significantly depart on average from the steady-state position, if the number of laws of motion of the dynamics becomes sufficiently high.

Employing the idea of a transition from the short run to the long run, in particular when based on Friedman-Phelps-type inflation theory as discussed here in Section 3, thus illegitimately restricts the possibility of the outcomes of the nonlinear dynamical world in which we live and may also exclude important aspects of a Keynesian analysis of wage–price dynamics as we will show in Chapter 5 on the Keynesian analysis of goods and labor market dynamics in a growing economy.

In the present chapter, we will, however, provide globally asymptotically stable dynamics for the medium-run representation of fluctuating inflation and unemployment rates that are linked to conventional IS-LM analysis only in the extreme case of a vertical LM-schedule (where interest-rate-oriented policy has no meaning) and that is also fairly unrelated to the monotonic full-employment path towards the steady state of the Solow growth model. The baseline model of the monetarist theory of inflation considered in this chapter therefore does not provide a bridge that relates the short run of IS-LM type (Section 4) with long-run growth (Section 2), and therefore does not properly describe the transition process between these two extremes of macroeconomic theorizing.

This closes our brief critical summary of the currently popular modeling approach of the textbook view of supply-driven growth in the longer run, demand-determined output, interest and unemployment rates in the short run, and Phillips curve inflation theory coupled with adjustments in inflationary expectations describing the transition from the short to the long run. These topics are usually taught by means of three different, nonintegrated types of macromodels even in quite recent textbooks, as the one of Blanchard (2006), despite its claim (see the preface to that book) to provide an integrated view of macroeconomics. On the contrary, these disintegrated model types – Keynesian IS-LM analysis, monetarist inflation theory and neoclassical growth theory – represent three partial modeling approaches with deficiencies in each component model and with a variety of problems that prevent their proper integration. By and large, the integrated view on macrodynamics is therefore missing in the traditional macroeconomic literature, which thus continues to ignore the need to provide baseline integrated models for the analysis of market economies on the macrolevel.

1.2 Neoclassical growth theory and the long run

The following brief discussion of the Solow (1956) growth model builds on Flaschel (1993, Ch.3) and Chiarella *et al.* (2000b, Ch.2). The Solow growth model is, of course, presented in numerous textbooks, old and new. A classic source for a detailed presentation of this model type is Jones (1975), and contemporary presentations and extensions are found in Romer (1996) and Barro and Sala-i-Martin (1995). The present book will not develop the Solovian growth theory into the now-fashionable direction of endogenous growth theory, but will aim at embedding it into a coherently formulated theory of AD–AS disequilibrium-cum-growth, leaving, however, the surely important issue of endogenous growth (along Schumpeterian lines) for future research on the potential of this type of analysis to also cope with waves of technological innovations, their diffusion and their decline.

1.2.1 The Solow model

Solow's (1956) one-good model of economic growth is based on full-employment throughout, and is made determinate with respect to its steady-state solution by the assumption (or if modeled, then by the implication) that growth adjusts to exogenously given labor force growth (plus productivity growth, if Harrod neutral technical change is added to it, see the following section). It provides a monotonic one-dimensional transition towards its steady-state solution for all initial values of capital-intensity or labor-intensity. It can be varied in many ways, including for instance differentiated saving habits and endogenous saving rates and endogenous technological change.

One variation of the Solow growth model is, however, rarely considered, namely its extension by an independent and in particular Keynesian investment function of firms, which is not closely related to the saving decisions of the households sector. This is the type of extension that we will pursue at the end of this book (in Ch.10) after demand side issues and portfolio approaches have been integrated with supply side issues in Part II. Without this integration, Solovian growth dynamics is not subject to any of the feedback mechanisms that we will discuss in this book, and thus in particular not plagued at all by unstable adjustment processes and the like.

The typical starting point of Solovian growth theory is the following set of assumptions (where in particular capital stock depreciation and technical change are still ignored for the time being):

$$Y = F(K, L^d) \quad \text{the neoclassical production function,} \tag{1.1}$$

$$S = sY, \ s = const. \quad \text{Harrod type savings function,} \tag{1.2}$$

$$\dot{K} = S \quad \text{capital stock growth driven by household savings decisions,} \tag{1.3}$$

$$\dot{L} = nL, \ n = const. \quad \text{labor force growth,} \tag{1.4}$$

$$L^d = L \quad \text{the full-employment assumption,} \tag{1.5}$$

$$\omega = F_L(K, L) \quad \text{the marginal productivity theory of employment.} \tag{1.6}$$

The notation in these equations is fairly standard (see the list of notations at the beginning of the book). We here use L^d to denote labor demand and $\omega = w/p$ to denote the real wage. Technology is described by means of a so-called neoclassical production function[1]

$$Y = F(K, L),$$

---

[1] See Jones (1975, Ch.2) for a detailed presentation of the mathematical conditions characterizing such a production function and also a detailed analysis of its properties. We here only recall that marginal products F_L, F_K are homogeneous of degree zero in both arguments, since the production function is assumed to be homogeneous of degree 1 and that $Y = F_L L + F_K K = \omega L + rK$ holds in such a situation with respect to the income distribution between labor and capital.

which exhibits constant returns to scale and marginal products of capital $F_K (\equiv r)$ and of labor F_L, which are positive and decreasing, so that $F_{KK} < 0, F_{LL} < 0.$[2]

There is only direct investment of savings into real capital formation in this model type – that is, Say's Law is assumed to hold true in its most simple form, namely

$$I \equiv S = sY$$

with savings being strictly proportional to output and income Y. Labor is growing at a given natural rate n and is fully employed, so that this model simply bases economic growth on actual factor growth without any demand-side restriction on the market for goods. Full-employment is assumed to follow from the equality of real wages ω with the marginal product of labor at the full-employment level, which means that the real wage always adjusts such that price-taking firms are maximizing their profits at the full-employment position and thus will clear the labor market. A perfectly flexible real wage ω thus is assumed to guarantee the full employment of the labor force at each moment of time.[3] The growing labor supply ($\dot{L} = nL$) is consequently always fully employed, and the profit-maximizing output can always be sold as there is no Keynesian problem of effective demand – all output that is not consumed is voluntarily invested into new capital formation.

It is obvious that Solow's growth model – despite many opposite statements in the literature – has not much in common with Harrod's or Domar's approach to economic dynamics, which this model intended to criticize. There are neither accelerating sales expectations nor capacity utilization problems based on an independent investment behavior. The problem of coordinating independent savings and investment behavior is thus absent from the model. No multiplier interacts with the accelerator principle to generate possibly unstable economic dynamics. Instead, its dynamics result solely from increases in factor supplies on the basis of the assumption of their full-employment.

Let us now consider some of the basic implications of Solow's growth model in its foregoing formulation. For the supply of new capital, we know from the foregoing that

$$\dot{K} = sF(K, L), \text{ where } L = L^d,$$

due to the full-employment assumption. Let us denote labor intensity L/K by l. Due to the assumption of constant returns to scale, we can reduce the dynamic analysis of this growth model to the movements of this ratio l, given by

$$\hat{l} = \dot{l}/l = n - \hat{K} = n - sF(K, L)/K = n - sF(1, l) = n - sf(l), \tag{1.7}$$

<hr />

2 One generally also assumes $F_{KL} (= F_{LK}) > 0$, i.e. the marginal product of one factor increases if more of the other factor becomes available.

3 See Jones (1975, Ch.2) – and the following discussion – for the details of this neoclassical theory of income distribution, which determines the shares of labor and capital by their marginal products *and* the assumption of their full-employment.

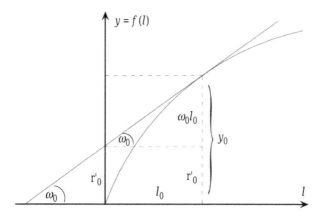

Figure 1.1 The Solow model; income distribution in the case of perfect competition, full-employment and neoclassical smooth factor substitution.[5]

where $f(\cdot) = F(1, \cdot)$ denotes the foregoing production function in its so-called intensive form (here expressed by means of labor intensity in the place of capital intensity $k = K/L$). The economic and mathematical conditions that are placed on the original production function $F(K, L)$ imply the following standard form (see Figure 1.1) for the function $y = f(l)$, where $y = Y/K$ the output–capital ratio.[4]

Because of the relationship $\omega = F_L(K, L) = F_L(1, K/L) = f'(l)$, this intensive form of the production function allows for a simple graphical presentation of the functional distribution of income between labor and capital and its variation if the relative factor supply term l is changing as shown in Figure 1.1 (see Jones(1975, Ch.2) for further details). The comparative statics associated with the Figure 1.1, characterizing the theory of income distribution behind Solovian growth, is thus very straightforward. It basically states that the factor of production which becomes the more abundant one (here measured by changes of the labor intensity l) will get a decreasing remuneration, here shown by the corresponding changes in ω and r.

Equation (1.7) is the so-called fundamental equation of Solow's growth model. In words, it simply states that the growth rate of labor intensity is positive if labor supply grows faster then the capital stock (and vice versa) – that is, labor intensity must rise or fall according to the difference that exists between labor force growth and the growth rate of the capital stock $sf(l)$.

This fundamental Equation (1.7) can easily be transformed into its more common form (which uses as dynamic variable the capital intensity expression

---

4 Jones uses capital intensity $k = 1/l$ for his presentation of the Solow growth model.
5 Note that $r = f(l) - f'(l)l = y - \omega l = F_K$ the rate of profit (a residual), see Jones (1975, Ch.1) and Sargent (1987, Chs.1, 5) for the details of such economic and also accounting relationships.

$k = K/L$ in the place of labor intensity $l = 1/k$) by making use of the relationships

$$\tilde{f}(k) = F(k, 1) = f(l)/l \text{ or } f(l) = \tilde{f}(k)/k,$$

which give (because of $\hat{k} = -\hat{l}$)

$$\hat{k} = sf(l) - n = s\tilde{f}(k)/k - n,$$

or simply

$$\dot{k} = s\tilde{f}(k) - nk.$$

The last law of motion gives rise to the following alternative characterization of Solow's fundamental equation and its components:

- nk is the amount of capital currently used per laborer that is needed to employ the current additions to the labor force nL without a change in the capital intensity k (the needed capital-widening to employ the growing labor force)
- $s\tilde{f}(k)$ is the amount of capital per laborer that is actually invested
- On this basis, the change in capital intensity k is then determined by the difference of these two terms (showing the resulting capital-deepening implied by the fundamental equation).

The comparative statics associated with Figure 1.1, characterizing the quantity side of the Solovian growth theory, is again a very simple one. Increases in natural growth increase the rate of growth of the economy as well as labor intensity and capital productivity, while increases in the savings rate of households do just the opposite.

Returning to the form (1.7) of the fundamental dynamic equation of Solow's growth model, the analysis of the stability of the steady-state position of this model is a simple matter, since the dynamics are only of dimension 1. A graphical presentation, as in Figure 1.2, is sufficient here to convince the reader of the validity of the important assertions of the Solow model. These assertions are:

- There is a unique steady-state value l_0 if it is, for example, assumed that the Inada conditions hold true; that is, $f(0) = 0, f'(0) = \infty, f(\infty) = \infty, f'(\infty) = 0$.
- The steady-state value is globally asymptotically stable – that is, the economy approaches n, the natural rate of growth, over time by an appropriate change in the labor intensity that is used in production.
- The steady-state values of labor intensity l_0, as well as of consumption per laborer $c = (1 - s)\tilde{f}(k)$,[6] depend on the rate of savings s, but the steady rate of growth of the economy is independent of it.

6 The consumption per a laborer c will be maximized when the savings rate s is chosen such that $n = \tilde{f}'(k)$ holds true (i.e. $S = sY = rK = Y - \omega L$), which gives the so-called golden rule of accumulation

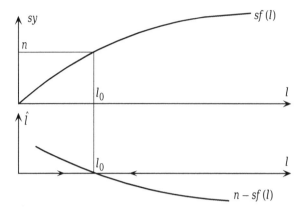

Figure 1.2 The one-dimensional quantity dynamics of the neoclassical growth model.

- In the steady-state we have

$$n = sf(l_0) = sy_0 = s/\sigma_0,$$

  which is the equality of Harrod's warranted rate of growth s/σ with the natural rate of growth n. There is thus no conflict between these two rates here.

The stability of the natural rate of growth path is achieved through variations in capital productivity y (or the capital–output ratio $v = 1/y$) by means of an appropriate change in labor or capital intensity, in the course of capital accumulation. From the perspective of supply, based on Say's Law ($I \equiv S$) and the full-employment of the supplied factors, there is thus no problem involved in the process of capital accumulation, since the factor that is more scarce in relation to the other (with regard to the steady-state ratio l_0) will always grow faster, so that a non-steady value of the labor intensity l will always be modified in the direction of its steady-state value l_0.

Yet, the foregoing analysis depends not only on the assumption that real wages ω are manipulated at each moment in time such that full-employment results. In addition to this counterfactual statement, it also depends on the classical view that goods supply will (always) create its appropriate goods demand, so that all income that is not consumed will be invested.

Adding capital stock depreciation at the rate δ to the model is not a big issue. For the ratio l, this addition gives rise to the extended fundamental equation

$$\hat{l} = n + \delta - sf(l), \text{ since } \dot{K} = sF(K,L) - \delta K,$$

(in which case investment is exactly equal to profits. In a model of differential swing, this result would correspond to the situation $s_w = 0, s_c = 1$ for the saving rate of workers (s_w) and capitalists (s_c), in the place of the uniform savings rate of the Solow model).

with $Y = F(K,L)$ being the gross national product of the economy. The addition of capital stock depreciation therefore only adds one further parameter to the model.

The same holds true if disembodied Harrod neutral technical change of the constant rate n_x is added to the Solow growth model ($x = Y/L$, the System of National Accounts measure of labor productivity). We denote the given natural rate of growth of the labor force by n_l and use n to denote the sum of these two given rates of growth, so that $n = n_l + n_x$. Harrod neutral technical change in the case of neoclassical smooth factor substitution is defined as

$$Y = F(K, \exp(n_x t)L)$$

and states that technical change in this economy would occur in a uniform way if the work effort of all laborers were to increase at a constant growth rate n_x, a situation that has been called labor-augmenting technical change in the literature; see Jones (1975) for a very detailed discussions of this issue. We note that Hicks neutral and Solow neutral technical change can be defined in similar ways (by making use of the expression $\exp(n_x t)$ in other places in the production function), but that Harrod neutral technical change is the only one among these three types that allows for a steady state solution, as it is derived in the following Section.

We shall continue to neglect depreciation and now approach neoclassical growth theory by using capital intensity in the place of labor intensity, which gives rise to

$$\hat{k} = s\tilde{f}(k) - nk, \ k = K/(\exp(n_x t)L), \ \text{since } \dot{K} = sF(K, \exp(n_x t)L).$$

Note that capital intensity has had to be redefined here in order to allow for a ratio that can be stationary in the steady state. This new measure, $k = K/(\exp(n_x t)L)$, is called capital intensity, measured in efficiency units in the literature, and is to be distinguished carefully from the System of National Accounts measure of capital intensity K/L. The above form of the Solovian fundamental equation follows immediately from the growth rate formula $\hat{k} = \hat{K} - (n_l + n_x)$ when the equation for $\dot{K}$ is taken into account. The Solow growth model is therefore again not changed very much by the addition of technical change (of Harrodian type), if account is taken of the facts that now we have to make use of

$$y = \frac{Y}{K}, \ x = \frac{Y}{\exp(n_x t)L}, \ l = \frac{\exp(n_x t)L}{K}, \ k = \frac{K}{\exp(n_x t)L}$$

when interpreting the model and the two Figures 1.1 and 1.2. Note in this regard also that the real wage ω must now be replaced by the wage share $v = wL/pY$ in Figure 1.1, while the definition of the rate of profit in this figure remains the same, namely $r = (Y - vY)/K$, but is now of course based on the wage share in the place the real wage in order to clearly see its stationarity in the steady state.

As the model is now formulated, it implies the following trend growth rates in the steady state by way of its stationary steady state solution:

- $\hat{Y} = n$ Output growth, explained by the sum of natural and productivity growth,
- $\hat{K} = n$ Capital stock growth, explained by the sum of natural and productivity growth,
- $\hat{\omega} = n_x$ Real wage growth, equal to productivity growth,
- $\hat{r} = 0$ No trend in the rate of profit (and the wage share),
- $\hat{I} = n$ A given share of investment in output growth.

This in turn implies that the System of National Accounts measure of capital productivity (the output–capital ratio) has no trend in the steady state (just as the rate of profit r and the wage share v), while that of actual labor productivity Y/L must then grow at the rate n_x, just as the real wage ω. Actual capital intensity K/L must grow at the rate n_x while the share of investment in national product is again a constant. These steady-state properties conform nicely to the stylized facts of the growth of capitalist economies as they were formulated by Kaldor; see Jones (1975). The Solow model augmented by Harrod neutral technical change thus, in particular, explains (in very basic terms, however) the observed systematic growth of capital employed per worker and also the growth rate of the real wages observed from a secular point of view. However, it is not only steady growth theory that allows for these and other stylized facts of long-run growth.

A further stylized fact of the evolution of capitalist economies is that, in the very long run, there is no trend in the rate of unemployment; however, the level of unemployment settles at a value significantly above zero (representing absolute full-employment) and the inflation rate at a value that remains positive in the very long run. NAIRU theories (on Non-Accelerating-Inflation Rates of Unemployment) which attempt to explain this fact will be considered, beginning with the next section, in various places in this book. If this rate can be considered to be determined outside the scope of the Solow model, the conclusions of this model type will, of course, remain intact with a positive NAIRU rate of unemployment (so-called full-employment) in the place of absolute full-employment.

Yet, it is highly questionable whether the NAIRU level can indeed be considered a given magnitude for the explanation of economic growth (see Chapter 6) and it may also be questioned whether steady-state analysis should be used to explain secular tendencies in capitalist economies or whether the long run is rather to be considered as referring to a historically unique long period in the evolution of such economies, like industrialization, the evolution of the welfare state and the like, referring to time spans that are generally considerably shorter than even one century see also Marglin (1984) in this regard. If such a perspective on the modeling of long-run growth is accepted, we may in addition postulate that such a period is characterized by a certain investment climate and thus be given by an investment demand schedule which is quite independent in its behavioral form from the schedule that characterizes aggregate savings per unit of capital. The latter

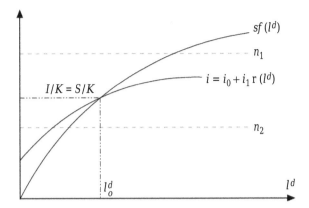

Figure 1.3 Investment-driven economic growth: leaden and golden ages.

is, of course, to be derived from households' decision making, while the former is in fact a consequence of firms' behavior which, up to certain episodes or sectors of the economy, is quite independent from the forces that shape the savings behavior of the households (though, of course, interacting with it).

1.2.2 Investment-driven growth

In order to show in as simple a way as possible that the logic of the Solow growth model need not at all apply to the explanation of growth in factual economies, we now assume as the investment schedule in this framework, besides the savings function we have already considered, the simple expression[7]

$$I/K = i_o + i_1 r, \quad r = (1-v)y, \quad y = Y/K, \quad v = \omega L^d/Y, \quad i_o, i_1 = const. > 0.$$

Here, investment per unit of capital thus depends solely on the rate of profit r of the economy (in a positive fashion) and investment itself exhibits an autonomous trend term i_o that may be related to an animal spirit explanations of investment behavior (of a particular historical episode of a capitalist economy). The addition of such an investment function to the Solow growth model is easily shown to give rise to the following graphical situation, where – for reasons of simplicity and also exposition – we have assumed that the parameter i_1 is chosen so small that the investment schedule is flatter than the one for savings, as shown in Figure 1.3.[8]

In Figure 1.3, we see, in contrast with Figure 1.2, that growth is no longer determined by the natural rate of labor force growth, but by the intersection of the

---

7 Here, we abstract again from depreciation and technical change ($n_2 = n_l = n$).
8 In terms of the following determination of the slope of $i(.)$, this amounts to assuming that $sf'(l^d) > -i(\cdot)f''(l^d)l^d$ holds true.

investment schedule with the savings schedule (both per unit of capital). In order to see this clearly, we must, however, first relate the rate of profit to the actual state of the labor intensity $l^d = L^d/K$ in order to be able to draw both the investment and the savings functions on the same diagram. This is easily done as follows. We have (due to the assumption of a price level that is always given by marginal wage costs)

$$r = f(l^d) - f'(l^d)l^d \quad \text{and thus} \quad r'(l^d) = -f''(l^d)l^d > 0,$$

that is, the rate of profit depends positively on the level of l^d, since the latter is strictly negatively correlated with the level of real wages (as we already know). The investment schedule can thus be written as

$$i(\cdot) = I/K = i_o + i_1 r(l^d) = g(l^d), \quad g'(l^d) > 0,$$

which is the function drawn in Figure 1.3. It has been drawn as strictly concave, but this needs not be the case, it would depend on the properties of the production function f. The intercept of the graph of the function with the vertical axis is given by the autonomous amount in the investment behavior (somehow determined by animal spirits outside the model), while its slope is always less than the corresponding one in the savings function.[9] We briefly note that the considered situation will lead to stable adjustments of labor intensity if there is movement out of the steady-state position.

Since $S/K = sf(l^d)$ is strictly increasing and takes on all values between zero and infinity, and since the investment function (based on l^d as well) is flatter than the savings function (and starts at zero with a positive value), there must be a unique and positive steady-state solution for the actual labor intensity $l_o^d \neq l_o$ where capital stock growth is the same considered from the perspective of savers and of investors and where profits assume the level $r_o = f(l_o^d) - f'(l_o^d)l_o^d$. Furthermore, at the steady state, we have that i_o, as one given trend in investment growth, is augmented by endogenously generated further investment growth $i_1 r_o$ and in sum gives $i_o + i_1 r_o$ as the resulting growth rate of the economy. This growth rate may be smaller (or larger) than n, the growth rate of the labor force, in which case workers are assumed to be repelled into (attracted from) segments of the economy (not modeled here), where they basically do not exercise pressure on the labor market and the rate of change of money wages.

Note here that we indeed do not go into a discussion of the formation of money wages – which is the subject of the following section – but simply assume that the price level of the economy is always determined, as in Keynes (1936), by perfect competition and thus through marginal wage costs, giving rise to the equality between real wages and the marginal product of labor even without

---

9 In the case of a Cobb-Douglas production function $Y = K^\alpha(L^d)^{1-\alpha}$, this amounts to assuming that $s > i_1\alpha$ holds true.

full-employment of the labor force ($l^d < l$ here in general). If the natural rate of growth n_1 applies, we have a so-called leaden age where the labor force grows at a faster rate than the capital stock, implying a progressively increasing rate of unemployment, which may be separated from what happens on the labor market by the assumption that such excess labor leaves this market and goes to other segments of the economy not explicitly considered by the model. We thus can have insufficient steady growth with respect to the labor market when the parameters i_o, i_1 are not large enough in order to lead to a common intersection with both the savings schedule and the horizontal n_1 line. Depressed investment behavior of this type thus allows for steady growth and Keynesian goods–market equilibrium simultaneously, but has severe implications for the labor market and the employment of the total labor force in an otherwise unchanged Solovian growth model.

The opposite situation of course holds in the case of a natural growth rate n_2, which gives rise to a situation of a golden growth age. Here, it must be assumed that labor is reallocated from peripheral sectors – not yet part of the labor market of the considered economy – in order to allow for such growth over a longer time horizon. These verbal additions to this Keynesian version of a Solow growth model in fact suggest that the natural growth rate n on the official labor market becomes an endogenous variable in the longer run and thus moves the horizontal lines shown in Figure 1.3 towards the intersection of the savings and the investment schedule. In view of this, we can summarize that the Keynesian version of the Solow growth model makes use of the parameters s, i_o, i_1 and the shape of the production function in order to explain the occurrence and the type of steady-state growth, while the rate n of natural growth is completely irrelevant for this explanation. Increasing the parameters s, i_o, i_1 through the appropriate use of economic policy will increase economic growth, which is no longer forced onto a particular path by the natural rate of growth of the labor force. Labor market policies therefore heavily depend for their success on what happens in the goods market and will therefore generally be quite impotent to solve labor market problems. Since saving rates may be considered as relatively stable outcomes of the consumption decision of households, it is therefore the investment decision and the investment climate into which it is embedded that shapes the growth path of a capitalist economy. Finally, since investment must also take account of the short-run situation of the considered economies, we have that there is no longer an unambiguous distinction between the forces that govern the long run and those responsible for short- and medium-run outcomes. This extension of the Solow growth model therefore shows that integrated macrodynamics becomes a must if considered from this wider perspective. There is no compelling theory of the long run that can be considered independently of the forces that shape the short run (and the medium run).

We summarize the findings of this section by the statement that the long-run position of the economy, in the sense of a path of balanced growth, obviously need not be of neoclassical type (purely supply-side determined), but may be determined primarily through the investment behavior of firms (in its interaction with the savings decision of the households). It is therefore not possible to determine the steady-state behavior of a capitalist economy without reference to the theory of the short- and medium-run one is pursuing – that is, disintegrating the long run from these other runs is not a sensible modeling strategy. With respect to further alternatives for formulating possible long-run positions of the economy, the reader is referred to Marglin (1984) and Dutt (1990), where it is shown in great detail that models of balanced growth can be of various origins, with the neoclassical one indeed being only one among others, and indeed not the most plausible one. It is the hypothesis of this chapter that the short-run considerations are the foundation of the medium run, which in turn must be expanded by factor growth and other considerations to lay the proper basis for the analysis of the long run. This is quite the opposite philosophy compared with what one finds in the popular textbook of Mankiw (1994) – as well as in many other textbooks – which therefore provides a perfectly formulated, but nevertheless fairly misleading presentation of the working of capitalist market economies, since they do not follow the logical consequences of what they present as their theory of the short run. The next section gives another example of this type, where certain elements of the short-run analysis are simply ignored in order to obtain the desired result of global asymptotic stability, now of the NAIRU full-employment position in the context of the interaction of unemployment, inflation and monetary policy, subjects that were considered as being of secondary importance and thus excluded from the neoclassical theory of steady economic growth of this section.[10]

1.3 Phillips curve transition dynamics in the medium run

In the preceding section, we have shown that there may be different theories of the long-run (balanced) position of the economy, where no choice can really be made on the basis of such long-run investigations alone. In this section, we now simply assume that there is given trend growth (of unspecified type) underlying the inflation dynamics that is now the focus of interest. With respect to labor supply (in efficiency units), capital stock growth and the growth rate of potential output, we now simply assume that $\hat{L} = \hat{K} = \hat{Y}^p$ are all equal to a given trend rate $\bar{g}$. Moreover, we assume for reasons of simplicity that, behind this situation, there is a fixed proportions technology with a constant rate of Harrod neutral technical change (and of a kind that is compatible with the Okun Law to be formulated in the following Section). The model of inflation dynamics that we will formulate on this basis has its origins in Frisch and Hof (1982) and Frisch (1983), and has been reformulated in Flaschel (2009, Ch.5).

---

10 See Flaschel (1993, Ch.8) and Chiarella and Flaschel (2000a, Ch.4ff). for extensions of the above Keynesian steady-state alternative to neoclassical growth, which include inflation dynamics and more; see also Gale (1983, Chs. 2, 3) for microfounded extensions from the neoclassical perspective, with questionable Keynesian features in his Chapter 3, as is argued in Flaschel (1993, Ch.8). These topics will be further pursued in Chapter 6.

We represent here, following Flaschel (2009), the monetarist baseline model in its original nonlinear form, which is simply given by a growth rate formulation of Okun's law, using the growth rate of the rate of employment in the place of its approximation – see Frisch and Hof (1982) – by a linear law of motion for the rate of unemployment. We shall see that the nonlinear version of the dynamics allows for interesting global propositions which indeed complete the linear dynamics in important ways, allowing for elegant mathematical proofs of the assertions. Thus, we will provide here a global analysis of basic monetarist propositions on the stability and also the vulnerability of the inflation dynamics of capitalist economies, where inflation inertia plays an important role, but where the breakdown of monetary impulses (money supply growth) into real growth and inflation is still regulated by very basic principles, concerning the relationship between inflation and real growth on the one hand, and between employment and real growth on the other. The three important 'parameters' of the Keynesian theory of goods and assets market equilibrium are missing here all; namely, the marginal propensity to consume, the marginal efficiency to invest and the state of liquidity preference. They do no matter in the following analysis of the interaction of unemployment and inflation, conceived as transitional dynamics to a balanced growth path with fully employed factor supplies, based on NAIRU concepts as the explanation of full factor utilization.

In this section, we will thus consider the baseline model of the monetarist theory of inflation which is here based on two important empirical regularities and, of course, on the quantity theory of money and a simple mechanism that describes the evolution of inflationary expectations. We will show that the implied dynamic structure will produce monotonic convergence or damped fluctuations for all positive rates of employment and all rates of inflation or deflation and will never leave the economic part of the phase space. We shall identify four regimes in this part (half-plane) of the whole phase space: inflationary booms, periods of stagflation, stagnation and disinflation and finally recovery with further disinflation of even deflation. These different regimes of the considered dynamics will all happen when damped fluctuations (stable nodes) characterize the situation close to the steady state. The baseline monetarist model of inflation to be considered is an excellent example of the construction of a necessarily nonlinear dynamical system that is to a certain degree rich in its implications and nevertheless still sufficiently simple to analyze even from the global point of view. It supports the Frischian paradigm of macroeconomic thinking which suggests that the private sector is basically of shock-absorber type and that persistent business fluctuations can therefore only be explained by persistent shocks hitting the economy over the course of time.

1.3.1 The model

In this section, we will briefly consider a baseline model of the monetarist theory of inflation in a closed economy that is based on two important empirical regularities, the quantity theory of money and an adaptive mechanism that describes the evolution of inflationary expectations. We will show that the implied dynamic structure will produce monotonic convergence or convergence with damped fluctuations back to the interior steady state for all positive rates of employment, in particular by always remaining in the economically feasible region of the phase space. We identify four regimes in this region of the phase space: inflationary booms, periods of stagflation, stagnation and disinflation and finally recovery with further disinflation of even deflation. These different scenarios of the considered dynamics may all happen when damped fluctuations (stable nodes) characterize the situation close to the steady state. This baseline monetarist model of inflation provides an excellent, yet simple, example of the view that macrodynamics proper leads us in a natural way to the consideration of a nonlinear dynamical system that in the case of this model type is fairly rich in its implications (nevertheless still simple enough to analyze even from the global point of view). The analysis here supports the Frischian paradigm of macroeconomic thinking which suggests that the private sector is basically of the shock-absorber type, even from the global point of view. We next model the monetarist view of more or less supply-side inertia and global return to the full-employment level of monetarist theory.[11] The baseline model of the monetarist theory of inflation, stagflation and disinflation consists of the four equations

$$\bar{\mu} = g + \pi, \tag{1.8}$$

$$\pi = \beta_w(e - \bar{e}) + \pi^e, \tag{1.9}$$

$$\hat{e} = b_e(g - \bar{g}), \tag{1.10}$$

$$\dot{\pi}^e = \beta_{\pi^e}(\pi - \pi^e), \tag{1.11}$$

where b_e, β_w, and β_{π^e} are positive speeds of adjustment. Equation (1.8) is the quantity theory of money $M = kpY$, $k = $ const. in growth rate form with $\bar{\mu} = \hat{M}$ the given growth rate of money supply, $g = \hat{Y}$ the growth rate of real output Y and $\pi = \hat{p}$ the inflation rate. It states that there is a strict bound for the evolution of real growth and nominal inflation. Accelerating inflation must lead the economy into a depression if the monetary authority keeps the growth rate of the money supply fixed, since the real growth rate is always given by the difference $\bar{\mu} - \pi$. The quantity theory of money – taken by itself – therefore already 'explains' turning points in inflation and economic growth (or, by the same token) deflation and economic decline.

Next, Equation (1.9) provides the now conventional type of price Phillips curve, based on sluggish adjustment of wage inflation (and – due to an assumed simple markup pricing rule – also of price inflation) to demand pressure on the labor market, measured by the deviation of the rate of employment e from the benchmark level $\bar{e}$, the representation of the Non–Accelerating–Inflation Rate

---

11   See Frisch (1983) for a detailed introduction to this type of model. Note also that one should set the parameter $b_e = 1$ in a fixed proportions technology (with no technical progress).

of (labor force) Utilization, or simply the NAIRU, here, however, measured in terms of employment and not with its complement: the rate of unemployment. This price Phillips curve is finally augmented in the usual way by a term that represents the expected rate of inflation, with a coefficient of unity. Sluggish wage–price adjustment, the NAIRU and expectation augmentation thus characterize the Phillips curve employed in our monetarist baseline model. Our modeling approach is to start from behavioral equations chosen to be as linear as possible, and thus we have specified only a constant speed of adjustment parameter in front of the demand pressure term $e - \bar{e}$ for the labor market.

Equation (1.10) is inspired by Okun (1970), from whom we depart (slightly), however, in that we assume an Okun's law of the form

$$e/\bar{e} = \alpha_v (u/\bar{u})^{b_e},$$

which states that changes of relative deviations of capacity utilization $u = Y/Y^p$ from the normal rate of capacity utilization $\bar{u}$ are translated with elasticity b_e into relative deviations of the rate of employment from the NAIRU rate of employment, i.e.

$$de/e = b_e du/u,$$

where $\bar{e}, \bar{u}, \alpha_v$ and b_e are given parameters. Just as with the price Phillips curve, we conceive this law as an empirical law which also incorporates the effects of technological change implying that the parameter b_e should lie between zero and one. In terms of rates of growth, the foregoing form of Okun's law immediately implies Equation (1.10), since

$$\hat{e} - \hat{\bar{e}} = \hat{e} = b_e(\hat{u} - \hat{\bar{u}}) = b_e \hat{u}$$
$$= b_e(\hat{Y} - \hat{Y}^p) = b_e(g - \bar{g})$$

must hold on the basis of the assumptions made. Note that, in addition, we assume $\bar{g}$ is constant. Okun's law (the strict correlation of rates of utilization on the market for labor and for goods) implies a simple, yet important nonlinearity for the baseline model of monetarist inflation theory, due to the fact that we have a growth rate (of e) on the left-hand side of Equation (1.10) and not just a time-derivative ($\dot{e}$). In textbook literature, one often makes use of the approximation

$$\frac{\dot{e}}{e} = \frac{-\dot{U}}{1 - U} \approx -\dot{U}, \quad U \text{ the unemployment rate.}$$

We shall, however, show that this approximation is neither helpful nor appropriate in this simple approach to growth and inflation.

Equation (1.11) finally provides the simplest adaptive rule for expectations formation, π^e, with respect to the rate of inflation. Note that the limit case $\beta_{\pi^e} = \infty$ for the adjustment speed β_{π^e} of inflationary expectations will be interpreted in the subsequent analysis as providing the situation of myopic perfect foresight, viz. $\pi^e = \pi := \hat{p}$.

Taken together, we have four equations for the determination of the growth rate g, inflation rate π, expected inflation rate π^e and the rate of employment e. Equation (1.8) states that a monetary impulse $\bar{\mu}$ must translate itself one-to-one into growth plus inflation. Inflation depends on the rate of employment e, which in turn depends on real growth. In this way, the division of the monetary impulse into inflation, growth and employment is determined, augmented by the fact that inflationary expectations are also involved in this process and here are generally determined by an adaptive process.

1.3.2 Local and global dynamic behavior

From Equations (1.8)–(1.11), we obtain the autonomous system of two nonlinear differential equations in the state variables e and π given by

$$\hat{e} = b_e(\bar{\mu} - \bar{g} - \pi) \text{ or } \dot{e} = b_e(\bar{\mu} - \bar{g} - \pi)e, \tag{1.12}$$

$$\dot{\pi} = \beta_w \dot{e} + \dot{\pi}^e = \beta_w e b_e(\bar{\mu} - \bar{g} - \pi) + \beta_{\pi^e}\beta_w(e - \bar{e}), \tag{1.13}$$

representing in reduced form the interaction of the rate of employment e with the rate of inflation π. We stress again that this system is a nonlinear one in a very simple way, due to the use of a growth rate in its first equation.

The unique steady state of these dynamics is given by

$$\pi_0 = \bar{\mu} - \bar{g},$$

$$e_0 = \bar{e}.$$

It is indeed uniquely determined, since $e_0 = 0$ implies $\dot{\pi} = -\beta_{\pi^e}\beta_w\bar{e}$ which is not a steady-state situation.

Local stability analysis derives from the Jacobian matrix J of partial derivatives of the system (1.12), (1.13) at the steady state, given by:

$$J = \begin{pmatrix} 0 & -b_e e_0 \\ \beta_{\pi^e}\beta_w & -\beta_w e_0 b_e \end{pmatrix}.$$

We immediately see that trace J is negative and the determinant of J positive and thus derive the result that the steady state of the dynamics is locally asymptotically stable under all circumstances. With respect to the discriminant $\Delta = \frac{(\text{trace } J)^2}{4} - \det J$, we furthermore have

$$4\Delta = \beta_w^2 e_0^2 b_e^2 - 4b_e e_0 \beta_{\pi^e}\beta_w$$

$$= b_e e_0 \beta_w(b_e e_0 \beta_w - 4\beta_{\pi^e}),$$

which is therefore negative if

$$\beta_{\pi^e} > \frac{b_e e_0 \beta_w}{4}$$

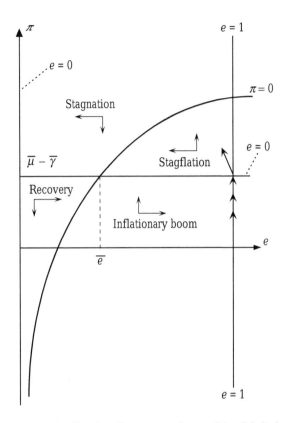

Figure 1.4 The baseline monetarist model of inflation, stagflation, disinflation and deflation.[12]

holds true. In this case, we thus conclude that the steady state is surrounded by damped fluctuations of the rate of employment and the rate of inflation.

The speed of adjustment of inflationary expectation (if increased) thus work against monotonic stability, while wage flexibility and a strong Okun connection between rates of utilization on goods and labor markets work in favor of it.

The isocline $\dot{e} = 0$ in Figure 1.4 is immediately obtained from the differential Equation (1.12). Above (below) this isocline we have falling (rising) rates of employment. For the other isocline, $\dot{\pi} = 0$, one easily obtains

$$\pi = \bar{\mu} - \bar{g} + (\beta_{\pi^e}/b_e)(1 - \bar{e}/e).$$

---

12 Note with respect to Figure 1.4 that its representation by means of the state variables e, π^e in the place of e, π would give rise to linear isoclines (with $\dot{\pi}^e = 0$ vertical and $\dot{e} = 0$ negatively sloped, including the vertical axis again of course). The movement off the isoclines would, however, be of the same type as shown in Figure 1.4, i.e. it is clockwise in orientation.

This curve is strictly concave and approaches $-\infty$ for $e \to 0$ and $\bar{\mu} - \bar{g} + \beta_{\pi} e / b_e$ for $e \to +\infty$. It is thus of the form shown in Figure 1.4. Above (to the left of) this curve, we have falling inflation rates and below (to its right) rising ones. The isoclines thus separate the phase space into four regions with adjustment directions as shown in Figure 1.4. Starting with the case of an inflationary boom, where both the rate of employment and of inflation are rising, we sooner or later must enter the phase of stagflation, since employment above the NAIRU level in interaction with adaptive inflationary expectations leads to accelerating inflation and thus to shrinking rates of growth as long as the growth rate of the money supply is left unchanged. Stagflation in turn comes to an end, not only because it stops the acceleration of inflation but also since the process of disinflation begins when the decline in employment rates outweighs the inertia of inflation rates caused by adaptive inflationary expectations formation. Further decreases in the employment rate speed up the ongoing disinflation until the economy starts growing again at a rate that exceeds the rate where Okun's law implies unchanged employment relationships. Recovery sets in and will sooner or later give rise again to an inflationary boom.

We note, with respect to Figure 1.4, that there are indeed always lower and upper turning points with respect to the evolution of inflation or deflation. This is due to the simple fact that the quantity theory of money implies a severely depressed real growth in the case of high inflation rates and rapidly increasing economic activity in the case of accelerating deflation. The Phillips curve mechanism should then always provide the link that stops increasing inflation by the slowdown in growth and decline in the employment caused by this increasing inflation. Accelerating deflation similarly is stopped by the increase in real growth and employment that it brings about. As shown, the dynamics is, however, not only viable in this sense, but indeed globally convergent (as we shall see in the following Section) to its unique steady state, which is governed by the NAIRU and the superneutrality result of the monetarist theory of inflation.

We have also already argued that there is always a lower turning point for the rate of employment of the dynamics (1.12), (1.13); see again Figure 1.4 and the $\dot{e} = 0$ isocline. With respect to an upper turning point of e, which must be ≤ 1, the model is, however, still incomplete. We resolve this incompleteness by modifying the law of motion (1.12) to

$$\hat{e} = \begin{cases} b_e(\bar{\mu} - \bar{g} - \pi) & \text{if } e < 1 \quad \text{or} \quad b_e(\bar{\mu} - \bar{g} - \pi) \leq 0, \\ 0 & \text{if } e = 1 \quad \text{and} \quad b_e(\bar{\mu} - \bar{g} - \pi) > 0. \end{cases}$$

This exactly provides the full-employment barrier $e = 1$ and the movement along it as long as $b_e(\bar{\mu} - \bar{g} - \pi) > 0$ holds, as shown in Figure 1.4. We thus obtain a second regime in this type of dynamics with only one law of motion, the regime of full-employment in the strict sense of the word. Note that the quantity theory here still explains the rate of growth of the economy by way of the rate of inflation that is implied by $\pi = \beta_w(1 - \bar{e}) + \pi^e$ at each moment in time at the full-employment ceiling. This assumes that firms can still pursue their production plans (which may be justified by allowing for overtime work of the employed workforce under these circumstances).

If the parameter β_{π^e}, the adjustment speed of inflationary expectations, is sufficiently high, we get, as was shown earlier, damped cyclical fluctuations around the steady state and, starting from the inflationary boom shown in the phase diagram bottom right, subsequent periods of stagflation, stagnation and finally disinflation and recovery (with further disinflation or even deflation). Unwise monetary policy can prolong the inflationary boom with its increasing rates of employment by increasing further and further $\bar{\mu}$, the growth rate of the money supply. This shifts both isoclines upwards (with intersection always on the $e = \bar{e}$ perpendicular line, called the long-run Phillips curve in this type of approach). Yet, we obtain accelerating inflation rates in this way and may expect that the monetary authority will eventually stop (or perhaps not even begin) this type of policy and return to moderate growth rates of the money supply. Depending on how low these driven growth rates are chosen, we get a radical return to low inflation rates with very low rates of employment in between or – when done in a stepwise fashion – a gradual decline in inflation rates coupled with not so strongly depressed labor markets. In this type of framework, 'cold turkey' or very cautious gradualism therefore represent two extreme strategies when accelerating inflation is to be stopped and brought down again to moderate levels.[13]

It is easy to show for the present model type also global asymptotic stability in the right-hand half-plane of $\mathbb{R}^2$, the economically feasible region of the phase space of the dynamics. For this purpose, one has to define a Liapunov function L, which in the present case is given by

$$L(e, \pi) = \int_{e_0}^{e} \beta_{\pi^e} \beta_w (x - \bar{e})/x \, dx + \int_{\pi_0}^{\pi} -b_e(\bar{\mu} - \bar{g} - y) \, dy.$$

This function has a single local as well as global minimum at (e_0, π_0) in the positive half plane of $\mathbb{R}^2$ and is characterized by closed level curves. Such a result is easily obtained by considering separately its two components, which are both strictly convex with minimum value e_o and π_o, respectively. Projecting the graph of the composed function into the half plane $\mathbb{R}^2$, where $e > 0$ holds true, thus gives rise to closed level curves surrounding the steady state that are characterized by higher values of L the farther away they are from the steady state.

---

13 We note here in passing that the dynamics as they are formulated imply that a sudden increase in the growth rate of the money supply cannot lead to jumps in the rate of employment or the rate of inflation. The only variable that can adjust immediately is the rate of growth of real output, which is not a very plausible feature of the model. In our view, this points to a variable that is left unconsidered in this baseline model, namely the short-term rate of interest, which indeed can perform such jumps and then cause sluggish adjustments in the real part of the economy. This interest rate effect will be included in the next section, together with an IS-LM-PC analysis of the dynamics of aggregate demand.

Using the vector $z(t) = (e(t), \pi(t))$ to denote the solution curve in the positive half plane, the function L fulfills

$$
\begin{aligned}
\dot{L} &= \frac{dL(z(t))}{dt} = L_e \dot{e} + L_\pi \dot{\pi} \\
&= \frac{\beta_{\pi^e} \beta_w (e - \bar{e})}{e} \cdot \dot{e} - b_e(\bar{\mu} - \bar{g} - \pi) \cdot \dot{\pi} \\
&= (\beta_{\pi^e} \beta_w (e - \bar{e}) b_e(\bar{\mu} - \bar{g} - \pi) - b_e(\bar{\mu} - \bar{g} - \pi)[\beta_w b_e(\bar{\mu} - \bar{g} - \pi)e \\
&\quad + \beta_{\pi^e} \beta_w (e - \bar{e})] \\
&= -b_e^2 \beta_w e(\bar{\mu} - \bar{g} - \pi)^2 \leq 0, \quad [= 0 \text{ iff } \pi = \bar{\mu} - \bar{g}].
\end{aligned}
$$

The derivative $\dot{L} \leq 0$ simply implies that the values of the function L are descending along the trajectories $z(t) = (e(t), \pi(t))$ of the system (1.12), (1.13), with the exception of the case where $\pi = \bar{\mu} - \bar{g}$ holds true. All level curves of the function L are thus crossed (nearly everywhere) towards lower values of L by the trajectories of the dynamics, which therefore must all approach the unique steady state of the considered dynamical system as time goes to infinity. This situation is illustrated in Figure 1.5.

Due to the fact that – viewed globally – the steady state (e_0, π_0) is the only sink in the graph of the Liapunov function L, we can thus assert that all trajectories must converge to the steady state (e_0, π_0), the deepest point in the graph of L, where L is zero. The level curves of L are generally crossed from outside to their inside area (apart from the isolated points where $\pi = \bar{\mu} - \bar{g}$ may hold), which means that the height measured by L will, apart from some isolated situations, always fall along the trajectories of the system (1.12), (1.13). Figure 1.4 shows the phase diagram of the dynamics. In the case of the approximation $\dot{e}/e \approx -\dot{U}$ and thus the linear from $\dot{U} = b_e(\bar{g} - g)$ of Okun's law, the $\dot{\pi} = 0$ isocline would be a straight line. This approximation has the disadvantage, however, that the baseline monetarist model of inflation would only give proper information on situations sufficiently close to the steady (which may not be true for stagflationary episodes, for example). The positive right half-plane would then not be an invariant set of the dynamics, since from the strict mathematical point of view, e could become negative (or U larger than 100 percent), which should be impossible for economic dynamics that are globally well defined. Our nonlinear dynamics, by contrast, cannot cross the vertical axis, as Figure 1.4 demonstrates by way of the $\dot{e} = 0$ isocline and thus must always exhibit a positive rate of employment.[14]

---

14 In fact, the dynamics cannot even approach the vertical axis, since this would create a further steady state (which would only be possible above $\bar{\mu} - \bar{g}$, but in fact is impossible due to what occurs on the vertical axis in this case).

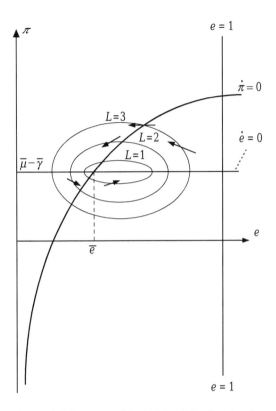

Figure 1.5 Contours of the height of the function L are crossed towards their interior and thus imply convergence to the steady state.

1.3.3 Accelerating inflation, stagflation and monetary policy

In Figure 1.6, we show an extreme case of the short-run trade-off that policy makers may face, the accelerating phase they induce when they insist on the level of employment reached thereby and the immediate beginning of stagflation when they stop increasing the growth rate of money supply used to preserve the high level of employment reached. We here assume that the initial situation is characterized by steady growth and zero inflation rates at the NAIRU rate of employment $\bar{e}$. The monetary authority then starts increasing the growth rate of the money supply to a level $\bar{\mu} - \bar{g} > 0$ as shown in Figure 1.6. As long as the resulting increase in growth, employment and inflation is not changing inflationary expectations, we have the short-run Phillips curve $\hat{p} = \beta_w(e - \bar{e}) + 0$ in action and we assume that this is the case until the full-employment ceiling $e = 1$ has been reached (at the point A).

Inflationary expectations then, however, are assumed to start to react to the increases in inflation taking place as the economy moves along the short-run Phillips curve and then creates an accelerating inflationary spiral along the

$e = 1$ locus as long as the monetary authority is assumed to defend this position of absolute full-employment. Such, however, is only possible by an accelerating increase in the growth rate of the money supply according to the conditions

$$\mu = \bar{g} + \beta_w(1 - \bar{e}) + \pi^e, \quad \dot{\pi}^e = \beta_{\pi^e}\beta_w(1 - \bar{e}),$$

so that such a monetary policy that cannot be maintained for ever.

Sooner or later, the monetary authority will stop increasing the growth rate of money supply (at point B) and will then allow the rate of employment to adjust in view of the high rate of inflation now in existence. The resulting situation is immediately of stagflationary type, as shown by the adjustment path passing from B to the point C in Figure 1.6. The stagflation – and the subsequent stagnation – generated in this way will become even more severe if the monetary authority starts radically decreasing the growth rate of the money supply back to moderate levels, by way of a 'cold turkey' strategy (in place of gradualism), with high unemployment rates, but faster adjustment to a new steady-state position with low inflation rates. The end result will in all cases be a rate of employment that is back at its NAIRU level and a rate of inflation given by the difference of money supply and real growth.

The question arises whether one can design a monetary policy rule by which a monotonic adjustment to the steady-state position – the unavoidable long-run position of the economy – is generated, and by which therefore the inertia in the process of adjusting wages and adjusting inflationary expectations can be circumvented to some extent, at least with respect to the overshooting mechanism shown in Figures 1.4 and 1.6. To achieve this end, we propose the rule for the growth rate of the money supply of the form

$$\mu = \bar{g} + \pi^e + \beta_\mu(\bar{e} - e), \quad \beta_\mu > 0.$$

This rule states that the money supply growth should be based on trend growth plus the currently expected rate of inflation and that the momentary authority departs from this benchmark to lower values if employment is above its NAIRU level and to higher values in the opposite case. On the basis of this rule, we get

$$g = \mu - \pi = \bar{g} + (\beta_\mu + \beta_w)(\bar{e} - e),$$

from which it follows that

$$\hat{e} = (\beta_\mu + \beta_w)(\bar{e} - e),$$

which implies a monotonic adjustment of the rate of employment towards its long-run level. This adjustment is faster the more flexible are wages and the stronger the monetary authority reacts to the deviations of the employment rate from its NAIRU level.

Remark on rational and other expectations: we briefly mention here the possibility of rational expectations, simply based on the myopic perfect foresight

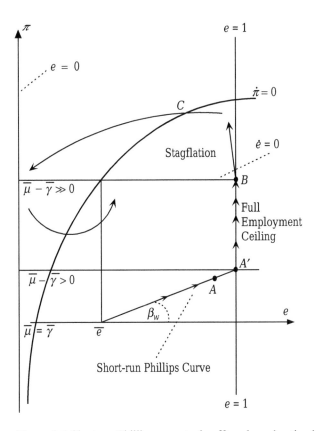

Figure 1.6 Short run Phillips curve trade-offs and accelerating inflation prepare the scene for more or less severe stagflationary episodes.[15]

rule $\bar{\pi}^e = \hat{p}$ (obtained in the limit case $\beta_{\pi e} = \infty$), in which case the structure of the dynamics basically degenerates. According to the Phillips curve (1.9), we then have $e = \bar{e}$ and thus $g = \bar{g}$ and therefore also $\pi = \pi^e = \bar{\mu} - \bar{g}$. Under such rational expectations, the real part of economy cannot depart from the steady state, while money is now superneutral also in the short run, which we conceive as a situation that is too narrow in structure to provide an adequate treatment of

---

15 With the line leading from $\bar{e}$ to point A as the trade-off between inflation and unemployment envisaged to exist for example by the former German chancellor Helmut Schmidt (at least up to the level of a 99 percent employment rate at point A) and with point A' even believed to be a stationary point for the macroeconomy by the former German chancellor Willi Brandt (preceding Helmut Schmidt as chancellor of the Federal Republic of Germany). It may be of interest here to note that the minister of finance, Alex Möller, in the government of Will Brandt left the government in 1971, since he feared becoming 'minister of inflation' because of the practices of this government.

the case of myopic perfect foresight. We note finally, but do not prove it here, that the assumption of regressive expectations in the place of adaptive or rational ones always implies monotonic convergence to the steady state in the place of the damped fluctuations discussed in the foregoing section. For detailed investigations and discussions of the relevance of such regimes of rational expectations, the reader is referred to the books by Sargent (1987) and Turnovsky (1995), for example. We will show in Part II that this type of degeneracy of the dynamics need not occur in a properly formulated Keynesian analysis of disequilibrium and growth with myopic perfect foresight on wage and price inflation. We will find there that inflationary inertia, in the present section caused by sluggishly adjusting wages and adaptively adjusting inflationary expectations, does not disappear even under myopic perfect foresight, due to expectations that concern the medium-run evolution of the economy.

1.3.4 Comments

Before closing this chapter on the analysis of the interaction of unemployment and inflation, let us briefly point to the central weaknesses of this approach. Due to the assumption of the strict form of the quantity theory of money, we have a very simple – in fact a too simple and (from an empirical point of view) implausible – explanation of lower and upper turning points in the case of inflation as well as of disinflation or deflation. Increases in inflation reduce in a one-to-one fashion the rate of growth of the economy and thus provide a very straightforward check to the inflationary process. Similarly, disinflation or deflation must increase the rate of growth of the economy also in this one-to-one fashion and thus brings to an end and even reverses this process in a very simple way. Yet, business fluctuations are not of this simple type that always guarantees in particular a safe recovery from recessions or depressions. Furthermore, money supply rules are no longer at the center of interest in the current discussions of monetary policy. Interest rate policy rules are now predominantly applied and investigated. In order to allow the discussion of such rules and their impact on the working of the economy, the interest rate must, however, play a role in the behavior of the private sector. A reintegration of the demand side of the goods market (as it is standard in the macroeconomic textbook literature) into the monetarist baseline picture must therefore be undertaken to really judge the propositions made in this section. The next section will then show on this basis that not much will remain of the monetarist propositions of this section when account is taken of the facts that the circular flow of income is characterized by multiplier effects, that real rate of interest dynamics act on this multiplier dynamics and there is also an interest-rate-dependent liquidity preference schedule to be employed in the analysis of the interaction between employment and inflation.

Summarizing, we may state that a model of the transition dynamics from a Keynesian short run (that is left implicit) to a neoclassical long run of the type of this section can be considered as a too simplified one, since it abstracts from all three important aspects of the Keynesian theory of effective demand, the marginal propensity to consume, the marginal efficiency to invest and liquidity preference. Using the quantity theory more or less implicitly as a theory of aggregate demand and of goods market equilibrium is in fact not a good substitute or proxy for aggregate consumption and investment demand and its various and differing determinants on the macrolevel. The three fundamental 'parameters' (marginal propensity to consume, marginal efficiency to invest and the state of liquidity preference) of Keynes' theory of effective goods demand thus appear to not be relevant for a proper analysis of the interaction of unemployment and inflation, here shown to be a simple transitional dynamics to a balanced growth path with fully employed factor supplies.[16]

We first show that this is not true if the IS-LM part of the model is taken as it is originally formulated in Dornbusch and Fischer (1994) – as well as in all other textbooks that include this type of analysis – as far as its medium-run dynamical features are concerned. These medium-run consequences are completely bypassed in Dornbusch and Fischer (1994/98), though they clearly state in an appendix to their Chapter 16 that the dynamic aggregate demand must include expected inflation as an item or determinant. They therefore seem to consider this omission to be of secondary importance, but we will attempt to demonstrate in this section that this is definitely not the case. In Blanchard (2003), the same result is achieved by the very arrangement of the chapters of his book, where PC dynamics are treated before the real rate of interest is introduced into investment behavior in the place of the originally only nominal one. Inflationary expectations and their role in the wage–price spiral are therefore discussed before they are introduced into the investment behavior of the employed model, which of course results in the same (generally misleading) stability scenario as in the earlier analysis of Dornbusch and Fischer (1994/98) that we present in the following Section.[17] IS-LM-PC dynamics proper, where expected inflation is not ignored in its impact on aggregate demand, is, however, often not viable and therefore not yet completely defined.

We have questioned the relevance of the Solow growth model as a model of capitalistic growth from a Keynesian perspective at the end of the preceding section and will question the relevance of the monetarist baseline model as a theory of the interaction of unemployment and inflation in a the same context and again from a Keynesian perspective in the next chapter. The Keynesian view of the interaction

---

16 See Section 1.6 in Flaschel (2009) for a discussion of the dynamic interaction of these parameters.

17 In their eighth edition, see for example the Australian edition of Dornbusch *et al.* (2002); these authors have rearranged the sequence of topics of their earlier editions in the spirit of Mankiw's (1994) macroeconomic textbook where the long run and the theory inflation are treated before aggregate demand issues are considered in depth. This seems to suggest that the theory of inflation is basically a supply-side issue which it is not, as we briefly argue in the final section of this chapter, see also Section 1.4.2 on Keynes' Notes on the Trade Cycle. This is also obvious once the modern treatment of interest rate policy rules is taken into account where a demand-side orientation is, at least implicitly, definitely present.

of real and financial markets in the short run (as it will be briefly described in the following Section) thus does not at all justify the view that the medium-run evolution of this interaction is properly portrayed by the monetarist baseline model of the present section, nor that the long-run evolution of this interaction has much in common with the stylized outcomes of the Solow growth model. Textbooks that claim that the disintegrated models of the present chapter can be integrated into a consistent whole without loss in their original substance therefore just claim too much in their attempt to offer a coherent view for the short, the medium and the long run to students of macroeconomics.

1.4 Short-run real-financial market interaction

1.4.1 The textbook model

Keynesian IS-LM analysis is presented in numerous textbooks, nowadays however, more on the basic than on the advanced textbook level, where – with respect to the latter – the traditional character of this type of analysis is often stressed. Flaschel (2009, Ch.2) provides a simple introduction into basic arguments of Keynes' revolution in the understanding of short-run macroeconomic equilibrium positions and what came out of this revolution in short-run analysis in the longer run; see Chapter 3 for alternative presentations in this regard. In this section, we shall briefly summarize Keynesian IS-LM analysis with the sole purpose of providing one possible description of the short-run determination of output and the rate of interest, on the basis of given wages and prices, and the implied levels of under- or overutilization in the use of labor and capital. To illustrate this well-known short-run situation on the market for labor and for goods here, serves the purpose of providing a conventional starting point for IS-LM-PC analysis proper, in Chapter 2, which – as we shall show there – is far from being well-presented in basic or advanced textbook literature, and to also provide a point of reference from which the achievements of later DAS–AD growth analysis, and, even more, the KMG growth dynamics, may be judged and understood.

The fairly standard graphical representation of short-run IS-LM equilibrium position and its consequences for the utilization of labor as well as capital – shown in Figure 1.7 – is based as the analysis of the preceding section on fixed proportions in production, now without any type of technical change however. We have a given output–employment ratio $\bar{x}$ and a given ratio between potential output Y^p and the capital stock K, represented by the parameter $\bar{y}$. We have also given money wages w and prices p in the considered situation, and on this basis the conventional determination of output and the nominal rate of interest as shown in the upper part of Figure 1.7. In this part of the figure, we also indicate that the dynamic adjustment of output and interest, via goods market and bond market disequilibrium processes, is in a straightforward way of stabilizing nature (if the rate of interest adjusts sufficiently fast) and thus leads the economy to the intersection of the IS and the LM curve where the goods and the asset markets are both in equilibrium.

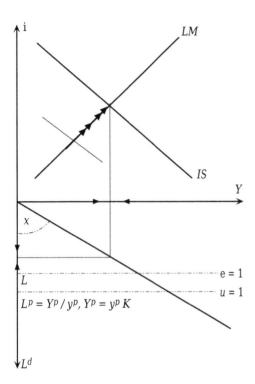

Figure 1.7 Keynesian IS-LM analysis and supply-side restrictions (signaling pressure towards wage or price inflation or deflation, respectively).

Fiscal or monetary shocks (or demand and supply side originating in the private sector of the economy) will move the IS or LM curve (as shown for a fiscal shock in Figure 1.7) and will lead to adjustment processes towards the new IS-LM equilibrium or intersection. In Figure 1.7, we have assumed in addition that financial markets adjust so fast that they are always in equilibrium. Adjustment towards the new equilibrium position, therefore, is always taking place along the LM-curve. In Figure 1.7, this means that fiscal expansion increases output and nominal interest simultaneously and is thus accompanied by a partial crowding out of investment expenditures.

In the lower part of Figure 1.7, we also show the two basic supply-side restrictions that may exist for this type of IS-LM analysis. We have on the one hand that L^d/L, with L the given labor supply, must always be less or equal than one, measuring the demand pressure on the labor market and signaling the potential for wage inflation or deflation. On the other hand, we have that L^d/L^p must also be always less or equal to one, measuring the demand pressure on the goods market and signaling the potential for price inflation of deflation. The situation shown therefore can be conceived as underlying the analysis of wage–price inflation undertaken in the preceding section, yet now based on IS-LM equilibrium analysis and the working of the well-known Keynes effect as well as the less-well-known Mundell effect, to be considered in detail in Chapter 2 of the book.

We here in this regard already state that the foregoing type of conventional IS-LM analysis will in no way support the analysis of the preceding section and will also cast considerable doubts on the validity of the neoclassical approach to long-run growth. Even the conventional type of analysis of short-run equilibrium positions of the macroeconomy and their disturbance by exogenous shocks does not support the medium-run and the long-run analysis of Mankiw (1994) type as we shall show in the remainder of this book, quite independent of the question of how the proper analysis of the temporary equilibrium positions of capitalist market economies should really be formulated, a topic which we will discuss in the Chapter 3 of this book.

We thus in sum find in this introductory chapter that there is indeed considerable uncertainty on how the short run, the medium run and the long run should really be modeled, and this of course in a way that makes them compatible with each other. To make progress in this direction is one of the main purposes of the present book. Chapter 3 shows in this regard that short-run analysis can indeed be conducted from various theoretical perspectives, leading possibly to a variety of longer-run extensions, while the remaining chapters of Part I start from traditional Keynesian IS-LM temporary equilibrium position and reformulate the conventional type of AD–AS analysis into a coherent type of DAD–AS dynamics with disequilibrium in the real markets, and equilibrium in the financial markets (still represented by a simple LM equilibrium schedule), including in the final chapter also economic growth, there however still of a fairly neoclassical or supply-side type, while the type of endogenous growth sketched in Section 1.2 will only become relevant in Part II.

1.4.2 Keynes' Notes on the trade cycle

> Since we claim to have shown in the preceding chapters what determines the volume of employment at any time, it follows, if we are right, that our theory must be capable of explaining the phenomena of the trade cycle.
>
> J. M. Keynes (1936, p.313)

Following this introductory remark of Keynes in his 'Notes on the trade cycle', we shall here briefly recapitulate his observations on the main source and the pattern of the cyclical fluctuations that characterize the evolution of capitalist economies in order to indicate an important perspective for the application of static IS-LM analysis. We only intend here to sketch some basic medium-run implications of the temporary equilibrium analysis, however. It will therefore not provide a thorough presentation or even elaboration of Keynes' ideas on this process. Yet, since most macroeconomics textbooks usually introduce IS-LM analysis without properly discussing its medium- and long-run dynamic implications, we hope that this brief overview may help to stimulate further interest in Keynes' particular approach to the analysis of the trade cycle – and the role that expectations play in his arguments.

There are three main elements that can be used from conventional IS-LM analysis for an analysis of the phenomenon of the business cycle:

- The marginal propensity to consume (γ),
- The marginal efficiency of (new) capital (η), and
- The state of liquidity preference (λ).

The marginal propensity to consume out of income is too well known to need further explanation here. Elements which may explain shifts in this propensity (and thus shifts in the IS-curve) are, among others:

- Changes in income distribution,
- Changes in perceived wealth and disposable income,
- Changes in the rate of time-discounting.

cf. Keynes (1936, Ch. 8,9). Shifts in the marginal propensity to consume decrease or increase the Keynesian multiplier and thus have expansionary or contractionary effects on the level of activity of the economy.

The marginal efficiency of capital, cf. Keynes (1936, Ch. 11), is defined in reference to certain time series $Q_1, \ldots, Q_n$ of prospective returns or yields of investment projects. Without going into the details of its definition,[18] it can be seen that such an approach makes investment heavily dependent on expectations of returns over a considerable amount of time. It follows that investment demand may be very volatile and consequently may be of central importance for an explanation of the trade cycle.

Multiplier effects (including its changes) may add to this volatility and its impacts. Nevertheless, in Keynes' view, they mainly transmit fluctuations in investment demand to those of income and employment, but do not by themselves explain the business cycle.

Changes in liquidity preference, cf. here Keynes (1936, Ch. 15), refer to the stock of accumulated savings and are – as investment demand – highly dependent on the 'state of confidence'. This, of course, is particularly true for the speculative motive for holding cash balances, which through sudden changes in expectations may give rise to 'discontinuous' changes in the rate of interest.

We may provisionally summarize the foregoing by the use of three additional parameters g, η and λ in the three behavioral relationships that underlie the usual IS-LM model, namely

$$C(\underset{+}{Y}, \underset{-}{r}, \underset{+}{\gamma}), \quad I(\underset{-}{r}, \underset{+}{\eta}), \quad \frac{M^d}{p}(\underset{+}{Y}, \underset{-}{r}, \underset{+}{\lambda}). \tag{1.14}$$

---

18 See Keynes (1936, pp. 135/6) for his original proposal of such a definition.

These parameters express the fact that the employed behavioral relationships may be subject to changes that are not explained by the IS-LM-model, but are added to it from the outside in an ad hoc fashion – due to the fact that an endogenous treatment in particular of the marginal efficiency of investment is at least a very demanding task.

> By a *cyclical* movement we mean that as the system progresses in, e.g. the upward direction, the forces propelling it upwards at first gather force and have a cumulative effect on one another but gradually lose their strength until at a certain point they tend to be replaced by forces operating in the opposite direction; which in turn gather force for a time and accentuate one another, until they too, having reached their maximum development, wane and give place to their opposite. We do not, however, merely mean by a *cyclical* movement that upward and downward tendencies, once started, do not persist for ever in the same direction but are ultimately reversed. We mean also that there is some recognizable degree of regularity in the time-sequence and duration of the upward and downward movements.
>
> There is, however, another characteristic of what we call the trade cycle which our explanation must cover if it is to be adequate; namely, the phenomenon of the *crisis* – the fact that the substitution of a downward for an upward tendency often takes place suddenly and violently, whereas there is, as a rule, no such sharp turning-point when an upward is substituted for a downward tendency.
>
> J. M. Keynes (1936, pp. 313/4)

Keynes then starts his discussion of such fluctuations in investment, income and, employment from the late stage of a boom period. In this stage of the boom, it may become apparent for investors – due to the past effects of capital accumulation on the abundance of physical capital and the costs of production – that their views on the marginal efficiency of capital demand a significant revision ($\eta \downarrow$). Such a revision of ideas – when it becomes generalized – may lead to a significant change in η and thus a fall in effective demand (via the multiplier process) – which in turn may aggravate the pessimism that has become established ($\eta \downarrow\downarrow$). The cumulative upward trends of the boom may thereby become reversed and turned into cumulative downward trends in income and employment.

It appears plausible that this decline (or collapse) in the marginal efficiency of capital (η) will give rise to an increase (or upward jump) in the liquidity preference parameter λ, i.e. a (sudden) increase in the demand for money. IS-LM analysis implies that this will lead to a (sharp) increase in the rate of interest i and consequently to a further decrease in investment and income. Negative expectations are thereby confirmed and strengthened. It follows that the parameters η and λ may interact in such a way that there results a collapse in economic activity. (Of course, milder forms – such as the recessions of the 1960s – are also conceivable in the above framework.)

The upper turning point for economic activity is thus explained by the interaction of three parameters of the model that bring to an end a boom that is gradually losing force – since the gradual change in η, λ has endogenous consequences (on I, Y, and r) that confirm the opinions which are responsible for this change in behavior. Finally, one effect of the boom may also have been that the marginal propensity to consume has risen (e.g., due to an increase of the share of wages in national income). The parameter γ may therefore also contribute to the decline in economic activity by its subsequent decline.

Let us assume, for our following discussion of the lower turning point in economic activity, that there has been a long period of economic prosperity, so that the aforesaid movements all work with sufficient strength and induce a depression of considerable strength. Economic activity now being low means that the rapid accumulation of 'capital' in the past has created a significant amount of idle capital goods. It is obvious that this excess capacity in production must disappear before there can be any recovery in the parameter that characterizes the marginal efficiency of capital. Therefore, a considerable amount of time will elapse, during which now-unprofitable investments of the past are eliminated in physical or in value form. Such a process of capital depreciation will not in general accelerate, since there is a floor to the level of gross investment (above zero) that helps maintain a low level of economic activity. Once the capital stock has been reduced so far to be in line again with the prevailing level of activity, a return to a more optimistic view on investment profitability becomes possible and may come about. The forces that have operated downward in the development of the depression may now come to help to allow a spreading optimism to gather force. Rising investment and thus rising income and economic activity confirm the positive change in the parameter η, eventually leading to a further increase in it. An improving state of confidence may give rise to a decline in λ, the liquidity preference parameter and thus to a decline in the rate of interest, giving further force to the spreading investment optimism. The resulting cumulative upward effects may, of course, in some cases be weak and thus only lead to a minor recovery, but may in other cases be strong enough to generate once again a boom of significant duration and strength.

This brief sketch of cumulative upward or downward working forces and the gradual appearance of counteracting elements that bring an end to such upward or downward tendencies must suffice here as an outline of the potential of IS-LM analysis to explain business fluctuations. The central role of the parameter η (in comparison to the other two parameters)[19] in the explanation of such fluctuations should be obvious from the statements just made.

No such analysis is possible when neoclassical models are used instead (because of their reliance on Say's law in the main). Business fluctuations in the market clearing approach are then, for example, explained by introducing local markets and misperceptions of agents into such a setup, see Barro (1990, Ch. 19), Sargent (1987, Ch. 18) for details, or by so-called 'real' business cycles, see Blanchard

---

19 Which play the role of amplifiers.

and Fischer (1989, Ch.7). We do not go into an analysis of such model types in the present book – nor into a discussion of recent developments of the New-Keynesian variety – but refer the reader in this regard to Chiarella, Flaschel, Franke and Semmler (2009), which provides alternative scenarios to these mainstream treatments of the macrodynamics of real or monetary economies.

Keynes' approach to explaining the trade cycle has not received much attention in the discussion on growth and instability that developed after the appearance of the 'General Theory'. This may in particular be due to the strong psychological influences that appear in his explanation of the cycle as, for example in the following statement (p. 317):

> … it is not so easy to revive the marginal efficiency of capital, determined, as it is, by the uncontrollable and disobedient psychology of the business world.

Instead of the foregoing speculative type of interaction of primarily psychologically determined magnitudes (the parameters η, γ, λ), dynamic economic analysis has turned to the analysis of interactions of a more mechanical type in the sequel: the multiplier and accelerator approaches and the like, later on replaced by models of inflation and stagflation as in Section 1.2 or those briefly mentioned in the preceding paragraph.

1.5 Outlook: towards integrated macrodynamics

We have reconsidered in this chapter conventional textbook presentations of the short run (income and interest rate determination), the medium run (the interaction of unemployment and inflation) and the long run (growth theory) of macroeconomic theorizing. We demonstrated that these three aspects of the evolution of capitalist economies are not really connected with each other and thus do not represent an integrated view of the working of the macroeconomy. This statement also holds in the case where Keynesian IS-LM is used with static inflationary expectations (as in Blanchard (2006), for example), since this does not change the qualitative features of the medium-run, see Chapter 2 Appendix 4. We thus basically have that the following fairly strange mixture of Keynesian, Monetarist and neoclassical views on the working of the macroeconomy characterizes the state of the art of textbook model building in the literature, a situation which is surely problematic from the scientific point of view.

Model I: Keynesian IS-LM Theory and the Short Run

$$Y = C(Y - T) + I(Y, i - \pi^e) + G$$
$$M = kpYm(i)$$
$$L^d = F^{-1}(Y)$$

Model II: Monetarist Inflation Theory and the Medium Run

$$Y = M/(kp), \quad i.e. \quad g = \hat{Y} = \hat{M} - \hat{p} = \bar{\mu} - \pi$$

$$\dot{p}/p = \hat{p} = \beta_w(e - \bar{e}) + \pi^e, \quad e = L^d/L$$

$$\hat{e} = \beta_e(g - \bar{g}), \quad g = \hat{Y}$$

$$\dot{\pi}^e = \beta_{\pi^e}(\hat{p} - \pi^e)$$

Model III: Neoclassical Growth Theory and the Long Run

$$Y = F(K, L^d)$$

$$L^d = L \quad via \quad \omega = w/p = F_L(K, L)$$

$$\dot{K} = S = sY, \quad s = 1 - c$$

$$\dot{L} = nL, \quad n = const$$

In the medium run, in IS-LM, by contrast, the role of inflationary expectations in aggregate demand is completely ignored, see Blanchard's (2006) IS-LM representation of the medium run. In addition, in the Solovian long-run analysis, financial markets and money demand no longer play any role, so that the model has then become completely un-Keynesian by assumption, since the multiplier theory is then made void of content by the assumption of Say's law (and the complete removal of the AD-curve from this model type).

We insist, however, on the sequence: from the Short run to the Medium run to the Long run as a modeling strategy and as a basis for understanding the working of the macroeconomy in its three runs, with no stability illusions, and with their

Table 1.1 The market-sector scheme of a closed economy

	Labor market	Goods market	Money market	Capital market	
Households	L	C	M^d	B^d	
Firms	L^d	$Y, I, \delta K$	$-$	B_f	Short Run
Government	$-$	G	M	B_g	
Prices	$w, \hat{w} = \dot{w}/w$	$p, \hat{p} = \dot{p}/p$	$p_m = 1$	r, p_b	Short or
Expectations	$-$	$\pi^e = \hat{p}^e$	$-$	$-$	Medium Run
Stocks	L^s	K	M	$B = B_f + B_g$	
Growth	$\hat{L} = \dot{L}/L$	$\hat{K} = \dot{K}/K$	$\hat{M} = \dot{M}/M$	$\hat{B} = \dot{B}/B$	Long Run
		$\hat{Y} = \dot{Y}/Y$			

coherent integration and proper implications. Our findings in this book will be that instability of the steady-state position is much more likely than the opposite and that – on this basis – more or less complex persistent fluctuations of quantities and prices are implied around (or also below) their steady-state positions by way of institutional or behavioral extrinsic nonlinearities far off the steady state. To approach such issues the modeling framework for the sectors and markets laid out in Table 1.1 will underpin our analysis.

This scheme of three interacting sectors on the two real and the two financial markets is to be supplemented with behavioral assumptions for the demand and supply schedules of the various agents of the model that then allow the short-run position of the economy (its temporary equilibrium) to be determined before its medium- and long-run evolution is considered, as indicated in the lower part of Table 1.1. The next chapter will do just this from the short- and the medium-run points of view by combining short-run Keynesian IS-LM analysis with medium-run Phillips curve and inflationary expectations dynamics.

References

Asada, T., Chiarella, C., Flaschel, P. and R. Franke (2003): *Open Economy Macrodynamics: an Integrated Disequilibrium Approach*. Heidelberg: Springer.

Barro, R. (1990): *Macroeconomics*. New York: Wiley and Sons.

Blanchard, O. and S. Fischer (1989): *Lectures on Macroeconomics*. Cambridge, MA: The MIT Press.

Blanchard, O. (2006): *Macroeconomics*. London: Pearson Prentice Hall.

Barro, R. and X. Sala-i-Martin (1995): *Economic Growth*. New York: McGraw Hill.

Blanchard, O. (2003): *Macroeconomics*. New York: Prentice Hall.

Chiarella, C. and P. Flaschel (2000a): *The Dynamics of Keynesian Monetary Growth: Macro Foundations*. Cambridge, UK: Cambridge University Press.

Chiarella, C., Flaschel, P., Franke, R., and W. Semmler (2009): *Financial Markets and the Macroeconomy. A Keynesian Perspective*. London: Routledge.

Chiarella, C., P. Flaschel, G. Groh, and W. Semmler (2000b): *Disequilibrium, Growth and Labor Market Dynamics: Macroperspectives*. Berlin: Springer.

Dornbusch, R. and S. Fischer (1994): *Macroeconomics*. New York: Mc Graw-Hill.

Dornbusch, R., Fischer, S. and R. Startz (2002): *Macroeconomics*. New York-Sydney: Mc Graw-Hill.

Dutt, A. (1990): *Growth, Distribution, and Uneven Development*. Cambridge: Cambridge University Press.

Flaschel, P. (1993): *Macrodynamics*. Bern: Peter Lang.

Flaschel, P. (2009): *The Macrodynamics of Capitalism: Elements for a Synthesis of Marx, Keynes and Schumpeter*. Heidelberg: Springer.

Frisch, H. (1983): *Theories of Inflation*. Cambridge, UK: Cambridge University Press.

Frisch, H. and F. Hof (1982): A textbook model of inflation and unemployment. *Kredit und Kapital*, 14, 159–179.

Gale, D. (1983): *Money: In Disequilibrium*. Cambridge: Cambridge University Press.

Goodwin, R.M. (1967): A growth cycle. In: C.H. Feinstein (ed.): *Socialism, Capitalism and Economic Growth*. Cambridge, UK: Cambridge University Press, 54–58.

Jones, H.G. (1975): *An Introduction to Modern Theories of Economic Growth*. London: Thomas Nelson & Sons.

Keynes, J.M. (1936): *The General Theory of Employment, Interest and Money*. New York: Macmillan.

Mankiw, N.G. (1994): *Macroeconomics*. New York: Worth Publishers.

Marglin, S. (1984): *Growth, Distribution, and Prices*. Cambridge, MA: Harvard University Press.

Okun, A.M. (1970): *The Political Economy of Prosperity*. Washington, D.C.: The Brookings Institution.

Romer, D. (1996): *Advanced Macroeconomics*. New York: McGraw-Hill.

Rose, H. (1967): On the non-linear theory of the employment cycle. *Review of Economic Studies*, 34, 153–173.

Sargent, T. (1987): *Macroeconomic Theory*. New York: Academic Press.

Solow, R. (1956): A contribution to the theory of economic growth. *The Quarterly Journal of Economics*, 70, 65–94.

Turnovsky, S. (1995): *Methods of Macroeconomic Dynamics*. Cambridge, MA: The MIT Press.

2 Neglected textbook results

IS-LM-PC inflation dynamics

In this chapter, we investigate the properties of the standard IS-LM-P(hillips) C(urve) textbook model and show that they are quite different from what is usually presented in models of this basic Keynesian type, for example in treatments such as Dornbusch and Fischer (1994, 1998), Mankiw (1994), Blanchard (2006) and Romer (1996). As compared with later chapters, we do not yet consider supply side dynamics from an advanced point of view, but only static markup pricing in combination with a textbook expectations augmented money wage Phillips Curve, which means that the real wage is kept constant during the cycles generated by the model. We also do not yet have factor growth included in the model and thus no capacity effect of investment in particular. Rational expectations, based on the assumption of myopic perfect foresight, here still imply the breakdown of the Keynesian demand-driven business cycle and still give the extreme result that the economy is always sitting in the steady state, with a consequent ineffectiveness of monetary and fiscal policy.

2.1 Feedback channels and stability issues

This chapter[1] reconsiders a prototype IS-LM-PC (Investment Saving-Liquidity preference Money supply-Philips Curve) textbook model of Keynesian output and interest rate determination coupled with wage, price and inflationary expectations inertia, similar to the one of Dornbusch and Fischer (1994, 1998), and indeed of various other macroeconomic textbooks that include sections on AS-dynamics (Aggregate Supply-dynamics).[2] These textbook models seem to imply that the features of such dynamics by and large support the monetarist propositions for the medium and the long run (in particular on the global asymptotic stability of the private sector, see appendices A1, A2 and A4 to this chapter), and thus appear to restrict the validity of Keynesian assertions solely to the short run.

---

1 This chapter is based on and extends work by Flaschel and Groh (1996, Ch.4, 1998), Chiarella, Flaschel, Groh and Semmler (2000, Ch.6), and Asada, Chiarella, Flaschel and Franke (2003, Ch.1) towards a complete analysis of the IS-LM-PC model of these earlier works.
2 See Blanchard (2006) for another prominent and recent example of this type of model.

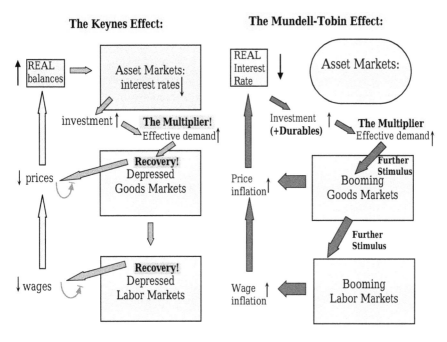

Figure 2.1 The Keynes-effect and the Mundell-Tobin feedback chains (during deflationary and inflationary episodes, respectively).

We first show that this is not true if the IS-LM part of the model is taken as it is formulated in Dornbusch and Fischer (1994, 1998) – as well as in all other textbooks that include this type of analysis – as far as its medium-run dynamical features are concerned. This is simply due to the joint working – both through the real rate of interest channel – of the so-called Keynes effect and the so-called Mundell(-Tobin (1975)) effect, where the latter is however generally neglected when the now traditional type of PC-dynamics (Phillips Curve-dynamics) is added and investigated (since it produces results in the standard textbook models that are not considered desirable). The two effects just mentioned can be illustrated – here for deflationary pressure both on the market for goods and for labor – as shown in Figure 2.1.

In the left-hand side of Figure 2.1[3], we illustrate the working of the Keynes-effect which basically says that falling wages and prices will increase real liquidity on the financial markets which tends to increase the demand for interest bearing assets. This in turn improves the investment demand on the market for goods and thus via the multiplier process the level of economic activity and employment

---

3 Note that the left-hand figure indicates that the fall in wages and prices must come to an end in this situation (with periods of rising prices and wages – not shown – in between).

whereby the fall in wages and prices is checked. Eventually, during this process, wages and prices will start rising again back to their equilibrium level, i.e. the Keynes-effect, though quite involved with respect to the markets concerned, may be able to restore full-employment again and may thus overcome the adverse shock that led to the initial fall in wages and prices. With regard to the Mundell-Tobin-effect, though working through the same channel, it operates in such a way that the expected real rate of interest, is on the one hand more direct, but on the other hand destabilizing. An expected increase of the rate of deflation will (the nominal interest rate now being given) increase the expected real rate of interest and thus exercise a negative influence on investment and on economic activity which may lead to further increases in deflation and thus an accelerating downturn of the economy.

The dynamics resulting from the joint working of the Keynes- and the Mundell-Tobin-effects is currently, and with respect to deflationary processes indeed considered as being, potentially of destabilizing type – in contrast to what is assumed in the older textbook literature – since it is definitely not viable. The model therefore is not yet completely defined if the zero bound for the nominal rate of interest is approached (see Section 2.7).

Such problematic consequences are, however, completely bypassed in for example Dornbusch and Fischer (1994, 1998) though they clearly state in an appendix to their Chapter 16 that their dynamic aggregate demand (AD) must include expected inflation as an item or determinant. They therefore seem to consider this omission to be of secondary importance under normal circumstances, whereas we will demonstrate in this chapter that quite the contrary will be the case.

In Blanchard (2006), the same result is achieved by the very arrangement of the chapters of that book, where PC-dynamics is treated before the real rate of interest is introduced into investment behavior in the place of the originally only nominal one. Inflationary expectations and their role in the wage–price spiral are therefore discussed before they are introduced into the investment behavior of the employed model, which of course results in the same – generally misleading – stability scenario as in the earlier analysis of Dornbusch and Fischer (1994, 1998) that we present in Appendix A2 of this chapter.[4]

IS-LM-PC dynamics proper – where expected inflation is not ignored in its impact on aggregate demand – is more often nonviable than viable and therefore

---

4 In their eighth edition, see for example the Australian edition of Dornbusch *et al.* (2002), these authors have rearranged the sequence of topics of their earlier editions in the spirit of Mankiw's (1994) macroeconomic textbook where the long run and the theory inflation are treated before aggregate demand issues are considered in depth. This seems to suggest that the theory of inflation is basically a supply-side issue which – as this chapter shows – it is not. This is also obvious once the modern treatment of interest rate policy rules is taken into account where a demand-side orientation is, at least implicitly, definitely present.

not yet completely defined.[5] We thus go on in this chapter and add to them a very basic nonlinearity, based on the empirical observation that the money wage Phillips curve used in such models cannot be linear in the large. Using as an example a simple kinked Phillips curve in the place of the linear one then adds on the one hand viability to the model for a large set of its parameter values and initial conditions and allows on the other hand for persistent business fluctuations when the steady state of the model is locally repelling and thus totally unstable with respect to the original dynamics.

There is a special case of the model where there is a continuum of stable steady states below natural employment at zero inflation, namely when the money supply is constant and wages do not fall in the resulting depression. Such a situation, on the one hand, prevents the economy from getting into a deflationary spiral that leads to its collapse, but, on the other hand, it does not possess a means that leads the economy out of the depression back to normal employment.

This, however, becomes possible when the money supply is growing, since this will generally lower the rate of interest and thus raise economic activity without any change in the wage and price level as long as this depressed situation persists. Depending on the size of the growth rate of the money supply the economy thereby returns more or less slowly to normal employment (and beyond!). It now depends on the speed of adjustment of inflationary expectations whether this ends in a convergence back to the 'natural employment' rate steady state or in a persistent cycle around it or – if monetary growth is too fast – in an unbounded inflationary boom that can only find its end when full-employment ceilings and turning points in aggregate demand are introduced into the model.

Prudent inflationary policy thus helps the economy out of its Keynesian depressions without causing accelerating upward instability, but it cannot prevent the occurrence of persistent business fluctuations if the characteristics of the private sector are of the assumed type. We thus find IS-LM-PC dynamics proper has only little to do with the globally asymptotically stable monetarist model of inflation, stagflation and disinflation that holds sway in the literature.

Taken together, we in fact allow in this chapter for two possible outcomes or different views on the working of modern market economies on the macrolevel. These indeed give rise to very different macrodynamic implications, even on the standard IS-LM-PC textbook level of macrodynamic model building as compared with the monetarist treatment of the Phillips Curve (PC) mechanism, in the monetarist baseline model. The basic, systematically destabilizing, feedback chains of this standard framework are simply ignored or – if taken note of – restricted to short discussions of basically comparative static type (e.g., on the adverse effects of deflation, as in Blanchard, 2006, p.408) or solely put into

---

5 This has already been demonstrated in terms of a critical condition in Tobin (1975). His work has initiated a number of further contributions – that still remain largely ignored – the most interesting of which being Groth (1993) and Scarth (1996, Ch.4); see also the literature that is quoted in Groth's work.

exercises (e.g., on 'destabilizing' price volatility, Romer, 1996, p.239), in the desire to always obtain convergence back to the steady state when the economy is not subject to external shocks. By contrast, we show in this chapter that such destabilizing feedback mechanisms form an integral part of any proper Keynesian IS-LM-PC analysis, in periods of inflation indeed even more than in periods where the threat of deflation is experienced. The relevance of these latter results can eventually, however, only be decided by an empirical analysis concerning the parameter sizes of the model for certain historical episodes and specific countries.

Generally ignored in this context is the fact that indeed even in the still dominant Keynesian IS-LM approach of the textbook literature there is not at all support for the Frisch paradigm on the exogeneity of the causes of persistent business cycle fluctuations.[6] Were the textbooks to really derive the consequences of their IS-LM temporary equilibrium analysis of output and interest determinations in their interaction with the contemporary presentations of the process of wage–price inflation (augmented by adjusting inflationary expectations), they would in general indeed arrive at an endogenous explanation of persistent business fluctuations in real activity and inflation.

Such fluctuations arise on the one hand from the generally ubiquitous local instability of the full-employment position of the given model, but are bounded on the other hand by at least one important institutional nonlinearity in money wage formation,[7] given (here in stylized form) by a kink in the money wage Phillips curve that implies (significant) upward wage flexibility and (strong) downward wage rigidity.[8] It will be shown that the combination of local instability of the steady state[9] with downward wage rigidity is able to create (see Section 2.6) persistent economic (real and nominal) fluctuations already on the deterministic level of analysis and can thus explain the existence of business fluctuations without any need to introduce recurrent outside shocks. Such shocks, when added, may modify the cycle and thus add to its descriptive relevance, but not really to its substance if account is taken of the fact that large shocks are rare on the macroeconomic level.

---

6 In contrast to most other textbook treatments of IS-LM dynamics, we stress in the present book the role of prominent locally destabilizing Keynesian feedback channels and the way they can be tamed by important extrinsic behavioral nonlinearities that keep the dynamics bounded. Exogenous shocks may come in later, but will not modify the fluctuations generated by the deterministic part of the models fundamentally with respect to phase lengths and amplitudes. This issue – and the calibration of our deterministic models to stylized facts of the business cycle – is pursued further in Chiarella, Flaschel and Franke (2005). In the present book, we primarily stay on the theoretical and qualitative level and thus do not pursue any further the empirical debate on the validity of the Frisch (1933) paradigm.

7 This mechanism, know as the kinked money wage Phillips curve, has been extensively analyzed in the work of some of the authors; see Chiarella, Flaschel, Franke and Semmler (2006) for various examples.

8 This mechanism had been already asserted to exist by Keynes (1936).

9 Which is to some extent an empirical issue and need not hold at all times or in all countries.

The resulting dynamic IS-LM-PC analysis indeed can handle both situations, the well-known Frisch (and Slutzky) paradigm and the less well-known Keynes (and Kalecki) paradigm[10] (as well as their synthesis),[11] depending in particular on the size of the adjustment speed parameters of wages and of inflationary expectations. This chapter therefore arrives – with a totally conventional and still very restrictive model type – at conclusions that provide a minimum framework for a modern theory of the business cycle.

In the next section, we present a detailed, but standard presentation of the traditional IS-LM model, here still supplemented by a simple horizontal aggregate supply schedule. Sections 2.3 and 2.4 then show that a traditionally specified dynamics of aggregate supply allows for various types of local behavior around the steady state, while the global considerations of Sections 2.5 and 2.6 will show that such IS-LM-PC dynamics is never globally stable and – if not locally asymptotically stable – will often give rise to persistent fluctuations in a corridor around the interior steady state. This occurs when the model makes use of the important asymmetry in the assumed money wage Phillips curve, here for simplicity given by strict downward money wage rigidity.

There are further bounds that need to be investigated for the IS-LM-PC dynamics considered in this chapter. On the one hand, there is the full-employment ceiling where all labor supply is in fact employed, where inflation would accelerate without any bound – if there is no downturn in aggregate demand due to forces not yet included in the model. On the other hand, there is an obvious floor to the nominal rate of interest, the zero interest bound, that is currently receiving a lot of attention in the literature, to be considered together with the full-employment ceiling in Section 2.7.

Section 2.8 extends our traditional IS-LM-PC approach to current formulations of monetary or interest rate policy rules, which use so-called Taylor rules in the place of traditional LM analysis. We show that the stability of the economy can be dramatically improved depending on the interest rate policy rule chosen by the central bank. Section 2.9 concludes. In three appendices, we finally provide examples that show that mainstream representations of Keynesian IS-LM-PC analysis often just miss the essential points of this analysis and thus do not really grasp the full potential of this not at all dated, though surely still underdeveloped approach.[12]

10 See again Frisch (1933), Slutzky (1937) and Keynes (1936, Ch.22), Kalecki (1935) for the original sources behind these two views on business cycle theory.
11 See Keynes (1936, Ch.22) and the appendices to this chapter.
12 In appendix A2 of this chapter, we consider the IS-LM-PC model of Dornbusch and Fischer (1994, 1998) – and indirectly also Blanchard's (2006) analysis of the medium-run – and show that it does not provide a correct representation of their Keynesian IS-LM analysis augmented by a conventional type of wage–price dynamics. See, however, Blanchard (2006, p. 408) for basically comparative-static considerations of the adverse effects of price deflation and Romer's (1996, p.239) exercise 5.15 on destabilizing price flexibility, to be considered in appendix A2 of this chapter.

2.2 Instantaneous real-financial market interaction

A standard approach to Keynesian IS-LM analysis (including a horizontal AS-schedule), in fact the one of Dornbusch and Fischer (1994, 1998), is given by the following 14 equations. These equations list everything that is assumed by this approach and can be easily condensed into 2 equations, representing goods and money market equilibrium or subsequently to a single AD curve and a trivial AS-curve, as shown in Figures 2.2 and 2.2.

$$\text{Consumption Function; } C = C(Y) = c(Y - \delta K - T), \ c \in (0,1), \quad (2.1)$$

$$\text{Investment Function; } I = I(i) = i_0 - i_1(i - \pi^e), \ i_0, i_1 > 0, \quad (2.2)$$

$$\text{Government Expenditure; } G = const., \quad (2.3)$$

$$\text{Goods Market Equilibrium; } Y = C + I + \delta K + G, \quad (2.4)$$

$$\text{Money Demand; } M^d/p = kY + h_0 - h_1 i, \ k, h_0, h_1 > 0, \quad (2.5)$$

$$\text{Money Market Equilibrium; } M = M^d, \quad (2.6)$$

$$\text{Walras' Law of Stocks; } 0 \equiv M^d - M + p_b(B^d - B), \quad (2.7)$$

$$\text{Bond Price; } p_b = 1/i, \quad (2.8)$$

$$\text{Employment; } L^d = Y/x, \quad (2.9)$$

$$\text{Potential Output; } Y^p = y^p K, \quad (2.10)$$

$$\text{NAIRU output level; } \bar{Y} = x\bar{L} < Y^f = xL, \quad (2.11)$$

$$\text{Nominal Wages; } w \quad \text{given in the short-run,} \quad (2.12)$$

$$\text{The Price Level; } p = (1+a)wL^d/Y = (1+a)w/x, \quad (2.13)$$

$$\text{Inflationary Expectations; } \pi^e \quad \text{given in the short-run.} \quad (2.14)$$

We assume in this model type standard consumption and investment functions, depending respectively on disposable income and the expected real rate of interest in the usual way. Government expenditures and taxes are given exogenously and the given capital stock depreciates with a given rate. Money demand is a positive function of economic transactions and a negative one of the nominal rate of interest. We assume that both the goods market and the money market clear at all times. Walras Law of Stocks allows us to ignore either the bonds or the money market. We have fixed proportions in the assumed production technology and assume given wages, given labor supply, given markups in pricing and finally given inflationary expectations.

The IS-LM diagram shows the position of demand constrained equilibrium output Y_o and the corresponding equilibrium rate of interest i_o. Equilibrium output is here assumed to be below full-employment output $\bar{Y}$ and full capacity

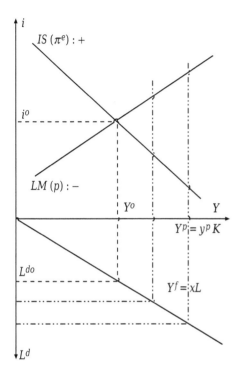

Figure 2.2 The IS-LM-diagram, Mundell-Tobin instability and the labor market (Y^p, Y^f potential and absolute full-employment output).

utilization output Y^p, that is we do not yet consider the topic of supply bottlenecks here. Our many assumptions shown in the foregoing section thus boil down to a simple graphical representation of this Keynesian short run equilibrium position, in fact the standard one of basic textbook approaches. Note, however, that accelerating inflation shifts the LM-curve to the left and – via changing expectations – the IS-curve to the right and thus not imply on the present level of the investigation a definite answer to the question of whether inflation loses momentum through shrinking economic activity (a dominant Keynes effect) and gains further momentum through increases in economic activity (a dominant Mundell-Tobin effect).

This situation moreover still has to be confronted with the supply side of the model as shown in Figure 2.3. Firms have been assumed to supply (below the capacity limits or their natural rate output levels) all demanded output with no change in output prices and thus have a horizontal supply schedule (based on given wages, given productivity and a given markup on unit wage costs). Equilibrium output thus remains here completely demand side determined and can be derived in this diagram by the intersection of the aggregate demand curve AD with the

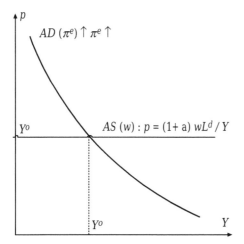

Figure 2.3 The Mundell-Tobin effect in the AD–AS diagram corresponding to the IS-LM-model given by (2.1)–(2.14).

horizontal aggregate supply curve, with the aggregate demand curve obtained in the usual way from IS-LM by varying prices and thus real balances.

Accelerating inflation shifts the AS-curve upwards and the AD-curve to the right (in the case of adapting expectations) and thus of course again gives no clear result of whether macroeconomic activity will be increasing or decreasing and may give further momentum to or provide a break for the ongoing inflationary process. Dynamic analysis has therefore to be used in order to decide whether the Keynes- or the Mundell-Tobin effect will determine the overall outcome and thus whether the economy is subject to stabilizing forces or not.

The result of this short run Keynesian theory of output and interest rate determination can be expressed algebraically in very simple and condensed terms, by means of the following two reduced form equations for these two equilibrium variables:

$$Y = a_0 + a_1 m + a_2 \pi^e, \quad m = M/p \quad a_1, a_2 > 0, \tag{2.15}$$

$$i = b_0 - b_1 m + b_2 \pi^e, \quad m = M/p, \quad b_1.b_2 > 0. \tag{2.16}$$

Equations (2.15) and (2.16) state that the equilibrium output rate Y is a positive function of real balances m, via the Keynes-effect, and also a positive function of expected inflation π^e, via the Mundell-Tobin-effect, while the equilibrium interest rate depends positively on the price level and thus negatively on real balances and positively on expected inflation, giving rise to a partial crowding out mechanism. Inflation is thus bad for economic activity, while expected inflation is good for it. This establishes to feedback channels that work in opposite directions and which must therefore be analyzed analytically in order to derive conditions under which one of them becomes the dominant.

In the foregoing discussion, we have assumed that the reader is familiar with this model type and its comparative statics. We will use the implications of this short run determination of output, interest and employment in the remainder of this chapter in condensed form only, as shown before, and thus in fact will not need all the parameters of the aforementioned model explicitly.

2.3 Medium-run IS-LM-PC dynamics

Solving the IS and LM equations of the preceding section for the IS-LM equilibrium Y and i provides us with the representation of these equilibrium values as

$$Y = \frac{-c(T + \delta K) + i_0 + i_1(m - h_0)/h_1 + i_1\pi^e + \delta K + G}{1 - c + i_1 k/h_1}$$

$$= a_o + a_1 m + a_2\pi^e, \tag{2.17}$$

$$i = \frac{k[-c(T + \delta K) + i_0 + i_1\pi^e + \delta K + G] + (1 - c)(h_0 - m)}{(1 - c)h_1 + i_1 k}$$

$$= b_o - b_1 m + b_2\pi^e. \tag{2.18}$$

We stress that the model so far has been a completely linear one which indeed allows for the explicit solution shown. Equation (2.17) summarizes the linear influence of real balances and expected inflation on output and gives formal expression to the working of the Keynes-effect (whereby falling money wages imply falling prices and thus a rightward shift of the LM curve which lowers the interest rate and increases output and the rate of employment) and the working of the Mundell-Tobin-effect (whereby increasing inflationary expectations lower the expected real rate of interest for each given nominal rate and thus shift the IS curve to the right thereby increasing output and the nominal rate of interest). This is the essence of the model of the short run that is used by Dornbusch and Fischer (1994, 1998) which they should use as a basis of their subsequent wage–price dynamical analysis. We have the Keynes-effect ($a_1 > 0$) of price level, wage level or real balances changes of the preceding section, but – due to the standard textbook formulations of the investment equation – also the so-called Mundell-Tobin-effect ($a_2 > 0$) of inflationary expectations π^e on aggregate economic activity.[13] The wage–price and inflationary expectations dynamics added to this traditional approach to income, employment and interest determination is also a

---

13 This effect is only mentioned in an appendix to Chapter 16 in Dornbusch and Fischer (1994/98) and neglected otherwise which, however, is not possible in their model where investment depends on the expected real rate of interest in a nonseparable way.

fairly traditional one and given by

$$\pi = \hat{p} = \hat{w} = \beta_w(Y - \bar{Y}) + \pi^e, \tag{2.19}$$

$$\dot{\pi}^e = \beta_{\pi^e}(\pi - \pi^e). \tag{2.20}$$

We have a NAIRU (Non-Accelerating-Inflation Rates of Unemployment) type, expectations augmented money wage Phillips curve which is transformed into a price-Phillips curve by the assumption of markup pricing with respect to average labor costs. This Phillips curve is supplemented by a backward looking scheme of adaptive expectations which in the case of the price level is of course a much more meaningful assumption than it would be with respect to behavior on the financial markets.

The following reduced form wage–price and inflationary expectations dynamics is based on the IS-LM theory of employment and the two building blocks for inflationary dynamics just considered which are identical to the ones used in the monetarist baseline model discussed in the preceding chapter. This baseline model is obtained here by just assuming $a_o, a_2 = 0$, while the IS-LM-PC analysis in Dornbusch and Fisher (1994, 1998) is based on $a_2 = 0$ which still provides the implications of the monetarist baseline model. Blanchard (2006, p.305) assumes instead static inflationary expectations ($\pi^e = const.$) which – since this suppresses the role of the Mundell effect – is just another way to ensure the validity of the monetarist baseline model and its implications. Thus we have

$$\hat{m} = \mu - \beta_w(Y - \bar{Y}) - \pi^e, \tag{2.21}$$

$$\dot{\pi}^e = \beta_{\pi^e}(\pi - \pi^e) = \beta_{\pi^e}\beta_w(Y - \bar{Y}), \tag{2.22}$$

$$Y = a_0 + a_1 m + a_2 \pi^e, \quad a_1, a_2 > 0. \tag{2.23}$$

Equations (2.21)–(2.23) constitute the full model of the standard textbook approach to medium-run wage–price dynamics. There are however two important distinctions with respect to its standard treatment in this literature:-

- The model is nonlinear (in the most basic way that is possible).[14]
- The model is based on $a_2 > 0$: a positive Mundell-Tobin-effect and not on $a_2 = 0$ as in Dornbusch-Fischer (1994/96), due to the assumptions on investment behavior made by these authors.

Of course, eq. (2.23) has to be inserted into eqs. (2.21)–(2.22) in order to obtain an autonomous differential equations system of dimension 2. We shall see that

---

14 Such a nonlinearity is also plausible in the Dornbusch and Fischer model discussed in Appendix A2 of this chapter, since the use of $\mu - \pi$ suggests that $\hat{Y}$ should have been used on its left hand side in the place of $\dot{Y}$ (which also would have restricted the dynamics of the preceding section to the right hand part of the phase plane).

this proper IS-LM-PC dynamics has only little in common with the dynamics considered in standard textbooks like that of Dornbusch and Fischer (1994, 1998).

2.4 Multiple steady states and local stability analysis

This section summarizes some local properties of the dynamics (2.21)–(2.22) around their two steady state positions, which are not difficult to obtain and which are therefore not proved in this section.[15] These propositions show that there is a need for global stability analysis in this traditional IS-LM-PC framework, a need that is totally ignored in the dominant textbook literature. The discussion of inflation dynamics in this type of literature is therefore generally erroneous and misleading.

Proposition 2.1 (Steady state analysis) There are two steady states of the dynamical system (2.21)–(2.22), one that is interior to the right half phase plane and thus economically meaningful

$$m_1^o = (\bar{Y} - a_o - a_2\mu)/a_1 > 0, \quad \pi_1^{eo} = \mu$$

and one that lies on its boundary:

$$m_2^o = 0, \quad \pi_2^{eo} = (\bar{Y} - a_0)/a_2 > 0$$

which – as an attractor – can be economically meaningful nevertheless ($Y^o = \bar{Y}$ in both cases).

Proposition 2.2 (Local stability analysis)
1. The Jacobian of the dynamical system (2.21)–(2.22) at the interior steady state is given by

$$J_1^o = \begin{pmatrix} -\beta_w a_1 m_1^o & -(\beta_w a_2 + 1)m_1^o \\ \beta_{\pi^e}\beta_w a_1 & \beta_{\pi^e}\beta_w a_2 \end{pmatrix}$$

which implies $\det J_1^o = \beta_{\pi^e}\beta_w a_1 m_1^o > 0$ (so there is no saddle point) and

$$trace\, J_1^o = \beta_w(\beta_{\pi^e} a_2 - a_1 m_1^o), \quad a_1 = \frac{i_1/h_1}{1-c+i_1k/h_1}, a_2 = \frac{i_1}{1-c+i_1k/h_1}$$

which is positive (implying local instability) if and only if $\beta_{\pi^e} - a_1 m_1^o/a_2 > 0$ holds true.[16]

---

15 We assume for the remainder of the chapter that $a_0 < \bar{Y}$. This assumption is not difficult to justify from the underlying IS-LM model.
16 See also Scarth (1996, Ch.4) in this regard where it is stressed that this type of instability – based on the Keynes-effect (represented by a_1) vs. the Mundell-Tobin-effect (represented by a_2) – is

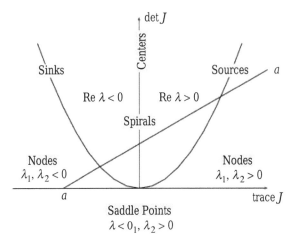

Figure 2.4 Local stability properties of the dynamical system (2.21)–(2.22) in terms of eigenvalues and matrix J characteristics.

2. The dynamical system (2.21)–(2.22) displays saddle point behavior around the border steady state (det $J_2^o < 0$) as is obvious from the Jacobian at this steady state, which is given by

$$J_2^o = \begin{pmatrix} \mu - \beta_w(a_o + a_2\pi_2^{eo} - \bar{Y}) - \pi_2^{e0} & 0 \\ \beta_{\pi^e}\beta_w a_1 & \beta_{\pi^e}\beta_w a_2 \end{pmatrix} = \begin{pmatrix} \mu - \pi_2^{e0} & 0 \\ \beta_{\pi^e}\beta_w a_1 & \beta_{\pi^e}\beta_w a_2 \end{pmatrix},$$

since $\mu < \pi_2^{eo}$ due to the negative slope of the $\dot{\pi}^e = 0$ isocline, see the next section.

The local results of this proposition for the interior steady state can be summarized graphically in the trace $J - \det J$ space as in Figure 2.4.[17] In Figure 2.4, the half line aa is given by

$$\beta_{\pi^e} \rightarrow (\text{trace } J(\beta_{\pi^e}), \det J(\beta_{\pi^e})), \quad \beta_{\pi^e} \in [0, \infty).$$

Note that the half line aa is parameterized by $\beta_{\pi^e} \in [0, \infty)$, since it is a relationship between trace $J(\beta_{\pi^e})$ and $\det J(\beta_{\pi^e})$. At the point of intersection with

independent of the degree of wage flexibility and solely dependent on the size of the parameter that characterizes the adjustment of inflationary expectations. This will change, however, if the Rose real-wage effect is taken into account, see Chapter 5 and Chiarella and Flaschel (2000, Ch.4) in this regard.

17 Note that the parabola separates cyclical behavior (above) from monotonic behavior (below).

the horizontal axis $\beta_{\pi^e} = 0$ and β_{π^e} increases to infinity as one moves to the right along the line *aa*.

The figure shows that the local dynamics will be characterized (in this order) by stable nodes, stable foci, unstable foci and unstable nodes as the parameter β_{π^e} is increased from zero to ∞. These results are due to the so-called Mundell-Tobin-effect which in contrast to the stabilizing Keynes-effect is destabilizing: increases in inflationary expectations stimulate the economy (ceteris paribus) and thus give a further push to already existing inflation, since they decrease the real rate of interest and thus increase effective demand. For sufficiently fast inflationary expectations, this positive feedback mechanism then overcomes the negative feedback provided by the Keynes-effect (as shown in Proposition 2.2 and the figure accompanying it).

Proposition 2.3 (Degenerate loss of stability)   The dynamical system (2.21)–(2.22) undergoes a degenerate Hopf-bifurcation (with a zero Liapunov coefficient) at the critical adjustment speed

$$\beta_{\pi^e}^H = a_1 m_1^o / a_2 = (\bar{Y} - a_o - a_2 \mu)/a_2 = \pi_2^{eo} - \pi_1^{eo}$$

of inflationary expectations.

Increasing the rate of money supply growth does therefore decrease the critical value of β_{π^e} in a one to one fashion. We also note that $\beta_{\pi^e}^H = (\bar{Y} - (1-c)(T + \delta K) - i_0)/i_1 + h_o/h_1 - \mu$ holds with respect to the underlying parameters of the model (if $T = G$ is assumed for simplicity). An increase in interest rate sensitivity in both investment or money demand thus for example decreases the bifurcation value at which the system losses its stability.

This proposition can easily be shown by means of the (complicated) formula for Liapunov coefficients supplied in Lux (1995) for dynamical systems of dimension 2, due to the very simple nonlinearity in the considered dynamics. These dynamics therefore do not fulfill the sufficient criteria for so-called super- or subcritical Hopf-bifurcation. We do not go into the details of this calculation here, as this result only says that we have to use other tools to get information on possible limit cycle behavior of the trajectories of these dynamics. Nevertheless it is important to know that the present very basic type of nonlinearity of the model does give rise solely to border type local bifurcations.

These are the local results that can be obtained for the dynamical system (2.21)–(2.22) and which show that this system is already locally far more complex than the model treated in Section 3 of Chapter 1 whose outcome is normally considered as representative for inflation dynamics of monetarist as well as of Keynesian type. In the following representations of these local results, we will denote the second (border) steady state by S_o and the interior steady state simply by (m_1^o, π_1^0).

2.5 Global analysis I: basic phase diagram properties

We approach the global features of the dynamical system (2.21)–(2.22) by means of its phase diagram, the isoclines of which are given by

$$\dot{m} = 0: \quad \pi^e = \frac{\bar{Y} - a_0 - a_1 m + \mu/\beta_w}{a_2 + 1/\beta_w} \quad \text{(and} \quad m = 0), \tag{2.24}$$

$$\dot{\pi}^e = 0: \quad \pi^e = \frac{\bar{Y} - a_0 - a_1 m}{a_2}. \tag{2.25}$$

Note that the first isocline includes the vertical axis of the phase plane, which is an invariant domain of the dynamics and thus cannot be left or crossed by them. Furthermore, the interior part of the $\dot{m} = 0$ isocline is an attractor with respect to the isolated movements of real balances m, and the $\dot{\pi}^e = 0$ isocline is a repeller with respect to the isolated movements of inflationary expectations π^e. On this basis, the phase portrait of the dynamics can be drawn as shown in Figure 2.5. We take note of the fact that the intersection of the $\dot{\pi}^e = 0$ isocline with the vertical axis determines the second steady state of the dynamics and that the positions of the two isoclines do not depend on the adjustment speed of inflationary expectations. Note that we leave the topic of floors and ceilings to the dynamics shown in Figure 2.5 to later sections of this chapter.[18] Note also that the upward inflationary and downward deflationary spirals that are possible in the unrestricted phase diagram shown in Figure 2.5 are discussed in Blanchard (2006, Ch.22, 23) under the heading 'pathologies'. Their occurrence is simultaneously prevented in the following by the assumption of downwardly rigid money wages (and replaced by the generation of persistent business fluctuations).

Note also that the areas above (respectively below) both isoclines show opposite directions with respect to the evolution of real balances and inflationary expectations and thus characterize the parts of the phase space where booms come to an end or where recovery starts again, respectively, since the downward arrows between the isoclines are clearly related to recessions or even depressions (rising i, falling π^e and $Y < \bar{Y}$) and the upward arrows between the isoclines with booms (falling i, rising π^e and $Y > \bar{Y}$). Note furthermore that the saddle point S_o of the dynamics gives rise to a separatrix S to the right of it (as shown). The depicted phase portrait, and numerical simulations of the dynamical system, see Figure 2.6, suggest the following proposition about the global properties of the dynamics of the system (2.21)–(2.22).

---

18 We briefly note that the $\dot{m}$-isocline is horizontal for $\beta_w = \infty$ and identical with the other isocline for $\beta_w = 0$.

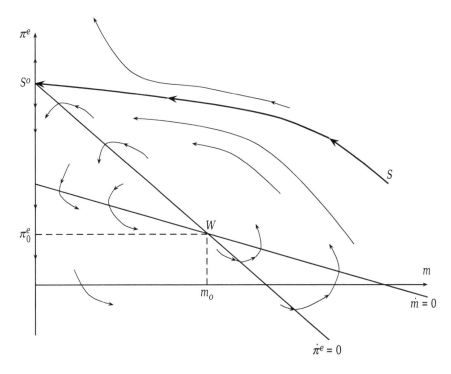

Figure 2.5 The phase portrait of the dynamical system (2.21)–(2.22).

Proposition 2.4 (Global stability features)
1. The dynamics of (2.21)–(2.22) are never globally stable.
2. If locally stable (at the interior steady state) the dynamics exhibit corridor stability (which generally seems to end with the separatrix S shown in Figure 2.5).
3. If locally unstable the system is (always) totally unstable (that is all trajectories either approach $(0, +\infty)$ via the saddle path dynamics shown in Figure 2.6 (a process of accelerating inflation) or give rise to a deflationary spiral which never ends.[19]
4. If $a_1 = 0$ holds (no Keynes-effect due to the liquidity trap) the system is explosive on both sides of the $\dot{\pi}^e = 0$ isocline and thus also exhibits a never ending deflationary process.

19 Contrast this with the monetarist baseline model of Chapter 1 where we have global asymptotic stability and trivial turning points in economic activity under all circumstances, see Also Appendix A1 of this chapter. Note furthermore that upper turning points may disappear if the Mundell-Tobin effect becomes too strong relative to the Keynes-effect, while lower turning points may disappear close to the liquidity trap (where the Keynes-effect disappears).

Since the model is too often not yet a viable one and thus not yet of economic interest, we do not prove the assertions of this proposition here (which to some extent are obvious, but which with respect to the size of the corridor and with respect to the total instability asserted under point 3 are not so obvious). Furthermore, the treatment of processes of inflation and deflation is far too symmetric still to be convincing with respect to actual economic dynamics. Finally, the situation of corridor stability is analyzed in detail and from a different angle (with more nonlinearities involved) in Groth (1993) and thus is already a known phenomenon in medium run IS-LM dynamics.

Figure 2.6 shows for the case of an unstable steady state (for $\beta_{\pi^e} = 0.2 > \beta_{\pi^e}^H$ and the parameter values $a_0 = 0.75, a_1 = 1, a_2 = 1, \bar{Y} = 0.95, \mu = 0.05, \beta_w = 0.5)$[20] the separatrix that in this case (as well as in all other cases of this type) connects the interior steady state W with the border steady state S_o (see Figure 2.5). This figure suggests, as already asserted in Proposition 2.4 – that the dynamics is globally unstable in all theses cases, since each trajectory that locally departs from the steady state (and which exhibits a lower turning point) will have the same format as the shown stable manifold S of the point S_o, but will wind around it and the point W until it is above this separatrix S for all times (where it then 'converges' to $(0, +\infty)$). Therefore the dynamics for $\beta_{\pi^e} > \beta_{\pi^e}^H$ are never bounded or viable and so must be augmented by forces that will keep the trajectories in an economically meaningful range.

Note that the dynamics need not be cyclical around the steady state as has been shown in Section 4. We conjecture that the separatrix will be strictly falling throughout (towards $(+\infty, -\infty)$) in those cases where the steady state is locally asymptotically stable in which case it cannot bend backwards as in the unstable situation considered in Figure 2.6. We assume in the following that the locally unstable case shown in Figure 2.6 is the relevant one for our further analysis of the dynamics and thus depart from the textbook tradition which normally focuses on an asymptotically stable steady state (or saddle-point stability of the rational expectations type).

Further simulations of the dynamics have shown that orbits will be closed at the Hopf-bifurcation point below the separatrix S and that the system has a considerable potential to recover from deflationary processes and accompanying depressions (if a_1 is not close to zero) which, however, may be very deep. Yet, the next section will show that we need not worry about the possibility of no lower turning point of the dynamics since there is an important institutional constraint in actual economies which is still missing, in the analysis of this section, and which prevents downward instability when added to the considered dynamics. Astonishingly, this simple institutional fact will also provide upward stability to situations that were previously purely explosive (as the one shown in Figure 2.6).

---

20 Note that the Hopf bifurcation value is in this situation given by $\beta_{\pi^e}^H = 0.15$.

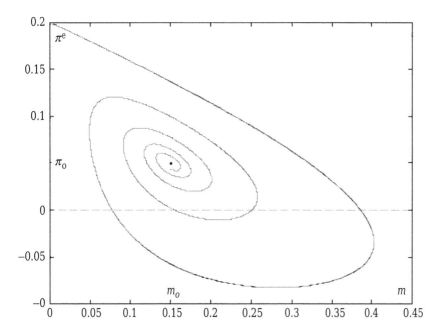

Figure 2.6 The separatrix S of (2.21)–(2.22) that connects the two steady states in the case of local instability of the interior steady state.[21]

2.6 Global analysis II: kinked money wage Phillips curves

Empirical observations, for example already in Phillips (1958), suggest that the Phillips curve cannot be linear, but will become fairly horizontal for large unemployment rates (low employment rates). This asymmetry has been reconsidered in a paper by Hoogenveen and Kuipers (2000) for several European countries, and has led there to the result that there is even a floor to money wage evolution at around a two percent level of wage inflation. This result may, however, be due to the strong nonlinearity in the type of function they assume as given for their parametric estimation, which forces a flattening of the money wage PC at low wage inflation rates. Chen and Flaschel (2005) have reconsidered this issue and found some evidence of a zero floor to money wage inflation in the case of the US economy. There may, however, be data problems for a detailed investigation of

---

21 We thank Thorsten Pampel for the calculation of Figure 2.6 as an application of a program he has developed for the numerical determination of stable manifolds of fixed points and more general situations; see Pampel (2001). The parameters for this simulation are those discussed in the previous paragraph. We briefly note here that the separatrix has a convex shape in the case of local stability of the steady state and thus must be linear in the border case, see Chiarella, Flaschel, Groh and Semmler (2000, p.20) for a numerical exploration of this case.

such a nonlinearity, since wages can be viewed in many indirect ways, not clearly measured in the wage compensation per hour.

Akerlof (2002), in his Nobel lecture, argues forcefully for the empirical fact of downward nominal wage rigidity and points to a number of recent empirical or experimental studies that strongly support this view. There are important policy consequences of this downward wage rigidity for monetary policy (see Akerlof (2002) and also Hoogenveen and Kuipers (2000)) which give the question of whether there exists a downward floor to money wage deflation significant weight in the macroeconomic literature on Keynesian disequilibrium analysis, as also the following analysis of our IS-LM-PC dynamics will clearly show.

We shall consider here a stylized, but not implausible example for the foregoing empirical observations, namely (in the absence of labor productivity growth) a kinked money wage Phillips curve that is given as

$$\hat{w} = \max\{\beta_w(Y - \bar{Y}) + \pi^e, f\},$$

where f is a given real number close to zero. We will explain and investigate the case $f = 0$ in the following qualitative analysis and leave the more general case of $f \neq 0$ for later numerical investigations of the model.

The kinked Phillips curve states that money wages behave as in the preceding section if their growth rate is positive, but stay constant if they are falling in the previous situations. So now there is thus no wage deflation possible. Of course, the kink could be smoothed or some wage deflation could be allowed for, but this will not significantly alter the conclusions of this section. We consider the kinked Phillips curve to be a much better description of reality than the one that is linear throughout.

The immediate consequence of this new form of the Phillips curve is that system (2.21)–(2.22) now only applies when $\beta_w(Y - \bar{Y}) + \pi^e \geq 0$ holds while it must be replaced by

$$\hat{m} = \mu - f, \tag{2.26}$$

$$\dot{\pi}^e = \beta_{\pi^e}(f - \pi^e), \tag{2.27}$$

when $\beta_w(Y - \bar{Y}) + \pi^e < f$.[22] We thus have now a system of differential equations which is only continuous (C^0), but which can be made a smooth system in an obvious way as already discussed. We call this system the patched system while we refer to the earlier dynamics as the unpatched one.

To explore the difference to the previous unpatched dynamics, let us consider the case $\mu = 0, f = 0$ first. In this case, there is the following simple, but radical modification of the dynamics (2.21)–(2.22) which now exhibits a continuum of depressed steady states as shown in Figure 2.7.[23]

---

22 The two systems are identical at the border line $\hat{w} = \beta_w(Y - \bar{Y}) + \pi^e = f$.
23 Note that there now exists a third steady state solution S_1 and that all points between W and S_1 are also steady states – due to the form of the lower part of the patched dynamical system for $\mu = 0$.

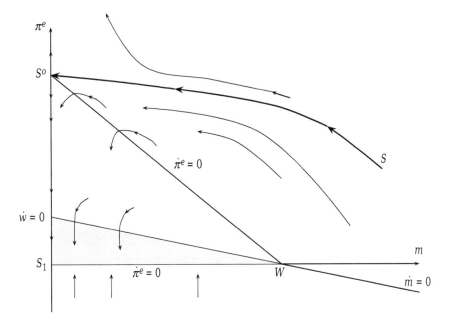

Figure 2.7 Stable Keynesian depressions, due to monetary policy that is too strict.

Depending on the size of the cycle in the inflationary region we end up (if we start below the separatrix S) in a stable depressed situation of less than 'natural' employment where wages and prices and inflationary expectations have become stationary and where there is no possibility of recovery since money wages do not fall by assumption in such a case. Downward money wage rigidity therefore causes stable depressions (of any possible size), but now of course excludes the possibility of deflationary spirals and economic collapse.

The foregoing result demonstrates in this simple textbook framework the consequences of Akerlof's (2002) observations on a monetary policy that is too tight in the presence of the radically kinked money wage Phillips curve. Is there anything that can improve the depicted situation and lead the economy back to normal employment (or beyond)? The simple answer to this question is that government should allow for (some) steady state inflation by allowing for a positive growth rate of the money supply in such an economy with a stationary steady state. This lifts the $\dot{m} = 0$ isocline above the $\dot{w} = 0$ locus and alters Figure 2.6 as discussed next (if the depicted assumption on the separatrix S holds).

As Figure 2.8 shows the domain below the separatrix S (in the non-negative orthant) is now an invariant domain D_o, that is no trajectory which starts in it can leave it. Note also that the domain below the $\dot{w} = 0$ isocline is governed by the dynamics (2.26)–(2.27) in the place of those of the preceding section. This, however, only alters the direction of the dynamics on the horizontal axes,

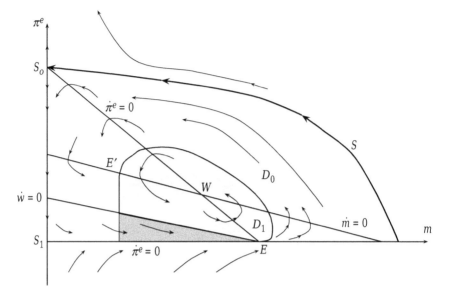

Figure 2.8 Persistent Keynesian business fluctuations in the case of moderate money
supply growth.

which is now also an isocline ($\dot{\pi}^e = 0$) of the patched dynamics (up to point E).
Note furthermore that the trajectory which starts at E (horizontally), followed up
to point E' and then continued vertically down the m-axis, also defines an invariant
domain D_1 of the patched dynamics which moreover is attracting for all trajectories
in the interior of D_o. We thus have that all orbits in D_o (with the exception of the
ones on the vertical axis) are either inside of D_1 or enter the domain D_1 (from its
left). This implies the following proposition.

Proposition 2.5 (Persistent fluctuations and corridor stability):[24]
1. There exist exactly three steady states, S_o, S_1, W, for the patched dynamics if
   $\mu > 0$ holds. These steady states are connected by the $\dot{\pi}^e = 0$ isocline.
2. Assume that the interior steady state W is locally repelling (high values of
   β_{π^e}). Then every trajectory in D_o converges to a persistent cycle around W
   (and in D_1).
3. Assume that the interior steady state W is locally attracting (for sufficiently
   low values of β_{π^e}). Then every trajectory in D_o either converges to the steady
   state W or a persistent cycle around it.

---

24 We add here that output and employment will stay positive along these dynamics if $a_0 > 0$ is
assumed and that the underlying IS-LM model can be specified in such a way that the nominal rate
of interest will also stay positive; see Section 2.8 on this matter.

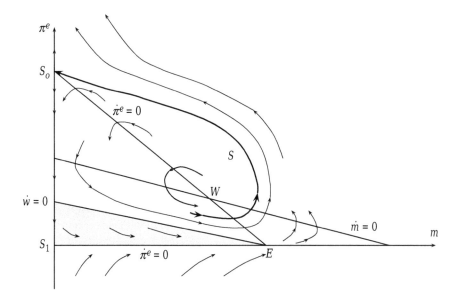

Figure 2.9 Strong monetary growth and the tendency towards hyperinflation (output ceilings neglected).

Proof An immediate implication of the Poincaré -Bendixson theorem, see Hirsch and Smale (1974), if one makes the kink in the Phillips curve smooth.

Remark We expect that the limit cycle of Figure 2.8 is uniquely determined and that all trajectories in situation 2 of Proposition 2.5 will in fact converge to the steady state (but we cannot prove this here). We stress that the introduction of a floor to the money wage dynamics is already sufficient to enforce lower as well as upper turning points for the considered dynamics for deviations from the steady state that stay in a certain corridor.

Note that the aforesaid proposition also holds if the separatrix S does not cut the horizontal axis at all as long as it does not bend backward.[25] There are, however, situations where the above proposition does not apply and they are of the type shown in Figure 2.9.

  In this figure, the separatrix of the unpatched system cycles around W before it approaches point S_o in a monotonic fashion, but it does not cut the horizontal axis

---

25 It has been observed from numerical simulations that the separatrix S will connect the points S_o, W in a cyclical or monotonic way in the case of local instability.

on the way.[26] This situation is the more likely the larger the policy parameter μ becomes. Increasing the speed of adjustment of inflationary expectations sufficiently (which makes them approach the horizontal axis below $\dot{w} = 0$ nearly vertically) then produces a situation where trajectories can escape from below S and thus end up in an inflationary spiral as in the unpatched system.

Proposition 2.6 (Unbounded inflationary dynamics)   Consider a situation where the separatrix S that connects the points W and S_o in the unpatched system does not cut the horizontal axis (based on a growth rate of the money supply that is sufficiently high). Then there exist adjustment speeds of inflationary expectations, chosen sufficiently high, where there is again no bound to inflation in the present specification of the model.

This situation implies that expansionary monetary policy used to overcome the stable depressions shown in Figure 2.7 must be exercised with care if it is desired not to end up in such an inflationary boom. Note that the possibility of such an occurrence implies that the model is still incomplete in this case and should be further revised in order to allow for the existence of absolute full-employment ceilings (which, however, cannot be done here due to space limitations).

2.7 Numerical and empirical aspects of IS-LM-PC analysis

We first present in this section some numerical phase plots of the phase space results shown in the preceding sections. These plots are meant to give numerical support to what has been derived analytically. At first, we will make use of the chosen state space variables in the plots shown. For empirical or policy analysis, it is, however, necessary (later on) to use the variables output Y, as a measure of the employment rate e or the unemployment rate $1 - e$, both in combination with the actual instead of the expected inflation rate as state variables of the model (in terms of which the model is however not so easily represented).

The Figures 2.10 show top left the situation of strictly downward rigid money wages ($f = 0$) and the stable limit cycle that is thereby created (and approached both from the inside and the outside). In the top right figure, we have relaxed the floor to money wage deflation from zero to 0.4 percent and can see the kink when this floor to wage deflation becomes operative. In both cases, we have a money supply growth rate of 5 percent. Setting this rate and the floor to money wage deflation both to zero then gives the situation on the bottom left figure which clearly corresponds to what is shown in Figure 2.7, while the figure on the bottom right corresponds to Figure 2.8, since we have removed the kink to the Wage PC and assumed a growth rate of the money supply of 30 percent in this repelling situation towards the occurrence of monotonic hyperinflation (see case A). In this figure bottom right, we also show a situation where money demand has been made

---

26 Note that the separatrix does not exist in the domain where the kink in the Phillips curve is operative.

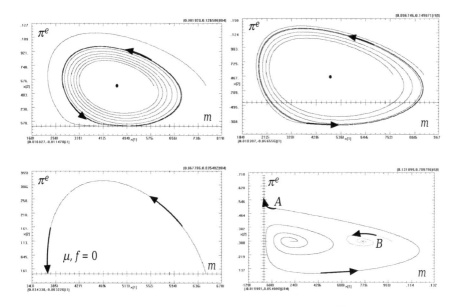

Figure 2.10 Some numerical explorations of the IS-LM-PC model.[27]
Top-left: $f = 0, \mu = 0.05$: stable limit cycle (with the assumed floor being operative), Top-right: $f = -0.04, \mu = 0.05$: stable limit cycle (with deflationary episodes), Bottom-left: $f = 0, \mu = 0$: shock-dependent stable depressions, Bottom-right: $f = -100, \mu = 0.3$: the trajectory towards hyperinflation (no output ceilings), $f = -100, \mu = 0.3$, and $h_1 = .02$: back to convergence via a strong Keynes-effect.

very inelastic and where therefore a strong Keynes effect is in operations, implying that the explosive trajectory in this figure is replaced by the convergent one in its right hand side (see case B).

We show in Figure 2.11 some eigenvalue diagrams for the parameter set of Figure 2.10 (where the steady state is locally unstable) with respect to some important parameters of the 2D dynamics. The role of the Mundell-Tobin effect and the Keynes-effect are shown in the top two panels of Figure 2.10 where the maximum of the real parts of the eigenvalues are shown as function of the speed parameter β_{π^e} of inflationary expectations and the interest rate sensitivity parameter h_1, respectively, and where we clearly see the destabilizing role of the first parameter and the stabilizing role of the second one (since the Keynes-effect becomes the stronger the smaller the parameter h_1 becomes). From the trace of the Jacobian of the dynamics at the steady state, see Proposition 2.2, we

27 The baseline parameter set for the simulations in this section is: $m = 649.980$, $\pi^e = 0.100$ (steady state initial values), $\beta_w = 0.2, \beta_{\pi^e} = 0.5, Y = 1, \mu = 0.05, c = 0.75, K = 1, T = .3, G = .3$, $k = 0.1$, $\delta = 0.1, i_0 = .2, i_1 = 0.1, h_0 = 0, h_1 = 0.1, f = 0$.

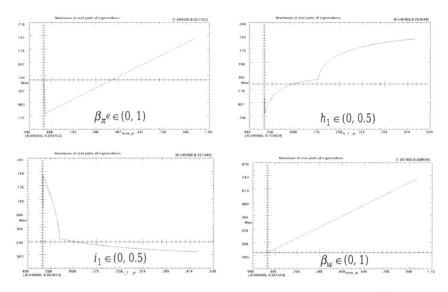

Figure 2.11 Eigenvalue diagrams for critical parameters of the 2D dynamics.[28]

obtain, however, that increasing wage flexibility (through increasing β_w) cannot bring stability back to the system, once we have a positive trace, which is clearly mirrored by the eigenvalue diagram in the bottom right panel. Real wages and thus wage flexibility do not yet play a role in the considered 2D dynamics, in contrast to what we will consider in the next chapter of the book. In the bottom left panel, we finally see that the parameter i_1 – which appears in front of the real rate of interest in the investment function – can be stabilizing if increased. Although an increase in i, makes both the Keynes- and the Mundell-Tobin effects stronger, it does so in an asymmetric way, depending on the shape of the effective demand function, and is thus not comparable to what happened in the case of wage flexibility considered in the bottom right-hand panel.

In the top panel of Figure 2.12, we show alternative limit cycles corresponding to a range of alternative floors in the evolution of money wages. As this figure shows, stricter floors to money wages strictly reduce the size of the cycle and thus make the economy less volatile, contrary to what is thought by those who advocate downwardly flexible money wages. Of course, these comparisons assume a give growth rate of the money supply, which is five percent in the situation currently being considered and thus still considerably higher than the highest floor to money

---

28 The parameters are as in Figure 2.10. Note with respect to Figure 2.11 that a situation close to a
   vertical LM-curve is the stable one as far as the Keynes-effect is concerned and that the parameter
   i_1 when increased is stabilizing though it works both on i and π^e in a seemingly symmetric fashion.
   Moreover, wage flexibility is of no help here in stabilizing the dynamics, due to fact that real wages
   are given by markup pricing.

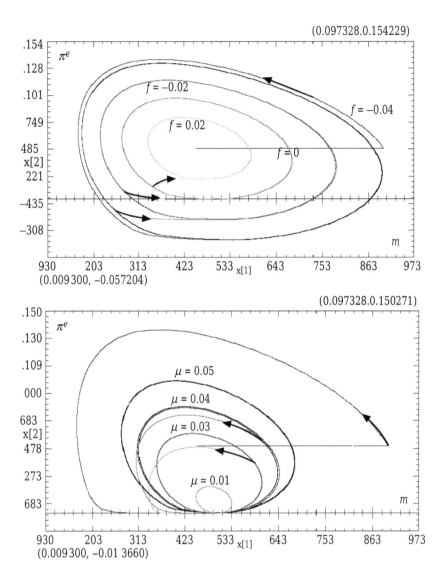

Figure 2.12 The role of floors to money wage flexibility. The upper figure shows the impact of various f for $\mu = 0.05$. The lower figure shows the strictness of the conduct of monetary policy by displaying the effect of various μ for $f = 0$ (the arrows indicate the switches that take place when the parameters are changed as described above).[29]

29 Parameters as in Figure 2.9.

wage inflation. This growth should not be approached by this floor, since stable depressions will then again be the outcome. This is so since the recovery phase becomes lost in such a situation, and the deepness of the depression will then depend on size of the shocks that hit the economy, in contrast to what holds for the limit cycle situations shown.

In the bottom panel of Figure 2.12, we assume a given zero floor to money wage inflation. We here vary the growth rate of the money supply and see that the limit cycle generated by the model is smaller the smaller is the growth rate of the money supply. Taking both panels of Figure 2.12 into consideration we arrive at the conclusion that the rate of money supply growth and the floor to money wage inflation (or deflation) should be close to each other in order to reduce the volatility of the economy, but not too close in order to still allow for economic recovery from the recession the economy then undergoes. These changes are not accompanied by significant lengthening of the cycle as one might expect from a more restrictive monetary policy (where restrictive is measured by the distance between the money supply growth rate and the wage floor).

In order to compare the outcome of the dynamical system, and in particular the persistent oscillation it may generate, it is helpful to use the (un-)employment rate and the rate of inflation as the state variables in the place of m and π^e due to their importance for economic policy considerations and due to the fact that their actual movement is easier to understand, explain and to compare with empirical observations than is the case for the original state variables. However, the dynamic outcomes are not easily investigated analytically in terms of the state variables Y and π in contrast to the situation based on the state variables m and π^e where only a growth rate term prevented the application of linear techniques of analysis.

There is, however, a linear relationship between the two sets of state variables which is easily obtained from the reduced form equations

$$Y = a_o + a_1 m + a_2 \pi^e, \quad \pi = \beta_w (Y - \bar{Y}) + \pi^e = \beta_w (a_o + a_1 m + a_2 \pi^e - \bar{Y}) + \pi^e.$$

These two equations imply in matrix notation that

$$\begin{pmatrix} Y \\ \pi \end{pmatrix} = \begin{pmatrix} a_1 & a_2 \\ \beta_w a_1 & \beta_w a_2 + 1 \end{pmatrix} \begin{pmatrix} m \\ \pi^e \end{pmatrix} + \begin{pmatrix} a_o \\ \beta_w (a_o - \bar{Y}) \end{pmatrix} \equiv A \begin{pmatrix} m \\ \pi^e \end{pmatrix} + b.$$

On the basis of this equation system we obtain by taking time derivatives

$$\begin{pmatrix} \dot{Y} \\ \dot{\pi} \end{pmatrix} = A \begin{pmatrix} \dot{m} \\ \dot{\pi}^e \end{pmatrix} = A \begin{pmatrix} (\mu - \pi) m \\ \beta_{\pi^e} \beta_w (Y - \bar{Y}) \end{pmatrix}, \qquad \det A > 0,$$

with real balances m being given by the IS-LM relationship:

$$m = \frac{Y - a_o + a_2 \beta_w (Y - \bar{Y}) - a_2 \pi}{a_1}, \qquad a_1 \neq 0,$$

that can be inserted into this reformulation of the IS-LM-PC dynamics in order to arrive at a system of differential equations in the state variables Y and π.[30] The dynamical system representation thus obtained is of course again an autonomous system of dimension 2, but more involved with respect to nonlinearities since these results from the insertion of the m expression into the new two laws of motion. It is, however, easy to show that $\det A$ is simply given by a_1 and that the two eigenvalues characterizing this matrix A are both real and positive. The matrix A is therefore invertible and the two steady states of the original dynamics are now given by[31]

$$Y_1^o = \bar{Y}, \pi_1^o = \mu, \quad \text{and} \quad Y_2^o = \bar{Y}, \pi_2^o = (\bar{Y} - a_o)/a_2.$$

Apart from this, the details of the Y, π phase diagram are, however, difficult to obtain, in particular the shape of the $\dot{Y} = 0$ isocline and also the global characteristics of the dynamics compared with those of the nearly linear m, π^e representation (and also the shape of the separatrices belonging to the second steady state which is now in the interior of the (Y, π) phase space).

For the specific kinked Phillips curve

$$\hat{w} = \max\{\beta_w(Y - \bar{Y}) + \pi^e, 0\}.$$

we obtain in the currently considered situation the correspondingly modified equations

$$\pi = 0, \; Y = a_o + a_1 m + a_2 \pi^e,$$
$$\hat{m} = \mu, \; \dot{\pi}^e = -\beta_{\pi^e} \pi^e,$$

as long as $\beta_w(Y - \bar{Y}) + \pi^e \leq 0$ with $Y = a_o + a_1 m + a_2 \pi^e$ holds true and there is a reswitching to the unconstrained dynamics if this condition turns positive again.

We now use the aforementioned variable transformation to actual rates of inflation and unemployment to study briefly the numerics of the dynamics in the phase space of the quantities $1 - e = (Y^f - Y)/Y^f$ and π where we use

---

30 The m equation is obtained by inserting the Phillips curve into the equation $Y = a_o + a_1 m + a_2 \pi^e$. Note here also that the resulting dynamical system is of the general form

$$\dot{Y} = \alpha_o + \alpha_1 \pi + \alpha_2 Y + \alpha_3 \pi Y + \alpha_4 \pi^2, \quad \dot{\pi} = \beta_o + \beta_1 Y,$$

in the case where the kink in the PC is not in operation ($\pi = 0$ otherwise).
31 In the economically meaningful steady state, we have

$$J_1^o = A \begin{pmatrix} 0 & -m_1^o \\ \beta_{\pi^e} \beta_w & 0 \end{pmatrix}, \quad \text{so that} \quad \det J_1^o > 0, \; \text{tr} J_1^o = \beta_w(a_2 \beta_{\pi^e} - a_1 m_1^o)$$

and thus obtain again the same stability results as in the case of the dynamics with the original state variables.

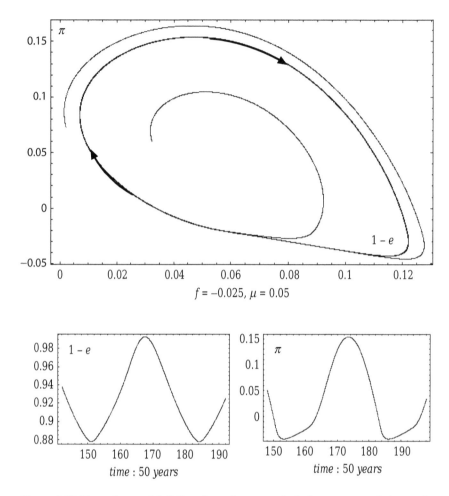

Figure 2.13 Unemployment inflation dynamics: numerical phase space and time series representations of the IS-LM-PC model ($f = -0.025, \mu = 0.05$).

$Y^f - Y$ as a measure of the level of unemployment, here strictly proportional to the unemployment rate due to the assumption of a given labor force and a given number of workhours per worker. Due to what is known about the unemployment inflation dynamics in standard treatments (see Mankiw (1994) for example) we would expect that the model should now show a clockwise rotation in the $1 - e, \pi$ phase space representation.

In Figure 2.13, we show a fifty-years-simulation run for the model and the basic parameter set chosen for it, yet now in the transformed variables, that is in the unemployment rate $1 - e$ and the inflation rate π. The floor to money wage inflation is here assumed to be -2.5 percent. This figure is to be compared with the corresponding empirical plots for the US economy after World War II which is shown in Figure 2.14 for a roughly similar time span of 50 years. Disregarding the business fluctuations in the empirical evolution of the US economy[32] one can see a similar long cycle in both the artificial model economy and the real US economy. This shows that our model, even in its great simplicity and with no time-varying constant parameters over the whole time span, can mirror in an important way certain long run fluctuations in the employment as well as in the inflation rate. It is therefore possible, even with the standard IS-LM-PC textbook model, to explain important regime changes in the interaction of unemployment and inflation for the US-economy in the post World War II period.[33]

2.8 Zero interest rate bounds and full-employment ceilings

In this section, we consider the two remaining bounds to the IS-LM-PC dynamics of this chapter, given by the two facts that the nominal rate of interest cannot become negative, and that (in a closed labor market) the rate of employment can at most become 1. Of course the rate of employment cannot become negative as well, but this is prevented here by assumption, since $Y = a_o + a_1 m + a_2 \pi^e$, $a_o > 0$ cannot become negative in the non-negative orthant of the phase space (where the occurrence of deflation is prevented by the kink in the money wage PC).

Let us first consider the case of a zero nominal rate of interest. According to the IS-LM model considered in Section 2.2 the rate of interest i the qualitative expression

$$i = b_o - b_1 m + b_2 \pi^e, b_o > 0$$

and thus get in the border case $i = 0$ the equation $\pi^e = (b_1 m - b_0)/b_2$, which is an upward sloping line in the considered phase space. Above this line, we always have the full IS-LM equilibrium solutions (since $i > 0$ is then applicable) and below this line, we have that employment is determined by $Y = a_o + a_2 \pi^e$, since the then relevant assumption $i = 0$ just removes the m term from the above IS-LM equilibrium equation (reducing it to a simple IS equation based on the investment function of the form $I = i_o + i_1 \pi^e$).

We now assume in the following discussion that the position of the LM curve in the IS-LM phase space is such that it cuts the horizontal axis to the left of the NAIRU employment rate for the steady state value of real balances considered in Figure 2.7, that is, we assume that deflationary wage pressure (possible only to the left of the point W in Figure 2.7) always occurs before the zero bound for the rate of interest i has been reached (which is reasonable from an empirical perspective).

---

32 These could be caused by systematic variations in the parameter of the model over the course of the cycle, see Subsection 1.1.

33 This result can also easily be checked by making use of the trend term time series of Hodrick-Prescott filtering (with $\lambda = 1600$) which remove the business cycle component from the considered time-series and which, when plotted against each other, give rise to a phase plot very similar to the one shown in Figure 2.13.

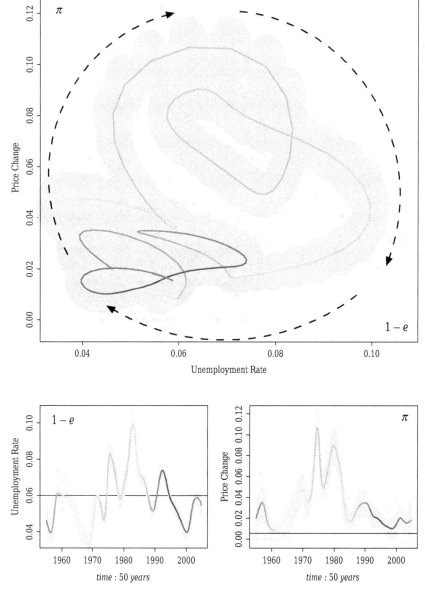

Figure 2.14 Unemployment inflation dynamics: empirical Phase space and time series representations for the US-economy.[34]

34 Unemployment/inflation dynamics (top panel) with an estimated smooth cycle. The grey areas show pointwise confidence regions (see Kauermann, Teuber and Flaschel (2009)). The bottom panels show data plotted against time. The numerical parameters are as before.

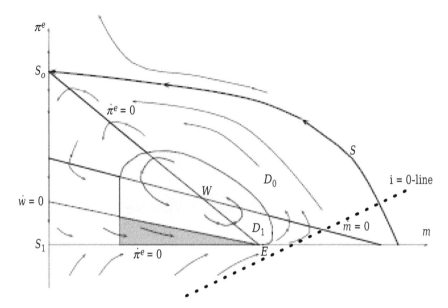

Figure 2.15 Persistent Keynesian business fluctuations above the zero interest rate floor.[35]

The upward sloping zero bound curve in the m, π^e phase space therefore always cuts the horizontal axis to the right of the noninflationary steady state value E as shown in the Figure 2.9 (where W now denotes the steady state value for a given $\mu > 0$). This curve is therefore completely irrelevant as long as it does not cut the domain D_1, which seems to be the likely case (unless there is a shock that moves the economy below the $i = 0$ line to the right of the point E).

There may, however, be parameter constellations where the dynamics enter the critical domain shown in Figure 2.15. As the figure shows this can only happen in that part of the phase space where both m and π^e are rising (where the symbol D_1, characterizing the dark, invariant area of the phase space is in fact situated). The dynamics then undergo the process of phase switching and are then given by

$$\hat{m} = \mu - \beta_w(Y - \bar{Y}) - \pi^e, \tag{2.28}$$

$$\dot{\pi}^e = \beta_{\pi^e}\beta_w(Y - \bar{Y}), \tag{2.29}$$

with

$$Y = a_0 + a_2\pi^e, \quad a_1, a_2 > 0.$$

---

35 This additional floor modifies the attracting domain of the considered limit cycle situation – if at all – only slightly and is thus far less important than the one for money wages in the present model context.

Since these dynamics can only be activated for values of π^e below μ and since we get for $\bar{Y} = a_o + a_2\pi^e$ a value of π^e that is larger than μ (due to the result that $\bar{Y} = a_o + a_1 m_1^o + a_2\mu$), we must have that the foregoing phase switching can only occur for values of Y (in the new dynamics) that are below $\bar{Y}$. The new law of motion for π^e then implies that π^e must be falling, which in turn implies a falling rate of employment Y and thus further declines in π^e and Y which only end when the value zero is reached for inflation and subsequently also for inflationary expectations due to the kink in the money wage Phillips curve. Note that this kink now comes into play below the horizontal line $0 = a_o + a_2\pi^e - \bar{Y}$ at another horizontal line $0 = \beta_w(a_o + a_2\pi^e - \bar{Y}) + \pi^e$ which is situated above the m axis and only relevant in the domain $i \leq 0$.

Furthermore, once the economy is caught in the aforesaid dynamics we not only have falling inflationary expectations throughout, but also always rising real balances as long as the monetary authority sticks to the growth rate $\mu > 0$ underlying the situation considered in Figure 2.9. This outcome follows, since the two terms in brackets in the expression

$$\hat{m} = (\mu - \pi^e) + \beta_w(\bar{Y} - Y) \tag{2.30}$$

are both positive and will remain positive in the situation under consideration and will thus lead to ever increasing balances without any effect on the nominal rate of interest, which remains zero throughout. The monetary authority will therefore sooner or later replace ineffective monetary growth by a zero growth rate (at the very latest when it holds all bonds) in which case not only inflation and inflationary expectations converge to zero, but also real balanced to a given value where the economy is fixed in a stable depression characterized by $Y = a_0$ and thus, see Section 2.2, by an output level given by the multiplier formula

$$Y = \frac{1}{1-c}(-c(T + \delta K) + i_o + \delta K + G).$$

This situation will remain unchanged as long as the autonomous part of investment and government expenditures stay in place, that is, as long as there is no further deepening of the considered crisis.

The question of course arises as to how the economy can be moved out of the zero interest bound trap, where increasing money supply only shifts the economy horizontally along the m-axis and where (some) wage deflation would only make the depression more severe since investment would then even decline further? The only answer seems to lie in a revitalization of aggregate demand, either through increased scrapping of the capital stock which makes investment in the remaining one more attractive or through increased consumption demand of the government which if sufficiently strong may move the economy back into the IS-LM part of the model above the $i = 0$ line. However, the present approach is still a very restrictive one and thus may not make it worthwhile to consider economic recovery from a zero interest rate bound (which here seldomly appears to become binding) in greater depth.

Let us come next to the full-employment ceiling $Y = 1 > \bar{Y}$ above the so-called NAIRU full-employment level. In this case, the dynamics switch to the following, since there is no way in the present model type to increase the number of the employed in this situation. We in addition assume that firms cannot provide the aggregate demand in the case $Y > 1$ and thus ration consumers or investors or the government with respect to their demand according to some rationing scheme. This excess demand, however, does not change the markup put by firms on average wage costs (in symmetry to the case of depressed situations on the market for goods). The resulting dynamical system is given by

$$\hat{m} = \mu - \beta_w(1 - \bar{Y}) - \pi^e, \tag{2.31}$$

$$\dot{\pi}^e = \beta_{\pi^e}\beta_w(1 - \bar{Y}) > 0, \tag{2.32}$$

with

$$Y = min(1, a_o + a_1 m + a_2\pi^e).$$

We immediately see that expected inflation (following the actual rate with a delay) will now increase without bound, while real balances m will shrink towards zero, since $\mu - \pi^e$ must become, and will remain, negative in such a situation. This process thus will end up in a hyperinflation if nothing else happens in this economy (and if $Y = a_o + a_1 m + a_2\pi^e < 1$ and later $< \bar{Y}$ is not generated endogenously).[36] In addition, the rate of interest i will approach the value $(kxL + h_o)/h - 1$ if all behavioral assumptions remain intact, while the real rate of interest will approach $-\infty$, clearly an indicator that the process will not continue in an undisturbed way. What will happen, however, lies outside the framework given by the equations of the model. It may be that real wages (fixed here by the constant markup on average wage costs) will start rising somehow, it may be that the central bank starts operating very restrictive monetary policies by fixing the nominal interest rate at a very high level, firms may cut down their investment expenditures due to expected significant real interest and / or real wage increases and the government might implement a very restrictive fiscal policy scenario. All this may dampen aggregate demand in such a way that the situation $Y < \bar{Y}$ becomes reestablished, inducing disinflation according to Figure 2.15 and thus a situation where the business cycle starts again towards the direction of lower inflation rates and rising real balances if some monetary growth is again allowed for in this situation. Again, a detailed analysis of these occurrence would demand a more refined model than the one currently under investigation and will thus not be conducted here.

We conclude that floors to nominal interest rates and ceilings to employment rates may cause problems for the working of the dynamics considered in

---

36 We note that the full-employment ceiling is not reached when the separatrix S lies completely below the parallel to the $\dot{\pi}^e = 0$ isocline in the situation considered in Figure 2.15 and that this $Y = 1$ curve will cut this separatrix twice in the opposite case. Note, however, that the movement will not necessarily be along this $Y = 1$ curve, due the switch in the laws of motion that takes place when this curve is reached.

this chapter and which must be overcome by the introduction of appropriate endogenous adjustment mechanisms that give rise to recovery from zero interest rates and that will enforce an upper turning point in the employment rate if the full-employment ceiling comes into play.

2.9 Policy rules for inflation targeting

Fair (2000) has shown that empirical observations may favor a type of Phillips curve that is based on the demand pressure in the market for goods in the place of the labor market, while wages basically follow price inflation with a lag. This is an interesting alternative to the price dynamics considered in this chapter, and could be used to formulate results similar to the ones shown in this chapter for a NAIRU rate of goods market behavior, see also Chiarella, Flaschel, Groh and Semmler (2000, Ch.6) in this regard. Stock and Watson (1997) estimate various types of Phillips curves and find that there is no relationship of Phillips (1958) type, but rather one between the cyclical components of inflation and unemployment. Chiarella and Flaschel (2000, Ch.6), extending work begun in Flaschel, Franke and Semmler (1997), show as in Fair (2000) that there should be two structural equations for money wage and price inflation in any fully specified macrodynamic model of the medium run (and just a simple markup approach to either wages or prices in order get a single law of motion for the rates of inflation characterizing the economy). This, however, in general implies that price level dynamics depend on demand pressure in the market for goods as well as for labor. There is therefore considerable scope for modification of the textbook model considered here as far as stability assertions on inflationary dynamics are concerned. It would indeed be interesting to see what these further aspects imply, on the one hand, for textbook stories and teaching and, on the other hand, for the stability scenarios obtained for these more advanced discussions of wage–price dynamics. We will return to these topics at the beginning of Chapter 5 on the proper Keynesian version of DAS–AD growth. Be that as it may, even the dynamics of the simple model considered in this chapter is far from being well understood both from the perspective of teaching and research, which in this area come very close to each other.

This also holds true for Laxton, Rose and Tambakis's (2000) discussion of the U.S. Phillips curve where they basically use the model presented in this chapter (in a discrete time framework with certain lags and leads). The basic difference between their approach and ours is that they use an interest rate policy rule (a Taylor rule) as a representation of the behavior of the monetary authority. The type of Taylor rule they employ is of the type[37]

$$ i = \pi^e + \alpha_{ip}(\pi^e - \bar{\pi}) + \alpha_{iy}(Y - \bar{Y}), \qquad \alpha_{ip}, \alpha_{iy} > 0. $$

---

37 Note here that standard Taylor rules employ π in the place of π^e which, however, only means that they in fact make use of another (composed) coefficient α_{iy} in the place of the coefficient here used.

This rule states that the central bank sets the (expected real) rate of interest according to the discrepancy that exists between the expected rate of inflation π^e and the target rate $\bar{\pi}$ of the central bank and the deviation of the actual rate of employment from the NAIRE-rate of employment and this in such a way that interest rates counteract what is observed as high or low economic activity and inflation. Of course, money supply must then be accommodated to money demand in order to allow this fixing of the nominal rate of interest. Using this equation in place of the conventional LM equation (which no longer is a binding constraint) in our model of stagflation then gives rise to only one law of motion, namely

$$\dot{\pi}^e = -\frac{\beta_{\pi^e}\beta_w}{1/a_2 + \alpha_{iy}}[\alpha_{ip}(\pi^e - \bar{\pi}) - (i - \pi^e)^o],$$

due to $Y = \bar{Y} - a_2(i - \pi^e - (i - \pi^e)^o)$ as the IS-curve relationship in such a situation. This follows easily by inserting the Taylor interest rate rule into the real rate IS-curve just shown and by solving this equation for the deviation of the employment rate from its NAIRU level. We note the astonishing result which, in contrast to what is found for interest rate smoothing in Proposition 2.7 below, states that an increase in the parameters $\beta_{\pi^e}, a_2, \beta_w$ will now improve the convergence to the steady state, and in particular that the Mundell-effect here works in favor of economic stability.

Employing this particular type of Taylor rule thus implies immediately monotonic global asymptotic stability of the new and single steady state position of the economy (see also Figure 2.10) here given by

$$\pi^{eo} = \bar{\pi} + (i - \pi^e)^o/\alpha_{ip}, \quad Y^o = \bar{Y}, \quad i^o = (i - \pi^e)^o + \pi^{eo},$$

where $(i - \pi^e)^o$ is given by the intersection of the IS-curve

$$Y = \frac{1}{1-c}(-c(T + \delta K) + i_o - i_1(i - \pi^e) + \delta K + G$$

with the NAIRE output configuration $\bar{Y} = \bar{y}\bar{L} < L$. Again, money supply will always be adjusted to money demand in the considered situation and will thus exercise no influence on the dynamics of the model with a Taylor rule in the place of a fixed money supply growth rule.

We note that the steady state value for the inflation rate here is larger than the target of the central bank (which is therefore not achieved) and that this upward deviation from the target becomes the larger (for a positive steady state real rate of interest) the more sluggish the response of the central bank is to the inflation gap $\pi^e - \bar{\pi}$. Therefore an aggressive stance by the central bank is called for to prevent a deviation from its target.

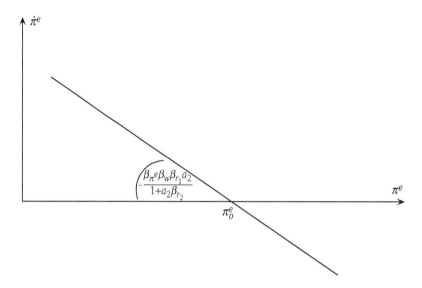

Figure 2.16 Global asymptotic stability for a specific choice of the Taylor interest rate
policy rule.

Next, we observe that adjustment to the long-run inflation rate is faster the
stronger is the adjustment of wages and inflationary expectations, and now the
stronger is the response of the monetary authority to the inflationary gap. There is
therefore some conflict between the level of inflation to be approached and the
speed with which this can be done. Finally, the stronger is the operation of the
Mundell-Tobin effect (the larger the parameter a_2) the faster will the economy
converge to its steady state position, while the opposite holds for the parameter
that characterizes the reaction of the central bank with respect to the output or
employment gap $Y - \bar{Y}$. In sum, we have the result that increasing wage flexibility
(with respect to demand pressure on the labor market), increasing speeds of adjustment of inflationary expectations and also increasing investment sensitivity (with
respect to the real rate of interest) now stabilizes the private sector of the economy,
which is quite the opposite as compared with the working of the economy under
a given money supply growth rule. We thus get the astonishing result that the
destabilizing force of the Mundell-Tobin effect can be completely neutralized and
in fact turned into a stabilizing force by adopting a specific rule for interest rate
formation. This shows that investigations as in Laxton, Rose and Tambakis (2000)
can be usefully related to standard textbook models and can thus be reflected even
on this level with new and interesting insights into economic stability.

Moreover we can achieve the result that monetary policy can reach its
inflationary target $\bar{\pi}$ if the Taylor rule we have employed so far is modified to

$$i = i^o - \bar{\pi} + \pi^e + \alpha_{ip}(\pi^e - \bar{\pi}) + \alpha_{iy}(Y - \bar{Y}),$$

with

$$i^o = (i - \pi^e)^o + \bar{\pi}.$$

If the central bank knows the steady state value of the real and thus of the nominal rate of interest (given its inflation target) it can even avoid any discrepancy between its target and the steady state inflation rate, since we then have

$$\dot{\pi}^e = -\frac{\beta_{\pi^e}\beta_w a_2}{1 + \alpha_{iy} a_2}[\alpha_{ip}(\pi^e - \bar{\pi})],$$

an appropriate adjustment of the steady state inflation rate to the target of the central bank. We note, however, that knowledge of the NAIRU as well as of the real rate of interest that is defined by this NAIRU is required in order to achieve such a result.

In the literature on Taylor rules, one often finds the type of rule given by

$$i^* = i_o - \bar{\pi} + \pi^e + \alpha_{ip}(\pi^e - \bar{\pi}) + \alpha_{iy}(Y - \bar{Y}), \tag{2.33}$$

$$\dot{i} = \alpha_{ii}(i^* - i), \tag{2.34}$$

where the rule considered so far only defines an interest target of the central bank and where there is interest rate smoothing with respect to this target level (with speed α_{ii}). For an infinite adjustment speed $\alpha_{ii} = \infty$, we are back to the situation so far considered. In the opposite case of $\alpha_{ii} = 0$, we have the situation of an interest rate peg, which provides an example of global instability, since there is then only the destabilizing Mundell effect present in the model. The foregoing extended rule therefore provides intermediate situations between global monotonic convergence and global monotonic divergence and thus should allow for a variety of stability scenarios.

Inserting the interest rate target of the central bank into the smoothing law of motion gives as reduced form the law of motion for the nominal rate of interest according to

$$\dot{i} = -\gamma_{ii}(i - i^o) + \gamma_{ip}(\pi^e - \bar{\pi}) + \gamma_{iy}(Y - \bar{Y}), \tag{2.35}$$

with

$$\gamma_{ii} = \alpha_{ii}, \gamma_{ip} = (1 + \alpha_{ip})\alpha_{ii}, \gamma_{iy} = \alpha_{iy}\alpha_{ii}. \tag{2.36}$$

This law of motion for the nominal rate of interest is again at work in an environment where there holds for the private sector of the economy

$$\dot{\pi}^e = \beta_{\pi^e}\beta_w(Y - \bar{Y}), \tag{2.37}$$

$$Y = a_o - a_2(i - \pi^e), \tag{2.38}$$

$$\bar{Y} = a_o - a_2(i - \pi^e)^o, \tag{2.39}$$

which in sum gives a (now linear) system of two independent differential equations. The steady state of theses dynamics is uniquely determined and given by

$$Y^o = \bar{Y}, \quad \pi^{eo} = \bar{\pi}, \quad (i - \pi^e)^o = (a_o - \bar{Y})/a_2, \quad i^o = (i - \pi^e)^o + \bar{\pi}.$$

The long run inflation rate is of course again given by the target rate of the monetary authority since the employment gap and the nominal interest rate gap here reduce to zero in the steady state.

For the isoclines of these linear 2D dynamics we get in this revised Taylor rule setting the two linear curves in the i, π^e phase space given by

$$\dot{\pi}^e = 0 : \quad i = \pi^e + (i - \pi^e)^o, \tag{2.40}$$

$$\dot{i} = 0 : \quad i = i^o + \frac{\gamma_{ip} + \gamma_{iy} a_2}{\gamma_{ii} + \gamma_{iy} a_2}(\pi^e - \bar{\pi}) = i^o + \frac{1 + \alpha_{ip} + \alpha_{iy} a_2}{1 + \alpha_{iy} a_2}(\pi^e - \bar{\pi}). \tag{2.41}$$

We thus obtain the phase diagram representation shown in Figure 2.17 with π^e and i as the state variables of the dynamics. In this representation, we again consider the case of basically monotonic convergence of the trajectories of the dynamics towards their steady state, two features for which we now derive the conditions for their existence. Note with respect to Figure 2.17 that we exclude negative interest rates from occurring. This can be achieved by assuming a floor to the evolution of nominal interest rates in the Taylor rule, or by using in this rule the growth rate of the nominal rate of interest in the place of its time derivative. Note furthermore that we ignore here the kink in the money wage Phillips curve and also the full-employment ceiling for reasons of simplicity.

Proposition 2.7: conditions for – monotonic – convergence
1. The Jacobian of the dynamics of (2.35), (2.37) at the steady state is given by

$$J = \begin{pmatrix} \beta_{\pi^e}\beta_w a_2 & -\beta_{\pi^e}\beta_w a_2 \\ \gamma_{ip} + \gamma_{iy} a_2 & -\gamma_{ii} - \gamma_{iy} a_2 \end{pmatrix}$$

2. We have $\det J = \beta_{\pi^e} a_2 \beta_w (\gamma_{ip} - \gamma_{ii}) > 0$ (no saddle) iff $\gamma_{ii} < \gamma_{ip}$ holds true (which holds, since $\alpha_{ip} > 0$).
3. We have trace $J < 0$ and thus convergence iff

$$\gamma_{iy} > \beta_{\pi^e}\beta_w - \gamma_{ii}/a_2, \quad i.e. \quad \alpha_{iy} > \beta_{\pi^e}\beta_w/\alpha_{ii} - 1/a_2$$

holds in addition.
4. We have finally monotonic convergence to the steady state (real and negative eigenvalues) if the reaction coefficient of the central bank to the employment gap is chosen sufficiently large.

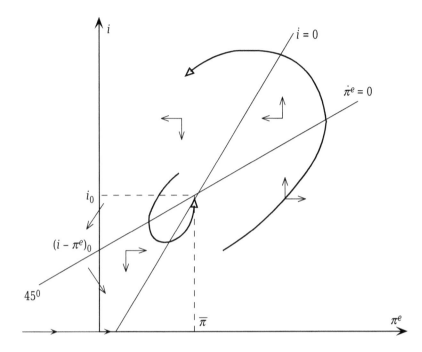

Figure 2.17 Global asymptotic stability for a Taylor interest rate policy rule with $\gamma_{ip} > \gamma_{ii}, \gamma_{iy} > \beta_{\pi^e}\beta_w - \gamma_{ii}/a_2.$[38]

We thus obtain that the central bank's strength of reaction to the output gap (and not at all to the inflation gap) is of central importance for asymptotic stability and also for monotonic convergence towards the steady state of this economy. It seems moreover that the limit case of $\alpha_{ii} = \infty$ cannot be considered as a continuous border case of the situation with some interest rate smoothing unless some further requirements are met. Finally, the destabilizing role of the parameters β_{π^e}, β_w is again of the expected type and not of the strange type we observed in the case with no interest rate smoothing.

2.10 Conclusions

In this chapter, we have shown that there are two omissions in the standard treatment or verbal reflection of IS-LM-PC dynamics from both the economic and the mathematical points of view, omissions that, however, are an integral part

---

38 Note that the slope of the steeper isocline does not depend on the parameter α_{ii}.

of any IS-LM-PC model and crucial for the dynamic implications of this type of analysis. These two components are:

- The necessity of employing a growth law in the formulation of these dynamics (the growth rate $\hat{m}$ of real balances in our formulation of the model.
- The necessity of including the expected rate of inflation into these dynamics if this effect is present in static IS-LM analysis ($a_2 > 0$) because of the assumed investment behavior.

Including a growth rate law of motion has the advantage that it restricts the dynamics to economically meaningful domains.[39] But including the Mundell-Tobin effect of inflationary expectations into aggregate demand behavior gives rise to economic problems as the system is then never globally stable in the economic domain and results in all possible stability scenarios (except saddlepoints) from a local point of view.

The outcome is that these corrected IS-LM-PC dynamics have only limited viability features when based solely on the growth rate nonlinearity. There is, however, a very basic nonlinearity that changes this situation drastically, namely the exclusion of deflationary processes via a kink in the Phillips curve at zero wage inflation. This kink indeed removes (by economic reasoning) the destabilizing Mundell-Tobin effect in the downward direction, since it removes the possibility of a deflationary spiral, and restricts the dynamics to the non-negative orthant ($Y, \pi \geq 0$) of the phase space (which we have used in a later reformulation of the dynamics). Furthermore, this kink also provides stability with persistent fluctuations in situations where the original system gave rise to upward inflationary spirals. However, there is still no total stability possible in these revised dynamics, but only corridor stability around the interior steady state position of the economy (while too high inflation will always lead to hyperinflation as the model is formulated). In addition, high growth rates of the money supply (imprudent monetary policy) may quickly lead the economy out of deep depressions, but may also imply the danger that the system then loses its stability corridor and ends up in an inflationary spiral from all starting positions (apart from the steady state position itself).

These are quite new aspects for the textbook treatment of IS-LM-PC dynamics, even compared with recent textbooks such as Blanchard (2006), but of course not new to those who have worked on the Tobin (1975) model of recessions and depressions, see Groth (1993) and Chiarella and Flaschel (2000) for a summary of this literature. By and large we consider this outcome as more Keynesian than monetarist, in contrast to the purely monetarist outcome of an economically illegitimate mathematical simplification of IS-LM-PC analysis to be discussed in

---

39 As shown in the appendices to this chapter, the dynamics are then globally asymptotically stable with a vertical $\pi^e = 0$ isocline.

an appendix to this chapter (the case of a vertical LM-schedule). We note here that the model needs further embellishment concerning the zero bound for nominal interest rates and the full-employment ceiling $Y = 1$. Both cases have been treated here only within the narrow framework of the given IS-LM-PC dynamics, but deserve further development in extended forms of these dynamics. The results of this chapter are indeed not limited solely to such textbook models, but can be usefully contrasted and integrated with even the most recent discussions of the wage–price dynamics of market economies.

The problem with Neoclassical Synthesis approaches to monetary macro-dynamics – in particular on the textbook level – quite generally is that they disintegrate short-run (IS-LM) from medium-run monetarist analysis (and also both from long run Solovian analysis) which leads them to stability propositions with regard to all these three runs, which, however, do not remain valid if the three runs are properly integrated. Keynesian analysis proper would instead add growth dynamics to the integrated IS-LM-PC approach considered in this chapter and should from this integrated perspective – as we will show in later chapters of the book – also take account of further feedback channels in such an environment, or also the eventually destabilizing effects of inventory adjustments if goods market disequilibrium is allowed for or a destabilizing wage–price spiral when certain conditions on adjustment speeds of wages versus prices and marginal propensities to consume and to invest hold. All these issues will be considered in detail in Part II, once we have expanded the IS-LM-PC analysis considered here to a dynamic AS–AD model that is no longer subjected to the deficiencies of the Neoclassical Synthesis type of integrated AS–AD dynamics. In Part II, however, we consider the AS-side of the economy in much more detail and in even further extended versions of Keynesian DAS–DAD (Disequilibrium AS–Disequilibrium AD) dynamics, and also consider there again the role of monetary policy from today's perspective that here has only been touched upon.

From the mathematical point we finally add that we have applied in this chapter (including the appendices that follow) most of the tools of the mathematical appendix of this book already in the still very basic frameworks of the present chapter, local and also global asymptotic stability in the case of the monetarist baseline model (given by a vertical LM-curve in this chapter) in particular by help of so-called Liapunov functions, and local (in-)stability by means of the Routh-Hurwitz conditions (and the Hopf-bifurcation theorem) and global stability in case of local instability by means of the Poincaré -Bendixson theorem. These tools for investigating local or global stability will find to some extent further application throughout the book and, in appropriately modified form, also for dimensions higher than 2. From the mathematical point of view we also observe that there is no easy way to discuss the cases where wage adjustment speeds or the speed of adjustment of inflationary expectations go to infinity. Both cases would establish $\pi^e = \hat{p}$ in the limit as an algebraic condition, implying that the economy is then always in the steady state, which is extremely different from its behavior before this limit case is reached and therefore not really convincing from the mathematical point of view (where nearly perfect inflationary expectations and perfect ones –

with respect to the short-run – should broadly speaking give rise to closely related economic dynamics and not a change in dynamic behavior that is completely at odds with the case of a very fast adjustment of inflationary expectations). We here, however, only state that such limit cases are subtle to treat and thus are not only a matter of the mathematical manipulation of the considered model types.

We stress in closing that the present analysis is a highly simplified one, since it does not allow for cyclical movements of the real wage. This will change in the ensuing AD–AS analyses of Keynesian macrodynamics, yet, at first in a conventional way that is, however, not consistently formulated and also not compatible with empirical observations. In the variant of this model type, we start from in Chapter 5 we succeed however in removing these failures from the conventional AD–AS model type (by making it a model of AD–D(isequilibrium)AS type.

References

Akerlof, G.A. (2002): Behavioral macroeconomics and macroeconomic behavior. *American Economic Review*, 92, 356–394.

Asada, T., C. Chiarella, P. Flaschel, and R. Franke (2003): *Open Economy Macrodynamics: An Integrated Disequilibrium Approach*. Heidelberg: Springer.

Blanchard, O. (2006): *Macroeconomics*. New York: Prentice Hall, Chapters 6–9.

Chen, P. and P. Flaschel (2005): Keynesian dynamics and the wage–price spiral: Identifying downward rigidities. *Computational Economics*, 25, 115–142.

Chiarella, C. and P. Flaschel (2000): *The Dynamics of Keynesian Monetary Growth: Macro Foundations*. Cambridge, UK: Cambridge University Press, Chapter 4.

Chiarella, C., P. Flaschel, and R. Franke (2005): *Foundations for a Disequilibrium Theory of the Business Cycle: Qualitative Analysis and Quantitative Assessment*. Cambridge, UK: Cambridge University Press.

Chiarella, C., P. Flaschel, G. Groh, and W. Semmler (2000): *Disequilibrium, Growth and Labor Market Dynamics: Macro Perspectives*. Berlin: Springer.

Chiarella, C., P. Flaschel, R. Franke, and W. Semmler (2006): *Quantitative and Empirical Analysis of Nonlinear Dynamic Macromodels Contributions to Economic Analysis* (Series Editors: B. Baltagi, E. Sadka and D. Wildasin). Amsterdam: Elsevier.

Crouch, R. (1972): *Macroeconomics*. New York: Harcourt Brace Jovanovich.

Dornbusch, R. and S. Fischer (1994, 1998): *Macroeconomics*. New York: McGraw-Hill, 6th and 7th Edition, Chapter 16.

Dornbusch, R., P. Bodman, M. Crosby, S. Fischer, and R. Startz (2002): *Macroeconomics*. Roseville, Australia: McGraw-Hill, Chapters 6 and 7.

Fair, R. (2000): Testing the NAIRU model for the United States. *The Review of Economics and Statistics*, 82, 64–71.

Flaschel, P. and G. Groh (1996): *Keynesianische Makroökonomik: Unterbeschäftigung, Inflation und Wachstum*. Heidelberg: Springer, Chapters 2–4.

Frisch, H. (1983): *Theories of Inflation*. Cambridge: Cambridge University Press, Chapter 4.

Frisch, R. (1933): Propagation problems and impulse problems in dynamic economics. *Essays in Honor of Gustav Cassel*. London: Allen & Unwin.

Groth, C. (1993): Some unfamiliar dynamics of a familiar macro model: A note. *Journal of Economics*, 58, 293–305.

Hirsch, M. and S. Smale (1974): *Differential Equations, Dynamical Systems and Linear Algebra*. London: Academic Press.

Hoogenveen, V.C. and S.K. Kuipers (2000): The long-run effects of low inflation rates. *Banca Nazionale del Lavoro Quarterly Review*, 53, 267–286.

Kalecki, M. (1935): A macrodynamic theory of the business cycle. *Econometrica*, 3, 327–344.

Kauermann, G., T. Teuber, and P. Flaschel (2009): *Estimating Loops and Cycles Using Penalized Splines*. Bielefeld University: Mimeo.

Keynes, J.M. (1936): *The General Theory of Employment, Interest and Money*. New York: Macmillan.

Laxton, D., D. Rose, and D. Tambakis (2000): The U.S. Phillips-curve: The case for asymmetry. *Journal of Economic Dynamics and Control*, 23, 1459–1485.

Lux, T. (1995): Corridor stability in Dendrino's model of regional factor movements. *Geographical Analysis*, 27, 360–368.

Mankiw, N.G. (1994): *Macroeconomics*. New York: Worth Publishers.

Pampel, T. (2001): Numerical approximation of connecting orbits with asymptotic rate. *Numerische Mathematik*, 90, 309–348.

Phillips, A.W. (1958): The relation between unemployment and the rate of change of money wage rates in the United Kingdom, 1861 – 1957. *Economica*, 25, 283–299.

Romer, D. (1996): *Advanced Macroeconomics*. New York: McGraw-Hill.

Scarth, W.M. (1996): *Macroeconomics: An Integration of New Classical and New Keynesian Insights*. Toronto: Harcourt Brace, Chapter 4.

Slutzky, E. (1937): The summation of random causes as the source of cyclic processes. *Econometrica*, 5, 105–146.

Solow, R.M. and J.B. Taylor (1998): *Inflation, Unemployment and Monetary Policy*. Cambridge, MA: The MIT Press.

Tobin, J. (1975): Keynesian models of recession and depression. *American Economic Review*, 65, 195–202.

Appendix: Stability analysis of some textbook models

A1. Monetarist IS-LM-PC dynamics – The special case of a vertical LM-curve

In this appendix, we consider the extreme case of a vertical LM-curve (no interest rate sensitivity of money demand) by assuming for the IS-LM model of Section 2.2 the special parameter values $h_o = h_1 = 0$. In this case, we can in fact transform the model into a phase space representation as it was used in Chapter 1 for the monetarist baseline model. In this way, we are able to make use of the state variables Y and π that were so difficult to handle in the general IS-LM-PC framework in Section 2.7.

Making use of the restricted monetarist type of money market equilibrium $m = M/p = kY$ we first of all get in this case the law of motion $\mu - \pi = \hat{Y}$. Furthermore, according to the Phillips curve, we have $\dot{\pi} = \beta_w \hat{Y} + \dot{\pi}^e$ where $\dot{\pi}^e$ as usual can be replaced by $\beta_{\pi^e} \beta_w (Y - \bar{Y})$. Taken together, these manipulations give the two laws of motion for Y and $\pi = \hat{p}$, namely

$$\hat{Y} = \mu - \pi \quad \text{or} \quad \dot{Y} = (\mu - \pi)Y, \tag{2.42}$$

$$\dot{\pi} = \beta_w(\mu - \pi)Y + \beta_{\pi^e}\beta_w(Y - \bar{Y}). \tag{2.43}$$

The model given by the dynamical system (2.42)–(2.43) is formally identical to the monetarist baseline model of Chapter 1 (now implied through a vertical LM-curve) that we recall can be written as

$$\dot{Y} = b(\mu - \bar{g} - \pi)Y \tag{2.44}$$

$$\dot{\pi} = \beta_w Yb(\mu - \bar{g} - \pi) + \beta_{\pi^e}\beta_w(Y - \bar{Y}), \tag{2.45}$$

and which therefore shares all the properties of this earlier model, based also on the quantity theory of money and there on Okun's law in the place of the linear production function $Y = Y/(xL)$ that is being used here. The analysis of Section 2.4 is thus also immediately applicable to the special case of IS-LM-PC dynamics currently under consideration and in fact can here be supplemented by a proposition on the global asymptotic stability of such a dynamics (highly desirable from a monetarist perspective) in the economically meaningful right half plane of the phase space where inflation can take on any real number, but where of course the rate of employment is restricted to positive values.

In terms of the state variables m and π^e mainly used in the body of the present chapter we then have the representation

$$\hat{m} = \mu - \beta_w(Y - \bar{Y}) - \pi^e, \tag{2.46}$$

$$\dot{\pi}^e = \beta_{\pi^e}\beta_w(Y - \bar{Y}), \tag{2.47}$$

with

$$Y = a_1 m, \quad a_1 > 0.$$

We know already from the monetarist model of Section 1.3 that upper and lower turning points no longer represent a problem at all and that in particular deflation cannot do any harm to the economy in this special case. In this regard, we now in addition prove the following proposition:

Proposition 2.8 (Global convergence to the steady state)   Assume as given an arbitrary initial situation for the rate of employment Y (> 0) and the rate of inflation or deflation π. Then, the trajectory starting from this position will converge to the steady state of the dynamics without violating the side condition $Y > 0$.[40]

---

40 The side condition $Y \leq 1$ can now simply be imposed on this model type. Furthermore, the side condition $r \geq 0$ is now of no relevance and can thus also be postulated to hold here too.

Proof   It is in fact easy to show for the restricted model type under consideration the global asymptotic stability of the now uniquely determined steady state $Y^o = \bar{Y}$ and $\pi^o = \mu$ in the right-hand side half-plane of $\mathbb{R}^2$, the economic part of the (Y, π) phase-space of the dynamics (where $Y > 0$ holds). For this purpose, one has to define a Liapunov function L given by

$$L(Y, \pi) = \int_{Y^o}^{Y} \beta_{\pi^e}\beta_w(x - \bar{Y})/x\,dx + \int_{\pi^o}^{\pi} -(\mu - y)\,dy.$$

This function has a single local as well as global minimum at (Y^0, π^0) in the positive half-plane of $\mathbb{R}^2$ and is characterized by closed level curves (where $L(Y, \pi) = const.$ holds true). This is easily obtained by considering separately the two functions it is composed of, which are both strictly convex with minimum value Y^o and π^o respectively. Projecting the graph of the composed function into the half-plane of $\mathbb{R}^2$ where $Y > 0$ holds true thus gives rise to closed level curves surrounding the steady state that is characterized by higher values of L the farther away they are from this steady state position. In order to not overload this appendix with technical analysis we do not go into the details of a graphical representation of such issues here, but refer the reader instead to Section 1.3 where a detailed application of the Liapunov function approach is provided in the context of a Solovian underemployment dynamics.

The function L furthermore fulfills along $z(t) = (Y(t), \pi(t))$

$$\dot{L} = \frac{dL(z(t))}{dt} = -(\mu - \pi) \cdot \dot{\pi} + \frac{\beta_{\pi^e}\beta_w(Y - \bar{Y})}{Y} \cdot \dot{Y}$$
$$= -\beta_w Y(\mu - \pi) \le 0 \quad (= 0 \text{ iff } \pi = \mu).$$

The fact that the derivative satisfies $\dot{L} \le 0$ simply means that the values of the function L are descending along the trajectories $z(t) = (Y(t), \pi(t))$ of the considered dynamical system, with the exception of the case where $\pi = \mu$ holds true. All level curves of the function L are thus crossed (nearly everywhere) towards lower values of L by the trajectories of the dynamics which therefore must all approach the unique steady state of the considered dynamical system as time goes to infinity.

Due to the fact that – viewed globally – the steady state (Y^0, π^0) is the only sink in the graph of the Liapunov function L we thus get the result that all trajectories must converge to the steady state (Y^0, π^0), the deepest point in the graph of L, where L is zero. The level curves of L are generally crossed from outside to their inside area (up to the isolated points where $\pi = \mu$ holds), which means that the height measured by L will (apart from some fluke occurrence) always fall along the trajectories of the dynamical system under investigation.

Remark   The speed of adjustment of inflationary expectation (if increased) is, according to what has been shown in Section 1.3, bad for monotonic stability while wage flexibility work in favor of it.[41] More flexible money wage adjustment is thus not a threat to economic stability as in IS-LM-PC dynamics proper, but indeed of help in reaching the steady state position more quickly.

Specializing the IS-LM-PC dynamics to the situation currently being considered thus gives rise to nice mathematical properties for the considered dynamics, yet unfortunately only in a situation without any empirical relevance, since money demand is of course known to be interest rate elastic and a vertical LM curve therefore remains only a theoretical possibility. We note furthermore that in the m, π^e space we will get a vertical $\dot{\pi}^e = 0$ isocline, thus implying from a different perspective that there cannot be a second steady state in this restricted IS-LM-PC analysis (which would indeed also violate the global stability assertion we have proved earlier).

The IS-LM-PC analysis of this chapter therefore does not at all support the propositions of the monetarist baseline model, but rather reveals that this model is only an uninteresting and extreme limit case. Furthermore, the use of Taylor interest rate policy rules nowadays suggests that inflation is a real phenomenon that is best controlled via a direct influence of monetary policy on real activity as was considered in Section 2.9. We conclude that the decomposition of aggregate demand into consumption, investment and government demand is of importance for the actual working of the economy and can be controlled by way of an interest rate policy rule as long as the economy is still working sufficiently above the zero interest rate bound.

A2. Distorted IS-LM-PC dynamics

In their presentation of the wage–price dynamics that appears to follow from Keynesian IS-LM equilibrium (as a theory of temporary equilibrium positions) when supplemented by a Phillips curve mechanism and adaptive expectations, Dornbusch and Fischer (1994, 1998)[42] make use of simplified IS-LM-PC dynamics of the form

$$\dot{Y} = a_1(\mu - \pi) + a_0 \bar{F}, \ (\mu = \hat{M} = const.), \tag{2.48}$$

$$\pi = \hat{p} = \hat{w} = \beta_w(Y - \bar{Y}) + \pi^e, \tag{2.49}$$

$$\dot{\pi}^e = \beta_{\pi^e}(\hat{p} - \pi^e). \tag{2.50}$$

---

41 This is not an obvious consequence of the above proof of global asymptotic stability, since the Liapunov function employed depends on the speed of adjustment parameters of the considered dynamics. We assert here, however, that the local analysis just quoted indeed characterizes monotonic vs. cyclical behavior also from the global perspective due to the simple nonlinearity involved in the dynamics under consideration.

42 These authors make use of a discrete time presentation of the model which, however, is not essential for the current discussion of their model.

This model is based on a dynamic theory of effective demand (2.48) where the time rate of change $\dot{Y}$ of IS-LM equilibrium output Y is postulated to depend positively on the growth rate of real balances M/p according to

$$\widehat{M/p} = \widehat{M} - \hat{p} = \mu - \pi$$

(due to the conventional Keynes-effect of static IS-LM theory) and on an exogenously given dynamic fiscal policy parameter $\bar{F}$. Equation (2.49) then adds again a linear expectations augmented natural rate (money wage and price level) Phillips curve, here based on output levels (actual and natural ones) in the place of rates of unemployment. Since this model is based on fixed proportions in production, a constant labor supply and on a constant markup on average wage costs, equation (2.49) can, however, easily be translated into one that shows rates of unemployment (or employment) in the place of Y. Furthermore, the assumption on markup-pricing immediately implies that wage and price inflation can again be identified and represented by a unique magnitude π. Equation (2.50) finally is the conventional adaptive expectations mechanism used in elementary inertia theories of inflation and stagflation.

The aforementioned model can be reduced to the form (π^e the expected rate of inflation)

$$\dot{Y} = a_1(\mu - \pi) + a_0\bar{F}, \tag{2.51}$$

$$\dot{\pi} = \beta_w a_1(\mu - \pi) + \beta_{\pi^e}\beta_w(Y - \bar{Y}) + \beta_w a_0\bar{F}, \tag{2.52}$$

which is a linear autonomous differential equations system of dimension 2 in the variables output (Y) and inflation (π).

These dynamics imply again everything one would wish to find in a basic model of monetarist wage–price dynamics with adaptive expectations, here, however, in the context of a system that is apparently of IS-LM-PC type. There is a unique and economically meaningful steady state $Y^o = \bar{Y}, \pi^o = \mu + a_0\bar{F}/a_1$ which reduces to $Y^o = \bar{Y}, \pi^o = \mu$ if fiscal policy is stationary. This steady state is globally asymptotically stable in the whole phase plane for all possible parameter values of the model. It is of a cyclical nature when adjustment of inflationary expectations is fast and converges monotonically otherwise. There hold the monetarist propositions on monetary policy, accelerating inflation, periods of inflation and stagflation, long run neutrality, changing expectations mechanisms and the like in this framework of medium run IS-LM dynamics.

A detailed discussion of all of these issues – which is straightforward due to the linearity of the model – is provided in Dornbusch and Fischer (1994, 1998) and will not be repeated here (since this model is of the type considered in appendix A1, see also Section 1.3). The model of Dornbusch and Fischer (1994, 1998, Ch.16) is, however, not a valid extension of their IS-LM analysis towards an inclusion of the dynamics of wages, prices and inflationary expectations.[43] This follows immediately from a visual inspection of their dynamical system (2.48)–(2.50) where one sees that growth rates are mixed up with time derivatives in (2.48) in order to get a linear dynamical system from an originally nonlinear one and the Mundell-Tobin-effect, but not the Keynes-effect, is again suppressed despite the fact that both effects work jointly through the same channel, namely the one that is provided by the expected real rate of interest in the assumed investment behavior.

A3. IS-LM-PC dynamics based on money illusion[44]

Romer (1996, Ch.5) provides a comparative discussion of the features and merits of traditional Keynesian theory that stresses some advantages of the macro ad hoc approach over the now fashionable, but restrictive, microfounded approach of the macroeconomic literature.[45] One advantage in this regard is that the macro-micro approach – as we would call it – can more rapidly proceed to a full analysis of market interactions on the macrolevel than the representative agent macro literature, the micro-macro approach in our terminology. The macro-micro approach of course also has considered microfoundations of the assumed behavior in detail, as can be seen for example from Crouch's (1972) macroeconomic textbook as well as many others. Yet, such macrofoundations are partial in nature, for example the consumption savings decision, the subsequent portfolio decision with respect to savings, the investment decision of firms etc. Justification of assumed aggregate behavior thus also characterizes the traditional approach to macrostatics and macrodynamics.

Coupled with a narrow view on the microfoundations of aggregate behavioral relationships one often also encounters the view – and Romer's (1996, Ch.5) is not really an exception in this regard – that traditional Keynesian analysis is of a fairly trivial type, based on some obvious comparative static exercises, but with no deep analysis of the interaction of the sectors and markets of the economy in particular over the medium- and the long run. Such a view is in fact more a caricature than reality of what is occurring in the macro-micro literature, in particular with respect to the many feedback channels of partly stabilizing and partly destabilizing nature known to exist in the Keynesian approach to macrodynamics. It is thus not astonishing to find – as in Romer's Chapter 5 – that the Keynes-effect rules the roost in such reflections on the traditional Keynesian approach, while an analysis of the baseline type we have conducted in this chapter is totally ignored.

However, Romer (1996, p.239) indeed provides a discussion also of the Mundell-Tobin-effect in his Chapter 5, though relegated to an exercise section.

---

43 Note also that, though globally asymptotically stable, the model is still incomplete since the right half of the phase plane is not an invariant set of these dynamics and so output can be become negative along trajectories that start in the economically meaningful domain.
44 Note that in Appendix A3 we use P to denote price and set $p = \ln P$.
45 See also our remarks on his Ch.5 in the 'general introduction' of our book.

The model he uses in this exercise is given by the following three equations, which apart from the interest rate i are expressed in terms of logarithms:-

$$y - \bar{y} = -a(i - \dot{p} - i^o), \tag{2.53}$$

$$m - p = \phi y - k(i - i^o), \tag{2.54}$$

$$\dot{p} = \theta(y - \bar{y}) + \eta \dot{p}. \tag{2.55}$$

The first equation, (2.53), is a logarithmic representation of the IS-equilibrium curve (in terms of deviations from the steady state $\bar{y}$ and i^o) where the real rate of interest effect is fully present, here already in actual terms, obviously due to the assumption of myopic perfect foresight (to be coupled with $\eta < 1$, see below). Equation, (2.54), provides the LM-curve, here based on a Cagan type money demand function represented in logarithmic terms. Equation (2.55) finally provides an expectations augmented price Phillips curve, also based on myopic perfect foresight, which means that $\eta \neq 1$ must be assumed (in fact even $\eta < 1$) in order to allow for deviations of actual output from the NAIRU level $\bar{y}$. We thus seem to have a model that is basically of the type considered in the body of this chapter, with both Keynes- and Mundell-Tobin-effect included and with money illusion of workers in the place of the adaptive expectations mechanism we have used there. However, there must be differences between this and our model type since the Romer model exhibits a single steady state $y^o = \bar{y}, i^o, p^o = m$ and is again linear in contrast to the model we have analyzed in this chapter (the model does not yet allow for steady state inflation, which, however, is not a crucial difference as compared to ours).

Let us briefly consider here the special case where $\phi = 0$ holds true. In this case, we get by substituting the PC into the IS-curve the expression

$$(1 - \eta)\dot{p} = -\theta a(i - i^o) + \theta a \dot{p}.$$

Making use of the LM-curve then gives

$$(1 - \eta - \theta a)\dot{p} = -\theta a(m - p)/k,$$

from which we finally obtain

$$\dot{p} = \frac{\theta a}{k(1 - \eta - \theta a)}(m - p).$$

Assuming for the adjustment speed θ in the PC the inequality $\theta < (1 - \eta)/a$ is obviously necessary and sufficient for global asymptotic stability of the price level dynamics determined by this model. We thus have obtained in sum a single law of motion, which is linear and exhibits a uniquely determined steady state level $p_o = m$ and which, since it is of dimension 1, is in a trivial way globally asymptotically stable under the assumed side condition.

Yet, as in the case of adaptive expectations, faster adjustment or here stronger influences of the accelerator term in the PC lead to global instability that moreover can here not be tamed by downward wage and price rigidity as far as situations to the right of the steady state are concerned. Yet, such results are not of interest in Romer's exercise, but instead the focus is on the situation where we have stability and nevertheless an increase in the adjustment speed of money wages and the price level. Increasing the parameter θ obviously increases the slope of the $\dot{p}$ equation. On the one hand it therefore makes the dynamic adjustment to its steady state level faster, but on the other hand makes the economy more volatile if it is subject to repeated shocks in money supply and so in its steady state position. There is thus a trade-off between adjustment speeds and volatility that should be reflected by monetary policy if it is subject to such a dynamic of the private sector.

However, more worrying from the perspective of this chapter is again the situation of only a single steady state solution and that a linear model seems to be sufficient to describe the IS-LM-PC dynamics of this chapter also from the global point of view. These difference need clarification and this is what we shall undertake in the remainder of this section of the appendix.

Turning first to the PC we get on the extensive form level (by removing logarithms or showing them explicitly and denoting the result with capital letters) the PC-equation $\hat{P} = \ln(Y/\bar{Y}) + \eta\hat{P}$. There is nothing problematic in this type of PC assumption, though it is of course of a special type (with money illusion now in place of adaptive expectations). The same holds with respect to money market equilibrium which on the extensive form level reads $M/P = Y^\phi \exp(-k(i - i^o))$. This is again a special functional shape. Doing the same with the IS-curve, however, implies: $Y/\bar{Y} = \exp(-a(i - \hat{P} - i_o))$ with i_o being determined by $\bar{Y} = \exp(-ai_o)$. The right-hand side, $\exp(-a(i - \hat{P}))$, is of course not a good representation of the summation of consumption, investment and government demand and can must be considered a local (formal) approximation of such an aggregate behavioral relationship. We thus see that the ensuing analysis is only local in nature and not very far reaching when compared with the one in the body of this chapter. Allowing for steady state inflation (by assuming $\dot{m} > 0$) would, however, reproduce the Proposition 2.2 in a one-dimensional setup. But that is all that can be obtained from the Romer (1996, p.239) example.

Again, an illegitimate, since only local in nature, reduction to linearity – though now with full presence of the real rate of interest rate channel in the IS-curve representation – removes nearly everything that is of interest in IS-LM-PC analysis proper and is also solely applicable in the case of stability. Including the kink in the money wage PC in the case of local instability would in fact give rise to the scenario shown in Figure 2.18, but to nothing more as compared to the nonlocal studies done in this chapter.

We conclude with the observation that the reduced form equation

$$Y - \bar{Y} = a_o + a_2(i - \pi^e), \quad (a_o, a_2 > 0)$$

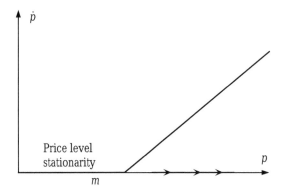

Figure 2.18 The localized Keynes and the Mundell-Tobin feedback chains with downward money wage rigidity.

is capable of representing an IS-curve from the global perspective (due to the additive nature of the components of aggregate demand) and thus can be used for a meaningful IS-LM-PC dynamics also from the global perspective, while the apparently similar equation

$$Y/\bar{Y} = a_o \exp(-a_2(i - \pi^e)), \quad (a_o, a_2 > 0)$$

is not, since it is not valid from the global perspective and since it cannot be used to obtain the results of this chapter.

A4. IS-LM-PC dynamics with static expectations

We started the analysis of the interaction of the (un)employment or output rate and the inflation rate from the static AD–AS representation of short run Keynesian goods and financial market equilibrium shown in Figure 2.3, which is reproduced here for convenience in Figure 2.19.

We then added a standard money wage Phillips curve (which made money wages a dynamically endogenous variable) and an adaptive revision of inflationary expectations as laws of motion, which then implied the dynamics that we have studied intensively in this chapter. Blanchard (2006) makes use throughout his book of the same model type, based, however, on a theory of money wages which makes this variable a statically endogenous one (while the theory of the price level is formally the sane as in this chapter and of markup pricing type). For money wages w Blanchard (2006, p.126) postulates the wage setting relationship

$$w = p^e h(U, \zeta) = p^e h(1 - e, \zeta) = p^e h((Y^f - Y)/Y^f, \zeta), \quad h_1 < 0$$

where p^e is the price level expected by workers, h_1 denotes the derivative of the function h with respect to its first argument and ζ is a vector of variables that may

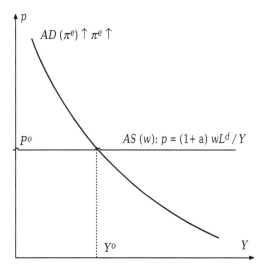

Figure 2.19 The Mundell-Tobin effect in an AD–AS representation of Keynesian IS-LM analysis, with given wages and markup pricing.

affect the outcome of the wage setting process. Combined with Blanchard's price setting relationship $p = (1 + a)w$ this gives

$$p = (1 + a)p^e \tilde{h}(e), \qquad (\tilde{h}'(e) > 0)$$

if we ignore the exogenous variables for simplicity. Dividing this equation by the past price level p_1 and using the relationship that $\ln(1 + x) \approx x$ for variables x sufficiently close to zero then gives

$$\hat{p} = \ln(1 + a) + \hat{p}^e + \ln \tilde{h}(e), \qquad \left((\ln \tilde{h})'(e) > 0\right).$$

This defines a reduced form price Phillips curve of qualitatively (from the mathematical perspective) the same type that we have used in the main body of this chapter. So we find that the analysis of this chapter is unchanged when this PC is used in the place of our standard PC, and made linear through an appropriate choice of the function $\tilde{h}(\cdot)$.

However, from the economic perspective we now have a somewhat different view on the working of the labor market with in particular an endogenous theory of the NAIRU, which is determined in Blanchard by $U^o = h(1/(1+a))$, that is in the aforesaid form of price PC by the equivalent expression $\ln(1 + a) = \ln \tilde{h}(e^o)$, describing the situation of myopic perfect foresight in the steady state of the economy. We conclude that the difference on the supply side of our IS-LM-PC model and Blanchard's (2006) analysis of inflation in the medium run is from a formal perspective negligible. Yet, our analysis of IS-LM-PC dynamics has

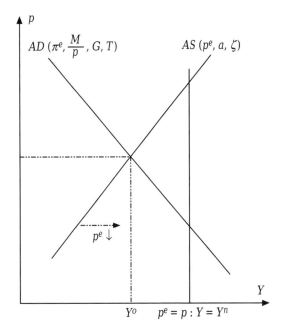

Figure 2.20 The AD–AS model of Blanchard (2006).

not much in common with the description of inflation dynamics in Blanchard (2006, Ch.9).

The reason for this difference is a simple one and is such that the analysis of the baseline monetarist model of Chapter 1.3 remains basically intact also in a Keynesian IS-LM-PC framework of the type chosen by Blanchard. This is assured in Blanchard's (2006) analysis of the forces that lead the economy from the short-to the medium run in his Chapters 3–9. In the short run, we have from his theory of aggregate supply an AD–AS model of the type illustrated in Figure 2.20, with the AD curve being the same as in our type of (identical) IS-LM analysis (where the negative slope of the AD curve is just a formal representation of the Keynes-effect involved in the working of the dynamics of the model).

Since Blanchard (2006) considers inflationary expectations and the real rate of interest that is based on them only after his full treatment of the short run, the medium run and the long run in his Chapter 14, in all preceding chapters he assumes that investment behavior depends solely on the nominal rate of interest. Inflationary expectations thus only shift the AS-curve, as shown in Figure 2.20 – but not yet the AD-curve, so that the position of this curve does not depend on π^e as shown in this figure and as was the basis of our analysis in this chapter. In the transition to the medium run, Blanchard is therefore able to assume a fixed AD schedule. In the situation shown in Figure 2.20, we then get that output is below its natural output level Y^n, so that the price level is below the one expected by workers who therefore revise their expectations in a downward direction. This shifts the AS-curve also in a downward direction. This process continues as long as output is below its natural level and the economy therefore converges in a monotonic way to this natural position where wage setting and price setting are compatible with correct anticipations of workers concerning the price level on the market for goods. Since the AD curve does not shift during this process this is a valid stability proof.

In Blanchard's (2006, Ch.9) analysis of inflation and the Phillips curve this analysis is repeated in terms of inflation rates, but with aggregate demand still given by $Y = Y(\frac{M}{p}, G, T)$ (see his page 189). Although there is now the consideration of inflation dynamics, expected inflation rates still do not enter the investment function and the stability result remains as already considered in his Chapter 7. From the perspective of the present chapter, this means that the model is treated under the assumption $a_2 = 0$, by which it becomes formally equivalent to the monetarist baseline model that we have considered in Section 1.3.

In the m, π^e phase space considered in Sections 2.3 and 2.4 the π^e-isocline is now a vertical line and there thus is no second steady state solution on the boundary of the right half plane of the phase space. The system is then globally asymptotically stable in this part of the phase space (as can easily be shown again by means of a suitably chosen Liapunov function, similar to the analysis in Appendix A1, since the dynamical system is simply given by

$$\hat{m} = \mu - \beta_w(a_1 m + a_o - \bar{Y}) - \pi^e,$$
$$\dot{\pi}^e = \beta_{\pi^e}\beta_w(a_1 m + a_o - \bar{Y}).$$

In the transformed Y, π phase space considered in Section 2.7, we obtain as the laws of motion in this special case

$$\begin{pmatrix} \dot{Y} \\ \dot{\pi} \end{pmatrix} = A \begin{pmatrix} (\mu - \pi)m \\ \beta_{\pi^e}\beta_w(Y - \bar{Y}) \end{pmatrix},$$

where

$$A = \begin{pmatrix} a_1 & 0 \\ \beta_w a_1 & 1 \end{pmatrix}, \quad m = \frac{Y - a_o}{a_1},$$

with m to be inserted into this reformulation of the IS-LM-PC dynamics in order to arrive at the system of differential equations

$$\dot{Y} = (\mu - \pi)(Y - a_o),$$
$$\dot{\pi} = \beta_w[(\mu - \pi)(Y - a_o) + \beta_{\pi^e}(Y - \bar{Y})],$$

in the state variables Y and π. This system is now simple enough to allow for a direct phase portrait representation as shown in Figure 2.21. We know already

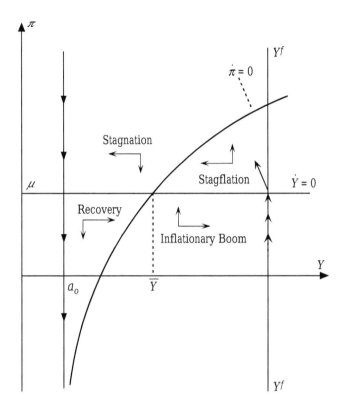

Figure 2.21 The output – inflation phase space representation of the Blanchard (2006) inflation model.

that it is possible to show global asymptotic stability for the dynamics depicted in Figure 2.21 as in the case of the monetarist baseline model of Section 1.4. Upper turning points in inflation are now guaranteed, since the intersection between the $\dot\pi = 0$ isocline and the full-employment output level bounds the highest value for the inflation rate that can be reached by the dynamics. A similar argument assures the existence of lower turning points during periods of disinflation or even deflation, since the $\dot\pi = 0$ isocline approaches the limit $Y = a_o$ when deflation tends to pass all bounds. Lower turning points in output dynamics are also guaranteed by the existence of the bounding $Y = a_o$ line for declines in output (where $m = 0$ holds), while upper turning points come into being at the latest through the full-employment ceiling Y^f as shown in Figure 2.21. These arguments provide intuitive reasons as to why the system is indeed globally stable in this special case (but do not prove its asymptotic stability however).

We recognize here that the situation of an IS- and AD-schedule that is not shifting with the expected rate of inflation represents a more advanced situation as compared with the vertical LM curve underlying the baseline monetarist model

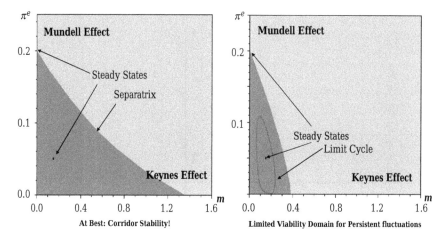

Figure 2.22 Corridor stability for local asymptotic stability as well as local instability and limit cycle results in textbook IS-LM-PC dynamics.

of Section 1.3, and also discussed in appendix A1. Yet, the fact remains that the investment function is assumed to depend on the real rate of interest, see Blanchard (2006, p.300), so that the term a_2 in the output equation is not zero both in the short- and the medium-run. Having recognized this explicitly, Blanchard then indirectly justifies his earlier stability results by just assuming static inflationary expectations in his brief stability analysis following this enhanced view of the investment behavior of firms. This however is just another inadequate assumption in a model of the interaction of employment and inflation of IS-LM-PC type, since it again suppresses the existence of the working of the Mundell-Tobin effect in the Keynesian approach to inflation dynamics that underlies Blanchard's (2006) textbook model as has been extensively discussed in the main body of the present chapter. In fact the Mundell-Tobin effect is in general totally ignored in the intermediate and advanced textbook literature.

It should be noted that the AD-curve is shifting in an inflationary or deflationary environment, and indeed in the opposite direction as compared with the shifts in the AS-schedule, not only under the pathological situations of deep depressions or high inflation as they are discussed in Blanchard's (2006) Chapters 22 and 23, but also always in the course of the normal working of the economy. Hence, it is not possible to speak of an integrated approach to macrodynamics unless these shifts are taken into account in the analysis of the medium run.

The foregoing statement is even more true if the analysis of the long run is pursued by means of Say's law ($I \equiv S$) and thus by means of a model type where the AD-schedule is not only manipulated appropriately in order to obtain desired stability results, but is in fact now completely absent from the modeling of capital accumulation and growth. As a consequence, neither the medium run nor the long run is treated in an integrated view in Blanchard's (2006) macroeconomic analysis, despite the claim that is made in Blanchard (2006, p.XIV).

Figure 2.22 summarizes the basic findings of the full model of IS-LM-PC inflation dynamics for the case of the Friedmanian neutral money supply rule used in the main body of this chapter. In the locally asymptotically stable case, the figure shows the corridor or the basin of attraction in the left hand panel (possibly reduced by downward money wage rigidity to the positive orthant of the phase plane shown). In the right-hand panel, the figure shows the same for the limit cycle that is generated through the kinked Phillips curve in the case of local instability of the interior steady state of the IS-LM-PC model. These outcomes are very different from those usually considered in the textbook literature on the medium-run behavior of macroeconomies, in particular compared to the corresponding analysis in Blanchard's (2006) discussion of the mediumrun, as has been shown in the foregoing.

3   Strange AS–AD outcomes
Rational expectations inflation theory

In this chapter, we will consider attempts to synthesize the medium- and long run with the real wage ω allowed to be dynamic. In the preceding chapter, we did the same for the short- and the medium run with a given real wage. Chapters 2 and 3 are therefore complementary to a certain degree, yet, as we will show, they give rise to an inconsistent whole when synthesized in the way it was done in the old Neoclassical Synthesis. When done in this way, it will be found that we have a Rose or real wage effect in the real part of the economy, but that the Mundell-effect considered in the preceding chapter is now only present in the nominal part of the model, which dichotomizes from the real part under the assumption of myopic perfect foresight and the attendant use of the jump-variable technique. This approach turns nominal into real rigidities and allows the Keynesian AD curve to only effect the nominal side of the AD–AS (Aggregate Demand–Aggregate Supply) growth dynamics.

3.1 The postulates of Classical economics

In this chapter, we will extend the Solow model of economic growth based on the neoclassical theory of income distribution by including features of the theory of inflation that we have considered in Chapters 1 and 2. We will see that as a consequence elements of the classical Goodwin employment cycle model will be introduced into this neoclassical framework, namely real wage dynamics that may repeatedly overshoot and undershoot the steady state position in the course of the convergence to the steady state path that this Solow-Goodwin type of analysis still guarantees. We shall in particular show that Goodwin type dynamics will come about in a stronger fashion if the elasticity of labor intensity with respect to real wage changes in the neoclassical theory of employment being used (based on the marginal productivity principle) becomes sufficiently low (approaches zero). In contrast, high (negative) elasticity of relative labor demand with respect to real wage changes will give rise to monotonic adjustments towards the steady state in this model type with Solovian capital accumulation and income distribution dynamics, now with under- or overemployment in the place of the full-employment assumption of the standard Solow model.

It therefore becomes an empirical question whether Solow- or Goodwin-like features dominate the dynamics of real wages and capital accumulation in this classical Solow-Goodwin extension of both Solow's and Goodwin's employment dynamics.

Due to the predominantly real formulation of the model, money and the price level dynamics are determined here only after the real dynamics and thus do not feed back into it. The monetary part of the model is therefore of a fairly trivial type. However, this simple dichotomizing structure with real dynamics determined first and nominal dynamics thereafter, indeed reappears in perfectly standard AD–AS textbook dynamics if the secondary assumption of myopic perfect foresight is introduced. The conventional type of Keynesian AD–AS-PC (AD–AS-Phillips Curve) dynamics is in the myopic perfect foresight case of this first Neoclassical Synthesis (the New-Keynesian approach being the second one) thus of a degenerate kind. These dynamics reduce under myopic perfect foresight to (neo-)classical real supply side dynamics without any influence of the Keynesian theory of income and interest determination. Instead, a price level dynamic of a Friedmanian type here derives from the IS-LM (Investment Saving-Liquidity preference Money supply) block of the model, by adjusting aggregate demand to aggregate supply via an unstable relationship between the price level and its rate of change. This unstable dynamic can then be stabilized by way of the jump-variable technique, here, however, accompanied by a subtle change of assumptions underlying this traditional AD–AS-PC approach (concerning a return to money-wage flexibility).

It follows from the foregoing discussion that not much remains in this old Neoclassical Synthesis of the Keynesian view about the working of the economy despite a strictly traditional formulation of the Keynesian part of the model. Supply side dynamics of classical or neoclassical type appear to be unavoidable if a seemingly innocent assumption is made about the forecasting of the short-term rate of goods price inflation. In Chapter 5 we will in addition show that this is due to a central logical inconsistency in this traditional type of a Neoclassical Synthesis, thus demonstrating that the conventional textbook view on the interaction of supply and demand side aspects is severely flawed, at least as far as their proper integration is concerned.

It must, however, be conceded here that this logical inconsistency, which becomes particularly striking if errors from prediction of the short-run inflation rate are removed from the model (in our opinion a secondary consideration from a Keynesian point of view), dates back to the discussion of the classical postulates in Keynes' (1936) 'General Theory'. In his Chapter 2, Keynes states with regard to the classical postulates:

> In emphasizing our point of departure from the classical system, we must not overlook an important point of agreement. For we shall maintain the first postulate as heretofore, subject only to the same qualifications as in the classical theory; and we must pause, for a moment, to consider what this involves.

It means that, with a given organisation, equipment and technique, real wages and the volume of output (and hence of employment) are uniquely correlated, so that, in general, an increase in employment can only occur to the accompaniment of a decline in the rate of real wages. Thus I am not disputing this vital fact which the classical economists have (rightly) asserted as indefeasible. In a given state of organisation, equipment and technique, the real wage earned by a unit of labour has a unique (inverse) correlation with the volume of employment. Thus if employment increases, then, in the short period, the reward per unit of labour in terms of wage-goods must, in general, decline and profits increase. This is simply the obverse of the familiar proposition that industry is normally working subject to decreasing returns in the short period during which equipment etc. is assumed to be constant; so that the marginal product in the wage-good industries (which governs real wages) necessarily diminishes as employment is increased. So long, indeed, as this proposition holds, any means of increasing employment must lead at the same time to a diminution of the marginal product and hence of the rate of wages measured in terms of this product.

Assuming the validity of the first classical postulate, however, is at the root of the problems we will establish in this chapter, since it means that the conventional static AS-curve of the textbook literature is a constituent part of the Keynesian approach to the theory of employment, inflation and growth. The bizarre result that we obtain in this regard is independent Solovian supply side unemployment growth dynamics and an appended AD curve that is always adjusting to supply side growth by determining a positive relationship between the price level and its rate of growth. This dichotomy is completely at odds with Keynes' understanding of the trade cycle (which is driven by marginal rates of substitution, marginal efficiencies of investment and liquidity preference as we have sketched it at the end of Chapter 1), since all of these parameters are then completely absent in the real dynamics of the model.

Our remedy for this absurd outcome of Keynesian AD–AS analysis (under myopic perfect foresight) will in fact be a simple one, but will give rise to a detailed overhaul of the conventional AD–AS growth dynamics in Part II. The inverse relationship discussed in the foregoing quotation from Keynes' General Theory is neither an empirically sensible assumption nor theoretically meaningful in any advanced reconsideration of the wage–price mechanism or of the wage–price spiral, since it applies a steady state condition to the analysis of the short run and thus gives rise to an overdeterminacy and the consequent logical inconsistencies. Prices may be equal to marginal wage costs (or the real wage, equal to the marginal product of labor), but this only holds in the limit and not at all moments of time. The consequences of this latter assumption in a Keynesian framework are the subject of the present chapter while the ways out of the inconsistencies that it creates are the subject of Part II.

3.2 AS dynamics and the quantity theory of money

The simplest approach to the determination of output, employment and prices with disequilibrium in the market for labor is given by coupling the static neoclassical theory of the aggregate supply relationship (based on given money wages) with the quantity theory of money as the constraint that acts on the nominal value of the output of firms. We then assume a neoclassical production function and that prices are given by marginal wage costs for each level of output and employment (that is the marginal product of labor must equal the real wage at each level of output and employment). Imposing the quantity theory of money on this relationship then gives rise to a unique determination of output (employment) and prices, generally below the full-employment level of the economy. This situation is represented graphically in Figure 3.1.

To this simple model of an underemployment equilibrium, we will add in the next section the dynamics of money wages (which shift the AS-schedule), the dynamics of the money supply (which shift the QT [Quantity theory]) and the dynamics of labor and capital stock growth (which shift both the AS-curve and the vertical full-employment position). These dynamic changes take place under the assumption of the perpetual validity of Says's law since we will assume that all savings are always invested and thus fully used to accumulate real capital. In this case aggregate demand must always be equal to aggregate supply, so that the output level determined in Figure 3.1 can always be sold on the market for goods. This classical theory of unemployment, inflation and growth thus has little in common with the IS-LM-PC dynamics considered in Chapter 2.

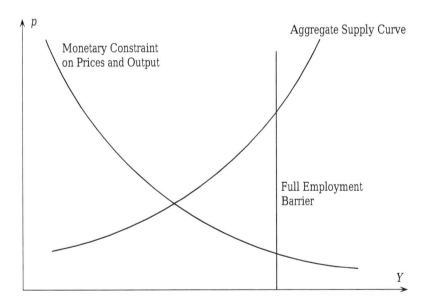

Figure 3.1 The so-called Classical model of output, prices (and employment).

In the course of this chapter, we will, however, demonstrate that the IS-LM-PC dynamics considered in the Chapter 2 will indeed give rise to such classical dynamics when its markup pricing rule is replaced by marginal wage cost pricing and if adaptive expectations are taken to their limit (by setting $\beta_{\pi^e} = \infty$), and so are replaced by the condition of myopic perfect foresight. Two seemingly minor modifications of the model of the preceding section (the acceptance of the first classical postulate by Keynes (1936) and no errors in place of a fast adjustment of expectations to current observations of inflation) thus seem to imply that the traditional Keynesian AD–AS-PC model of employment, inflation and growth collapses as far as its central role in the determination of output and interest is concerned and gives way to a classical view on employment and growth with an appended theory of price inflation that can be (but must not be) manipulated according to the methodology of the rational expectations school.

We will, however, see in Chapter 5 that the 'villain' in this classical revolution of the traditional Keynesian approach is the assumption that firms are always on their supply schedule. The latter is surely a problematic assumption from an advanced Keynesian perspective and which indeed is to be coupled with a hidden change in the assumption on money wage behavior in order to allow at all the bizarre outcomes of this chapter on traditional Keynesian AD–AS growth dynamics.

3.3 Employment cycles in neoclassical monetary growth

In this section, we generalize the Solow model by adding (somewhat) sluggish nominal wage adjustment similar to the way it was used in the monetarist baseline model where the monetarist theory of inflation and stagflation was formulated and analyzed. We will also preserve the simple quantity approach to inflation and deflation of this model type, but will now use the alternative expectational mechanism of myopic perfect foresight that was only briefly considered there. The changes concern Okun's law and the theory of production where we now assume a neoclassical two-factor production function (with capital and labor as inputs) and the marginal productivity theory as in the original Solow model. We assume furthermore extremely classical saving habits, namely that all wages are consumed and all profits are invested (all investment is financed by retained earnings, so that debt financing and interest is still excluded from this model type). Furthermore there is not yet a government sector included in the model. Instead of the given trend in output growth of the monetarist baseline model we now thus have capital stock fluctuations according to the rate of profit realized at each moment in time (equal to profits per unit of capital). In addition, labor supply is growing at a given natural rate as in the original Solow dynamics. These are the building blocks of the AS inflation dynamics to be considered and analyzed in this and the following sections.

Taken together, we thus have the following equations for the Solow dynamics with monetarist wage–price dynamics based on the usual expectations augmented money wage Phillips curve and the quantity theory of money, but with prices equal to marginal wage costs in the place of the Samuelson-Solow type marked up wage

Phillips curve. Note, however, that price inflation is determined by the quantity theory of money as a complement to output growth, which means that the condition 'prices equal wage costs' must be interpreted here as a theory of employment and not as a theory of the price level. Note that the following assumes extremely classical (differentiated) saving habits (all wages are consumed, all profits are invested) and thus in particular Say's Law that total output always meets a goods demand of equal size. The alternative assumption of a uniform savings rate out of wages and profits, $s = s_w = s_c > 0$, will be used later when the Keynesian AD–AS approach is compared to the neoclassical employment dynamics of this section. The model is given by:[1]

$$Y = F(K, L^d) \quad \text{the neoclassical theory of production,} \tag{3.1}$$

$$\omega = \frac{w}{p} = F_L(K, L^d) \quad \text{the marginal productivity theory of}$$
$$\text{employment,} \tag{3.2}$$

$$C = \omega L^d \quad \text{workers' consumption } (s_w = 0), \tag{3.3}$$

$$I = \Pi = Y - \delta K - \omega L^d \quad \text{profits and investment } (s_c = 1), \tag{3.4}$$

$$Y \equiv C + I + \delta K \quad \text{Say's Law,} \tag{3.5}$$

$$\hat{w} = h(e) + \pi^e, \ h' > 0, \ h(\bar{e}) = 0 \quad \text{the money wage Phillips curve,} \tag{3.6}$$

$$\pi^e = \hat{p}_+ \quad \text{myopic perfect foresight,} \tag{3.7}$$

$$\hat{K} = r = (Y - \delta K - \omega L^d)/K \quad \text{capital stock growth,} \tag{3.8}$$

$$\hat{L} = n = const. \quad \text{labor force growth,} \tag{3.9}$$

$$\bar{\mu} = \hat{M} = \hat{Y} + \hat{p} \quad \text{money growth, output growth and inflation.} \tag{3.10}$$

Equations (3.1) and (3.2) determine the standard AS-curve of the textbook literature, while the following two equations for consumption and investment imply Say's law, equation (3.5), for goods market behavior. Equations (3.6) and (3.7) represent the conventional approach to labor market dynamics here under myopic perfect foresight. Equations (3.8) and (3.9) give the laws of motion for factor growth (which in sum determine output growth) and finally equation (3.10) is a simple growth rule for money supply which on the basis of output growth determines the rate of goods price inflation in this economy. Note that this final law of motion (for goods prices) implies that real wages are a given magnitude at each moment in time, which in turn implies that the AS-curve is used here to determine output and employment and not the price level at each moment in time.

---

1 With regard to the $\hat{p}_+$ notation in equation (3.7) this involves basically the right hand growth rate of p; see Sargent (1987) pp. 2,3 for a more detailed discussion.

Since we have analyzed the case of adaptive expectations in the case of the monetarist theory of inflation as well as for IS-LM-PC dynamics in the Chapter 2 extensively, we here immediately consider the situation of myopic perfect foresight (in which $\beta_{\pi^e} = \infty$), which in the case of the monetarist base model as well as in Keynesian IS-LM-PC dynamics gave rise to a collapse of the model's structure in that only steady state situations are then admissible under this assumption. Money was then thus superneutral also in the short run and monetary policy completely ineffective as a means of lowering the rate of unemployment. Note, however, that the case of adaptive expectations is not easy to analyze in the present situation, since it involves the calculation of the growth rate of output $\hat{Y}$ which is not a simple expression of the state variables of the model. Note finally again that the present model – just as the full-employment Solow growth model – is based on Say's Law throughout since output is always fully allocated to either consumption or investment demand.

In order to obtain the intensive form representation we switch to the variables $y = Y/K = f(l^d)$, $l^d = L^d/K$ (see Section 1.2 on the Solow growth model in Chapter 1).[2] Due to the conventionally assumed properties of the neoclassical production function on the extensive form level we obtain the inverse relationship between real wages and the labor intensity realized by firms of the form

$$\omega = F_L(K, L^d) = F_L(1, L^d/K) = F_L(1, l^d) = f'(l^d) > 0, f'' < 0$$

or, by inverting this relationship we have

$$l^d = l^d(\omega), \quad l^{d'} < 0, l^d = L^d/K$$

and thus get a negative reaction of actual labor intensity l^d with respect to changes in real wages ω. We basically have just another representation of the downward sloping real wage equal to the marginal product of labor schedule of static neoclassical theory or the upward sloping AS-schedule of this type of approach, if note is taken of the fact that real wages and the price level are inversely related for any given level of money wages. For the rate of profit $r = (Y - \delta K - \omega L^d)/K$ we have in addition that

$$r(\omega) = f(l^d(\omega)) - \delta - \omega l^d(\omega) \quad \text{or} \quad r(l^d) = f(l^d) - \delta - f'(l^d)l^d$$

and thus

$$\rho'(l^d) = f'(l^d) - f'(l^d) - f''(l^d)l^d = -f''(l^d)l^d > 0 \quad \text{or} \quad \rho'(\omega) < 0$$

due to $l^{d'}(\omega) < 0$.

Making use of the aforementioned relationships allows the reduction of the model to a system of differential equations in the two variables ω, the real wage,

---

2 cf. also Jones (1975, Ch.2).

and $l = L/K$, the full-employment labor intensity. The system so obtained is independent of the nominal side of the dynamics due to the assumption of myopic perfect foresight which in contrast to the monetarist baseline model of Chapter 1 implies that the quantity theory of money is not at all a restriction on the real dynamics of the economy and that in fact the evolution of price inflation is irrelevant for the real part of the model. Instead, depending on the growth rate of real output that is generated by the real dynamics, we have an appended theory of price inflation of no real importance. For the real dynamics we instead obtain the interdependent system of differential equations

$$\hat{\omega} = \hat{w} - \hat{p} = h(l^d(\omega)/l), \tag{3.11}$$

$$\hat{l} = \hat{L} - \hat{K} = n - (f(l^d(\omega)) - \delta - \omega l^d(\omega)) = n - r(\omega), \tag{3.12}$$

with both l^d and r depending negatively on the real wage ω.

The real wage dynamics are thus driven by the level of employment, which as stated depends negatively on the real wage, in its relation to the full-employment level, both expressed in per unit of capital form. The full-employment labor intensity in turn is determined by the difference of labor force and capital stock growth, the latter being determined by the rate of profit generated by the level of real wages.

Note here again that we make use of the neoclassical production in intensive form $y = Y/K = F(1, l^d) = f(l^d)$ in the expression for the growth rate of the capital stock and that we have abbreviated the Phillips curve demand pressure term by a function h which, as far as the method of proof used below is concerned, can in fact be any function which is negative to the left of the steady state value of the rate of employment and positive to its right. The only additional condition on the function h is that it indeed allows for a meaningful steady state solution.

The interior steady state of the system of differential equations (3.11) and (3.12) is given by $n = r(\omega_0)$ and $l_0 = l^d(\omega_0)/h^{-1}(0)$ with $h^{-1}(0) = V_o$ being the steady state value of the rate of employment e. We assume that the profit function $r(\omega)$ is such that the natural rate of growth is contained in its mathematical image[3] (which is the case for all typical neoclassical production functions). Note again that this profit function has the derivative given by

$$\rho'(\omega) = f'(l^d(\omega))l^{d'}(\omega) - \omega l^{d'}(\omega) - l^d(\omega) = -l^d(\omega) < 0,$$

since $\omega = f'(l^d(\omega))$ because of the assumed marginal productivity theory. The interior steady state solution for ω is therefore uniquely determined, as is the subsequently determined solution for l. There is a further steady state at the origin of the $\mathbb{R}^2$ plane which due to the global asymptotic stability results for the positive orthant of $\mathbb{R}^2$ – shown in Figure 3.3 – need not concern us here.

---

3 That is in the range of values of r obtained as ω varies over its economic domain.

The Jacobian of the dynamical system (3.11) and (3.12) evaluated at the steady state is

$$J = \begin{pmatrix} \omega h' l^{d'}/l & -\omega h' V_0/l \\ -\rho' l & 0 \end{pmatrix} = \begin{pmatrix} - & - \\ + & 0 \end{pmatrix}.$$

This matrix structure fulfills the conditions of Olech's theorem in its growth rate form, see Flaschel (1984) for details, which implies that the dynamical system is globally asymptotically stable in the positive orthant of $\mathbb{R}^2$. This result will be proved below by means of a suitably chose Liapunov function, to be defined on the positive orthant of $\mathbb{R}^2$ In order to see whether convergence toward the steady state is accompanied by cyclical movements or not, we need to consider the relationship between $\det J$ and trace J shown in Figure 3.2, where

$$4 \det J = 4(-\rho')h'\omega V_o, \quad (\text{trace } J)^2 = (h')^2(l^{d'}\omega/l^d)^2 V_o^2 = (h')^2 \epsilon^2 V_o^2.$$

with ϵ denoting the elasticity of the $l^d(\omega)$ relationship. The combinations of $\det J$ and $tr\,J$ that lie above the parabola (and of course to the left of the vertical axis) are those for which damped cycles occur. Note, that this calculation is only valid at the steady state and that it is here applied to the dynamical system (3.11), (3.12) written in terms of its derivatives $\dot{\omega}$, $\dot{l}$ rather than to its growth rate formulation in terms of $\hat{a}$, $\hat{l}$, that is the dynamical system

$$\dot{\omega} = \omega h(l^d_{(\omega)}/l), \tag{3.13}$$

$$\dot{l} = l(n - r(\omega)). \tag{3.14}$$

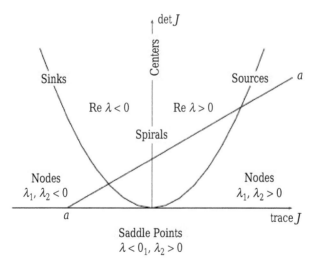

Figure 3.2 Stability features of the dynamical system (3.11), (3.12) based on determinant / trace-configurations (with the parabola being given by $\det J = (trace\,J)^2/4$).

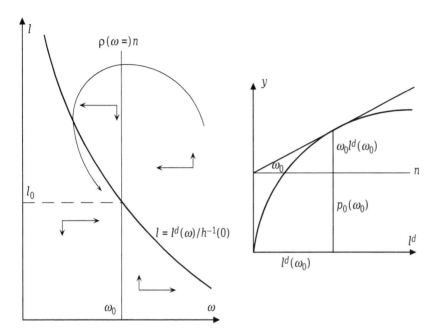

Figure 3.3 The Solow-Goodwin dynamics for a wage-elastic employment function.

Note also with respect to Figure 3.3 that the $\dot{l} = 0$ isocline that separates upward from downward movements of the full-employment labor intensity ratio is vertical and thus simply determined by a single value of the real wage, while higher (lower) real wages increase (decrease) labor intensity by corresponding reactions of capital stock growth. The $\hat{\omega} = 0$ isocline, by contrast, is downward sloping due to the mathematical expression that determines its shape ($h^{-1}(0) = \bar{e} = V_o$). Higher levels of the full-employment labor intensity imply employment rates below the NAIRU and thus falling real wages, while the opposite holds true below the $\hat{\omega} = 0$ isocline. The relationship between output per unit of capital and its distribution between capital and labor is shown on the right hand side of Figure 3.3, illustrating again that higher real wages are negatively correlated with output and the rate of profit, the latter a classical relationship already detected by Ricardo at the beginning of the nineteenth century.

In order to get cyclical movements we require

$$4 \det J > (\operatorname{tr} J)^2 \quad \text{or} \quad 4(-\rho')\omega\bar{e} > h'\epsilon^2, \tag{3.15}$$

where

$$\epsilon = \frac{dl^d / l^d}{d\omega / \omega} = l^{d'}(\omega)\omega / l^d. \tag{3.16}$$

We consequently arrive at the conclusion that the slope of the Phillips–curve h' and the elasticity $\epsilon(\omega)$ of the $l^d(\omega)$ curve are of decisive importance for the generation of cyclical movements, which are more likely the flatter is the Phillips curve h or the smaller the elasticity expression $\epsilon(\omega)$ for the neoclassical theory of employment.

We will obtain larger and longer fluctuations around the steady state in Figure 3.3 when we reduce the real-wage elasticity of labor demand sufficiently and (in the limit) Goodwin type closed orbit fluctuations when elasticity becomes zero (implying fixed proportions in production). In the next section, we shall start from this case of fixed proportions in production and the Goodwin growth cycle model in its original formulation in order to subsequently consider its relationship to the model of the present section in a phase diagram of Goodwinian type, that is with the rate of employment in place of labor intensity on the vertical axis.

3.4 Employment cycles in Classical real growth

It is no exaggeration to state that the Goodwin (1967) growth cycle model represents just as important a prototype model as the original Solow (1956) growth model with its monotonic full-employment path in the place of fluctuating employment rates, yet with smooth factor substitution in the place of Goodwin's fixed proportions technology. Indeed, Solow himself has expressed his admiration for this compact growth cycle model, see Solow (1990), where he discusses its background, its strength and its weaknesses as well as its empirical importance. Yet, despite its importance, Goodwin's model remains largely neglected in mainstream economics and in the textbook literature.

Figure 3.4 provides in graphical terms the basic elements needed to derive Goodwin's (1967) classical growth cycle model of labor market and real wage dynamics. We see an overshooting mechanism in an environment where we still abstract from technical change, and are implicitly assuming a fixed proportions technology. We have top left a real wage Phillips-Curve (PC), relating the rate of growth $\hat{\omega}$ of real wages with the state of the labor market, expressed by the rate of employment e. This PC has been drawn as strictly convex, but at the minimum need only fulfill the following three conditions in order to obtain the conclusions of this prototype growth cycle model:[4]

- There is a uniquely determined Non-Accelerating-Inflation Rate of Utilization (NAIRU) $\bar{e}$ of the labor force.[5]
- The PC curve exhibits negative values below this rate, and thus implies falling real wages in this domain.
- The PC shows positive values to the right of the NAIRU, implying rising real wages on this side.

---

4 Continuity of this curve is of course assumed in addition. Note also that we have $\epsilon = 1/-\alpha$ in the case of a Cobb-Douglas production function $y = f(l) = l^{1-\alpha}$.

5 Note that we reinterpret the NAIRU of the literature here in terms of the rate of employment (or utilization) e of the labor force, not in terms of the level of unemployment.

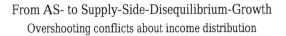

From AS- to Supply-Side-Disequilibrium-Growth
Overshooting conflicts about income distribution

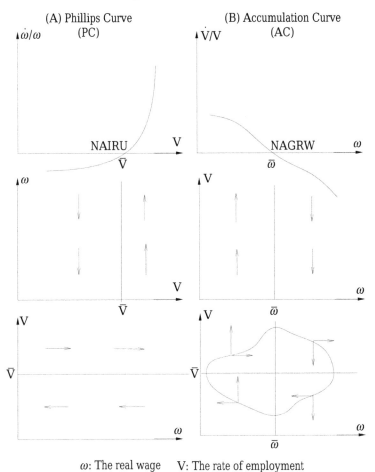

ω: The real wage   V: The rate of employment

Figure 3.4 The basic elements of the Goodwin growth cycle model ($V = e$ the rate of employment).

Thus, in the following analysis, we do not require that the real wage PC, which satisfies a relationship of the form

$$\hat{\omega} = PC(e),$$

as far as its dependence on the rate of employment e is concerned, be monotonically increasing as is generally assumed in the literature and as it is shown in the Figure 3.4.[6] The type of PC assumed here is exactly the one we have used in the Solow-Goodwin synthesis of the preceding section.

Corresponding to the real wage Phillips Curve just described we assume as second building block of our model an Accumulation Curve (AC) which postulates that the rate of change, $\hat{e}$, of the rate of employment is a function of the level of real wages, again with a benchmark value, a Non-Accelerating-Growth Rate of (real) Wages $\bar{\omega}$ (NAGRW), which separates regimes of rising from regimes of falling rates of employment, due to their impact on profitability and thus the rate of investment. As before, all conclusions of the classical growth cycle model hold under the foregoing three conditions, and thus again, we do not demand monotonicity of the curve shown at the top right in Figure 3.3. The accumulation curve is derived in the Goodwin (1967) approach by assuming (as in the preceding section) the extreme type of classical saving habits, fixed proportions in production, full capacity utilization with respect to the capital stock (due to Say's Law again) and a constant rate of natural growth (see below for the inclusion of technical change). On this basis we obtain for e the dynamical law

$$\hat{e} = \hat{L}^d - \hat{L} = \hat{K} - n = r - n = y - \delta - \frac{\omega}{x} y - n = AC(\omega), \tag{3.17}$$

where y again denotes the now given output-capital ratio Y/K and x the given state of labor productivity Y/L^d. The accumulation curve shown in Figure 3.3 thus is simply a linear one on the basis of the present derivation, but as stated can have in fact any shape in the domains where it is positive or negative, respectively.

On the basis of the two curves shown in the top two panels of Figure 3.3 one gets the adjustments of the rate of employment and of real wages as shown in the middle panels of this figure. In order to then obtain the dynamic consequences for the interaction of real wages with the rate of employment (bottom right panel) one has to mirror the implications of the PC part of the model along the 45° degree line (bottom left panel). The phase space in the bottom right panel then simply integrates the neighboring situations, as shown by the arrows.

The further implication of the model, that all curves, in the positive part of the phase space shown, must be closed orbits, can of course not be proven by such simple graphical arguments. In order to obtain this result in an intuitively understandable way, one has to consider a Liapunov function of the type

$$L(\omega, e) = G(\omega) + H(e) = -\int_{\bar{\omega}}^{\omega} AC(\tilde{\omega})/\tilde{\omega}\, d\tilde{\omega} + \int_{\bar{e}}^{e} PC(\tilde{e})/\tilde{e}\, d\tilde{e}, \tag{3.18}$$

with $PC(e)$ in fact given by $h(e)$ according to the preceding section and $AC(\omega)$ given by $y - \delta - \omega y/x - n$ according to the above analysis. The graph of this

---

6 Note that a real wage PC has been obtained from the conventional money wage PC (augmented by inflationary expectations of course) by assuming myopic perfect foresight with regard to the expected rate of inflation.

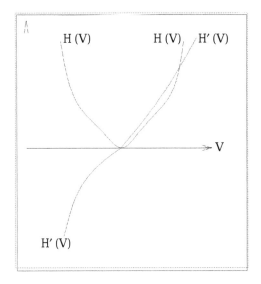

Figure 3.5 Building a Liapunov function for Goodwin's center type dynamics ($V = e$).

function has the form of a 3D global sink, under the assumptions made, with its minimum at $\bar{\omega}, \bar{e}$ and with all level curves (where the function assumes a given value) closed. This is simply due to the fact that the functions G and H are both 2D sinks (with argument ω, e respectively, see the Figure 3.5 for an example), since their derivatives are negative on the left-hand side and positive on the right-hand side of the steady state values ω, e respectively.

Projected into the ω, e phase space, the closed curves that are thereby obtained from the level curves of the Liapunov-function are just the orbits or trajectories of the considered Goodwin real wage – rate of employment dynamics, since it is easily shown (see below) that L is constant along the trajectories of the dynamical system under investigation. Figure 3.6 illustrates an example of such a situation.[7]

In order to prove that all trajectories of the interacting PC, AC dynamics are indeed closed curves one only needs to calculate $\dot{L}$, the time-derivative of the defined Liapunov-function along the orbits or trajectories of these dynamics. By differentiating (3.18) with respect to time one immediately obtains

$$\dot{L} = L_{\omega}\dot{\omega} + L_e\dot{e} = -AC(\omega)\hat{\omega} + PC(e)\hat{e} = -AC(\omega)PC(e) + PC(e)AC(\omega) \equiv 0. \tag{3.19}$$

7 Note that these assertions apply to all the trajectories in the positive orthant shown, while all other trajectories are unimportant from an economic point of view. For further investigations of Goodwin's growth cycle mechanism, the reader is referred to Flaschel (1993) and Flaschel, Franke and Semmler (1997).

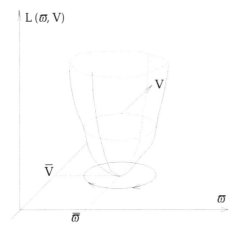

Figure 3.6 The Liapunov function and the implied closed orbit structure ($V = e$).

It is clear from Figure 3.6 that $\dot{L} = 0$ gives a closed curve at a fixed height on the L axis, which when projected onto the (ω, V) plane will yield a closed curve. We stress again that this proof applies to very general situations as far as functional shapes of the PC-AC curves are concerned, but some modification is required for systems which do not rely on the simple cross-dual[8] nature of the AC-PC interaction as shown in Figure 3.4.[9]

We thus have the result that all trajectories generated by the interaction of PC and AC dynamics represent periodic motions of the real wage and the rate of employment as the one shown in the bottom right panel of Figures 3.4. We do not describe the overshooting dynamics here in detail, as this has been done many times already.[10] The overshooting occurs in a growing economy if there is labor force growth or Harrod neutral technical change, and it should also be applicable (not necessarily with periodic motions throughout) to modern representations of technical change, see Desai and Shah (1981) for an early attempt along Kennedy-Weizsäcker lines (see Jones (1975)) which implied convergence to the steady state for this model of economic growth.

Goodwin's growth cycle model has often been criticized as representing a structurally unstable model of cyclical growth. Indeed, many small perturbations of the structure of the model will destroy the closed orbit structure of its trajectories and lead, for example, to explosive or implosive fluctuations instead.

---

8 By cross-dual we here refer to a two-dimensional dynamical system in which one variable enters into the rate of change of the other and vice versa.

9 See Flaschel, Franke and Semmler (1997) for the consideration of cross-dual macrodynamics on various levels of generality.

10 See for example Flaschel (1993, Ch.4) in this regard.

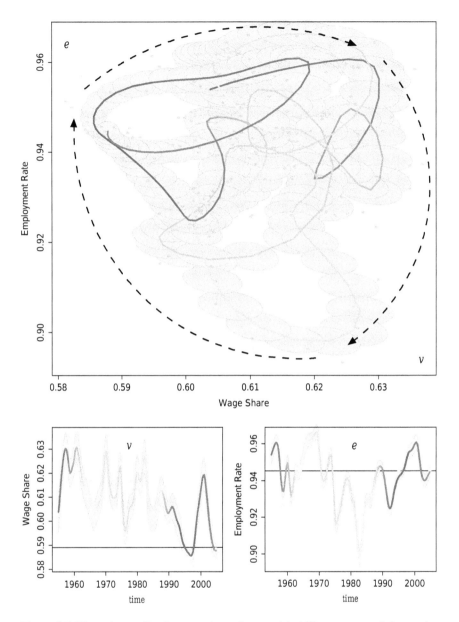

Figure 3.7 Wage share – Employment dynamics: empirical Phase space and time series representations for the US-economy.[11,12]

11 Wage share / employment rate dynamics (top plot) with an estimated smooth cycle. The grey areas show pointwise confidence regions. The bottom panels show data plotted against time. Numerical parameters are as before.

12 This figure can be usefully compared with its companion figure in Chapter 2, the employment inflation phase diagram.

Yet, such a change in qualitative mathematical properties does not necessarily imply that the economics of the model has been changed in a significant way. To provide an example for this claim, an important extension of the aforesaid model was introduced in the preceding section, by which we attempted to demonstrate to the reader (and continue that attempt in this section) that Solow's and Goodwin's models are in fact only two sides of the same coin.

In closing this section, we show in Figure 3.7 the empirical phase plot, with data of the U.S. economy, of the Goodwin profit squeeze dynamics with the wage share in place of the real wage. We leave open here the question as to whether the long phase cycle that is shown in the figure is the result of a Goodwin growth cycle model enhanced by neoclassical substitution between capital and labor and stochastic shocks or is more of a Rose (1967) limit cycle type, based on a repelling steady state position which is kept viable by the assumption of increasing wage flexibility far off the steady state.

3.5 Neoclassical employment dynamics from a Classical perspective

We now return to the Solow-Goodwin synthesis of Section 3.3 (with its assumption of extremely classical saving habits)[13] and seek to show here that there is a Goodwin type representation of these dynamics, in terms of the real wage and the rate of employment, that can easily be compared to the limit case of fixed proportions in production considered by Goodwin. We will thereby also increase our understanding of the Solow-Goodwin synthesis. A Goodwin-like reformulation of the dynamics (3.11), (3.12) considered in the Section 3.3 is given by the representation[14]

$$\hat{\omega} = h(e), \tag{3.20}$$

$$\hat{e} = \frac{l^{d'}(\omega)}{l^d(\omega)}\dot{\omega} - (n - r(\omega)),$$

$$= \epsilon(\omega)\hat{\omega} + g(\omega) = \epsilon(\omega)h(e) + g(\omega), \tag{3.21}$$

where we have used the relation $e = l^d/l$ and set $g(\omega) = r(\omega) - n$ so that $g'(\omega) = -l^d(\omega) < 0$ holds true and where $\epsilon(\omega)$ is defined in equation (3.16). We note in addition that steady state values are calculated according to $e_o = h^{-1}(0) \in (0, 1)$ and $\omega_o = r^{-1}(n)$. The real wage PC is here used in its original form, since a growth law for the rate of employment could be calculated from the marginal productivity theory of employment as shown above.

---

13 The case $s = s_w = s_c$ will be considered when AD–AS growth dynamics is analyzed, while differentiated saving habits á la Kaldor are left for future research.
14 Note here that the PC-curve of Figure 3.4 is here given by the function h and the AC-curve by $\hat{e} = \epsilon h(e) - (n - r(\omega))$. The latter curve is therefore now shifting with the rate of employment e, if $\epsilon \neq 0$ holds and thus no longer of the type shown in Figure 3.4.

By means of the Liapunov-function

$$L(\omega, e) = \int_{e_o}^{e} \frac{h(x)}{x} dx - \int_{\omega_o}^{\omega} \frac{g(y)}{y} dy,$$

which is again of the shape shown in Figure 3.4, we can readily calculate

$$\dot{L} = h(e)\dot{e} - g(\omega)\dot{\omega} = h(e)g(\omega) - g(\omega)h(e) + \epsilon(\omega)h(e)^2 = \epsilon(\omega)h(e)^2 \leq 0,$$

and

$$\dot{L} = 0 \text{ iff } e = e_o,$$

which now allows us to prove the global asymptotic stability of the steady state solution with respect to the positive orthant of $\mathbb{R}^2$ where the Liapunov function is always well-defined.[15] By Liapunov's direct method[16] in place of Olech's theorem we thus again get the result that all trajectories starting in the positive domain of the phase space will converge to the interior steady state of the dynamical system (3.20), (3.21). This is due to the fact that the Liapunov function is again of the type shown in Figure 3.6 and due to the fact that – up to isolated situations given by $e = e_o$ – this Liapunov function is now falling along the trajectories of the synthesized Solow-Goodwin dynamics until the global sink of the shown graph of the L–function has been reached.

Remark: In the case of a Cobb-Douglas production function $Y = K^\alpha (L^d)^{1-\alpha}$ we have $f(l^d) = (l^d)^{1-\alpha}$ and $f'(l^d) = (1 - \alpha)(l^d)^{-\alpha} = \omega$, implying that

$$l^d = (\frac{\omega}{1-\alpha})^{-1/alpha} \quad \text{and} \quad \epsilon = \frac{l^{d'}\omega}{l^d} = -\frac{1}{\alpha}, \quad \alpha \in (0, 1).$$

Thus in the case of the Cobb-Douglas function the considered elasticity is a constant between -1 and $-\infty$. We will use this simplified situation in the phase portrait to be considered in Figure 3.8 below. This of course only holds as long as we have $\epsilon < 0$. Compared with the original Goodwin model considered in this section (the case when $\epsilon = 0$ and where motions stay on the level curves and thus must become closed orbits) we have that negative elasticity of the labor demand schedule will imply that the level curves of the Liapunov-function are now (nearly everywhere) crossed from outside to the inside by the orbits of the Solow-Goodwin dynamics which therefore must move to lower and lower level curves and thus to the deepest point in the global 3D sink shown in Figure 3.6.

---

15 We note here that the shape of the function L as well as the size of $\dot{L}$ depends on both ϵ and h, which does not allow us to conclude anything definite on the speed of convergence towards the steady state and the extent to which this is accompanied by cyclical behavior.

16 See theorem 3 in the mathematical appendix or theorem 2 in Hirsch and Smale (1974, p.196) applied to the set $P = L^{-1}([0, c]), c > 0$ ($\epsilon = 0$ the original Goodwin case).

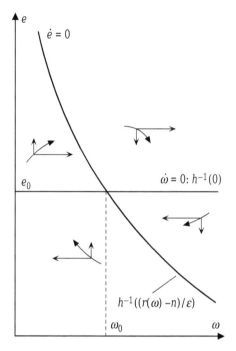

Figure 3.8 The phase portrait of the Solow-Goodwin growth dynamics.

The Figure 3.8 below finally shows the phase portrait of the dynamical system (3.20), (3.21) considered in the preceding Section from the perspective of Liapunov's direct method. We know from there that every trajectory in the positive orthant of $\mathbb{R}^2$ will converge to the interior steady state solution in the cyclical fashion shown. However, it is easy to show by means of the Jacobian J at the steady state, given by

$$J = \begin{pmatrix} 0 & h'(e_0)\omega_0 \\ \rho'(\omega_o)e_0 & \epsilon h'(e_0)e_0 \end{pmatrix} = \begin{pmatrix} 0 & + \\ - & - \end{pmatrix},$$

that monotonic adjustment towards the steady state (a stable node) must come about when the parameter ϵ or the slope of the function h are made sufficiently large, that is when the employment function is very elastic or the wage adjustment speed sufficiently large. This result demonstrates that this model type supports neoclassical labor market policies despite its partially classical nature. Moreover, persistent cyclical motion is not easily derived from such a model type, since this would demand the establishment of local instability combined with global stability which is not too easily realized with such supply side dynamics.[17] Destabilizing

---

17 A counterexample is given when one makes the assumption that workers demand more than the rate of inflation close to the steady state and less far away from it; see Flaschel (1984) for an approach in this direction.

forces close to the steady state are easily obtained on fairly traditional grounds when one turns to the dynamics of aggregate demand, which is the topic of the next section and which was the subject of the Chapter 2, though from a different angle.

We have seen in Chapter 1 that the monetarist theory of inflation, which is generally used to represent the medium run evolution of the considered economy, combines a strict ceiling on nominal growth (or the sum of real growth and inflation) with inertia in wage level adjustments and inflationary expectations to derive the fundamental conclusion that prudent monetary policy can avoid the occurrence of this inertial adjustment and that labor market policy (via increasing labor market flexibility) can speed up the process of convergence towards the steady state.[18] Yet, if inertia characterizes wage and inflationary expectations adjustments there may be periods of stagflation and subsequent long stagnation needed to adjust wages and inflationary expectations such that the NAIRU rate of unemployment is established and inflation again becomes steady. These are the costs of inflation in this model type if policy makers have followed a strategy of easy money in order to have unacceptably low unemployment rates on the labor market, low that is compared with the NAIRU.

We conclude for this synthesis of Solow's and Goodwin's approach to economic growth that Solow adds stability to the Goodwin cycle, while Goodwin causes Solovian adjustment paths to cycle, if (for example) the reaction of real wages to unemployment is sufficiently slow. These two important prototype models are therefore in no way in opposition to each other, but clearly show that there is a bridge between Classical and Neoclassical ideas as far as the labor market is concerned and that it will depend on empirical judgments (in particular on reaction speeds, elasticities and other parameter values discussed) to decide which of these approaches will ultimately give the more convincing picture of economic dynamics.[19]

In the Solow-Goodwin model type, we have not yet paid much attention to inflationary processes and the nominal side of the economy. Here, the conflict over income distribution (represented by a real wage Phillips curve) and its consequences for real economic growth have interacted with each other to generate a possibly cyclical process of real adjustment to an endogenously generated NAIRU rate of employment and a level of the real wage that is compatible with steady real growth. The question was therefore not so much the danger of price inflation, but instead the danger of over- and undershooting adjustments in income distribution that on the one hand generated too little and on the other hand too much real growth compared to the steady growth path of the economy. Nominal issues were of no importance, and if included would simply imply an adjustment

---

18 In fact, the steady state is never left when expectations become of the myopic perfect foresight variety, which represents another possibility to overcome the inertia characterizing labor market adjustments.

19 Adding Harrod neutral technical change to this Solow-Goodwin synthesis will give rise to a model that exhibits in its steady growth solution all of the Kaldorian stylized facts (see Jones (1975, Ch.1) for their enumeration), including a steady state rate of unemployment not contained in Kaldor's list of the stylized facts of economic growth.

of the rate of inflation towards the difference between monetary and real growth as presented in the initial formulation of the model.

One can even go one step further and completely abandon the role of the quantity theory of money as a restriction, here only on the rate of price inflation of the economy. Assume an economy where bills of exchange are used as medium of exchange and fully accepted by the agents of the economy. Assume furthermore as a revised theory for price inflation that this rate is set by firms in order to achieve a given target rate of profit $\bar{r}$, for example according to

$$\hat{p} = \beta_p(\bar{r} - r).$$

Whenever the actual rate of profit falls below the targeted level $\bar{r}$ there is price inflation and price deflation in the opposite case. Money is fully endogenous by assumption, which in addition implies that the rate of growth of the money supply is given by $\mu = \hat{Y} + \hat{p}$. This alternative approach to price and money wage inflation again implies that nominal magnitudes do no matter for the real dynamics. Again, monetarist considerations do not matter for the discussion of the core dynamics of the economy. Labor market and employment theories here must address the issue of a real wage Phillips curve and the elasticities present in the production function of the economy in order to achieve a more flexible adjustment of the economy towards its steady state growth path.[20]

We shall show in the next section that such conclusions also apply to the standard AD–AS textbook model of economic growth, where there is a fully integrated Keynesian IS-LM block in the place of the strict quantity theory of money or a fully endogenous money supply. We stress, however, that this will be due again to the assumption of myopic perfect foresight instead and will be altered to some extent when adaptive expectations are used. Yet, myopic perfect foresight has not at all the implications that happened to hold for the monetarist theory of inflation, neither in the model of the present and the last section, and nor in the Keynesian AD–AS growth dynamics to be considered next.

3.6 AD–AS dynamics under myopic perfect foresight

In this section, we investigate the traditional model of AS–AD growth, now normally considered as the first Neoclassical Synthesis in the development of Keynesian demand and supply side analysis. This synthesis marries the Hicksian IS-LM model with the standard AS-schedule, which was not rejected as invalid

---

20 On the basis of such an approach, one can enrich the Solow model with Harrod neutral technical change (and the Kaldorian stylized facts it implies) by two further stylized facts, namely that the steady state rate of employment is positive and that this also holds for the steady state rate of inflation. The latter will be the case if it is assumed that target rate of profit $\bar{r}$ is higher than the steady state rate of profit of the model, which is determined in the real part of the dynamics. The further stylized fact implied by the Goodwin extension of the Solow model, that of a clockwise movement in the interaction of income distribution and employment rate dynamics, must be extended to the case of technical change before it can really be evaluated.

in Keynes' (1936) critique of the neoclassical approach and which therefore still appears to be a natural candidate for the representation of supply side dynamics in a Keynesian framework. Yet, combining the AS-schedule with IS-LM and PC analysis – under myopic perfect foresight – seems to give rise to bizarre outcomes from a Keynesian perspective, since they seem to imply that the real dynamics becomes completely independent of aggregate demand side forces (stage A of this Neoclassical Synthesis), while the nominal dynamics becomes completely subordinate to these real dynamics and are subject to centrifugal forces if these are not tamed by the rational expectations approach to saddlepoint instability (the Neoclassical Synthesis stage B).

AD–AS growth with adaptively formed or myopic perfect foresight expectations is investigated in detail in Sargent (1987, Ch.5). It is more or less explicitly stated there that the adaptive case has the usual inertia problems of the monetarist base model of our Chapter 1 and thus repeats for Keynesian IS-LM analysis what is true if Keynesian goods demand does not matter and the quantity theory of money strictly regulates the nominal growth path of the economy. It has been shown in Flaschel (1993, Ch.6) and in more detail in Franke (1996) that this does not generally hold true, since the model undergoes a Hopf bifurcation for adjustment speeds of adaptive expectations sufficiently fast and thus loses its local asymptotic stability and also its global stability if such adjustment speeds are further increased. The analysis of cycles and growth – when based on the conventional Keynesian IS-LM model – is thus not always a complete one, due basically to the fact that the Keynes-effect and the Mundell-effect work in opposition to each other through the real rate of interest effect present in the Keynesian investment schedule.

We have considered these two feedback channels in detail in the preceding chapter on Keynesian IS-LM-PC analysis, representing the extension of IS-LM analysis by the Phillips curve and the expectation schemes we used in Chapter 1 for the monetarist base model. Briefly summarized, the foregoing two effects are thus characterized as stabilizing (the Keynes-effect), since price inflation leads to nominal interest rate increases, declining aggregated demand and economic activity and therefore produce a counter force to further price increases, and destabilizing (the Mundell-effect), since inflation here (ceteris paribus) decrease the real rate of interest and thus give a further push to the increase in economic activity already under way. However, Mundell-effects – though reconsidered from time to time (in particular in the presence of a zero bound on nominal interest rates) – are basically ignored in textbook literature and other approaches to Keynesian dynamics, since they give rise to the problem of how to handle Keynesian AD–AS growth when the steady state of such a model type is surrounded by centrifugal forces.[21]

---

21 Groth's (1993) paper stresses the unfamiliar nature of such an occurrence and proves that even when locally asymptotically stable there may nevertheless be global instability and thus corridor stability.

In the present section, we make use of Sargent's (1987, Ch.5) AD–AS growth model only for the case of myopic perfect foresight (as in the preceding sections of this chapter) and will show that the resulting Keynesian AD–AS growth dynamics then simply give rise to the globally asymptotically stable Solow-Goodwin dynamics discussed in the previous section, coupled with a law of motion for nominal wages and prices that is purely explosive when solved by way of historical conditions and a predetermined price level. This indicates that the jump-variable technique of Sargent and Wallace (1973) may find application here to remove the nominal instability of wages and prices by jumps in their levels that would allow these variables to converge back to their steady state values, in the case of unanticipated or anticipated monetary or fiscal shocks, respectively. Yet, in the considered Phillips curve, nominal wages have been assumed to adjust only sluggishly in the light of the demand pressure and the cost pressure terms. The model is thus manipulated in a strange way in order to obtain neoclassical or monetarist conclusions from a conventional Keynesian setup. Further details can be found in Flaschel (1993, Ch.7) and Flaschel, Franke and Semmler (1997, Part III).

A way around the foregoing conundrums and problems has been given in Chiarella and Flaschel (2000) by the introduction of the Keynes-Metzler-Goodwin (KMG) approach to cyclical growth, which is based on sluggish prices, wages and quantities with fluctuating rates of capacity utilization of both labor and capital. This approach in our view provides the consistent formulation of Keynesian AD–AS growth now (as should be the case with disequilibrium) on both the market for labor and for goods, with both factors of production faltering in depressions and gaining in booms. The KMG approach to disequilibrium and growth will be introduced here in Chapter 7. However, in the present chapter we still only consider the dynamics that comes about when conventional equilibrium AD–AS growth is coupled with the assumption of myopic perfect foresight to show that Keynesian analysis can be (mis-)used and reduced to supply side dynamics of classical and neoclassical type if appropriately manipulated, with bizarre outcomes on the adjustment of nominal variables to say the least.

The Keynesian AD–AS model (of the old Neoclassical Synthesis) on which Sargent's (1987) analysis of perfect foresight is based is described by the following set of equations:[22, 23]

$$Y = F(K, L^d), \tag{3.22}$$

$$w/p = F_L(K, L^d), \tag{3.23}$$

$$C = c(Y - T - \delta K), \quad 1 > c > 0, \tau = T/K = const., \tag{3.24}$$

---

22 The assumptions on trend growth are, following Sargent, made for reasons of simplicity in order to avoid further laws of motion that describe the adjustment of the various trend terms.

23 Note that we use $i(\cdot)$ to denote the investment function and just i by itself to denote the nominal interest rate.

$$I/K = i((F_K(K, L^d) - \delta) - (i - \pi^e)) + n, \quad (i > 0) \tag{3.25}$$

$$Y = C + I + \delta K + G, \quad \gamma = G/K = const., \tag{3.26}$$

$$M = pm^d(Y, i) = pY \exp(-\alpha i) = pYe^{-\alpha i}, \quad (\alpha > 0) \tag{3.27}$$

$$\hat{M} = \mu \quad (\text{here} = n) \tag{3.28}$$

$$\hat{w} = \beta_w(L^d/L - 1) + \pi^e, \quad (\beta_w > 0) \tag{3.29}$$

$$\pi^e = \hat{p}_+, \tag{3.30}$$

$$\hat{K} = i(\cdot) + n, \quad (\text{and:} \quad \hat{L} = n = const.). \tag{3.31}$$

The model given by equations (3.22)–(3.31) ignores the market for bonds (and equities) by virtue of Walras' Law of Stocks. Its behavioral assumptions, apart from one, are well known from the textbook literature.[24] The new assumption is that of myopic perfect foresight which is here formulated by means of the right hand time derivative $\dot{p}_+$[25] of the price level p at the present moment of time and which replaces the traditional assumption of adaptive inflationary expectations. It is interesting to note that this assumption that $\pi^e = \hat{p}_+ = \dot{p}_+/p$ can be obtained (at least formally) from the adaptive expectations case $\dot{\pi}^e/\beta_{\pi^e} = \hat{p}_+ - \pi^e$, by setting $\beta_{\pi^e} = \infty$. Thus from a mathematical point of view, the case of perfect foresight can be considered as a limit case of the adaptive mechanism which should therefore reflect to some extent the properties of this more 'old-fashioned' type of approach to expectations formation if these expectations are formed in a sufficiently fast way. This should in a Keynesian approach (under appropriate assumptions) make the difference between actual and expected inflation as small as desirable, since small errors in short-term inflationary expectations should not matter very much for a Keynesian theory of the business cycle.

Before proceeding to an analysis of the dynamic model (3.22)–(3.31), there is one remark to be made with respect to its (implicit) subdivision of its endogenous variables into static and dynamic ones. Dynamically endogenous variables are those whose time derivative (but not the variable itself) is considered as endogenous at time t, that is instantaneously determined in each point in

---

24 The model exhibits a neoclassical production function (3.22), the 'marginal productivity theory of employment' (3.23), a standard consumption function (3.24), a particular form of investment behavior (3.25), a special, but customary form of liquidity preference function (3.27), and a money-wage Phillips-curve (3.28). It is closed by various exogenous and endogenous growth equations, concerning assumptions on factor and money supply, see Flaschel (1993, Ch.6 and 7) for details.

25 It should be noted that the use of right-hand derivatives in this context is not meant to indicate that the class of admissible functions is extended to those having differing left- and right-hand side derivative everywhere. In fact, the points where jumps are permitted to occur are determined exogenously – and even restricted to the 'present' point-in-time in general (that is to the treatment of initial conditions whether predetermined or not). At all other points in time at least the usual assumption of absolute continuity is made with regard to the construction of the solution curves of the dynamical system (3.22)–(3.31).

time. Consequently, it is (or seems to be) assumed in the above model, see the formulation of the Phillips curve in (3.29) – that the change in money wage is determined endogenously at each moment t (by the rate of employment $e = L^d/L$), while the money wage itself is considered as given for each such t. However, such is not the case in Sargent's treatment of the model with myopic perfect foresight.[26]

In our view, it is important to have a *disjoint* classification into statically endogenous variables (Y, C, I, L^d, i, p) and dynamically endogenous variables (w, K) in a continuous time model such as the aforementianed one. In this way, we would avoid treating both the current and the future money wage, that is w_t and w_{t+1} or $(w_{t+1} - w_t)/w_t$ in discrete time or $w(t)$ and $\dot{w}(t)$ in continuous time, as being both endogenously determined at each moment t. Variables which allow for equilibrium at each moment of time are considered to adjust with infinite speed to the new equilibrium in the case of a disturbance of their former position. Statically endogenous variables thus fulfill dynamical laws which are intentionally left implicit by the very nature of the approach adopted. These dynamical laws consequently cannot be used to describe the evolution of the system, that is these variables cannot appear in the form of time rates of change in the equations which describe this evolution, since such rates do not mirror the true behavior of these variables (which is composed of discontinuous and continuous types of reaction). It is therefore in particular not sensible to formulate differential equations for such variables *in addition* to their static determination by equilibrium conditions and thus to group such a statically endogenous variable among the dynamically endogenous ones at one and the same time. Yet, Sargent's methodology in the case of perfect foresight is precisely of this (in our view problematic) type, at least as far as the treatment of the wage level w and the price level p is concerned.

In this and the next section, we shall study Sargent's methodology, which in its structure is well known and widely accepted, but which nevertheless is not a consistent procedure in the present context. We shall see that his results are indeed based on an (arbitrary) regrouping of the endogenous variables of the following form: Y, C, I, L, i, w as statically endogenous and $K, \omega = w/p, p$ as dynamically endogenous. This regrouping is combined with a further subdivision of the latter variables into predetermined ones (fixed by initial conditions) and nonpredetermined ones (determined by terminal conditions) in order to overcome a knife edge situation that turns out to be present in the dynamics of the variables K, ω, p of this modified model of Keynesian dynamics.

To allow for the existence of steady-states (which are needed as starting-points and reference paths in his analysis) Sargent (1987, p.113) assumes, as already indicated above, that the functions F, C and $m^d(\cdot, i)$ are homogeneous of degree 1. Dividing by K and expressing the resulting ratios by means of lower case letters

---

26 The choice of the symbol 't' for time is in conflict with our subsequent use of t for taxes per capital T/K. Since it is, however, always obvious when t is used for 'taxes' or to denote time we do not introduce a different symbol for one of these two quantities.

one then obtains the equivalent model[27],[28]

$$y = f(l^d), f'(l^d) > 0, \tag{3.32}$$

$$w/p = f'(l^d), f''(l^d) < 0, \tag{3.33}$$

$$c = c(y - \tau - \delta), \quad \tau = const., \tag{3.34}$$

$$\hat{K} = i(f(l^d) - f'(l^d)l^d - \delta - (i - \pi^e)) + n, \tag{3.35}$$

$$y = c + \hat{K} + n + \delta + \gamma, \quad \gamma = const., \tag{3.36}$$

$$ml = y \exp(-\alpha i), \quad m = M/L, \quad l = L/K, \tag{3.37}$$

$$\hat{M} = \mu \quad (= n = \hat{L} \text{ here}), \tag{3.38}$$

$$\hat{w} = \beta_w(l^d/l - 1) + \pi^e, \quad l = L/K, \tag{3.39}$$

$$\pi^e = \hat{p}_+, \tag{3.40}$$

$$\hat{l} = n - \hat{K} = -i(\cdot). \tag{3.41}$$

Given initial conditions (and in fact also one terminal condition) and given the time paths for the exogenous variables M, G and T, the model (3.32)–(3.41) will generate (under suitable assumptions) time paths of its endogenous variables, since the statically endogenous variables y, i, c, l^d, i, w^{29} can all be expressed as functions of the dynamic variables K, w and p by means of the implicit function theorem. Assuming in addition, the assumption $\hat{M} = n(= \hat{L})$ and the choice of special initial conditions for the dynamic variables allows in particular for full-employment steady-state behavior with

$$\hat{w} = \pi^e = \hat{p} = 0, \quad \hat{K} = \hat{L}^d = \hat{Y} = n.$$

The interior steady state of the model is in fact given by

$$y^o = \frac{n + \gamma + \delta - c(\delta + \tau)}{1 - c}, \quad l^{do} = f^{-1}(y^o) = l^o \quad (\bar{e} = 1),$$

as far as factor utilization rates are concerned (which are thus demand determined). The long-run value of y therefore defines a vertical line in the IS-LM temporary equilibrium phase diagram (with the understanding that the IS and LM curve will both adjust in time towards an intersection point on this vertical line; see also Sargent (1987, Ch.5).

---

27 See Sargent (1987, p.114)
28 Note, that the ratios t, g are treated as exogenous in Sargent's text. This means that he employs the special assumption that the growth rates of T and G equal $\hat{K}$.
29 See the foregoing remark and our following discussion of Sargent's reverted treatment of nominal and real wages w, ω.

For income distribution we then obtain

$$\omega^o = f'(l^o), r^o = y^o - \delta - \omega^o l^o = i^o,$$

with all rates of inflation being zero in the steady state. Finally, real balances are given by $m^o = ky^o \exp(-\alpha_r i^o)$. With regard to such reference paths, Sargent (1987, p.117) then describes in verbal terms possible effects, if such a steady state is disturbed at some moment t by a *once-and-for-all jump in money supply* M (engineered via an open-market operation that leaves $\hat{M}$ unaltered). On the assumption of myopic perfect foresight, namely equation (3.30), Sargent (1987, p.120 ff.) here obtains, in contrast to the situation of an in general cyclical adjustment toward (or away from) long-run neutrality caused by such shocks in the case of adaptive expectations, the following two results in comparison to the steady state reference situation initially assumed to prevail:

Hyper-Neutrality: an unexpected jump in the money supply M^s (that leaves $\hat{M}_+$ unchanged) implies an instantaneous jump in prices p and wages w *and* leaves all other variables unaltered.

Hyper-Anticipation: a jump in M of this type that is expected at time t to occur at time $t + \theta$. $(\theta > 0)$ is reflected (from t onwards, with correct anticipation of the rate of inflation) in all earlier values of the price level p (and w and i) and will give rise to strict neutrality from $t + \theta$ onwards.

Sargent's (1987, Ch.5) attempt to derive Friedmanian hypotheses from a complete model of Keynesian dynamics represents an approach which is very demanding, in particular since it attempts to show propositions that raise severe problems for Keynesian economics on its, i.e. the opponents' ground, by making use of assumptions which are typical for Keynesian model building. As we shall see in the following, these assumptions will no longer give rise to an overall stable private sector of the considered economy, a fact which then will allow, under suitable additional specifications, that the price level (and other nominal magnitudes) can react in the way that is asserted in the aforementioned two propositions.

There are, however, two still puzzling facts[30] surrounding these assertions in the context of a completely specified model of Keynesian dynamics. The differential equation that is derived for the evolution of the price (and the wage) level of this model is solved by imposing on it (in an ad hoc manner) an, in general, fairly complicated stability requirement. This is done solely by assumption, and leaves the reader totally uninformed about the general validity of such a procedure with respect to more complex (nonlinear) behavioral assumptions and more complicated disturbances of the given time paths of the exogenous variables.

---

30 Despite the long tradition and the wide acceptance of this approach. It is therefore hoped that the reader will at least feel a little bit puzzled by this particular application of the jump variable technique in the context of a full-fledged IS-LM model of monetary growth and of capital accumulation. We do not deny here, however, that such forward-looking behavior, and its formalization, can make sense in appropriately chosen Keynesian models of the medium run.

Furthermore, the variable w which was *assumed* to be exogenously given at each point in time t is now able to perform jumps, in order to allow for the claimed hyper-neutrality.

These two theorems thus look very strange when viewed from the standpoint of a conventional Keynesian (IS-LM) monetary growth dynamics (with an integrated wage–price sector) which is based on given wages at each moment of time and which treats the price level in some approaches as an equilibrium variable and in other approaches as a predetermined magnitude, but never as a variable which is governed by future events solely.

A thorough explanation of this 'bifurcation' in the model's implications, in comparison to the case of adaptive expectations which imply normal looking damped or explosive cycles, will be worked out in the following section.

The basic observation to be made in the case of perfect foresight is that eq. (3.39) can then be reduced to

$$\hat{\omega} = \beta_w(l^d/l - 1), \quad (\omega = w/p) \tag{3.42}$$

which gives the first differential equation of this new model. And for $\hat{l} = n - \hat{K}$ we can compute by means of equations (3.32), (3.34), (3.36) and (3.41) that

$$\hat{l} = n - [f(l^d) - c(f(l^d) - \tau - \delta) - \gamma - \delta] \tag{3.43}$$

as the second differential equation for this system. Inverting equation (3.33) to obtain $l^d = (f')^{-1}(\omega)$ then shows that (3.42) and (3.43) form an autonomous system of ordinary differential equations in the variables ω and l (since, following Sargent, t and g are assumed to be given). This system can be solved in the usual way for each given pair of initial conditions. Its stationary solution is given by

$$(1 - c)f(l_o^d) = n - c\tau + (1 - c)\delta + \gamma, \quad l_o^d = l_o = (f')^{-1}(\omega_o).$$

This steady state solution is uniquely determined and positive. Applying Olech's Theorem (see the mathematical appendix) the stationary solution can easily be shown to be globally asymptotically stable, since the Jacobian J of the system (3.42),(3.43) is characterized by

$$J = \begin{pmatrix} - & - \\ + & 0 \end{pmatrix}$$

in the positive orthant of $\mathbb{R}^2$. For each given vector $(\omega_0, l_0) \in \mathbb{R}^2_+$ of initial conditions (at time $t = t_0$) we have therefore a uniquely determined positive solution path $(\omega(t), l(t)), t_0 \le t < \infty$, which converges to (ω_o, l_o) as $t \to \infty$.[31]

---

31 Note that the rate of profit must remain positive throughout implying that the share of wages will always be less than 1.

The results obtained here are of the same type as those obtained for real part of the Solow-Goodwin model and can also be proved by use of a Liapunov function. The full details of the dynamics of (3.42), (3.43) thus need not be discussed any further here.

In the way just described, we can solve for all real variables of Sargent's dynamic model. Note, however, that ω has now become a dynamically endogenous variable, which by its very treatment is *assumed* to evolve in a continuous fashion (which includes the present time t_o). This treatment of the variable ω (together with the unambiguously continuous behavior of K or l) implies that the variables l^d, y, c, i (and L^d, Y etc.) must now all be continuous functions of time (compare equations (3.33), (3.32), (3.34),(3.36)), so they are no longer capable of performing jumps in response to a sudden change in the money supply M. This is a trivial consequence of the *assumed* change in the treatment of the variable ω.

Instead of our aforesaid procedure, Sargent (1987, pp.120,121) specializes to the particular case of a Cobb–Douglas production function $f(l^d) = (l^d)^{1-\alpha}$ and a log-linear Phillips–curve $\beta_w(l^d/l - 1) = \gamma \ln(l^d/l)$ which allows him to give an explicit solution for the variable l^d (or L^d) on the basis of a given time path $K(t)$. This, however, seems to be an inadmissible procedure, since L^d and K (or l^d and l) are mutually interdependent in their evolution. And from the integral formulation (3.38) which he obtains (on p.121) by this method Sargent finally concludes that L^d and therefore the above set of variables cannot respond at time t to the imposition of shocks at time t, without noticing that this is already a trivial consequence of treating ω and l (or K) as continuous solutions of the differential equations (3.42), (3.43). These variables *cannot jump because of the very method chosen* and not because of a dubious integration procedure which tries to demonstrate that they must remain fixed in the light of a sudden jump in money supply!

3.7 Appended price dynamics and rational expectations?

In this section, we study the nominal part of the dynamics which is completely subordinate to the real dynamics and which in fact allows for a variety of dynamic outcomes.

3.7.1 Only predetermined variables and nominal instability

The dynamical evolution we have considered so far is *completely independent* of the assumed investment behavior (3.35), the money market equilibrium (3.37), and any possible solution path for prices $p(t)$. Therefore the task of equations (3.35) and (3.37) of the model given by equations (3.32)–(3.41) in the case of perfect foresight is simply to determine the rate of inflation $\hat{p}$ and the rate of interest i in such a way that goods market and money market equilibrium is ensured for all t.

To obtain such an outcome Sargent proceeds in the following way. He assumes for the money demand function $m^d(y, i)$ the special form $e^{-\alpha i}y$, as already shown ealier. The equation for money market equilibrium can then be solved explicitly for the rate of interest i to yield

$$i = (\ln p + \ln K - \ln M + \ln y)/\alpha. \tag{3.44}$$

The variable i is subject to jumps, which ensure equilibrium in the money market whenever a jump in money supply M occurs. Inserting equation (3.44) into equation (3.35) and noting that $i(\cdot) + n$ is predetermined through (3.36) we have

$$i(\cdot) + n = f(l^d) - c(f(l^d) - \tau - \delta) - \gamma - \delta,$$

from which we can obtain an implicit differential equation for the variable p. This equation can be made an explicit one by inverting the (here linear) function $i(\cdot)$ to obtain

$$f(l^d) - f'(l^d)l^d - \delta - (i - \hat{p}) = i^{-1}[(1 - c)(f(l^d) - \delta) + c\tau - \gamma - n],$$

from which

$$\hat{p} = i^{-1}[(1 - c)(f(l^d) - \delta) + c\tau - \gamma - n] - (f(l^d) - f'(l^d)l^d - \delta)$$
$$+ (\ln M - \ln K - \ln p - \ln f(l^d))/(-\alpha). \tag{3.45}$$

This is the third and final dynamical law of Sargent's perfect foresight model (recall that it and equation (3.44) are but an equivalent expression for goods market and money market equilibrium). Noting that all terms apart from $M(t)$ and $p(t)$ depend on $\omega(t)$ and $l(t)$ through equations (3.42), (3.43) and (3.35) and using $h(\omega(t), l(t))$ to denote this dependence, the differential equation (3.45) can be more succinctly expressed as

$$\hat{p} = h(\omega(t), l(t)) + (\ln M(t))/(-\alpha) - (\ln p)/(-\alpha) = h(t) - (\ln M(t))/\alpha + \ln p/\alpha. \tag{3.46}$$

This third differential equation again makes plain that the evolution of the price level has no influence on the real variables of the system, but is simply an appendage to the motion of these latter variables. The assumption of perfect foresight ($\beta_{\pi^e} = \infty$) has completely voided the model (3.32) – (3.41) of its Keynesian features and given it an outlook of a very (neo-)classical type.

At first sight the law of motion governing the evolution of the price level appears to be a very complicated one, since it is given by a lengthy expression and does not represent an autonomous law of motion, but is driven by the real dynamics in quite an involved way. Reformulating it as shown before, however, reveals that it implies that inflation depends positively on the price level and is thus subject to centrifugal forces, though the real part of the model has been shown to be globally asymptotically stable and thus converges to the real steady state from all economically meaningful positions. Yet, this stable real growth path is surrounded by explosive movements of the price level (that do not feed back into the real dynamics), which appears bizarre from an economic point of view.

3.7.2 Real wage continuity, p-jumps and nominal stability

Our main concern in the remainder of this section is not the change in the model's structure at $\beta_{\pi^e} = \infty$ that has just been discussed, but rather the treatment of the differential equation (3.46) which Sargent uses to prove his assertions on hyper-neutrality and hyper-anticipation.[32] In Sargent and Wallace (1973), it was argued by means of a special example that one should abandon in the case of perfect foresight the requirement that the price level $p(t)$ be a continuous function of time *and* that one should adopt instead a forward looking solution procedure in such situations, which in our case becomes

$$\ln p(t) = -e^{t/\alpha} \int_t^\infty e^{-s/\alpha}[h(s) + (\ln M(s))/(-\alpha)]ds, \quad t \in [t_0, \infty). \quad (3.47)$$

This explicit solution of (3.46) is the only one that is asymptotically stable, since it suppresses the explosive $ce^{t/\alpha}$ term (recall that $\alpha > 0$) of the general solution of the differential equation (3.46) (see Sargent (1987, p.127) for further details).

The rationale behind this approach is the following one: if the public knows the whole future development of the function h as it is implied by the evolution of the variables ω and l (namely of the real part of the model as considered earlier) *and* if it knows the future development of the money supply M (and of G and T), then it can make use of the explicit formula (3.47) to predict what the price level should and thereby also will prevail at time t such that at the same time myopic perfect foresight and a stable reaction to monetary shocks is always guaranteed. Using the special solution (3.47) guarantees that the price level p will converge to '1', in contrast to all other solution paths q of (3.46) which will behave in a purely explosive or purely implosive manner (approach zero in the latter case) in their deviation $x(= q/p)$ from this reference solution, due to the fact that x satisfies the differential equation

$$\hat{x} = \frac{1}{\alpha} \ln x.$$

This last dynamic equation describes a similar instability to that of Harrod's model of knife-edge growth. Yet, in contrast to Harrod's reflection of such an occurrence the assumed economic agents have become meanwhile much more capable in reflecting the world (model) they live in, since they manage to see through this instability and avoid it by simply choosing the foregoing particular type of the solution of the linear inhomogeneous differential equation (3.46). Centrifugal forces here exist anywhere off the steady state as in this earlier model of unstable growth, but these forces can no longer create any harm – due to the perfect behavior of agents in managing such totally unstable situations. It follows that Sen's (1970)

---

32 On this point, the reader may compare with the preceding section.

model of Harrod's approach has been misleading to that extent as it also relied on the supposedly 'stupid' assumption of adaptive expectations. Assuming instead myopic perfect foresight for this model, too, would in this case immediately imply that the economy cannot leave the steady state.

Agents in Sargent's IS-LM growth model do not only have such myopic perfect foresight ($\pi_t^e = \hat{p}_t$, but they in addition have to be able to choose from a continuum of possibilities of such perfect foresight paths the one that is asymptotically stable in the light of the shock that hit the economy. In the present situation, there is fortunately only one such viable perfect foresight price path which then provides the relevant theory of the price level. It has already been demonstrated by Friedman (1979) for a much simpler macroeconomic model that such a procedure can hardly be justified by a detailed microeconomic reasoning. Furthermore, as can be seen by applying Minford and Peel's (1983, Ch.2) methodological considerations to Sargent's macrodynamic model, also purely verbal arguments (which appeal to forces not included in the model to justify the imposition of the terminal condition employed in the solution (3.47)) will look very strange in the context of this Solovian underemployment model of monetary growth.

The abandonment of the requirement that the price level $p(t)$ be continuous at all t is motivated in Sargent and Wallace (1973) only by the instability phenomena that otherwise will develop, and the elimination of the term $ce^{t/\alpha}$ is justified by the assumption that individuals will not expect an ever-accelerating inflation of deflation if M *is constant in time*.[33]

The fact that the assumption of continuity with respect to initial conditions, when solving (3.46), leads to an economically implausible behavior of the model's variables[34] may be due to the particular approach chosen for the presentation of "Keynesian" dynamics under perfect foresight. This problem will be reconsidered in the next chapter. In any case, formula (3.47) is the basis of the *hyper-neutrality proposition* and the *hyper-anticipation* proposition, which can be summarized in the following way:

1. Suppose that at time t it becomes known that money supply $M(s), s \geq t$ has been misconceived and is given by $M(s) \cdot \Phi$ from then on instead. Comparing (3.47) before and after this change in opinion (both for the same point in time t) implies that their difference is exactly $+\Phi$ (see Sargent (1987, p.124) for details). This means that p (or $\ln p$) jumps in the same way as M (or $\ln M$) does, which furthermore implies that the money wage w must jump in the same fashion, too, since $\omega = w/p$ is already fixed at time t by assumption.
2. Suppose, on the other hand, that it becomes known at time t that such a change in money supply will occur at time $t + \theta, \theta > 0$. The new function for $(\ln)M(s)$ must then be introduced into the price formula (3.47) at time t

---

33 An assumption which in the present model must be applied to the ratio M/L.
34 This is of 'saddle-point'-type: the real sector is asymptotically stable, while the thereby implied determination of nominal values is unstable.

already, which implies a jump at t in comparison to the price–formation rule which prevailed up to t. The price–level then indeed must react before this monetary policy comes into effect. (see again Sargent (1987, p.124) for the details of this calculation which in addition show that the situation of point 1 must, of course, again apply from time $t + \theta$ onwards).

It is immediately obvious that point 1 is but a special case of point 2. We stress again, that both cases demand a thorough justification that (3.47) is *the* economically meaningful solution to equation (3.46) *in a meaningful economic model* and that the whole procedure heavily depends on the special assumptions necessary to derive the differential equation (3.46) and the integral which solves it.[35]

Closing this section, Sargent's perfect foresight case may now be characterized as follows. Equation (3.43) would describe a Solow–type growth model if the real wage rate were always flexible enough to guarantee full-employment $l^d = l$. However, because of the assumed Phillips curve, this is not the case. Employment l^d is therefore in general different from full-employment and evolves according to $\hat{\omega} = -\beta_w(l^d/l - 1)$ and $\omega = f'(l^d)$, see equations (3.33) and (3.39), giving rise to a Solovian underemployment growth model. A third differential equation (3.46) concerning the price level p finally follows from adjusting the money-market rate of interest and on this basis investment plans to this predetermined Solovian growth path. If this equation is solved in the conventional way (from initial time) by a continuous function $p(t)$, instead of (3.47) we would obtain the solution

$$\ln p(t) = e^{t/\alpha} \left(\ln p(t_0) + \int_0^t e^{-s/\alpha}[h(s) + (\ln M(s))/(-\alpha)]ds \right). \tag{3.48}$$

This type of solution is unstable with regard to once-and-for-all disturbances of the steady-state by open market operations, a very unpleasant fact for an otherwise stable Solow-type model. It is therefore replaced by the solution (3.47), whereby this strange behavior is made to disappear and the aforesaid propositions are obtained. This is indeed a classical revolution within a Keynesian model. Again, only one new assumption seems to be necessary to overthrow completely the conventional (that is the Keynesian) approach to goods-market and money-market equilibrium. Investment is now again adjusted to savings, and not the other way round as in Keynes' revolution of the Classical model of his time. This would be far more than only the Neoclassical Synthesis as in Sargent (1987, Chapters 1,2), but in fact the (neo-)classical counterrevolution to the Keynesian revolution – if this approach to monetary growth is correct.

Doubts about the solution procedure introduced by Sargent and Wallace (1973) were expressed early in the development of the literature using it. For instance

---

35 The above Lucas–Sargent propositions will, for example, no longer be true if the log-linear dependence of the rate of interest on p and M is dispensed with (see Snower (1984) for details).

Blanchard (1981) in adopting this procedure in his now famous model of stock market dynamics writes

> Following a standard if not entirely convincing practice, I shall assume that q always adjusts so as to leave the economy on the stable path to equilibrium.

For a detailed critique of the technique, we refer the reader to Section 1.6 of Chiarella and Flaschel (2000) and to Chiarella, Flaschel, Franke and Semmler (2009, Ch.2). In the current context, these doubts can be crystallized in the following observation. First, the money wage w is suddenly again treated in a classical manner as a statically endogenous variable, at least in the case where jumps in the price level occur. It thus implicitly employs two wage-reaction functions, one for the continuous case at the precise point where the price jump occurs (the above type of Phillips curve) and one for the discontinuous case (the classical assumption of perfectly flexible wages). The classical features of these Keynesian dynamics therefore seem to rest at least on a partial return to pre-Keynesian assumption as far as the flexibility of the nominal wage level is concerned.

Second, when we initiated our consideration of the model (3.32)–(3.41) for the case $\beta_{\pi^e} = \infty$, it seemed to us that a certain mathematical bifurcation must be involved when the change β_{π^e} large but finite, to $\beta_{\pi^e} = \infty$ occurs. Our conclusion, however, now is that it is in fact the economics of the model which undergoes a severe bifurcation at this point, while the mathematics is merely appropriately manipulated to justify this bifurcation in economic thinking.

Further critical observations on the economic validity of the jump-variable technique will be the subject of the following subsection.

3.8 A critique of rational expectations

The instability of the price level $p(t)$ in an otherwise stable surrounding is given as the reason why solution (3.47) of the dynamic law (3.46) is preferred to the solution (3.48). This is clearly stated in Sargent and Wallace (1973) with regard to the simple Cagan model of price level dynamics and it holds true in the same way for Sargent's (1987) dynamic analysis of a Keynesian model. However, in our view, this device for dealing with certain problems of monetary growth models creates more difficulties that it helps to solve.

To demonstrate this point, we consider again formula (3.47) now rewritten as

$$\ln p(t) = -e^{t/\alpha} \int_t^\infty e^{-s/\alpha} [h(s) + (\ln M(s))/(-\alpha) + \varepsilon(s)] ds. \tag{3.49}$$

Assume that $M(s)$ and $h(s)$ represent the correct behavior of the exogenous policy variable M and of the function h (as it results from the dynamics of the variables ω, l or the real sector of the economy) over the whole future. Assume furthermore, that the "belief-term" $\varepsilon(s)$ that we now have included in this formula has the same simple functional properties as they are postulated in Sargent (1987) for the given money supply function M.[36] An explicit treatment of this belief term will now be of use in judging the content of the forecasting formula (3.49).

It may be argued that it is not sensible (and practicable) for individuals to operate with a formula such as equation (3.49) for the price-level which extends over an infinite horizon and which has as its background a growing system (possibly of a cyclical nature, but with natural growth n as its asymptotic growth rate). A special choice of the 'belief-term' $\varepsilon(s)$, however, avoids this sort of criticism. All that is needed for Sargent's kind of perfect foresight to prevail, say over the time interval $[t_0, T]$[37] is that $\varepsilon(s)$ be zero during this interval of time. It is thus sufficient that individuals perceive the money supply correctly over the interval $[t_0, T)$ in order to allow for myopic perfect foresight, $\pi^e = \hat{p}_+$, during this time interval. Thereafter everything may be wrong (for example, because individuals have trivialized the 'tail' of this formula), but this will only make the model inapplicable from time T onwards. In this way, the model may be used as a model of the medium run.

Indeed, differentiation of (3.49) with regard to t immediately shows that the differential equation (3.46), namely

$$\hat{p} = -\frac{1}{2}e^{t/\alpha} \int_t^\infty e^{-s/\alpha}[h(s) + (\ln M(s))/(-\alpha) + \varepsilon(s)]ds + h(t)$$

$$+ (\ln M(t))/(-\alpha) + \varepsilon(t)$$

$$= (-\ln p(t))/(-\alpha) + h(t) + (\ln M(t))/(-\alpha) + \varepsilon(t),$$

will be satisfied at all points in this interval of time. Furthermore, an economically meaningful rate of interest which guarantees money-market equilibrium can always be associated with (3.49) as long as the price-level (3.49) fulfills the inequality $M/(pK) < y$, where y is meant to be an upper bound to the evolution of real balances per unit of capital. Yet, it is not our intent here to justify this model with regard to its validity for such medium run analysis. Instead, we shall now show that the inclusion of such an belief term reveals serious problems for this way of solving the model (3.32) - (3.40), problems which in the end indicate that the model itself is not yet well formulated as an economic model.

Inserting the belief term $\varepsilon(s)$ into Sargent's price equation (3.47) represents but a simple generalization of his discussion of unanticipated monetary shocks, since the function ε will be revised in some way or another at least whenever a point in time t is reached where $\varepsilon(t) \neq 0$ holds true, meaning that this belief has then finally become obvious (notice here, that the additional assumption $\varepsilon_{t_+} = 0$ is then necessary in order to imply the Lucas–Sargent proposition for such a case). However the observation of an error at time t may induce individuals to revise

---

36 Assumptions which guarantee Sargent's mathematical methodology [as they are examined in Calvo (1977)] are not central for the discussion that follows.

37 Taking t_0 the present point in time.

their whole expectations M^* of the money supply M after time t giving rise to a completely new belief function $\varepsilon = M^* - M$ from t onwards.[38] Such a (from the theoretical point of view-arbitrary) revision of expectations regarding the whole future will imply that the price level will jump by an (again from a theoretical point of view) unknown amount. Within the domain of the aforesaid inequality, this says that the determination of the price level $p(t)$ in Sargent's model is completely arbitrary and subject to uncontrollable beliefs about the future, for instance with regard to periods $[T, \infty), T > t$ as considered earlier. This implies that there are many paths for the price level which are consistent with a given steady-state of the real sector.

The actual jump that occurs at a point in time t where expectations about policy actions at that point have to be revised is completely indeterminate, unless very special assumptions (as in Sargent's Chapter 5) are made with regard to the revision that will be induced for the function ε for values $s \geq t$. This is the content of Sargent's theory of the price level for a Keynesian model with myopic perfect foresight. This level is now mainly the result of economic speculation about the future, subject only to the side condition that such speculations must be locally correct with regard to the point in time that actually prevails and must suffice (but how?) for the economic limits that exist for such jumps in the general level of prices.

There are further serious problems which question the meaningfulness of this approach to perfect foresight:[39]

1. Consider for reference as in Sargent (1987, p.123) the steady state path with $\hat{M} = n$ and $\hat{w} = \hat{p} = \pi^e = 0$. Assume that unexpected jumps in the money supply of the type

$$f(s) = \ln M(s) \rightarrow \tilde{f}(t) = \begin{cases} \ln M(s), & s < t, \\ \ln M(s) + \Phi, & s \geq t, \end{cases}$$

occur at times $t = t_0 + 1, t_0 + 2, \ldots$ without any upper limit. The Lucas–Sargent proposition then implies $p(t), w(t) \rightarrow \infty$, yet this is not reflected in expected and actual rates of inflation since $\pi^e = 0$ and $\hat{p} = 0$ for all $t \geq t_0$. The effect on inflation of a money supply of the smooth type shown in the left-hand panel of Figure 3.9 therefore cannot in general be approximated by a money supply function of the step-wise type shown in the right-hand panel of Figure 3.9 if the step function in the right-hand panel approaches the smooth path in the left-hand panel in any meaningful way.

38 Subject again to the side condition $\varepsilon_{t_+} = 0$.
39 See Flaschel, Franke and Semmler (1997), Chiarella, Flaschel, Groh and Semmler (2000), Asada, Chiarella, Flaschel and Franke (2003) and in particular Chiarella, Flaschel, Franke and Semmler (2009) for extended discussions of such and further problems of the jump variable technique of the Rational Expectations school.

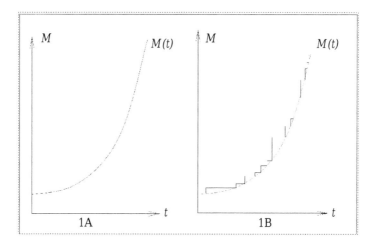

Figure 3.9 The nonequivalence of approximately equivalent smooth and stepwise money supply paths.

Should we really believe that these two types of money supplies will generate completely different evolutions of inflation, no matter how close is the approximation of the smooth supply rule by the step function?[40]

2. To ensure the solvability of the model, open market operations cannot be performed at each moment $t \geq t_o$. Nevertheless what are the economic reasons which exclude jumps in money-supply except for a discrete set of points in a continuous time model that in principle should be open to such operations at each moment t?

3. With regard to the foregoing steady-state situation ($\pi^e \equiv 0$), the Phillips–curve (3.39) of this model degenerates to $\hat{w} = \beta_w(l^d/l - 1) < \infty$. For the money wage w and this Phillips–curve it is stated in Sargent (1987, p.47): 'all that we require is that the value of dw/dt implied by any such relationship be finite so that w cannot jump at a point in time as a result of its interactions with other endogenous or exogenous variables'. Despite all this, the money wage w is in fact allowed to jump in Sargent's perfect foresight case. The quoted logic thus cannot hold true universally. The explanation for this is that there is another implicit change involved in the employed model when $0 < \beta_w < \infty$ (adaptive expectations) is replaced by $\beta_w = \infty$ (perfect foresight), since the latter case in fact makes use of a real wage Phillips–curve $\hat{\omega} = \beta_w(l^d/l - 1)$

---

40 Mathematically speaking, it is of course not startling to see that "C_0-convergence on the M^s-level" does not imply "C_1-convergence on the p-level." However, the economics of this model does demand something of this kind, for example, by means of a redefinition of the rate of inflation in terms of a moving average or by means of a reformulated theory of price-level changes.

solely, and assumes a classical money–wage equation given by $w = \omega \cdot p$, where ω (but not p) is a continuous function of time for all $t \geq t_0$.

We conclude that Sargent's model (3.22)–(3.31) (or (3.32)–(3.41) in intensive form) is neither consistent by itself nor consistently applied by Sargent (in the case $\beta_w = \infty$), since, on the one hand, its determination of the price level is not without ambiguities and methodological flaws and since, on the other hand, its Keynesian Phillips–curve has implicitly been replaced by a real-wage Phillips-curve with $w = \omega \cdot p$ as the new equation for the determination of money wages. This variation of the original model and the new approach (3.47) to price level determination provide the scenario for short-run neutrality assertions and the like which originally appeared so odd from the methodological viewpoint of ordinary dynamical analysis. This approach may be termed as a classical revolt, but not a revolution in 'Keynesian Economics'. The task of explaining to students Friedmanian conclusions by means of a full-fledged model of Keynesian dynamics remains consequently still to be undertaken and demands a further analysis of such much neglected, both simple and yet very demanding, models of monetary growth.

We conclude here that the jump-variable technique cannot be applied in a logically consistent way to the real markets of Keynesian AD–AS growth analysis with their sluggish wage adjustments. We will return to such a critique of treating problems of myopic perfect foresight in a standard Keynesian textbook model later in the book; we also refer the reader to various chapters in Flaschel, Franke and Semmler (1997) and Chiarella and Flaschel (2000) on this matter. The basic problem here is that aggregate demand boils down to a theory of inflation with no real effects if marginal productivity theory strictly holds in the short run, that is if firms output decisions are always on their supply schedule. We believe that this postulate is not as strict as it is usually applied, but that instead (based on a relaxation of this postulate) the wage price dynamics (also often called supply side characteristics of the economy) should receive greater attention in order to really get supply-side dynamics with interesting features and that are also of descriptive relevance.

As open questions, we here simply pose the following ones: 1.) Can nominal wage continuity be coupled also with price-level jumps and bounded dynamics? 2.) Is there scope for interest rate policy in the conventional AD–AS model under myopic perfect foresight? These two problems for this type of analysis further suggest that the conventional AD–AS growth model is not a good prototype for the study of Keynesian macrodynamics.

3.9 Outlook: gradual price adjustment processes

We close this chapter with the observation that a Keynesian type of AD–AS analysis should not give rise to the kind of results discussed in the last two sections simply on the basis of no errors with respect to the short-run evolution of the rate of price inflation. In a proper Keynesian approach to disequilibrium and growth, we should have besides delayed wage adjustment also delayed price and quantity adjustment, implying that firms are in general off their supply curve and also do not know the point of effective demand with certainty. Excess capacity (positive or negative) thus generally concerns both labor and capital and leads to at least somewhat sluggish adjustments on these real markets.

Yet, with marginal productivity then only holding in the steady state of these disequilibrium AD–AS dynamics and with both wage and price levels confined to react continuously, the whole approach we have investigated in the preceding two sections becomes redundant. There is then no longer a breakdown in the Keynesian structure of the model by which it merely allows the determination of the rate of interest and the price level on the basis of a predetermined level of goods supply such that goods market equilibrium is established. It then turns out that IS-LM analysis continues to determine the real dynamics, even in the case of myopic perfect foresight, so giving rise to a Keynesian theory of economic fluctuations in real as well as in nominal variables.

It is the aim of Chapter 6 to formulate and demonstrate these assertions in detail, based on what has already been shown in Chiarella and Flaschel (2000). In the following chapters, we will, however, first show that not only the dynamic AS analysis considered in this chapter, but also dynamic AD analysis is not well understood in the literature, when (as here) wage–price dynamics is added. We therefore have considered in this chapter and will explore further in subsequent chapters the deficiencies in formulating the dynamics of aggregate supply as well as aggregate demand before we start to integrate what we can learn from Chapters 2 and 3.

With a view to the feedback chains to be discussed in Part II, let us finally consider the following modification of the AD–AS growth analysis of Sargent (1987, Ch.5), thereby supplying already some of the elements for the proper Keynesian analysis of disequilibrium and growth to be introduced in Chapter 7. Assume first of all the extension of the money wage PC of the considered AD–AS model of the form

$$\hat{w} = \beta_w(L^d/L - 1) + \kappa_w\hat{p} + (1 - \kappa_w)\hat{p}_o. \tag{3.50}$$

Equation (3.50) states that wage earners still have perfect foresight on current price inflation, but use in addition the steady state rate of inflation in their estimation of inflation over the medium run. We assume again that the steady state rate of inflation is zero. The weighted average of short-run and long-run inflation used as cost-pressure term in the wage PC then reduces to $\kappa_w\hat{p}$ for $\kappa_w \in (0, 1)$.

As the price level PC for the considered AD–AS model assume[41]

$$\hat{p} = \beta_p \left(\frac{I - S}{K}\right) + \kappa_p\hat{w} + (1 - \kappa_p)\hat{w}_o. \tag{3.51}$$

---

41 Such a price dynamics will be further extended and refined in the chapters to come.

This equation shows that firms also have perfect foresight, in their case on current wage inflation, but also use in addition the steady state rate of wage inflation in their estimation of wage inflation over the medium run. We assume again that the steady state rate of wage (and price) inflation is zero. The weighted average of short- and long-run inflation used as cost-pressure term in the price PC then reduces to $\kappa_p \hat{w}$ for $\kappa_p \in (0, 1)$. We stress the 1 in both PC's refers to the Non-Accelerating-Inflation Rate of Utilization (NAIRU) of both labor and capital, respectively.

From these two PC's for labor and goods market dynamics we obtain as law of motion for the real wage $\omega = w/p$ the differential equation

$$\hat{\omega} = \frac{1}{1 - \kappa_w \kappa_p} \left((1 - \kappa_p)\beta_w(L^d/L - 1) - (1 - \kappa_w)\beta_p \left(\frac{I - S}{K} \right) \right). \tag{3.52}$$

In view of what will be considered in Part II, we here abstract from Keynes- and Mundell-effects and assume that the real rate of interest of the considered AD–AS growth model is a constant (guaranteed by way of an appropriate Taylor interest rate policy rule in the place of the constant growth rate of the money supply of the original approach) which moreover is equal to the steady state value of this rate that is compatible with zero inflation rates for both wages and prices. Finally, as already indicated by the formulation of the price PC, we now allow for goods market disequilibrium in the short-run where savings per unit of capital are given by $y - \delta - c(y - \delta - t) - g$ and investment per unit of capital by $i(r(\omega) - (r_o - \hat{p}_o))$.[42] We have, based on the wage and price decisions modeled earlier at each moment in time, a given level of real wages ω and due to this a given level of employment per unit of capital $l^d(\omega)$, $l^{d'} < 0$ as in the Solow-Goodwin model of this chapter. Furthermore, also the profit rate function $r(\omega)$ of course again fulfills $r' < 0$. These assumptions and conditions give rise to a dynamical system of the form

$$\hat{\omega} = \frac{1}{1 - \kappa_w \kappa_p}((1 - \kappa_p)\beta_w(l^d(\omega)/l - 1)$$

$$- (1 - \kappa_w)\beta_p(i(r(\omega) - (r_o - \hat{p}_o)) - (1 - c)f(l^d(\omega)) - \delta + c(\delta + \tau) - \gamma)), \tag{3.53}$$

$$\hat{l} = n - ((1 - c)f(l^d(\omega)) - \delta + c(\delta + \tau) - \gamma), \tag{3.54}$$

if savings determine capital accumulation (while investment in its departure from savings only determines the rate of inflation).

The matrix of partial derivatives at the interior steady state of the dynamics (which is the same as the one of the Sargent AD–AS growth model) is

---

42 Both the savings and the investment function will become richer with respect to the arguments involved in them in Chapter 7 where, however, neoclassical smooth factor substitution, and thus the dependence of l^d on ω, is no longer considered.

characterized by

$$J = \begin{pmatrix} \pm & - \\ + & 0 \end{pmatrix},$$

and is thus always locally unstable if the parameter β_p characterizing price adjustment speed is sufficiently large compared with wage adjustment speed β_w. We shall assume here that this is indeed the case. In a seminal paper Rose (1967) has proved in a related approach global stability of the overall dynamics by assuming that wage adjustment speed depends on the disequilibrium in the labor market and approaches infinity when this disequilibrium becomes very large; we refer the reader to Flaschel, Franke and Semmler (1997) and Chiarella and Flaschel (2000) for details. This assumption is also sufficient here to prove global stability by constructing a domain in the economic phase space that cannot be left by the trajectories generated by the dynamics. Due to the local instability of the steady state (which of course lies in this domain) we then get by the Poincaré-Bendixson theorem. (see the mathematical appendix at the end of the book) that all trajectories in this invariant domain will converge to a limit cycle and thus a persistent economic fluctuation in the state variables real wage ω and full-employment labor intensity l.

We only use this brief sketch of Rose's theory of the business cycle here to introduce the concept of the so-called Rose-effects, so named to celebrate this seminal paper. These effects will be present in all macrodynamic models that assume that excess demand, or simply aggregate demand, depends on income distribution and that consider the effects of wage versus price flexibility. Such models have here served the purpose of showing that the (neo-)classical growth dynamics can indeed give rise to local instability but nevertheless global stability if aggregate demand enters the picture to some extent. In the general setup to be presented in Chapter 5, the Rose-effects can be represented as shown in Figure 3.10, a representation that shows the Rose type fluctuations that can be generated where aggregate demand always depends negatively on real wages and where sufficient price flexibility is needed to stabilize the steady state and sufficient wage flexibility far off the steady state to guarantee global stability and the establishment of persistent fluctuations.

By normal Rose effects, we denote situations where aggregate demand changes due to real wage changes are combined with flexibilities in wage and price dynamics such that the end result is a slowing down and finally a reversal of such real wage changes. Figure 3.7 (left-hand panel) illustrates the normal Rose effect, one of the two possibilities for such an occurrence. It assumes that investment responds more strongly (positively) to real wage decreases in a depressed economy than consumption (which is assumed to respond negatively). Combined with wages that respond more strongly than prices to disequilibrium (and wage earners being more short-sighted with respect to inflation than firms), we then get that there will be a slowdown in real wage decreases until aggregate demand has recovered by so much that a boom is generated, which eventually leads the economy back

Normal Rose Effects:

Adverse Rose Effects:

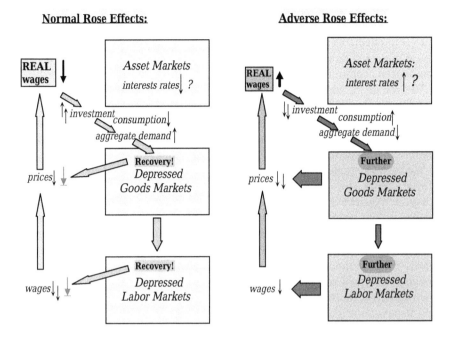

Figure 3.10 Normal and adverse Rose effects in demand determined growth dynamics.

to 'full' employment (with damped fluctuations in real wages and the rate of employment around this 'full' employment level). Real wage decreases thus in this case revive the economy and finally bring an end to such falls in real wages. The same, of course, holds for real wage increases which would be hold in check by falling aggregate demand.

Real wage decreases are, however, problematic should investment respond less than consumption, because this would imply then a decrease in aggregate demand which, when wages are more flexible than prices, leads to further real wage decreases and further reduced aggregate demand without any possibility for a reversal of such a situation. This situation would thus provide an example of persistent adverse real wage adjustment and is illustrated in Figure 3.7 (right-hand panel) showing the situation where aggregate demand depends negatively on the real wage, but where prices are more flexible than wages. In this case, real wages rise in the depression, reducing aggregate demand and implying a further rise in real wages and so on.

This brief introduction into the feedback mechanisms must suffice here, but will be continued in Chapter 7 of the book, where the Keynes-Metzler-Goodwin approach to disequilibrium and growth is introduced and investigated, the contours of which will became slowly visible from what has been discussed here and in the following chapters. In the Chapter 5, we will focus on the feedback chains known as the Keynes-effect and the Mundell-effect in the literature before we come to an integration of all these effects (augmented by the inclusion of the Metzlerian inventory accelerator mechanism) in Chapter 7. Equilibrium assumptions are in this way systematically replaced by disequilibrium adjustment processes, giving rise to more and more elaborate delayed feedback chains that are hidden by the equilibrium conditions of conventional AD–AS growth dynamics.

The foregoing approach to Rose type dynamics will thus be generalized in Chapter 6, where besides the K(eynes)M(etzler)G(oodwin) dynamics also the K(eynes)W(icksell)G(oodwin) type of dynamics will be briefly introduced and discussed. KWG approaches to macrodynamics will be also considered (for reasons of comparison) in Part III of the book.

We have shown in this chapter in this respect that Solow-Goodwin dynamics is of vital interest, since it is close to the neoclassical interpretation of Keynesian AD–AS growth dynamics. Yet, we have also stressed that this type of AD–AS growth dynamics is too exceptional in order to be really convincing from a Keynesian perspective. However, considering the dynamics of aggregate supply points to the need to discuss wage–price dynamics with more and more care and rigor, which brings forth interesting new aspects on stability issues as we have tried to sketch in this final section of this chapter. We have here discussed such wage–price dynamics in a basically supply side determined framework, but will extend this discussion of the wage–price spiral to the inclusion of demand side issues in the chapters to come. Having here, however, demonstrated that smooth factor substitution (just like endogenous technical change as considered in Desai and Shah (1981)) basically adds stability to the Goodwin growth cycle model (without altering its cyclical overshooting features of elasticities of substitution do not become too high) we will suppress such effects in the remainder of the book, in order to concentrate on economic implications in the simplest technological environment possible. Smooth factor substitution can be added at any stage of the discussion later on and will not significantly alter the economic results achieved (if not too elastic), but basically improve the stability of the considered adjustment processes, as shown for the model of Chapter 4 in Chiarella and Flaschel (2000).

References

Asada, T., C. Chiarella, P. Flaschel, and R. Franke (2003): *Open Economy Macrodynamics: An Integrated Disequilibrium Approach*. Heidelberg: Springer.

Blanchard, O. (1981): Output, the stock market, and interest rates. *American Economic Review*, 71, 132–143.

Calvo, G.A. (1977): The stability of models of money and perfect foresight: A comment. *Econometrica*, 45, 1737–39.

Chiarella, C. and P. Flaschel (2000): *The Dynamics of Keynesian Monetary Growth: Macro Foundations*. Cambridge, UK: Cambridge University Press, Chapter 4.

Chiarella, C., P. Flaschel, G. Groh and W. Semmler (2000): *Disequilibrium, Growth and Labor Market Dynamics*. Heidelberg: Springer.

Chiarella, C., P. Flaschel, R. Franke, and W. Semmler (2009): *Financial Markets and the Macroeconomy: A Keynesian Perspective*. London: Routledge.

Desai, M. and A. Shah (1981): Growth cycles with induced technical change. *The Economic Journal*, 91, 1006–1010.

Flaschel, P. (1984): Some stability properties of Goodwin's growth cycle model. *Zeitschrift für Nationalökonomie*, 44, 63–69.

Flaschel, P. (1993): *Macrodynamics: Income Distribution, Effective Demand and Cyclical Growth*. Bern: Peter Lang, Chapters 2 and 3.

Flaschel, P., R. Franke, and W. Semmler (1997): *Dynamic Macroeconomics: Instability, Fluctuations and Growth in Monetary Economies*. Cambridge, MA: The MIT Press.

Franke, R. (1996): A Metzlerian model of inventory growth cycles. *Structural Change and Economic Dynamics*, 7, 243–262ñ.

Friedman, B.M. (1979): Optimal expectations and the extreme information assumptions of "rational expectations" macromodels. *Journal of Monetary Economics*, 5, 23–41.

Goodwin, R.M. (1967): A growth cycle. In: C.H. Feinstein (ed.): *Socialism, Capitalism and Economic Growth*. Cambridge: Cambridge University Press, 54–58.

Groth, C. (1993): Some unfamiliar dynamics of a familiar macro model: A note. *Journal of Economics*, 58, 293–305.

Hirsch, M.W. and S. Smale (1974): *Differential Equations, Dynamical Systems, and Linear Algebra*. New York: Academic Press.

Jones, H.G. (1975): *An Introduction to Modern Theories of Economic Growth*. London: Thomas Nelson & Sons.

Keynes, J.M. (1936): *The General Theory of Employment, Interest and Money*. New York: Macmillan.

Minford, P. and D. Peel (1983): *Rational Expectations and the New Macroeconomics*. Oxford: Martin Robertson.

Rose, H. (1967): On the non-linear theory of the employment cycle. *Review of Economic Studies*, 34, 153–173.

Sargent, T. (1987): *Macroeconomic Theory*. New York: Academic Press.

Sargent, T. and N. Wallace (1973): The stability of models of money and growth with perfect foresight. *Econometrica*, 41, 1043–1048.

Sen, A., ed. (1970): *Growth Economics*. London: Penguin Economics Readings.

Snower, D.J. (1984): Rational expectations, nonlinearities, and the effectiveness of monetary policy. *Oxford Economic Papers*, 36, 177–199.

Solow, R. (1956): A contribution to the theory of economic growth. *Quarterly Journal of Economics*, 70, 65–94.

Solow, R. (1990): Goodwin's growth cycle: Reminiscence and rumination. In: K.Velupillai (ed.): *Nonlinear and Multisectoral Macrodynamics*. London: Macmillan, 31–41.

4 Taking Stock

Keynesian Dynamics and the AD–AS Framework

(by Amitava Dutt and Peter Skott)

4.1 Introduction

Along with various coauthors, Chiarella and Flaschel have been engaged over the last 15 years in a research program on integrated Keynesian disequilibrium dynamics (IKDD). The results have been impressive. Using sophisticated mathematical and computational techniques, the research has greatly increased our understanding of Keynesian models and the very complex dynamics that these models may generate.

The contrast between the IKDD and New Keynesian approach (NK) is striking. The IKDD follows an 'old Keynesian tradition' of formal mathematical model building. The simple static predecessor is the *IS-LM* model or its cousin, the AD–AS model. This chapter[1] discusses the merits of this old Keynesian tradition and the relation between this tradition (and IKDD) and the post Keynesian and New Keynesian approaches.

Section 2 outlines a standard version of the AD–AS model and shows that it can be given a logically consistent Marshallian interpretation. It also shows that the model does not, as claimed by some critics, suffer from internal logical contradictions. Section 3 discusses some alleged shortcomings of the model. Section 4 considers the NK alternative - focusing on two main issues, microeconomic foundations and the treatment of stability - and comments on the IKDD treatment of expectations. Section 5 introduces post Keynesian and other arguments for the relevance of aggregate demand, not just in the short run but also as an influence on real outcomes in the medium and the long run. Section 6, finally, ends with a few concluding remarks.

4.2 The AD–AS framework

Several turn-of-the-century assessments of the state of macroeconomics regard the discipline as healthy. There may have been fierce debates and controversies,

---

1 This chapter was written by Amitava Dutt and Peter Skott and relies heavily on Dutt and Skott (2006), but also draws on Skott (2006). The reader should note that the notation used in this chapter is not always consistent with that of the rest of the book.

but these debates mainly served to highlight deficiencies of existing models and to stimulate the creation of new improved hybrid models. The history of macroeconomics, according to Blanchard (2000, p.1375) is 'one of a surprisingly steady accumulation of knowledge', and 'progress in macroeconomics may well be the success story of twentieth century economics'. Woodford's (1999) assessment gives slightly more weight to the disagreements and revolutions in the second half of the twentieth century. But Woodford also sees convergence, and he concludes that 'modern macroeconomic models are intertemporal general equilibrium models derived from the same foundations of optimizing behavior on the part of households and firms as are employed in other branches of economics' (p.31). We disagree with these assessments. In our view, a large part of what has happened in macroeconomics since the late 1960s has been a wasteful detour. A generation of macroeconomists has grown up learning tools that may be sophisticated, but the usefulness of these tools is questionable. Moreover, a great deal of damage may be, and has been, done when the tools are applied to real-world situations. For all their limitations, the simple models of the old Keynesian school using the Aggregate Demand–Aggregate Supply (AD–AS) framework provide a better starting point for serious analysis than that is provided by more recent models in the New Keynesian (NK) or Real Business Cycle (RBC) traditions which have come to dominate modern macroeconomics.

Following Keynes, the AD–AS approach visualizes the economy as a whole, that is, the theory is 'general' rather than 'partial'.[2] Keynes's (1936/1973) derivation of a fix-wage general equilibrium in Chapters 1–18 of *The General Theory of Employment, Interest and Money* (GT) was an enormous intellectual achievement, and the one stressed by both Blanchard and Woodford in their accounts of the Keynesian revolution. The AD–AS framework gives a reasonable representation of the analytical skeleton behind this fix-wage general equilibrium. The strength of the AD–AS apparatus is precisely the explicit attempt to integrate the analysis of goods, labor and financial markets.

The AD–AS framework divides the economy into two parts – the 'demand side' and the 'supply side' – and examines their interaction using accounting identities, equilibrium conditions and behavioral and institutional equations. The 'demand side' typically examines factors relating to the demand for goods and the demand and supply of assets. The 'supply side' typically examines factors

---

2 According to the preface to the French edition of the GT, written three years after the English publication, Keynes (1936/1973, p.xxxii) explains:

> I have called my theory a general theory. I mean by this that I am chiefly concerned with the behavior of the economic system as a whole, – with aggregate incomes, aggregate profits, aggregate output, aggregate employment, aggregate investment, aggregate saving rather than with the incomes, profits, output, employment, investment and saving of particular industries, firms and individuals. And I argue that important mistakes have been made through extending to the system as a whole conclusions which have been arrived at in respect of a part of it taken in isolation.

relating to output and pricing decisions of producers, and factor markets. The framework ensures that neither demand nor supply side factors are overlooked in the analysis and that macroeconomic outcomes depend on the interaction between the different markets. The particular partitioning into 'aggregate demand' and 'aggregate supply' along with the choice of terminology may provide the pedagogic advantage of making macroeconomic analysis possible in terms of the same tools as the simplest microeconomic model of the market. But this advantage comes at a high price. The aggregate demand and supply curves embody complex interactions and are clearly not the same as the microeconomic curves which take a partial view of the economy. The analogy therefore is spurious, and forgetting this has led to a great deal of confusion in the literature, as briefly discussed later.

The basic AD–AS model is well-known, of course, but to ease the exposition it is helpful to state a simple version of it explicitly. There are two equilibrium conditions

$$Y = C + I + G, \tag{4.1}$$

$$M/P = L, \tag{4.2}$$

where, in standard notation, Y is real output, C, I and G, denote real consumption, investment and government expenditure, M the supply of money, P the price level, and L the real demand for money, and six behavioral or institutional equations

$$C = C(Y), \tag{4.3}$$

$$I = I(r), \tag{4.4}$$

$$L = L(Y, r), \tag{4.5}$$

$$Y = F(N), \tag{4.6}$$

$$W/P^e = F'(N), \tag{4.7}$$

$$W = W_0, \tag{4.8}$$

where $0 < C' < 1, I' < 0, L_1 > 0, L_2 < 0, F' > 0$ and $F' < N$, and where r is the rate of interest, N the level of employment, W the money wage, and P^e is the price expected by firms. Equations (4.3) through (4.6) are standard consumption, investment, money demand and production functions. Since C, I and L are used to denote desired amounts in equations (4.3) through (4.5), equations (4.1) and (4.2) are equilibrium conditions (rather than accounting identities) showing that output is equal to the demand for it and that the money supply in real terms is equal to the demand for it. Behind these equilibrium conditions lie dynamic adjustment processes with excess demand for goods leading to an increase in

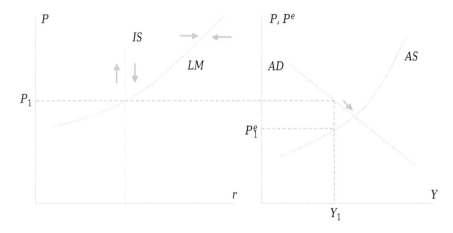

Figure 4.1 From IS-LM to AS–AD.

P and excess demand for money leading to an increase in r.[3] Equation (4.6) is the profit maximizing condition of firms that are assumed to be price takers in perfectly competitive markets; since there is a production lag and firms make production plans prior to knowing what price they will receive for their goods, the price that is relevant for their production decision is the expected price. The levels of M, G and W are given exogenously. To stress that this is the case for the money wage, equation (4.7) states that the money wage is given at the exogenous level W_0.

Our interpretation of the model is Marshallian, and we examine the behavior of the economy in two different 'runs'. The expected price and the level of output are given in the 'market' (or 'ultra-short') run. In the 'short' run, expected price changes in response to its deviations from the actual price, and this change is accompanied by changes in the level of production; in a short-run, equilibrium expectations are being met and the expected and actual price coincide.

In the market run, given P^e, and given W from equation (4.8), N is determined by equation (4.7), and Y by equation (4.6). For this level of Y, substitution of equations (4.3) and (4.4) into equation (4.1) yields a value of r which satisfies that equation, irrespective of the price level. The *IS* curve in Figure 4.1, which shows

3 The dynamics can be explicitly formalized by the equations

$$dP/dt = \beta_G[C + I + G - Y],$$

$$dr/dt = \beta_A[L - (M/P)],$$

where t denotes time and β_i are speed of adjustment parameters for the goods and asset markets.

equilibrium in the goods market in (P, r) -space , is vertical at this level of r.[4] The vertical arrows show the direction of price adjustments when the economy is out of goods market equilibrium. In addition for the given level of Y, substitution of equation (4.5) into equation (4.2) yields a positive LM relation between P and r, which represents money (and assets) market equilibrium. The horizontal arrows show the direction of interest adjustments when the economy is out of money-market equilibrium. The intersection of the *IS* and *LM* curves gives the market-run equilibrium values of P and r. The equilibrium value of r is determined by the position of the vertical *IS* curve, and the *LM* curve determines the value of P. With off-equilibrium dynamics given by the equations in note 2, it is readily seen that the market-run equilibrium is stable for a given Y.

In the short run, P^e is allowed to change in response to unfulfilled expectations. When P^e changes to a new level, firms adjust their employment and output levels. This adjustment is captured by the AS curve, which shows the profit-maximizing level of output produced by the firms for a given P^e. When Y changes, the *IS* and *LM* curves shift in (r, P)-space and determine a new market-run equilibrium of r and P. The level of P which clears goods and money markets for each level of Y is shown along the AD curve. A higher level of Y increases the level of saving, so that goods market equilibrium requires an increase in investment, a fall in r and hence a leftward shift of the *IS* curve. A higher level of Y increases the real demand for money, so that money market equilibrium requires a fall in P (or an increase in r), so that the LM curve shifts to the right in (r, P)-space. Consequently, a higher Y implies a lower P for market-run equilibrium, explaining the negative slope of the AD curve.

The short-run dynamics shown in Figure 4.1 can be described as follows. Starting from an initial level of expected price, P_1^e, output is determined at Y_1 (as shown by the AS curve) and price at P_1 (as shown by the AD curve). Since $P_1 > P_1^e$, if firms revise their price expectations adaptively, P^e rises, making Y expand along the AS curve and the market-run equilibrium move along the AD curve (representing shifts in the *IS* and *LM* curve) as shown by the arrow. This adjustment will continue till the economy arrives at the short-run equilibrium at the intersection of the AD and AS curves, where $P = P^e$.[5]

Three comments about this model are in order. First, the Marshallian interpretation of the model finds a great deal of exegetical support in Keynes's own work and in the writings of many Keynesians. Clower (1989), for instance, notes the

---

4 If we introduce real balance effects which make C (and, possibly, I) depend positively on M/P, the *IS* curve would be negatively sloped rather than vertical. We abstract from this complication here, but refer to it later.

5 The stability of short-run equilibrium can be verified by representing the dynamics of expected price by the equation

$$dP^e/dt = \beta_E[P - P^e],$$

where $\beta_E > 0$ is the speed of expectations adjustment parameter.

Marshallian aspects of Keynes' GT, although not as precisely as done in our model (see Dutt, 1992a).

Second, the Marshallian interpretation is important for the internal consistency of the economic argument. It has been argued by Barro (1994), Fields and Hart (1990), Colander (1995) and Bhaduri, Laski and Riese (1999) that the AD–AS model embodies two mutually-contradictory approaches to pricing and production by firms. According to this criticism, the AD curve is based on *IS* and *LM* curves, but the analysis assumes that firms fix the price (having the ability to do so) and that equilibrium levels of r and Y are determined from equations (4.1) and (4.2), using (4.3) through (4.5). The story told is that firms fix their price and adjust their output in response to changes in demand conditions. The AS curve, on the other hand, assumes price taking behavior on the part of firms operating in purely competitive markets with demand constraints, producing to maximize profits given the money wage and the production function. While some textbook versions of the AD–AS model do suffer from this inconsistency, our Marshallian model is free of it. The equations of the model are similar to those of the standard textbook version,[6] but in our interpretation, the AD and AS curves both embody profit maximization and price-taking behavior: the AD curve in our interpretation shows equilibrium price for a given level of output and not, as the standard AD curve, the equilibrium value of Y for different levels of P.[7]

Third, the model can easily be recast using Keynes's own 'AD–AS diagram' with employment and the value of output (price times quantity) on the axes (he did not actually draw this diagram in GT, but described it in words in Chapter 3).[8] Keynes's Aggregate Supply function is given by $W_0 F(N)/F'(N)$ and is derived from equations (4.6), (4.7) and (4.8): its curve shows the expected value of output at each level of employment consistent with profit maximizing behavior. The Aggregate Demand function is derived from equations (4.1) through (4.6), and its curve shows the actual equilibrium proceeds (PY) for any given level of N. The level of N determines Y from equation (4.6), and given this Y, P is determined as shown in the *IS-LM* diagram of Figure 4.1, which determines the equilibrium level of PY. The value of aggregate demand at the intersection between the supply and demand curves defines 'the effective demand' (GT, p.25).

By construction, expectations are being met at the point of effective demand. In Chapter 5 of GT, however, Keynes discusses the formation and revision of short-period expectations, showing how firms produce a certain level of output with a certain level of employment, given short period expectations, and then adjust these expectations if they are not fulfilled. Though he does not explicitly analyze this process, we can do so by using the expected proceeds curve,

---

6 For a discussion of the history of the AD–AS model, including that of its emergence and spread in macroeconomic textbooks, see Dutt (2002).

7 See Dutt and Skott (1996) for further discussion of the internal-consistency criticisms.

8 He probably used this type of diagram, rather than that in (P, Y) space, because aggregate price level and real output were not in common use in his day, while value of output and total employment, involving fewer aggregation problems, were.

given by $P^e Y = P^e F(N)$, for a given P^e from equation (4.6): it shows what firms expect the value of output to be for a given price expectation. The intersection of this curve with the curve for the Aggregate Supply function determines the market-run equilibrium level of employment since it satisfies equation (4.7). For the market-run equilibrium employment level, one can read off actual proceeds from the Aggregate Demand function. If actual proceeds are different from expected proceeds, P^e will change, shifting the expected proceeds curve, till the economy arrives at short-run equilibrium at the intersection of all three curves.[9] For most of the GT, however, Keynes confines attention to short-run equilibrium in which actual and expected price are equal, thereby concealing the Marshallian adjustment process, because it was not central to his demonstration of the possibility of unemployment short-run equilibrium.[10]

4.3 Shortcomings

An AD–AS model of the type just described has many well-known weaknesses and limitations, of which three are relevant for our purposes.

The criticisms that have received the most attention concern the alleged lack of microeconomic foundations of the model. NKs (along with new classical economists and RBC theorists), who have been vocal in this criticism, wish to supplant the model with models based on explicit optimization. We shall take up the issue of optimizing microfoundations in Section 4.4 where we discuss the NK approach. However the behavioral approach of the AD–AS model has also been criticized from another angle. Many post-Keynesian economists, but also some impeccably mainstream old Keynesians, have suggested that the model is too mechanical and does not take into account uncertainty and

---

9 Keynes's Aggregate Demand function does not actually use the simultaneous equations approach to solving P, focusing only on goods-market equilibrium without taking into account asset markets explicitly. An alternative formulation of the model, which focuses only on the goods market, but allows consumption demand to respond to price changes due to either the real balance effect or distribution shifts, can easily be developed. See Dutt (1987) for a version in which changes in price affect the value of output through changes in income distribution between wages and profits.

10 The *Treatise on Money* had concentrated on the Marshallian ultra-short run (or market run) equilibrium:

> My so-called 'fundamental equations' were an instantaneous picture taken on the assumption of a given output. They attempted to show how, assuming the given output, forces could develop which involved a profit-disequilibrium, and thus required a change in the level of output. But the dynamic development, as distinct from the instantaneous picture, was left incomplete and extremely confused
>
> (Keynes, 1936/1973, p.xxii).

Skott (1989a, 1989b) develops a model of cyclical growth using the Marshallian (or Keynes-of-the-Treatise) ultra-short run equilibrium as the basic building block; see also Skott (1983) for a discussion of this Marshallian approach and the relation between the *Treatise on Money* and the GT.

expectations in a serious manner.[11] It is beyond the scope of the present chapter to address this important issue in any detail, but in our view, 'mechanical' mathematical formalization can be extremely useful. This formalization needs to be supplemented by verbal descriptions and empirical analysis, and less formal discussions of possible outcomes may also come into play if the relations determining the evolution of the system are not capable of being formalized in a precise manner. Even this informal discussion, however, will often benefit from using more formal analyses as points of reference and by suggesting where and how the results of the models may need to be modified. Models which modify these 'mechanical' models to incorporate informal discussions of changes in expectations can and have been developed.[12]

A second set of criticisms claims that the AD–AS model omits many important features of reality and that some of its implications are not consistent with empirical observation. Assumptions of imperfect competition, for instance, should replace perfect competition, and the money supply should not be treated as an exogenous variable in an economy with modern monetary institutions.[13] The consumption function should also take into account income distributional effects on consumption, increases in aggregate demand should provide a direct stimulus to investment, and the distinction between nominal and real rates of interest may be critical (not least for the reactions of aggregate demand to changes in money wages and the stability of full-employment). These (and other) modifications may complicate the model and affect some of its properties, but in principle their introduction is quite straightforward and the resulting model can still be depicted with AD and AS curves (see, for instance, Dutt and Skott, 1996, and Section 4.5.1 in this chapter). The modifications, moreover, help to address some of the empirical criticisms of the AD–AS model. The simple model, for instance, predicts a counter-cyclical movement of the real wage. This implication, which finds little support in the data (as noted early on by Dunlop, 1938, Tarshis, 1939), no longer holds in versions of the model that include imperfect competition (perhaps with markup pricing à la Kalecki, 1971) and some combination of nondiminishing returns to labor and/or a counter-cyclical pattern in the markup.

A third set of problems with the AD–AS model concerns the unsatisfactory treatment of dynamics. There is a lack of integration between the analysis of the short-run and more long-term issues, and even when it comes to the treatment of the short run, the analysis often relies on unstated or questionable

---

11 For a review of post Keynesian contributions see Dutt and Amadeo (1990). For more mainstream discussions, see Hicks (1980–81), Tobin (1975) and Meltzer (1988).

12 For instance, Kregel's (1976) informal discussion of the interaction between Keynes's short-period and long-period expectations has been formalized in Dutt (1997) to produce path-dependent equilibria.

13 See, for instance, Moore (1988). New Keynesians have also abandoned the exogenous-money assumption, but rather than stressing the nature of monetary institutions, they focus on the specific policy rule adopted by the Central Bank in the US and elsewhere (e.g. Romer, 2000, Woodford 2003)).

assumptions concerning the process leading to a short-run Keynesian equilibrium. Our own foregoing presentation is quite explicit in its assumptions (footnotes 3 and 5) but, perhaps unrealistically, it presumes that the adjustment to market-run equilibrium is 'very fast' relative to the adjustments of price expectations. The adjustment to market-run equilibrium could therefore be based on given price expectations, and in the analysis of adjustments to short-run equilibrium it could be assumed that there is continuous market equilibrium during the adjustment process.[14]

The shortcomings of simple AD–AS models with respect to dynamics may be a legacy of Keynes's own focus on short-run equilibria in GT. The assumption of fulfilled expectations facilitated the presentation of the fix-wage general equilibrium.[15] Unfortunately, it makes it hard to discuss the stability issues, and from today's perspective – having before us a well-developed theory of general equilibrium – the truly revolutionary and provocative message of the GT concerns the destabilizing effects of money wage flexibility, rather than the existence of a fix-wage equilibrium with unemployment.

The AD–AS model does not address the stability issue – it takes the money wage as given – but can serve as a starting point. The model can be easily extended in a way which makes it have the implications presented in the typical textbook: (i) that unemployment can exist in the model, because the money wage is exogenously fixed; (ii) that if one allows the money wage to fall in response to the existence of unemployment, the AS curve, given by $P = W/F'(F^{-1}(Y))$ is shifted downwards; and that (iii) this leads to an expansion of output and employment along the negatively-sloped AD curve and moves the economy to the 'natural rate of unemployment' (corresponding to the absence of Keynesian involuntary unemployment). The mechanism behind this adjustment is the 'Keynes effect' by which a reduction in wage and price increases the real supply of money, lowers the interest rate, and increases investment and aggregate demand. This effect can be supplemented by the real balance effect by which the rise in real balances directly stimulates the aggregate demand for goods.

---

14 In the context of our simple specification, however, it is easy to prove that local stability carries over to the case where P, P^e and r are all treated as state variables, with their dynamics shown by the equations in notes 2 and 4.

15 In a set of lecture notes from 1937, Keynes argues as follows:

> When one is dealing with aggregates, aggregate effective demand at time A has no corresponding aggregate income at time B. All one can compare is the expected and actual income resulting to an entrepreneur from a particular decision. Actual investment may differ through unintended stock changes, price changes, alteration of decision. The difference, if any, is due to a mistake in the short-period expectation and the importance of the difference lies in the fact that this difference will be one of the relevant factors in determining subsequent effective demand.
>
> I began, as I have said, by regarding this difference as important. But eventually I felt it to be of secondary importance, emphasis on it obscuring the real argument. For the theory of effective demand is substantially the same if we assume that short-period expectations are always fulfilled.
>
> (Keynes 1973, p.181)

This standard analysis is at odds with Keynes's own argument in GT where, in Chapter 19, he insisted that involuntary unemployment would not be eliminated by increased wage flexibility. Falling money wages will influence the economy in a number of ways but, on balance, are unlikely to stimulate output.[16] Keynes's analysis of the effects of changes in money wages may have been sketchy, but the logic behind potential instability is impeccable. The real balance effect was overlooked by Keynes, but has been found to be empirically insignificant, and the expansionary effects of a decline in money wages due to the Keynes effect may be more than offset by the adverse influences of debt deflation, distributional shifts and expectations of continuing reductions of wages and prices.[17]

These complicating factors can be addressed by an informal discussion of the diverse effects of money wage changes, using the AD–AS model as the starting point. This is basically what Keynes did in Chapter 19 of GT. The analysis and the destabilizing effects can be illustrated using the AD–AS diagram (see Dutt and Amadeo, 1990). For instance, debt deflation problems can make the AD curve upward-sloping and, in addition, money-wage reductions can shift the AD curve to the left (because of a higher propensity to consume out of wage income than non-wage income), both of which prevent the economy from converging to the 'natural' level of output.

Old Keynesians were well aware of the stability problem (e.g. Hicks (1974), Tobin (1975)), but the treatment of dynamics in Keynesian models of a 1970s vintage was unsatisfactory. There was a lack of integration between the analysis of the short-run and more long-term issues, and even the short run analysis often relied on unstated assumptions concerning the process leading to a short-run Keynesian equilibrium. Models of IKDD analyze these dynamic issues using new and powerful mathematical tools. The aim has been to construct a framework in which 'contributions to the non-market clearing paradigm could be reformulated on a common basis and extended systematically, leading successively to more and more coherent integrated models of disequilibrium growth with progressively richer interactions between markets and sectors' (Chiarella and Flaschel, 2000, p.xix).

Starting from a simple AS–AD framework, IKDD models analyze the interaction between multiple feedback mechanisms. Agents respond to disequilibrium signals in a range of markets, and the analysis demonstrates that it is essential to look at interactions across these markets. Secondly, local instability is confirmed as the most likely outcome, but plausible nonlinearities ensure that the movements of the variables remain bounded and economically meaningful. Thus, the analysis demonstrates that the Keynesian models can generate very complex dynamics and that local instability is a likely outcome for plausible specifications.

16 Hicks (1974) used the term Keynes's 'wage theorem' to denote the benchmark result that variations in money wages have no net effects on real output and employment in a closed economy'.
17 Post Keynesians have stressed additional problems arising from the role of uncertainty, the financial situation of firms and the effects of an endogenous money supply.

4.4 The New Keynesian detour and the IKDD alternative

The New Keynesian approach can be characterized as one which attempts to derive Keynesian conclusions with respect to the existence of unemployment equilibrium and/or the effectiveness of aggregate demand policy, while using a standard neoclassical methodology.

Unemployment equilibrium can be explained in terms of the optimizing behavior of agents in models that depart from Walrasian perfect competition by introducing perceived demand curves for imperfectly competitive firms, asymmetric information, efficiency wages, credit rationing, and the like.[18] Some of these models are very insightful, but they largely fail to address the issue of involuntary unemployment in Keynes's sense. Keynes explicitly defined 'voluntary unemployment' to include all frictional and structural unemployment, that is, to include unemployment caused by minimum wage legislation and excessive union wage demands, for instance. By extension, Keynes's notion of voluntary unemployment also includes structural unemployment generated by the various departures from perfect competition that have been invoked by the NK approach. Structural unemployment of this kind may be theoretically interesting and empirically significant, but it is not the kind of unemployment addressed by Keynes. His involuntary unemployment is defined in terms of inadequate aggregate demand and the failure of the market mechanism to ensure the adjustment of aggregate demand to the level of aggregate supply associated with a structurally determined (minimum) rate of unemployment. It is the deviation from a structural unemployment rate that makes demand policy desirable.

In NK models, the effectiveness of aggregate demand policy is confined to the short run and derives from nominal wage and price rigidities. Some of the early NK models were of the spanner-in-the-works variety which merely introduced nominal wage and price rigidities into new classical or RBC models with rational expectations. However the NK methodology requires that such rigidities be based on optimizing behavior: 'rather than postulating that prices and wages respond mechanically to some measure of market disequilibrium, they are set optimally, that is, so as to best serve the interests of the parties assumed to set them, according to the information available at the time' (Woodford 2003, p.7). Thus, prices and wages are set in a forward-looking manner, expectations are assumed to be rational, and preferences are regarded as structural and invariant to changes in policy.

Our comments on the NK approach focus on two issues: the obsession with microeconomic foundations based on explicit optimization, and the treatment of stability issues. The two issues are related since the obsession with optimization stands in the way of serious stability analysis. Following that, we turn to the IKDD alternative to discuss how it deals with expectations in its analysis of stability issues.

---

18 Some contributions are adventurous enough to depart from optimization to invoke 'near' rationality! See Akerlof and Yellen (1987).

4.4.1 Optimization

We may first note that microfoundations and optimization are not the same. Micro-foundations requires clear and plausible accounts of how individual decision-makers make decisions based on their goals and environments without necessarily requiring the use of explicit optimization based on precise objective functions and constraints. Moreover, optimization can be used to depict the behavior of institutions like firms and labor unions who are not individuals. The provision of microfoundations of macroeconomics has much to recommend it, for instance, in order to avoid ascribing internally-inconsistent behavior of decision-makers and overlooking possible free-rider problems in making groups behave like individuals. However, microfoundations need to take into account in an appropriate manner the macroeconomic environment in which individuals make decisions, by providing what has been called the macroeconomic foundations of microeconomics. We next turn to optimization itself.

Optimization can sometimes be very useful as a simple way of describing goal-oriented behavior (indeed, both our simple AD–AS model and Keynes's own analysis included the assumption of profit maximizing firms). Nevertheless insisting on optimization can also result in problems. The problems with the optimization approach are largely well known and a brief summary of some of the main points will suffice.

The cognitive limitations and bounded rationality of all real-world decision makers have been stressed by many authors, most notably perhaps by Simon, and a more recent literature has documented the existence of systematic departures from optimizing behavior (see Kahneman, 2000, and Camerer *et al.*, 2004). From this perspective, the NK demand for optimizing microeconomic foundations is remarkable primarily because of the highly restrictive form that it takes.[19]

Aggregation represents another problem for the optimizing approach. To obtain definite results, any theory of the economy as a whole has to engage in aggregation. Thus, there can be no attempt at full disaggregation in the agent space, as in Arrow-Debreu models of general equilibrium, and it is well known that even if all individual agents were fully rational and maximized well-behaved utility functions subject to standard constraints, aggregate variables do not behave as if determined by an optimizing representative agent (see, for instance, Kirman, 1992). Aggregation problems therefore imply that the use of an optimizing representative agent in NK models has little to recommend itself.

---

19 It can be argued that problems related to information gathering and computational ability need not undermine the neoclassical optimizing hypothesis, because this hypothesis does not assume rationality in an empirical sense (whatever that means), but simply uses the organizing framework of analyzing behavior in terms of the optimization of some objective function subject to some constraints (see Boland, 1981). This argument, however, suggests that there is no overriding justification for insisting on the use of the optimizing approach (for instance, based on some notion of the rationality of economic agents), and that a nonoptimizing approach need not be inferior to the neoclassical one.

The existence of social norms and conventions provides a further reason to eschew the mechanical application of optimization methods based on exogenously given and constant preferences. The role of relative wages and norms of fairness in Keynes' GT analysis of wage formation presents an example of this perspective. The existence of norms and conventions may be a source of 'conditional stability' in Keynesian models of uncertainty (Crotty, 1994) but norms and conventions also change over time, both endogenously and as a result of exogenous shocks. We shall return to these issues in Section 4.5.

A more subtle danger of the optimization approach is that it may predispose the analysis to slide from individual 'rationality' to systemic 'rationality'. Some economists may view optimization as simply an organizing principle (see footnote 19), but countless examples suggest that an optimization approach may generate (sometimes unconsciously) a slippery slope in which individual optimization eventually leads to social optimality. Sargent (1993), for instance, is able to assume bounded rationality and yet produce, eventually, his unique, new classical equilibrium. As a second example, many of the problems caused by efficiency wage considerations can be 'solved' when credit markets function efficiently (again, with clever institutions). A history of how a focus on individual optimization in neoclassical economics inexorably, albeit tortuously, has led to presumptions of social optimality awaits an author, if one does not exist already.

A serious problem, finally, arises from the bounded rationality of the theorist. Carrying the straightjacket of optimization – especially in its dynamic versions – reduces the ability of the theory to incorporate many important aspects of reality in a tractable manner, and therefore encourages the theorist to ignore them. One may insist on treating all agents in a model as fully optimizing, but there is a cost to meeting this demand. Simplifications then need to be made in other areas in order to keep the model tractable; the number of distinct agents, for instance, may have to be kept very small and the nature of the interaction between the agents very simple.

All useful models represent drastically stylized pictures of a complex reality. The art of model building consists in choosing appropriate simplifying assumptions, and in our view the insistence on fully optimizing behavior represents a suboptimal 'corner solution' to the modeling problem: the gains from explicit optimization are often minimal and the costs of the required simplifications in other areas high. Thus, over the last 30 years macroeconomists have struggled to solve problems of intertemporal optimization. These optimization problems grossly simplify real-world decision problems, and the astounding implicit presumption has been that agents in the real world solve (or act as if they had solved) these much more complex problems. The neglect of aggregation problems and the use of representative agents in models that purport to provide microeconomic foundations only serve to make the picture even more bizarre. In fact, the contemporary approach with its sophisticated and perfectly rational representative agents would seem to embody a good example of how not to use mathematics: mathematical models arguably are useful, primarily because they allow a clear analysis of complex interactions between agents, each of whom may follow relatively simple (but possibly changing) behavioral rules.

4.4.2 Stability and rational expectations

NK models may include nonclearing labor markets and allow for real effects of aggregate demand policy. However it is assumed that, in the absence of shocks, the economy converges to an equilibrium position, and cyclical fluctuations are generated by introducing stochastic shocks into models with a stable equilibrium solution. If only prices and wages were flexible, there would be no Keynesian problems of effective demand.

The stability concerns that were at the center of Keynes's message have been largely forgotten.[20] Is there a NK answer to these stability concerns? Not really. Stability is simply assumed in NK models, and most of the feedback mechanisms analyzed by IKDD models are left out of the NK analysis. The NK models typically involve saddlepoints and jump variables, and the presumption of stability is used to pin down the outcome in the short run. Agents have rational expectations, and the jump variables seek out the stable saddlepath. Thus, to the extent that there is an answer, it comes from the NK focus on microfoundations and rational expectations, and from the implicit rejection of the old Keynesian analysis because of its alleged deficiencies in these areas.

Rational expectations have been used before Muth and Lucas, although without using that name. Keynes' own GT approach of assuming that short-period expectations are fulfilled is an example of rational expectations in the sense of perfect foresight, and Harrod's (1939) warranted growth path also represents a rational expectations path. But the extension of rational expectations to all models – and not just steady growth paths or Robinsonian mythical ages – lacks both theoretical and empirical foundations. We confine our attention to a few observations about theory.

The theoretical argument relies on the claim that the systematic deviations characterizing other specifications would lead to changes in expectation formation. This claim has some force and, indeed, changing expectations may be an important source of instability (as suggested by the role of 'animal spirits' in Keynesian analyzes). But the claim does not justify a focus on rational expectations. It has been notoriously difficult to get convergence to rational expectations even in simple models of rational learning, and the real-world learning process takes place within a complex overall environment and one that is subject to constant and profound technical and institutional change (Frydman and Phelps, 1983).

---

20 The Japanese stagnation in the 1990s may have alerted the profession to some stability issues, and the 'liquidity trap' has made a comeback (e.g. Krugman 1998, Nakatani and Skott 2007). The liquidity trap arises because of an inability of monetary policy to reduce interest rates, that is, to change intertemporal prices. It seems to have escaped attention, however, that the liquidity trap and the problem of intertemporal prices are indicative of the general stability problem. Money-wage reductions fail to solve the unemployment problem because '[a]ccording to Keynes' diagnosis, it is fundamentally the *intertemporal relative values* observed or implicit in the actual vector that are "wrong" ', and, *"although the most eye-catching symptom of maladjustment is the great excess supply in the labor markets, ... the burden of adjustment should not be thrown on this market."* (Leijonhufvud, 1968, pp.338 and 336; italics in original)

These changes in the environment may lead to shifts in expectations; indeed, some institutional or structural change is often invoked to justify expectations that would otherwise seem unreasonable, viz. the appeal to a 'new economy' during the stock market boom of the 1990s. However, structural and institutional changes of this kind count against rational expectations, since the learning processes underlying the claims in favor of rational expectations fare better in a stable environment, and the learning argument is particularly vulnerable with respect to some of the key variables of macroeconomic interest – saving for retirement, for instance, or educational choices (investment in human capital) – where essentially each agent makes only a single decision.[21, 22]

4.4.3 Dynamics and expectations in IKDD models

Models in the IKDD framework have departed from the New Keynesian optimizing approach and used behavioral equations and dynamic adjustment mechanisms along 'old' Keynesian lines. As noted earlier, these models use sophisticated mathematical and computational techniques to formalize many of the arguments of the old Keynesian approach and the stability properties are analyzed rigorously. These models, moreover, avoid a 'rational expectations perfect foresight methodology according to which variables, when out of steady-state equilibrium, are allowed to jump to their stable paths in order to ensure convergence back to steady state' (Flaschel, Franke and Semmler, 1997, p.xi). We consider this a promising approach, but have reservations with respect to some of the behavioral and institutional assumptions. In this section, we look briefly at technical aspects relating to the treatment of expectations; Section 4.5 takes up some broader issues.

Some IKDD writings suggest that the absence of perfect foresight is consistent with myopic perfect foresight, not just at a particular moment but at all times along a complete dynamic trajectory. We find this claim surprising.

If one leaves a world of complete perfect foresight, there must be times when expectations fail to be met. Disappointed medium- or long-run expectations must

---

21 A dismissal of stability concerns cannot be justified by reference to Walrasian general equilibrium theory. In fact, the realization that stability had not and probably could not be established under reasonable assumptions may have been a critical factor behind the virtual abandonment in microeconomics of all research on Walrasian general equilibrium theory (Kirman, 1989, Katzner 2004). Joan Robinson's criticism of tâtonnement-based stability should have provided additional impetus for this shift, but her criticism was not widely understood (e.g. Robinson (1962, pp. 23–29), Skott (2005b)).

22 Not all New Keynesian contributions ignore stability issues. A notable exception is the work of Hahn and Solow (1995), who develop an overlapping-generations model and introduce real money balances using a variant of the Clower constraint to show that wage–price flexibility can result in macroeconomic instability. They also show that wage and price sluggishness as explained by standard NK techniques can be stabilizing but also prevent the economy from attaining full-employment. However, their model becomes extremely unwieldy, primarily due to its optimizing assumptions and they have to resort to simulation techniques to examine the behavior of the economy.

show up in the form of disappointed short-run expectations at some moment, and an assumption of myopic perfect foresight concerning all variables at all times would seem to imply globally perfect foresight. Thus, we are not convinced that

> "Keynesian IS-LM dynamics proper (demand driven growth and business fluctuations) must remain intact if (generally minor) errors in inflationary expectations are excluded from consideration"
>
> (Asada *et al.*, 2006, p. 96)

On the contrary, it is not surprising if an economy with myopic foresight at all times behaves in a way that differs qualitatively from economies without myopic perfect foresight.

Asada *et al.* (2006) get around the problem – and the qualitative difference between economies with and without myopic perfect foresight at all times – by introducing a new variable, the 'inflationary climate'. Wage and price formation, they assume, depend on the inflationary climate as well as on the (perfectly foreseen) current rate of inflation. The inflationary climate is seen as an expression of inflation expectations for the medium-run expectations, and it is suggested that

> Inflationary expectations over the medium run, $\hat{\pi}^c$, i.e. the inflationary climate in which current wage and price inflation is operating, may be adaptively following the actual rate of inflation (by use of some exponential weighting scheme), may be based on a rolling sample (with hump-shaped weighting schemes), or on other possibilities for updating expectations. For simplicity of exposition we shall here make use of the conventional adaptive expectations mechanism.
>
> (Asada *et al.*, 2006, P. 102)

This interpretation of $\hat{\pi}^c$ as an expectational variable may be hard to sustain: why should the current inflation rate lead anyone to adjust his or her medium-run expectations (the 'inflationary climate') if the current rate is exactly as expected?[23, 24] What matters from a technical perspective, however, is the

---

23 Adjustments to the inflation climate may occur, even in the absence of surprises, if the inflation climate is defined as

$$\pi^c(t) = \int_0^\infty \pi^e(\tau)\rho e^{-\rho(\tau-t)}d\tau.$$

In this case, an unchanged trajectory of future expected inflation rates implies that

$$\dot{\pi}^c(t) = \rho(\pi^c(t) - \pi(t)).$$

But this specification, which corresponds to a negative adjustment parameter in the adaptive specification, is very different from the one used by Asada *et al.* (2006).

24 Disappointed expectations could show up as unanticipated changes in inventories rather than as unanticipated inflation. But if the surprises manifest themselves in quantity movements, presumably adjustments in the inflation climate should be related to these quantity movements, rather than to the deviations between the current inflation rate and the inflationary climate.

existence of an inertial element in wage and price formation. If there is myopic perfect foresight, it is essential that something prevents wage and price setters from acting fully on their foresight. That something need not be adaptive medium-run inflation expectations; an alternative source might be institutional features of the economy, including staggered wage contracts, as in some NK formulations. The precise source of the inertial element may be irrelevant for the analysis of the dynamic properties of the model. The source becomes important, however, if one wants to evaluate the model in relation to real-world economies and discuss the robustness of the specification to various shocks or changes in policy rules.

4.5 Post-Keynesian, Structuralist and Neo-Marxian alternatives

The AD–AS tradition – including the recent work on 'integrated Keynesian disequilibrium dynamics' by Chiarella and Flaschel and their associates – rightly stresses the need to consider dynamic interactions across markets, and it is justifiably critical of optimization methodology. But theories in the AD–AS tradition need to be developed not just in terms of more advanced mathematical analysis of the dynamic interactions but also in terms of a renewed attention to the behavioral and institutional assumptions and their implications for the specification of the various equations.

The behavioral foundations have not been neglected in the Keynesian literature, as is evident from even a cursory look at Keynes's own analysis or the efforts of many old Keynesians. Nonetheless, some of the presumptions of the AD–AS tradition seem questionable from a heterodox perspective. A post Keynesian approach questions the limited role of aggregate demand in determining medium- and long-run growth patterns in AD–AS models; a neo-Marxian approach suggests a greater focus on income distribution and its interaction with the rate of accumulation and the movements in the 'reserve army of labor'; a structuralist approach (see Taylor, 1991, 2004) emphasizes the need to examine how the structural and institutional characteristics of economies determine their dynamics.

It is beyond the scope of this chapter to discuss the behavioral alternatives in any detail. We shall confine ourselves to a few of examples of what we have in mind. The examples concern a simple model of the short run using the AD–AS framework, and assumptions that affect the role of aggregate demand in the medium and long run. We shall focus on the medium- and long-run steady states of these model rather than on the stability of their steady states.

4.5.1 A short-run AD–AS model

We examine a simple AD–AS model of the short-run determination of output and price using elements of post-Keynesian, structuralist and neo-Marxian approaches to macroeconomics.[25] The model uses standard goods and money market equilibrium conditions given by equations (4.1) and (4.2) above. We assume that wage income is entirely consumed whereas a fraction s of non-wage (or what can be called profit) income is saved, as is common in all three approaches.[26] Hence we replace equation (4.3) of the previous model with

$$C = \frac{W}{P}N + (1-s)\left(Y - \frac{W}{P}N\right) \qquad (4.3')$$

We introduce expectations explicitly in the investment function and write

$$I = I(r, E), \qquad (4.4')$$

where E denotes the state of long-term expectations. In this chapter, we treat E as a parameter, and thus it adds very little to the model, but we include it since E may have a strong influence on investment, as emphasized by Keynes and the post-Keynesians; the effect of the interest rate, on the other hand, may be weak. We leave the demand for money equation (4.5) unchanged, although it would make sense to include E as an argument in the function. We replace the production function with diminishing returns to labor given by equation (4.6) above with a fixed coefficients production function which states that output is produced with capital and labor. With the stock of capital given in the short run, and with firms maintaining excess capacity and hiring labor according to the needs of production we have

$$N = a_0 Y, \qquad (4.6')$$

where a_0 is the fixed unit labor requirement. Firms are assumed to operate in an oligopolistic environment and set their price as a markup on labor costs, so that

$$P = (1+z)Wa_0, \qquad (4.7')$$

where z is the fixed markup rate. This approach, used initially by Kalecki (1971), is now adopted by some standard mainstream textbooks and is extensively used by post-Keynesian and structuralists. The equation can be derived from optimization; eschewing formal optimization, a post-Keynesian explanation may suggest that firms ignore 'soft' information about demand and set their price using 'hard' information regarding costs, while a structuralist justification relies on empirical

---

25 This type of model has been extensively used in the post-Keynesian and structuralist literatures. We draw here on the version discussed in Dutt and Skott (1996).

26 Differential saving propensities need not be the result of heterogeneity among households, 'capitalist households' (rentiers) having a higher saving propensity than 'worker households'. This kind of heterogeneity may play a role, but Kaldor's 'Neo-Pasinetti Theorem' provides an alternative explanation (Kaldor 1966b, Skott 1981).

studies of firms within specific structural environments. The markup is influenced by the degree of concentration, as emphasized by Kalecki, but can also incorporate neo-Marxian notions of class struggle as also mentioned by Kalecki. Finally, we keep the money wage fixed assuming that there is enough unemployed labor, therefore maintaining equation (4.8).

The two adjustment variables in the short run are Y, which responds positively to excess demand in the goods market, and M, which responds positively to excess demand in the money market. The first adjustment follows from a simple quantity adjustment story while the second one follows the post-Keynesian horizontalist or endogenous money view according to which the excess demand for money leads to an expansion of loans which create bank deposits, at an interest rate, r_0, determined by the Central Bank's target rate and the markup charged by banks (see, for instance, Moore, 1988).

The AD–AS curves can be derived as follows. Equations (4.3′), (4.4′), (4.6′), (4.8) and the new equation $r = r_0$, can be substituted into equation (4.1) to obtain the AD curve. The negative slope of this curve is explained by the fact that a higher P reduces the real wage, redistributes income away from wage earners, reduces consumption demand, and induces firms to reduce output. The role of equation (4.2) is simply to determine the demand for money. The AS curve is given by equation (4.7′) and is horizontal. Equilibrium output and price are determined at the intersection of the AD and AS curves.

This version of an AD–AS model – like the textbook specification in Section 4.2 – has many shortcomings and is only a starting point for further analysis. Arguably, however, it provides a better representation of key structural characteristics of a modern economy. Moreover, it demonstrates in a simple manner some of the potential destabilizing forces at work in the economy. If unemployment results in a fall in the money wage, W, this results in a fall in the price level, and if the markup, z, is unchanged, both the AD and AS curves will move down by the same amount, keeping output and employment the same. If, however, the fall in the money wage leads to a fall in the real wage, or an increase in z, the AS curve shifts down less than the AD curve, which reduces output and employment and

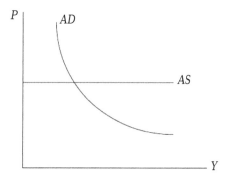

Figure 4.2 Structuralist AD–AS schedules.

increases unemployment. These kinds of destabilizing forces have been explored in the IKDD models.

4.5.2 The medium run: fairness and the 'natural rate of unemployment'

If the adjustment of the economy in the face of unemployment is stable, it will tend towards the 'natural rate of unemployment' of the economy. The existence of such a rate has been a mainstay of NK models, and most of the IKDD extensions of the AD–AS models share this feature; the natural rate of unemployment may not be asymptotically stable in the models, but cycles take place around a structurally determined long run.[27] The existence of a natural rate of unemployment implies that aggregate demand plays (almost) no role in the determination of the trend of output and the average long-run value of the unemployment rate. We find this aspect of the models questionable, both empirically and theoretically.

Money wages may be sticky, partly because workers care about relative wages (as suggested by Keynes). This argument implies a rejection of a traditional view of preferences as defined over the agent's own consumption. Instead, a notion of fairness becomes central, and the behavioral literature has provided strong support for the role of 'fairness' in wage formation (see, for instance, Bewley, 1998, Fehr and Gächter, 2000, Akerlof and Yellen, 1990). The literature also shows that changes in nominal wages are relevant for the perceived fairness of the wage offer. The relevance of nominal changes implies a kind of 'money illusion'. As a result, there is no natural rate of unemployment. Instead, a downward sloping Phillips curve emerges, and demand policies may affect real output and employment in the medium and long run (Shafir *et al.*, 1997, Akerlof *et al.*, 1996).

A more radical conclusion can be obtained if it is recognized that norms of fairness may change over time and that the prevailing wage norms are strongly influenced by the actual wage patterns in the past. Thus, according to Kahneman *et al.* (1986, p.730–1) notions of fairness tend to adjust gradually to actual outcomes:[28]

> ... the reference transaction provides a basis for fairness judgments because it is normal, not because it is just. Psychological studies of adaptation suggest that any stable state of affairs tends to become accepted eventually, at least in the sense that alternatives to it no longer readily come to mind. Terms of exchange that are initially seen as unfair may in time acquire the status of

---

27 The empirical section of Chapter 7 has a brief discussion of hysteresis in European unemployment but basically uses a Hodrick-Prescott filter to generate a time-varying NAIRU.
28 The conventional aspect of fairness is implicit in many discussions of these issues. Keynes (1930b), for instance, expressed his sympathy with the view that 'there is a large arbitrary element in the relative rates of remuneration, and the factors of production get what they do, not because in any

reference transaction. Thus, the gap between the behavior that people consider fair and the behavior that they expect in the market-place tends to be rather small.

Skott (1999, 2005a) shows that this conventional aspect of wage norms may lead to employment hysteresis, even in models that exclude money illusion of any kind.[29] If inflationary expectations are formed adaptively and adjustments in wage norms take a simple linear form, the models generate a downward-sloping Phillips curve. In general, however, aggregate demand policy will affect output in the medium run, but there will be no well-behaved Phillips relation, vertical or downward–sloping, between employment and the inflation rate.

These examples illustrate how lessons from behavioral economics may cast doubt on the natural rate hypothesis.[30] Theoretical doubts might not carry a lot of weight if the empirical evidence was overwhelming, but this is not the case. Even strong supporters of the framework concede that the applicability of the theory may be limited. Thus, Gordon (1997, p.28) concludes that

> Within the postwar experience of the United States, the modest fluctuations in the NAIRU seem plausible in magnitude and timing. When applied to Europe or to the United States in the Great Depression, however, fluctuations in the NAIRU seem too large to be plausible and seem mainly to mimic movements in the actual unemployment rate.

From a Popperian perspective, Gordon's reading of the evidence must imply that the theory should be rejected.

4.5.3 The long run: growth, accumulation and technological change

Models of the long run, which introduce capital accumulation, technological change and labor supply growth are generally of two varieties.

---

strict sense they precisely earn it, but because past events have led to these rates being customary and usual' (quoted from Keynes 1930b/1981, p.7). Marshall (1887) noted that fairness must be defined 'with reference to the methods of industry, the habits of life and the character of the people' (p.212). Fairness, he argues, requires that a worker

> … ought to be paid for his work at the usual rate for his trade and neighborhood; so that he may live in that way to which he and his neighbors in his rank of life have been accustomed.
>
> (p.213; italics added)

Similar views have been advocated by Hicks (1974) and Solow (1990).

29 Here we use the term hysteresis in a broad sense to include zero-root models, and not just models with 'remanence' (see Cross, 1988).

30 Other theoretical and arguments against the natural rate hypothesis are discussed in, for instance, Cross (1988, 1995).

By far the more popular one is the one in which aggregate demand disappears from the scene and aggregate supply determines growth. In fact, neoclassical growth theory following Solow (1956), and new growth theory, following Romer (1986) and others, abstracts entirely from the AD side, assuming perpetual full-employment and investment being determined identically by saving. The debate between neoclassical and new growth theory revolves around whether or not the marginal product of the produced factor of production, capital, falls to zero as the capital-labor ratio rises indefinitely and, therefore, whether long-run growth is affected by the saving rate and other economic variables. The neglect of AD is usually not explicitly explained in these models, but it is implicitly assumed that wage and price flexibility will remove unemployment in the medium run or, failing that, that government aggregate demand policy will do the job. Thus, the long-run growth path is independent of AD factors.

A less popular variety, with roots in the Keynesian theories of Harrod (1939), Robinson (1962) and others, focuses on AD as determining growth. In these models, growth is determined by the interaction between aggregate demand and supply factors (including, for instance, firms' pricing decisions). Some work in this tradition has included the labor market explicitly and linked the long-run rate of growth of output to the growth of the labor supply in efficiency units (see, for instance, Kaldor 1957, Skott 1989a, Dutt 1992b). Most models, however, do not impose the requirement that the unemployment rate be constant in the long run but simply assume that the labor supply does not constrain the rate of growth (see Marglin, 1984, Dutt, 1984, Taylor, 1991). These models have many interesting implications, including the possibility that a more equal distribution of income can increase the rate of growth and that technological change can have immiserizing effects, and the assumption of no labor constraints can be defended by pointing to the existence of large amounts of hidden unemployment in the primary and tertiary sectors in most countries, developed as well as less developed, until some time in the post World War II period. For the more recent period, however, the hidden-unemployment argument may not be persuasive, at least for advanced industrial countries. Most of the OECD (Organization for Economic Cooperation and Development) economies arguably have become 'mature' in Kaldor's (1966a) sense: they certainly have unemployment, both open and disguised, but it would be misleading to treat the labor supply to the modern sector as perfectly elastic and to disregard the labor constraints on the long-run rate of growth. Even under conditions of maturity, however, the rate of growth may be influenced by aggregate demand.

As argued in Section 4.5.2, the rate of employment can not be taken as independent of the demand side, even in the medium run, and this dependence of employment on aggregate demand opens up ways in which demand may also influence the rate of growth in the long run.

One channel runs through migration. Even if a country has exhausted its domestic reserves of hidden unemployment, the possibility of immigration provides an international reserve army and, immigration laws permitting, the growth rate of the country need not be limited by its labor supply. Immigration laws respond to economic conditions (as evidenced, for instance, by the change in attitudes of European countries between the 1960s and the more recent period), and the employment rate can therefore have a significant effect on the rate of growth of the labor force.[31]

Induced technical progress represents a second possible channel. Labor shortages provide an incentive for firms to seek out new labor saving techniques, and this technology channel suggests that the rate of growth of the labor supply in efficiency units may be positively related to the employment rate. Both the employment and technology channels imply that insofar as aggregate demand policy influences the rate of employment, it also affects the long-run rate of growth (Flaschel and Skott, 2006).[32]

A more radical approach is pursued by Dutt (2006) who considers a range of models in which the rate of labor productivity growth responds to labor market conditions, with tight labor markets speeding up labor-saving technological change. One of the models makes the employment rate affect both changes in the 'autonomous' investment parameter (to capture the effects of unemployment and wage reductions on aggregate demand through the Keynes effect) and the rate of labor productivity growth. Since the same rate of employment makes investment and labor productivity growth stationary, the result is a zero root model in which a change in the level of autonomous demand (for instance, government expenditure) has a permanent effect on the long-run rate of growth. The economy converges to its long-run rate of growth, at which the economy grows with unemployment at its 'natural' rate, but the long-run rate of growth itself is affected by aggregate demand. AD and AS grow at the same rate, but the growth rate of the economy is not independent of factors determining AD.

4.6 Conclusion

We have argued in this chapter that the older Keynesian tradition based on the aggregate demand–aggregate supply framework provides a more suitable and promising framework for building macroeconomics than the currently-dominant approach, including its New Keynesian variant. This is so for a number of reasons.

Contrary to what has been argued by a number of critics, first, the traditional aggregate demand–aggregate supply approach is internally consistent, at least in its Marshallian interpretation, as well as consistent with Keynes's own analysis.

Second, it has the strength of explicitly including the major markets and sectors of the economy and examining their interactions. In this sense, it is a general, rather than a partial, theory. Walrasian general equilibrium theory may also be

---

31 This channel may be reinforced by the effects of unemployment on changes in the labor force participation rate; women's participation rate and the average retirement age, for instance, may respond gradually to labor market conditions.

32 Verdoorn's-law effects in which learning by doing generates a positive impact of the rate of growth of output on productivity growth imply an additional stimulus from faster immigration to productivity growth.

general in this sense, but is different in several ways, including the perspective on behavioral foundations.

Third, the aggregate demand–aggregate supply approach does not insist on optimizing microfoundations. The AD–AS model is not necessarily inconsistent with optimizing behavior, but the approach is eclectic. It starts with some basic and commonly-used accounting identities, adds rules of behavior of individuals or groups in specific institutional settings, and examines their consequences for the performance and evolution of the system. The theorist must be prepared to explain and defend the choice of behavioral rules, but an appeal to optimization is neither necessary nor sufficient for a successful defense. This eclecticism, we have argued, is a strength, and the New Keynesian methodological position is flawed. New Keynesian macroeconomics has produced interesting insights, but the insistence on optimizing microfoundations means that these insights have come at the cost of neglecting a variety of important issues, including the analysis of stability.

Fourth, it is true that a great deal of analysis using the aggregate demand–aggregate supply framework is mechanical and fails to capture important aspects of reality, and its extensions to medium- and long-run issues typically ignore the role of aggregate demand. However, unencumbered by the straightjacket of optimizing microfoundations, the approach provides a useful starting point for the analysis of dynamic macroeconomic interactions. In developing this analysis, the approach can draw on insights from the post-Keynesian, neo-Marxian and structuralist traditions, as well as from the burgeoning literature on behavioral economics.

References

Akerlof, G.A. and J.L. Yellen (1987): Rational models of irrational behavior, *American Economic Review*, May, 137–142.

Akerlof, G.A. and J.L. Yellen (1990): The fair wage-effort hypothesis and unemployment. *Quarterly Journal of Economics*, 105, 254–283.

Akerlof, G.A., W.T. Dickens, and G.L. Perry (1996): The macroeconomics of low inflation. *Brookings Papers on Economic Activity*, 1–59.

Asada, T., P. Chen, C. Chiarella, and P. Flaschel, P. (2006): Keynesian dynamics and the wage–price spiral: A baseline disequilibrium model. *Journal of Macroeconomics*, 28, 90–130.

Barro, R.J. (1994): The aggregate-supply/aggregate-demand model. *Eastern Economic Journal*, Winter, 1–6.

Bewley, T. (1998): Why not cut pay. *European Economic Review*, 42, 459–490.

Bhaduri, A., K. Laski, and M. Riese (1999): Effective demand versus profit maximization in aggregate demand/supply analysis from a dynamic perspective. *Banca Nazionale del Lavoro Quaterly Review*, 52(210), 281–293.

Blanchard, O. (2000) What do we know about macroeconomics that Fisher and Wicksell did not? *Quarterly Journal of Economics*, 115, 1375–1409.

Boland, L.A. (1981): On the futility of criticizing the neoclassical maximization hypothesis. *American Economic Review*, 71(5), December, 1031–1036.

Camerer, C.F., G. Loewenstein, and M. Rabin (2004): *Advances in Behavioral Economics*, Princeton: Princeton University Press.

Chiarella, C. and Flaschel, P. (2000) *The Dynamics of Keynesian Monetary Growth*. Cambridge: Cambridge University Press.

Clower, R. W. (1989): Keynes's General Theory: The Marshallian connection. In: D.A. Walker (ed.): *Perspectives on the History of Economic Thought, Vol II*. Aldershot: Edward Elgar.

Colander, D. (1995): The stories we tell: A reconsideration of AS/AD analysis. *Journal of Economic Perspectives*, Summer, 169–188.

Cross, R. ed. (1988): *Hysteresis and the Natural Rate Hypothesis*. Oxford: Basil Blackwell.

Cross, R. ed. (1995): *The Natural Rate of Unemployment: Reflections on 25 Years of the Hypothesis*. Cambridge: Cambridge University Press.

Crotty, J. (1994): Are Keynesian uncertainty and macrotheory compatible? Conventional decision making, institutional structures, and conditional stability in Keynesian macromodels. In: G. Dymski and R. Pollin (eds): *New Perspectives in Monetary Macroeconomics: Explorations in the Tradition of Hyman Minsky*. Ann Arbor: University of Michigan Press, 105–142.

Dunlop, J.G. (1938): The movement of real and money wage rates. *Economic Journal*, 413–434.

Dutt, A.K. (1984): Stagnation, income distribution and monopoly power. *Cambridge Journal of Economics*, 8(1), March, 25–40.

Dutt, A.K. (1987): Keynes with a perfectly competitive goods market. *Australian Economic Papers*, 26, 275–293.

Dutt, A.K. (1992a): Keynes, market forms, and competition. In: Bill Gerrard and John Hillard (eds.): *The Philosophy and Economics of J M Keynes*. Aldershot: Edward Elgar.

Dutt, A.K. (1992b): Conflict inflation, distribution, cyclical accumulation and crises. *European Journal of Political Economy*, 8, 579–597.

Dutt, A.K. (1997): Equilibrium, path dependence and hysteresis in post-Keynesian models. In P. Arestis and M. Sawyer (eds.): *Essays in Honour of G. C. Harcourt, Vol 2: Markets, Unemployment and Economic Policy*. London: Routledge, 238–253.

Dutt, A.K. (2002): Aggregate demand and aggregate supply: A history. *History of Political Economy*, Summer, 34(2), 321–363.

Dutt, A.K. (2006): Aggregate demand, aggregate supply and economic growth. *International Review of Applied Economics*, 20(3), 319–336.

Dutt, A.K. and Amadeo, E.J. (1990): *Keynes's Third Alternative? The neo-Ricardian Keynesians and the Post Keynesians*. Aldershot: Edward Elgar.

Dutt, A.K. and Skott, P. (1996): Keynesian theory and the aggregate-supply/ aggregate-demand framework: A defense. *Eastern Economic Journal*, 22(3), Summer, 313–331.

Dutt, A.K. and Skott, P. (2006): Keynesian theory and the AD–AS framework: A reconsideration. In: C. Chiarella, P. Flaschel, R. Franke and W. Semmler (eds): *Quantitative and Empirical Analysis of Nonlinear Dynamic Macromodels*. Elsevier, 149–172.

Fehr, E. and S. Gächter (2000): Fairness and retaliation: The economics of reciprocity, *Journal of Economic Perspectives*, 14, 159–181.

Fields, T.W. and W.R. Hart (1990): Some pitfalls in the conventional treatment of aggregate demand. *Southern Economic Journal*, 676–684.

Flaschel, P. and P. Skott (2006): Steindlian models of growth and stagnation. *Metroeconomica*, 57(3), 303–338.

Flaschel, P., R. Franke, and W. Semmler (1997): *Dynamic Macroeconomics Instability, Fluctuations, and Growth in Monetary Economies*. Cambridge, MA: MIT Press.

Frydman, R. and E. S. Phelps, eds. (1983): *Individual Forecasting and Aggregate Outcomes: 'Rational Expectations' Examined*. Cambridge: Cambridge University Press.

Gordon, R.J. (1997): The time-varying NAIRU and its implications for economic policy. *Journal of Economic Perspectives*, 11, 11–32.

Hahn, F. and R.M. Solow (1995): *A Critical Essay on Modern Macroeconomic Theory*. Cambridge, Mass.: MIT Press.

Harrod, R.F. (1939): An essay in dynamic theory. *Economic Journal*, 49, 14–33.

Hicks, J. (1974): *The Crisis in Keynesian Economics*. Oxford: Blackwell.

Hicks, J. (1980–81): IS-LM: An explanation, *Journal of Post Keynesian Economics*, 3, Winter, 139–154.

Kahneman, D. (ed.) (2000) *Choices, Values and Frames*. Cambridge: Cambridge University Press.

Kahneman, D., J.L. Knetsch, and R. Thaler (1986): Fairness as a constraint on profit seeking: Entitlements in the market. *American Economic Review*, 76, 728–741.

Kaldor, N. (1957) A model of economic growth. *Economic Journal*, 67, 591–624.

Kaldor, N. (1966a): *Causes of the Slow Rate of Economic Growth in the United Kingdom*. Cambridge: Cambridge University Press.

Kaldor, N. (1966b) Marginal productivity and the macroeconomic theories of distribution. *Review of Economic Studies*, 33, 309–319.

Kalecki, M. (1971): *Selected Essays on the Dynamics of the Capitalist Economy*. Cambridge: Cambridge University Press.

Katzner, D.W. (2004): *The Current Non-Status of General Equilibrium Theory*, UMass Working Paper 2004-10.

Keynes, J.M. (1930a): *A Treatise on Money*. London and Basingstoke: Macmillan.

Keynes, J.M. (1930b): *The Question of High Wages, The Political Quarterly*. Reprinted in Collected Writings, Vol 20: Activities 1929–1931, London and Basingstoke: Macmillan, 1981.

Keynes, J.M. (1936 / 1973): *The General Theory of Employment, Interest and Money*. London: Macmillan.

Keynes, J.M. (1973): *Collected Writings, Vol. 14: The General Theory and After – Part II Defence and Development*. London and Basingstoke: Macmillan.

Kirman, A.P. (1989): The intrinsic limits of modern economic theory: The Emperor has no clothes. *Economic Journal*, 99, 126–139.

Kirman, A.P. (1992): Whom or what does the representative individual represent? *Journal of Economic Perspectives*, 6, 117–136.

Kregel, J. (1976): Economic methodology in the face of uncertainty: The modeling methods of Keynes and the post-Keynesians. *Economic Journal*, 86, 209–225.

Krugman, P.R. (1998): It's Baaack: Japan's slump and the return of the liquidity trap. *Brookings Papers on Economic Activity,* 2, 137–187.

Leijonhufvud, A. (1968): *On Keynesian Economics and the Economics of Keynes*. Oxford University Press.

Marglin S.A. (1984): *Growth, Distribution and Prices*. Cambridge, Mass.: Harvard University Press.

Marshall, A. (1887): A fair rate of wages. In: A.C. Pigou (ed.): *1956, Memorials of Alfred Marshall*. New York: Kelley & Millman, 212–226.

Meltzer, A.H. (1988): *Keynes's Monetary Theory. A Different Interpretation*. Cambridge: Cambridge University Press.

Moore, B.J. (1988): *Horizontalists and Verticalists*, Cambridge: Cambridge University Press.

Nakatani, T. and P. Skott (2007) Japanese growth and stagnation: A Keynesian perspective. *Structural Change and Economic Dynamics*, 18, 306–332.

Robinson, J. (1962): *Essays in the Theory of Economic Growth*. London: Macmillan.

Romer, D. (2000): Keynesian macroeconomics without the LM curve. *Journal of Economic Perspectives*, 14(2), Spring, 149–169.

Romer, P.M. (1986): Increasing returns and long-run growth. *Journal of Political Economy*, 94, 1102–1137.

Sargent, T.J. (1993): *Bounded Rationality in Macroeconomics*, Oxford: Oxford University Press.

Shafir, E., P. Diamond, and A. Tversky (1997): Money illusion. *Quarterly Journal of Economics*, 112, 341–374.

Skott, P. (1981) On the 'Kaldorian' Saving Function. *Kyklos*, 34, 563–581.

Skott, P. (1983): An essay on Keynes and general equilibrium theory. *Thames Papers in Political Economy*, Summer, 1–43.

Skott, P. (1989a): *Conflict and Effective Demand in Economic Growth*. Cambridge: Cambridge University Press.

Skott, P. (1989b): Effective demand, class struggle and cyclical growth. *International Economic Review*, 30, 231–247.

Skott, P. (1999): Wage formation and the (non-) existence of the NAIRU. *Economic Issues*, 4, 77–92.

Skott, P. (2005a): Fairness as a source of hysteresis in employment and relative wages. *Journal of Economic Behavior and Organization*, 57, 305–331.

Skott, P. (2005b): Equilibrium, stability and economic growth. In: B. Gibson (ed.): *Joan Robinson: A Centennial Celebration*. Northampton, MA: Edward Elgar, 175–196.

Skott, P. (2006): Comments on integrated Keynesian disequilibrium dynamics. *Journal of Macroeconomics*, 28, 131–135.

Solow, R.M. (1956): A contribution to the theory of economic growth. *Quarterly Journal of Economics*, 70, 65–94.

Solow, R. (1990): *The Labor Market as a Social Institution*. Oxford: Blackwell.

Tarshis, L. (1939): Changes in real and money wages. *Economic Journal*, 150–154.

Taylor, L. (1991): *Distribution, Growth and Inflation: Lectures in Structuralist Macroeconomics*. Cambridge, Mass.: MIT Press.

Taylor, L. (2004): *Reconstructing Macroeconomics*, Cambridge, Mass.: Harvard University Press.

Tobin, J. (1975): Keynesian models of recession and depression. *American Economic Review*, 65, 195–202.

Woodford, M. (1999): *Revolution and Evolution in Twentieth-Century Macroeconomics*. Unpublished, Princeton University.

Woodford, M. (2003): *Interest and Prices: Foundations of a Theory of Monetary Policy*. Princeton and Oxford: Princeton University Press.

Part II

Matured Keynesian AD–AS model building

5 New Keynesian equilibrium vs. Keynesian disequilibrium dynamics

Two competing approaches

5.1 Introduction

During the last decade Dynamic Stochastic General Equilibrium (DSGE) models along the lines of Erceg, Henderson and Levin (2000), Smets and Wouters (2003) and Christiano, Eichenbaum and Evans (2005) have become the workhorse framework for the study of monetary policy and inflation in the academic literature. However, despite its popularity, this approach – where the dynamics of the economy is derived from neoclassical microfoundations, the assumption of rational expectations and the condition of general equilibrium – has been starkly questioned from both the theoretical and empirical point of view by numerous researchers like Mankiw (2001), Estrella and Fuhrer (2002) and Solow (2004), among others. The criticisms focus primarily on the highly unrealistic assumptions concerning the alleged 'rationality' in the forward-looking behavior of the economic agents, and its failure to explain important empirical stylized facts.

Indeed, besides the 'dynamic inconsistencies' concerning, among other things, the interactions between key macroeconomic variables such as the inflation rate and the output gap resulting from the assumed purely forward-looking and 'rational' (in Muth's (1961) mathematical sense) behavior of the economic agents (see e.g. Estrella and Fuhrer (2002), as well as Rudd and Whelan (2005)), one of the major shortcomings related with the rational expectations assumption is its lack of economic content, which reduces the determination of the model's solution (and the determinacy conditions of the system, on which see Blanchard and Kahn (1980) and Sims (2001)) to not much more than a purely mathematical exercise.

We show this[1] by reconsidering the baseline New Keynesian model with staggered wages and prices introduced by Erceg, Henderson and Levin (2000) and discussed in Woodford (2003, Ch.4) and Galí (2008, Ch.6) concerning the determinacy conditions of this model. As we will show, the role of important

---

[1] This chapter is based on Flaschel, P. and C.R. Proaño, (2009): 'Determinacy and Stability Analysis in New Keynesian and Keynesian Macrodynamics', CEMM, Bielefeld University: Working Paper, http://www.wiwi.uni-bielefeld.de/nc/cemm.

feedback channels such as the real wage channel (investigated in Chiarella and Flaschel (2000) and later work) in the shaping of the cyclical adjustment processes and their inflationary consequences is almost nonexistent in the New Keynesian framework, since there determinacy is achieved by the specification of a Taylor interest rate rule with parameters values which imply a certain combination of unstable/stable roots for the Jacobian matrix of the dynamics.

By contrast, a closely related reformulation of the 4D New Keynesian baseline model in terms of a wage–price spiral with only model consistent – but not *rational* – expectations enables a thorough theoretical analysis of this and other feedback channels and the related stability issues possible in a world without rational expectations – in the sense of Muth's (1961) theory. As discussed in Section 5.3, such a framework can be proven to be globally asymptotically stable for conventional types of interest rate policy rules and much more attractive in its deterministic properties than the purely forward-looking 4D baseline New Keynesian approach with its fairly trivial deterministic core (in the case of determinacy), since it integrates different possible scenarios concerning real interest rate effects, real wage effects and a nominal interest rate policy rules.

In this alternative model, we use from the beginning continuous-time as the modeling framework, since that allows for a straightforward stability analysis even in high order dynamical systems (which nevertheless can be simulated adequately with a step length of 1/365). Within this modeling approach, also built on the assumptions of gradually adjusting wages and prices, we can of course consider limit cases where wages, prices or expectations adjust with infinite speed, but these are more a matter of theoretical curiosity than of fundamental importance. As we will show, while the determination of the local stability properties of the (D)AS–AD model is by far no less mathematically demanding than the determinacy analysis of the New Keynesian 4D model, the structure of the former allows us to investigate a large variety of aspects – such as the role of different macroeconomic channels for the dynamic stability of an economy – not analyzed in the New Keynesian framework.

The remainder of this chapter is organized as follows. Based on the intuition made by Foley (1975), Sims (1998) and more recently by Flaschel and Proaño (2009) which suggests that period models should feature qualitatively similar dynamics (and thus stability properties) as their continuous time analogues, in Section 5.2, we reformulate the deterministic structure of the discrete-time New Keynesian model with staggered wages and prices in a continuous-time representation and use it to show how determinacy analysis of this model type can be undertaken, confirming Galí's (2008,Ch.6) numerical results in an analytical manner. In contrast, in Section 5.3, we discuss an alternative macroeconomic framework based on gradual adjustments of wages and prices to disequilibrium situations in the real markets, and show how the analysis of the stability properties of different macroeconomic channels can be performed in that framework. In Section 5.4, we compare both approaches and draw some concluding remarks from this study.

5.2 New Keynesian (Equilibrium) macrodynamics

As it was previously pointed out, the representation of the dynamics of the economy in New Keynesian DSGE models is derived from first principles (which result from neoclassical microfoundations implying a rational, forward- looking maximizing behavior by firms and households) and the condition of general equilibrium holding at every moment in time.[2]

In the following, we focus on the New Keynesian model with staggered wages and prices developed by Erceg *et al.* (2000), since it represents in our view (due to the staggered nature of the wage and price setting) the baseline situation to be considered as the natural starting point of a Keynesian version of the New Neoclassical Synthesis (as our own matured approach to be discussed in the following Section), rather than as one of its two limit cases (staggered price setting with full wage flexibility or viceversa), with which it may nevertheless be compared.

5.2.1 The New Keynesian model with staggered wages and prices

We begin directly from Galí's (2008, Ch.6) presentation of the loglinearly reduced form of the New Keynesian model with staggered wages and prices in order to discuss on this basis analytically the determinacy properties of this model type. The loglinear representation of this New Keynesian model employed in Galí (2008, Ch.6) reads:

$$\pi_t^w \overset{\text{WPC}}{=} \beta(h)\pi_{t+h}^w + h\kappa_w \tilde{y}_t - h\lambda_w \tilde{\omega}_t, \quad \pi_t^w = (w_t - w_{t-h})/h \tag{5.1}$$

$$\pi_t^p \overset{\text{PPC}}{=} \beta(h)\pi_{t+h}^p + h\kappa_p \tilde{y}_t + h\lambda_p \tilde{\omega}_t, \quad \pi_t^p = (p_t - p_{t-h})/h \tag{5.2}$$

$$\tilde{y}_t \overset{\text{IS}}{=} \tilde{y}_{t+h} - h\sigma^{-1}(i_t - \pi_{t+h}^p - r^n) \tag{5.3}$$

$$i_t \overset{\text{TR}}{=} r^n + \phi_p \pi_t^p + \phi_w \pi_t^w + \phi_y \tilde{y}_t \tag{5.4}$$

with

$$\tilde{\omega}_t \equiv \tilde{\omega}_{t-h} + h(\pi_t^w - \pi_t^p) - \Delta\omega_{t+h}^n$$

as the identity relating the changes in the real wage gap $\tilde{\omega}_t = \omega_t - \omega_t^n$ (ω_t^n being the natural real wage) to wage inflation, price inflation, and the change in the natural real wage $\Delta\omega_t^n$. Note here also that $\beta(h) := \frac{1}{1+h\rho}$ is the discount factor that

2 See also Walsh (2003) for a textbook introduction to the New Keynesian model with staggered wages and prices.

applies to the period length h, and that there holds on this basis $\frac{1-\beta(h)}{\beta(h)} = h\rho$, or; $1/\beta(h) = 1 + h\rho$, when solved for the discount rate ρ of the New Keynesian model, which will be of importance in the Section that follows.

Eq. (5.1) describes a New Keynesian Wage Phillips Curve (WPC), and eq. (5.2), analogously, describes a New Keynesian Price Phillips Curve (PPC), all parameters being positive, see Galí (2008) for their derivation. We assume as in Galí (2008, p.128) that the conditions stated there for the existence of a zero steady state solution are fulfilled, namely that a) $\Delta\omega_t^n = 0$ for all t and that b) the intercept in the nominal interest rate rule adjusts always in a one-to-one fashion to variations in the natural rate of interest. The dynamic IS equation (derived by combining the goods markets clearing condition $y_t = c_t$ with the Euler equation of the households) is given by eq. (5.3), with $\tilde{y}_t \equiv y_t - y_t^n$ as the output gap (y_t^n being the equilibrium level of output attainable in the absence of both wage and price rigidities) and r^n as the natural rate of interest. Finally, eq. (5.4) describes a generalized type of contemporaneous Taylor interest rate policy rule (TR), whereafter the nominal interest rate is assumed to be a function of the natural rate of interest, of the wage inflation, the price inflation as well as of the output gap, see Galí (2008, 6.2) for details.

Note that we have in this formulation of the model, three forward looking variables and one equation that is updating the historically given real wage. For the model to be determinate, we thus need the existence of three unstable eigenvalues (three variables that can jump to the 1D stable submanifold) and one eigenvalue that is negative (corresponding to the stable submanifold). In contrast to Galí (2008, fn.6), we use annualized rates, obtained by dividing the corresponding period differences through the period length h (usually 1/4 year in the literature). We show herewith which parameters change with the data frequency or just the iteration step-size h when the model is simulated. We thus use the conventional scaling for the rates here under consideration, but allow for changes in the data collection frequency or iteration frequency.[3] We consequently consider the equations (5.1)–(5.4) from an applied perspective, i.e. we take them as starting point for an empirically motivated study of the influence of the data frequency (quarterly, monthly or weekly) on the size of the parameter values to be estimated.

5.2.2 Determinacy analysis

In principle, period analysis and continuous-time model building should provide qualitatively the same results, which means that the model should not depend in its fundamental qualitative properties on the length of the period h, in particular when frequencies of empirical relevance are considered. In this respect, Foley (1975, p.310) proposes as a methodological precept concerning macroeconomic

---

3 For two analyzes of the consequences of such a discrepancy for the resulting dynamics of macroeconomic models see Aadland and Huang (2004) as well as Flaschel and Proaño (2009).

period models that '*No substantive prediction or explanation in a well-defined macroeconomic period model should depend on the real time length of the period.*'[4] We therefore expect that it reflects the properties of its continuous-time analogue, abbreviated by $\dot{x} = J_o x$.

In the linear case, this can be motivated further by the following type of argument: consider the mathematically equivalent discrete and continuous-time models (I denoting the identity matrix):

$$x_{t+1} = Ax_t \quad \text{and} \quad \dot{x} = (A - I)x = Jx$$

which follow the literature by assuming an unspecified time unit 1.

Our foregoing arguments suggest that we should generalize such an approach and rewrite it with a variable period length as follows:

$$x_{t+h} - x_t = hJx_t \quad \text{and} \quad \dot{x} = Jx.$$

This gives for their system matrices the relationships

$$A = hJ + I.$$

According to Foley's postulate both J and A should be stable matrices if period- as well as continuous-time analysis is used for macroeconomic analysis in such a linear framework, i.e. all eigenvalues of J should have negative real parts, while the eigenvalues of A should all be within the unit circle. Graphically, this implies the situation shown in Figure 5.1 (which shows that, if J's eigenvalues do not yet lie inside the unit circle shown, that they have to be moved into it by a proper choice of the time unit and thus the matrix hJ.)

If the eigenvalues of the matrix J of the continuous time case are such that they lie outside the solid circle shown, but, for example, within a circle of radius 2, the discrete time matrix $J + I$ would – in contrast to the continuous time case – have unstable roots (on the basis of a period length $h = 1$ that generally is left implicit in such approaches). The system $x_{t+1} = Ax_t$, $A = J + I$ then has eigenvalues outside the unit circle (which is obtained by shifting the shown solid unit circle by 1 to the right (into the dotted one). Choosing $h = 1/2$ would, however, then already be sufficient to move all eigenvalues $\lambda(A) = h\lambda(J) + 1$ of $A = hJ + I$ into this unit circle, since all eigenvalues of hJ are moved by this change in period length

---

4 Furthermore, from the view point of economic model building, Sims (1998, p.318) analyzes a variety
   of models featuring real and nominal stickiness 'formulated in continuous time to avoid the need to
   use the uninterpretable "one period" delays that plague the discrete time models in this literature.' As
   a general statement and conclusion, related to Foley's (1975) observation, we, however, would assert
   that New Keynesian period models with stable/unstable eigenvalue structures that differ from their
   continuous-time analogue should be questioned with respect to their relevance from the theoretical
   and – even more – from the empirical point of view. Period models, if meaningful, thus depend on
   their continuous-time analogues in the validity of their results.

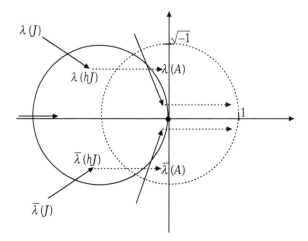

Figure 5.1 A choice of the period length that guarantees equivalence of continuous and discrete time analysis.

into the solid unit circle shown in Figure 5.1, since J's eigenvalues have all been assumed to have negative real parts and are thus moved towards the origin of the space of complex numbers when the period length h is reduced.

We also note here already (in view of the New Keynesian approach to be considered next) that matrices J with eigenvalues with only positive real parts will always give rise to totally unstable matrices $A = hJ + I$, since the real parts are augmented by '1' in such a situation. We will, however, show in the next section that the here considered simple h-dependence of the eigenvalues of the matrix A: $\lambda(A) = h\lambda(J) + 1$, – in this linear setup – does not apply to baseline New Keynesian models, since they – though linear – depend nonlinearly on their period length h and are only directly comparable to the foregoing in the special case $h = 1$. Comparisons for larger period lengths h are therefore not so easy and demand other means in order to compare determinacy in both continuous- and discrete-time.

The New Keynesian model reformulated in this way represents an implicitly formulated system of difference equations, where all variables with index $t + h$ are expected variables or should be interpreted as representing perfect foresight in the deterministic skeleton of the considered dynamics. Making use again of the TR and the PPC, see equations (5.1)–(5.4) and using the foregoing representation of $\tilde{\omega}_t$, it can be made an explicit system of difference equations as follows (with $\eta = \sigma^{-1}$):

$$\pi_{t+h}^{w} = \frac{\pi_{t}^{w} - h\kappa_w \tilde{y}_t + h\lambda_w \tilde{\omega}_t}{\beta(h)} = \pi_t^w + h\rho\pi_t^w - h\frac{\kappa_w \tilde{y}_t - \lambda_w \tilde{\omega}_{t-h} - h\lambda_w(\pi_t^w - \pi_t^p)}{\beta(h)}$$

$$(5.5)$$

$$\pi_{t+h}^p = \frac{\pi_t^p - h\kappa_p\tilde{y}_t - h\lambda_p\tilde{\omega}_t}{\beta(h)} = \pi_t^p + h\rho\pi_t^p - h\frac{\kappa_p\tilde{y}_t + \lambda_p\tilde{\omega}_{t-h} + h\lambda_p(\pi_t^w - \pi_t^p)}{\beta(h)}$$

(5.6)

$$\tilde{y}_{t+h} = \tilde{y}_t + h\eta\left[\phi_w\pi_t^w + \left(\phi_p - \frac{1}{\beta(h)}\right)\pi_t^p\right.$$

$$\left. + \phi_y\tilde{y}_t + h\frac{\kappa_p\tilde{y}_t + \lambda_p\tilde{\omega}_{t-h} + h\lambda_p(\pi_t^w - \pi_t^p)}{\beta(h)}\right]$$

(5.7)

$$\tilde{\omega}_t = \tilde{\omega}_{t-h} + h(\pi_t^w - \pi_t^p)$$

(5.8)

which we can represent in brief through the following matrix equation:

$$x_{t+h} = x_t + h(J_o + hJ_1(h))x_t = x_t + hA(h)x_t = (I + hA(h))x_t.$$

where J_o collects the terms that are linear in h and which therefore will characterize the continuous-time limit case.

The reformulation of this 4D New Keynesian model in continuous-time can also be justified on the empirical basis that while the actual data generating process (DGP) at the macrolevel, even in the real markets, is by and large of a daily one (concerning averages over the day), the corresponding data collection process (DCP) on the economy-wide goods and labor markets is (due to technological and suitability issues) often of a much lower frequency, namely on a monthly or quarterly basis. In the majority of theoretical New Keynesian models, this issue has not been addressed properly, leaving the underlying length of the 'one-period delay' unspecified or assuming that the DGP and the DCP are equivalent, with the DGP being set equal to the DCP. However, this modeling strategy leads to the highly questionable implication that all wage and price changes occur in clustered or completely synchronized fashion at the beginning and the end of each considered period (the beginning of the next one). Though in reality micro price and wage changes may be staggered with considerable period lengths in between (at the firms' level), this surely does not hold at the macrolevel, where due to the aggregation of overlapping staggered wage and price decisions the assumption of a quasi continuous-time like behavior is more realistic for the macroeconomic time series.[5]

The New Keynesian baseline model with both staggered wage and price setting, the 'Keynesian' version of the New Neoclassical Synthesis, reads thus in its loglinearly approximated form, see Erceg *et al.* (2000), Woodford

---

5 Consequently, in our view the notion that aggregate wage levels and price levels are adjusting only gradually at each moment in time (since they are macro-variables which do not perform noticeable jumps on a daily time scale, which we consider as the relevant time unit for the macro data *generating* process) should be accepted in modern models of the Keynesian variety (but also older ones).

(2003, pp.225ff.) and Galí (2008, Ch.6):[6]

$$\dot{\pi}^w = \rho\pi^w - \kappa_w\tilde{y} + \lambda_w\tilde{\omega} \tag{5.9}$$

$$\dot{\pi}^p = \rho\pi^p - \kappa_p\tilde{y} - \lambda_p\tilde{\omega} \tag{5.10}$$

$$\dot{\tilde{y}} = \eta\phi_w\pi^w + \eta(\phi_p - 1)\pi^p + \eta\phi_y\tilde{y} \tag{5.11}$$

$$\dot{\tilde{\omega}} = \pi^w - \pi^p \tag{5.12}$$

With respect to this model type, it is asserted in Galí (2008, p.128) – and illustrated numerically in his Figure 6.1 – that the New Keynesian model is – in the case $\phi_y = 0$ considered below – determinate (exhibits three unstable and one stable root) for all policy parameters ϕ_p, ϕ_w when the following form of the Taylor principle holds: $\phi_w + \phi_p > 1$. To investigate this assertion one has to consider the eigenvalues of the system matrix J_o of our system of differential equations.[7]

$$J_o = \begin{pmatrix} \rho & 0 & -\kappa_w & \lambda_w \\ 0 & \rho & -\kappa_p & -\lambda_p \\ \eta\phi_w & \eta(\phi_p - 1) & \eta\phi_y & 0 \\ 1 & -1 & 0 & 0 \end{pmatrix}$$

Let us start with the case $\rho = 0$. Let γ_j $(j = 1, 2, 3, 4)$ be the roots of the characteristic polynomial $p(\gamma) = \gamma^4 + a_1\gamma^3 + a_2\gamma^2 + a_3\gamma + a_4$ of the matrix J_o. Then, we have[8]

$$a_1 = -\gamma_1 - \gamma_2 - \gamma_3 - \gamma_4 = -\text{trace } J_o = -\phi_y\eta \leq 0$$

$$a_2 = \gamma_1\gamma_2 + \gamma_1\gamma_3 + \gamma_1\gamma_4 + \gamma_2\gamma_3 + \gamma_2\gamma_4 + \gamma_3\gamma_4$$

$$= \text{ sum of the principal second-order minors of } J_o$$

$$= -(\lambda_w + \lambda_p) + (\phi_w\kappa_w + (\phi_p - 1)\kappa_p)\eta$$

$$a_3 = -\gamma_1\gamma_2\gamma_3 - \gamma_1\gamma_2\gamma_4 - \gamma_1\gamma_3\gamma_4 - \gamma_2\gamma_3\gamma_4$$

$$= -(\text{sum of the principal third-order minors of) } J_o$$

---

6 Note that there holds $1/\beta(h) = 1 + h\rho = 1$ in the limit.

7 We show in this section that this determinacy condition is in fact sufficient and necessary for the 4D New Keynesian model for all positive values of the parameter ϕ_y in front of the output gap in the case of the continuous time version of the model (and thus also for period lengths h that are chosen sufficiently small), *provided that* $\rho = 0$ holds.

8 The following eigenvalue representation of the coefficients of a characteristic polynomial $p(\gamma)$ is a direct consequence of the fundamental theorem of algebra on the n complex roots of complex polynomials of degree n, since there holds: $p(\gamma) = \prod_{i=1}^{n}(\gamma - \gamma_i)$.

$$= \phi_y(\lambda_w + \lambda_p)\eta \geq 0$$

$$a_4 = \gamma_1\gamma_2\gamma_3\gamma_4 = \det J_o = (1 - \phi_p - \phi_w)(\kappa_w\lambda_p + \lambda_w\kappa_p)\eta$$

On the basis of these expressions for the four eigenvalues γ_i of the matrix J_o, we can easily prove the following lemma:

Lemma Assume $a_1 < 0, a_3 > 0$ for the coefficients of the characteristic polynomial of the matrix J_o. Then: all eigenvalues $\gamma = a + b\sqrt{-1}$ with $a = 0$ also satisfy $b = 0$.

Proof Assume that there is a pair of eigenvalues $\gamma_1 = b\sqrt{-1}, \gamma_2 = -b\sqrt{-1}$. We then get for the coefficients a_1, a_3 of the characteristic polynomial of the matrix J_o the expressions:

$$a_1 = -\gamma_3 - \gamma_4, \quad a_3 = -\gamma_1\gamma_2\gamma_3 - \gamma_1\gamma_2\gamma_4 = b^2(-\gamma_3 - \gamma_4)$$

which contradicts the signs we have assumed to apply to these two coefficients if $b \neq 0$ holds. □

On this basis one can derive the following proposition 2:

Proposition 1 Assume that $\rho \geq 0$ and that $\phi_y > 0$. Then: the characteristic equation $|\lambda I - J_o| = 0$ has 3 roots with positive real parts and 1 negative root if and only if the generalized Taylor principle $\phi_p + \phi_w > 1$ holds true.

Proof We consider first the case where $\phi_y = 0$ and assume for the time being in addition that $\phi_p + \phi_w = 1$ holds. In this case, we have $a_1 = a_3 = a_4 = 0$ and get from this that two roots (γ_1, γ_2) of the matrix J_o must be zero and the other two a) real and of opposite sign or b) purely imaginary. Let us now move away from this special case to a second case and consider $\phi_y > 0$ (assumed, however, to be sufficiently small). In this case, we have $a_1 < 0, a_3 > 0$, and $a_4 = 0$. There is then still one zero root (γ_1), but the other zero root must now be positive in case a.) and negative in case b), due to $a_3 = -\gamma_2\gamma_3\gamma_4 > 0$. In the latter case, we have in addition that the purely imaginary roots we started from must exhibit a positive real part now, since the trace of J_o would be negative otherwise. The end result is in both cases that there are now two eigenvalues with positive real parts (complex eigenvalues in the case b), and one which is negative.[9]

Assume now moreover that $\phi_p + \phi_w > 1$ holds (sufficiently close to 1). Since $a_4 < 0$ holds in this case we have that the remaining zero eigenvalue must have become positive. The considered case therefore implies for the matrix J_o the

---

9 In the case $a_2 = 0$ we have initially 4 zero eigenvalues, but get here from $\phi_y > 0$ and therefore from $a_1 < 0, a_3 > 0$ the sign distribution $0, -, +, +$ for the real parts of eigenvalues (where the two positive signs may be arising from real or conjugate complex eigenvalues).

existence of 3 unstable roots and 1 stable one, as was illustrated by Galí (2008, Figure 6.1), there for the case $\rho > 0$.[10]

In order to show that this result can be extended to arbitrarily large parameter variations (when $\phi_p + \phi_w > 1$ holds) and not only holds for the small variations so far considered, we simply have to note that the assumption $a_4 = \det J_o < 0$ prevents that the real parts of the eigenvalues can change sign, since they also cannot cross the imaginary axis due to what was shown in the lemma.

In the case $\det J_o > 0$, by contrast, we cannot have determinacy since this case only allows for an even number of stable as well as unstable roots. We, however, can conclude from what was shown in the foregoing that this case is always characterized by the existence of two unstable and two stable roots.   □

The employed proof strategy is summarized in Figure 5.1 by the arrows on its left-hand side and the two choices of points A_+, A_- in the (in)determinacy regions of the parameter space.

Note that the foregoing proof implies that Galí's (2008) result – shown in his Figure 6.1 – in fact holds for all positive ϕ_y if $\rho = 0$ is assumed. His case $\phi_y = 0$ is, however, not yet covered by the above Proposition 1 and its proof. For the case $\rho > 0$, $\phi_y > 0$ (numerically investigated in Galí's Figure 6.2), the reader is referred to Flaschel *et al.* (2008).

It should be noted, however, that the determinacy analysis undertaken here concerns a loglinear approximation of the true nonlinear model – where rational expectations must be of a global nature – which need not be mirrored through the rational expectations' paths generated by the loglinear approximation. It may therefore well be that the paths that are generated through computer algorithms in the loglinearized version have not much in common with the corresponding ones of the true model.

The foregoing determinacy analysis, however, opens up the question whether rational expectations models as the New Keynesian model discussed here deliver an adequate representation of the functioning of the economy, and whether such an expectation formation scheme should have such a predominant role in macroeconomics. Indeed, a theory which reduces the complexity of the interaction between economic agents to a purely mathematical exercise – where the convergence of the economy after a shock back towards a uniquely determined steady state is also uniquely determined by purely mathematical arguments – should not be considered as the most adequate representation of a real economy. Additionally, as discussed for example by Fuhrer (2004), models with such a 'mathematically rational' and forward-looking behavior need further – ad hoc – assumptions such as habit formation and consumption, investment adjustment

---

10 In order to show that this result can be extended to arbitrarily large parameter variations (when $\phi_p + \phi_w > 1$ holds) and not only holds for the small variations so far considered, we simply have to note that the assumption $a_4 = \det J_o < 0$ prevents that the real parts of the eigenvalues can change sign, since they also cannot cross the imaginary axis due to what was shown in the lemma.

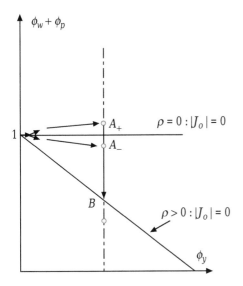

Figure 5.2 A comparison of $\rho = 0$ with the case $\rho > 0$.

costs, 'rule-of-thumb' type of behavior in the wage and price setting, etc., and therefore the incorporation of 'epicycles' in order to reconcile their theoretical predictions with empirical stylized facts.

There is thus a need for alternative baseline scenarios which can be communicated across scientific approaches, can be investigated in detail with respect to their theoretical properties in their original nonlinear format, and which – when applied to actual economies – remain controllable from the theoretical point of view as far as the basic feedback chains they contain are concerned. As stated by Fuhrer (2004):

> In a way, this takes us back to the very old models
> — With decent long-run, theory-grounded properties
> — But dynamics from a-theoretic sources.

In the following section, we provide our alternative to the New Keynesian scenario we have investigated here by means of an extension of the AD–AS model of the Old Neoclassical Synthesis that primarily improves the AS side, the nominal side, of this traditional integrated Keynesian AS–AD approach (and which allows for the impact of wage–price dynamics on the AD side of the model in addition). We call this model type (D)AS–AD where the additional 'D' stands for 'Disequilibrium'. We attempt to show that this matured Keynesian approach can compete with the New Neoclassical Synthesis with respect to an understanding of the basic feedback mechanisms that characterize the working of the macroeconomy, their stability properties and their empirical validity.

5.3 Keynesian (Disequilibrium)AS–AD Macrodynamics

In this section, we discuss a traditionally oriented alternative to the New Keynesian model of the preceding section in the spirit of Chen, Chiarella, Flaschel and Semmler (2006) which, though being based on a quite different philosophy, shares significant similarities with the 4D New Keynesian model previously discussed.[11]

In particular, it is also our view that in a properly formulated Keynesian model both nominal wage- and price levels should react in a sluggish manner to the state of economic activity. However, we do not found our theoretical formulation on utility/profit maximization under monopolistic competition and Calvo (1983) as is done with staggered wage and price setting schemes in New Keynesian models. Rather we assume instead that the gradual adjustment of wages and prices occurs as a reaction to disequilibrium situations in the goods and labor markets, as also done in previous work; see Chiarella and Flaschel (2000), Chiarella, Flaschel and Franke (2005), Chen *et al.* (2006) and Proaño, Flaschel, Ernst and Semmler (2006). We consider, as already discussed in the previous section, a quasi-continuous time modeling framework as the appropriate one for the study of economic phenomena at the aggregate level. In such a setting, the assumption of goods and labor market equilibrium *at every point in time* is difficult to defend, given the assumed sluggishness of wages and prices, so disequilibrium situations in the real markets will represent a core feature of our approach, where they, among other things, are the main determinants of wage and price inflation.

Using this alternative framework based on the gradual adjustments of wages and prices to disequilibrium situations in the goods and labor markets, we will be able to study the role of different macroeconomic transmission channels in the economy, by means of a thorough analysis of the local stability conditions of the steady state of this model, in a clearer and economics-based fashion than it is the case in the determinacy analysis of the 4D New Keynesian model we discussed in the previous section.

5.3.1 A Keynesian (D)AS–AD model

Despite our criticism concerning, among other things, the use of the rational expectations assumption in the 4D New Keynesian model of Section 5.2, our alternative framework features many common elements with this model, in particular as far as the formal structure of the Wage- and Price Phillips Curve equations are concerned. Indeed, the output gap and the wage share also enter our wage and price Phillips Curve equations, the latter variable, however, not being a result of utility/profit maximization of households and firms, respectively, but rather due to wage bargaining and price setting situations as they are for instance

---

11 In a plenary lecture at the 'Computing in Economics and Finance' conference in 2007, Volker Wieland compared as two possible approaches simple Traditional Keynesian (TK) models with New Keynesian (NK) models. In view of this lecture, the present chapter can be considered as an attempt towards the formulation of more advanced models of the TK type.

discussed in Blanchard and Katz (1999) in their microfoundation of the wage Phillips curve, see also Flaschel and Krolzig (2006) in this regard.

Concerning the modeling of inflationary expectations and the 'rationality' of the agents of our theoretical framework, we assume that the economic agents have a hybrid expectations formation scheme, see Chiarella and Flaschel (1996), based on short-run cross-over and model consistent expectations and the concept of an inflationary climate (within which the short run is embedded) which is updated adaptively. We use simultaneous dating and cross-over wage and price expectations in the formulated wage–price spiral, in place of the forward- looking self-reference that characterizes the New Keynesian approach on both the labor and the goods market, and – as stated – in addition hybrid ones that give inertia to our formulation of wage–price dynamics.

Under these modifications, with the inclusion of a conventional IS equation[12] and a standard monetary policy rule, the deterministic part of the model of the preceding section reads (with a neoclassical dating of inflationary expectations now and thus without the need to put an h in front of the terms that drive wage and price inflation):[13]

$$\pi_{t+h}^w = \tilde{\pi}_{t+h}^p + \beta_{wy} y_t - \beta_{w\omega}\theta_t, \quad \pi_{t+h}^w = (w_{t+h} - w_t)/(w_t h)$$

$$\pi_{t+h}^p = \tilde{\pi}_{t+h}^w + \beta_{py} y_t + \beta_{p\omega}\theta_t, \quad \pi_{t+h}^p = (p_{t+h} - p_t)/(p_t h)$$

$$y_{t+h} = y_t - h\alpha_{yi}(i_t - \pi_{t+h}^p - i_0)$$

$$i_t = i_0 + \beta_{ip}\pi_t^p + \beta_{iy} y_t$$

As just discussed, for the impact of price inflation on wage inflation (and v.v) we assume in addition that it is not only of a temporary nature, but subject also to some inertia, here measured by an index for the inflation climate in which the economy is currently operating. It is natural to assume that such a medium-run climate expression π^c is updated in adaptive fashion, i.e. in the simplest approach that it satisfies a law of motion of the following type

$$\pi_{t+h}^c = \pi_t^c + h\beta_{\pi^c}(\pi_t^p - \pi_t^c) \tag{5.13}$$

We define on this basis the still undefined variables $\tilde{\pi}_{t+h}^p, \tilde{\pi}_{t+h}^w$ by the expressions

$$\tilde{\pi}_{t+h}^p = \alpha_p \pi_{t+h}^p + (1 - \alpha_p)\pi_{t+h}^c, \quad \tilde{\pi}_{t+h}^w = \alpha_w \pi_{t+h}^w + (1 - \alpha_w)\pi_{t+h}^c \tag{5.14}$$

with $\alpha_p, \alpha_w \in (0, 1)$.

---

12 See e.g. Woodford (2003). For simplicity, we abstract from an explicit modeling of the labor market and assume that the employment dynamics can also be represented by the output gap dynamics, see Chen *et al.* (2006) and Proaño (2007) for alternative modeling approaches of the employment dynamics in the (D)AS–AD framework.

13 Note that we use as in the New Keynesian models the log of the output level as quantity variable and a zero target rate of inflation of the Central Bank.

In continuous time, the system can then be summarized as follows – if π^w and π^p are used to denote the forward rate of inflation of wages and prices, i.e. the right hand derivatives of $\ln w$ and $\ln p$:

$$\pi^w = \alpha_w \pi^p + (1 - \alpha_w)\pi^c + \beta_{wy}y - \beta_{w\omega}\theta \tag{5.15}$$

$$\pi^p = \alpha_p \pi^w + (1 - \alpha_p)\pi^c + \beta_{py}y + \beta_{p\omega}\theta \tag{5.16}$$

$$\dot{y} = -\alpha_{yi}\{(\beta_{ip} - 1)\pi^p + \beta_{iy}y\} \tag{5.17}$$

$$\dot{\pi}^c = \beta_{\pi^c}(\pi^p - \pi^c) \tag{5.18}$$

$$\dot{\theta} = \pi^w - \pi^p \tag{5.19}$$

where β_{wy}, $\beta_{w\omega}$, β_{py}, $\beta_{p\omega}$, β_{iy}, and α_{yi} are positive parameters and $0 < \alpha_w < 1$, $0 < \alpha_p < 1$, $0 < \beta_{\pi^c} < 1$, $\beta_{ip} > 1$.
We can rewrite equations (5.15) and (5.16) as follows:

$$\begin{pmatrix} 1 & -\alpha_w \\ -\alpha_p & 1 \end{pmatrix} \begin{pmatrix} \pi^w \\ \pi^p \end{pmatrix} = \begin{pmatrix} (1 - \alpha_w)\pi^c + \beta_{wy}y - \beta_{w\omega}\theta \\ (1 - \alpha_p)\pi^c + \beta_{py}y + \beta_{p\omega}\theta \end{pmatrix}$$

Solving this equation, we obtain the following relationships.

$$\pi^w = \frac{1}{1 - \alpha_p\alpha_w} \begin{vmatrix} (1 - \alpha_w)\pi^c + \beta_{wy}y - \beta_{w\omega}\theta & -\alpha_w \\ (1 - \alpha_p)\pi^c + \beta_{py}y + \beta_{p\omega}\theta & 1 \end{vmatrix}$$

$$= \alpha\{(\beta_{wy} + \alpha_w\beta_{py})y + (\alpha_w\beta_{p\omega} - \beta_{w\omega})\theta\} + \pi_c = \pi^w(y, \theta) + \pi^c \tag{5.20}$$

$$\pi^p = \frac{1}{1 - \alpha_p\alpha_w} \begin{vmatrix} 1 & (1 - \alpha_w)\pi^c + \beta_{wy}y - \beta_{w\omega}\theta \\ -\alpha_p & (1 - \alpha_p)\pi^c + \beta_{py}y + \beta_{p\omega}\theta \end{vmatrix}$$

$$= \alpha\{(\beta_{py} + \alpha_p\beta_{wy})y + (\beta_{p\omega} - \alpha_p\beta_{w\omega})\theta\} + \pi^c = \pi^p(y, \theta) + \pi^c \tag{5.21}$$

where $\alpha = 1/(1 - \alpha_p\alpha_w) > 1$. Substituting equations (5.20) and (5.21) into equations (5.17)–(5.19), we obtain the following three-dimensional linear dynamical system:

$$\dot{y} = -\alpha_{yi}[(\beta_{ip} - 1)(\pi^p(y, \theta) + \pi^c) + \beta_{iy}y] = F_1(y, \pi^c, \theta) \tag{5.22}$$

$$\dot{\pi}^c = \beta_{\pi^c}\pi^p(y, \theta) = F_2(y, \theta) \tag{5.23}$$

$$\dot{\theta} = \dot{\theta}(y, \theta) = \pi^w(y, \theta) - \pi^p(y, \theta) = F_3(y, \theta) \tag{5.24}$$

and it exhibits (as the one in the preceding section) the origin as the steady state.
The Jacobian matrix J of this simple 2-D dynamical system at the interior steady state is characterized by:

$$J = \begin{pmatrix} \partial\dot{y}/\partial y & \partial\dot{y}/\partial\omega \\ \partial\dot{\omega}/\partial y & \partial\dot{\omega}/\partial\omega \end{pmatrix} = \begin{pmatrix} -\pm \\ \pm & 0 \end{pmatrix}$$

Table 5.1 Four baseline real wage adjustment scenarios

	Wage-led goods market	Profit-led goods market
Labor market-led	$\begin{pmatrix} - & + \\ + & 0 \end{pmatrix}$	$\begin{pmatrix} - & - \\ + & 0 \end{pmatrix}$
real wage adjustment	– Divergent or convergent –	– Convergent –
Goods market-led	$\begin{pmatrix} - & + \\ - & 0 \end{pmatrix}$	$\begin{pmatrix} - & - \\ - & 0 \end{pmatrix}$
real wage adjustment	– Convergent –	– Divergent of convergent –

As it can be easily observed, the foregoing Jacobian matrix allows for four different scenarios which can be jointly summarized as in Table 5.1.

As illustrated there, there exist two cases where the Rose (1967) real wage channel operates in a stabilizing manner: in the first case, the goods markets (represented in our analysis by *the output gap in the Price Phillips Curve* equation) depend negatively on the real wage – a situation usually referred to as 'a profit-led goods market' – and the dynamics of the real wage are determined primarily by the nominal wage adjustments and therefore by the developments in the labor market (represented here by *the output gap in the Wage Phillips Curve* equation). In this case, labor market-led real wage increases *receive a check* through the implied negative effect on goods markets activity levels. In the second case, the goods markets depend positively on the real wage (a wage-led goods market), and the price level dynamics, and therefore the goods markets, primarily determine the behavior of the real wages.[14]

It should be clear that an identification of an economic by means of these four cases cannot be done a priori, since the concerned partial effects depend directly on the model parameters (which are additionally likely to be state- and/or time-varying), see Chen *et al.* (2006) and Proaño (2009) for an empirical analysis of the (D)AS–AD model.

Our traditional Keynesian model therefore exhibits an interesting feedback structure – the Rose (1967) real wage channel – that is rarely considered in the literature from the theoretical or the empirical point of view. Furthermore, our alternative – traditional – Keynesian dynamics also overcomes the trivial explanation of turning points in economic activity of the monetarist baseline models (with its narrow quantity theory driven inflation ceiling, see Flaschel *et al.* (2008, Ch.1)) and remains – just as these simpler models – under certain mild assumptions globally asymptotically stable in a setup which integrates real interest rate effects and a nominal interest rate policy rule with the real wage feedback channel of our Keynesian approach to the wage–price spiral, allowing

---

14 Note here that also the cost-pressure parameters play a role here and may influence the critical stability condition that characterizes the real wage channel, see Flaschel and Krolzig (2006) for details.

us moreover to address modern issues of monetary policy, as they are typical for the New Keynesian approaches, as well as other types of issues which are more related with the distributive cycle, see Proaño, Diallo, Flaschel and Teuber (2009).

5.3.2 Local stability analysis

In the following, we discuss – in contrast to the determinacy analysis of the New Keynesian model discuss in the previous section – the local stability conditions of the steady state of the Disequilibrium AS–AD model of this section. As it will be shown, the local stability analysis of this second system relies on much more economic grounds than the determinacy analysis required by rational expectations models, and delivers therefore a much deeper economic insight on the workings of the economy.

The equilibrium solution of this system such that $\dot{y} = \dot{\pi}^c = \dot{\theta} = 0$ is determined by

$$\tilde{J}\begin{pmatrix} y \\ \pi^c \\ \theta \end{pmatrix} = \begin{pmatrix} 0 \\ 0 \\ 0 \end{pmatrix} \tag{5.25}$$

where

$$\tilde{J} = \begin{pmatrix} -\alpha_{yi}G_{11} & -\alpha_{yi}G_{12} & -\alpha_{yi}G_{13} \\ \beta_{\pi^c}\alpha G_{21} & 0 & \beta_{\pi^c}\alpha G_{23} \\ \alpha G_{31} & 0 & \alpha G_{33} \end{pmatrix} \tag{5.26}$$

is the Jacobian matrix of this system such that

$$G_{11} = (\beta_{ip} - 1)\alpha(\beta_{py} + \alpha_p\beta_{wy}) + \beta_{iy} > 0,$$

$$G_{12} = \beta_{ip} - 1 > 0,$$

$$G_{13} = (\beta_{ip} - 1)\alpha(\beta_{p\omega} - \alpha_p\beta_{w\omega}),$$

$$G_{21} = (\beta_{py} + \alpha_p\beta_{wy}) > 0,$$

$$G_{23} = \beta_{p\omega} - \alpha_p\beta_{w\omega}, \quad G_{31} = (1 - \alpha_p)\beta_{wy} - (1 - \alpha_w)\beta_{py},$$

$$G_{33} = -\{(1 - \alpha_p)\beta_{w\omega} + (1 - \alpha_w)\beta_{p\omega}\} < 0.$$

Since

$$\det\tilde{J} = -\alpha^2\alpha_{yi}\beta_{\pi^c}\begin{vmatrix} G_{11} & G_{12} & G_{13} \\ G_{21} & 0 & G_{23} \\ G_{31} & 0 & G_{33} \end{vmatrix} = \alpha^2\alpha_{yi}\beta_{\pi^c}\underset{(+)\;(+)\;(-)}{G_{12}}(\underset{(?)\;\;(?)}{G_{21}G_{33} - G_{23}G_{31}})$$

$$= -\alpha^2\alpha_{yi}\beta_{\pi^c}\underset{(+)}{G_{12}}\{(1 - \alpha_p)(\beta_{py}\beta_{w\omega} + \beta_{p\omega}\beta_{wy}) + (1 - \alpha_w)\alpha_p(\beta_{wy}\beta_{p\omega}$$

$$+ \beta_{w\omega}\beta_{py})\} < 0, \tag{5.27}$$

we have the unique equilibrium solution $y* = \theta* = \pi^c* = \pi^w* = \pi^p* = 0$.

The characteristic equation of this system becomes as follows.

$$|\lambda I - \tilde{J}| = \lambda^3 + b_1\lambda^2 + b_2\lambda + b_3 = 0 \tag{5.28}$$

Let $\lambda_j (j = 1, 2, 3)$ be the characteristic roots of eq. (5.28). Then, the Routh-Hurwitz conditions for local stability of the steady state (see Hirsch and Smale 1974), are

$$b_1 = -\lambda_1 - \lambda_2 - \lambda_3 = -\text{trace } \tilde{J} = \underset{(+)}{\alpha_{yi} G_{11}} - \underset{(-)}{\alpha G_{33}} > 0 \tag{5.29}$$

$b_2 = \lambda_1\lambda_2 + \lambda_1\lambda_3 + \lambda_2\lambda_3 = $ sum of all principal second-order minors of $\tilde{J}$

$$= \alpha \begin{vmatrix} 0 & \beta_{\pi^c} G_{23} \\ 0 & G_{33} \end{vmatrix} - \alpha\alpha_{yi} \begin{vmatrix} G_{11} & G_{13} \\ G_{31} & G_{33} \end{vmatrix} - \alpha\alpha_{yi}\beta_{\pi^c} \begin{vmatrix} G_{11} & G_{12} \\ G_{31} & 0 \end{vmatrix} = C + D\beta_{\pi^c}; \tag{5.30}$$

$$b_3 = -\lambda_1\lambda_2\lambda_3 = -\det \tilde{J} > 0 \tag{5.31}$$

with

$$C = \alpha\alpha_{yi}(-G_{11}G_{33} + G_{13}G_{31}) = \alpha^2\alpha_{yi}(\beta_{ip} - 1)[(1 - \alpha_p)\{(\beta_{py} + \beta_{iy})\beta_{w\omega}$$
$$+ \beta_{p\omega}\beta_{wy}\} + (1 - \alpha_w)\{\alpha_p(\beta_{wy}\beta_{p\omega} + \beta_{w\omega}\beta_{py}) + \beta_{iy}\beta_{p\omega}\}] > 0,$$
$$D = \alpha\alpha_{yi}G_{12}G_{31} = \alpha\alpha_{yi}(\beta_{ip} - 1)\{(1 - \alpha_p)\beta_{wy} - (1 - \alpha_w)\beta_{py}\}$$

Finally, for the last Routh-Hurwitz condition we have

$$b_1b_2 - b_3 = -(\lambda_1 + \lambda_2)(\lambda_1 + \lambda_3)(\lambda_2 + \lambda_3) = E - H\beta_{\pi^c} \tag{5.32}$$

with

$$E = b_1 C = \alpha^2\alpha_{yi}(\beta_{ip} - 1)[\alpha_{yi}\{(\beta_{ip} - 1)\alpha(\beta_{py} + \alpha_p\beta_{wy}) + \beta_{iy}\}$$
$$+ \alpha\{(1 - \alpha_p)\beta_{w\omega} + (1 - \alpha_w)\beta_{p\omega}\}][(1 - \alpha_p)\{(\beta_{py} + \beta_{iy})\beta_{w\omega} + \beta_{p\omega}\beta_{wy}\}$$
$$+ (1 - \alpha_w)\{\alpha_p(\beta_{wy}\beta_{p\omega} + \beta_{w\omega}\beta_{py}) + \beta_{iy}\beta_{p\omega}] > 0,$$
$$H = b_3 - b_1 D = \alpha^2\alpha_{yi}(\beta_{ip} - 1)[(1 - \alpha_p)(\beta_{py}\beta_{w\omega} + \beta_{p\omega}\beta_{wy})$$
$$+ \alpha_p(1 - \alpha_w)(\beta_{wy}\beta_{p\omega} + \beta_{w\omega}\beta_{py}) + [\alpha_{yi}\{(\beta_{ip} - 1)(\beta_{py} + \alpha_p\beta_{wy}) + \beta_{iy}\}$$
$$+ \{(1 - \alpha_p)\beta_{w\omega} + (1 - \alpha_w)\beta_{p\omega}\}][(1 - \alpha_w)\beta_{py} - (1 - \alpha_p)\beta_{wy}]]$$

For the Jacobian J of these dynamics we get – under the assumptions of an active monetary policy rule ($\beta_{ip} > 1$) and $\partial\dot{\theta}_y/\partial y > 0$ (which implies a procyclicity of real wages with respect to economic activity) –:

$$J = \begin{pmatrix} - & - & ? \\ + & 0 & ? \\ + & 0 & - \end{pmatrix} \tag{5.33}$$

It can be shown that the steady state of this alternative dynamical system is locally stable if the following proposition holds:[15]

Proposition 2 The interior steady state of the dynamical system (5.22)–(5.24) is locally asymptotically stable if the growth rate of real wages depends positively on economic activity, if monetary policy is active with respect to the inflation gap (which overcomes the destabilizing Mundell effect in this model type) and if the state of the business cycle operates on the interest rate setting policy of the Central Bank with sufficient strength.

Sketch of Proof Exploiting the linear dependencies within the considered dynamics and its Jacobian, one can show for the characteristic polynomial of the matrix J:

$$\lambda^3 + b_1\lambda^2 + b_2\lambda + b_3, \quad \text{the conditions} \quad b_1, b_3 > 0.$$

Furthermore, the parameter β_{iy} only appears in the entry J_{11} of the matrix J. Making it sufficiently large (assuming thus an active monetary policy) therefore will obviously ensure that b_2 and $b_1 b_2 - b_3 > 0$ hold true in addition. This stability result even holds for all choices of the parameter β_{iy}, i.e. we have – in the case of a law of motion of real wages that is labor market led – always global stability of the considered dynamics if the interest rate is reacting to the inflation gap with a strength that is larger than one. □

But what if the growth rate of real wages depends negatively on economic activity and where the dynamics of real wages is therefore goods market led? In order to investigate this case, assume to begin $H > 0$. A sufficient (but not necessary) condition for $H > 0$ to be satisfied is $(1 - \alpha_w)\beta_{py} \geq (1 - \alpha_p)\beta_{wy}$, which describes the case of a goods market led real wage dynamics (the opposite case of the first condition of Proposition 3). Let us now define the value $\beta_{\pi^c}^0$ as $\beta_{\pi^c}^0 = E/H > 0$. Then, under $H > 0$, we have the following proposition

Proposition 3
(1) Suppose that $\beta_{\pi^c}^0 < 1$. Then, the characteristic equation (5.28) has

(i) Three roots with negative real parts for all $\beta_{\pi^c} \in (0, \beta_{\pi^c}^0)$
(ii) A set of pure imaginary roots and a negative real root at $\beta_{\pi^c} = \beta_{\pi^c}^0$
(iii) Two roots with positive real parts and a negative real root for all $\beta_{\pi^c} \in (\beta_{\pi^c}^0, 1)$

(2) Suppose that $\beta_{\pi^c}^0 \geq 1$. Then, the characteristic equation (5.28) has three roots with negative real parts for all $\beta_{\pi^c} \in (0, 1)$

15 The proofs of the Proposition 3 can be obtained on request from the authors.

Proof

(1)   (i)   Suppose that the parameter β_{π^c} is fixed at $\beta_{\pi^c} \in (0, \beta_{\pi^c}^0)$. Then, we have a set of inequalities $b_1 > 0$, $b_3 > 0$, and $b_1 b_2 - b_3 > 0$, which means that all of the Routh-Hurwitz conditions for stable roots are satisfied (cf. Gandolfo 1996, p.221 and Asada, Chiarella, Flaschel and Franke 2003, p.519).

   (ii)   Suppose that β_{π^c} is fixed at $\beta_{\pi^c} = \beta_{\pi^c}^0$. Then, we have $b_1 b_2 - b_3 = 0$ and $b_2 = b_3/b_1 > 0$. In this case, three roots of eq. (5.28) become $\lambda_1 = i\sqrt{b_2}$, $\lambda_2 = -i\sqrt{b_2}$, and $\lambda_3 = -b_1 < 0$, where $i = \sqrt{-1}$ (cf. Asada 1995, p.248 and Asada, Chiarella, Flaschel and Franke 2003, p.522).

   (iii)   Suppose that β_{π^c} is fixed at $\beta_{\pi^c} \in (\beta_{\pi^c}^0, 1)$. Then, we have a set of inequalities $b_1 > 0$, $b_3 > 0$, and $b_1 b_2 - b_3 < 0$. These inequalities imply that $\lambda_1 + \lambda_2 + \lambda_3 < 0$, $\lambda_1 \lambda_2 \lambda_3 < 0$, and $(\lambda_1 + \lambda_2)(\lambda_1 + \lambda_3)(\lambda_2 + \lambda_3) > 0$ (cf. equations (5.29), (5.31), and (5.33)). This proves the assertion (iii).

(2)   In case of $\beta_{\pi^c}^0 > 1$, all of the Routh-Hurwitz conditions for stable roots ($b_1 > 0$, $b_3 > 0$, and $b_1 b_2 - b_3 > 0$) are satisfied for all $\beta_{\pi^c} \in (0, 1)$.   □

Remark   The point $\beta_{\pi^c} = \beta_{\pi^c}^0$ is a degenerated 'Hopf Bifurcation point' in a system of linear differential equations (S_2).

Corollary of Proposition 3

1   Suppose that $\beta_{\pi^c}^0 < 1$. Then, we have the following properties.

   (i)   The equilibrium point of the system (S_2) is asymptotically stable for all $\beta_{\pi^c} \in (0, \beta_{\pi^c}^0)$, and it is unstable for all $\beta_{\pi^c} \in (\beta_{\pi^c}^0, 1)$.

   (ii)   Even if the equilibrium point of the system (S_2) is unstable, it does not become totally unstable, but it becomes a saddle point.

   (iii)   Cyclical fluctuations occur in the system (S_2) at some range of the parameter value β_{π^c} which is sufficiently close to $\beta_{\pi^c}^0$. In particular, a family of closed orbits exists at $\beta_{\pi^c} = \beta_{\pi^c}^0$.

2   Suppose that $\beta_{\pi^c}^0 > 1$. Then, the equilibrium point of the system (S_2) is asymptotically stable for all $\beta_{\pi^c} \in (0, 1)$.

Proof   These results directly follow from Proposition 3. For instance, let us consider the following numerical example.

$$\beta_{wy} = \beta_{v\omega} = \beta_{py} = \beta_{p\omega} = \beta_{iy} = \alpha_{yi} = 1, \quad \alpha_w = \alpha_p = 0.5. \tag{5.34}$$

Then, we have $\beta_{\pi^c}^0 \cong 2.2 + 5(\beta_{ip} - 1) > 1$ for all $\beta_{ip} > 1$.

In this case, the equilibrium point of the system (S_2) is asymptotically stable for all $\beta_{\pi^c} \in (0, 1)$. $\qquad\qquad\qquad\qquad\qquad\qquad\qquad\qquad\qquad\square$

It should be clear that in this conceivable, but limited situation of $\beta_{\pi^c} > \beta_{\pi^c}^0$ values strong monetary policy reactions with respect to the parameter β_{iy} or meaningful behavioral nonlinearities off the steady state may be needed in addition in order to make the dynamics bounded or viable if it departs by too much from the steady state, see for example Chen *et al.* (2006).[16]

The foregiong stability investigations imply that we will always get asymptotic stability if $(1 - \alpha_p)\beta_{wy} - (1 - \alpha_w)\beta_{py} > 0$ holds true, i.e. in the case of a labor market led real wage dynamics, since we then have $D > 0, H < 0$. The labor market led case thus is completely unambiguous as far as stability results are concerned.

5.4 Concluding remarks

In this chapter, we compared two alternative theoretical approaches to macroeconomics, focusing on their determinacy/stability conditions and the implications of such analysis for the understanding of the functioning of an economic system.

The approach to determinacy analysis of the 4D New Keynesian model pursued in Section 5.2 made use of the notion that the intrinsic dynamics and determinacy properties of a dynamic model should be invariant to the assumed frequency of the decision making of the economic agents in the discrete time version of the model, and therefore, should not depend on whether such a model is formulated in continuous- or discrete time.[17] On this basis, the approach pursued there made determinacy analysis of New Keynesian models with staggered wages and prices as studied for example in Woodford (2003) much more tractable, because it allowed us to circumvent the calculation of the significantly more complicated conditions which hold for the corresponding discrete time case, see for example the mathematical appendices in Woodford (2003) for the difficulties that exist already in the 3D case.

However, in view of this New Keynesian approach to macroeconomic model building, we intended to highlight the fact that the solution method implied by the rational expectations assumption in this type of model lacks economic insight to a significant extent. As we showed, the analysis of the determinacy conditions even of simple rational expectations models such as the 4D New Keynesian model discussed here, resembles much more a mathematical exercise than an economic analysis.

Furthermore, there are additional issues related to the appropriateness of the New Keynesian approach as the workhorse framework in macroeconomics. On the

---

16 The reader is referred to this and other earlier works for more details on such dynamical systems and further empirical investigations of this model prototype.

17 For counterfactual examples where the determinacy properties of the rational expectations equilibrium in an economy do depend on the decision frequency assumed, see Hintermaier (2005).

one hand there is the validity of its use of the word Keynesian as a label; there is in fact no IS-curve, representing Keynesian demand rationing on the market for goods, as the model is formulated, but simply a Walrasian type of notional goods demand and on this basis the assumption of goods market equilibrium. On the other hand, the theory of rational expectations has also very little to do with Keynes' (1936) views on the difficulties of expectations formation, in particular for the evaluation of long-term investment projects. Finally, Keynes' liquidity preference theory is no longer a subject to which attention is paid here, due to the disappearance (irrelevance) of the LM schedule, which is at best present in the background of a simple to handle Taylor interest rate policy rule.

However, liquidity preference matters as the recent crises in financial markets show. Therefore, when compared with Keynes' (1936, Ch. 22) 'Notes on the Trade Cycle' and its important constituent parts – the marginal propensity to consume out of rationed income, the marginal efficiency of investment (and the expected cash flow that is underlying it) and the parameters that shape liquidity preference – , not much of this is left in the New Keynesian approach to macrodynamics, in particular concerning the systematic forces within the business cycle and its turning points as they are discussed in Keynes' (1936, Ch.22). Moreover, as previously discussed, in the New Keynesian framework further important feedback channels such as the real wage channel – investigated in Chiarella and Flaschel (2000) and later work – is almost nonexistent, since there determinacy is achieved by the specification of a Taylor rule with parameters values which imply a certain combination of unstable/stable roots for the Jacobian matrix of the dynamics.

Furthermore, while the *microfoundation* of economic behavior is per se an important desideratum to be reflected also by behaviorally oriented macrodynamics, the use of 'representative' consumers and firms for the explanation of macroeconomic phenomena is too simplistic and also too narrow to allow a proper treatment of what is *really* interesting on the behavior of economic agents – the interaction of heterogenous agents –, and it is also not detailed enough to discuss the various feedback channels present in the real world. *Market Clearing*, the next ingredient of such approaches, may, however, be a questionable device for studying the macroeconomy in particular on its real side. The data generating process is too fast in order to allow for period models with a *uniform* period length of a quarter or more. In continuous time, however, it is much too heroic to assume market clearing at all moments in time, but real markets are then only adjusting towards moving equilibria in such an framework.

Yet, neither microfoundations per se nor market clearing assumptions are the true dividing line between the approaches we are advocating and the ones considered in this section. It is the ad hoc, that is not behaviorally microfounded assumption of *Rational Expectations* that by the chosen analytical method makes the world in general loglinear (by construction) and the generated dynamics convergent (by assumption) to its unique steady state which is the root of the discontent that this chapter tries to make explicit. Indeed, agents are heterogeneous, form heterogeneous expectations along other lines than suggested by the rational expectations theory, and have differentiated short- and long-term views about the economy.

We conclude that the New Keynesian approach to macrodynamics creates more theoretical and empirical problems than it helps to solve, therefore not (yet) representing a theoretically and empirically convincing strategy for the study of the fluctuating growth that we observe in capitalist economies. The alternative theoretical framework discussed in Section 5.3, in contrast, features a number of advantages which, in our opinion, facilitate to a significant extent the analysis and understanding of the role of the different macroeconomic channels working in an economy, such as the disequilibrium specification of the dynamics of the economy[18] and the alternative (and maybe more realistic, but on all accounts more tractable) specification of expectations formation, that allows already in its deterministic setup for a meaningful theory of the business cycle with monotonic convergence or damped fluctuations in economic activity towards its steady state.

References

Aadland, D. and K. Huang (2004): Consistent high-frequency calibration. *Journal of Economic Dynamics and Control*, 28, 2277–2295.

Asada, T. (1995): Kaldorian dynamics in an open economy. *Journal of Economics*, 62, 239–269.

Asada, T., C. Chiarella, P. Flaschel, and R. Franke (2003): *Open Economy Macrodynamics: An Integrated Disequilibrium Approach*. Berlin: Springer.

Blanchard, O.J., and C.M. Kahn (1980): The solution of linear difference models under rational expectations. *Econometrica*, 48, 1305–1312.

Blanchard, O.J. and L. Katz (1999): Wage dynamics: Reconciling theory and evidence. *American Economic Review*, 89, 69–74.

Calvo, G. (1983): Staggered prices in a utility maximizing framework. *Journal of Monetary Economics*, 12, 383–398.

Chen, P., C. Chiarella, P. Flaschel, and W. Semmler (2006): Keynesian macrodynamics and the Phillips curve:. An estimated baseline macro-model for the U.S. economy. In: C. Chiarella, P. Flaschel, R. Franke and W. Semmler (eds.): *Quantitative and Empirical Analysis of Nonlinear Dynamic Macromodels*. Amsterdam: Elsevier.

Chiarella, C. and P. Flaschel (1996): Real and monetary cycles in models of Keynes-Wicksell type. *Journal of Economic Behavior and Organization*, 30, 327–351.

Chiarella, C. and P. Flaschel (2000): *The Dynamics of Keynesian Monetary Growth: Macro Foundations*. Cambridge, UK: Cambridge University Press.

Chiarella, C., P. Flaschel, and R. Franke (2005): *Foundations for a Disequilibrium Theory of the Business Cycle: Qualitative Analysis and Quantitative Assessment*. Cambridge, UK: Cambridge University Press.

Christiano, L.J., Eichenbaum, M. and C.L. Evans (2005): Nominal rigidities and the dynamic effects of a shock to monetary policy. *Journal of Political Economy*, 113, 1–45.

---

18 The proper approach to follow given that fluctuations of macroeconomic aggregates occur on a daily basis and not on a quarterly basis as implicitly assumed in many macroeconomic models.

Erceg, C., D.W. Henderson, and A.T. Levin (2000): Optimal monetary policy with staggered wage and price contracts. *Journal of Monetary Economics*, 46, 281–313.

Estrella, A. and J. Fuhrer (2002): Dynamical Inconsistencies: Counterfactual implications of a class of rational expectations models. *American Economic Review*, 92, 1013–1028.

Flaschel, P. and H.-M. Krolzig (2006): Wage and price Phillips curves: An empirical analysis of destabilizing wage–price spirals. In: C. Chiarella, P. Flaschel, R. Franke and W. Semmler (eds.): *Quantitative and Empirical Analysis of Nonlinear Dynamic Macromodels*. Amsterdam: Elsevier.

Flaschel, P. and C.R. Proaño (2009): The J2 status of "Chaos" in macroeconomic period models. *Studies in Nonlinear Dynamics and Econometrics*, 13(2), Article 2.

Flaschel, P., G. Groh, C.R. Proaño, and W. Semmler (2008): *Topics in Applied Macroeconomic Theory*. Heidelberg: Springer Publishing House.

Flaschel, P., R. Franke, and C.R. Proaño (2008): On equilibrium determinacy in new Keynesian models with staggered wages and prices. *The B.E. Journal of Macroeconomics*, 8(1), Art.31 (Topics).

Foley, D. (1975): On two specifications of asset equilibrium in macro-economic model. *Journal of Political Economy*, 83, 303–324.

Fuhrer, J. (2004): Comments on "Empirical and policy performance of a forward-looking monetary model" by A. Onatstu and N. Williams; presented at the FRB San Francisco conference on "Interest rates and monetary policy", March 19–20, 2004. http://www.frbsf.org/economics/conferences/0403/jeff_fuhrer.pdf

Galí, J. (2008): *Monetary Policy and the Business Cycle: A New Keynesian Approach*. Princeton: Princeton University Press.

Galí, J. and M. Gertler (1999): Inflation dynamics: A structural econometric analysis. *Journal of Monetary Economics*, 44, 195–222.

Galí, G. and J. López-Salido (2005): Robustness of the estimates of the hybrid New Keynesian Phillips curve. *Journal of Monetary Economics,* 52, 1107–1118.

Gandolfo, G. (1996): *Economic Dynamics*. Berlin: Springer.

Goodwin, R.M. (1967): A growth cycle. In: C.H. Feinstein (ed.): *Socialism, Capitalism and Economic Growth*. Cambridge, UK: Cambridge University Press, 54–58.

Hintermeier, T. (2005): A sunspot paradox. *Economic Letters*, 87, 285–290.

Hirsch, M.W. and S. Smale (1974): *Differential Equations, Dynamical Systems, and Linear Algebra*. New York: Academic Press.

Keynes, J.M. (1936): *The General Theory of Employment, Interest and Money*. New York: Macmillan.

Lucas, R. (1976): Econometric policy evaluation: A critique. *Carnegie-Rochester Conference Series on Public Policy*, 1, 19–46.

Mankiw, G. (2001): The inexorable and mysterious tradeoff between inflation and unemployment, *Economic Journal*, 111, 45–61.

Muth, J.F. (1961). Rational expectations and the theory of price movements, *Econometrica*, 29, 315–335.

Proaño, C.R. (2007): Gradual Wage–Price Adjustments, Labor Market Frictions and Monetary Policy Rules, Macroeconomic Policy Institute (IMK) Working Paper 09/2007.

Proaño, C.R. (2009): Gradual wage–price adjustments and Keynesian macrodynamics: Theoretical formulation and cross-country evidence, Chapter 7. In: Asada, T., C. Chiarella, P. Flaschel, and R. Franke (eds): *Lectures on Monetary Macrodynamics*, London: Routledge.

Proaño, C.R., Flaschel, P, Diallo, M. and Teuber, T. (2009): *Macroeconomic Activity, Real Wage Dynamics and Monetary Policy: Some Empirical and Theoretical Considerations.* Unpublished manuscript.

Proaño, C.R., Flaschel, P., Ernst, E. and W. Semmler (2006): *Disequilibrium macroeconomic dynamics, income distribution and wage-price Phillips curves.* Evidence from the U.S. and the Euro area. Düsseldorf: IMK Working Paper No. 4.

Rose, H. (1967): On the non-linear theory of employment. *Review of Economic Studies*, 34, 153–173.

Rudd, J. and K. Whelan (2005): New tests of the new-Keynesian Phillips curve. *Journal of Monetary Economics*, 52, 1167–1181.

Sims, C. (1998): Stickiness. *Carnegie-Rochester Conference Series on Public Policy*, 49, 317–356.

Sims, C. (2001): Solving linear rational expectations models. *Journal of Computational Economics*, 20(1–2), 1–20.

Smets, F. and R. Wouters (2003): An estimated dynamic stochastic general equilibrium model for the euro area, *Journal of the European Economic Association*, 1(5), 1123–1175.

Solow, R. (2004): Introduction: The Tobin approach to monetary economics. *Journal of Money,*

Credit and Banking, 36, 657–663.

Walsh, C. (2003): *Monetary Theory and Policy.* 2nd Edition. Cambridge: MIT Press.

Woodford, M. (2003): *Interest and Prices: Foundations of a Theory of Monetary Policy.* Princeton: Princeton University Press.

6 Beyond neoclassical syntheses

A baseline DAS–AD model

6.1 Neoclassical syntheses

In this chapter,[1] we reformulate and extend the traditional AS–AD (Aggregate Supply–Aggregate Demand) growth dynamics of the Neoclassical Synthesis, stage I with its traditional microfoundations, as it is for example treated in detail in Sargent (1987, Ch.5). Our extension in the first instance does not replace the LM (Liquidity preference–Money supply) curve with a now standard Taylor rule, as is done in the New Keynesian approaches (however, the Taylor rule is treated in Section 6.5). The model exhibits sticky wages as well as sticky prices, underutilized labor as well as capital, myopic perfect foresight of current wage and price inflation rates and adaptively formed medium-run expectations concerning the investment and inflation climate in which the economy is operating. The resulting nonlinear 5D dynamics of labor and goods market disequilibrium (at first – in comparison with the old Neoclassical Synthesis – with a conventional LM treatment of the financial part of the economy) avoids the striking anomalies of the conventional model of the Neoclassical Synthesis, stage I. Instead, it exhibits Keynesian feedback dynamics proper with, in particular, asymptotic stability of its unique interior steady state solution for low adjustment speeds of wages, prices and expectations. The loss of stability occurs cyclically, by way of Hopf bifurcations, when these adjustment speeds are made sufficiently large, leading eventually to purely explosive dynamics.

Locally, we thus obtain and prove in detail (in the case of an interest rate policy rule in the place of the LM curve) – for a certain range of parameter values – the existence of damped or persistent fluctuations in the rates of capacity utilization of both labor and capital, and of wage and price inflation rates accompanied by interest rate fluctuations that (due to the conventional working of the Keynes-effect or later also in the case of an interest rate policy rule) move in line with the goods price level (or the inflation gap). Our modification and extension of traditional AS–AD growth dynamics, as investigated from the orthodox point of

---

1 This chapter provides foundations for a disequilibrium approach to AS–AD model building. This DAS–AD approach was introduced in Chiarella, Flaschel, Groh and Semmler (2003) and significantly extended in particular in Asada, Chen, Chiarella and Flaschel (2006), on which this chapter is based.

view in detail in Sargent (1987), see also Chiarella, Flaschel and Franke (2005, Ch.2), thus provides us with a Keynesian theory of the business cycle.[2] This is so even in the case of myopic perfect foresight, where the structure of the traditional approach dichotomizes into independent supply-side real dynamics – that cannot be influenced by monetary policy at all – and subsequently determined inflation dynamics that are purely explosive if the price level is taken as a predetermined variable. These dynamics are turned into a convergent process by an application of the jump variable technique of the Rational Expectations (RE) school (with unmotivated jumps in the money wage level, however). In our new type of Keynesian labor and goods market dynamics, we can, by contrast, treat myopic perfect foresight of both firms and wage earners without any need for the methodology of the rational expectations approach to unstable saddlepoint dynamics.

If the model loses asymptotic stability for higher adjustment speeds, it does so in a cyclical fashion, by way of so-called Hopf-bifurcations, which may give rise to persistent fluctuations around the steady state. However, this loss of stability (generated if some of the speed of adjustment parameters become sufficiently large) is only of a local nature (with respect to parameter changes), since eventually, purely explosive behavior is the generally observed outcome, as is verified by means of numerical simulations. The model developed thus far cannot therefore be considered as being complete in such circumstances, since some additional mechanism is required to bound the fluctuations to economically viable regions. Downward money wage rigidity is the mechanism we use for this purpose. Extended in this way, we therefore obtain and study a baseline model of the D(isequilibrium)AS–AD variety with a rich set of stability implications and a variety of patterns of the fluctuations that it can generate.

The dynamic outcomes of this baseline DAS–AD model can be usefully contrasted with those of the currently fashionable baseline or extended New Keynesian alternative (the Neoclassical Synthesis, Stage II) that in our view is more limited in scope, at least as far as interacting Keynesian feedback mechanisms and thereby implied dynamic possibilities are concerned. This comparison reveals in particular that one does not always end up with the typical (and in our view strange) dynamics of rational expectation models, due to certain types of forward looking behavior, if myopic perfect foresight is of cross-over type in the considered wage–price spiral, is based on neoclassical dating of expectations, and is coupled with plausible backward looking behavior for the medium-run evolution of the economy. Furthermore, our dual Phillips curves approach to the wage–price spiral indeed also performs quite well from the empirical point of view,[3] and

---

2 Yet one, as must be stressed with respect to the results obtained in this chapter, with generally a long phase length for the implied cycles, due to the central role that is played by income distribution in the generation of the cycle and due to the lack of any fluctuations in the marginal propensity to consume, in investment efficiency and in the parameters characterizing the state of liquidity preference.

3 See Flaschel and Krolzig (2006), Flaschel, Kauermann and Semmler (2007) and Chen and Flaschel (2006).

in particular, does not give rise to the situation observed for the New Keynesian Phillips curve(s), found in the literature to be completely at odds with the facts.[4] In our approach, standard Keynesian feedback mechanisms are coupled with a wage–price spiral having a considerable degree of inertia, with the result that these feedback mechanisms work by and large (as is known from partial analysis) in their interaction with the added wage and price level dynamics.

In Section 6.2, we briefly reconsider the fully integrated Keynesian AS–AD model of the Neoclassical Synthesis, Stage I, and briefly indicate again that it gives rise to an inconsistent real / nominal dichotomy under myopic perfect foresight – with appended explosive nominal dynamics, subsequently tamed by means of the jump variable technique. Money wage levels must then, however, be allowed to jump just as the price level, despite the presence of a conventional money wage Phillips curve, in order to overcome the observed nominal instability by means of the assumption of rational expectations (which indeed makes this solution procedure an inconsistent one in the chosen framework). We conclude that this model type – though still heavily used at the intermediate textbook level, see Blanchard (2006) – is not suitable for a Keynesian approach to economic dynamics which (at least as a limit case of fast adaptive expectations) should allow for myopic perfect foresight on inflation rates without much change in its implications under normal circumstances.[5]

Section 6.3 then proposes our new and nevertheless traditional (matured) approach to Keynesian dynamics, by taking note of the empirical facts that both labor and capital can be under- or overutilized, that both wages and prices adjust only gradually to such disequilibria and that there are certain climate expressions surrounding the current state of the economy which add sufficient inertia to the dynamics. This organic structural reformulation of the model of the old Neoclassical Synthesis completely avoids its anomalies without representing a break with respect to the Keynesian part of the model, though the AS-curve in the narrow sense (of the old Neoclassical Synthesis) is still present in the steady state of the model, but only of secondary importance in the adjustment processes surrounding this steady state.

The resulting 5D dynamical model is briefly analyzed with respect to its stability features in Section 6.4 and shown to give rise to local asymptotic stability when certain Keynesian feedback chains – to some extent well known to be destabilizing from a partial perspective – are made sufficiently weak, including a real wage adjustment mechanism that is not so well established in the literature. The informal stability analysis presented there is made rigorous (for the case of an interest rate policy rule) in an appendix, where the calculation of the Routh-Hurwitz conditions for the relevant Jacobians is considered in great detail and where the occurrence

---

4 In this connection, see for example Mankiw (2001) and with much more emphasis Eller and Gordon (2003), whereas Galí, Gertler and Lopez-Salido (2003) argue in favor of a hybrid form of the Phillips Curve in order to defend the New Phillips curve.

5 See Chiarella, Flaschel and Franke (2005, Ch.2) for the case of adaptive expectations formation.

of Hopf bifurcations (i.e. cyclical loss of stability) is also shown. Preparing the grounds for this appendix, Section 6.5 replaces the LM curve view of financial markets in conventional AS–AD by a classic Taylor interest rate policy rule and also extends the wage and price Phillips curves of our baseline model such that they can be compared in a nearly one to one fashion with the New Keynesian approach towards staggered price as well as wage setting.

Section 6.6 then provides some numerical explorations of the model, which in particular illustrate the role of wage and price flexibility with respect to their corresponding measures of demand pressure. This analysis does not always support the economic arguments based on the partial feedback structures considered in Sections 6.3 and 6.4. In particular, although aggregate demand always depends negatively on the real wage, under certain conditions, increasing wage flexibility may not lead to more stability. In such situations, downward money wage rigidity can indeed assist in stabilizing the economy and this in a way that creates economically still simple, but mathematically complex dynamics due to the 'squeezed' working of the economy during the low inflation regime. Section 6.7 concludes.

6.2 Traditional AD–AS with myopic perfect foresight—a reminder

In this section, we briefly discuss the traditional AS–AD growth dynamics with prices set equal to marginal wage costs and nominal wage inflation driven by an expectations-augmented Phillips curve. Introducing myopic perfect foresight (i.e. the assumption of no errors with respect to the short-run rate of price inflation) into such a Phillips curve alters the dynamics implied by the model in a radical way, in fact towards a globally stable (neo-)classical real growth dynamics with real wage rigidity and thus fluctuating rates of under- or overemployment. Furthermore, price level dynamics no longer feed back into these real dynamics and are now unstable in the large. The accepted approach in the literature is then to go on from myopic perfect foresight to 'rational expectations' and to construct a purely forward looking solution (which incorporates the whole future of the economy) by way of the so-called jump-variable technique of Sargent and Wallace (1973). However, in our view, this does not represent a consistent solution to the dynamic results obtained in this model type under myopic perfect foresight, as we shall argue in this chapter.

The case of myopic perfect foresight in a dynamic AD–AS model of business fluctuations and growth has been considered in very detailed form in Sargent (1987, Ch.5). The model of Sargent's (1987, Ch.5) so-called Keynesian dynamics is given by a standard combination of AD based on IS-LM (Investment Saving-Liquidity preference Money supply) and AS based on the condition that prices always equal marginal wage costs, plus finally an expectations augmented money wage Phillips Curve or WPC. The specific features that characterize this textbook treatment of AS–AD–WPC are that investment includes profitability considerations besides the real rate of interest, that a reduced form PC is not immediately employed in this dynamic analysis, and most importantly that expectations are rational (i.e. of the myopic perfect foresight variety in the deterministic context). Consumption is based on current disposable income in the traditional way, the LM curve is of standard type and there is neoclassical smooth factor substitution along with the assumption that prices are set according to the marginal productivity principle – and thus optimal from the viewpoint of the firm. These more or less standard ingredients give rise to the following set of equations that determine the statically endogenous variables: consumption (C), investment (I), government expenditure (G), output (Y), interest (r), prices (p), taxes (T), the profit rate (ρ), employment (L^d) and the rate of employment (e). These statically endogenous variables feed into the dynamically endogenous variables: the capital stock (K), labor supply (L) and the nominal wage level (w), for which laws of motion are also provided in the equations shown below. The equations are

$$C = c(Y + rB/p - \delta K - T), \tag{6.1}$$

$$I/K = i(\rho - (r - \pi)) + n, \quad \rho = \frac{Y - \delta K - \omega L^d}{K}, \quad \omega = \frac{w}{p}, \tag{6.2}$$

$$G = gK, \quad g = \text{const.}, \tag{6.3}$$

$$Y \overset{IS}{=} C + I + \delta K + G, \tag{6.4}$$

$$M \overset{LM}{=} p(h_1 Y + h_2(r_0 - r)W), \tag{6.5}$$

$$Y = F(K, L^d), \tag{6.6}$$

$$p \overset{AS}{=} w/F_L(K, L^d), \tag{6.7}$$

$$\hat{w} \overset{PC}{=} \beta_w(e - \bar{e}) + \pi, \quad e = L^d/L, \tag{6.8}$$

$$\pi \overset{MPF}{=} \hat{p}, \tag{6.9}$$

$$\hat{K} = I/K, \tag{6.10}$$

$$\hat{L} = n \quad (= \hat{M} \quad \text{for analytical simplicity}). \tag{6.11}$$

We make the simplifying assumptions that all behavior is based on linear relationships in order to concentrate on the intrinsic nonlinearities of this type of AS–AD–WPC growth model. Furthermore, following Sargent (1987, Ch.5), we assume that $t = (T - rB/p)/K$ is a given magnitude and thus, like real government expenditure per unit of capital, g, a parameter of the model. This excludes feedbacks from government bond accumulation and thus from the government budget equation on real economic activity. We thus concentrate on the working of the private sector with minimal interference from the side of fiscal policy, which is not an issue in this chapter. The model is fully backed-up by budget equations as in Sargent (1987): pure equity financing of firms, money and bond financing of the government budget deficit and money, bond and equity accumulation in the sector of private households. There is flow consistency, since the new inflow of money and bonds is always accepted by private households. Finally, Walras' Law of Stocks and the perfect substitute assumption for government bonds and equities ensure that equity price dynamics remain implicit. The LM–curve is thus the main representation of the financial part of the model, which is therefore still of a very simple type at this stage of its development.

The treatment of the resulting dynamics turns out to be not very difficult. In fact, equations (6.8) and (6.9) imply a real–wage dynamics of the type:

$$\hat{\omega} = \beta_w(l^d/l - \bar{e}), \quad l^d = L^d/K, l = L/K.$$

From $\dot{K} = I = S = Y - \delta K - C - G$ and $\dot{L} = nL$ we furthermore get

$$\hat{l} = n - (y - \delta - c(y - \delta - t) - g) = n - (1 - c)y - (1 - c)\delta + ct - g,$$

with $y = Y/K = F(1, l^d) = f(l^d)$.
Finally, by eq. (6.7) we obtain

$$\omega = f'(l^d), \text{ i.e. }, \quad l^d = (f')^{-1}(\omega) = h(\omega), \quad h' < 0.$$

Hence, the real dynamics of the model can be represented by the following autonomous 2D dynamical system:

$$\hat{\omega} = \beta_w(h(\omega)/l - \bar{e}),$$

$$\hat{l} = n - (1 - c)\delta - g + ct - (1 - c)f(h(\omega)).$$

It is easy to show, see e.g., Flaschel (2009), that this system is well defined in the positive orthant of the phase space, has a unique interior steady-state, which moreover is globally asymptotically stable in the considered domain. In fact, this is just a Solow (1956) growth dynamics with a real–wage Phillips curve (real wage rigidity) and thus classical under- or overemployment dynamics if $\bar{e} < 1$!). There may be a full-employment ceiling in this model type, but this is an issue of secondary importance here.

The unique interior steady state is given by

$$y_o = \frac{1}{1 - c}[(1 - c)\delta + n + g - ct] = \frac{1}{1 - c}[n + g - t] + \delta + t,$$

$$l_o^d = f^{-1}(y_o), \quad \omega_o = f'(l_o^d), \quad l_o = l_o^d/\bar{e},$$

$$m_o = h_1 y_o, \quad \hat{p}_o = 0, \quad r_o = \rho_o = f(l_o^d) - \delta - \omega_o l_o^d.$$

Keynes' (1936) GT approach is almost entirely absent in this type of analysis, which seems to be Keynesian in nature (AS–AD), but which – due to the neglect of short-run errors in inflation forecasting – has become in fact of very (neo-)classical type. The marginal propensity of consume, the stabilizing element in Keynesian theory, is still present, but neither investment nor money demand plays a role in the real dynamics we have obtained from equations (6.1)–(6.11). Volatile investment decisions and financial markets are thus simply irrelevant for the real dynamics of this AS–AD growth model when *myopic* perfect foresight on the current rate of price inflation is assumed. What, then, remains for the role of traditional Keynesian 'troublemakers', the marginal efficiency of investment and liquidity preference schedule? The answer again is, in technical terms, a very simple one:

We have for given $\omega = \omega(t) = (w/p)(t)$ as implied by the real dynamics (due to the $I = S$ assumption):

$$(1-c)f(h(\omega))-(1-c)\delta+ct-g=i(f(l)-\delta-\omega h(\omega)-r+\hat{p})+n, \quad i.e.$$

$$\hat{p}=\frac{1}{i}[(1-c)f(h(\omega))-(1-c)\delta+ct-g-n]-(f(l)-\delta-\omega h(\omega))+$$

$$r=g(\omega,l)+r,$$

with an added reduced-form LM-equation of the type

$$r=(h_1f(h(\omega))-m)/h_2+r_0, \quad m=\frac{M}{pK}.$$

The foregoing equations imply

$$\hat{m}=\hat{l}(\omega)-g(\omega,l)-r_o+\frac{m-h_1f(h(\omega))}{h_2},$$

as the nonautonomous[6] differential equation for the evolution of real money balances, as the reduced form representation of the nominal dynamics.[7] Due to this feedback chain, $\hat{m}$ depends positively on the level of m and it seems as if the jump–variable technique needs to be implemented in order to tame such explosive nominal processes; see Flaschel (2009), Turnovsky (1997) and Flaschel, Franke and Semmler (1997) for details on this technique. Advocates of the jump–variable technique, therefore are led to conclude that investment efficiency and liquidity preference only play a role in appended purely nominal processes and this solely in a stabilizing way, though with initially accelerating phases in the case of anticipated monetary and other shocks. A truly Neoclassical Synthesis.

By contrast, we believe that Keynesian IS-LM growth dynamics proper (demand driven growth and business fluctuations) must remain intact if (generally minor) errors in inflationary expectations are excluded from consideration in order to reduce the dimension and to simplify the analysis of the dynamical system to be considered. A correctly formulated Keynesian approach to economic dynamics and fluctuating growth should not give rise to such a strange dichotomized system

---

6 Since the independent (ω, l) block will feed into the RHS as a time function.
7 Note that we have $g(\omega, l) = -\rho_o$ in the steady state.

with classical real and purely nominal IS-LM inflation dynamics, here in fact of the most basic jump variable type, namely

$$\hat{m} = \frac{m - h_1 y_o}{h_2} \quad \left[\hat{p} = -\frac{(M/K)_o \frac{1}{p} - h_1 y_o}{h_2}\right],$$

if it is assumed for simplicity that the real part is already at its steady state. This dynamic equation is of the same kind as the one for the Cagan monetary model and can be treated with respect to its forward-looking solution in the same way, as it is discussed in detail for example in Turnovsky (1997, 3.3/4), i.e. the nominal dynamics assumed to hold under the jump-variable hypothesis in AS–AD–WPC is then of a very well-known type.

However, the basic fact that the AS–AD–WPC model under myopic perfect foresight is not a consistently formulated one and also not consistently solved arises from its ad hoc assumption that nominal wages must here jump with the price level $p(w = \omega p)$, since the real wage ω is now moving continuously in time according to the derived real wage dynamics. The level of money wages is thus now capable of adjusting instantaneously, which is in contradiction to the assumption of only sluggishly adjusting nominal wages according to the assumed money wage PC.[8] Furthermore, a properly formulated Keynesian growth dynamics should – besides allowing for un- or overemployed labor – also allow for un- or overemployment of the capital stock, at least in certain episodes. Thus the price level, like the wage level, should better and alternatively be assumed to adjust somewhat sluggishly; see also Barro (1994) in this regard. We will come back to this observation after the next section which is devoted to new developments in the area of Keynesian dynamics, the so-called New Keynesian approach of the macrodynamic literature.

The conclusion of this section is that the Neoclassical Synthesis, Stage I, must be considered a failure on logical grounds and not a valid attempt 'to formalize for students the relationships among the various hypotheses advanced in Milton Friedman's AEA presidential address (1968)', see Sargent (1987, p.117).

6.3 Matured Keynesian model building: the DAS–AD baseline case

We have already remarked that a Keynesian model of aggregate demand fluctuations should (independently of whether justification can be found in Keynes' General Theory) allow for under- (or over-)utilized labor as well as capital in order to be general enough from the descriptive point of view. As Barro (1994), for example, observes IS-LM is (or should be) based on imperfectly flexible wages *and* prices and thus on the consideration of wage as well as price Phillips Curves. This is precisely what we will do in the following, augmented by

---

8 See Flaschel (2009) and Flaschel, Franke and Semmler (1997) for further investigations along these lines.

the observation that medium-run aspects count both in wage and price adjustment as well as in investment behavior, here still expressed in simple terms by the introduction of the concept of an inflation as well as an investment climate. These economic climate terms are based on past observation, while we have model-consistent expectations with respect to short-run wage and price inflation. The modification of the traditional AS–AD model of Section 6.2 that we shall introduce now thus treats expectations in a hybrid way, myopic perfect foresight on the current rates of wage and price inflation on the one hand and an adaptive updating of economic climate expressions, with an exponential weighting scheme, on the other hand.

In light of the foregoing discussion, we assume here two Phillips Curves or PCs in the place of only one. In this way, we provide wage and price dynamics separately, both based on measures of demand pressure $e - \bar{e}, u - \bar{u}$, in the market for labor and for goods, respectively. We denote by e the rate of employment on the labor market and by $\bar{e}$ the NAIRU-level of this rate, and similarly by u the rate of capacity utilization of the capital stock and $\bar{u}$ the normal rate of capacity utilization of firms. These demand pressure influences on wage and price dynamics, or on the formation of wage and price inflation, $\hat{w}, \hat{p}$, are both augmented by a weighted average of cost-pressure terms based on forward-looking perfectly foreseen price and wage inflation rates, respectively, and a backward looking measure of the prevailing inflationary climate, symbolized by π^c. Cost pressure perceived by workers is thus a weighted average of the currently evolving price inflation rate $\hat{p}$ and some longer-run concept of price inflation, π^c, based on past observations. Similarly, cost pressure perceived by firms is given by a weighted average of the currently evolving (perfectly foreseen) wage inflation rate $\hat{w}$ and again the measure of the inflationary climate in which the economy is operating. We thus arrive at the following two Phillips Curves for wage and price inflation, formulated here in a fairly symmetric way.

Structural form of the wage–price dynamics (the DAS component):

$$\hat{w} = \beta_w(e - \bar{e}) + \kappa_w \hat{p} + (1 - \kappa_w)\pi^c,$$
$$\hat{p} = \beta_p(u - \bar{u}) + \kappa_p \hat{w} + (1 - \kappa_p)\pi^c.$$

Inflationary expectations over the medium run, π^c, i.e. the *inflationary climate* in which current wage and price inflation is operating, may be adaptively following the actual rate of inflation (by use of some exponential weighting scheme), may be based on a rolling sample (with hump-shaped weighting schemes), or on other possibilities for updating expectations. For simplicity of exposition, we shall make use of the conventional adaptive expectations mechanism here. Besides demand pressure, we thus use (as cost pressure expressions) in the two PC's weighted averages of this economic climate and the (foreseen) relevant cost pressure term for wage setting and price setting. In this way we get two PC's with very analogous building blocks, which despite their traditional outlook turn out to have interesting and novel implications. These two Phillips curves have been estimated for the US-economy in various ways in Flaschel and Krolzig (2006), Flaschel, Kauermann and Semmler (2007) and Chen and Flaschel (2006) and found to represent a significant improvement over single reduced-form price Phillips curves, with wage flexibility being greater than price flexibility with respect to demand pressure in the market for goods and for labor, respectively. Such a finding is not possible in the conventional framework of a single reduced-form Phillips curve.

Note that for our current version, the inflationary climate variable does not matter for the *evolution of the real wage* $\omega = w/p$, the law of motion of which is given by:

$$\hat{\omega} = \kappa[(1 - \kappa_p)\beta_w(e - \bar{e}) - (1 - \kappa_w)\beta_p(u - \bar{u})], \quad \kappa = 1/(1 - \kappa_w\kappa_p).$$

This follows easily from the obviously equivalent representation of the above two PC's:

$$\hat{w} - \pi^c = \beta_w(e - \bar{e}) + \kappa_w(\hat{p} - \pi^c),$$
$$\hat{p} - \pi^c = \beta_p(u - \bar{u}) + \kappa_p(\hat{w} - \pi^c),$$

by solving for the variables $\hat{w} - \pi^c$ and $\hat{p} - \pi^c$. It also implies the two cross-markets or *reduced form PC's* are given by:

$$\hat{p} = \kappa[\beta_p(u - \bar{u}) + \kappa_p\beta_w(e - \bar{e})] + \pi^c, \tag{6.12}$$
$$\hat{w} = \kappa[\beta_w(e - \bar{e}) + \kappa_w\beta_p(u - \bar{u})] + \pi^c, \tag{6.13}$$

which represent *a considerable generalization of* the conventional view of a single-market price PC with only one measure of demand pressure, the one in the labor market. This traditional expectations-augmented PC formally resembles the aforesaid reduced form $\hat{p}$-equation if Okun's Law holds in the sense of a strict positive correlation between $u - \bar{u}$, $u = Y/Y^p$ and $e - \bar{e}$, $e = L^d/L$, our measures of demand pressures on the market for goods and for labor. Yet, the coefficient in front of the traditional PC would even in this situation be a mixture of all of the $\beta's$ and $\kappa's$ of the two originally given PC's and thus represent a synthesis of goods and labor market characteristics.

With respect to the investment climate, we proceed similarly and assume that this climate is adaptively following the current risk premium $\epsilon(= \rho - (r - \hat{p}))$, the excess of the actual profit rate over the actual real rate of interest (which is perfectly foreseen). This gives[9]

$$\dot{\epsilon}^m = \beta_{\epsilon^m}(\epsilon - \epsilon^m), \quad \epsilon = \rho + \hat{p} - r,$$

which is directly comparable to

$$\dot{\pi}^c = \beta_{\pi^c}(\pi - \pi^c), \quad \pi = \hat{p}.$$

---

9 Chiarella, Flaschel, Groh and Semmler (2003) in response to Velupillai (2003), have used a slightly different expression for the updating of the investment climate, in this regard see the introductory observation in Section 6.6.

We believe that it is very natural to assume that economic climate expressions evolve sluggishly towards their observed short-run counterparts. It is, however, easily possible to introduce also forward looking components into the updating of the climate expressions, for example, based on the p^* concept of central banks and related potential output calculations. The investment function of the model of this section is now given simply by $i(\epsilon^m)$ in the place of $i(\epsilon)$.

We have now covered all modifications needed to overcome the extreme conclusions of the traditional AS–AD approach under myopic perfect foresight as they were sketched in Section 6.2. The model simply incorporates sluggish price adjustment besides sluggish wage adjustment and makes use of certain delays in the cost pressure terms of its wage and price PC and in its investment function. In the Sargent (1987) approach to Keynesian dynamics the $\beta_{\epsilon^m}, \beta_{\pi^c}, \beta_p$ are all set equal to infinity and $\bar{U}_c$ set equal to one, which implies that only current inflation rate and excess profitabilities matter for the evolution of the economy and that prices are perfectly flexible, so that full capacity utilization, not only normal capacity utilization, is always achieved. This limit case has, however, little in common with the properties of the model of this section.

This brings us to one point that still needs definition and explanation, namely the concept of the rate of capacity utilization that we will be using in the presence of neoclassical smooth factor substitution, but Keynesian over- or underemployment of the capital stock. Actual use of productive capacity is of course defined in reference to actual output Y. As measure of potential output Y^p, we associate with actual output Y the profit-maximizing output with respect to currently given wages and prices. Capacity utilization u is therefore measured relative to the profit maximizing output level and thus given by[10]

$$u = Y/Y^p \quad \text{with} \quad Y^p = F(K, L^p), \quad \omega = F_L(K, L^p).$$

where Y is determined from the IS-LM equilibrium block in the usual way. We have assumed in the price PC as normal rate of capacity utilization a rate that is less than one and thus assume in general that demand pressure leads to price inflation, before potential output has been reached, in line with what is assumed in the wage PC and demand pressure on the labor market. The idea behind this assumption is that there is imperfect competition on the market for goods so that firms raise prices before profits become zero at the margin.

Sargent (1987, Ch.5) not only assumes myopic perfect foresight ($\beta_{\pi^c} = \infty$), but also always the perfect – but empirically questionable – establishment of the condition that the price level is given by marginal wage costs ($\beta_p = \infty, \bar{u} = 1$). This 'limit case' of the dynamic AS–AD model of this section does not represent a meaningful model, in particular since its dynamic properties are not at all closely related to situations of very fast adjustment of prices and climate expressions to currently correctly observed inflation rates and excess profitability.

---

10 In intensive form expressions the following gives rise to $u = y/y^p$ with $y^p = f((f')^{-1}(\omega))$ in terms of the notation we introduced in Section 6.2.

There is still another motivation available for the imperfect price level adjustment we are assuming. For reasons of simplicity, we consider here the case of a Cobb-Douglas production function, given by $Y = K^\alpha L^{1-\alpha}$. According to the foregoing we have

$$p = w/F_L(K, L^p) = w/[(1-\alpha)K^\alpha(L^p)^{-\alpha}]$$

which for given wages and prices defines potential employment. Similarly, we define competitive prices as the level of prices p_c such that

$$p_c = w/F_L(K, L^d) = w/[(1-\alpha)K^\alpha(L^d)^{-\alpha}].$$

From these definitions we get the relationship

$$\frac{p}{p_c} = \frac{(1-\alpha)K^\alpha(L^d)^{-\alpha}}{(1-\alpha)K^\alpha(L^p)^{-\alpha}} = (L^p/L^d)^\alpha.$$

Due to this we obtain from the definitions of L^d, L^p and their implication $Y/Y^p = (L^d/L^p)^{1-\alpha}$ an expression that relates the above price ratio to the rate of capacity utilization as defined in this section:

$$\frac{p}{p_c} = \left(\frac{Y}{Y^p}\right)^{\frac{-\alpha}{1-\alpha}} \quad \text{or} \quad \frac{p_c}{p} = \left(\frac{Y}{Y^p}\right)^{\frac{\alpha}{1-\alpha}} = (u)^{\frac{\alpha}{1-\alpha}}.$$

We thus get that (for $\bar{u} = 1$) upward adjustment of the rate of capacity utilization to full capacity utilization is positively correlated with downward adjustment of actual prices to their competitive value and vice versa. In particular, in the special case $\alpha = 0.5$ we would get as reformulated price dynamics (see equation 6.12 with $\bar{u}$ being replaced by $(p_c/p)_o$):

$$\hat{p} = \beta_p(p_c/p - (p_c/p)_o) + \kappa_p\hat{w} + (1-\kappa_p)\pi^c,$$

which resembles the New Phillips curve of the New Keynesian approach as far as the reflection of demand pressure forces by means of real marginal wage costs are concerned. Price inflation is thus increasing when competitive prices (and thus nominal marginal wage costs) are above the actual ones and decreasing otherwise (neglecting the cost-push terms for the moment). This shows that our understanding of the rate of capacity utilization in the framework of neoclassical smooth factor substitution is related to demand pressure terms as used in New Keynesian approaches[11] and thus further motivating its adoption. Actual prices

---

11 See also Powell and Murphy (1997) for a closely related approach there applied to an empirical study of the Australian economy. We would like to stress here that this property of our model represents an important further similarity with the New Keynesian approach, yet, here in a form that gives substitution (with moderate elasticity of substitution) no major role to play in the overall dynamics.

will fall if they are above marginal wage costs to a sufficient degree. However, our approach suggests that actual prices start rising before marginal wage costs are in fact established, i.e. in particular, we have that actual prices are always higher than the competitive ones in the steady state.

We note that the steady state of the now considered Keynesian dynamics is the same as the one of the dynamics of Section 6.2 (with $\epsilon_o^m = 0, u_o = \bar{u}, e_o = \bar{e}, y_o^p = y_o/u_o, l_o^p = f^{-1}(y_o^p)$ in addition). Furthermore, the dynamical equations considered above have of course to be augmented by the ones that have remained unchanged by the modifications just considered. The intensive form of all resulting static and dynamic equations is presented in the following section from which we then start the stability analysis of the baseline model of the next section. The modifications of the AS–AD model of Section 6.2 proposed in the present section imply that it no longer dichotomizes and there is no need here to apply the poorly motivated jump-variable technique. Instead, the steady state of the dynamics is locally asymptotically stable under conditions that are reasonable from a Keynesian perspective, loses its asymptotic stability by way of cycles (by way of so-called Hopf-bifurcations) and becomes sooner or later globally unstable if (generally speaking) adjustment speeds become too high.

We no longer have state variables in the model that can be considered as being not predetermined, but in fact can reduce the dynamics to an autonomous system in the five predetermined state variables: the real wage, real balances per unit of capital, full-employment labor intensity and the expressions for the inflation and the investment climate. When the model is subject to explosive forces, it requires extrinsic nonlinearities in economic behavior, assumed to come into affect far off the steady state, that bound the dynamics to an economically meaningful domain in the 5D state space. Chen, Chiarella, Flaschel and Hung (2006) provide details of such an approach and its numerical investigation.

Summing up, we can state that we have arrived at a model type that is much more complex, but also much more convincing, that the labor market dynamics of the traditional AS–AD dynamics of the Neoclassical Synthesis, Stage I. We now have five in the place of only three laws of motion, which incorporate myopic perfect foresight without any significant impact on the resulting Keynesian dynamics. We can handle factor utilization problems both for labor and capital without necessarily assuming a fixed proportions technology, i.e. we can treat AS–AD growth with neoclassical smooth factor substitution. We have sluggish wage as well as price adjustment processes with cost pressure terms that are both forward and backward looking and that allow for the distinction between temporary and permanent inflationary shocks. We have a unique interior steady state solution of (one must stress) supply side type, generally surrounded by business fluctuations of Keynesian short-run as well as medium-run type. Our DAS–AD growth dynamics therefore exhibits a variety of features that are much more in line with a Keynesian understanding of the features of the trade cycle than is the case for the conventional modelling of AS–AD growth dynamics.

Taken together the model of this section consists of the following five laws of motion for real wages, real balances, the investment climate, labor intensity and the inflationary climate:

$$\hat{\omega} = \kappa[(1 - \kappa_p)\beta_w(l^d/l - \bar{e}) - (1 - \kappa_w)\beta_p(y/y^p - \bar{u})], \tag{6.14}$$

$$\hat{m} = -\hat{p} - i\epsilon^m, \tag{6.15}$$

$$\dot{\epsilon}^m = \beta_{\epsilon^m}(\rho + \hat{p} - r - \epsilon^m), \tag{6.16}$$

$$\hat{l} = -i\epsilon^m, \tag{6.17}$$

$$\dot{\pi}^c = \beta_{\pi^c}(\hat{p} - \pi^c), \tag{6.18}$$

with $\hat{p} = \kappa[\beta_p(y/y^p(\omega) - \bar{u}) + \kappa_p\beta_w(l^d/l - \bar{e})] + \pi^c$.

Here we already employ reduced-form expressions throughout and consider the dynamics of the real wage, ω, real balances per unit of capital, m, the investment climate ϵ^m, labor intensity, l, and the inflationary climate, π^c on the basis of the simplifying assumptions that natural growth n determines also the trend growth term in the investment function as well as money supply growth. The foregoing dynamical system is to be supplemented by the following static relationships for output, potential output and employment (all per unit of capital) and the rate of interest and the rate of profit:

$$y = \frac{1}{1 - c}[i\epsilon^m + n + g - t] + \delta + t, \tag{6.19}$$

$$y^p = f((f')^{-1}(\omega)), \quad F(1, L^p/K) = f(l^p) = y^p, F_L(1, L^p/K))$$
$$= f'(l^p) = \omega, \tag{6.20}$$

$$l^d = f^{-1}(y), \tag{6.21}$$

$$r = r_o + (h_1 y - m)/h_2, \tag{6.22}$$

$$\rho = y - \delta - \omega l^d, \tag{6.23}$$

which have to be inserted into the right-hand sides in order to obtain an autonomous system of 5 differential equations that is nonlinear in a natural or intrinsic way. We note, however, that there are many items that reappear in various equations, or are similar to each other, implying that stability analysis can exploit a variety of linear dependencies in the calculation of the conditions for local asymptotic stability. This dynamical system will be investigated in the next section in somewhat informal terms and, with slight modifications, in a rigorous way in the appendix to this book.

As the model is now formulated it exhibits – besides the well-known real rate of interest channel (giving rise to destabilizing Mundell-effects that are traditionally tamed by the application of the jump variable technique – another real feedback channel, see Figure 6.1, which we have called the Rose real wage effect (based on the work of Rose (1967)) in Chiarella and Flaschel (2000). This channel is completely absent from the considered New Keynesian approach, and it is in a

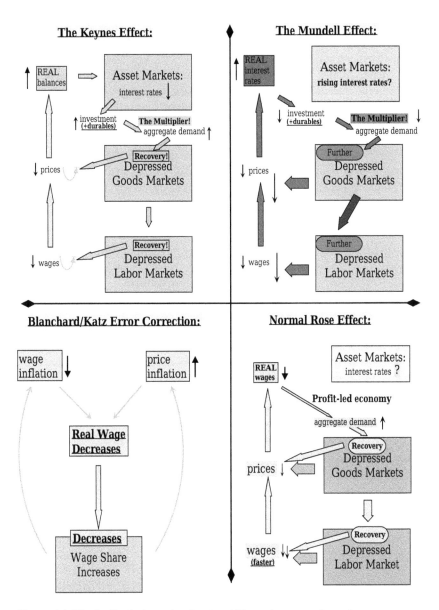

Figure 6.1 The feedback channels of matured Keynesian macrodynamics.

weak form present in the model of the Neoclassical Synthesis, Stage I, due to the inclusion of the rate of profit into the considered investment function. The Rose effect only gives rise to a clearly distinguishable and significant feedback channel, however, if wage and price flexibilities are both finite and if aggregate demand depends on the income distribution between wages and profits. In the traditional

AS–AD model of Section 6.2, it only gives rise to a directly stabilizing dependence of the growth rate of real wages on their level, while in our mature form of this AS–AD analysis it works through the interaction of the law of motion (6.14) for real wages, the investment climate and the IS-curve we have derived on this basis. The real marginal costs effect of the New Keynesian approach is present here in addition, in the denominator of the expression we are using for rate of capacity utilization, $(u = y/y^p)$ and contributes to some extent to stability should the Rose effect by itself be destabilizing.

We thus have now two feedback channels interacting in our extended DAS–AD dynamics which in specific ways exhibit stabilizing as well as destabilizing features (Keynes vs. Mundell effects and normal vs. adverse Rose effects). A variety of further feedback channels of Keynesian macrodynamics are investigated in Chiarella, Flaschel, Groh and Semmler (2000). The careful analysis of these channels and the partial insights that can be related with them form the basis of the 5D stability analysis of the next section and the appendix to this book. Such an analysis differs radically from the always convergent jump-variable analysis of the rational expectations school in models of the Neoclassical Synthesis, Stage I and Stage II and many other approaches to macrodynamics.

In Figure 6.1, we summarize the basic feedback channels of our approach to DAS–AD dynamics. We have the textbook Keynes-effect or stabilizing nominal rate of interest rate channel top-left and the therewith interacting destabilizing Mundell- or inflationary expectations effect which together with the Keynes-effect works through the (expected) real rate of interest channel. In addition, we have Rose (1967)-effects working though the real wage channel. Figure 6.1 indicates that the real wage channel will be stabilizing when investment reacts more strongly than consumption to real wage changes (which is the case in our model type, since here consumption does not depend at all on the real wage) if this is coupled with wages being more flexible than prices, in the sense that eq. (6.14) then establishes a positive link between economic activity and induced real wage changes. However, if this latter relationship becomes a negative one, due to a sufficient degree of price level flexibility, this will destabilize the economy, since shrinking economic activity due to real wage increases will then indeed induce further real wage increases, due to a price level that is falling faster than the wage level in this state of depressed markets for goods and for labor (representing an adverse type of Rose-effect). We stress here that the degree of forward looking behavior in both the wage and the price level dynamics is also important, since these weights also enter the crucial eq. (6.14) describing the dynamics of real wages for any changing states of economic activity. Figure 6.1 finally also shows the Blanchard and Katz wage share correction mechanism (bottom left) which will be added to the considered dynamics in Section 6.6.

6.4 Local stability analysis: the feedback-guided approach

In this section, we illustrate an important method used to prove local asymptotic stability of the interior steady state of the considered dynamical system, through partial motivations from the feedback chains that characterize our baseline model of Keynesian macrodynamics. Since the model is an extension of the traditional AS–AD growth model we know that there is a real rate of interest effect involved, first analyzed by formal methods in Tobin (1975), see also Groth (1993). There is therefore the stabilizing Keynes-effect based on activity-reducing nominal interest rate increases following price level increases, which provides a check to further price increases. Secondly, if the expected real rate of interest is driving investment and consumption decisions (increases leading to decreased aggregate demand), there is the stimulating (partial) effect of increases in the expected rate of inflation that may lead to further inflation and further increases in expected inflation under appropriate conditions. This is the Mundell-effect that works opposite to the Keynes-effect, but also through the real rate of interest channel as just seen; we refer the reader again to Figure 6.1.

The Keynes-effect is the stronger the smaller the parameter h_2 characterizing the interest rate sensitivity of money demand becomes, since the reduced-form LM equation reads:

$$r = r_o + (h_1 y - m)/h_2, \quad y = Y/K, m = M/(pK).$$

The Mundell-effect is the stronger the faster the inflationary climate adjusts to the present level of price inflation, since we have

$$\dot{\pi}^c = \beta_{\pi^c}(\hat{p} - \pi^c) = \beta_{\pi^c}\kappa[\beta_p(u - \bar{u}) + \kappa_p\beta_w(e - \bar{e})],$$

and since both rates of capacity utilization depend positively on the investment climate ϵ^m which in turn (see equation 6.16) is driven by excess profitability $\epsilon = \rho + \hat{p} - r$. Excess profitability in turn depends positively on the inflation rate and thus on the inflationary climate as the reduced-form price Phillips curve shows.

There is – as we already know – a further potentially (at least partially) destabilizing feedback mechanism as the model is formulated. Excess profitability depends positively on the rate of return on capital ρ and thus negatively on the real wage ω. We thus get – since consumption does not yet depend on the real wage – that real wage increases depress economic activity (though with the delay that is caused by our concept of an investment climate transmitting excess profitability to investment behavior). From our reduced-form real wage dynamics

$$\hat{\omega} = \kappa[(1 - \kappa_p)\beta_w(e - \bar{e}) - (1 - \kappa_w)\beta_p(u - \bar{u})],$$

we thus obtain that price flexibility should be bad for economic stability due to the minus sign in front of the parameter β_p while the opposite should hold true for the parameter that characterizes wage flexibility. This is a situation already investigated in Rose (1967). It gives the reason for our statement that wage flexibility gives rise to normal, and price flexibility to adverse, Rose effects as far as real wage adjustments are concerned. Besides real rate of interest effect, establishing opposing Keynes- and Mundell-effects, we thus have also another real adjustment process in the considered model where now wage and price flexibility are in opposition to each other, see Chiarella and Flaschel (2000) and Chiarella, Flaschel, Groh and Semmler (2000) for further discussion of these as well as other feedback mechanisms in Keynesian growth dynamics.

There is still another adjustment speed parameter in the model, the one (β_{ϵ^m}) that determines how fast the investment climate is updated in the light of current excess profitability. This parameter will play no decisive role in the stability investigations that follow, but will become important in the more detailed and rigorous stability analysis to be considered in the appendix to the book. In the present stability analysis we will, however, focus on the role played by $h_2, \beta_w, \beta_p, \beta_{\pi^c}$ in order to provide one example of asymptotic stability of the interior steady state position by appropriate choices of these parameter values, basically in line with the aforesaid feedback channels of partial Keynesian macrodynamics.

The foregoing adds to the understanding of the dynamical system (6.14) – (6.18) whose stability properties are now briefly investigated by means of varying adjustment speed parameters. With the feedback scenarios considered earlier in mind, we first observe that the inflationary climate can be frozen at its steady state value, here $\pi_o^c = \hat{M} - n = 0$, if $\beta_{\pi^c} = 0$ is assumed. The system thereby becomes 4D and it can indeed be further reduced to 3D if in addition $\beta_w = 0$ is assumed, since this decouples the *l*-dynamics from the remaining dynamical system with state variables ω, m, ϵ^m.

We intentionally will consider the stability of these 3D subdynamics – and its subsequent extensions – in very informal terms here, leaving rigorous calculations of stability criteria to the appendix (there however for the case of an interest rate policy rule in the place of our standard LM-curve). In this way, we hope to demonstrate to the reader how one can proceed in a systematic way from low to high dimensional analysis in such stability investigations. This method has been already applied to various other often much more complicated dynamical systems, see Asada, Chiarella, Flaschel and Franke (2003) for a variety of typical examples.

Proposition 1 Assume that $\beta_{\pi^c} = 0, \beta_w = 0$ holds. Assume furthermore that the parameters h_2, β_p are chosen sufficiently small and that the κ_w, κ_p parameters do not equal 1. Then: the interior steady state of the reduced 3D dynamical system

$$\hat{\omega} = -\kappa(1 - \kappa_w)\beta_p(y/y^p(\omega) - \bar{u}),$$

$$\hat{m} = -i\epsilon^m - \kappa\beta_p(y/y^p(\omega) - \bar{u}),$$

$$\dot{\epsilon}^m = \beta_{\epsilon^m}(\rho + \kappa\beta_p(y/y^p(\omega) - \bar{u}) - r - \epsilon^m),$$

is locally asymptotically stable.

Sketch of proof The assumptions made imply that the Mundell-effect is absent from the reduced dynamics, since inflationary expectations are kept constant, and that the destabilizing component of the Rose-effect is weak. Due to the further assumption of a strong Keynes-effect, the steady state of the system is thus surrounded by centripetal forces,

Proposition 2 Assume in addition that the parameter β_w is now positive and chosen sufficiently small. Then: the interior steady state of the implied 4D dynamical system (where the law of motion for l has now been incorporated)

$$\hat{\omega} = \kappa[(1 - \kappa_p)\beta_w(l^d/l - \bar{e}) - (1 - \kappa_w)\beta_p(y/y^p - \bar{u})],$$

$$\hat{m} = -i\epsilon^m - \kappa[\beta_p(y/y^p - \bar{u}) + \kappa_p\beta_w(l^d/l - \bar{e})],$$

$$\dot{\epsilon}^m = \beta_{\epsilon^m}(\rho + \kappa[\beta_p(y/y^p(\omega) - \bar{u}) + \kappa_p\beta_w(l^d/l - \bar{e})], -r - \epsilon^m),$$

$$\hat{l} = -i\epsilon^m,$$

is locally asymptotically stable.

Sketch of proof In the considered situation we do not apply the Routh-Hurwitz conditions to 4D dynamical systems, as in the appendix to this chapter, but instead proceed by simple continuity arguments. Eigenvalues are continuous functions of the parameters of the model. It therefore suffices to show that the determinant of the Jacobian matrix of the 4D dynamics that is generated when the parameter β_w is made positive is positive in sign. The zero eigenvalue of the case $\beta_w = 0$ must then become negative and the three other eigenvalues continue to exhibit negative real parts if the parameter β_w is changing by a small amount solely. We conjecture – in view what is shown in the appendix in the case of an interest rate policy rule – that this proposition holds for all changes of the parameter β_w.

Proposition 3 Assume in addition that the parameters β_{π^c} is now positive and chosen sufficiently small. Then: the interior steady state of the full 5D dynamical system (where the differential equation for π^c is now included)

$$\hat{\omega} = \kappa[(1 - \kappa_p)\beta_w(l^d/l - \bar{e}) - (1 - \kappa_w)\beta_p(y/y^p - \bar{u})],$$

$$\hat{m} = -\pi^c - i\epsilon^m - \kappa[\beta_p(y/y^p - \bar{u}) + \kappa_p\beta_w(l^d/l - \bar{e})],$$

$$\dot{\epsilon}^m = \beta_{\epsilon^m}(\rho + \kappa[\beta_p(y/y^p(\omega) - \bar{u}) + \kappa_p\beta_w(l^d/l - \bar{e})] + \pi^c - r - \epsilon^m),$$

$$\hat{l} = -i\epsilon^m,$$

$$\dot{\pi}^c = \beta_{\pi^c}(\kappa[\beta_p(y/y^p(\omega) - \bar{u}) + \kappa_p\beta_w(l^d/l - \bar{e})]),$$

is locally asymptotically stable.

Sketch of proof[12]   As for Proposition 2, now simply making use of the rows corresponding to the laws of motion for l and m in order to reduce the row corresponding to the law of motion for π^c to the form $(0, 0, 0, 0, -)$, again without change in the sign of the determinants of the accompanying Jacobians, allows us to show here that the determinant of the full 5D dynamics is always negative. The fifth eigenvalue must therefore change from zero to a negative value if the parameter β_π is made slightly positive (but not too large), while the remaining real parts of eigenvalues do not experience a change in sign. A weak Mundell-effect does consequently not disturb the proven asymptotic stability.

We stress again that the parameters β_p and β_{π^c} have been chosen such that adverse Rose and destabilizing Mundell-effects are both weak and accompanied by a strongly stabilizing Keynes-effect.

We formulate as a corollary to Proposition 3 that, due to the always negative sign of the just considered 5D determinant, loss of stability can only occur by way of Hopf-bifurcations, i.e. through the generation of cycles in the real-nominal interactions of the model.

Corollary   Assume an asymptotically stable steady state on the basis of Proposition 3. Then: the interior steady state of the full 5D dynamical system will lose its stability (generally) by way of a sub- or supercritical Hopf-bifurcation if the parameters β_p or β_{π^c} are chosen sufficiently large.

Since the model is in a natural way a nonlinear one, we know from the Hopf-bifurcation theorem[13] that usually loss of stability will occur through the death of an unstable limit cycle (the subcritical case) or the birth of a stable one (the supercritical case), when destabilizing parameters pass through their bifurcation values. Such loss of stability is here possible if prices become sufficiently flexible compared to wage flexibility, leading to an adverse type of real wage adjustment, or if the inflationary climate expression is updated sufficiently fast, i.e. if the system loses the inflationary inertia – we have built into it – to a sufficient degree. These are typical feedback structures of a properly formulated Keynesian dynamics that may give rise to global instability, directly in the case of subcritical Hopf-bifurcations and sooner or later in the case of supercritical bifurcations, and thus give rise to the need to add further *extrinsic behavioral nonlinearities* to the model in order to bound the generated business fluctuations. Such issues will be briefly explored in the following section and are further considered in companion papers to the present chapter, there, from the numerical as well as the empirical perspective, see Chen, Chiarella, Flaschel and Hung (2006) and Chen, Chiarella, Flaschel and Semmler (2006).

We conclude from this section that a properly specified Keynesian disequilibrium dynamics – with labor and capital both over- or underutilized in the

---

12 A detailed rigorous proof can be found in Asada, Chen, Chiarella and Flaschel (2006).
13 See the mathematical appendix in Asada, Chiarella, Flaschel and Franke (2003) for details.

course of the generated business fluctuations – integrates important feedback channels based on partial perspectives into a consistent whole, where all behavioral and budget restrictions fully specified. We can have damped oscillations, persistent fluctuations or even explosive oscillations in such a framework. The latter necessitate the introduction of certain behavioral nonlinearities in order to allow for viable business fluctuations. However, a variety of well-known stabilizing or destabilizing feedback channels of Keynesian macrodynamics are still excluded from the present stage of the modelling of Keynesian macro-dynamics, such as wealth effects in consumption or Fisher debt effects in investment behavior, all of which define the agenda for future extensions of this model type.[14]

6.5 Real wage adjustment corrections and nominal interest rate policy rules

We have considered in Section 6.3 the New Keynesian approach to wage and price dynamics and have compared this approach already briefly with the two Phillips curve wage–price spirals of this chapter there (without use of real wage gaps in this baseline DAS–AD model). We recapitulate this extended wage–price spiral here briefly and include thereby Blanchard and Katz (1999) type error correction terms into our baseline DAS–AD dynamics, together with a Taylor interest rate policy rule now in the place of the LM-curve representation of the financial markets of Section 6.4, in order to fully show how our matured Keynesian AS–AD dynamics is differentiated from the New Keynesian approach when both approaches make use of two Phillips curves and an interest rate policy rule. In the New Keynesian model of wage and price dynamics, we had:

$$d\ln w_t \overset{NWPC}{=} E_t(d\ln w_{t+1}) + \beta_{wy}\ln Y_t - \beta_{w\omega}\ln\omega_t,$$

$$d\ln p_t \overset{NPPC}{=} E_t(d\ln p_{t+1}) + \beta_{py}\ln Y_t + \beta_{p\omega}\ln\omega_t.$$

Current wage and price inflation depend on expected future wage and price inflation, respectively, and in the usual way on output gaps, augmented by a negative (positive) dependence on the real wage gap in the case of the wage (price) Phillips curve. Assuming again a deterministic framework and myopic perfect foresight allows us to suppress the expectations operator.

In order to get from these two laws of motion the corresponding Phillips curves of our matured, but conventional DAS–AD dynamics, we use neoclassical dating of expectations in a crossover fashion, i.e. perfectly foreseen wage inflation in the price Phillips curve and perfectly foreseen price inflation in the wage Phillips curve, now coupled with hybrid expectations formation as in the DAS–AD model of the preceding sections. We, furthermore, replace the output gap in the NWPC

14 See Chiarella, Flaschel, Groh and Semmler (2000) for a survey on such feedback channels.

by the employment rate gap and by the capacity utilization gap in the NPPC as in the matured Keynesian macrodynamics introduced in Section 6.4. Finally, we now also use real wage gaps in the MWPC and the MPPC, here based on microfoundations of Blanchard and Katz type, as in the paper by Flaschel and Krolzig (2006). In this way, we arrive at the following general form of our M(atured)WPC and M(atured)PPC, formally discriminated from the New Keynesian case of both staggered wage and price setting solely by a different treatment of wage and price inflation expectations.

$$d\ln w_{t+1} \overset{MWPC}{=} \kappa_w d\ln p_{t+1} + (1-\kappa_w)\pi_t^c + \beta_{we}(e_t-\bar{e}) - \beta_{w\omega}(\ln\omega_t - \ln\omega_o),$$

$$d\ln p_{t+1} \overset{MPPC}{=} \kappa_p d\ln w_{t+1} + (1-\kappa_p)\pi_t^c + \beta_{pu}(u_t-\bar{u}) + \beta_{p\omega}(\ln\omega_t - \ln\omega_o).$$

In continuous time, these wage and price dynamics read

$$\hat{w} = \kappa_w\hat{p} + (1-\kappa_w)\pi^c + \beta_{we}(e-\bar{e}) - \beta_{w\omega}(\ln\omega - \ln\omega_o),$$

$$\hat{p} = \kappa_p\hat{w} + (1-\kappa_p)\pi^c + \beta_{pu}(u-\bar{u}) + \beta_{p\omega}(\ln\omega - \ln\omega_o).$$

Reformulated as reduced-form expressions, these equations give rise to the following linear system of differential equations ($\theta = \ln\omega$):

$$\hat{w} = \frac{1}{1-\kappa_w\kappa_p}[\beta_{we}(e-\bar{e}) - \beta_{w\omega}(\theta-\theta_o) + \kappa_w(\beta_{pu}(u-\bar{u}) + \beta_{p\omega}(\theta-\theta_o))] + \pi^c,$$

$$\hat{p} = \frac{1}{1-\kappa_w\kappa_p}[\beta_{pu}(u-\bar{u}) + \beta_{p\omega}(\theta-\theta_o) + \kappa_p(\beta_{we}(e-\bar{e}) - \beta_{w\omega}(\theta-\theta_o))] + \pi^c,$$

$$\dot{\theta} = \frac{1}{1-\kappa_w\kappa_p}[(1-\kappa_p)(\beta_{we}(e-\bar{e}) - \beta_{w\omega}(\theta-\theta_o)),$$

$$-(1-\kappa_w)(\beta_{pu}(u-\bar{u}) + \beta_{w\omega}(\theta-\theta_o))].$$

As monetary policy we now in addition employ a Taylor interest rate rule, in the place of an LM-curve, given by:

$$r^* = (r_o - \bar{\pi}) + \hat{p} + \alpha_p(\hat{p}-\bar{\pi}) + \alpha_u(u-\bar{u}), \tag{6.24}$$

$$\dot{r} = \alpha_r(r^*-r). \tag{6.25}$$

These equations describe the interest rate target r^* and the interest rate smoothing dynamics chosen by the central bank. The target rate of the central bank r^* is made here dependent on the steady state real rate of interest, augmented by actual inflation towards to a specific nominal rate of interest, and is as usually dependent on the inflation gap with respect to the target inflation rate $\bar{\pi}$ and the capacity utilization gap (our measure of the output gap). With respect to this interest rate target, there is then interest rate smoothing with strength α_r. Inserting r^* and rearranging terms we get from this latter expression the following form of a Taylor rule

$$\dot{r} = -\gamma_r(r - r_o) + \gamma_p(\hat{p} - \bar{\pi}) + \gamma_u(u - \bar{u}),$$

where we have $\gamma_r = \alpha_r, \gamma_p = \alpha_r(1 + \alpha_p), i.e. \alpha_p = \gamma_p/\alpha_r - 1$ and $\gamma_u = \alpha_r \alpha_u$.

Since the interest rate is temporarily fixed by the central bank, we must have an endogenous money supply now and get that the law of motion of the original model

$$\hat{m} = -\hat{p} - i\epsilon^m,$$

does now no longer feed back into the rest of the dynamics.

Taken together the revised AS–AD model of this section consists of the following five laws of motion for the log of real wages, the nominal rate of interest, the investment climate, labor intensity and the inflationary climate:

$$\dot{\theta} = \frac{1}{1 - \kappa_w \kappa_p}[(1 - \kappa_p)(\beta_{we}(e - \bar{e}) - \beta_{w\omega}(\theta - \theta_o)),$$

$$- (1 - \kappa_w)(\beta_{pu}(u - \bar{u}) + \beta_{w\omega}(\theta - \theta_o))],$$

$$\dot{r} = -\gamma_r(r - r_o) + \gamma_p(\hat{p} - \bar{\pi}) + \gamma_u(u - \bar{u}),$$

$$\dot{\epsilon}^m = \beta_{\epsilon^m}(\epsilon - \epsilon^m),$$

$$\hat{l} = -i\epsilon^m,$$

$$\dot{\pi}^c = \beta_{\pi^c}(\hat{p} - \pi^c),$$

with $\hat{p} = \frac{1}{1 - \kappa_w \kappa_p}[\beta_{pu}(u - \bar{u}) + \beta_{p\omega}(\theta - \theta_o) + \kappa_p(\beta_{we}(e - \bar{e}) - \beta_{w\omega}(\theta - \theta_o))]$.

This dynamical system is to be supplemented by the following static relationships for output, potential output and employment (all per unit of capital), the rate of interest and the rate of profit:

$$y = \frac{1}{1 - c}[i\epsilon^m + n + g - t] + \delta + t,$$

$$y^p = f((f')^{-1}(\exp\theta)), \quad F(1, L^p/K) = f(l^p) = y^p, F_L(1, L^p/K) = f'(l^p) = \omega,$$

$$l^d = f^{-1}(y),$$

$$u = y/y^p, \quad e = l^d/l,$$

$$\rho = y - \delta - \omega l^d, \quad \epsilon = \rho - (r - \hat{p}),$$

$$r_o = \rho_o + \bar{\pi},$$

which have to be inserted into the right-hand sides of the dynamics in order to obtain an autonomous system of 5 differential equations that is nonlinear in a natural or intrinsic way.

The interior steady state solution of the above dynamics is given by:

$$y_o = \frac{1}{1-c}[n+g-t]+\delta+t, \quad l_o^d = f^{-1}(y_o), \quad l_o = l_o^d/\bar{e}, \quad y_o^p = y_o/\bar{u},$$

$$l_o^p = f^{-1}(y_o^p),$$

$$\omega_o = f'(l_o^p), \quad \hat{p}_o = \pi_o^c = \bar{\pi}, \quad \rho_o = f(l_o^d)-\delta-\omega_o l_o^d, \quad r_o = \rho_o+\hat{p}_o,$$

$$\epsilon_o = \epsilon_o^m = 0.$$

Note that income distribution in the steady state is still determined by marginal productivity theory, since it does not yet play a role in aggregate demand in the steady state.

Despite formal similarities in the building blocks of the New Keynesian AS–AD dynamics and the above matured Keynesian DAS–AD dynamics, the resulting reduced form laws of motion, see Section 6.3, have not much in common in their structure and nothing in common in the applied solution strategies. The New Keynesian model has four forward-looking variables and thus demands for its determinacy four unstable roots, while our approach only exhibits myopic perfect foresight of a crossover type and thus allows again, with respect to its all variables, for predeterminacy and for stability results as in the preceding section and as shown in the mathematical appendix of this book.

We note in this regard that there are many items that reappear in various equations, implying that stability analysis can exploit a variety of linear dependencies in the calculation of the conditions for local asymptotic stability. Using such linear dependencies and the knowledge we have about the feedback structure of the dynamics we can then show the following proposition:

Proposition 4 Assume that the parameters $\beta_{pu}, \beta_{p\omega}$ in the price PC are not chosen too large and that the parameters κ_p, β_{pm} and i, γ_r are chosen sufficiently small. Then: the interior steady state of the above 5D dynamical system is locally asymptotically stable.

Proof See Asada, Chen, Chiarella and Flaschel (2006).

We thus see that the assumption about the price PC, the Mundell effect, the degree of interest rate smoothing and the speed with respect to which investment is adjusted to profitability changes can be decisive for the stability of the dynamics. However, this is only one set of sufficient stability conditions for the considered dynamics, which and not all a necessary selection yet. Further combination of the working of destabilizing Mundell-effects, Rose real-wage effects and the strength the inflation targeting process may be found that ensure stability, yet relevant parameter choices can also be found where the dynamics are not viable without the addition of extra behavioral nonlinearities, a topic that is considered in the next section by means of numerical simulations of the dynamics (in the case of an LM-curve as well of a Taylor interest rate rule).

6.6 On the role of downward money-wage rigidities

Let us now turn to some numerical simulations of our matured Keynesian analysis of the working of the wage–price spiral. In Figure 6.2 we show the maximum real parts of eigenvalues as functions of the crucial adjustment speeds of prices and wages with respect to the demand pressure on their corresponding markets. We see from these graphs that increasing wage flexibility is initially

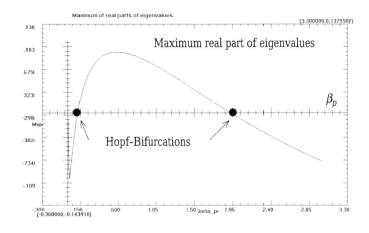

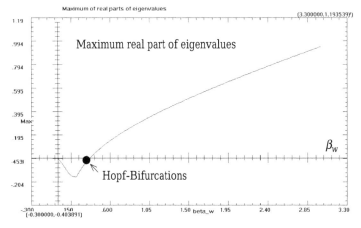

Figure 6.2 Loss of stability and reestablishment of stability by way of Hopf-bifurcations.

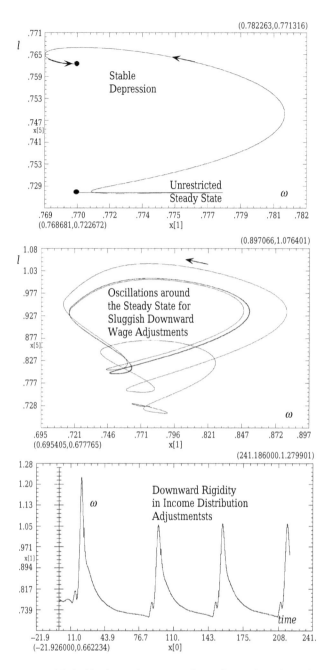

Figure 6.3 Stable depressions or persistent fluctuations through downwardly rigid money wages (phase length approximately sixty years).[15]

15 The parameter set used was: $\omega(0) = 0.770$, $m(0) = 9.088$, $\epsilon^m(0) = 0$, $\ell(0) = 0.727$, $\pi^c(0) = 0$, $\beta_\omega = 0.5$, $\beta_p = 0.5$, $\beta_{\pi^c} = 0.32$, $\beta_{\epsilon^m} = 0.3$, $\alpha = 0.3$, $\kappa_w = 0.5$, $\kappa_p = 0.5$, $s_c = 0.2$, $t^n = 0.25$, $\delta = 0.05$, $n = 0.05$, $g = 0.3$, $\bar{u} = 1.0$, $\bar{e} = 1.0$, $h_1 = 0.1$, $h_2 = 0.1$, $i = 0.25$, *wage-floor* $= 0.0$, $w_{shock} = 1.01$.

stabilizing and increasing price flexibility destabilizing (as expected from our partial consideration of the real wage channel). However fairly soon the role played by these parameters becomes reversed, approaching thereafter in fact a second Hopf-bifurcation point in each case. Thus, sooner or later, the partial insights gained from our consideration of Rose-effects are overturned and further wage flexibility and price flexibility then start to do just the opposite of what these partial arguments would suggest. This shows that a 5D dynamical system (and the numerous local asymptotic stability conditions it exhibits) can be much more complicated than is suggested by partial formal or even verbal economic reasoning.

Starting from this observation, we now consider situations where the loss of stability has become a total one, giving rise to economic fluctuations, the amplitude of which increases without bound. From the perspective of previous work of ours[16]– and the reversal in the stability features just observed – we expect that complete or partial downward rigidity of money wages may be the cure in such a situation, in line with what has been suggested already by Keynes (1936), since wage adjustment is then destabilizing, while price adjustment is not. We thus now consider situations where money wages can fall at most with the rate $f \leq 0$, which alters our WPC in an obvious way, leading to a kink in it if the floor f is reached. Figure 6.3 provides a typical outcome of the dynamics if downwardly rigid money wages are added to an explosive situation where the economy is not at all a viable one and in fact subject to immediate breakdown without such rigidity.

If the money wage Phillips curve is augmented by the assumption that money wages can rise as described, but cannot fall at all, we get a situation of a continuum of steady states (for money supply growth equal to natural growth $\hat{M} = n$ and thus no steady state inflation). This is due to the zero root hysteresis that then occurs, and the thereby implied strong result that the economy will then converge rapidly to the situation of a stable depression where wages become stationary. This stable depression depends in its depth on the initial shock the economy was subject to and is indeed a persistent one, since money wages do not fall (whereby on the one hand economic breakdown is avoided, at the cost of more or less massive underemployment on the other hand). If, by contrast, money wages can fall, but will do so at most at the rate of for example −0.01, the steady state instead remains uniquely determined (as shown in this chapter) and – though surrounded by strongly explosive forces – it is not totally unstable, due to the limit cycle situation that is then generated by the operation of the floor to the speed of money wage declines. This type of floor makes depressions much longer than recoveries, but avoids the situation where the economy can be trapped in a stable depression as in the case of complete downward rigidity of money wages. The two situations just discussed are illustrated by the Figure 6.3 in the real wage and labor intensity phase subspace of the full 5D dynamics. In this figure, the

16 See e.g. Chiarella and Flaschel (2000).

latter situation is also augmented by a time series plot for the real wage with its characteristic asymmetry between booms and depressions, with a total phase length of around sixty years of the generated income distribution dynamics. This is in broad agreement with observed empirical phase plots of this sort, for example, for the U.S. economy, see Chen, Chiarella, Flaschel and Hung (2006). Money supply policy rules can dampen the fluctuations shown, but are in general too weak to allow for a disappearance of such endogenously generated and very persistent business cycles in the private sector.

Note that the employment rate of an economy is inversely related to the fluctuations in the full-employment labor intensity ratio l that is shown in Figure 6.3. A high value of l therefore signifies a low employment rate and thus the situation of a long-lasting depression from where the economy is slowly recovering. Normal employment, by contrast, is given when the state variable l exhibits a low value and is accompanied by the instability the economy is subject to if the kink in the money wage PC is not in operation. The economy is then in a very volatile state, which is, however, moving into a new depression the more the kink in the money wage PC comes into operation again. The working of the kink is clearly shown in the bottom figure of Figures 6.3 where we have only sluggishly falling real wages until a new recovery phase sets in.

It is one important implication of such a downward floor to the speed of money wage declines that it can easily generate complex dynamics from the mathematical point of view. This is due to the fact that the economy is hitting the kink often in slightly distinct situations after each unstable recovery and thus works each time through the depression phase in a different way, leading to a clearly distinguishable upswing thereafter. Such a situation is exemplified in Figure 6.4 where the irregularity of the fluctuations in the real wage ω is shown over a time horizon of four thousand years in the top figure. In the bottom figure, we in addition show the projection of the cycle into the $\omega - l$ phase plane. One can see there the small corridor through which the dynamics are squeezed on the left-hand side for low real wages and the in principle explosive fluctuations that are generated thereafter, but kept under control again and in an increasing manner through the kink in the money wage PC.

An indication of the range of complex behavior can be obtained by considering bifurcation diagrams (showing the local maxima and minima of a state variable as one parameter of the model is increased along the horizontal axis). In Figure 6.5, we show such a diagram for ω with respect to the savings rate $s(= 1 - c)$. As s increases the bifurcation diagram indicates that two-cycles for ω give way to periods of complex behavior interspersed with period of high order cycles. Of course, average savings ratios above 25 percent are not too likely from the economic point of view, so that the economic range for the savings parameter is significantly smaller than the one shown in Figure 6.5. Visible is, however, that higher savings ratios increase the tension in our model economy. This also holds true for the case of an interest rate policy, as shown in Figure 6.6, where we in fact would get convergence for saving rates below $s = 0.03$ percent solely.

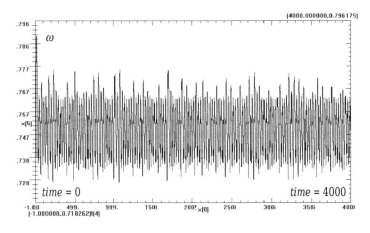

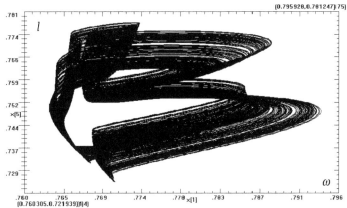

Figure 6.4 Mathematically complex dynamics with basically economically similar long-term fluctuations in growth and income distribution[17].

In Figure 6.6,[18] we instead show for a higher savings rate period doubling situations (top-left and bottom-left) that can be reduced to simple limit cycles (top-right) by increasing the strength of the reaction of the Central Bank with respect to the inflation gap. Yet, due to the fast adjustment of the inflationary

17 The parameter set used was: $\omega(0) = 0.770$, $m(0) = 9.088$, $\epsilon^m(0) = 0$, $\ell(0) = 0.727$, $\pi^c(0) = 0$, $\beta_\omega = 0.2$, $\beta_p = 0.5$, $\beta_{\pi^c} = 1.1$, $\beta_{\epsilon^m} = 0.3$, $\alpha = 0.3$, $\kappa_w = 0.7$, $\kappa_p = 0.3$, $s_c = 0.2$, $t^n = 0.25$, $\delta = 0.05$, $n = 0.05$, $g = 0.3$, $\bar{u} = 1.0$, $\bar{e} = 1.0$, $h_1 = 0.1$, $h_2 = 0.1$, $i = 1$, *wage-floor* $= -0.0049$, $w_{shock} = 1.01$.
18 The parameter set here is: $\beta_w = 0.2$, $\beta_p = 0.1$, $\beta_{pi^m} = 0.72$, $\beta_{\epsilon^m} = 0.8$, $\gamma_{rr} = 0.1$, $\gamma_{rp} = 0.7$, $\gamma_{ru} = 0.1$, $\alpha = 0.3$, $\kappa_w = 0.5$, $\kappa_p = 0.5$, $s = 0.1$, $t^n = 0.3$, $\delta = 0.05$, $n = 0.05$, $g = 0.3$, $\bar{u} = 1.0$, $\bar{e} = 1.0$, $\bar{\pi} = 0$, $i = 0.2$.

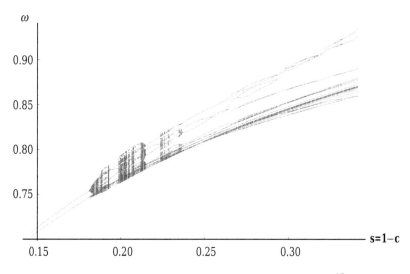

Figure 6.5 Mathematically complex dynamics: Bifurcation diagram.[17]

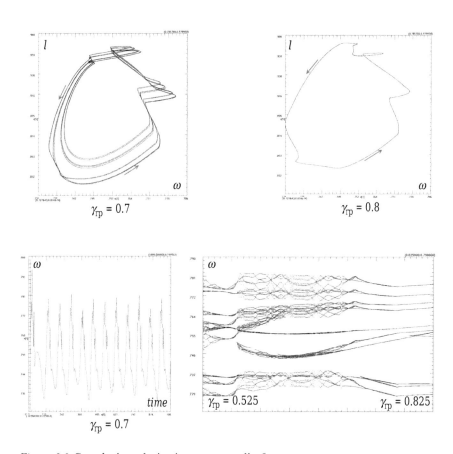

Figure 6.6 Complexity reducing interest rate policy?

climate with respect to current inflation rates that is here assumed, not much more can be achieved by monetary policy in the considered case. Figure 6.6, bottom-right shows in this respect again a bifurcation diagram which indicates complex types of limit cycle behavior for parameter values γ_{rp} below 0.7, but thereafter the establishment of simpler limit cycles which cannot made simpler, however, or even turned into convergent dynamics as the parameter γ_{rp} is further increased, even when increased much beyond 0.825 (not shown in this figure). Monetary policy may reduce dynamic complexity to a certain degree, but may be incapable to turn persistent business fluctuations generated in the private sector of the economy into damped oscillations.

Underlying Figure 6.6 is a floor parameter $f = 0.02$, i.e. wage inflation cannot even be reduced below two percent. In addition, we, however, here assume that wages regain their assumed flexibility if the rate of employment falls below 80 percent. Without this latter assumption cycles would be much larger than shown in Figure 6.6, i.e, here we have a case where a return to wage flexibility in deep depressions improves the stability of the dynamics, though the floor to money wage inflation in between is indeed of help, since its removal would lead to explosive business fluctuations. A wage Phillips curve with three regimes (two regime changes) as investigated empirically in Filardo (1998) may therefore be better than one with only two in a situation where partial Rose effects indicate that wage flexibility is stabilizing while price flexibility is not.

6.7 Conclusion

In this chapter, we have been able to generate damped business fluctuations, persistent oscillations or even complex dynamics from a matured, but conventional synthesis of Keynesian AS–AD dynamics with an advanced description of its wage–price module as a wage–price spiral, when in addition simple (plausible) regime changes in the money wage Phillips curve are taken into account. There are thus no fancy nonlinearities necessary in a by and large conventional type of AS–AD disequilibrium dynamics in order to obtain interesting dynamic outcomes. Some further stability may be achieved through monetary policy to a certain degree. However, the cycle generating mechanisms in the private sector are often too strong to be overcome completely by the mechanisms analyzed in this chapter. This is so since in a situation of possibly fairly explosive dynamics the downward money wage rigidity provides a stabilizing influence on the dangers for economic breakdown arising from inflationary or deflationary spirals and their implications, but not on other broader destabilizing tendencies.

We stress that we have achieved viable or bounded dynamics through behavioral assumptions that concern the private sector and not – as in the New Keynesian approach of Section 6.3 – only by way of an interest rate policy of the Central Bank that is sufficiently advanced and active such that all roots of the Jacobian of the dynamics become unstable. In the latter case, boundedness comes about by assumption in a totally unstable linear(ized) environment and not by changes in agents' behavior when the economy departs too much from the steady state.

References

Asada, T., C. Chiarella, P. Flaschel and R. Franke (2003): *Open Economy Macrodynamics: An Integrated Disequilibrium Approach.* Heidelberg: Springer.

Asada, T., P. Chen, C. Chiarella, and P. Flaschel (2006): Keynesian dynamics and the wage-price spiral: A baseline disequilibrium model. *Journal of Macroeconomics*, 28, 90–130

Barro, X. (1994): The aggregate supply/aggregate demand model. *Eastern Economic Journal*, 20, 1–6.

Blanchard, O. and X. Katz (1999): Wage dynamics: Reconciling theory and evidence. *American Economic Review, Papers and Proceedings*, 89, 69–74.

Blanchard, O. (2006): *Macroeconomics.* London: Pearson Prentice Hall.

Chen, P. and P. Flaschel (2006): Measuring the interaction of wage and price Phillips curves for the U.S. economy. *Studies in Nonlinear Dynamics and Econometrics*, 10, 1–35.

Chen, P., C. Chiarella, P. Flaschel, and H. Hung (2006): Keynesian disequilibrium dynamics: Convergence, roads to instability and the emergence of complex business fluctuations. *UTS: School of Finance and Economics, working paper 46.*

Chen, P., C. Chiarella, P. Flaschel, and W. Semmler (2006): Keynesian Macrodynamics and the Phillips curve: An estimated baseline macro-model for the U.S. economy. In: C. Chiarella, P. Flaschel, R. Franke and W. Semmler (eds.): *Quantitative and Empirical Analysis of Non linear Dynamic Macromodels: Contributions to Economic Analysis.* Amsterdam: Elsevier, 229–284.

Chiarella, C., P. Flaschel, G. Groh, and W. Semmler (2003): AS–AD, KMG growth and beyond: A reply to Velupillai. *Journal of Economics*, 78, 96–104.

Chiarella, C. and P. Flaschel (2000): *The Dynamics of Keynesian Monetary Growth: Macro Foundations.* Cambridge, UK: Cambridge University Press.

Chiarella, C., P. Flaschel, and R. Franke (2005) *Foundations for a Disequilibrium Theory of the Business Cycle: Qualitative Analysis and Quantitative Assessment.* Cambridge, UK: Cambridge University Press.

Chiarella, C., P. Flaschel, G. Groh and W. Semmler (2000): *Disequilibrium, Growth and Labor Market Dynamics: Macro Perspectives.* Heidelberg: Springer.

Chiarella, C., P. Flaschel, G. Groh and W. Semmler (2003): AS-AD, KMG Growth and Beyond: A Reply to Velupillai. *Journal of Economics*, 78, 96–104.

Eller, J.W. and R.J. Gordon (2003): Nesting the new Keynesian Phillips curve within the mainstream model of U.S: Inflation Dynamics. *Paper presented at the CEPR Conference: The Phillips curve revisited.* Berlin: June 2003.

Filardo, A. (1998): New evidence on the output cost of fighting inflation. *Economic Review.* Kansas: Federal Bank of Kansas City, 33–61.

Flaschel, P. (2009): *The Macrodynamics of Capitalism: Elements for a Synthesis of Marx, Keynes and Schumpeter.* Heidelberg: Springer.

Flaschel, P. and H-M. Krolzig (2006): Wage-price Phillips curves and macroeconomic stability: Basic structural form, estimation and analysis. In: C. Chiarella, P. Flaschel, R. FrankeandW.Semmler (eds.): *Quantitative and Empirical Analysis of Nonlinear Dynamic Macromodels: Contributions to Economic Analysis.* Amsterdam: Elsevier, 7–47.

Flaschel, P., R. Franke, and W. Semmler (1997): *Dynamic Macroeconomics: Instability, Fluctuations and Growth in Monetary Economies.* Cambridge, MA: The MIT Press.

Flaschel, P., G. Kauermann, and W. Semmler (2007): Testing wage and price Phillips curves for the United States. *Metroeconomica*, 58, 550–581.

Galí, J., M. Gertler, and J.D. Lopez-Salido (2003): Robustness of the estimates of the hybrid new Keynesian Phillips curve. *Paper presented at the CEPR Conference: The Phillips curve revisited*. Berlin: June 2003.

Gandolfo, G. (1996): *Economic Dynamics*. Berlin: Springer.

Groth, C. (1993): Some unfamiliar dynamics of a familiar macromodel. *Journal of Economics*, 58, 293–305.

Keynes, J.M. (1936): *The General Theory of Employment, Interest and Money*. New York: Macmillan.

Mankiw, G. (2001): The inexorable and mysterious tradeoff between inflation and unemployment. *Economic Journal*, 111, 45–61.

Powell, A. and C. Murphy (1997): *Inside a Modern Macroeconometric Model: A Guide to the Murphy Model*. Heidelberg: Springer.

Rose, H. (1967): On the non-linear theory of the employment cycle. *Review of Economic Studies*, 34, 153–173.

Sargent, T. (1987): *Macroeconomic Theory*. New York: Academic Press.

Sargent, T. and N. Wallace (1973): The stability of models of money and growth with perfect foresight. *Econometrica*, 41, 1043–1048.

Solow, R. (1956): A contribution to the theory of economic growth. *The Quarterly Journal of Economics*, 70, 65–94.

Tobin, J. (1975): Keynesian models of recession and depression. *American Economic Review*, 65, 195–202.

Turnovsky, S. (1997): *Methods of Macroeconomic Dynamics*. Cambridge, MA: The MIT Press.

Velupillai, K. (2003): Book review. *Journal of Economics*, 78, 326–332.

Appendix I: Behavioral foundations

Wage dynamics: theoretical foundation

This subsection builds on the paper by Blanchard and Katz (1999) and briefly summarizes their theoretical motivation of a money-wage Phillips curve which is closely related to our dynamic equation in Section 6.3.[19] Blanchard and Katz assume – following the suggestions of standard models of wage setting – that real wage expectations of workers, $\omega^e = w_t - p_t^e$, are basically determined by the reservation wage, $\bar{\omega}_t$, current labor productivity, $y_t - l_t^d$, and the rate of unemployment, U_t^l:

$$\omega_t^e = \theta\bar{\omega}_t + (1-\theta)(y_t - l_t^d) - \beta_w U_t^l.$$

Expected real wages are thus a Cobb-Douglas average of the reservation wage and output per worker, but are departing from this normal level of expectations by the state of the demand pressure on the labor market. The reservation wage in turn is

---

19 In this section, lower case letters (including w and p) indicate logarithms.

determined as a Cobb-Douglas average of past real wages, $\omega_{t-1} = w_{t-1} - p_{t-1}$, and current labor productivity, augmented by a factor $a < 0$:

$$\bar{\omega}_t = a + \lambda \omega_{t-1} + (1 - \lambda)(y_t - l_t^d)$$

Inserting the second into the first equation results in

$$\omega_t^e = \theta a + \theta \lambda \omega_{t-1} + (1 - \theta \lambda)(y_t - l_t^d) - \beta_w U_t^l,$$

which gives after some rearrangements

$$\Delta w_t = p_t^e - p_{t-1} + \theta a - (1 - \theta \lambda)[(w_{t-1} - p_{t-1}) - (y_t - l_t^d)] - \beta_w U_t^l$$
$$= \Delta p_t^e + \theta a - (1 - \theta \lambda) u_{t-1} + (1 - \theta \lambda)(\Delta y_t - \Delta l_t^d) - \beta_w U_t^l$$

where Δp_t^e denotes the expected rate of inflation, u_{t-1} the past (log) wage share and $\Delta y_t - \Delta l_t^d$ the current growth rate of labor productivity. This is the growth law for nominal wages that flows from the theoretical models referred to in Blanchard and Katz (1999).

In this paper, we proposed to operationalize this theoretical approach to money-wage inflation by replacing the short-run cost push term Δp_t^e by the weighted average $\kappa_w \Delta p_t^e + (1 - \kappa_w)\pi_t$, where Δp_t^e is determined by myopic perfect foresight. Thus, temporary changes in the correctly anticipated rate of inflation do not have full impact on temporary wage inflation, which is also driven by lagged inflation rates via the inflationary climate variable π_t. Adding inertia to the theory of wage inflation introduced a distinction between the temporary and persistent cost effects to this equation. Furthermore we have that $\Delta y_t - \Delta l_t^d = n_x$ due to the assumed fixed proportions technology. Altogether, we end up with an equation for wage inflation of the type presented in Section 6.3, though now with a specific interpretation of the model's parameters from the perspective of efficiency wage or bargaining models.[20]

Price dynamics: theoretical foundation

We follow here again Blanchard and Katz (1999) and start from the assumption of normal cost pricing, here under the additional assumption of our paper of fixed proportions in production and Harrod neutral technological change. We therefore

---

20 Note that the parameter in front of u_{t-1} can now not be interpreted as a speed of adjustment coefficient. Note furthermore that Blanchard and Katz (1999) assume that, in the steady state, the wage share is determined by the firms' markup $u = -\mu$ (both in logs) to be discussed in the next subsection. Therefore, the NAIRU can be determined endogenously on the labor market by $\bar{U}^l = \beta_w^{-1}[\theta a - (1 - \theta \lambda)\bar{\mu} - \theta \lambda(\Delta y_t - \Delta l_t^d)]$. The NAIRU of their model therefore depends on both labor and goods market characteristics in contrast to the NAIRU levels for labor and capital employed in our approach.

consider as rule for normal prices

$$p_t = \mu_t + w_t + l_t^d - y_t, \quad \text{i.e.} \quad \Delta p_t = \Delta \mu_t + \Delta w_t - n_x,$$

where μ_t represents a markup on the unit wage costs of firms and where again myopic perfect foresight, here with respect to wage setting is assumed. We assume furthermore that the markup is variable and responding to the demand pressure in the market for goods $\bar{U}^c - U_t^c$, depending in addition negatively on the current level of the markup μ_t in its deviation from the normal level $\bar{\mu}$. Firms therefore depart from their normal cost pricing rule according to the state of demand on the market for goods, and this the stronger the lower the level of the currently prevailing markup has been (markup smoothing). For sake of concreteness let us here assume that the following behavioral relationship holds:

$$\Delta \mu_t = \beta_p(\bar{U}^c - U_{t-1}^c) + \gamma(\bar{\mu} - \mu_{t-1}),$$

where $\gamma > 0$. Inserted into the formula for price inflation this in sum gives:

$$\Delta p_t = \beta_p(\bar{U}^c - U_{t-1}^c) + \gamma(\bar{\mu} - \mu_{t-1}) + (\Delta w_t - n_x)$$

In terms of the logged wage share $u_t = -\mu_t$ we get

$$\Delta p_t = \beta_p(\bar{U}^c - U_{t-1}^c) + \gamma(u_{t-1} - \bar{u}) + (\Delta w_t - n_x).$$

As in the preceding subsection of the paper, we again add persistence the cost pressure term $\Delta w_t - n_x$ now in the price Phillips curve in the form of the inflationary climate expression π and thereby obtain in sum the equation of Section 6.3.

Appendix II: Proof to Section 6.6

In this appendix, we provide the stability proof for the case where the LM-curve is replaced by an interest rate policy rule and thus moved to the background of the model. For the convenience of the reader, we first provide a short summary of the model before we start our stability investigation.

The model

The static relationships supplementing the laws of motion introduced in Section 6.6 and their partial derivatives are reformulated for the subsequent proof as follows:

$$y = \frac{1}{1-c}[i_1 \epsilon^c + n + g - t] + \delta + t = y(\epsilon^c); \quad y_{\epsilon^c} = dy/d\epsilon^c = \frac{1}{1-c}i_1 > 0,$$

$$(6.26)$$

$$y^p = f((f')^{-1}(\exp\theta)) = y^p(\theta); \quad y_\theta^p = dy^p/d\theta = (f'(l^p)/f''(l^p))(\exp\theta) < 0,$$

$$(6.27)$$

$$l^d = f^{-1}(y(\epsilon^c)) = l^d(\epsilon^c); \quad l^d_{\epsilon^c} = dl^d/d\epsilon^c = y_{\epsilon^c}/f' > 0, \tag{6.28}$$

$$u = y(\epsilon^c)/y^p(\theta) = u(\epsilon^c, \theta); \quad u_{\epsilon^c} = \partial u/\partial \epsilon^c = y_{\epsilon^c}/y^p > 0,$$

$$u_\theta = \partial u/\partial \theta = -yy^p_\theta/(y^p)^2 > 0, \tag{6.29}$$

$$e = l^d(\epsilon^c)/l = e(\epsilon^c, l); \quad e_{\epsilon^c} = \partial e/\partial \epsilon^c = l^d_{\epsilon^c}/l > 0,$$

$$e_l = \partial e/\partial l = -l^d/l^2 < 0, \tag{6.30}$$

$$r = y - \delta - \omega l^d = y(\epsilon^c) - \delta - (\exp\theta)l^d(\epsilon^c) = r(\epsilon^c, \theta);$$

$$r_{\epsilon^c} = \partial r/\partial \epsilon^c = \{1 - (\exp\theta)/f'(l^d)\}y_{\epsilon^c} = \{1 - f'(l^p)/f'(l^d)\}y_{\epsilon^c} > 0 \text{ if } l^d < l^p,$$

$$r_\theta = \partial r/\partial \theta = -(\exp\theta)l^d < 0, \tag{6.31}$$

$$i^0 = r^0 + \bar{\pi}, \tag{6.32}$$

$$\hat{p} = \frac{1}{1 - \kappa_w \kappa_p}[\beta_{pu}\{u(\epsilon^c, \theta) - \bar{u}\} + \beta_{p\omega}(\theta - \theta^0) + \kappa_p\{\beta_{we}(e(\epsilon^c, l) - \bar{e})$$

$$- \beta_{w\omega}(\theta - \theta^0)\}] + \pi^c = f(\theta, \epsilon^c, l) + \pi^c,$$

$$f_\theta = \partial f/\partial \theta = \frac{1}{1 - \kappa_w \kappa_p}(\beta_{pu}u_\theta + \beta_{p\omega} - \kappa_p\beta_{w\omega})$$

$$f_{\epsilon^c} = \partial f/\partial \epsilon^c = \frac{1}{1 - \kappa_w \kappa_p}(\beta_{pu}u_{\epsilon^c} + \kappa_p\beta_{we}e_{\epsilon^c}) > 0,$$

$$f_l = \partial f/\partial l = \frac{1}{1 - \kappa_w \kappa_p}\kappa_p\beta_{we}e_l < 0 \tag{6.33}$$

because of the inequalities $0 < \kappa_w < 1$ and $0 < \kappa_p < 1$.
    In this case, we have

$$\epsilon = r - (i - \hat{p}) = r(\epsilon^c, \theta) - i + f(\theta, \epsilon^c, l) + \pi^c = \epsilon(\theta, i, \epsilon^c, l, \pi^c)$$

$$\epsilon_\theta = \partial\epsilon/\partial\theta = \underset{(-)}{r_\theta} + \underset{(?)}{f_\theta}, \quad \epsilon_i = \partial\epsilon/\partial i = -1 < 0, \quad \epsilon_{\epsilon^c} = \partial\epsilon/\partial\epsilon^c = r_{\epsilon^c} + f_{\epsilon^c} > 0$$

$$\epsilon_l = \partial\epsilon/\partial l = f_l < 0, \quad \epsilon_{\pi^c} = \partial\epsilon/\partial\pi^c = 1 > 0. \tag{6.34}$$

We will make the following two assumptions in the derivation of the propositions of this appendix:

Assumption 1   The parameters β_{pu} and $\beta_{p\omega}$ are not extremely large so that we can have $\epsilon_\theta = r_\theta + f_\theta < 0$. Substituting the foregoing static relationships into the dynamic equations of Section 6.6, we have the following five-dimensional system of nonlinear differential equations.

(i) $\quad \dot{\theta} \;=\; \frac{1}{1-\kappa_w\kappa_p}[(1-\kappa_p)\{\beta_{we}(e(\epsilon^c,l)-\bar{e})-\beta_{w\omega}(\theta-\theta^0)\}$
$\qquad\qquad -(1-\kappa_w)\{\beta_{pu}(u(\epsilon^c,\theta)-\bar{u})+\beta_{w\omega}(\theta-\theta^0)\}] = F_1(\theta,\epsilon^c,l),$

(ii) $\quad \dot{i} \;=\; -\gamma_i(i-i^0)+\gamma_p\{f(\theta,\epsilon^c,l)+\pi^c-\bar{\pi}\}+\gamma_u\{u(\epsilon^c,\theta)-\bar{u}\}$
$\qquad\quad = F_2(\theta,i,\epsilon^c,l,\pi^c),$

(iii) $\quad \dot{\epsilon}^c = \beta_{\epsilon^c}\{\epsilon(\theta,i,\epsilon^c,l,\pi^c)-\epsilon^c\} = F_3(\theta,i,\epsilon^c,l,\pi^c),$

(iv) $\quad \dot{l} \;=\; -i_1\epsilon^c l = F_4(\epsilon^c,l),$

(v) $\quad \dot{\pi}^c = \beta_{\pi^c}f(\theta,\epsilon^c,l) = F_5(\theta,\epsilon^c,l).$

$$(6.35)$$

The equilibrium solution of this system is given in Section 6.6. We assume that

Assumption 2 At the equilibrium point, we have $l^d < l^p$ so that $r_{\epsilon^c} > 0$ holds true.

Five-dimensional analysis of local stability

Now, let us investigate the local stability/instability of the equilibrium point of the system (6.35). We can write the Jacobian matrix of this system *at the equilibrium point* as follows

$$J = \begin{bmatrix} F_{11} & 0 & F_{13} & F_{14} & 0 \\ F_{21} & -\gamma_i & F_{23} & F_{24} & \gamma_p \\ \beta_{\epsilon^c}(r_\theta+f_\theta) & -\beta_{\epsilon^c} & -\beta_{\epsilon^c}(1-r_{\epsilon^c}-f_{\epsilon^c}) & \beta_{\epsilon^c}f_l & \beta_{\epsilon^c} \\ 0 & 0 & -i_1l^0 & 0 & 0 \\ \beta_{\pi^c}f_\theta & 0 & \beta_{\pi^c}f_{\epsilon^c} & \beta_{\pi^c}f_l & 0 \end{bmatrix}, \quad (6.36)$$

where

$$F_{11} = \frac{-1}{1-\kappa_w\kappa_p}[\underset{(+)}{(2-\kappa_p-\kappa_w)\beta_{w\omega}}+(1-\kappa_w)\beta_{pu}\,u_\theta] < 0,$$

$$F_{13} = \frac{1}{1-\kappa_w\kappa_p}[\underset{(+)}{(1-\kappa_p)\beta_{we}\,u_{\epsilon^c}}-\underset{(+)}{(1-\kappa_w)\beta_{pu}\,u_{\epsilon^c}}],$$

$$F_{14} = \frac{1}{1-\kappa_w\kappa_p}[\underset{(-)}{(1-\kappa_p)\beta_{we}\,e_l}] < 0,$$

$$F_{21} = \underset{(?)}{\gamma_p f_\theta}+\underset{(+)}{\gamma_u\,u_\theta},$$

$$F_{23} = \underset{(+)}{\gamma_p f_{\epsilon^c}}+\underset{(+)}{\gamma_u\,u_{\epsilon^c}} > 0,$$

$$F_{24} = \underset{(-)}{\gamma_p\,f_l} < 0.$$

The sign pattern of the matrix J becomes as follows

$$sign\, J = \begin{bmatrix} -\ 0 & ? & -\ 0 \\ ? & -\ + & -\ + \\ -\ - & ? & -\ + \\ 0\ 0 & - & 0\ 0 \\ ?\ 0 & + & -\ 0 \end{bmatrix}. \tag{6.37}$$

The characteristic equation of this system can be written as

$$\Gamma(\lambda) = \lambda^5 + a_1\lambda^4 + a_2\lambda^3 + a_3\lambda^2 + a_4\lambda + a_5 = 0, \tag{6.38}$$

where coefficients $a_i, i = 1, \ldots, 5$ are given as follows.

$$a_1 = -traceJ = \underset{(-)}{-F_{11}+\gamma_i} + \underset{(+)}{\beta_{\epsilon^c}}(1-\underset{(+)}{r_{\epsilon^c}} - f_{\epsilon^c}) = a_1(\beta_{\epsilon^c}), \tag{6.39}$$

$a_2 = $ sum of all principal second-order minors of J

$$= \begin{vmatrix} F_{11} & 0 \\ F_{21} & -\gamma_i \end{vmatrix} + \beta_{\epsilon^c}\begin{vmatrix} F_{11} & F_{13} \\ r_\theta + f_\theta & -(1-r_{\epsilon^c}-f_{\epsilon^c}) \end{vmatrix} + \begin{vmatrix} F_{11} & F_{14} \\ 0 & 0 \end{vmatrix} + \begin{vmatrix} F_{11} & 0 \\ \beta_{\pi^c}f_\theta & 0 \end{vmatrix}$$

$$+ \beta_{\epsilon^c}\begin{vmatrix} -\gamma_i & F_{23} \\ -1 & r_{\epsilon^c}+f_{\epsilon^c}-1 \end{vmatrix} + \begin{vmatrix} -\gamma_i & F_{24} \\ 0 & 0 \end{vmatrix} + \begin{vmatrix} -\gamma_i & \gamma_p \\ 0 & 0 \end{vmatrix}$$

$$+ \beta_{\epsilon^c}\begin{vmatrix} -(1-r_{\epsilon^c}-f_{\epsilon^c})\, f_l & \\ -i_1 l^0 & 0 \end{vmatrix} + \beta_{\epsilon^c}\beta_{\pi^c}\begin{vmatrix} -(1-r_{\epsilon^c}-f_{\epsilon^c}) & 1 \\ f_{\epsilon^c} & 0 \end{vmatrix} + \begin{vmatrix} 0 & 0 \\ \beta_{\pi^c}f_l & 0 \end{vmatrix},$$

$$= \underset{(-)}{-F_{11}\gamma_i} + \beta_{\epsilon^c}\{\underset{(-)}{-F_{11}(1-r_{\epsilon^c}-f_{\epsilon^c})} - \underset{(?)}{F_{13}(r_\theta+f_\theta)} + \underset{(-)}{\gamma_i(1-r_{\epsilon^c}-f_{\epsilon^c})} + \underset{(+)}{F_{23}}$$

$$+ \underset{(-)}{i_1 l^0 f_l} - \underset{(+)}{\beta_{\pi^c}f_{\epsilon^c}}\} = a_2(\beta_{\epsilon^c}, \beta_{\pi^c}). \tag{6.40}$$

$a_3 = -($sum of all principal third-order minors of J),

$$= -\beta_{\epsilon^c}\begin{vmatrix} F_{11} & 0 & F_{13} \\ F_{21} & -\gamma_i & F_{23} \\ r_\theta+f_\theta & -1 & -(1-r_{\epsilon^c}-f_{\epsilon^c}) \end{vmatrix} - \begin{vmatrix} F_{11} & 0 & F_{14} \\ F_{21} & -\gamma_i & F_{24} \\ 0 & 0 & 0 \end{vmatrix} - \begin{vmatrix} F_{11} & 0 & 0 \\ F_{21} & -\gamma_i & \gamma_p \\ \beta_{\pi^c}f_\theta & 0 & 0 \end{vmatrix}$$

$$- \beta_{\epsilon^c}\begin{vmatrix} F_{11} & F_{13} & F_{14} \\ r_\theta+f_\theta & -(1-r_{\epsilon^c}-f_{\epsilon^c}) & f_l \\ 0 & -i_1 l^0 & 0 \end{vmatrix} - \beta_{\epsilon^c}\beta_{\pi^c}\begin{vmatrix} F_{11} & F_{13} & 0 \\ r_\theta+f_\theta & -(1-r_{\epsilon^c}-f_{\epsilon^c}) & 1 \\ f_\theta & f_{\epsilon^c} & 0 \end{vmatrix}$$

$$- \begin{vmatrix} F_{11} & F_{14} & 0 \\ 0 & 0 & 0 \\ \beta_{\pi^c}f_\theta & \beta_{\pi^c}f_l & 0 \end{vmatrix} - \beta_{\epsilon^c}\begin{vmatrix} -\gamma_i & F_{23} & F_{24} \\ -1 & -(1-r_{\epsilon^c}-f_{\epsilon^c}) & f_l \\ 0 & -i_1 l^0 & 0 \end{vmatrix}$$

$$-\beta_{\epsilon^c}\beta_{\pi^c}\begin{vmatrix} -\gamma_i & F_{23} & \gamma_p \\ -1 & -(1-r_{\epsilon^c}-f_{\epsilon^c}) & 1 \\ 0 & f_{\epsilon^c} & 0 \end{vmatrix} - \begin{vmatrix} -\gamma_i & F_{24} & \gamma_p \\ 0 & 0 & 0 \\ 0 & \beta_{\pi^c}f_l & 0 \end{vmatrix}$$

$$-\beta_{\epsilon^c}\beta_{\pi^c}\begin{vmatrix} -(1-r_{\epsilon^c}-f_{\epsilon^c})f_l & 1 \\ -i_1 l^0 & 0 & 0 \\ f_{\epsilon^c} & f_l & 0 \end{vmatrix}$$

$$= \beta_{\epsilon^c}[-F_{11}\,\gamma_i(1-r_{\epsilon^c}-f_{\epsilon^c})+F_{13}F_{21}-F_{13}\,\gamma_i(r_\theta+f_\theta) \qquad (6.41)$$
$$\phantom{= \beta_{\epsilon^c}[}_{(-)} \phantom{F_{11}\,\gamma_i(1-r_{\epsilon^c}-f_{\epsilon^c})}_{(?)\ \ (?)} \phantom{F_{13}F_{21}}_{(?)} \phantom{-F_{13}\,\gamma_i(r_\theta}_{(-)}$$

$$- F_{11}F_{23}+F_{14}\,i_1 l^0(r_\theta+f_\theta)-F_{11}\,i_1 l^0\,f_l - F_{24}\,i_1 l^0 + \gamma_i i_1 l^0\,f_l$$
$$_{(-)\ (+)} \phantom{F_{14}\,i_1 l^0}_{(-)} _{(-)} \phantom{-F_{11}\,i_1 l^0\,f_l}_{(-)} \phantom{-F_{24}\,i_1 l^0}_{(-)\ (-)} _{(-)}$$

$$+ \beta_{\pi^c}\{-F_{13}\,f_\theta +F_{11}f_{\epsilon^c}+\gamma_p f_{\epsilon^c}-\gamma_i f_{\epsilon^c}+f_l\,i_1 l^0\}] = a_3(\beta_{\epsilon^c},\beta_{\pi^c})$$
$$\phantom{+ \beta_{\pi^c}\{}_{(?)\ (+)} \phantom{-F_{13}\,f_\theta}_{(-)\ (+)} \phantom{+F_{11}f_{\epsilon^c}+\gamma_p f_{\epsilon^c}}_{(+)} \phantom{-\gamma_i f_{\epsilon^c}}_{(+)\ (-)}$$

a_4 = sum of all fourth-order minors of J

$$= \beta_{\epsilon^c}\beta_{\pi^c}i_1 l^0 \left\{ \begin{vmatrix} -\gamma_i & F_{23} & F_{24} & \gamma_p \\ -1 & -(1-r_{\epsilon^c}-f_{\epsilon^c}) & f_l & 1 \\ 0 & -1 & 0 & 0 \\ 0 & f_{\epsilon^c} & f_l & 0 \end{vmatrix} \right.$$

$$+ \begin{vmatrix} F_{11} & F_{13} & F_{14} & 0 \\ r_\theta+f_\theta & -(1-r_{\epsilon^c}-f_{\epsilon^c}) & f_l & 1 \\ 0 & -1 & 0 & 0 \\ f_\theta & f_{\epsilon^c} & f_l & 0 \end{vmatrix} + (1/i_1 l^0)\begin{vmatrix} F_{11} & 0 & F_{13} & 0 \\ F_{21} & -\gamma_i & F_{23} & \gamma_p \\ r_\theta+f_\theta & -1 & -(1-r_{\epsilon^c}-f_{\epsilon^c}) & 1 \\ f_\theta & 0 & f_{\epsilon^c} & 0 \end{vmatrix}$$

$$+ \begin{vmatrix} F_{11} & 0 & F_{13} & F_{14} \\ F_{21} & -\gamma_i & F_{23} & \gamma_p \\ r_\theta+f_\theta & -1 & -(1-r_{\epsilon^c}-f_{\epsilon^c}) & f_l \\ 0 & 0 & -1 & 0 \end{vmatrix} \right\}$$

$$= \beta_{\epsilon^c}\beta_{\pi^c}i_1 l^0 \left\{ \begin{vmatrix} -\gamma_i & F_{24} & \gamma_p \\ -1 & f_l & 1 \\ 0 & f_l & 0 \end{vmatrix} + \begin{vmatrix} F_{11} & F_{13} & F_{14} \\ 0 & -1 & 0 \\ f_\theta & f_{\epsilon^c} & f_l \end{vmatrix} \right.$$

$$+ (1/i_1 l^0)F_{11}\begin{vmatrix} -\gamma_i & F_{23} & \gamma_p \\ -1 & 1-r_{\epsilon^c}-f_{\epsilon^c} & 1 \\ 0 & f_{\epsilon^c} & 0 \end{vmatrix}$$

$$+ (1/i_1 l^0)F_{13}\begin{vmatrix} F_{21} & -\gamma_i & \gamma_p \\ r_\theta+f_\theta & -1 & 1 \\ f_\theta & 0 & 0 \end{vmatrix} + \begin{vmatrix} F_{11} & 0 & F_{14} \\ F_{21} & -\gamma_i & \gamma_p \\ r_\theta+f_\theta & -1 & f_l \end{vmatrix} \right\}$$

$$= \beta_{\epsilon^c}\beta_{\pi^c}i_1 l^0\{-f_l(\gamma_p-\gamma_i)-F_{11}f_l+F_{14}f_\theta-(1/i_1 l^0)F_{11}f_{\epsilon^c}(\gamma_p-\gamma_i)$$

$$+(1/i_1 l^0)F_{13}f_\theta(\gamma_p - \gamma_i) - F_{11}\gamma_i f_l - F_{14}F_{21} + F_{14}\gamma_i(r_\theta + f_\theta) + F_{11}\gamma_p\}$$

$$= \beta_{\epsilon^c}\beta_{\pi^c}i_1 l^0[-\underset{(-)}{f_l}\{\underset{(-)}{(\gamma_p - \gamma_i)} + F_{11}(1+\gamma_i)\} + F_{14}\{\underset{(-)}{-F_{21}} + \underset{(?)}{r_\theta}\underset{(-)}{\gamma_i} + (1+\gamma_i)\underset{(?)}{f_\theta}\}$$

$$+ \{\underset{(-)}{-F_{11}(f_{\epsilon^c}/i_1 l^0)} + \underset{(+)}{(F_{13}/i_1 l^0)}\underset{(?)}{f_\theta}\underset{(?)}{}\}(\gamma_p - \gamma_i) + \underset{(-)}{F_{11}\gamma_p}] = a_4(\beta_{\epsilon^c}, \beta_{\pi^c}). \qquad (6.42)$$

$$a_5 = -\det J = -\beta_{\epsilon^c}\beta_{\pi^c}i_1 l^0 \begin{vmatrix} F_{11} & 0 & F_{13} & F_{14} & 0 \\ F_{21} & -\gamma_i & F_{23} & F_{24} & \gamma_p \\ r_\theta + f_\theta & -1 & -(1-r_{\epsilon^c}-f_{\epsilon^c}) & f_l & 1 \\ 0 & 0 & -1 & 0 & 0 \\ f_\theta & 0 & f_{\epsilon^c} & f_l & 0 \end{vmatrix}$$

$$= -\beta_{\epsilon^c}\beta_{\pi^c}i_1 l^0 \begin{vmatrix} F_{11} & 0 & F_{14} & 0 \\ F_{21} & -\gamma_i & F_{24} & \gamma_p \\ r_\theta + f_\theta & -1 & f_l & 1 \\ f_\theta & 0 & f_l & 0 \end{vmatrix}$$

$$= \beta_{\epsilon^c}\beta_{\pi^c}i_1 l^0 \left\{ -F_{11} \begin{vmatrix} -\gamma_i & F_{24} & \gamma_p \\ -1 & f_l & 1 \\ 0 & f_l & 0 \end{vmatrix} - F_{14} \begin{vmatrix} F_{21} & -\gamma_i & \gamma_p \\ r_\theta + f_\theta & -1 & 1 \\ f_\theta & 0 & 0 \end{vmatrix} \right\}$$

$$= \beta_{\epsilon^c}\beta_{\pi^c}i_1 l^0 (\underset{(-)}{F_{11}}\underset{(-)}{f_l} - \underset{(-)}{F_{14}}\underset{(?)}{f_\theta})(\gamma_p - \gamma_i) = a_5(\beta_{\epsilon^c}, \beta_{\pi^c}). \qquad (6.43)$$

Routh-Hurwitz conditions

We can define the Routh-Hurwitz terms Δ_j $(j = 1, 2, \cdots, 5)$ as follows

(i) $\quad \Delta_1 \; = a_1 = a_1(\beta_{\epsilon^c}),$

(ii) $\quad \Delta_2 \; = \begin{vmatrix} a_1 & a_3 \\ 1 & a_2 \end{vmatrix} = a_1 a_2 - a_3 = \Delta_2(\beta_{\epsilon^c}, \beta_{\pi^c}),$

(iii) $\quad \Delta_3 = \begin{vmatrix} a_1 & a_3 & a_5 \\ 1 & a_2 & a_4 \\ 0 & a_1 & a_3 \end{vmatrix} = a_3 \Delta_2 + a_1(a_5 - a_1 a_4),$

$\qquad\qquad\quad = a_1 a_2 a_3 - a_1^2 a_4 - a_3^2 + a_1 a_5 = \Delta_3(\beta_{\epsilon^c}, \beta_{\pi^c}),$

(iv) $\quad \Delta_4 = \begin{vmatrix} a_1 & a_3 & a_5 & 0 \\ 1 & a_2 & a_4 & 0 \\ 0 & a_1 & a_3 & a_5 \\ 0 & 1 & a_2 & a_4 \end{vmatrix} = a_4 \Delta_3 - a_5 \begin{vmatrix} a_1 & a_3 & a_5 \\ 1 & a_2 & a_4 \\ 0 & 1 & a_2 \end{vmatrix},$

$\qquad\qquad\quad = a_4 \Delta_3 + a_5(-a_1 a_2^2 - a_5 + a_2 a_3 + a_1 a_4),$

$\qquad\qquad\quad = a_4 \Delta_3 + a_5(a_1 a_4 - a_5 - a_2 \Delta_2) = \Delta_4(\beta_{\epsilon^c}, \beta_{\pi^c}),$

$$(6.44)$$

$$(v) \quad \Delta_5 = \begin{vmatrix} a_1 & a_3 & a_5 & 0 & 0 \\ 1 & a_2 & a_4 & 0 & 0 \\ 0 & a_1 & a_3 & a_5 & 0 \\ 0 & 1 & a_2 & a_4 & 0 \\ 0 & 0 & a_1 & a_3 & a_5 \end{vmatrix} = a_5 \Delta_4 = \Delta_5(\beta_{\epsilon^c}, \beta_{\pi^c}),$$

It is well known that the equilibrium point of the five dimensional dynamical system (6.35) is locally stable if and only if the following Routh-Hurwitz conditions for stable roots are satisfied

$$\Delta_j > 0 \quad \text{for all } j \in \{1, 2, \cdots, 5\}. \tag{RH}$$

It is also well known that the set of conditions RH can be expressed in any of the four following alternative forms, which are called Lienard-Chipart conditions (cf. Gandolfo (1996, p.223))

$$
\begin{aligned}
&\text{(a) } a_5 > 0, \quad a_3 > 0, \quad a_1 > 0, \quad \Delta_3 > 0, \quad \Delta_5 > 0, \\
&\text{(b) } a_5 > 0, \quad a_3 > 0, \quad a_1 > 0, \quad \Delta_2 > 0, \quad \Delta_4 > 0, \\
&\text{(c) } a_5 > 0, \quad a_4 > 0, \quad a_2 > 0, \quad \Delta_1 > 0, \quad \Delta_3 > 0, \quad \Delta_5 > 0, \\
&\text{(d) } a_5 > 0, \quad a_4 > 0, \quad a_2 > 0, \quad \Delta_2 > 0, \quad \Delta_4 > 0.
\end{aligned} \tag{LC}
$$

It follows from Lienard-Chipart conditions that the following conditions are *necessary* (but not sufficient) conditions for local asymptotic stability.

$$a_j > 0 \quad \text{for all } j \in \{1, 2, \cdots, 5\} \tag{6.45}$$

From the relationships $\gamma_i = \alpha_i$ and $\gamma_p = \alpha_i(1 + \alpha_p)$ we always have

$$\gamma_p - \gamma_i = \alpha_i \alpha_p > 0, \tag{6.46}$$

which means that we have the following expressions

$$a_4 = \beta_{\epsilon^c} \beta_{\pi^c} i_1 l^0 [\underset{(-)}{- f_l} \{\alpha_i \alpha_p + \underset{(-)}{F_{11}(1 + \alpha_i)}\} + F_{14}\{\underset{(-)}{-F_{21}} + \underset{(?)}{r_\theta} \underset{(-)}{\alpha_i} + \underset{(?)}{(1 + \alpha_i) f_\theta}\}$$

$$+ \{\underset{(-)}{-F_{11}(f_{\epsilon^c}/i_1 l^0)} + \underset{(+)}{(F_{13}/i_1 l^0)} \underset{(?)}{f_\theta}\} \underset{(?)}{\alpha_i \alpha_p} + \underset{(-)}{F_{11} \alpha_i(1 + \alpha_p)}], \tag{6.47}$$

$$a_5 = \beta_{\epsilon^c} \beta_{\pi^c} i_1 l^0 (\underset{(-)}{F_{11}} \underset{(-)}{f_l} - \underset{(-)}{F_{14}} \underset{(?)}{f_\theta}) \alpha_i \alpha_p, \tag{6.48}$$

where $(f_{\epsilon^c}/i_1 l^0)$ and $(F_{13}/i_1 l^0)$ are *independent* of the parameter $i_1 > 0$. We can easily see that the following relationships are satisfied

(i) $f_l = 0$ if $\kappa_p = 0$,
(ii) $f_\theta = 0$ and $F_{21} > 0$ if $\kappa_p = \beta_{pu} = \beta_{p\omega} = 0$.

Therefore, we can obtain the following results

$$a_4 = \beta_{\epsilon^c}\beta_{\pi^c}i_1 l^0 [F_{14}(-F_{21}+r_\theta\,\alpha_i)+\alpha_i F_{11}\{-(f_r/i_1 l^0)+1+\alpha_p\}]$$
$$\qquad\qquad\quad (-)\qquad (+)\quad (-)\qquad\quad (-)\qquad\quad (+)$$

if $\kappa_p = \beta_{pu} = \beta_{p\omega} = 0$,

$$a_5 = -\beta_{\epsilon^c}\beta_{\pi^c}i_1 l^0\,F_{14}\,\beta_{p\omega}\alpha_i\alpha_p > 0 \text{ for all } (\beta_{\epsilon^c},\beta_{\pi^c},i_1,\beta_{p\omega}) > (0,0,0,0)$$
$$\qquad (-)$$

if $\kappa_p = 0$.

Lemmas and propositions

Now, let us assume as follows

Assumption 3   The parameters $\kappa_p > 0$, $\beta_{pu} > 0$, $\beta_{p\omega} > 0$, and $\gamma_i = \alpha_i > 0$ are sufficiently small.

Lemma 1   Under assumptions $1 - 3$, we have $a_4 > 0$ and $a_5 > 0$ for all $(\beta_{\epsilon^c},\beta_{\pi^c},i_1) > (0,0,0)$.

Proof   This result follows directly from the equations (25), (26) and **Assumption 3** by continuity.   □

Lemma 2   Under assumptions $1 - 3$, we have $a_1 > 0$, $a_2 > 0$, $a_3 > 0$, $\Delta_2 > 0$, $\Delta_3 > 0$, and $\Delta_4 > 0$ for all $\beta_{\epsilon^c} > 0$ if $\beta_{\pi^c} > 0$ and $i_1 > 0$ are sufficiently small.

Proof   We can easily see that the following equalities are satisfied

$$\lim_{i_1\to 0} y_{\epsilon^c} = \lim_{i_1\to 0} l^d_{\epsilon^c} = \lim_{i_1\to 0} u_{\epsilon^c} = \lim_{i_1\to 0} e_{\epsilon^c} = \lim_{i_1\to 0} r_{\epsilon^c} = \lim_{i_1\to 0} f_{\epsilon^c} = \lim_{i_1\to 0} F_{13}$$
$$= \lim_{i_1\to 0} F_{23} = 0. \tag{6.49}$$

Therefore, we have the following inequalities from the equations (6.44)

$$\lim_{i_1\to 0} a_1(\beta_{\epsilon^c}) = -F_{11}+\gamma_i+\beta_{\epsilon^c} > 0 \quad \text{for all } \beta_{\epsilon^c} \geq 0,$$
$$\qquad\qquad\qquad\quad (-)$$

$$\lim_{i_1\to 0} a_2(\beta_{\epsilon^c},0) = -F_{11}\gamma_i+\beta_{\epsilon^c}(-F_{11}+\gamma_i) > 0 \quad \text{for all } \beta_{\epsilon^c} \geq 0,$$
$$\qquad\qquad\qquad\quad (-)\qquad\qquad (-)$$

$$\lim_{i_1\to 0} a_3(\beta_{\epsilon^c},0) = -\beta_{\epsilon^c}F_{11}\gamma_i > 0 \quad \text{for all } \beta_{\epsilon^c} > 0,$$
$$\qquad\qquad\qquad\quad (-)$$

$$\lim_{i_1\to 0} \Delta_2(\beta_{\epsilon^c},0) = (\gamma_i-F_{11})\{\beta^2_{\epsilon^c}+(\gamma_i-F_{11})\beta_{\epsilon^c}-F_{11}\gamma_i\} > 0 \quad \text{for all } \beta_{\epsilon^c} \geq 0,$$
$$\qquad\qquad\qquad\quad (-)\qquad\qquad (-)\qquad\qquad (-)$$

$$\lim_{i_1\to 0} \Delta_3(\beta_{\epsilon^c},0) = \lim_{i_1\to 0}\{a_3(\beta_{\epsilon^c},0)\Delta_2(\beta_{\epsilon^c},0)\} > 0 \quad \text{for all } \beta_{\epsilon^c} > 0.$$

These inequalities imply that we have $a_1 > 0,\quad a_2 > 0,\quad a_3 > 0,\quad \Delta_2 > 0$, and $\Delta_3 > 0$ for all $\beta_{\epsilon^c} > 0$ if $\beta_{\pi^c} > 0$ and $i > 0$ are sufficiently small (by continuity).

Next, let us turn to the analysis of the term Δ_4. Substituting Eq. (6.44)(iii) into Eq. (6.44)(iv), we obtain

$$\Delta_4(\beta_{\epsilon^c},\beta_{\pi^c}) = a_4(a_3\Delta_2 + a_1a_5 - a_1^2a_4) + a_1a_4a_5 - a_5^2 - a_2a_5\Delta_2,$$

$$= (a_3a_4 - a_2a_5)\Delta_2 + a_1a_4(2a_5 - a_1a_4) - a_5^2,$$

$$= \beta_{\epsilon^c}\beta_{\pi^c}i_1 l^0 [(a_3\tilde{a}_4 - a_2\tilde{a}_5)\Delta_2(\beta_{\epsilon^c},\beta_{\pi^m})$$

$$+ a_1\tilde{a}_4(2a_5 - a_1a_4) - \tilde{a}_5a_5],$$

$$= \beta_{\epsilon^c}\beta_{\pi^c}i_1 l^0 \phi(\beta_{\epsilon^c},\beta_{\pi^c}), \qquad (6.50)$$

where $\tilde{a}_j = a_j/\beta_{\epsilon^c}\beta_{\pi^c}i_1 l^0 (j = 4, 5)$. We can easily see that

$$\lim_{i_1\to 0}\phi(\beta_{\epsilon^c},0) = [\lim_{i_1\to 0}\{a_3(\beta_{\epsilon^c},0)\tilde{a}_4 - a_2(\beta_{\pi^c},0)\tilde{a}_5\}]\{\lim_{i_1\to 0}\Delta_2(\beta_{\epsilon^c},0)\},$$

$$(6.51)$$

where $\lim_{i_1\to 0}\Delta_2(\beta_{\epsilon^c},0) > 0$ is satisfied for all $\beta_{\epsilon^c} \geq 0$ because of Eq. (6.56).

From equations (6.49), (6.50), (6.51), and (6.55) we can obtain the following result if $\kappa_p = \beta_{pu} = \beta_{p\omega} = 0$

$$\lim_{i_1\to 0}\{a_3(\beta_{\epsilon^c},0)\tilde{a}_4 - a_2(\beta_{\epsilon^c},0)\tilde{a}_5\}$$

$$= -\beta_{\epsilon^c}F_{11}\alpha_i[F_{14}(-F_{21}+r_\theta\,\alpha_i)+\alpha_iF_{11}\{-(f_r/i_1 l^0)+1+\alpha_p\}], \quad (6.52)$$
$$(-)(-)(+)(-)(-)(+)$$

which will be positive for all $\beta_{\epsilon^c} > 0$ if $\gamma_i = \alpha_i > 0$ is sufficiently small. From equations (6.50), (6.51) and (6.52) we have $\Delta_4 > 0$ for all $\beta_{\epsilon^c} > 0$ if $\beta_{\pi^c} > 0$ and $i_1 > 0$ are sufficiently small under assumptions $1 - 3$ by continuity reasons. This completes the proof of Lemma 2.　□

The following two propositions are our main results.

Proposition 1
(i) Under assumptions $1 - 3$, the equilibrium point of the system (6.35) is locally asymptotically stable for all $\beta_{\epsilon^c} > 0$ if $\beta_{\pi^c} > 0$ and $i_1 > 0$ are sufficiently small.
(ii) Suppose that $\beta_{\epsilon^c} > 0$. Then, the equilibrium point of the system (6.35) is locally unstable for all sufficiently large values of $\beta_{\pi^c} > 0$.

Proof
(i) Lemma 1 and Lemma 2 imply that all of the conditions (LC)(b) (or alternatively, all of the conditions (LC)(d)) are satisfied for all $\beta_{\epsilon^c} > 0$ under assumptions $1 - 3$ if $\beta_{\pi^c} > 0$ and $i_1 > 0$ are sufficiently small.

(ii) Suppose that $\beta_{\epsilon^c} > 0$. Then, we have $a_2 < 0$ for all sufficiently large values of $\beta_{\pi^c} > 0$. In this case, one of the necessary conditions for local stability in (20) is violated.   □

Proposition 2   We posit assumptions $1-3$ and assume that $i_1 > 0$ is sufficiently small. Furthermore, β_{ϵ^c} is fixed at an arbitrary positive value, and we select $\beta_{\pi^m} > 0$ as a bifurcation parameter. Then, there exists at least one bifurcation point $\beta_{\pi^c}^0$ at which the local stability of the equilibrium point of the system (6.35) is lost as the parameter β_{π^c} is increased. At the bifurcation point, the characteristic equation (6.38) has at least one pair of pure imaginary roots, and there is no real root $\lambda = 0$.

Proof   Existence of the bifurcation point $\beta_{\pi^c}^0$, at which the local stability of the system is lost, is obvious from Proposition 1 by continuity. By the very nature of the bifurcation point, the characteristic equation (6.38) must have at least one root with zero real part at $\beta_{\pi^c} = \beta_{\pi^c}^0$. But, we can exclude a real root $\lambda = 0$, because we have $\Gamma(0) = a_5 > 0$.   □

Remark   In general, the following two cases are possible.

(A) At the bifurcation point, the characteristic equation (6.38) has a pair of purely imaginary roots and three roots with negative real parts.

(B) At the bifurcation point, the characteristic equation (6.38) has two pairs of purely imaginary roots and one negative real root.

The case (A) corresponds to the so called 'Hopf bifurcation', and in this case, we can establish the existence of the closed orbits at some parameter values β_{π^c} which are sufficiently close to the bifurcation value (cf. Gandolfo (1996, Ch.25) and in Asada, Chiarella, Flaschel and Franke (2003) the mathematical appendix). On the other hand, in the case (B) one of the conditions for Hopf bifurcations is not satisfied. The case (A) will be more likely to occur than the case (B), and case (B) will occur only by accident. Even in the case (B), however, the existence of the cyclical fluctuations is ensured at some range of the parameter values β_{π^c} which are sufficiently close to the bifurcation value, because of the existence of two pairs of the complex roots.

7 DAS–DAD dynamics

Respecification and estimation of the model

Christian Proaño

7.1 Introduction

As was discussed in Chapter 5 and previously pointed out by Mankiw (2001) and Solow (2004), among many others, the New Keynesian DSGE (Dynamic Stochastic General Equilibrium) approach features a number of important short-comings at both the theoretical and empirical level, therefore, not (yet) representing a theoretically and empirically convincing strategy for the study of the fluctuating growth of modern economies. At the empirical level, the so-called 'dynamic inconsistencies' (Estrella and Fuhrer 2002) and the related poor performance of empirical estimates of New Keynesian Wage- and Price Phillips Curve equations (Rudd and Whelan 2005) have been used to underpin these criticisms. Mankiw (2001), for example, states that 'although the new Keynesian Phillips curve has many virtues, it also has one striking vice: it is completely at odds with the facts'.

Alternatively, in Chiarella and Flaschel (1996) and Chiarella and Flaschel (2000) a theoretical macroeconomic framework where wages and prices react sluggishly to disequilibrium situations in both the goods and labor markets has been proposed. As it will be discussed in this chapter, despite of the apparent similarity that the gradual wage and price inflation adjustment equations along the lines of Chiarella and Flaschel (2000) share with their recent New Keynesian and DSGE analogues (which, among other things, also include elements of forward- and backward-looking behavior concerning the inflation dynamics of the economy), their approach is based on the notion of nonclearing goods and labor markets, and therefore of underutilized labor and capital stock. Therefore, this alternative approach to the modeling of wage and price inflation dynamics thus permits an interesting comparison with New Keynesian framework which, knowingly, models the dynamics of wage and price inflation as the result of the reoptimization by the economic agents under a staggered wage and price setting mostly in the line of Rotemberg (1982) and Calvo (1983).

In this chapter,[1] the semistructural baseline Disequilibrium AS–AD model discussed in Chen, Chiarella, Flaschel, and Semmler (2006) is discussed and estimated using aggregate macroeconomic time series not only of the U.S. economy, but also of the U.K., Germany and France. On this basis, some of the questions to be addressed in this chapter are: to what extent is this semistructural Keynesian macroeconomic model able to fit the behavior of wages, prices and other macroeconomic variables in the major industrialized economies? Are there significant differences in wage and price inflation (the wage–price spiral) among these economies observable over the past twenty years? What are the implications of the wage–price spiral for the dynamics of income distribution in those economies?

The remainder of this chapter is organized as follows. In Section 7.2, the macroeconomic framework developed in Chen, Chiarella, Flaschel, and Semmler (2006) is briefly discussed and its main conceptual differences from to the New Keynesian approach are highlighted. Section 7.3 provides against this background a feedback guided stability analysis of the implied 4-dimensional dynamical system. In Section 7.4, the model is estimated by means of GMM (Generalized Methods of Moments) with aggregate time series of the U.S., the U.K., Germany and France in order to find out sign and size restrictions for its behavioral equations and to study which feedback mechanisms may have primarily influenced these economies in the past twenty years. Section 7.5 focuses on the eigenvalue stability analysis of the system. Section 7.6 concludes.

7.2 A baseline semistructural macromodel

As will be discussed in more detail in the following Section, the framework developed in Chen *et al.* (2006) builds on gradual wage and price inflation adjustments as recent New Keynesian macroeconometric models, but assumes, in contrast to those models, that such adjustments are not the result of the agents' reoptimization to new economic conditions, but occur instead as a reaction to disequilibrium situations in both the goods and labor markets.

7.2.1 The goods and labor markets

Since the focus of this theoretical framework is indeed the modeling of the wage–price dynamics, the goods and labor markets are modeled in a rather parsimonious manner. Concerning the goods markets dynamics, a dynamic IS-equation is assumed (see also Rudebusch and Svensson (1999) in this regard), where the growth rate of output gap (represented by the growth rate of the capacity utilization

---

1 This chapter is a revised version of Proaño (2008, Ch.2): 'essays on Gradual Wage–Price Adjustments, Monetary Unions and Open Economy Macrodynamics', PhD Thesis, Bielefeld University, see also Ch.4 in Flaschel, Groh, Proaño and Semmler (2008) for related considerations.

rate of firms u) is determined by

$$\hat{u} = -\alpha_u(u - u_o) + \alpha_v(v - v_o) - \alpha_r((i - \hat{p}) - (i_o - \pi_o)), \tag{7.1}$$

Eq. (7.1) has three important characteristics; (i) it reflects the dependence of output changes on aggregate income (and thus on the previous rate of capacity utilization) by assuming a negative, i.e. stable dynamic multiplier relationship in this respect, (ii) it shows the joint dependence of consumption and investment on the real wage – which joint parameter may in the aggregate be positive ($\alpha_v > 0$) or negative ($\alpha_v < 0$), depending on whether consumption or investment is more responsive to real wage changes[2] – and finally, (iii) it shows the negative influence of the real rate of interest on the evolution of economic activity.

Concerning the labor market dynamics, a simple empirical relationship is assumed which links the output and the employment rate (measured in hours work) as follows:

$$e_h = u^b.$$

Consequently, the growth rate of employment rate (in hours worked) is accordingly given by

$$\hat{e}^h = b\,\hat{u}. \tag{7.2}$$

Employment in hours is in fact the relevant measure for the labor input of firms and therefore for the aggregate production function in the economy. Nevertheless, due to the lack of available time series of this variable for the European economies (this series is available only for the U.S.) and for the sake of comparability of the parameter estimates in the next section, it will be assumed here that the dynamics of employment rate in hours and the employment rate measured in the number of persons are equivalent, so that eq. (7.2) in fact describes the dynamics of actual employment rate e, so that $\hat{e} = b\,\hat{u}$ holds.

7.2.2 The wage–price dynamics

As stated before, the core of the theoretical framework of this chapter, which allows for nonclearing labor and goods markets and therefore for under- or overutilized labor and capital stock, is the wage–price dynamics module, as being specified through two separate Phillips Curves, each one led by its own measure of demand pressure (or capacity bottlenecks).

The approach of specifying two separate Wage- and Price-Phillips Curves is not altogether new: while Barro (1994) observes that Keynesian macroeconomics

---

2 This simplifying formulation helps to avoid the estimation of separate equations for consumption and investment.

are (or should be) based on imperfectly flexible wages and prices and thus on the consideration of wage as well as price Phillips Curves equations, Fair (2000) criticizes the low accuracy of reduced-form price equations. In the same study, Fair estimates two separate wage and price equations for the United States, using nevertheless a single demand pressure term, the NAIRU gap. In contrast, by the modeling of wage and price dynamics separately from each other, each one determined by its own measures of demand pressure in the market for labor and for goods, namely $e - e_o$ and $u - u_o$, respectively,[3] the identification problem pointed out by Sims (1987) for the estimation of separate wage and price equations with the same explanatory variables is circumvented.[4] By these means, the dynamics of the real wages in the economy can be analyzed and converse effects which might result from different developments on labor and goods markets can be identified.

More specifically, the structural form of the wage–price dynamics is given by:

$$\hat{w} = \beta_{we}(e - e_o) - \beta_{wv}\ln(v/v_o) + \kappa_{wp}\hat{p} + (1 - \kappa_{wp})\pi_c + \kappa_{wz}\hat{z}, \qquad (7.3)$$

$$\hat{p} = \beta_{pu}(u - u_o) + \beta_{pv}\ln(v/v_o) + \kappa_{pw}(\hat{w} - \hat{z}) + (1 - \kappa_{pw})\pi_c. \qquad (7.4)$$

where $\hat{w} = \dot{w}/w$ and $\hat{p} = \dot{p}/p$ denote the growth rates of nominal wages and prices, respectively, that is, the wage and price inflation rates. The demand pressure terms $e - e_o$ and $u - u_o$ in the wage and price Phillips Curves are augmented by three additional terms: the log deviation of the wage share v from its steady state level v_o (the error correction term discussed in Blanchard and Katz (1999, p.71)), a weighted average of corresponding expected cost-pressure terms, assumed to be model-consistent, with forward looking, cross-over wage and price inflation rates $\hat{w}$ and $\hat{p}$, respectively, and a backward looking measure of the prevailing inertial inflation in the economy (the 'inflationary climate', so to say) symbolized by π_c, and labor productivity growth $\hat{z}$ (which is expected to influence wages in a positive and prices in a negative manner, due to the associated easing in production cost pressure). Concerning the latter variable we assume for simplicity that it is always equal to the growth rate of trend productivity, namely $\hat{z} = g_z =$ const.[5]

Concerning the inertial inflation term, this may be formed adaptively following the actual rate of inflation (by use of some linear or exponential weighting scheme), a rolling sample (with bell-shaped weighting schemes), or other possibilities for updating expectations. For simplicity of exposition, the use of a conventional adaptive expectations mechanism will be assumed in the theoretical part of this

3 e_o being the NAIRU-equivalent level of the employment rate and u the rate of capacity utilization of the capital stock – knowingly closely linked with the output gap – (u_o being its normal level).
4 See Erceg, Henderson, and Levin (2000) and Sbordone (2004) for other alternative approaches.
5 Even though explicitly formulated, we will assume in the theoretical framework of this chapter $g_z = 0$ for simplicity and leave the modeling of the labor productivity growth for future research.

chapter, namely

$$\dot{\pi}_c = \beta_{\pi_c}(\hat{p} - \pi_c). \tag{7.5}$$

Note that here the Chiarella and Flaschel (1996) approach differs again from the standard New Keynesian framework based on the work by Rotemberg (1982) and Calvo (1983). Instead of assuming that the aggregate price (and wage) inflation is determined in a profit maximizing manner solely by the expected future path of nominal marginal costs, or in the hybrid variant discussed in Galí, Gertler, and López-Salido (2001), which includes the effects of lagged inflation, it assumes that instead of last period inflation, the medium run inflationary development in the economy is taken into account by the economic agents.

The microfoundations of the wage Phillips curve are thus of the same type as in Blanchard and Katz (1999) – see also Flaschel and Krolzig (2006) – which can be reformulated as expressed as in eq. (7.3) and eq. (7.4) with the unemployment gap in the place of the logarithm of the output gap if hybrid expectations formation is in addition embedded into their approach. Concerning the price Phillips curve, a similar procedure can be applied, based on desired markups of firms. Along these lines, an economic motivation for the inclusion of – indeed the logarithm of – the real wage (or wage share) with negative sign in the wage PC and with positive sign in the price PC is obtained, without any need for loglinear approximations. Furthermore, the employment- and the output gap are incorporated in these two wage- and price-Phillips Curves equations, respectively, in the place of a single measure (the log of the output gap). This wage–price module is thus consistent with standard models of unemployment based on efficiency wages, matching and competitive wage determination, and can be considered as a valid alternative to the – at least empirically questionable – New Keynesian formulation of wage–price dynamics.

Note additionally that model-consistent expectations with respect to short-run wage and price inflation are assumed, which are incorporated into the Phillips curves in a cross-over manner, with perfectly foreseen price- in the wage- and wage inflation in the price-inflation adjustment equations. It should be stressed that forward-looking behavior is indeed incorporated here, without the need for an application of the jump variable technique of the Rational Expectations (RE) school in general and of the New Keynesian approach in particular.[6]

Slightly different versions of the two Phillips curves given by eq. (7.3) and eq. (7.4) have been estimated for the U.S. economy in various ways in Flaschel and Krolzig (2006), Flaschel, Kauermann, and Semmler (2007), Chen and Flaschel (2006) and Chen, Chiarella, Flaschel, and Semmler (2006), and have been found to represent a significant improvement over the conventional single reduced-form

---

6 For a detailed comparison with the New Keynesian alternative to this model type see Chiarella, Flaschel, and Franke (2005).

Phillips curve. A particular finding of these studies is that wage flexibility is larger than price flexibility with respect to their demand pressure measures in the labor and goods markets,[7] respectively, and that workers are more short-sighted than firms with respect to their cost pressure terms.

The corresponding across-markets or *reduced-form Phillips Curve* equations resulting from eqs. (7.1) and (7.2) are given by (with $\kappa = 1/(1 - \kappa_{wp}\kappa_{pw})$):

$$\hat{w} = \kappa \left[\beta_{we}(e - e_o) - \beta_{wv} \ln(v/v_o) + \kappa_{wp}(\beta_{pu}(u - u_o) + \beta_{pv} \ln(v/v_o)) \right.$$

$$\left. + (\kappa_{wz} - \kappa_{wp}\kappa_{pw})g_z \right] + \pi_c, \tag{7.6}$$

$$\hat{p} = \kappa \left[\beta_{pu}(u - u_o) + \beta_{pv} \ln(v/v_o) + \kappa_{pw}(\beta_{we}(e - e_o) - \beta_{wv} \ln(v/v_o)) \right.$$

$$\left. + \kappa_{pw}(\kappa_{wz} - 1)g_z \right] + \pi_c, \tag{7.7}$$

with pass-through terms behind the κ_{wp}, κ_{pw}-parameters, representing a considerable generalization of the conventional view of a single-market price PC with only one measure of demand pressure, namely the one in the labor market.

Note that for this current version of the wage–price spiral, the inflationary climate variable π_c does not matter for the evolution of the labor share $v = w/(pz)$, which law of motion is given by :

$$\hat{v} = \hat{w} - \hat{p} - \hat{z}$$

$$= \kappa \left[(1 - \kappa_{pw})(\beta_{we}(e - e_o) - \beta_{wv} \ln(v/v_o)) - (1 - \kappa_{wp})(\beta_{pu}(u - u_o) \right.$$

$$\left. + \beta_{pv} \ln(v/v_o)) + (\kappa_{wz} - 1)(1 - \kappa_{pw})g_z \right]. \tag{7.8}$$

Eq. (7.8) shows the ambiguity of the stabilizing nature of the real wage channel discussed by Rose (1967) which arises – despite the incorporation of specific measures of demand and cost pressure on both the labor and the goods markets – if the dynamics of the employment rate are linked to the behavior of output and if inflationary cross-over expectations are incorporated in both Phillips curves. Indeed, as illustrated in Figure 7.1, a real wage increase can act, taken by itself, in a stabilizing or destabilizing manner, depending on whether the output dynamics depend positively or negatively on the real wage (i.e. if consumption reacts more strongly than investment or vice versa) *and* on whether price flexibility is larger than nominal wage flexibility with respect to its own demand pressure measure.

---

7 For lack of better terms, we associate the degree of wage and price flexibility with the size of the parameters β_{we} and β_{pu}, though of course the extent of these flexibilities will also depend on the size of the fluctuations of the excess demand expression in the market for labor and for goods.

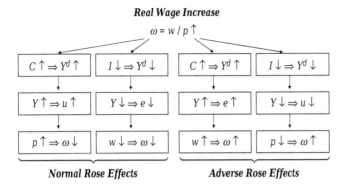

Figure 7.1 Normal (convergent) and adverse (divergent) rose effects: the real wage channel of Keynesian macrodynamics.

These four different scenarios can be jointly summarized as in Table 7.1. As Table 7.1 clearly shows, the combination of these four possibilities sets up four different scenarios where the dynamics of the real wage (in their interaction with the goods and labor markets) might turn out to be *per se* convergent or divergent. As it can be observed in Figure 7.1, there exist two cases where the Rose (1967) real wage channel operates in a stabilizing manner: in the first case, aggregate goods demand (approximated in this framework by the capacity utilization rate) depends negatively on the real wage, which can be denoted in a closed economy as the profit-led case[8] – and the dynamics of the real wage are led primarily by the nominal wage dynamics and therefore by the developments in the labor market. In the second case, aggregate demand depends positively on the real wage, and the price inflation dynamics (and therefore the goods markets) determine primarily the behavior of the real wages.[9]

7.2.3 Monetary policy

Concerning monetary policy, the nominal interest rate is made endogenous by using a simple Taylor rule as is customary in the literature, see e.g., Svensson (1999). Indeed, as Romer (2000, p.154–55) states, 'Even in Germany, where there

---

8 In an open economy, other macroeconomic channels, such as the real exchange rate channel, would also be influenced by the real wage and in turn influence aggregate demand dynamics, so that the designation 'profit led' would not be appropriate anymore. Nevertheless, since we restrict our theoretical analysis to closed economies (or relatively closed as in our econometric analysis of the United States and the euro area), we will adhere to the designation used in Table 7.1.

9 Note here that the cost-pressure parameters also play a role and may influence the critical stability condition of the real wage channel, see Flaschel and Krolzig (2006) for details.

Table 7.1 Four baseline real wage adjustment scenarios

	Wage-led goods demand	Profit-led goods demand
Labor market-led real wage adjustment	Adverse (Divergent)	Normal (Convergent)
Goods market-led real wage adjustment	Normal (Convergent)	Adverse (Divergent)

were money targets beginning in 1975 and where those targets paid a major role in the official policy discussions, policy from the 1970s through the 1990s was better described by an interest rate rule aimed at macroeconomic policy objectives than by money targeting.'[10] The target rate of the monetary authorities and the law of motion resulting from an interest rate smoothing behavior by the central bank are defined as

$$i_\text{T} = (i_o - \pi_o) + \hat{p} + \phi_\pi(\hat{p} - \pi_o) + \phi_y(u - u_o)$$

$$\dot{i} = \alpha_i(i_\text{T} - i).$$

The target rate of the Central Bank i_T is thus assumed here to depend on the steady state real rate of interest $i_o - \pi_o$ augmented by actual inflation back to a nominal rate, and as usual also on the inflation and on the output gap (approximated here by the deviation of the capacity utilization rate from its steady state level).[11] With respect to this target, there are interest rate smoothing dynamics with strength α_i. Inserting i_T and rearranging terms we obtain from this expression the following dynamic law for the nominal interest rate

$$\dot{i} = -\alpha_i(i - i_o) + \gamma_{ip}(\hat{p} - \pi_o) + \gamma_y(u - u_o) \tag{7.9}$$

where we have: $\gamma_{ip} = \alpha_i(1 + \phi_\pi)$, i.e., $\phi_\pi = \gamma_{ip}/\alpha_i - 1$ and $\gamma_{iu} = \alpha_i\phi_y$.

Furthermore, the actual (perfectly foreseen) rate of inflation $\hat{p}$ is used to measure the inflation gap with respect to the inflation target π_o of the central bank. Note finally that a new kind of gap, namely the labor share gap, could have included into the aforesaid Taylor rule, since in this model aggregate demand depends on income distribution (and therefore on the labor share), so that the state of income distribution matters to the dynamics of the model and thus should also play a role in the decisions of the central bank. However, this has not been done here.

---

10 See also Clarida and Gertler (1997).
11 All of the employed gaps are measured relative to the steady state of the model, in order to allow for an interest rate policy that is consistent with it.

Taken together, the model of this section consists of the following five laws of motion (with the derived reduced-form expressions as far as the wage–price spiral is concerned):[12]

The Model

$$\hat{v} \overset{LaborShare}{=} \kappa[(1 - \kappa_{pw})(\beta_{we}(e - e_o) - \beta_{wv} \ln(v/v_o))$$
$$- (1 - \kappa_{wp})(\beta_{pu}(u - u_o) + \beta_{pv} \ln(v/v_o)) + \kappa_{vz} g_z], \qquad (7.10)$$
$$\text{with } \kappa_{vz} = (\kappa_{wz} - 1)(1 - \kappa_{pw})$$

$$\hat{u} \overset{Dyn.IS}{=} -\alpha_u(u - u_o) + \alpha_v(v - v_o) - \alpha_r((i - \hat{p})$$
$$- (i_o - \pi_o)), \qquad (7.11)$$

$$\dot{i} \overset{T.Rule}{=} -\alpha_i(i - i_o) + \gamma_{ip}(\hat{p} - \pi_o) + \gamma_{iu}(u - u_o), \qquad (7.12)$$

$$\dot{\pi}_c \overset{I.Climate}{=} \beta_{\pi_c}(\hat{p} - \pi_c) \qquad (7.13)$$

$$\hat{e} \overset{O.Law}{=} b\,\hat{u}, \qquad (7.14)$$

Note that the law of motion given by eq. (7.10) for the labor share: $\hat{v} = \hat{w} - \hat{p} - \hat{z}$ makes use of the same explanatory variables as the New Keynesian approach but features no accompanying sign reversal concerning the influence of output and wage gaps, as is the case in the 4D-baseline New Keynesian models as discussed e.g., in Walsh (2003). Together with the IS goods market dynamics (7.11), the Taylor Rule (7.12), the law of motion (7.13) that describes the updating of the inflationary climate expression, and finally Okun's Law (7.14) as the link between the goods and the labor markets, eq. (7.10) represents a simple theoretical framework which nevertheless features the main transmission channels operating in modern economies. Note that the model can be reduced to a 4D-system if the actual level of employment is recovered from eq. (7.14) by making use of the original formulation of Okun's Law (see the equation preceding eq. (7.2)), the resulting functional relationship is inserted in the remaining equations of the system. We can thus prescind from eq. (7.14) (and the influence of e as an endogenous variable) in the stability analysis to be discussed in the following Section.

In order to get an autonomous nonlinear system of differential equations in the state variables labor share v, output gap u, the nominal rate of interest i, and the inflationary climate expression π_c, we have to make use of eq. (7.7) (the reduced-form price Phillips Curve equation). This then has to be inserted into the remaining laws of motion in various places.

---

12 As the model is formulated, we have no real anchor for the steady state rate of interest (via investment behavior and the rate of profit it implies in the steady state) and thus have to assume that it is the monetary authority that enforces a certain steady state value for the nominal rate of interest.

With respect to the empirically motivated restructuring of the original theoretical framework, the model is as pragmatic as the approach employed by Rudebusch and Svensson (1999). By and large, it represents a working alternative to the New Keynesian approach, in particular, when the current critique of the latter approach is taken into account. It overcomes the weaknesses and the logical inconsistencies of the old Neoclassical Synthesis, see Asada, Chen, Chiarella, and Flaschel (2006), and it does so in a minimal way from a mature, but still traditionally oriented Keynesian perspective (and is thus not really 'New'). It preserves the problematic stability features of the real rate of interest channel, where the stabilizing Keynes effect or the interest rate policy of the central bank is interacting with the destabilizing, expectations driven Mundell effect. It preserves the real wage effect of the old Neoclassical Synthesis, where – due to an unambiguously negative dependence of aggregate demand on the real wage – it was the case that price flexibility was destabilizing, while wage flexibility was not. This real wage channel, summarized in the Figure 7.1, is not normally discussed in the New Keynesian literature due to the specific form of wage–price and IS (Investment Saving) dynamics there considered.

7.3 4D Feedback-guided stability analysis

In this section, the local stability properties of the interior steady state of the dynamical system given by eqs. (7.10)–(7.13) (with eq. (7.7) inserted wherever needed) are analyzed through partial considerations from the feedback chains that characterize this empirically oriented baseline model of Keynesian macrodynamics. The Jacobian of the 4D-dynamic system, evaluated at its interior steady state, is

$$J = \begin{pmatrix} - & \pm & 0 & 0 \\ \pm & - & - & + \\ \pm & + & - & + \\ \pm & + & 0 & 0 \end{pmatrix}.$$

Since the model is an extension of the standard AS–AD (Aggregate Supply–Aggregate Demand) growth model, we know from the literature that the real rate of interest, first analyzed by formal methods in Tobin (1975) (see also Groth (1992)), typically affects, in a negative manner, the dynamics of the economic activity (J_{23}). Additionally, there is the activity stimulating (partial) effect of increases in the rate of inflation (as part of the real rate of interest channel) that may lead to accelerating inflation under appropriate conditions (J_{24}). This transmission mechanism is known as the Mundell effect. The stronger the Mundell Effect, the faster the inflationary climate adjusts to the present level of price inflation. This is due to the positive influence of this climate variable both on price as well as on wage inflation and from there on rates of employment of both capital and labor. Concerning the Keynes effect, due to the use of a Taylor rule in the place of the conventional LM (Liquidity reference Money supply) curve, it is implemented here in a more direct way towards the stabilization of the economy (coupling nominal interest rates directly with the rate of price inflation), and it works the stronger the larger the choice of the parameters γ_{ip}, γ_{iu}.

As it is formulated, the theoretical model also features further potentially (at least partially) destabilizing feedback mechanisms due to the Mundell- and Rose-effects in the goods-market dynamics and the converse Blanchard-Katz error correction terms in the reduced form price Phillips curve. There is first of all J_{12}, see eq. (7.10), the still undetermined influence of the output gap (the rate of capacity utilization) on the labor share, which depends on the signs and values of the parameter estimates of the two structural Phillips curves, and therefore on the cross-over expectations formation of the economic agents. In the second place, see eq. (7.11), we have J_{21}, the ambiguous influence of the labor share on (the dynamics of) the rate of capacity utilization. This should be a negative relationship if investment is more responsive than consumption to real wage increases and a positive relationship in the opposite case. Concerning also the effects of the labor share on capacity utilization, we have aggregate price inflation determined by the reduced form price Phillips curve given by eq. (7.7). Thus, there is an additional, though ambiguous, channel through which the labor share affects the dynamics of the output gap on the one hand and the inflationary climate of the economy (J_{41}) through eq. (7.13) on the other hand. Mundell-type, Rose-type and Blanchard-Katz error-correction feedback channels therefore make the dynamics indeterminate on the theoretical level.

The feedback channels just discussed will be the focus of interest in the following stability analysis of the D(isequilibrium)AS–AD dynamics. Reduced-form expressions have been employed in the above system of differential equations whenever possible. Thereby a dynamical system in four state variables was obtained that is in a natural or intrinsic way nonlinear (due to its reliance on growth rate formulations). We can see furthermore that there are many items that reappear in various equations, or are similar to each other, implying that stability analysis can exploit a variety of linear dependencies in the calculation of the conditions for local asymptotic stability. A rigorous proof of the local asymptotic stability for the original model version and its loss by way of Hopf bifurcations can be found in Asada, Chen, Chiarella, and Flaschel (2006).

In order to focus on the interrelation between wage–price and output gap dynamics, we make use of the following proposition.

Proposition 1 Assume that the parameter β_{π^c} is not only close to zero but in fact equal to zero. This decouples the dynamics of π^c from the rest of the system and the system becomes 3D. Assume furthermore that the partial derivative of the second law of motion J_{22} depends negatively on v, and that $(1 - \kappa_{pw})\beta_{we} > (1 - \kappa_{wp})\beta_u$ holds, and that the interest rate smoothing parameter α_i is chosen sufficiently small in addition. Then: the interior steady state of the implied 3D dynamical system

$$\hat{v} = \kappa[(1 - \kappa_{pw})(\beta_{we}(e(u) - e_o) - \beta_{wv}\ln(v/v_o))$$
$$- (1 - \kappa_{wp})(\beta_{pu}(u - u_o) + \beta_{pv}\ln(v/v_o))], \tag{7.15}$$

$$\hat{u} = -\alpha_u(u - u_o) - \alpha_v(v - v_o) - \alpha_r((i - \hat{p}) - (i_o - \pi_o)), \qquad (7.16)$$

$$\hat{i} = -\alpha_i(i - i_o) + \gamma_{ip}(\hat{p} - \pi_o) + \gamma_{iu}(u - u_o), \qquad (7.17)$$

is locally asymptotically stable.

Sketch of proof   In the considered situation, we have for the Jacobian of the reduced dynamics at the steady state:

$$J = \begin{pmatrix} - & + & 0 \\ - & - & - \\ 0 & + & - \end{pmatrix}.$$

According to the Routh-Hurwitz stability conditions for the characteristic polynomial of the considered 3D-dynamical system, asymptotic local stability of a steady state is fulfilled when:

$$a_i > 0, \quad i = 1, 2, 3 \quad \text{and} \quad a_1 a_2 - a_3 > 0,$$

where: $a_1 = -\text{trace}(J)$, $a_2 = \sum_{k=1}^{3} J_k$ with

$$J_1 = \begin{vmatrix} J_{22} & J_{23} \\ J_{32} & J_{33} \end{vmatrix}, \; J_2 = \begin{vmatrix} J_{11} & J_{13} \\ J_{31} & J_{33} \end{vmatrix}, \; J_3 = \begin{vmatrix} J_{11} & J_{12} \\ J_{21} & J_{22} \end{vmatrix},$$

and: $a_3 = -\det(J)$. The determinant of this Jacobian is obviously negative if the parameter α_i is chosen sufficiently small. The sum of the minors of order 2: a_2 is unambiguously positive. The validity of the full set of Routh-Hurwitz conditions then easily follows, since trace $J = -a_1$ is obviously negative. ∎

Proposition 2   Assume now that the parameter $\beta_{\pi c}$ is positive, but its specific value is chosen sufficiently small. Assume furthermore that α_i is sufficiently small, and that $\gamma_{ip} > 1$. Then: the interior steady state of the resulting 4D-dynamical system (where the state variable π^c is now included)

$$\hat{v} = \kappa[(1 - \kappa_{pw})(\beta_{we}(e(u) - e_o) - \beta_{wv} \ln(v/v_o))$$
$$- (1 - \kappa_{wp})(\beta_{pu}(u - u_o) + \beta_{pv} \ln(v/v_o))], \qquad (7.18)$$

$$\hat{u} = -\alpha_u(u - u_o) - \alpha_v(v - v_o) - \alpha_i((i - \hat{p}) - (i_o - \pi_o)), \qquad (7.19)$$

$$\hat{i} = -\alpha_i(i - i_o) + \gamma_{ip}(\hat{p} - \pi_o) + \gamma_{iu}(u - u_o), \qquad (7.20)$$

$$\dot{\pi}^c = \beta_{\pi c}(\hat{p} - \pi^c) \qquad (7.21)$$

is locally asymptotically stable.

Sketch of proof Under the mentioned stated assumptions, the Jacobian of the 4D-system is equal to:

$$J = \begin{pmatrix} - & + & 0 & 0 \\ - & - & - & + \\ 0 & + & - & + \\ 0 & + & 0 & - \end{pmatrix}.$$

We can clearly see that J_{34} describes the reaction of the nominal interest rate with respect to inflation. According to the Taylor (1993) principle, as long as $\gamma_{ip} > 1$, monetary policy stabilizes the economy. Together with sufficiently small β_{π^c} and α_i, the incorporation of the inflationary climate as a state variable in the dynamical system does not disturb the local stability properties of the system. ∎

Summing up, we can state that a weak Mundell effect; the neglect of Blanchard-Katz error correction terms; a negative dependence of aggregate demand on real wages, coupled with larger nominal wage- than price level flexibility; and a Taylor rule that stresses inflation targeting are here (for example) the basic ingredients that allow for the proof of local asymptotic stability of the interior steady state of the dynamics (7.10)–(7.13).

In order to investigate in more detail the stability properties concerning variations in the parameter values, in the next section the theoretical model discussed here will be estimated with aggregate data of major industrialized economies in order to obtain empirical parameter values. These in turn will serve as baseline parameters in the eigenvalue analysis in the following Section.

7.4 Econometric analysis

In this section, the estimation results of the theoretical model of the previous section obtained with aggregate time series data of the U.S., the U.K., Germany and France are reported. The objective of these estimations is twofold. On the one hand, they are supposed to demonstrate the consistency of the theoretical model discussed in the previous section with aggregate empirical data and, on the other, to highlight the main similarities and differences of the determinants of wage and price inflation dynamics in these economies.

7.4.1 Model estimation

As discussed in the previous section, the law of motion for the real wage rate given by eq. (7.10) represents a reduced form expression of the two structural equations for $\hat{w}_t$ and $\hat{p}_t$. Noting again that the inflation climate variable is defined in the estimated model as a linearly declining function of the past twelve price inflation rates, the dynamics of the system (7.3)–(7.9) can be then reformulated as:

$$\hat{w}_t = \beta_{we}(e_{t-1} - e_o) - \beta_{wv} \ln(v_{t-1}/v_o) + \kappa_{wp}\hat{p}_t + (1 - \kappa_{wp})\pi_t^{12} + \kappa_{wz}\hat{z}_t$$
$$(7.22)$$

$$\hat{p}_t = \beta_{pu}(u_{t-1} - u_o) + \beta_{pv}\ln(v_{t-1}/v_o) + \kappa_{pw}(\hat{w}_t - \hat{z}_t) + (1 - \kappa_{pw})\pi_t^{12}$$

$$\ln u_t = \ln u_{t-1} + \alpha_u(u_{t-1} - u_o) - \alpha_{ui}(i_{t-1} - \hat{p}_t) + \alpha_{uv}(v_t - v_o)$$

$$\hat{e}_t = \alpha_{eu-1}\hat{u}_{t-1} + \alpha_{eu-2}\hat{u}_{t-2} + \alpha_{eu-3}\hat{u}_{t-3}$$

$$i_t = \phi_i i_{t-1} + (1 - \phi_i)\phi_{ip}\hat{p}_t + (1 - \phi_i)\phi_{iu}(u_{t-1} - u_o) + \epsilon_{it},$$

with sample means denoted by a subscript o (with the exception of e_o, which is supposed to represent the (eventually time-varying) NAIRU (Non-Accelerating Inflation Rate of Unemployment) equivalent employment rate). We estimate this model with time series of the U.S., the UK, Germany and France. The corresponding time series stem from the Federal Reserve Bank of St. Louis data set (see http://research.stlouisfed.org/fred2/) for the U.S. and the OECD (Organization for Economic Cooperation and Development) database for the European countries (where also estimates for the U.S. NAIRU are available). The data is quarterly, seasonally adjusted and concerns the period from 1980:1 to 2004:4. The logarithms of wages and prices are denoted by $\ln(w_t)$ and $\ln(p_t)$, respectively. Their first differences (backwardly dated), i.e. the current rate of wage and price inflation, are denoted $\hat{w}_t$ and $\hat{p}_t$.

As stated above, in eq. (7.22), $e - e_o$ represents the deviation of the employment rate from its NAIRU consistent level, and not the deviation of the former from its sample mean, as it is the case with the other variables. This differentiation is particularly important for the estimation of the European countries, since while the U.S. unemployment rate has fluctuated, roughly speaking, around a constant level (what would suggest a somewhat constant or at least a not all too varying NAIRU) over the last two decades, the European employment (unemployment) rate has displayed a persistent downwards (upwards) trend over the same period.

This particular European phenomenon has been explained by Layard, Nickell, and Jackman (1991) and Ljungqvist and Sargent (1998) by an overproportional increase in the number of long-term unemployed (i.e. workers with an unemployment duration over 12 months) with respect to short-term unemployed (workers with an unemployment duration of less than 12 months) and the phenomenon of hysteresis especially in the first group. One main explanation for the persistence in long-term unemployment is that human capital, and therefore the productivity of the unemployed, tend to diminish over time, which makes the long-term unemployed less 'hirable' for firms, see Pissarides (1992) and Blanchard and Summers (1991). Because the long-term unemployed become less relevant, and primarily the short-term unemployed are taken into account in the determination of nominal wages, the potential downward pressure on wages resulting from the unemployment of the former diminishes, with the result of a higher level of the NAIRU.[13] When long-term unemployment is high, the aggregate unemployment rate of an economy thus, 'becomes a poor indicator of effective labor supply,

---

13 See Blanchard and Wolfers (2000).

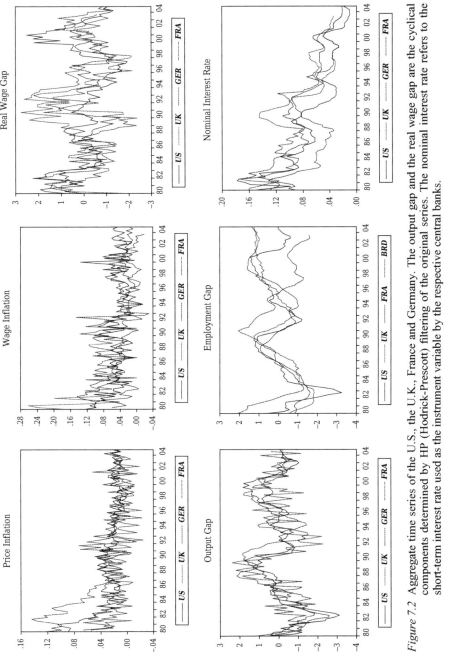

Figure 7.2 Aggregate time series of the U.S., the U.K., France and Germany. The output gap and the real wage gap are the cyclical components determined by HP (Hodrick-Prescott) filtering of the original series. The nominal interest rate refers to the short-term interest rate used as the instrument variable by the respective central banks.

Table 7.2 Phillips-Perron unit root test results

| | | | Sample: 1980: 1–2004: 4 | | |
Country	Variable	Lag length	Determ.	Adj. Test Stat.	Prob.*
U.S.	$\hat{p}_t$	1	–	−2.106	0.034
	$\hat{w}_t$	1	–	−2.589	0.010
	$d(e_t)$	–	–	−4.909	0.000
	$d(u_t)$	1	–	−7.122	0.000
	i	1	–	−1.856	0.061
U.K.	$\hat{p}_t$	1	–	−5.289	0.000
	$\hat{w}_t$	1	–	−3.139	0.002
	$d(e_t)$	1	–	−8.576	0.000
	$d(u_t)$	1	–	−23.695	0.000
	i	1	–	−1.697	0.085
Germany	$\hat{p}_t$	1	–	−3.788	0.000
	$\hat{w}_t$	1	–	−4.386	0.000
	$d(e_t)$	1	–	−3.657	0.000
	$d(u_t)$	1	–	−7.969	0.000
	i	1	–	−1.405	0.148
France	$\hat{p}_t$	1	–	−2.316	0.021
	$\hat{w}_t$	1	–	−2.376	0.018
	$d(e_t)$	1	–	−2.977	0.003
	$d(u_t)$	1	–	−8.494	0.000
	i	1	–	−1.550	0.113

*McKinnon (1996) one-sided p-values.

and the macroeconomic adjustment mechanisms – such as downward pressure on wages and inflation when unemployment is high – will then not operate effectively.'[14] Indeed, Llaudes (2005) for example, by using a modified wage Phillips curve which incorporates the different influences of long-and short-term unemployed in the wage determination, finds empirical evidence of the fact that for some OECD countries the long-term unemployed have only a negligible influence on the wage determination.

In order to test for stationarity, Phillips-Perron unit root tests were carried out for each series in order to account, not only for residual autocorrelation as is done by the standard ADF (Augmented Dickey Fuller) Tests, but also for possible residual heteroskedasticity when testing for stationarity. The Phillips-Perron test specifications and results are shown in Table 7.2. As it can be observed there, the applied unit root tests confirm the stationarity of all series with the exception of the short term nominal interest rate i in all countries. Nevertheless, although the Phillips-Perron test on these series cannot reject the null of a unit root, there

14 OECD (2002, p.189).

is no reason to expect these time series to be unit root processes. Indeed, it is reasonable to expect these rates to be constrained to certain limited ranges. Due to the general low power of the unit root tests, these results can be interpreted as providing only a hint of the possibility that the nominal interest rates exhibit a strong autocorrelation.

The discrete time version of the structural model formulated in the foregoing Section was estimated by means of instrumental variables system GMM (Generalized Method of Moments).[15] The use of an instrumental variables estimator such as GMM is indeed adequate since it allows for eventual regressor endogeneity to be accounted in the case that some of the explaining variables are not completely exogenous. Additionally, since among the explaining variables contained in our general specification there are also expected future variables, the use of an instrument set composed solely by lagged variables allows for the approximation of expected values of those forward-looking variables on the basis of the information available at time t. In order to test for the validity of the overidentifying restrictions (since we have more instrumental variables as coefficients to be estimated) we calculate the J-statistics as proposed by Hansen (1982).

The weighting matrix in the GMM objective function was chosen to allow for the resulting GMM estimates to be robust against possible heteroskedasticity and serial correlation of an unknown form in the error terms. Concerning the instrumental variables used in our estimations, since at time t only past values are contained in the information sets of the economic agents, for all five equations, besides the strictly exogenous variables, the last four lagged values of the employment rate, the labor share (detrended by the Hodrick-Prescott Filter) and the growth rate of labor productivity were incorporated. In order to test for the validity of the overidentifying restrictions, the J-statistics for both system estimations were calculated. We present and discuss the structural parameter estimates for the analyzed economies (t-statistics in brackets), as well as the J-statistics (p-values in brackets) in the next subsections.

Before discussing the estimation results for each country individually, it should be pointed out at a general level, that the GMM parameter estimates shown in the following tables deliver an empirical support for the theoretical Keynesian disequilibrium model specified in the previous section. This confirms for the U.K., Germany and France some of the empirical findings of Flaschel and Krolzig (2006) and Flaschel, Kauermann, and Semmler (2007) for the U.S. economy. Especially, the specification of cross-over inflation expectation terms, with the wage inflation

---

15 As stated in Wooldridge (2001, p.92), a GMM estimation possesses several advantages in comparison to more traditional estimation methods such as OLS (Ordinary Least Squares) and 2SLS (Two Stage Least Squares). This is especially true in time series models, where heteroskedasticity in the residuals is a common feature: 'the optimal GMM estimator is asymptotically no less efficient than two-stage least squares under homoskedasticity, and GMM is generally better under heteroskedasticity.' This and the additional robustness property of GMM estimates, of not relying on a specific assumption with respect to the distribution of the residuals, make the GMM methodology appropriate and advantageous for our estimation.

entering in the price Phillips curve and the price inflation entering in the wage Phillips Curve, as well as the inclusion of lagged price inflation (as a proxy for the inflationary climate term) in both equations seems to be supported by the data. Nevertheless, the role of this term in the wage and price inflation determination in the two analyzed economies seems to be somewhat heterogeneous: while, for example, in the estimated wage Phillips curves for the U.S. and the U.K. the influence of the perfectly foreseen actual price inflation κ_{wp} is around 0.4, and Germany and France it is around 0.8; in the estimated price Phillips curves the corresponding parameter κ_{pw} is around 0.10 for all economies with the exception of the U.K., where this parameter is around 0.35. The lagged price inflation thus seems to have a predominant role in the price determination by the firms, while actual price inflation apparently influences to a higher extent the dynamics of wage inflation.

Also along the lines of Flaschel and Krolzig (2006) and Flaschel, Kauermann, and Semmler (2007) the empirical evidence from the analyzed countries suggests that wage flexibility is larger than price flexibility (towards their demand pressure terms in the labor and goods markets, respectively) by and large, in all economies. Concerning the (log of the) wage share, namely the Blanchard-Katz error correction terms, we find by and large statistically significant and numerically similar coefficients in both wage and price adjustment equations with a similar influence on the price inflation dynamics in all analyzed economies and a larger effect of this variable on the wage dynamics in the European countries, confirming (from a qualitative perspective) the empirical findings of Blanchard and Katz (1999).

Next, the estimations of the individual countries are discussed in detail.

Estimation results: U.S. economy

As stated before, the theoretical model specification discussed in the previous section is confirmed by parameter estimates shown in Table 7.3 for the U.S. economy. As expected, we find a large responsiveness of wage inflation towards the labor market gap, which is higher than the responsiveness of price inflation towards the goods markets gap. Concerning the (log of the) wage share, statistically significant coefficients (with the expected negative sign in the wage inflation- and the positive sign in the price inflation equations) were estimated. This result contradicts the findings of Blanchard and Katz (1999), which found these coefficients to be significant only in Europe.

Concerning the effect of the wage share in the dynamic IS equation represented by the coefficient α_{uv}, a negative and statistically significant influence was found which supports the standard notion that real wage increases lead to a deacceleration of the economy due to its effects on aggregate investment and on net exports. With respect to the labor market dynamics, the sum of the estimated lagged coefficients of $\hat{u}$ is quite close to 0.3, what also confirms Okun's (1970) notion about the relationship between goods and labor markets. This result is consistent across all estimated economies with the exception of Germany.

Table 7.3 GMM parameter estimates: U.S.

		Estimation sample: 1980: 1–2004: 4					
		Kernel: Bartlett, Bandwidth: Andrews (2.59)					
$\hat{w}$	β_{we}	β_{wv}	κ_{wp}	κ_{wz}	const.	$\bar{R}^2$	DW
	0.948	−0.234	0.350	0.278	0.016	0.354	1.871
	[12.055]	[5.824]	[3.152]	[8.809]	[11.457]		
$\hat{p}$	β_{pu}	β_{pv}	κ_{pw}	const.		$\bar{R}^2$	DW
	0.293	0.116	0.046	–		0.763	1.263
	[13.277]	[5.107]	[3.167]				
$\hat{u}_t$	α_u	α_{ui}	α_{uv}	const.		$\bar{R}^2$	DW
	−0.077	−0.040	−0.176	0.002		0.902	1.521
	[9.028]	[4.256]	[8.163]	[3.511]			
$\hat{e}$	α_{eu-1}	α_{eu-2}	α_{eu-3}	α_{eu-4}		$\bar{R}^2$	DW
	0.202	0.114	0.040	–		0.387	1.638
	[22.780]	[8.204]	[3.884]				
i	ϕ_i	ϕ_{ip}	ϕ_{iu}			$\bar{R}^2$	DW
	0.831	2.173	0.423			0.929	1.916
	[71.464]	[36.152]	[5.113]				

Determinant Residual Covariance: 7.95E-21
J-Statistic [p-val]: 0.373 [0.975]

Estimation results: U.K.

Concerning the model estimation with U.K. time series shown in Table 7.4, it corroborates the overall formulation of the theoretical model and the related sign restrictions on the variables of the system, delivering by and large similar structural coefficients to those of the U.S. economy.

The main differences between the U.K. and the U.S. are the significantly lower values of κ_{wp}, α_{uu} and α_{uv}, as well as the larger value of κ_{pw}. Besides of these differences, an interesting finding in the U.K. estimation is the remarkable similarity in all coefficients in the wage and price inflation equations, what follows from the fact that these two macrovariables have exhibited in the U.K. a quite similar dynamic behavior in the last twenty years.

Estimation results: Germany

With respect to the Germany estimation, Table 7.5 shows three main findings which highlight the differences in the dynamics of wage and price inflation in the German economy with respect to the U.S. and the U.K.

In the first place, we have at first glance a counterintuitive finding that wage flexibility towards the labor market gap is indeed of a comparable dimension to

Table 7.4 GMM parameter estimates: U.K.

				Estimation sample: 1980: 1–2004: 4				
				Kernel: Bartlett, Bandwidth: Andrews: 2.62				
$\hat{w}$	β_{we}	β_{wv}	κ_{wp}	κ_{wz}	const.	$\bar{R}^2$	DW
	0.345	−0.212	0.289	0.360	0.010	0.589	1.183
	[15.84]	[16.678]	[21.971]	[21.784]	[20.998]		
$\hat{p}$	β_{pu}	β_{pv}	κ_{pw}	const.		$\bar{R}^2$	DW
	0.357	0.219	0.383	–		0.353	2.338
	[4.647]	[7.081]	[16.262]				
$\hat{u}_t$	α_u	α_{ui}	α_{uv}	const.		$\bar{R}^2$	DW
	−0.361	−0.015	−0.095	–		0.426	1.995
	[23.217]	[4.089]	[12.046]				
$\hat{e}$	α_{eu-1}	α_{eu-2}	α_{eu-3}	α_{eu-4}		$\bar{R}^2$	DW
	0.124	0.057	0.122			0.266	1.396
	[33.624]	[9.420]	[26.413]				
i	ϕ_i	ϕ_{ip}	ϕ_{iu}			$\bar{R}^2$	DW
	0.949	0.249	1.181			0.934	1.805
	[221.371]	[4.460]	[6.703]				

Determinant Residual Covariance: 1.91E-21
J-Statistic [p-val]: 0.241 [0.961]

that in the U.S. This, however, becomes understandable when one recalls that it is indeed the deviation of the actual employment rate to its NAIRU-consistent- and not to its long-run average level the variable included in the wage adjustment equation. In the second place, we find a quite high numerical value of β_{wv}, the effect of income distribution on wage inflation, compared with those in the other economies, showing the significant influence of trade unions in the German wage setting. And lastly, the relatively low value of β_{pu} should also be highlighted, which is indeed the lowest among all analyzed countries.

Concerning the dynamics of the capacity utilization rate, particularly interesting is the high numerical value of α_{uv}, which is the reaction coefficient of $\hat{u}$ with respect to the wage share for the German economy. This value, though, should be interpreted not as coming about from the importance of income distribution for the goods markets dynamics, but rather from the clear export-orientation of the German economy. Under this interpretation, a higher wage share leads to a slowdown of economic activity not due to the predominant decrease of investment over consumption, but rather due to the loss of competitiveness in the international goods markets. And finally, concerning Germany's employment rate dynamics, there are the low values of α_{eu} for several estimated lags, which clearly show the decoupling of the labor and the goods markets in the German economy.

Table 7.5 GMM parameter estimates: Germany

			Estimation sample: 1981: 2–2003: 4				
			Kernel: Bartlett, Bandwidth: Andrews (2.06)				
$\hat{w}$	β_{we}	β_{wv}	κ_{wp}	κ_{wz}	const.	$\bar{R}^2$	DW
	0.809	−0.887	1.149	0.190	0.001	0.371	2.035
	[22.012]	[45.026]	[50.048]	[12.076]	[2.543]		
$\hat{p}$	β_{pu}	β_{pv}	κ_{pw}		const.	$\bar{R}^2$	DW
	0.086	0.199	0.124		0.005	0.427	2.166
	[30.861]	[27.069]	[47.469]		[48.653]		
$\hat{u}_t$	α_u	α_{ui}	α_{uv}		const.	$\bar{R}^2$	DW
	−0.157	−0.044	−0.784		0.002	0.893	1.804
	[57.542]	[7.691]	[75.529]		[7.369]		
$\hat{e}$	α_{eu-1}	α_{eu-2}	α_{eu-3}	α_{eu-4}		$\bar{R}^2$	DW
	0.042	0.031	0.051	–		0.341	0.976
	[31.334]	[25.827]	[32.280]				
i	ϕ_i	ϕ_{ip}	ϕ_{iu}		const.	$\bar{R}^2$	DW
	0.926	0.631	1.195		0.002	0.966	1.309
	[438.31]	[10.827]	[35.775]		[26.713]		

Determinant Residual Covariance: 1.03E-20
J-Statistic [p-val]: 0.476 [0.754]

Estimation results: France

The estimated French parameter values (shown in Table 7.6), are also consistent with the parameter values obtained from the other economies, corroborating again the empirical validity of the present model specification.

Particularly we find highly significant coefficients of the cross-over inflation expectations terms in both wage and price inflation adjustment equations. Again, the coefficient κ_{wp} is found to be higher than κ_{pw}, as it was the case in all analyzed countries with the U.K. as the sole exception.

The main particularity in Table 7.6 is, however, that the estimation with French aggregate data delivers the Blanchard-Katz error correction terms coefficients with the lowest numerical values (though statistically significant) of all economies, and that the corresponding coefficient of the wage share in the goods markets equation is also the lowest estimated. Income distribution, though, seems to play a lesser role for both the dynamics of wage and price inflation in a direct manner as well as in an indirect manner through its effect on the dynamics of the capacity utilization rate.

7.5 Eigenvalue stability analysis

After having obtained empirical numerical values for the parameters of the theoretical model, in this section the effect of parameter value variations – and

Table 7.6 GMM parameter estimates: France

		Estimation sample: 1980: 1–2004: 4					
		Kernel: Bartlett, Bandwidth: Andrews (4.87)					

$\hat{w}$	β_{we}	β_{wv}	κ_{wp}	κ_{wz}	const.	$\bar{R}^2$	DW
	0.354	0.109	0.745	0.025	0.027	0.767	1.434
	[16.701]	[5.627]	[23.770]	[1.628]	[27.857]		
$\hat{p}$	β_{pu}	β_{pv}	κ_{pw}	const.		$\bar{R}^2$	DW
	0.403	0.158	0.070	–		0.888	1.172
	[31.699]	[12.668]	[7.028]				
$\hat{u}_t$	α_u	α_{ui}	α_{uv}	const.		$\bar{R}^2$	DW
	−0.113	−0.026	−0.047	0.001		0.906	1.609
	[17.295]	[9.983]	[25.074]	[7.605]			
$\hat{e}$	α_{eu-1}	α_{eu-2}	α_{eu-3}	α_{eu-4}		$\bar{R}^2$	DW
	0.209	0.188	0.106	–		0.436	0.689
	[31.442]	[25.941]	[12.588]				
i	ϕ_i	ϕ_{ip}	ϕ_{iu}			$\bar{R}^2$	DW
	0.935	1.236	1.649			0.958	1.716
	[214.86]	[20.367]	[7.697]				

Determinant Residual Covariance: 2.00E-21
J-Statistic [p-val]: 0.217 [0.975]

especially of wage- and price flexibility – for the stability of the economic system is further investigated.[16] For this, following Chen, Chiarella, Flaschel, and Semmler (2006), we focus on the effect of parameter variations for the maximum value of the real parts of the eigenvalues of the model using exemplarily the estimated parameters of the U.S. economy.[17]

These maximum eigenvalue diagrams concerning variations in the structural parameters of the wage–price module are depicted in Figure 7.3. They clearly show in a graphical manner what was indeed proven in the local stability analysis of Section 7.3, namely the relevance of the cross-over inflation expectations terms κ_{pw} and κ_{wp} in both wage and price Phillips Curves, of the degree of price flexibility to goods markets disequilibria β_{pu} as well as of the adjustment speed of the inflationary climate variable β_{π^c} for the stability of the system.

Indeed, in Figure 7.3 we can clearly observe that higher values of these parameters lead ceteris paribus to a loss of local stability of the steady state of

---

16 The calculations underlying the plots in this section were performed using the SND package described in Chiarella, Flaschel, Khomin, and Zhu (2002).
17 An analogous analysis was also performed using the estimated parameters of the other countries which led to similar conclusions. These graphs are available upon request.

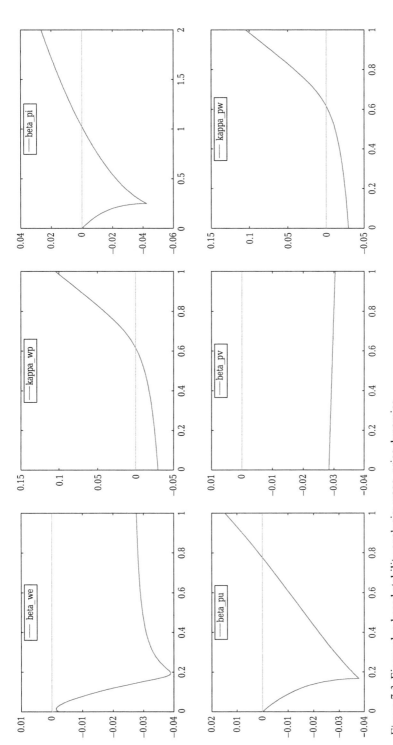

Figure 7.3 Eigenvalue-based stability analysis: wage–price dynamics.

the system. This leads to the conclusion that a somehow sluggish adjustment of the system variables is indeed needed to ensure local stability if the dynamics of the system are not driven by the rational expectations assumption, where possible unstable paths are simply not possible by definition.[18]

Concerning the parameters determining the goods markets dynamics, the second panel in the first row of Figure 7.4 shows the destabilizing influence of Mundell-Effect, which would increase for higher values of the goods markets real interest rate sensitivity parameter α_{ur}. As expected, the monetary policy parameters, shown in the second row of Figure 7.4, confirm two standard notions in the monetary policy literature (see e.g. Woodford (2003)): first, that a too large interest rate smoothing term might reduce the effectiveness of monetary policy and, second, that the validity of the Taylor principle, i.e. of a sufficiently active interest rate policy (what implies $\phi_\phi = \gamma_{ip}/\alpha_i - 1 > 0$) is central for the stability of the economy.

7.6 Concluding remarks

In this chapter, a significant extension and modification of the traditional approach to AS–AD growth dynamics developed by Chen, Chiarella, Flaschel, and Semmler (2006) was discussed and estimated with aggregate time series of the main industrialized countries.

The various estimations of the structural model equations for the different economies, besides confirming the theoretical sign restrictions of the dynamical system, delivered some interesting insights into the similarities and differences of both economies with respect to the analyzed macroeconomic variables. In the first place, a remarkable similarity in nearly all of the estimated coefficients in the structural equations was found. The analyzed economies seem thus to share more common characteristics than is commonly believed, specially concerning the wage inflation reaction to labor market developments, once a proxy for the rate of short-term unemployed rather than the aggregate unemployment rate is taken into account.

Taken together, these results deliver a different perspective on the dynamics of wage and price inflation. While the alternative New Keynesian approach is based on the assumption that primarily future expected values are relevant for the respective wage and price determination, the estimation results of this chapter deliver empirical support for an alternative specification of the wage–price inflation dynamics. Indeed, the cross-over expectation formation (where current price (wage) inflation influences the current wage (price) inflation rate) as well as the inflationary climate cannot be rejected as significant explanatory variables in the wage and price Phillips Curves. In sum, the system estimates for all analyzed countries discussed in the previous section provide empirical evidence that supports the theoretical sign restrictions in all economies. They, moreover, provide more clear answers with respect to the role of income distribution in the

---

18 See Flaschel, Groh, Proaño, and Semmler (2008, Ch.1) for an extensive discussion of this issue.

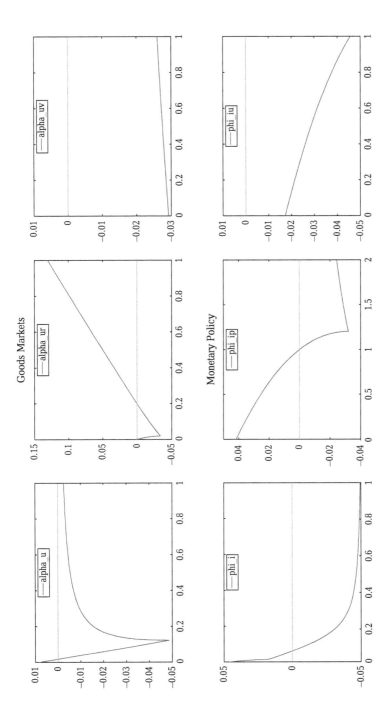

Figure 7.4 Eigenvalue stability analysis: goods markets dynamics and monetary policy.

considered disequilibrium AS–AD or DAS–AD dynamics. In particular, they also confirm the orthodox point of view that economic activity is likely to depend negatively on real unit wage costs. We have also a stabilizing effect of real wages on the dynamics of income distribution, in the sense that the growth rate of the real wages depends – through Blanchard-Katz error correction terms – negatively on its own level.

More empirical work is indeed needed in order to check for the model's parameter stability and so to account Lucas' (1976) Critique. However, given the empirical cross-country evidence discussed in this chapter, this framework (which may be called a disequilibrium approach to business cycle modeling of mature Keynesian type) seems to provide an interesting alternative to the DSGE (Dynamic Stochastic General Equilibrium) framework for the study of monetary policy and inflation dynamics.

References

Asada, T., P. Chen, C. Chiarella, and P. Flaschel (2006): "Keynesian Dynamics and the Wage-Price Spiral. A Baseline Disequilibrium Model," *Journal of Macroeconomics*, 28, 90–130.

Barro, R. (1994): "The Aggregate Supply / Aggregate Demand Model," *Eastern Economic Journal*, 20, 1–6.

Blanchard, O. J., and L. Katz (1999): "Wage Dynamics: Reconciling Theory and Evidence," *American Economic Review*, 89, 69–74, Papers and Proceedings of the One Hundred Eleventh Annual Meeting of the American Economic Association (May, 1999).

Blanchard, O. J., and L. H. Summers (1991): "Hysteresis and Unemployment," in *New Keynesian Economics. Coordination Failures and Real Rigidities*, ed. by G. N. Mankiw, and D. Romer, vol. 2, pp. 235–243. MIT Press, London.

Blanchard, O. J., and J. Wolfers (2000): "The Role of Shocks and Institutions in the Rise of European Unemployment: The Aggregate Evidence," *The Economic Journal*, 110(462), 1–33.

Calvo, G. A. (1983): "Staggered Prices in a Utility Maximizing Framework," *Journal of Monetary Economics*, 12, 383–398.

Chen, P., and P. Flaschel (2006): "Measuring the Interaction of Wage and Price Phillips Curves for the U.S. Economy," *Studies in Nonlinear Dynamics and Econometrics*, 10, 1–35.

Chen, P., C. Chiarella, P. Flaschel, and W. Semmler (2006): "Keynesian Macrodynamics and the Phillips Curve. An Estimated Baseline Macromodel for the U.S. Economy," in *Quantitative and Empirical Analysis of Nonlinear Dynamic Macromodels*, ed. by C. Chiarella, P. Flaschel, R. Franke, and W. Semmler, Amsterdam, Elsevier.

Chiarella, C., and P. Flaschel (1996): "Real and Monetary Cycles in Models of Keynes-Wicksell Type," *Journal of Economic Behavior and Organization*, 30, 327–351.

——— (2000): *The Dynamics of Keynesian Monetary Growth: Macro Foundations*. Cambridge University Press, Cambridge, U.K.

Chiarella, C., P. Flaschel, and R. Franke (2005): *Foundations for a Disequilibrium Theory of the Business Cycle. Qualitative Analysis and Quantitative Assesment*. Cambridge University Press, Cambridge, U.K.

Chiarella, C., P. Flaschel, A. Khomin, and P. Zhu (2002): *The SND Package. Applications to Keynesian Monetary Growth Dynamics*, vol. 22 of *Dynamic Economic Theory*. Peter Lang, Frankfurt am Main.

Clarida, R., and M. Gertler (1997): "How the Bundesbank Conducts Monetary Policy," in *Reducing Inflation: Motivation and Strategy*, ed. by C. D. Romer, and D. H. Romer, pp. 363–406. Chicago University Press, Chicago.

Erceg, C. J., D. W. Henderson, and A. T. Levin (2000): "Optimal Monetary Policy with Staggered Wages and Prices," *Journal of Monetary Economics*, 46, 281–313.

Fair, R. (2000): "Testing the NAIRU Model for the United States," *The Review of Economics and Statistics*, 82, 64–71.

Flaschel, P., and H.-M. Krolzig (2006): "Wage-Price Phillips Curves and Macroeconomic Stability. Basic Structural Form, Estimation and Analysis," in *Quantitative and Empirical Analysis of Nonlinear Dynamic Macromodels*, ed. by C. Chiarella, P. Flaschel, R. Franke, and W. Semmler, Amsterdam. Elsevier.

Flaschel, P., G. Groh, C. Proaño, and W. Semmler (2008): *Topics in Applied Macrodynamics Theory*. Springer, Berlin, forthcoming.

Flaschel, P., G. Kauermann, and W. Semmler (2007): "Testing Wage and Price Phillips Curves for the United States," *Metroeconomica*, 58, 550–581.

Galí, J., M. Gertler, and J. D. López-Salido (2001): "European Inflation Dynamics," *European Economic Review*, 45, 1237–1270.

Groth, C. (1992): "Some Unfamiliar Dynamics in a Familiar Macromodel," *Journal of Economics*, 58, 293–305.

Hansen, L. P. (1982): "Large Sample Properties of Generalized Method of Moments Estimators," *Econometrica*, 50(4), 1029–1054.

Layard, R., S. Nickell, and R. Jackman (1991): *Unemployment: Macroeconomic Performance and the Labor Market*. Oxford University Press, Oxford.

Ljungqvist, L., and T. J. Sargent (1998): "The European Unemployment Dilemma," *Journal of Political Economy*, 106(3), 514–550.

Llaudes, R. (2005): "The Phillips Curve and Long-Term Unemployment," Working Paper 441, European Central Bank.

Lucas, R. E. J. (1976): "Econometric Policy Evaluation: A Critique," *Carnegie-Rochester Conference Series on Public Policy*, 1, 19–46.

Mankiw, G. (2001): "The Inexorable and Mysterious Tradeoff between Inflation and Unemployment," *Economic Journal*, 111, 45–61.

OECD (2002): "The Ins and Outs of Long-Term Unemployment," in *OECD Employment Outlook*, pp. 189–239. OECD.

Okun, A. M. (1970): *The Political Economy of Prosperity*. The Brookings Institution.

Pissarides, C. (1992): "Loss of Skill During Unemployment and the Persistence of Unemployment Shocks," *Quarterly Journal of Economics*, 107(4), 1371–1391.

Romer, D. (2000): "Keynesian Macroeconomics without the LM Curve," *The Journal of Economic Perspectives*, 14(2), 149–169.

Rose, H. (1967): "On the Non-Linear Theory of Employment," *Review of Economic Studies*, 34, 153–173.

Rotemberg, J. (1982): "Monopolistic Price Adjustment and Aggregate Output," *Review of Economic Studies*, 49, 517–531.

Rudebusch, G. D., and L. E. Svensson (1999): "Policy Rules for Inflation Targeting," in *Monetary Policy Rules*, ed. by J. B. Taylor, chap. 15. The University of Chicago Press, Chicago.

Sbordone, A. M. (2004): "A Limited Information Approach to Simultaneous Estimation of Wage and Price Dynamics," Rutgers University, mimeo.

Sims, C. (1987): "Discussion of Olivier J. Blanchard, Aggregate and Individual Price Adjustment," *BPEA*, 1, 117–20.

Taylor, J. B. (1993): "Discretion versus Policy Rules in Practice," *Carnegie-Rochester Conference Series on Public policy*, 39, 195–214.

Tobin, J. (1975): "Keynesian Models of Recession and Depression," *American Economic Review*, 45, 195–202.

Walsh, C. E. (2003): *Monetary Theory and Policy*. MIT Press, Cambridge, MA.

Woodford, M. (2003): *Interest and Prices. Foundations of a Theory of Monetary Policy*. Princeton University Press, Princeton.

Wooldridge, J. M. (2001): "Applications of Generalized Method of Moments Estimation," *Journal of Economic Perspectives*, 15(4), 87–100.

8 Applied DAD–DAS modelling
Elaboration and calibration

8.1 Introduction

This chapter is related to current work on modern macroeconomic modelling in a, broadly speaking, Keynesian (but not new-Keynesian) tradition. It particularly draws on the disequilibrium approach advanced in Chiarella *et al.* (2005), which refers to Keynes, Metzler, Goodwin and Taylor as its patron saints. 'Goodwin' indicates that income distribution plays a crucial role in the dynamics. In the form of the wage share, it is determined by the interplay of a wage as well as a price Phillips curve, and in turn impacts positively on aggregate demand *via* workers' consumption and negatively *via* profit-oriented investment. The Metzlerian part is a consequence of goods market disequilibrium, which is absorbed by inventories, while the evolution of the latter feeds back on planned inventory investment and thus aggregate supply. 'Taylor' takes account of monetary policy and follows the general consensus reached over the last decade that the central bank adopts an interest rate rule, most often specified as a variant of the Taylor rule responding to inflation and the output gap.

Though modelled in a parsimonious way, when combined with sales and inflation expectations the dynamic system obtained in the end is six-dimensional. This means limited prospects for an analytical treatment, so that the model has to be studied by means of numerical simulations, an endeavor for which numerical values have to be assigned to the parameters. Chiarella *et al.* (2005, Chapters 5 and 6) use calibration methods for the parameter search, which amounts to an extensive investigation that requires judgement and dealing with a great variety of details.[1]

The 'Keynes-Metzler-Goodwin-Taylor model' cannot be easily estimated by econometric methods since, briefly, some components are too differentiated and some of the disequilibrium adjustment rules include composed variables whose empirical counterparts, or their behavior, are problematic. A good strategy, if one

---

1 For each of the topics sketched in the first paragraph many small-scale macrodynamic models have been put forward in the literature. Besides Chiarella *et al.* (2005), however, we do not know of other disequilibrium modelling approaches that address these themes simultaneously, with a similar degree of complexity and with similarly meticulous care.

nevertheless wants to try an estimation, is to take a step backward and simplify the model at the cost of sacrificing some of its structure. The equations thus arising will no longer meet all standards one can demand from a consistent theoretical model, although they still have more structure than many other theoretically motivated estimation equations. In effect, what such a simplification will arrive at can be best described as a *semistructural* model.

This route has been taken in a recent working paper by Proaño, Flaschel, Ernst and Semmler (2005;[2] PFES henceforth). They drop the Metzlerian feedbacks and the explicit distinction between workers' and rentiers' income, and regarding expectations an exogenous time path of the model's so-called inflation climate is specified. In this way, they set up five equations to be estimated, which determine wage inflation, price inflation, capacity utilization, the employment rate and the interest rate. As their theoretical background the authors appeal to a wage and price Phillips curve, to the IS (Investment Saving) concept, Okun's law and the Taylor rule respectively. The results from their GMM (Generalized Method of Moments) estimation appear very promising; all coefficients of interest come out significant and with the correct sign.

Here we take the PFES estimation as a point of departure.[3] The contribution here goes beyond this characterization of the data, widens the perspective of the separate components of the model, and seeks to study the interaction of these individual parts when, using some auxiliary assumptions, they are combined and form a closed dynamical system again (the estimation equations themselves do not yet constitute a dynamical system proper). We can then simulate this (augmented) model with the estimated coefficients and ask the first question: does its dynamics make economic sense, qualitatively as well as in terms of quantitative relationships? This is in fact the starting point for a numerical investigation of its own.

Our analysis in this chapter proceeds as follows. Section 8.2 is a recapitulation of the PFES estimation. Section 8.3 arranges, and augments, its equations such that a closed dynamical system is obtained, where we set up a four-dimensional deterministic differential equations system and a system of stochastic difference equations. Section 8.4 begins with a set of impulse-response functions of this economy. The finding of extreme slow convergence motivates a respecification of the adjustments of the model's inflation climate. This gives us an alternative empirical time path of this variable, on whose basis the PFES equations are re-estimated. In fact, substituting the new coefficients into the dynamic model yields far more satisfactory impulse-response functions, which is also supported by a complementary VAR (vector autoregression) estimation. In addition,

---

2 Revised and (in various directions) extended versions of this paper are given by the contributions on which Ch.7 of the present book is based, see the introductory section of this chapter.
3 PFES is concerned with the U.S. economy and data for a Euro zone. After the estimation, special emphasis is put on a comparison of the results for the two economies. By contrast, the present chapter exclusively deals with the U.S. data.

the variabilities of the main variables in the stochastic model turn out to be well compatible with the statistics of their empirical counterparts.

Section 8.5 is devoted to a deeper analysis of the properties of the system and the numerical coefficients on which we thus settle down. Section 8.5.1 designs an experiment that in a stylized impulse-response manner seeks to reflect the increasing pressure under which the position of workers has come in recent years. Here as well as in the subsections to follow the distinction between a profit-led and wage-led regime becomes relevant. This notion means that a rise in the wage share induces a negative reaction of capacity utilization (as estimated) or a positive reaction, respectively. Sections 8.2 and 8.3 investigate whether *ceteris paribus* variations of a parameter are stabilizing or destabilizing. In the eigenvalue analysis in Section 8.2, these terms refer to the (deterministic) model's steady state position, whether these changes may render it stable or unstable. Section 8.3 is concerned with the stochastic economy, where the expressions refer to a decrease or increase of the standard deviations of the model-generated time series. As an upshot of these investigations, both sections present a table that succinctly classifies the parameters in the wage–price dynamics as stabilizing, destabilizing or ambiguous. Section 8.6 concludes.

8.2 Econometric estimation: the point of departure

The semistructural Keynes-Goodwin model that was estimated in PFES refers to quarterly data. It integrates five building blocks.

1 *A wage Phillips curve (WPC):* While the main driving variable is the employment rate, nominal wages are in addition negatively affected by the wage share. As benchmark terms, wage inflation takes the growth of labour productivity into account, and it moves with the contemporaneous rate of price inflation and a variable that represents a general inflation climate in the economy.

2 *A price Phillips curve (PPC):* Besides capacity utilization as the main driving variable, again the wage share takes effect; in this relationship in a positive manner. Cost push terms are contemporaneous wage inflation and the inflation climate, whereas productivity growth may have a negative effect. The contemporaneous cross rates of inflation in WPC and PPC reflect the idea of myopic perfect foresight in the nominal variables.

3 *An IS relationship:* Utilization, *via* aggregate demand, is supposed to be determined by two lags of itself, the real interest rate, and also by income distribution in the form of the wage share. On an *a priori* basis the latter influence is ambiguous; a rise in the wage share lowers profits and so reduces investment demand, on the other hand, it increases the component of consumption demand that is paid out of wages. If the first effect dominates the economy is said to be *profit-led*, in the other case, it is said to be *wage-led*.

4 *Okun's law:* Employment is linked to capacity utilization by a growth rate version of Okun's law, such that the change in the employment rate depends on three lags of the changes in utilization.

Table 8.1 Quarterly data for the econometric estimation

Variable	Description
e	Employment rate
i	Federal funds rate
p	Implicit GDP price deflator
u	Capacity utilization in the manufacturing sector
v	Wage share (real compensation per unit of output)
w	Compensation per hour
z	Output per hour
π^{12}	Moving average of price inflation over the past 12 quarters with linearly declining weights, which serves to represent the inflation climate

Note: US economy; wages, output and hours refer to the nonfarm business sector.

5 *Taylor rule:* According to the now standard view on central banks, monetary policy is described by an interest rate reaction function. Specifically, a version of the Taylor rule responding to inflation and output is employed that includes an interest rate smoothing motive.

Table 8.1 lists the quarterly time series of the US economy on which the estimation is based. Denoting logarithms of a time series x_t as $\ln(x_t)$ and the first (backward) differences in logs as $d\ln(x_t)$, PFES settle down on the following specification:

$$d\ln(w_t) = \beta_{we}e_{t-1} - \beta_{wv}\ln(v_{t-1}) + \kappa_{wp}d\ln(p_t) + \kappa_{w\pi}\pi_t^{12}$$
$$+ \kappa_{wz}d\ln(z_t) + c_w + \varepsilon_{wt} \tag{8.1}$$

$$d\ln(p_t) = \beta_{pu}u_{t-1} + \beta_{pv}\ln(v_{t-1}) + \kappa_{pw}d\ln(w_t) + \kappa_{p\pi}\pi_t^{12}$$
$$- \kappa_{pz}d\ln(z_t) + c_p + \varepsilon_{pt} \tag{8.2}$$

$$u_t = \beta_{uu1}u_{t-1} + \beta_{uu2}u_{t-2} - \beta_{ui}(i_{t-1} - d\ln(p_t)) + \gamma_{uv}v_{t-1} + c_u + \varepsilon_{ut} \tag{8.3}$$

$$d\ln(e_t) = \beta_{eu1}d\ln(u_{t-1}) + \beta_{eu2}d\ln(u_{t-2}) + \beta_{eu3}d\ln(u_{t-3}) + \varepsilon_{et} \tag{8.4}$$

$$i_t = \beta_{ii}i_{t-1} + \beta_{ip}d\ln(p_t) + \beta_{ip}u_t + c_i + \varepsilon_{it} \tag{8.5}$$

On theoretical grounds, the coefficients β are non-negative and the κ's are to be thought of as weights between 0 and 1 (the precise sense of these weights is made explicit below). The single letter $\gamma = \gamma_{uv}$ for the coefficient on the wage share in the IS equation (8.3) is chosen in order to indicate that this effect is theoretically ambiguous, a negative or positive sign characterizing the economy as, respectively, profit-led and wage-led. The constants c capture the steady state relationships between the variables.

The estimation by PFES treated (8.1)–(8.5) as a system and applied the GMM to it.[4] The coefficient κ_{pw} was set equal to zero after observing that this restriction raises the complementary weight $\kappa_{p\pi}$ to, even precisely, unity.[5] All other coefficients came out strongly significant and with the desired sign, or in the desired range. In addition, κ_{wp} and $\kappa_{w\pi}$ (nearly) add up to unity, as they should (see next section). In detail, for the sample period 1961:4–2004:4 the following point estimates for the reaction coefficients were obtained:[6]

$$
\begin{aligned}
&\kappa_{wp} = 0.47 && \kappa_{w\pi} = 0.51 && \kappa_{wz} = 0.23 \\
&\beta_{we} = 0.60 && \beta_{wv} = 0.27 \\
&\kappa_{pw} = 0.00 && \kappa_{p\pi} = 1.00 && \kappa_{pz} = 0.06 \\
&\beta_{pu} = 0.38 && \beta_{pv} = 0.25 && && \text{(8.6)} \\
&\beta_{uu1} = 1.13 && \beta_{uu2} = -0.23 && \beta_{ui} = 0.05 && \gamma_{uv} = -0.10 \\
&\beta_{eu1} = 0.17 && \beta_{eu2} = 0.12 && \beta_{eu3} = 0.05 \\
&\beta_{ii} = 0.92 && \beta_{ip} = 0.11 && \beta_{iu} = 0.11
\end{aligned}
$$

Regarding the order of magnitude of the coefficients that connect levels and rates of change, it has to be noted that all growth rates are annualized, i.e. the first differences in logs in (8.1)–(8.5) are multiplied by four.

Since the reaction and weight coefficients are not only significant but, on an *a priori* basis, also make perfect economic sense, the estimation appears to be a great success that lends full support to the present Keynes-Goodwin modelling framework. Of course, this is not the end of the story, and in a next step we have to take a wider perspective at the model at large, which is more than just the sum total of its separate parts. Accordingly, we have to turn to the interaction of the individual parts and inquire into the dynamic properties to which the numerical coefficients in (8.6) may give rise.

Here, the first thing to recognize is that eqs (8.1)–(8.5) are so far only our raw materials. They still have to be processed in such a way that they form a closed dynamic system of its own, which requires a few additional specifications and theoretical assumptions. This transformation is the subject of Section 8.3, which is concerned with a somewhat simplified formulation in continuous time as well as with a more extensive discrete-time version.

---

4 Besides the strictly exogenous variables, the following instruments were used: the contemporaneous and lagged first differences of an 'employment rate' constructed from hours, the real interest rate, the lagged nominal interest rate, lagged productivity growth, and four lags of the employment rate, the first differences in utilization, and the wage share (detrended by the Hodrick-Prescott filter).

5 It should be remarked that undoing the restriction $\kappa_{pw} = 0$ leads to the disconcerting results that β_{pu} becomes negative and the standard error of (8.2) increases, although the rest of the system remains unaffected.

6 The constants can be omitted since PFES do not discuss their implications for a steady state solution, i.e. a stationary point of system (8.1)–(8.5).

The common task to both model variants includes the following six points: (*a*) Derive the motions of the wage share v and labour productivity z, which are unexplained in (8.1)–(8.5), from the motions of the other variables in the system. (*b*) Modify the determination of the inflation climate, so that it is theoretically more appealing and gets rid of the twelve quarterly lags. (*c*) Make the constants in the regression equations explicit. (*d*) Give more structure to the weight coefficients κ. (*e*) Maintain the growth rate formulation of Okun's law but augment it with a level variable, which helps ensure uniqueness of the equilibrium position. (*f*) Respecify, in fact simplify, the interest rate reaction function, since the recent literature (discussed in the following Section) gives good reasons to consider a high persistence coefficient like $\beta_{ii} = 0.92$ as spurious.

8.3 Transforming the estimated equations into a closed dynamic system

8.3.1 Output and employment adjustments

Because of the easy growth rate formulations for composed variables, it is convenient to begin the modelling in continuous and in a deterministic setting. The time derivative of a dynamic variable $x = x(t)$ is denoted $\dot{x} = dx/dt$, and its growth rate $\hat{x} = \dot{x}/x$. The underlying unit of time is to be thought of as a year. Hence, a term $\hat{x}$ in the continuous-time framework approximately equals $4 \cdot d \ln(x_t)$ if it is related to its counterpart in the quarterly model (8.1)–(8.5). The steady state value of x is designated x^o.

Let us first consider the changes of the rate of capacity utilization as they are described in (8.3). It will be seen in a moment that in a continuous-time formulation the coefficients there obtained have to be rescaled. To limit the changes in notation to a minimum, it is useful to denote utilization from now on by y, instead of u.[7] To translate the corresponding equation (8.3) into continuous time we disregard the second lag of utilization in this equation. Before, still in discrete time, we reestimate the entire five-equations system with just one lag u_{t-1} in (8.3). While the coefficients in the other equations remain practically unaltered, the coefficient on lagged utilization decreases below unity, $\beta_{uu1} = 0.90$. On this basis, and turning to the new symbol y for the utilization rate, we can subtract y_{t-1} from both sides of the equation. The coefficient $\tilde{\beta}_{yy}$ in the resulting equation, $y_t - y_{t-1} = -\tilde{\beta}_{yy}y_{t-1} +$ rest, is then given by $\tilde{\beta}_{yy} = 1 - 0.90 = 0.10$.

For the continuous-time analogue, it still has to be noted that these differences in utilization are quarterly. Therefore, we divide both sides of the equation by 0.25; identify the expression $(y_t - y_{t-1})/0.25$ with the time derivative $\dot{y}$ in the continuous-time framework; disregard the lags on the right-hand side of the

---

7 The new letter may also be indicative of the two options that we introduce in the following Section when we have to be more explicit about the precise concept of capacity (one of the options will correspond to the output gap which in the literature is usually denoted as y).

equation; refer to the percentage deviations $(v - v^o)/v^o$ of the wage share from its steady state value v^o (instead of the reference to, just, v in (8.3)); and replace $\tilde{\beta}_{yy}$, β_{ui}, γ_{uv}, with $\beta_{yy} = \tilde{\beta}_{yy}/0.25$, $\beta_{yi} = \beta_{ui}/0.25$ and $\gamma_{yv} = v^o\gamma_{uv}/0.25$, respectively. Besides the wage share, we also compare utilization and the real interest rate on the right-hand side to their equilibrium values, which are likewise denoted by a superscript 'o'.[8] For convenience, we may furthermore, locally around equilibrium utilization $y = 1$, work with the growth rate $\hat{y}$ instead of the derivative $\dot{y}$ (which as just noted we obtained from $(y_t - y_{t-1})/0.25$). Taken together, the changes in utilization are described by the equation

$$\hat{y} = -\beta_{yy}(y - 1) - \beta_{yi}[i - \hat{p} - (i^o - \hat{p}^o)] + \gamma_{yv}(v - v^o)/v^o \tag{8.7}$$

As eq. (8.7) views output as demand-driven, employment has to adjust accordingly. In this respect, the estimation has not referred to an explicit production function but (8.4) has specified the changes in the rate (not the volume) of employment as an empirical regularity, as a version of Okun's law with distributed lags. For its translation into continuous time, the lags on the right-hand collapse and we get $\hat{e} = \beta_{ey}\hat{y}$. It will, however, be seen in the following Section that together with the other dynamic equations this would give rise to a continuum of equilibrium points. The critical issue is not so much multiplicity as such, but the feature that the equilibrium values of several variables will generally depart from their target or benchmark values. To avoid this inconsistency, we add to the changes in utilization the influence of a level variable.[9]

A conceptually attractive variable for that purpose is the wage share. Our idea is that in times of rising capacity utilization the creation of new jobs is a little delayed if wages are already relatively high. To evaluate the current wage share as relatively high or low, its steady state value v^o is used as a benchmark. This leads us to augment Okun's law as

$$\hat{e} = \beta_{ey}\hat{y} - \beta_{ev}(v - v^o)/v^o \tag{8.8}$$

where β_{ey} is a small 'error correction' coefficient. In fact, when in the estimation of (8.1)–(8.5) we include $\ln v$ in various lags or leads in (8.4) and also allow for autocorrelation in the residuals, the coefficient persistently comes out negative, though it is extremely small with t-statistics between 1.2 and 1.6. We therefore regard a weak influence of the wage share in (8.8) as an acceptable rough-and-ready device to ensure uniqueness of the steady state in a simple way. Concretely, in the numerical investigations later on we will set β_{ev} as low as 0.01.

---

8 The sum of the products of these values with the corresponding reaction coefficients should be close to the constant c_u in (8.3).

9 Just for the continuous-time model it would be possible to circumvent this problem by integrating the growth rate equation $\hat{e} = \beta_{ey}\hat{y}$ as $e/e^o = y^{\beta_{ey}}$, where e^o is the given 'natural' rate of employment. In the discrete-time model, however, we wish to maintain the three lags of the changes in utilization on the right-hand side of (8.4), whereby the uniqueness problem crops up again. Since in other respects we want the two model versions to be as close as possible, we introduce the level variable into the Okun equation already here.

The coefficient β_{ey}, on the other hand, corresponds to the β_{euj} ($j = 1, 2, 3$) in (8.4). We will choose for β_{ey} a value slightly less than the sum of the latter three coefficients, $\beta_{ey} = 0.30$. Note that this is well in the range of Okun's rule of thumb that the unemployment rate changes inversely 1:3 with the output gap; production must rise by three percent in order to reduce the unemployment rate by one percentage point.

8.3.2 Labour productivity as an endogenous variable

It should first of all be made explicit that although the models considers variable growth rates of labour productivity, it neglects the distinction between movements in hours and the number of jobs. We just write L for 'employment' and leave it open whether the employment rate e is conceived of as hours worked over hours that the labour force would work under 'normal' conditions, or the ratio $z = Y/L$ is a ratio of output to the number of current jobs. Nevertheless, since 'output-employment ratio' in the latter case would be an unfamiliar expression, we continue to call z labour productivity.[10]

If the time path of the labour force L^s and productive capacity Y^c were specified for the estimation equations, (8.3) and (8.4) would also determine the volumes of output Y and employment L, and thus productivity z. The productivity growth rate would then be no exogenous variable (as $\hat{z} = d \ln z_t$ was treated in the estimation) but determined from within the system. Since L^s and Y^c are exogenous or at least predetermined for the firms, once they decide on Y and L, labour productivity is a residual for them. Therefore, we wish to determine $\hat{z}$ as an endogenous variable from the other equations of the system. To this end some auxiliary assumptions are introduced, which amount to statements about L^s and Y^c and which are formulated in such a way that no additional dynamic state variable will enter the stage. The price to be paid for this simplification is that the employment part of the model has no fully structural (or satisfactory) interpretation.

It may be emphasized that if we have an expression for productivity growth $\hat{z}$, we also have a law of motion for the wage share $v = wL/pY = (w/p)/z$, by way of the growth rates $\hat{v} = \hat{w} - \hat{p} - \hat{z}$. While $\hat{z}$ could disappear again if the influence of labour productivity in the wage Phillips curve is suitably specified, it will be seen that such a convenient device is not supported by the estimation results. Hence, the variations of $\hat{z}$ are a more than peripheral part of the model.

As an initial step in the determination of the productivity growth rate, observe that if the changes of productive capacity Y^c in the expression for utilization $y = Y/Y^c$, and the changes of the labour force L^s in the employment rate $e = L/L^s$, are given, then, with $\hat{y} = \hat{Y} - \hat{Y}^c$ and $\hat{e} = \hat{L} - \hat{L}^s$, productivity growth results as

$$\hat{z} = \hat{Y} - \hat{L} = (\hat{y} + \hat{Y}^c) - (\hat{e} + \hat{L}^s)$$

---

10 An explicit distinction between hours and employment and econometric estimations of gradual adjustments of each of the two variables can be found in Franke (2006, Section 8.6).

Two options could be considered to integrate this open expression into the present framework. In a first specification, productive capacity Y^c could be viewed as being given by the firms' stock of fixed capital, $Y^c = u^n K$, where the constant u^n is the output-capital ratio that would prevail under 'normal' conditions (in the presence of Harrod-neutral technical progress). In this way, $\hat{Y} = \hat{y} + \hat{Y}^c = \hat{y} + \hat{K}$. Here, on the one hand, we could introduce more structure into the model by not only making aggregate demand explicit but also the component of net investment ($I = \hat{K}$). According to what has been said earlier, however, this treatment is ruled out since, to say the least, it would require a generalization of eq. (8.3) and the estimation of additional coefficients.

On the other hand, the labour force L^s may not be regarded as an exogenously growing part of the population but as responding to the general economic climate. While this is certainly a relevant phenomenon, these adjustments will take some time in the real world.[11] As a theoretical short-cut we might nevertheless proxy the economic climate by the growth rate of the capital stock, less the (constant) growth rate of trend productivity g_z, and assume that the adjustments of the labour force are instantaneous, which provides us with $\hat{L}^s = \hat{K} - g_z$. With these specifications, the foregoing equation for the actual growth rate of labour productivity becomes

$$\hat{z} = \hat{y} - \hat{e} + g_z \qquad (8.9)$$

If this assumption on the labour force is felt to be too restrictive, one can alternatively proxy productive capacity by the concept of potential output, which grows at a constant rate $\hat{Y}^c = g^o$. In fact, $(y - 1)$ could then be referred to as the output gap, which is the usual representation of economic activity in most of the (more or less new-Keynesian) small-scale models of the 'new consensus in macroeconomics'. Suppose furthermore that also the labour force grows at a constant rate, $\hat{L}^s = g_\ell$. The two rates g^o and g_ℓ are linked by the growth rate g_z of trend productivity; without suggesting any causal direction the steady state relationship between output, labour force and productivity reads $g^o - g_\ell - g_z = 0$.[12] The implication for the changes in actual productivity is $\hat{z} = (\hat{y} + g^o) - (\hat{e} + g_\ell) = \hat{y} - \hat{e} + (g^o - g_\ell) = \hat{y} - \hat{e} + g_z$, which coincides with (8.9). In any case, eq. (8.9) will be part of our closure of the estimated dynamic system.

---

11 It is, however, remarkable that the correlation of the labour force with output has become much stronger over the past 15 or 20 years, with a lag of only 2 quarters; see Franke (2006, Section 4.3).

12 From a neoclassical point of view, the evolution of labour supply is an autonomous process and, given the rate of technical progress, establishes the growth potential of the economy, to which firms adjust in long-run equilibrium. Thus, $g^o = g_\ell + g_z$. A more Keynesian perspective is that g^o, in the end, derives from the (long-term) animal spirits of the firms, and it is the labour force (through migration or discouraged and encouraged workers, for example) that in the long-run adjusts to it, yielding $g_\ell = g^o - g_z$. Both interpretations are possible here.

8.3.3 Wage and price Phillips curves

The wage and price Phillips curves have to take the role of κ_{wp}, $\kappa_{w\pi}$, κ_{wz} and κ_{pw}, $\kappa_{p\pi}$, κ_{pz} as weights into account. In eq. (8.1), we explicitly demand that the weights on current inflation (κ_{wp}) and the inflation climate ($\kappa_{w\pi}$) add up to one. The inflation climate itself, whose twelve-quarter moving average specification will be modified below, is from now on denoted as π^c. Regarding the coefficient κ_{wz} on labour productivity growth, the steady state condition $\hat{v} = \hat{w} - \hat{p} - \hat{z} = 0$ has to be observed. Hence, with $\pi^c = \hat{p}$ in this position, (8.1) implies $\hat{p} + \hat{z} = \hat{w} = \kappa_{wp}\hat{p} + (1 - \kappa_{wp})\pi^c + \kappa_{wz}\hat{z} + (1 - \kappa_{wz})\cdot$ something else. A meaningful 'something else' is the growth rate of trend productivity, g_z. In this way, (8.1) becomes a fully structural wage Phillips curve,

$$\hat{w} = [\kappa_{wz}\hat{z} + (1 - \kappa_{wz})g_z] + [\kappa_{wp}\hat{p} + (1 - \kappa_{wp})\pi^c] + f_w(e, v)$$

$$f_w(e, v) = \beta_{we}(e - e^o) - \beta_{wv}(v - v^o)/v^o \tag{8.10}$$

The two terms in square brackets provide a benchmark for neutral wage adjustments, in the sense that wages increase in line with productivity and (current and expected) prices. The functional expression f_w summarizes the two driving variables, employment and the wage share. As already indicated in footnote 9 earlier, e^o is here treated as an exogenously given 'natural' rate of employment, the counterpart of the usual NAIRU specification.

The negative influence of the wage share in (8.10) can be given an immediate intuitive interpretation. It sees this Phillips curve as arising from a wage bargaining process where the parties also have an eye on the general distribution of total income. At relatively low values of the wage share, workers seek to catch up to what is considered a normal, or 'fair', level, and they succeed in including this aspect in the wage bargaining. By the same token, workers are somewhat restrained in their wage claims if v is currently above normal.

Another theoretical (and perhaps more fashionable) underpinning could be borrowed from Blanchard and Katz (2000). They specify a wage curve argument in which the tighter the labour market, the higher the level of the real wage (rather than its rate of change!), given the workers' reservation wage. The wage share enters this scenario in a logarithmic form by assuming that the reservation wage depends on labour productivity and lagged wages.[13] A detailed translation of this approach into eq. (8.10) is given in Chiarella *et al.* (2005, pp. 170f). Blanchard and Katz quote evidence from macroeconomic as well regional data that (their counterpart for) the coefficient β_{wv} is close to zero (this holds for the United States, in contrast to most European countries). It is one remarkable result of the PFES estimation with U.S. data that it yields a coefficient that, with the proper sign, is significantly bounded away from zero.

We thus turn to the price Phillips curve. When assigning the weights in this relationship, it has to be noted that benchmark inflation is formed as a weighted

---

13 This is why PFES specified the wage share as logarithms in their estimations.

average, not of the inflation climate π^c and wage inflation, but of π^c and wage inflation corrected for productivity growth. Regarding the latter, it is only natural to assume that the growth of actual and trend productivity is weighted in the same manner as in the wage Phillips curve. Equation (8.2) thus becomes

$$\hat{p} = \kappa_{pw}\{\hat{w} - [\kappa_{wz}\hat{z} + (1 - \kappa_{wz})g_z]\} + (1 - \kappa_{pw})\pi^c + f_p(y, v)$$

$$f_p(y, v) = \beta_{py}(y - 1) + \beta_{pv}(v - v^o)/v^o \tag{8.11}$$

The positive influence of the wage share in the equation can be explained by a target markup rate μ that firms may wish to realize.[14] Besides the other arguments in (8.11), firms raise prices if labour costs are currently so high that $pY < (1+\mu)wL$, which is equivalent to $(1+\mu)wL/pY - 1 = (1+\mu)v - 1 > 0$. If the target markup is consistent with equilibrium income distribution, $1+\mu = 1/v^o$ and we obtain the wage share deviations specified in (8.11).

Since the rates of wage and price inflation appear on both sides of (8.10) and (8.11), the equations still have to be solved for the reduced-form expressions of the two inflation rates. They are computed as

$$\hat{w} = \kappa_{wz}\hat{z} + (1 - \kappa_{wz})g_z + \pi^c + \kappa[f_w(e, v) + \kappa_{wp}f_p(y, v)] \tag{8.12}$$

$$\hat{p} = \pi^c + \kappa\,[f_p(y, v) + \kappa_{pw}f_w(e, v)], \quad \text{where } \kappa := 1/(1 - \kappa_{wp}\kappa_{pw}) \tag{8.13}$$

With (8.12) and (8.13) we can begin to derive the law of motion for the wage share. Logarithmic differentiation of v now yields $\hat{v} = \hat{w} - \hat{p} - \hat{z} = \kappa[(1 - \kappa_{pw})f_w - (1 - \kappa_{wp})f_p] - (1 - \kappa_{wz})(\hat{z} - g_z)$. The difference between actual and trend productivity growth, in turn, is given by eq. (8.9), $\hat{z} - g_z = \hat{y} - \hat{e}$. Using (8.8) for $\hat{e}$, we provisionally obtain

$$\hat{v} = \kappa[(1 - \kappa_{pw})f_w(e, v) - (1 - \kappa_{wp})f_p(y, v)] - (1 - \kappa_{wz})[(1 - \beta_{ey})\hat{y}$$

$$+ \beta_{ev}(v - v^o)/v^o] \tag{8.14}$$

It remains to substitute (8.7) for $\hat{y}$ in the last square bracket. Before, however, we have to introduce our respecification of the interest rate, which also enters this equation.

The last square bracket in (8.14) is rather unfamiliar in this context and promises to produce some complicated effects in the determination of income distribution, in addition to those already represented by the first square bracket (recall from (8.6) that $\kappa_{wz} = 0.23$). One may suspect that the influence of not only utilization but also its rate of change in (8.14) is the mere product of an awkward specification detail. Obviously, we can immediately get rid of the disturbing term

---

by postulating $\kappa_{wz} = 1$, and probably no one would have indicted this assumption if it had been introduced right at the start. Unfortunately, we are no longer allowed to choose this way out if we are to take the econometric investigation seriously, because if the system is re-estimated with κ_{wz} confined to one, the fit in eq. (8.1) deteriorates drastically: the standard error of the regression equation (8.1) increases from 0.0208 to 0.0314 (while, interestingly, the estimated β_{wv} more than doubles).

It is noteworthy that in the core expression governing the motions of the wage share, the first square bracket in (8.14), the inflation climate cancels out. π^c nevertheless takes effect on the economy through eq. (8.13) for the rate of price inflation, which enters the dynamic IS equation that determines $\hat{y}$ in (8.7). Hence, with $\kappa_{wz} < 1$, the climate variable has also a direct impact on the wage share in (8.14).

While in the estimation approach the inflation climate is given by the twelve-quarter moving average, PFES make the theoretical background of this simplifying specification explicit as an adaptive expectations mechanism. Here, we generalize this hypothesis by combining these adjustments with regressive expectations: this is conceptually richer and, as will be seen next, can generate more satisfactory dynamics. Introducing an adjustment speed β_π and another weight parameter κ_π between 0 and 1, we have

$$\dot{\pi}^c = \beta_\pi [\kappa_\pi (\hat{p} - \pi^c) + (1 - \kappa_\pi)(\pi^\star - \pi^c)] \tag{8.15}$$

$\pi^\star$ is to be thought of as the target rate of inflation of the central bank. It is publicly known and agents have some faith that monetary policy will succeed in bringing inflation back to this target. The degree of their confidence *vis-à-vis* the trend-chasing adaptive expectations component is measured by $(1 - \kappa_\pi)$, which can also be referred to as the central bank's credibility. Following the framework in PFES, we will begin the analysis with zero credibility, $\kappa_\pi = 1$, and will afterwards study the effects from increasing the weight of the regressive expectations, when $\kappa_\pi < 1$.

8.3.4 Reconsidering the monetary policy rule

The last variable to consider is the rate of interest set by the central bank. Estimations of a Taylor rule variant as in (8.5) typically produce a good fit on the basis of a high persistence parameter, which in PFES comes out as $\beta_{ii} = 0.92$ per quarter. These inertia were often taken as support for the notion that the central bank adopts an interest rate smoothing device. Recent research, however, casts doubts on this view. Keeping the discussion of the literature to a minimum, note first that the interpretation neglects the following aspects.

1   At the time when the central bank sets the interest rate, it has only preliminary information about the data, in particular, about the output gap ($y - 1$ in our model). The deviations from the final, revised data used in the econometric

studies are nonnegligible, and especially for the output gap, these measurement errors are strongly autocorrelated.

2 The natural rate of interest entering the Taylor rule will not be a constant, but the assumptions of the central bank about it will, likewise, move in an autocorrelated manner.

3 Actual monetary policy follows a rule only as a guide. Thus, deviations from the rule during episodes are an appropriate response to special circumstances, not evidence of partial adjustment (for example, the credit crunch shock 1992–93; the worldwide financial crisis 1998–99; or commodity price scares 1988–89 and 1994–95).[15]

In this perspective, the lagged interest rate in the estimations may just be a proxy for these serially correlated shocks, so that policy rule estimations with their typically high inertia are not a proven description of actual central bank behavior. Conversely, it may even be said that any estimation of a relatively straightforward formulation of a rule *should* exhibit a considerable degree of autocorrelation in the residuals; as a rough-and-ready statistic, at least a lower Durbin-Watson than the value of 1.71 one obtains in eq. (8.5).

On these grounds, we choose to return to the original Taylor rule without a partial adjustment mechanism, for whose policy coefficients we can draw on evidence from the literature. Specifically, we borrow a result from Rudebusch (2001, Section 6). With a maximum likelihood estimation of the federal funds rate 1987–1999, he establishes for the demeaned quarterly data,

$$i_t = 1.24\hat{p}_t^{(4)} + 0.33y_t + \quad \xi_t, \xi_t = 0.92\xi_{t-1} + \omega_t \quad (\sigma_\omega = 0.35\%, \bar{R}^2 = 0.96) \tag{8.16}$$

($\hat{p}_t^{(4)}$ is the average of the last four quarter-to-quarter inflation rates, which is often employed in this kind of estimations). By combining (8.16) with the other equations, we do not need to worry about the latter's numerical coefficients. As a matter of fact, the system character of the estimation of (8.1)–(8.5) is extremely weak once the instrumental variables are chosen as they have been. In particular, eliminating the interest rate equation from the system has been found to have only a minimal bearing on the coefficients in the remaining equations.

It may be argued that the decision to discard (8.5) is not entirely convincing since rules like (8.5) and (8.16) are too difficult to distinguish; when empirically

---

15 It may suffice here to refer to Rudebusch's (2001, pp. 19f) quotation of Chairman Alan Greenspan's testimony to Congress on 22, June 1994: 'Households and businesses became much more reluctant to borrow and spend and lenders to extend credit—a phenomenon often referred to as the "credit crunch." In an endeavor to defuse these financial strains, we moved short-term rates lower in a long series of steps that ended in the late summer of 1992, and we held them at unusually low levels through the end of 1993—both absolutely and, importantly, relative to inflation.' Thus, as Rudebusch emphasizes, this episode appears better described as a persistent 'credit crunch' shock than as a sluggish partial adjustment to a known desired rate.

taken on their own, they are observationally equivalent. The problem is excellently illustrated by the fact that the autocorrelation coefficient of 0.92 for the random perturbations in (8.16) coincides with the estimated coefficient β_{ii} on the lagged interest rate in (8.6). One can, however, go one step further and invoke information contained in the term structure. Thus, Rudebusch (2001) demonstrates that a slow partial adjustment of the short rate to new information by the Fed should imply the existence of predictable future variation in the short rate that is not present with serially correlated shocks. In his study he reveals a general lack of predictive information in the yield curve about changes in the short rate, which suggests the absence of policy inertia.

These investigations were extended in Rudebusch and Wu (2003), where they rigorously analyze the issue in a combined model that includes the macro variables as well as a no-arbitrage term structure, and also allows for both types of policy rule dynamics—partial adjustment and persistent shocks. Letting 'the data judge between these interpretations', they find there is little term structure evidence suggesting interest rate smoothing in the Federal Reserve's policy actions.

We conclude from these arguments that even a simple rule like (8.16) is to be preferred to (8.5). Therefore, using the same nominal equilibrium rate of interest i^o as in (8.7) and the same target rate of inflation $\pi^\star = \hat{p}^o$ as in (8.15), we employ the interest rate reaction function,

$$i = i^o + \beta_{ip}(\hat{p} - \pi^\star) + \beta_{iy}(y - 1) \tag{8.17}$$

where the numerical order of magnitude of the policy coefficients derives from (8.16). A side effect of replacing (8.5) with (8.16) is that we save one dynamic variable when setting up the differential equations system. For an analytical treatment of its Jacobian matrix to study stability this is, however, of no great help since, of course, the influence of the rule is still present, and several of the other entries in the matrix are already complicated enough.

8.3.5 The 4D differential equations system

The laws of motion set up in the previous sections can be summarized in a system of four differential equations, where the state variables are the wage share v, capacity utilization y, the employment rate e and the inflation climate π^c. For a compact representation which nevertheless makes the variables involved explicit, we define the functional expressions h_p for the rate of price inflation $\hat{p}$ in (8.13) and h_r for the real rate of interest $r := i - \hat{p}$ from (8.17) and (8.13),

$$h_p = h_p(v, y, e, \pi^c) := \pi^c + \kappa[f_p(y, v) + \kappa_{pw}f_w(e, v)]$$

$$h_r = h_r(v, y, e, \pi^c) := (\beta_{ip} - 1)h_p(v, y, e, \pi^c) + \beta_{iy}(y - 1) + i^o - \beta_{ip}\pi^\star$$

Furthermore, refer to the right-hand side of (8.7) for the growth rate of utilization $\hat{y}$ as

$$h_y = h_y(v, y, e, \pi^c) := -\beta_{yy}(y-1) - \beta_{yi}h_r(v, y, e, \pi^c) + \gamma_{yv}(v - v^o)/v^o$$
$$+ \beta_{yi}(i^o - \pi^\star)$$

and abbreviate the first square bracket (including κ) in (8.14) for the changes in the wage share $\hat{v}$ as

$$h_v = h_v(v, y, e) := \kappa[(1 - \kappa_{pw})f_w(e, v) - (1 - \kappa_{wp})f_p(y, v)]$$

On this basis, the autonomous system to be investigated in continuous time reads

$$\dot{v} = v[h_v - (1 - \kappa_{wz})(1 - \beta_{ey})h_y - (1 - \kappa_{wz})\beta_{ev}(v - v^o)/v^o] \qquad (8.18)$$

$$\dot{y} = yh_y \qquad (8.19)$$

$$\dot{e} = e\beta_{ey}h_y - e\beta_{ev}(v - v^o)/v^o \qquad (8.20)$$

$$\dot{\pi}^c = \beta_\pi[\kappa_\pi h_p + (1 - \kappa_\pi)\pi^\star - \pi^c] \qquad (8.21)$$

Since the adjustment principles were directly specified in deviation form, it is obvious that $v = v^o$, $y = 1$, $e = e^o$, $\pi^c = \pi^\star$ constitute a stationary point of (8.18)–(8.21). Equating the right-hand sides of these equations to zero and dividing by v, y and e, respectively, we have a system of four linear equations which, except for a fluke, are linear independent. This establishes the (generic) uniqueness of the economy's steady state position. Referring to the introduction of eq. (8.8), which modified the original specification of Okun's law, it has to be stressed that linear independence relies on a nonzero coefficient β_{ev} in (8.20); otherwise (8.19) and (8.20) provide the same information and a continuum of equilibria would be obtained. Because they imply values of, for example, y and $\hat{p}$ different from 1 and $\pi^\star$, whereas the latter serve as benchmark or target values in the price Phillips curve and the Taylor rule, these stationary points would not be consistent states of equilibrium, so that stability of this set (rather than a specific point) of equilibria would not be a meaningful property, either.

8.3.6 The discrete-time formulation

Unfortunately, formulating the model in discrete time is a bit cumbersome and, if carefully justified, requires considering a number of details and cross-references. One might, however, proceed immediately to the final set of equations at which we arrive. They are presented in such a form that they can be directly translated into a source code for the computer simulations.

The discrete-time version of the model can retain the lags in the IS equation (8.3) and Okun's law (8.4). While for studying the impulse-response properties of the system the dynamic equations are deterministic (except for the one-time shock at $t = 0$), we are also interested in the system's behavior when it is continuously subjected to exogenous random forces. In the latter respect, the five random shocks that correspond to the ε-residuals in the estimation (8.1)–(8.5) are considered. The dating $t = 0, 1, 2, \ldots$ of the variables refers to the quarters $t = 0, 1, 2, \ldots$, but all rates of change continue to be annualized. As in the continuous-time formulations above, each variable on the right-hand side of the equations is specified as a deviation from its steady state value, thus absorbing the constant in the estimation equations.

The equation determining utilization derives from eq. (8.3) and its lags. In a likewise manner, the equation governing the changes in the employment rate reiterates (8.4), with the minor wage share correction term from (8.8). The wage and price Phillips curves are as in eqs (8.10) and (8.11). Conforming to (8.1) and (8.2), the employment rate, utilization and the wage share enter as one-quarter lags, and the productivity growth rate is contemporaneous. It then only remains to add the disturbances $\varepsilon_{w,t}$ and $\varepsilon_{p,t}$, respectively. The resulting reduced-form expressions, with the corresponding dating, read like (8.12) and (8.13), where the terms $\varepsilon_{w,t}$ and $\varepsilon_{p,t}$ are to be included analogous to f_w and f_p in these equations. The discrete-time version of the differential equation (8.15) for the inflation climate is obtained by transforming the time derivative $\dot{\pi}^c$ to $(\pi_t^c - \pi_{t-1}^c)/h$, with $h = 0.25$. For simplicity, the rates of change of productivity and the wage share use the continuous-time growth rate formulae.

The Taylor rule is taken over from (8.16). For the stochastic simulations, the inflation gap refers to the mean of the last four inflation rates (which almost coincides with the four-quarter rates of inflation); see eq. (8.33). This smoothing effect is meaningful to protect against quarterly outliers, but it is not necessarily needed in the noiseless setting of the impulse-response exercises. Since under the special circumstances of just one shock to a tranquil steady state position we wish the central bank to react without delay to the impulse, the inflation gap is based on the contemporaneous quarter-to-quarter rate of inflation in this case; see (8.32).

Arranging these equations in a suitable order the system can be written in recursive form, which is done in (8.22)–(8.31). Note that the contemporaneous dating of inflation in the utilization equation (8.24) together with the contemporaneous dating of productivity growth $\hat{z}_t$ in the wage Phillips curve require us to compute $\hat{p}_t$ before y_t, and $\hat{w}_t$ after y_t; the latter because of (8.28). Hence the wage and price inflation rates are no longer determined in two successive equations. In the stochastic version, the $\varepsilon_{x,t}$-terms ($x = p, y, e, w, i$) are supposed to be i.i.d. serially uncorrelated random shocks; or they specify the impulse shock at $t = 0$ and are zero otherwise. On the whole, we have:

$$\pi^c = \pi_{t-1}^c + 0.25 \cdot \beta_\pi [\kappa_\pi \hat{p}_{t-1} + (1 - \kappa_\pi)\pi^\star - \pi_{t-1}^c] \tag{8.22}$$

$$\hat{p}_t = \pi_t^c + \kappa[\beta_{py}(y_{t-1} - 1) + \kappa_{pw}\beta_{we}(e_{t-1} - e^o) + (\beta_{pv} - \kappa_{pw}\beta_{wv}) \tag{8.23}$$

$$(v_{t-1} - v^o)/v^o] + \kappa[\varepsilon_{p,t} + \kappa_{pw}\varepsilon_{w,t}]$$

$$y_t = 1 + \beta_{yy1}(y_{t-1} - 1) + \beta_{yy2}(y_{t-2} - 1) \tag{8.24}$$
$$- \beta_{yi}[i_{t-1} - \hat{p}_t - (i^o - \pi^\star)] + \gamma_{yv}(v_{t-1} - v^o)/v^o + \varepsilon_{y,t}$$

$$\hat{y}_t = 4(y_t - y_{t-1})/y_{t-1} \tag{8.25}$$

$$\hat{e}_t = \beta_{ey1}\hat{y}_{t-1} + \beta_{ey2}\hat{y}_{t-2} + \beta_{ey3}\hat{y}_{t-3} - \beta_{ev}(v - v^o)/v^o + \varepsilon_{e,t} \tag{8.26}$$

$$e_t = (1 + 0.25\hat{e}_t)e_{t-1} \tag{8.27}$$

$$\hat{z}_t = g_z + \hat{y}_t - \hat{e}_t \tag{8.28}$$

$$\hat{w}_t = \kappa_{wz}\hat{z}_t + (1 - \kappa_{wz})g_z + \pi_t^c + \kappa[\beta_{we}(e_{t-1} - e^o) + \kappa_{wp}\beta_{py}(y_{t-1} - 1) \tag{8.29}$$
$$+ (\kappa_{wp}\beta_{pv} - \beta_{wv})(v_{t-1} - v^o)/v^o] + \kappa[\varepsilon_{w,t} + \kappa_{wp}\varepsilon_{p,t}]$$

$$\hat{v}_t = \hat{w}_t - \hat{p}_t - \hat{z}_t \tag{8.30}$$

$$v_t = (1 + 0.25\hat{v}_t)v_{t-1} \tag{8.31}$$

and finally the two specifications of the Taylor rule for the impulse-response and stochastic experiments,

$$i_t = i^o + \alpha_p(\hat{p}_t - \pi^\star) + \alpha_y(y_t - 1) \tag{8.32}$$

$$i_t = i^o + \alpha_p(\hat{p}_t^{(4)} - \pi^\star) + \alpha_y(y_t - 1) + \eta_{i,t} \quad (\hat{p}_t^{(4)} = 0.25 \cdot \sum_{j=0}^{3} \hat{p}_{t-j})$$

$$\eta_{i,t} = \rho_i\eta_{i,t-1} + \varepsilon_{i,t} \tag{8.33}$$

The system can be simply iterated forward once a history of utilization y_{0-j} and inflation rates $\hat{p}_{0-j}$ ($j = 0, \ldots, 3$) is given, and initial values for the wage share v_0, the employment rate e_0, the inflation climate π_0^c, and the disturbance η_0 in the Taylor rule (8.33).

8.4 An improvement of the numerical coefficients

8.4.1 A rough-and-ready calibration of the inflation climate

Since the disequilibrium reactions in both the continuous-time and discrete-time model versions refer to the deviations of the variables from their equilibrium values, the dynamics are independent of the numerical specification of the steady state position. For concreteness, we may choose the following values for the target rate of inflation, the nominal interest rate, the employment rate, the wage share and trend productivity growth,

$$\pi^\star = 2.5\% \quad i^o = 5.0\% \quad e^o = 94\% \quad v^o = 65\% \quad g_z = 2.0\% \tag{8.34}$$

The steady state values of the other variables are easily derived from here.

To study the implications of the PFES estimation, the numerical parameter values from (8.6) can be directly plugged into the discrete-time system (8.22)–(8.32), (8.33). Only four modifications are made: (*i*) symbol u is replaced with y; (*ii*) the weight κ_{pz} appearing in (8.2) becomes obsolete since the benchmark inflation term in the model's price Philips curve takes the weights of actual and trend productivity in the wage Phillips curve into account; (*iii*) as discussed in Section 8.4, the interest rate smoothing approach to the Taylor rule in (8.5) is discarded in favor of the Rudebusch (2001) estimation of eq. (8.16) with the autocorrelated disturbances; (*iv*) following the discussion of Okun's law in Section 8.1, we choose a small value like 0.01 for the additional parameter β_{ev} in eq. (8.26).

It therefore only remains to determine the coefficients β_π and κ_π for the adjustments of the inflation climate in (8.22). PFES are explicit in interpreting their climate variable π_t^{12} as a proxy for the outcome of an adaptive expectations mechanism. Accordingly, the regressive expectations are to be neglected here and κ_π is to be put equal to one. Regarding the adjustment speed β_π, we simulate eq. (8.22) with the historical inflation data under alternative values of β_π, and select the one that minimizes the root mean square deviation between our endogenously determined climate π_t^c and the auxiliary π_t^{12} entering the PFES Phillips curves. The minimization problem is solved by $\beta_\pi = 0.65$, at which the two series are indeed as close as 0.35 percentage points.

To see whether the estimated values are not only plausible each one for itself but also meaningful in the interaction of all the variables in the system, we examine a standard impulse-response function. For a Keynesian demand-driven model, this should be a demand shock. Correspondingly, we set the initial shock to the utilization equation (8.24) equal to the standard error of the estimation equation (8.3), that is, $\varepsilon_{y,t} = 0.77\%$ in (8.24) for period $t = 0$, and zero again thereafter (as all the other ε-terms). The resulting adjustment paths of utilization, price inflation and the wage share back to their steady state values are depicted in Figure 8.1.

The time paths of y_t and v_t almost coincide with the paths from another experiment, which will be discussed in a moment. The reactions of utilization are quite in line with what is well-known from a great variety of VAR responses to a demand shock: a return back to normal in a few years, with a weak subsequent overshooting. Adjustments of the wage share are far less often studied in the literature, but convergence of this variable occurs at the same time scale.

The behavior of the rate of inflation $\hat{p}_t$ is, however, completely different. As the upper thin line in the middle panel of Figure 8.1 demonstrates, the monotonic convergence of this time series after it has reached its peak at $t = 3.25$ is extremely slow. It actually takes 83 years until price inflation enters a corridor of ± 0.096 percent around the steady state value of 2.50 percent, which is 10 percent of the maximal deviation in the third year. Convergence of wage inflation, by the way, is not much faster: $\hat{w}_t$ reaches the corresponding corridor after 67 years. All the more remarkable is the balancing of these slow adjustments, which leads the wage share back to its equilibrium value within ten years.

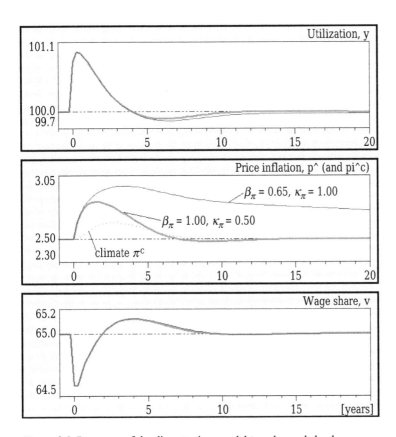

Figure 8.1 Response of the discrete-time model to a demand shock.

Clearly, the sluggish convergence of $\hat{p}_t$ and $\hat{w}_t$ is not an acceptable property of a model that places strong emphasis on the wage–price dynamics. It is an immediate idea to put the blame on the inflation climate, which may be suspected to react much too hesitatingly. The improvement by employing a faster speed of adjustment β_π is, however, rather limited. For example, even if β_π is increased from 0.65 to 2.00, the convergence time of price inflation as it was just specified is still 26.75 years.

Because of their built-in mean reverting tendencies, it is certainly more promising to activate the regressive expectations in the climate's adjustment equation (8.22), that is, to reduce the weight parameter κ_π below unity. A few explorations suffice to verify this intuition not only qualitatively but also quantitatively; convergence can indeed be decisively accelerated in this way. Concretely, we have a closer look at $\kappa_\pi = 0.50$ and $\beta_\pi = 1.00$. These values have already been extensively used in the numerical investigations of the structural models in Chiarella *et al.* (2005, Chapters 5–7 and 9). There they have been introduced on an *a priori* basis, and possibly several of the other parameters of the model had to 'adjust' to these values in the calibration studies. By contrast, here the other parameters are already given by the econometric estimation and we adjust κ_π and β_π to them, on the basis of an evaluation of the implied impulse-response properties.

The result of this modification of κ_π and β_π are the bold lines in Figure 8.1. While, as already said, the differences in the two time series of utilization and the wage share are hardly visible, convergence of the rate of price inflation now occurs at a reasonable speed. We add that apart from a short transitional stage of three quarters, wage inflation behaves in a like fashion.

The dotted line in the middle panel of Figure 8.1 illustrates the role of the inflation climate π_t^c for the improved adjustment pattern. In comparison to the case of purely adaptive expectations ($\kappa_\pi = 1$), where right after the start π_t^c follows $\hat{p}_t$ relatively closely (not shown in the diagram), the restrained reactions of π_t^c under $\kappa_\pi = 0.50$ attenuate the effects of the initial shock in size as well as duration; the inflation rate peaks at a value of 2.82 percent, as opposed to the previous 2.96 percent, already at $t = 1.50$. Even more important is the feature that after the turning point the climate has a greater potential to pull inflation downward. Whereas under $\kappa_\pi = 1$ the climate seeks to keep track of inflation, under $\kappa_\pi = 0.50$ inflation could almost be said to follow the climate in this phase. This characterization is supported by the observation that the original adjustment speed of π_t^c produces quite similar trajectories, when $\kappa_\pi = 0.50$ and $\beta_\pi = 0.65$. So it is really the weight parameter κ_π that is responsible for the faster convergence of wage and price inflation.

8.4.2 Re-estimation of the Phillips curves

Having decided to settle down on $\kappa_\pi = 0.50$ and $\beta_\pi = 1.00$ in the adjustments of the inflation climate, we should return to the econometric estimation of equations (8.1)–(8.5) and ask how strongly its parameters are modified if π_t^{12} is replaced with the climate π_t^c constructed from (8.22) and actual price inflation. For easier reference, this climate series may be called the endogenous inflation climate (although the parameters κ_π and β_π were exogenously chosen). Since in the GMM system estimations, eqs (8.3)–(8.5) for utilization, employment and the interest rate are just marginally affected by this revision, we can concentrate on the two Phillips curves (8.1) and (8.2). The results are summarized in Table 8.2, where rows (a)–(c) report the GMM estimations and row (d) is based on nonlinear least squares.[16]

Row (a) reiterates the estimation from PFES in Section 8.2 (writing y instead of u). The only alteration in row (b) is the substitution of the endogenous climate for π^{12}. In particular, the coefficients on π^c and $d\ln p$ in the wage Phillips curve, and π^c and $d\ln w$ in the price Phillips curve, are still unconstrained.

---

16 Nonlinear only in the respect that the sums of the coefficients on π^c and the corresponding inflation variable are constrained to one.

Table 8.2 Re-estimation of the wage and price Phillips curves (8.1), (8.2).

Dep.	Regressors									
Var.	π^{12}	π^c	$d\ln p$	$d\ln w$	e_{-1}	y_{-1}	$\ln v_{-1}$	$d\ln z$	R^2	DW
$d\ln w$:										
(a)	0.51	—	0.47	—	0.60	—	−0.27	0.23	0.51	1.99
(b)	—	0.77	0.35	—	0.58	—	−0.24	0.24	0.51	2.02
(c)	—	0.58	0.42	—	0.51	—	−0.23	0.24	0.51	2.02
(d)	—	0.61	0.39	—	0.52	—	−0.22	0.22	0.51	2.00
$d\ln p$:										
(a)	1.00	—	—	—	—	0.38	0.25	−0.06	0.76	1.36
(b)	—	0.75	—	0.46	—	0.08	0.23	−0.15	0.76	1.75
(c)	—	0.45	—	0.55	—	0.00	0.27	−0.21	0.70	1.79
(d)	—	0.88	—	0.12	—	0.14	0.26	−0.12	0.82	1.32

Note: Rows (a)–(c) are from GMM system estimations of (8.1)–(8.5) with the same instrumental variables as listed in fn 4, (d) are nonlinear least squares; (a) are the results from PFES and in (c) the coefficients on π^c and $d\ln p$, or $d\ln w$ respectively, are constrained to sum up to one. Constants are omitted. All nonzero estimates have highly significant t-statistics.

Comparing (a) and (b), the changes in the wage Phillips curve are seen to be limited, only the coefficient on $d\ln p$ decreases somewhat. The latter is partly undone in row (c) when the coefficients on the inflation rates π^c and $d\ln p$ are required to sum up to one. In this case, the responsiveness of wage inflation to variations in the employment rate shows a moderate decline. Interestingly, these results are quite independent of the system approach; the ordinary single equations least squares approach yields practically the same numerical values and summary statistics.

The differences from the PFES results are more severe in the second part of Table 8.2. First of all, the introduction of the endogenous inflation climate together with dropping the zero constraint on $d\ln w$ decreases the coefficient on utilization from 0.38 to 0.08. Moreover, with the constraint on the weights of π^c and $d\ln w$, this coefficient even vanishes. Besides the more satisfactory concept of the inflation climate variable, rows (b) and (c) are also econometrically more trustworthy than (a) because of the reduction of serial correlation in the residuals, as indicated by the increase in the Durbin-Watson statistic.[17] The lower Durbin-Watson in the least squares estimation in (d), although it produces the highest R^2, underlines the necessity of including the instrumental variables.[18]

As already in the wage Phillips curve, a remarkable feature is the role of the wage share. Its coefficients (β_{wv} and β_{pv}) always come out significant and with the correct sign, and they are even scarcely affected by the specification of the inflation

17 As a matter of fact, the important point is not so much the change in the climate variable but the inclusion of $d\ln w$ in the regressors. The coefficients on π^{12} and $d\ln w$ obtained from this estimation are 0.25 and 0.82, respectively, while with −0.06 the coefficient on y_{-1} turns slightly negative (all coefficients with significant t-values) and the Durbin-Watson rises up to 1.93.
18 Incidentally, estimation by two-stage least squares leads to results similar to those in Table 8.2.

climate in the estimations. This consistency is strong support for the theoretical approach (8.10) and (8.11) to the Phillips curves.

These Phillips curves are additionally corroborated in another, less obvious detail, namely, the compatibility of the coefficients on the productivity growth rates in the two curves. If the coefficient on $\hat{z}$ in the price Phillips curve is designated β_{pz} then, according to (8.11), it is given by $\beta_{pz} = -\kappa_{pw}\kappa_{wz}$. From row (c), the latter are estimated as $\kappa_{pw} = 0.55$ and $\kappa_{wz} = 0.24$. Their signed product, $-\kappa_{pw}\kappa_{wz} = -0.13$, is close to the estimate of $\beta_{pz} = -0.15$ in row (b) in the second part of Table 8.2. It differs more from $\beta_{pz} = -0.21$ in (c), but the specification of the influence of the growth rate of labour productivity in (8.11) can still be considered to be acceptable.

On the basis of Table 8.2 and the results discussed in the previous sections, we will employ the following set of numerical parameters for the simulations of the discrete-time system (8.22)–(8.32) or (8.33), respectively:

$$
\begin{aligned}
&\text{Climate:} & \beta_\pi &= 1.00 & \kappa_\pi &= 0.50 \\
&\text{WPC:} & \kappa_{wp} &= 0.42 & \beta_{we} &= 0.51 & \beta_{wv} &= 0.23 & \kappa_{wz} &= 0.24 \\
&\text{PPC:} & \kappa_{pw} &= 0.55 & \beta_{py} &= 0.00 & \beta_{pv} &= 0.27 \\
&\text{IS:} & \beta_{yy1} &= 1.13 & \beta_{yy2} &= -0.23 & \beta_{yi} &= 0.05 & \gamma_{yv} &= -0.10 & (8.35) \\
&\text{Okun:} & \beta_{ey1} &= 0.17 & \beta_{ey2} &= 0.12 & \beta_{ey3} &= 0.05 & \beta_{ev} &= 0.01 \\
&\text{Taylor:} & \beta_{ip} &= 1.24 & \beta_{iy} &= 0.33 & \rho_i &= 0.92
\end{aligned}
$$

8.4.3 Impulse-response functions as a more detailed evaluation criterion

Though the econometric estimation with the improvements in Table 8.2 appears rather reliable, one may feel uneasy about a price Phillips curve without economic activity playing an active role.[19] The uneasiness would be justified if $\beta_{py} = 0$ would give rise to some unfamiliar dynamic phenomena. To check this, let us re-examine the demand shock impulse-response function from above with the new parameters from (8.35). To begin with, consider the impact reactions in the same quarter $t = 0$ in which the shock $\varepsilon_{y,t}$ in (8.24) occurs. The main effect is a lower wage share, which is brought about by the change in labour productivity. The argument is that the (strong) increase in the growth rate $\hat{y}_0$ (strongly) raises the productivity growth rate, which immediately, with factor κ_{wz}, translates into higher wage inflation $\hat{w}_0$ in (8.29). Since $\kappa_{wz} < 1$, the change in $\hat{z}_0$ dominates the change in $\hat{w}_0$ in (8.30) for $\hat{v}_0$, so that the wage share v_0 falls.

---

19 At least if the curve is not thought to be derived from an infinite horizon optimization as in the new-Keynesian models, where price inflation responds to marginal cost, which in turn is often proxied by a wage share variable. Then, however, also future values of the wage share would have to show up on the right-hand side of the Phillips curve.

In the next quarter, $t = 1$, the inflation climate in (8.22) is not yet affected, but the lower wage share has a negative effect on the subsequent equation, which determines price inflation. This is due to the fact that the composed coefficient on v_{t-1} in (8.23) results to be positive, $\beta_{pv} - \kappa_{pw}\beta_{wv} = 0.27 - 0.55 \cdot 0.23 > 0$. Owing to $\beta_{py} = 0$, this is the only change in (8.23). As a consequence, the positive demand shock in $t = 0$ causes a *fall* in the rate of inflation one quarter later. This stands in contrast to what we have obtained in Figure 8.1, and may seem counterintuitive.

In fact, the reaction is reminiscent of what is known in the literature as the 'price puzzle'. There it refers to monetary policy where it has been observed that a contractionary innovation by the central bank tends to increase, rather than decrease, the rate of price inflation.[20] It is easily verified that a negative interest rate shock in our model produces the same result, a fall in y and a rise in $\hat{p}$. Hence, it can be said that our model with the estimated parameters from (8.35) does reproduce the price puzzle, and because of the (weak or even) vanishing influence of output in the price Phillips curve and the, as it turns out, positive influence of the wage share on price inflation, the model also provides a theoretical explanation for it.

Nevertheless, the rate of price inflation starts increasing in quarter $t = 2$. This is because y increases further in $t = 1$ and now also raises the employment rate e. The strong shock to $\hat{z}$ was only transitory, and wage inflation $\hat{w}_1$ in (8.29) returns close to normal. Thus, $\hat{p}_1 < \hat{p}^o$ is the greatest deviation from the steady state values in the growth rate formula (8.30) for the wage share. The resulting increase in v together with the increase in e then leads to $\hat{p}_2 > \hat{p}_1$ in the subsequent quarter. The adjustment process has now gathered momentum and, with respect to six selected variables, Figure 8.2 shows how it unfolds in the following periods.

The speed of convergence is the same as in Figure 8.1, which is the first litmus test that the numerical coefficients have to pass. Another and more ambitious criterion to evaluate the adjustment paths of the variables is a comparison with the impulse-response functions that one obtains from an atheoretical vector autoregression. Since we are interested here in the trajectories of y, $\hat{p}$, $\hat{w}$, v and i (with a slight delay, the employment rate e moves quite in line with y), we estimated a VAR with four lags in the six variables y, e, $\hat{p}$, $\hat{w}$, v, i and computed the response of the variables to a one standard deviation innovation to y. The outcome over the first ten years is shown in Figure 8.3. Because the shock to y is of the same size as our demand shock in Figure 8.2, the two figures can be directly compared.

The overall impression of this comparison is a fine qualitative match of the responses in the model and from the VAR. The initial reaction of the variables are in the same direction and the adjustment patterns regarding turning points, overshooting and speed of convergence are quite the same.[21] In particular,

---

20 For a documentation of this feature, see, e.g., Gordon and Leeper (1994) or Christiano *et al.* (1998).
21 Except that the VAR implies slower convergence for the interest rate, which not the least is due to the rate's high coefficient of 0.91 on the first lag of itself. This is a general problem of all VARs including a rate of interest.

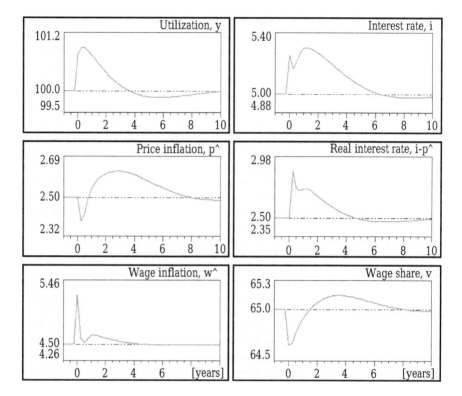

Figure 8.2 Response of the model to a demand shock, with parameters from (8.35).

the VAR displays the same kind of price puzzle in the middle-left panel and the wage share falls at the beginning, where even the size of the initial reactions of the two variables is the same.[22] The main quantitative differences of Figure 8.3 from Figure 8.2 are the higher amplitude of the upper turning points of $\hat{p}$, $\hat{w}$ and i (but not v) after 9, 8 and 7 quarters, respectively, and the moderate impact reaction of wage inflation when we compare it to the fierce reaction in our model, which we have seen originates with the sudden change in the productivity growth rate.

The positive aspects of the match are nonetheless predominant, so that the qualitative and to some extent even quantitative properties of the model's impulse-response functions in Figure 8.2 can be taken as strong support for the model and its parameters in (8.35).

---

22 The feature that in Figure 8.3 the three variables v, $\hat{w}$ and i react immediately at $t = 0$, while $\hat{p}$ only changes at $t = 1$, is a consequence of the chosen ordering of the variables in the VAR, which is made explicit in the note to Figure 8.3. Thus all variables ranked after y are affected by the impulse to y still in the same quarter, where sign and size of the reaction is given by their covariance with y.

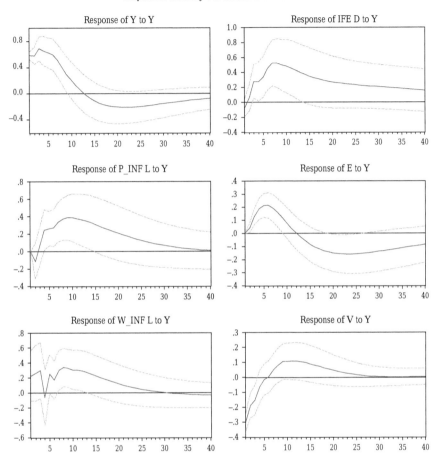

Response to Cholesky One S.D. Innovations ± 2 S.E.

Figure 8.3 VAR impulse-response functions to a demand shock.

Note: Time in quarters, all variables measured in percentage points. Cholesky ordering of the variables: e, $\hat{p}$ (p_infl), y, $\hat{w}$ (w_infl), v, i (ifed).

8.4.4 Variabilities in the stochastic economy

A guideline for calibrating (instead of estimating) the shock-driven models of the real business cycle school was to simulate the stochastic dynamics and check whether several of its summary statistics can approximate their empirical counterparts. Almost exclusive interest in this respect attached to the standard deviations of the variables that the models seek to explain. In the present section, we want to take up this type of evaluation where, however, we have already decided upon the numerical values of the coefficients in the deterministic part of the model. Only the specification of the random forces needs a short additional discussion.

Ideally, the random disturbances in the stochastic system (8.22)–(8.33) should be modelled in accordance with the properties of the residuals from the econometric estimation. A first attenuation of this idea has already been mentioned earlier, namely, that we neglect possible cross correlations between the disturbances as they may be indicated by the residual correlation matrix. For simplicity, we furthermore assume that besides being i.i.d., the error terms are also normally distributed. Naturally, their variances may then be given by those of the estimated residuals in the corresponding estimation equations.

Before proceeding with them, the determination of the employment rate should be reconsidered. The problem is easier to see in the (deterministic) continuous-time version (8.18)–(8.21). In a first comment on it we have already pointed out that a zero coefficient β_{ev} in the Okun equation (8.20) would imply a zero eigenvalue of the Jacobian matrix and thus give rise to continuum of stationary points. The set is stable if the other eigenvalues have negative real parts. If under these circumstances a shock perturbs the economy from such an equilibrium point, it will return to the equilibrium set but generally to a different equilibrium point.

Although a positive coefficient β_{ev} was introduced to avoid this undesirable feature, one serious consequence still remains. As long as β_{ev} is not much different from zero, one eigenvalue of the Jacobian is close to zero, too. Hence, even if Re $\lambda < 0$ for all eigenvalues λ, convergence to the (now unique) equilibrium will be slow. Without going into the technical details, things are completely analogous in the discrete-time system with its distributed lags (instead of zero, the critical eigenvalue is here a unit root).

On the other hand, after calibrating the coefficients of the inflation climate adjustments, slow convergence was no longer a problem in the impulse-response functions that we have studied. The reason is that there the employment rate e was not driven too far from its equilibrium value. Things are different, however, if e itself is subjected to a shock. With a small value of β_{ev} like the chosen 0.01 in (8.35), convergence actually takes several hundred years.

This problem makes itself also felt in the stochastic economy. The unit root of the discrete-time system under $\beta_{ev} = 0$ signifies that the stochastic process exhibits random walk behavior if the disturbances $\varepsilon_{e,t}$ in (8.26) are active, which technically means that the variances of the variables are unbounded for $t \to \infty$. The variances are bounded if $\beta_{ev} > 0$ (and, as we have seen, the system is stable), but they are rather large as long as β_{ev} is small. On the other hand, the diverging forces can be (mostly) bypassed if the employment rate is exempted from the stochastic shocks.

These remarks show that the specification of Okun's law, even if the *ad-hoc* remedy of $\beta_{ev} > 0$ is accepted, is still a weak point in the present framework. For the moment being, we may leave it at that and help ourselves by putting the random forces acting on it to rest. Regarding the other stochastic terms $\varepsilon_{x,t}$ in the system, we follow what has been said in the foregoing and adopt the standard deviations

Table 8.3 Standard deviations of the time series

	Standard deviations of					
	y	e	$\hat{w}$	$\hat{p}$	v	i
Empirical benchmarks:	2.15	1.47	1.50	1.42	0.95	2.17
Stochastic economy:	2.37	0.79	1.68	1.50	1.12	2.13

$\sigma = \sigma(\varepsilon_{x,t})$ of the corresponding estimated residuals for them ($x = w, p, y, i$). The numerical coefficients from (8.35) are thus complemented by the following standard deviations,

$$\sigma(\varepsilon_{p,t}) = 1.32\% \quad \sigma(\varepsilon_{w,t}) = 2.08\%$$

$$\sigma(\varepsilon_{y,t}) = 0.77\% \quad \sigma(\varepsilon_{e,t}) = 0.00\% \quad \sigma(\varepsilon_{i,t}) = 0.35\% \tag{8.36}$$

We are thus ready to check whether the variabilities of the single variables that the model brings about are sufficiently reasonable. It only remains to make the empirical benchmarks explicit to which the standard deviations of the model-generated time series are to be compared. The standard deviations for utilization, the employment rate and the wage share are computed from the same series as in the econometric estimation. Regarding the nominal variables we hold the idea that in the high inflation times in the 1970s and at the beginning of the 1980s, additional forces were at work that are not present in our model. We seek to remove them by applying a flexible detrending procedure to empirical wage and price inflation and the rate of interest, although we use it in a very moderate way. Specifically, we adopt the Hodrick-Prescott filter with a smoothing parameter as high as $\lambda = 102,400$, instead of the usual $\lambda = 1,600$ for quarterly data.[23] Considering four-quarter inflation rates $\hat{w}$ and $\hat{p}$, the standard deviations reported in the first row of Table 8.3 are obtained.[24]

The second row of the table shows the outcome of a model simulation over 1000 years. Five out of the six standard deviations are of the same order of magnitude as their benchmark values. The only exception is the variability of the employment rate, which is certainly too low. This is another hint that the modelling of the

---

23 As is well known, the trend would tend to a straight line as $\lambda \to \infty$. It is astonishing that Hodrick and Prescott's recommendation $\lambda = 1,600$ has practically never been discussed in the business cycle literature. We only know of Gordon (2003, p. 218) as one exception, who expresses a profound skepticism when he characterizes this value as implying 'implausibly large accelerations and decelerations of the trend *within* each cycle' (emphasis added). Franke (2006, Section 3.1.2) finds this feature fully confirmed. On the basis of the results presented there, we decide to settle down on $\lambda = 102,400$.

24 Detrending empirical wage and price inflation with $\lambda = 1,600$ would reduce their standard deviations further to 1.13 and 0.98, respectively. Note that here, too, wage inflation is more variable than price inflation.

employment dynamics needs to be improved. Nevertheless, this shortcoming does not impair the ordering of wage and price inflation, according to which the rate of wage inflation should turn out be more variable than the rate of price inflation. On the whole, the model-generated variabilities shown in Table 8.3 are encouraging and can be taken as further corroboration of the model.

8.5 Working with the model

While the formulation of Okun's law has been identified as the weakest of the model, a more appropriate specification of the employment dynamics is beyond the scope of this chapter. This deficiency has, however, turned out to be of secondary importance that does not seriously affect the other parts of the model. On the whole, the analysis so far has established a certain credibility of the model's qualitative as well as quantitative dynamics. It is therefore justified to study already the model as it presently stands in greater depth and infer some conclusions from it.

8.5.1 A cutback in workers' ambitions

In many industrialized countries, the position of workers has come under severe pressure in the last one or two decades. In this section, we design an experiment that allows us to study, in a stylized vacuum, the consequences of such a shift in the general economic climate.

The experiment is again of an impulse-response type in an otherwise determinis-tic setting. Suppose the economy smoothly grows on its steady state path and then, all of a sudden, the benchmark wage share v^o unanimously drops in all components of the model, from 66 percent to 65 percent, say. The other equilibrium values, in particular the natural rate of employment e^o, are assumed to be unaffected by this change.

The wage share v^o as a benchmark plays a role in three parts of the model. First in the wage bargaining processes, where the fall of v^o directly reflects the weaker position of workers since v enters the structural wage Phillips curve with a negative coefficient. Hence, wage increases initially decelerate. Second, in the price Phillips curve the reduction of v^o can be interpreted as a higher markup firms are striving for, the immediate effect being a faster rise of prices. To be exact, these tendencies of lower wage inflation and higher price inflation are maintained in the reduced-form expressions (8.29) and (8.23) for the two rates of inflation.

In the IS curve (8.24), which is the third point, two aspects are to be distinguished. On the one hand, shareholders and managers demand higher profit margins and if they cannot be currently realized, firms cut back on their investment expenditures. On the other hand, also in their consumption demand workers are aware of the general deterioration of their position. To make the scenario not overly pessimistic, let us leave aside the possibility of precautionary saving and assume that, as long as the present wage share still exceeds the new v^o,

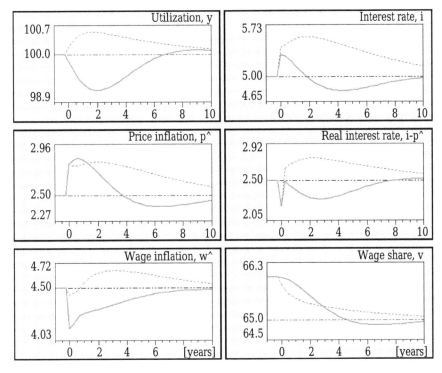

Figure 8.4 Response of the model to a sudden decrease of v^o from 66% to 65%.

Note: Dotted lines are based on $\gamma_{yv} = +0.10$, as opposed to the estimated coefficient $\gamma_{yv} = -0.10$ for the bold lines.

they consume proportionately more.[25] Nevertheless, in our profit-led economy with $\gamma_{yv} = -0.10 < 0$ the 'investment strike' of firms dominates. Hence, the fall of v^o has a contractionary effect on output.

The adjustment process that has thus been set in motion is depicted by the bold lines in Figure 8.4. The decline of the wage share to its new and lower equilibrium value is achieved by lower rates of wage inflation and higher rates of price inflation. Their deviations from the steady state values are, however, quite limited, so that the reduction of the wage share is gradual and it takes about four years until it has completed its adjustment. The initial decline in economic activity (relative to potential output) continues for two years, when utilization has fallen to 99.1 percent. As the subsequent recovery is quite slow, we can summarize that on the whole the adjustments to the new equilibrium position take five or six years, at the cost of a mild recession and only weak nominal disturbances.

---

25 This is certainly another place where a more structural modelling is desirable that explicitly distinguishes between the disposable incomes of workers and (interest and) profit earners.

By changing the sign of the coefficient γ_{yv} from negative to positive in the IS curve, Figure 8.4 also considers what happens if the economy were wage-led (see the dotted lines). Maintaining the hypothesis that the gap $(v - v^o)$, which at $t = 0$ has become positive, induces workers to raise their consumption, this time the output effect is positive. The expansion is, however, less pronounced than the contraction in the previous scenario. This is due to the fact that although the rise in price inflation is similarly moderate, the return of $\hat{p}$ to the target rate of inflation takes more time than before. This feature together with the initial positive output response implies a higher, and longer lasting, increase in the interest rate, such that also the real rate of interest is above its equilibrium value, which is a negative counter-effect on output.

It may also be noted that apart from a negligible intermezzo at the beginning, the rate of wage inflation does not decrease in this experiment, but it rises. The wage share can nevertheless adjust in a downward direction since prices are rising faster than wages. The first reactions in v are even stronger than in the profit-led economy, but convergence slows down afterwards.

Of course, the kind of experiment reflects the present change in economy and society in a very simplistic manner. It might, however, be a starting point for richer stories to tell which, in particular, may include some of the agents' long-term expectations and the overall consumer sentiment. Because of the crucial role it assigns to income distribution, our model can serve here as a workhorse to explore important feedback effects beyond the standard supply-side arguments.

8.5.2 Wage and price flexibility: eigenvalue analysis

In the theoretical discussion of the model, PFES put special emphasis on the feedback effects arising from variations in income distribution, where labour productivity is neglected for simplicity and the reasoning is in terms of the real wage rate. Giving their credit to Rose (1967), they point out that the real wage channel has ambiguous stability implications. On the one hand, the stability effects depend on the relative flexibilities with which prices and wages respond to the utilization measures on the respective markets. On the other hand, they are affected by the way in which output responds to changes in the wage share, or real wages for that matter, which concerns the distinction of profit-led and wage-led economies. Thus, the real wage rate can act in a stabilizing or destabilizing manner, where each case itself can be brought about by two completely different sets of conditions.

Let us concentrate on the destabilizing real wage channel and let it be understood that the following statements on rising or falling levels of the variables mean that they rise or fall relative to a trend. Consider an increase of the real wage rate w/p, which raises consumption C of workers and depresses investment I (and perhaps also consumption out of rentiers' income). If, as in our estimation earlier with $\gamma_{yv} < 0$, the economy is profit-led (PL), the latter effect is dominant. Capacity utilization y as well as the employment rate e decrease, and so do prices and wages. In a situation that may be called goods market led (GML), when prices

$$w/p \uparrow \overset{PL}{\Rightarrow} C \uparrow, I \downarrow\downarrow \implies y \downarrow, e \downarrow \overset{GML}{\Rightarrow} p \downarrow\downarrow, w \downarrow \implies w/p \uparrow$$

$$w/p \uparrow \overset{WL}{\Rightarrow} C \uparrow\uparrow, I \downarrow \implies y \uparrow, e \uparrow \overset{LML}{\Rightarrow} p \uparrow, w \uparrow\uparrow \implies w/p \uparrow$$

Figure 8.5 Adverse real wage effects.

react more vigorously to y than wages to e, real wages will nevertheless increase. On the whole, as sketched in the upper part of Figure 8.5, a positive feedback loop comes into being, which has a destabilizing influence on the economy.

If these forces together are sufficiently strong, they may even succeed in desta-bilizing the economy as a whole. By this expression, we presently mean that the steady state of the deterministic part of the discrete-time system (8.22)–(8.32), or the differential equations system (8.18)–(8.21), would no longer be attractive then. The positive feedback loop can be made arbitrarily strong by sufficiently increasing the coefficient β_{py} in the price Phillips curve relative to β_{we} in the wage Phillips curve (the responsiveness of prices to utilization relative to the responsiveness of wages to the employment rate) and by sufficiently decreasing the (negative) param-eter γ_{yv} in the IS curve. In a profit-led economy, it can thus be said that β_{py} tends to be destabilizing (i.e. rising values of this coefficient), while β_{we} and γ_{yv} tend to be stabilizing since increasing them may sufficiently weaken this mechanism in relation to other feedbacks in the economy with a stabilizing potential.

In contrast, assume the economy is wage-led (WL, by $\gamma_{yv} > 0$) and wage and price adjustments are labour market led (LML), such that now wages are markedly more flexible than prices. After an initial increase of real wages, the signs of the reactions of y, e and then p, w are reversed in this scenario; all of these variables are increasing and the lower part of Figure 8.5 makes clear that the real wage rate increases, too. As a consequence, the parameters change their role: higher values of β_{py} are stabilizing, and β_{we}, γ_{yv} tend to be destabilizing.

As elementary as this feedback argument is, it provides us with the insight that higher price or wage flexibility cannot be generally characterized, or recommended, as stabilizing. A crucial factor that has to be taken into account for that are the reactions of output, whether they constitute a profit-led or wage-led regime, and how strong such a regime is.

It is easily verified that normal real wage effects, where $w/p \downarrow$ at the end of the chains sketched in Figure 8.5, are obtained if in a profit-led regime the nominal adjustments are labour market led, or if in a wage-led regime they are goods market led.

While this discussion is fairly general, it can be made more specific by investigating the stability properties of our numerical economy. To save us dealing with the technical effort caused by the distributed lags in the discrete-time system, we use the convenient differential equations (8.18)–(8.21) for this kind of analysis.[26] That is, we set up the Jacobian matrix of this four-dimensional system, which is straightforward, and compute the eigenvalues, which must all have negative real parts for the steady state to be (locally asymptotically) stable.

We cannot take over all of the parameters from (8.35); some of them have to be adjusted to the continuous-time setting, which are the coefficients in the determination of output and the employment rate. According to the remarks on eq. (8.7) for the growth rate of utilization, the adjustment speed β_{yy} is given by $\beta_{yy} = (1 - \beta_{yy1} - \beta_{yy2})/0.25$, and β_{yi} and γ_{yv} are obtained from dividing their discrete-time counterpart in (8.35) by 0.25, or multiplying it by $v^o/0.25$, respectively. As remarked on eq. (8.8) for the growth rate of the employment rate, β_{ey} in this equation is given by the sum of $\beta_{ey1}, \beta_{ey2}, \beta_{ey3}$ from (8.35). Underlying the eigenvalue analysis of (8.18)–(8.21) are, therefore, the following numerical coefficients,

Climate, WPC, PPC, Taylor as in (8.35)

$$\text{IS} : \beta_{yy} = 0.40 \beta_{yi} = 0.20 \gamma_{yv} = -0.26 \qquad (8.37)$$

$$\text{Okun} : \beta_{ey} = 0.30 \beta_{ev} = 0.01$$

We first of all make sure that the steady state position of this continuous-time system continues to be stable. From the discussion of Okun's law and the role of the coefficient β_{ev} in its specification, we already know that the leading eigenvalue λ (the one with maximum real part), which turns out to be real, is not much smaller than zero ($\lambda = -0.0070$, to be exact).

Ceteris paribus variations of the central parameter γ_{yv} confirm the intuition from above that both too strongly profit-led and too strongly wage-led regimes are destabilizing, though an unstable economy itself requires fairly extreme values of the parameter; the steady state is stable if $-1.513 < \gamma_{yv} < 2.008$, and unstable outside this interval. This is a noteworthy observation for model builders in a Kalecki-Steindl tradition, for whom the distinction between profit-led and wage-led regimes plays an important role and who tend to view wage-led regimes as being more favorable for stability. Nevertheless, we have more to say on this in the next section.

The result that, within the feedback loops considered in Figure 8.5, the wage and price flexibilities β_{we} and β_{py} have opposite effects in profit-led and wage-led regimes carries over to the total economy. The left part of Figure 8.6 illustrates this by means of parameter diagrams for these coefficients, which indicate that all pairs (β_{we}, β_{py}) in the dotted area give rise to a stable equilibrium, and all pairs outside to an unstable equilibrium. To make the effects stand out, the diagrams assume that the profit-led and wage-led regimes are constituted by the switching values just mentioned, i.e. by $\gamma_{yv} = -1.5$ and $\gamma_{yv} = +2.0$, respectively. The upper-left panel shows that in such a profit-led economy, more wage flexibility (higher

---

26 Besides, transforming (8.22)–(8.32) into a well-defined difference equations system analogous to (8.18)–(8.21) would not be a trivial task, either.

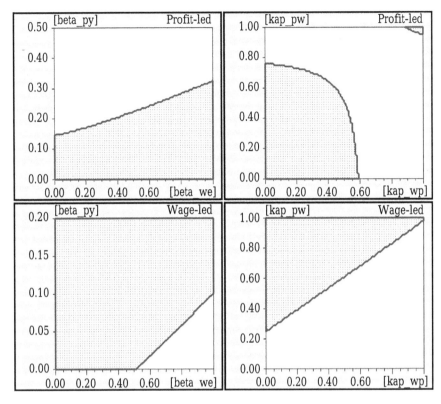

Figure 8.6 Parameter diagrams under profit-led and wage-led conditions.

Note: Parameter combinations in the dotted area induce stability of the steady state position. Profit-led and wage-led scenarios are here given by $\gamma_{yv} = -1.5$ and $\gamma_{yv} = +2.0$, respectively.

values of β_{we}) can make an unstable equilibrium stable, and more price flexibility (higher values of β_{py}) can destabilize it. By contrast, in the wage-led economy more wage flexibility is destabilizing, and more price flexibility is stabilizing.

The influence of the wage share in the wage as well as the price Phillips curve is conducive to stability, a property that holds in profit-led and wage-led economies alike. Computing the same type of diagrams (not shown) for the corresponding coefficients, pairs (β_{wv}, β_{pv}) in a neighborhood of the origin are found to render the steady state unstable, while sufficiently large values of them render it stable. In fact, the (β_{wv}, β_{pv})-parameter diagrams do not look very different for $\gamma_{yv} = -1.5$ and $\gamma_{yv} = 2.0$.[27]

---

27 This nice result should, however, not be overrated. Within a richer structural framework, these parameter diagrams may lose their unambiguity; see Chiarella *et al.* (2005, Figure 7.8 on p. 316).

Table 8.4 Characterization of parameters as stabilizing and destabilizing the steady state position

	β_{we}	β_{py}	β_{wv}	β_{pv}	κ_{wp}	κ_{pw}	κ_{wz}	β_{π}	κ_{π}
Profit-led :	S	D	S	S	D	D	S	NE	NE
Wage-led :	D	S	S	S	D	S	NE	NE	NE

Note: S and D mean that a *ceteris paribus* increase of the parameter tends to stabilize or destabilize the equilibrium, respectively; NE that it has largely negligible effects.

The right part of Figure 8.6 is concerned with effects from κ_{wp} and κ_{pw}. These parameters may be easily forgotten in a discussion on stability, since they 'only' serve to obtain an expression for benchmark inflation and weight current inflation rates against the inflation climate for that purpose. The two diagrams on the right part of the figure point out that this neglect would be unwarranted: both parameters have an impact on stability just as much as the familiar wage and price flexibilities β_{we} and β_{py}. Moreover, their role is not as symmetric as the role of β_{we} and β_{py}. In the profit-led economy, κ_{wp} and κ_{pw} are both destabilizing, whereas in the wage-led economy κ_{wp} maintains its destabilizing potential and κ_{pw} becomes stabilizing. Interesting is also the small stability region in the top-right corner of the upper diagram, from which it is seen that, under the given circumstances, not only sufficiently low but also sufficiently strong (common) weights may stabilize the steady state.

Table 8.4 succinctly summarizes the effects just described. It also contains information about the remaining three parameters κ_{wz}, β_{π}, κ_{π} in the two Phillips curves, which was obtained by similar parameter diagrams. The negligible effects from variations of β_{π} and κ_{π} are perhaps a bit surprising. From the discussion of the slow convergence of the economy under $\kappa_{\pi} = 1$, increases of this parameter toward unity might have been expected to have some destabilizing potential; and in many low-dimensional models with purely adaptive expectations, a faster adjustment speed usually turned out to be destabilizing, too.

Given that the stability results here presented are based on values of γ_{yv} that are far lower or higher than the estimated $\gamma_{yv} = -0.10$, the relevance of the analysis may be questioned. We think it is nevertheless useful. First, a side result which so far we have failed to emphasize is that the stability region around our set of numerical parameters is quite large. Stability of the steady state is thus not sensitive to larger changes of the parameters that might result from other estimations, which in more less sophisticated ways could try to incorporate the inflation climate coefficients κ_{π} and β_{π}.

Second, the identification of positive or negative feedback loops such as in Figure 8.5 is an important possibility to explain why certain parameters are

---

For a real wage feedback diagram similar to Figure 8.5 earlier, which also includes effects from β_{we} and β_{py} (some of which are destabilizing!), see pp. 310f., *ibid*.

stabilizing or destabilizing. These arguments ultimately refer to the stability properties of a state of equilibrium, and the eigenvalue analysis can verify or falsify conjectures deriving from those feedback mechanisms. A third point is that the extreme values of γ_{yv} underlying Figure 8.6 served to obtain clear-cut pictures of the parameters' stabilizing or stabilizing potential. The idea is that, under more reliable values of γ_{yv}, these effects still find some reflection when the stability investigation is extended and a less rigorous notion is used of what is considered to be (de)stabilizing. This brings us back to the stochastic economy.

8.5.3 Wage and price flexibility: variabilities in the stochastic economy

So far, the discussion of stabilizing and destabilizing parameters referred to the deterministic part of the model, where variations of them may turn an unstable equilibrium into a stable one and *vice versa*. In mainstream macroeconomics, however, stability of the equilibrium point is usually presupposed,[28] or, especially in (quasi-) linear models, it is a direct consequence of an econometric estimation method. These models are shock-driven, and obviously our model together with its estimation belongs to the same category. In this perspective, an expression like stabilization refers to the stochastic economy and the variabilities of certain state variables, meaning that a parameter variation reduces the standard deviation of the time series of that variables.

We have already made all preparations in Section 8.4 to simulate our stochastic economy. Table 8.3 has also documented that, with the exception of the employment rate, the model-generated standard deviations conform quite well to the empirical statistics. We are therefore ready to vary selected parameters and compare the resulting standard deviations with those of the baseline scenario from Table 8.3.[29]

Instead of the extreme values of γ_{yv} in the previous section, let a profit-led and wage-led regime be constituted by the estimated value $\gamma_{yv} = -0.10$ and, respectively, by $\gamma_{yv} = 0.10$. The bold face figures in the upper part of Table 8.5 reproduce the standard deviations from Table 8.3 (where the employment rate is now omitted). The outcome of a *ceteris paribus* change of γ_{yv} from -0.10 to 0.10 in the baseline case is given by the bold face figures in the lower part of the table. This modification is stabilizing in the sense that it reduces the standard deviations of utilization and the wage share, but these effects are not universal. The standard deviations of the two rates of inflation slightly rise, though this may not be reckoned significant, and that of the interest rate increases more distinctly.[30]

---

28 In the rational expectations models, it is the reduced-form representation of the motions of the predetermined variables that is stable.
29 Since for each set of parameters the same sequences of random shocks are used, it suffices to run a single experiment over 4,000 quarters.
30 The latter may appear somewhat surprising given that the interest rate is determined by the Taylor rule and the variability of y decreases more than the variability of $\hat{p}$ increases. The phenomenon

Table 8.5 Variabilities in the stochastic model under *ceteris paribus* variations of the wage–price parameters

	Standard deviations of				
	y	$\hat{p}$	$\hat{w}$	v	i
Profit-led ($\gamma_{yv} = -0.10$)					
baseline:	2.37	1.50	1.68	1.12	2.13
$\beta_{we} = 1.00$ (0.51):	2.41	1.70	1.91	1.26	2.38
$\beta_{py} = 0.38$ (0.00):	2.79	2.72	2.77	1.31	3.98
$\beta_{wv} = 0.50$ (0.23):	2.25	1.45	1.78	0.98	2.18
$\beta_{pv} = 0.50$ (0.27):	2.24	1.73	1.70	0.96	2.27
$\kappa_{wp} = 0.80$ (0.42):	2.56	2.18	2.48	1.33	2.84
$\kappa_{pw} = 0.80$ (0.55):	2.40	2.09	2.14	1.04	2.91
$\kappa_{wz} = 0.50$ (0.24):	2.20	1.48	1.76	0.90	2.12
$\beta_{\pi} = 1.50$ (1.00):	2.36	1.35	1.57	1.12	1.98
$\kappa_{\pi} = 0.80$ (0.50):	2.39	2.09	2.12	1.13	2.72
Wage-led ($\gamma_{yv} = +0.10$)					
baseline:	1.90	1.53	1.70	0.90	2.29
$\beta_{we} = 1.00$ (0.51):	2.03	1.84	1.98	1.07	2.76
$\beta_{py} = 0.38$ (0.00):	1.69	2.02	2.04	0.78	2.85
$\beta_{wv} = 0.50$ (0.23):	1.86	1.44	1.66	0.78	2.13
$\beta_{pv} = 0.50$ (0.27):	1.84	1.70	1.77	0.76	2.44
$\kappa_{wp} = 0.80$ (0.42):	2.01	2.30	2.64	1.10	3.27
$\kappa_{pw} = 0.80$ (0.55):	1.83	2.07	2.07	0.80	2.87
$\kappa_{wz} = 0.50$ (0.24):	1.98	1.55	1.81	0.83	2.32
$\beta_{\pi} = 1.50$ (1.00):	1.90	1.65	1.80	0.90	2.41
$\kappa_{\pi} = 0.80$ (0.50):	1.91	2.32	2.35	0.90	3.20

Note: Estimated values in parentheses.

Nevertheless, contrasting the profit-led with the wage-led baseline case, the latter can be said to bring about a stabilization in utilization y and the wage share v, at the price of, if at all, a weak destabilization in $\hat{p}$, $\hat{w}$ and i.

Knowing from the eigenvalue analysis that too low as well as too high values of γ_{yv} destabilize the steady state position, we may also examine other values of this parameter. In fact, we find destabilization (in the present sense) in both directions, where significant effects are already observed at far less extreme variations. For example, $\gamma_{yv} = -0.20$ increases the standard deviation of utilization

must have something to do with the serial correlation of the disturbances in the rule and the interest rate inertia it causes. Perhaps a certain phase shift of $\hat{p}$ versus y affects persistence in such a way that, under $\gamma_{yv} = 0.10$, the more extreme values of the interest rate are favored. An even more astonishing case is the increase of β_{wv} in the profit-led regime in Table 8.5, where the variabilities of both y and $\hat{p}$ decrease but that of i increases.

Table 8.6 Characterization of parameters as stabilizing and destabilizing in the stochastic economy

	β_{we}	β_{py}	β_{wv}	β_{pv}	κ_{wp}	κ_{pw}	κ_{wz}	β_{π}	κ_{π}
Effects on (y, v)									
Profit-led :	D	D	S	S	D	A	S	NE	NE
Wage-led :	D	S	S	S	D	S	A	NE	NE
Effects on $(\hat{p}, \hat{w}, i)$									
Profit-led :	D	DD	A	D	D	D	NE	S	D
Wage-led :	D	D	S	D	DD	D	NE	D	DD

Note: D (DD), S, A, NE means that a *ceteris paribus* increase of the parameter is (strongly) destabilizing, stabilizing, ambiguous or has largely negligible effects; that is, it increases (D, DD) or decreases (S) the variabilities of the corresponding group of variables.

to $sd(y_t) = 3.90$ and $\gamma_{yv} = 0.30$ increases it to $sd(y_t) = 3.35$, while the standard deviations of the other variables increase, too.

Concentrating on the two regimes $\gamma_{yv} = -0.10$ and $\gamma_{yv} = 0.10$, Table 8.5 presents the variabilities resulting from *ceteris paribus* variations of all of the parameters in the Phillips curves. We have explored several values for each coefficient, for positive and negative deviations from the estimated value alike. Within the range considered, the effects on the standard deviations are usually monotonic and they have the opposite sign if the coefficient is decreased instead of increased. So the reported coefficients are sufficiently representative.

A general feature of the experiments is that (by and large) the changes in the standard deviations of utilization and the wage share on the one hand, and of wage inflation, price inflation and the interest rate on the other hand, go in the same direction. There are indeed parameters where the variabilities of the two groups of variables go in opposite directions; most notably, this is the case for β_{pv} in both regimes and for β_{py} in the wage-led regime. Hence, in contrast to the eigenvalue approach, the notion of (de)stabilization is here multifaceted.

The distinction between the two groups of variables helps to organize the information in Table 8.5. It is also used in the qualitative summary of Table 8.6, which will therefore be more convenient for a brief overview. This classification of the parameters as stabilizing, destabilizing and ambiguous, in the profit-led case as possibly opposed to the wage-led case, is the upshot of our investigation of the properties of the stochastic model.

Besides, the sometimes different effects on (y, v) and $(\hat{p}, \hat{w}, i)$, it is interesting to compare Table 8.6 with Table 8.4, where the characterization of (de)stabilization was based on the eigenvalue analysis. In particular, the evaluation of wage and price flexibilities is now revised. According to Table 8.6, higher wage flexibility is destabilizing, for all variables and not only in the wage-led but also the profit-led regime. Higher price flexibility continues to be stabilizing in the wage-led case, but this only applies to y and v, whereas the nominal magnitudes become more volatile in both regimes.[31] These finding are worth emphasizing as they are ground for caution against inexpensive recommendations of more wage (and perhaps also price) flexibility.

8.6 Conclusion

This chapter has started out from a recent econometric estimation by PFES that seeks to take into account some central features of models in the tradition of, especially, Keynes and Goodwin. We rearranged and slightly augmented the estimation equations to obtain a closed dynamic system, which thus constitutes a semistructural Keynes-Goodwin model. Since it was found that the specification of the model's inflation climate by PFES causes unacceptably slow convergence in the impulse-response functions, we generalized the adjustment mechanism for this variable. Proposing plausible parameters in that rule and constructing the corresponding empirical climate series, the system was then re-estimated. The generalized rule together with the new coefficients produced a kind of dynamic behavior that could be described as highly satisfactory. This holds for the impulse-response functions considered and for the variabilities in the model-generated time series in the stochastic environment.

Generally, we may claim that these results set a standard for the dynamic behavior of macrodynamic systems as it is implied by econometric estimation, which many other models of the same scale still have to meet. It was therefore justified to study some of the model's properties in greater depth. Of course, the results here obtained cannot be claimed to be the end of the story, but they constitute important benchmarks to which the results from other models or future research can be fruitfully related. On the other hand, even if its semistructural nature is accepted, the model has one weak point that in any case urges for improvement. This is the specification of Okun's law that basically links the change of the employment rate e to the changes of utilization y. As convenient as it is, the specification implies that if for some reason y and e move too much out of line, the latter will exhibit (near) random walk behavior. In addition, the variability of e is too low in relation to that of y. Another feature that should be mentioned in this context is our problematic identification of the number of jobs (in the concept of the employment rate) and the number of hours worked (in the concept of labour productivity). Instead of a slight modification in an equation for the composed variable $e =$ labour employed/labour supplied, one may think about two separate adjustment equations for jobs and hours. In this way, a further utilization variable generally varying over the business cycle would enter the stage: actual hours per worker employed. Estimations of these adjustments have been recently carried out by Franke (2006, Section 6). Together with a suitable hypothesis on the supply side on the labour market, we intend to incorporate this module into the present framework in future research.

---

31 Similar differences from Table 8.4 can be observed for the weight parameter κ_{pw}.

References

Blanchard, O.J. and L. Katz (2000): Wage dynamics: reconciling theory and evidence. *American Economic Review*, 90, P.P, 69–74.

Brayton, F., J.M. Roberts, and J.C. Williams (1999): What's happened to the Phillips curve? *Finance and Economics Discussion Series*, 1999–49; Board of Governors of the Federal Reserve System.

Chiarella C., P. Flaschel, and R. Franke (2005): *Foundations for a Disequilibrium Theory of the Business Cycle: Qualitative Analysis and Quantitative Assessment.* Cambridge: Cambridge University Press.

Christiano, L., M. Eichenbaum, and C.L. Evans (1998): Monetary policy shocks: What have we learned and to what end? In: J.B. Taylor and M. Woodford (eds.): *Handbook of Macroeconomics, Volume 1A*. Amsterdam: Elsevier, 65–148.

Franke, R. (2006): Technical Report: Themes on Okun's law and beyond. *SCEPA, New School for Social Research*, New York.

Gordon, D.B. and E. Leeper (1994): The dynamic impacts of monetary policy: An exercise in tentative identification. *Journal of Political Economy*, 102, 1128–1147.

Gordon, R.J. (2003): Exploding productivity growth: Context, causes, and implications. *Brookings Papers on Economic Activity*, no. 2, 207–279.

Proaño, C., P. Flaschel, E. Ernst, and W. Semmler (2005): Comparing U.S. and Euro area wage and price inflation dynamics. *Revised version of a paper presented at the Conference on Macroeconomics and Macroeconomic Policies*. Berlin, Oct. 2005.

Rose, H. (1967): On the non-linear theory of employment. *Review of Economic Studies*, 34, 153–173.

Rudebusch, G. (2001): Term structure evidence on interest rate smoothing and monetary policy inertia. Federal Reserve Bank of San Francisco, mimeo; published in *Journal of Monetary Economics*, 49(2002), 1161–1187.

Rudebusch, G.D. and T. Wu (2003): A macro-finance model of the term structure, monetary policy, and the economy. *Federal Reserve Bank of San Francisco*, mimeo.

9 Sophisticatedly simple expectations in the Phillips curve and optimal monetary policy

9.1 Introduction

The Taylor rule has captured general attention as a useful, simple device for monetary policy. On the one hand, it appears to be a rather reliable description of recent behavior of the U.S. Federal Reserve and central banks in other countries. At a theoretical level, on the other hand, when the preferences of the central bank are represented by a (quadratic) loss function that penalizes inflation, output, and interest rate variability, numerous studies have found that Taylor rules with a suitable responsiveness to inflation and output perform nearly as well as the optimal policy in the model. As they are furthermore more robust across different models than the model-specific optimal rules, Taylor rules are an obvious pivotal scheme to refer to.

A basic problem is nevertheless the reconciliation of historical and optimal policy rules, i.e. Taylor rules with optimally chosen policy coefficients. While estimations of the Taylor rule suggest that monetary policy can be characterized as having reacted in a moderate fashion to inflation and output gaps, it has been observed by many authors that optimal rules derived in empirical models of the economy tend to recommend significantly stronger reactions.[1]

Taking it for granted, in the light of the general acclaim, that at least in the USA monetary policy has approximated some sort of optimum, a better match of theoretical prediction and real-world policy requires modifications of the macroeconomic model or the objective function. In the literature, variations of the latter have been quite limited (for good reasons). Regarding modelling in general, the introduction of data uncertainty on the part of the central bank has been most promising.[2] Especially if the central bank is exposed to measurement errors of the output gap, which typically exhibit high serial correlation, the response to output fluctuations has been found to be substantially mitigated. There is also a

---

1 This not only holds for backward-looking models, which is discussed later in this chapter, but also for forward-looking models; see Rudebusch (2002b) as an example in a standard new-Keynesian framework, and Lansing and Trehan (2001, 2003) for a 'neoclassical' variant.
2 Important contributions are Swanson (2000), McCallum (2001), Rudebusch (2001), Smets (2002), Orphanides (2003), Orphanides and Williams (2003).

certain tendency for lower policy coefficients on the inflation gap, but this effect is weaker and in our view not sufficient to explain their low estimates.

There may be some scattered models in the literature that indeed give rise to a realistic inflation gap coefficient, too, as part of the optimal Taylor rule. So the reconciliation problem does appear to have a satisfactory solution, an example being the paper by Smets (2002, see Table 2 on p. 123). Unfortunately, the result is almost noted in passing, and it is not worked out what feature of the model specification or its estimation is, in the first instance, responsible for this.

Before presenting our interpretation of Smet's finding, it should be clarified that we are concerned with small-scale models of the determination of inflation and output, which represent the private sector by a price Phillips curve and a dynamic (as it is often called) IS equation. Our interest is furthermore restricted to backward-looking models. One reason is that their feedback mechanisms are more transparent than in the forward-looking models, and that therefore also many policymakers feel more comfortable with a backward-looking framework.[3] Another reason is, however, given by econometric problems. While backward-looking Phillips curves and IS equations are easily estimated with reasonable success, recent econometric work has produced severe evidence against their new-Keynesian rational expectations counterparts; see Rudd and Whelan (2001) for the new-Keynesian Phillips curves, and Fuhrer and Rudebusch (2004) regarding the Euler equation for output.

Rudd and Whelan (2001, p. 20) are particularly explicit about the theoretical evaluation of their results, stating that they provide 'a clear warning against the use of the new-Keynesian Phillips curve (or hybrid variants that place a large weight on forward-looking expectations) for policy analysis'. The implication of these models, that current inflation summarizes the entire sequence of expected future output gaps or marginal costs, may well influence the optimal conduct of monetary policy. Noting this, they conclude, 'Given that this prediction is soundly rejected by the data, the use of these models for policy analysis strikes us as questionable at best'. Thus, 'it may be that the research agenda on inflation dynamics needs to move away from the sticky-price models that underly the new-Keynesian Phillips curve, and towards other mechanisms that can generate the degree—and type—of inflation persistence that we observe in the data' (p. 20). In fact, we view the present chapter as a contribution to such a shift in the research agenda, which should be useful even if one does not fully share Rudd and Whelan's harsh assessment.

A useful backward-looking reference model for our purpose is the quarterly estimated model by Rudebusch and Svensson (1999). In particular, it contains an accelerationist Phillips curve, whose coefficients ($\alpha_{\pi k}$) on the four lags ($k = 1, \ldots, 4$) of inflation sum up to unity. This model is well known for its vigorous

---

3 The point that this simple structure appears to roughly capture the views about the dynamics of the economy held by many monetary policymakers has been made by Rudebusch and Svensson (1999, p. 206).

responses in optimized Taylor rules. Smets' model is a slight modification of the Rudebusch-Svensson model, which only differs from it by the incorporation of measurement errors and by less persistence in inflation, i.e. the sum of its $\alpha_{\pi k}$ is less than one. With the benefit of hindsight, after having completed our own investigations, we can claim it is indeed the latter feature that plays a key role for the low optimal inflation gap coefficient at which Smets arrives.

The model that we wish to put forward in this chapter has originally been designed independently of these considerations. Starting out from the Rudebusch-Svensson model, it focusses on the formation of expectations in the Phillips curve. It refers to previous work (Franke, 2005) on a reinterpretation of the new-Keynesian Phillips curve and points out that the expectation variable on its right-hand side is not an inflation forecast for the next quarter (or year), but this variable reflects the firms' heterogeneous (and appropriately discounted) beliefs about inflation over the whole future. The variable is therefore viewed as representing the general 'inflation climate' in the economy.

Life is breathed into this concept by the dynamic process that governs its adjustments over time. While the adjustments are gradual, they do not only respond to current inflation but also to output and output changes, and they take the central bank's target rate of inflation into account. We think of this updating procedure as being brought about by firms that are not rational in the abstract sense of the theory, but adaptive in the common sense that they react in reasonable ways to the arrival of new information in an uncertain environment. The adjustment module will therefore be called the *adaptive inflation climate*. This kind of modelling is intended to follow Zellner's (1992, 2002) famous KISS principle, which is to be read as 'keep it sophisticatedly simple'. The expectations of the heterogeneous firms are certainly less elaborate than rational expectations, but also less naive than adaptive expectations. Hence, we would rather like to characterize the firms' expectations as sophisticatedly simple.

Numerical values for the four structural coefficients entering the updating process have been derived in Franke (2005). If after some algebraic manipulation the Phillips curve is rewritten in a reduced form with an infinite series of lagged inflation rates, it turns out that, similar to Smets' model, its inflation persistence is less than one. Incidentally, this is equivalent to a positive value of a coefficient representing the credibility of the central bank, which measures the extent to which the inflation climate is anchored on target inflation, and which is implicitly zero in Rudebusch and Svensson's accelerationist Phillips curve.

The main concern of this chapter is to demonstrate that it is just the lower inflation persistence that substantially decreases the coefficient on the inflation gap in an optimized Taylor rule, and that also quotes the central bank to achieve a sizable reduction of the variability in inflation, output and the interest rate. On the other hand, in conformity with the results quoted before, measurement errors are shown to be the main reason for a lower policy coefficient on the output gap.[4]

---

4 However, borrowing from the literature we model this data uncertainty different from Smets (2002).

Thus, the combination of data uncertainty and lower inflation persistence in the Phillips curve, or higher credibility of the central bank, brings the model's optimal policy responses closer to reality. If anything, it might be objected that the optimal inflation gap coefficient that we obtain is too low, though it will be argued that the general view of the 'Taylor principle', according to which it should be greater than one, may be modified.

The remainder of the chapter is organized as follows. Section 2 is an extensive discussion of the properties of the Rudebusch-Svensson model, in its original form and if the central bank's measurements of inflation and the output gap are subjected to noise. Besides the (usual) evaluation of monetary policy on the basis of large samples, we will also study here the phenomenon of small variability, when a single economy is simulated over a fifty-year period 'only'. Section 3 introduces our adaptive inflation climate. Since the treatment of expectations in the Phillips curve is the only point in which our model deviates from Rudebusch and Svensson, all the differences in the results can be ascribed to this concept. As a preparatory step in the analysis, we compare the impulse-response functions of the two models. This will provide a better understanding of the results of the monetary policy experiments, which are subsequently conducted in strict analogy to Section 2. The important role of inflation persistence, or central bank credibility, is additionally highlighted by constructing a hybrid version of the expectations in the Rudebusch-Svensson model and ours, where upon the continuous change of a parameter one model turns into the other. Lastly, Section 3 considers the issue of interest rate smoothing, which we had neglected before. Section 4 concludes.

9.2 The Rudebusch-Svensson model

9.2.1 Formulation of the model

The model that Rudebusch and Svensson (RS, henceforth) use for their investigations of optimal monetary policy is a simple backward-looking model of output and inflation. It is nevertheless well suited for this purpose, since it appears to roughly capture the views that many policymakers hold about the dynamics of the economy (RS, 1999, p. 206). The private sector is described by two equations for the quarterly changes of the output gap y_t and the (annualized) quarterly rate of inflation π_t. An IS (Investment Saving) curve relates the output gap to two of its own lags and an approximate *ex post* real interest rate, which is specified as the difference between the average funds rate and average inflation over the previous four quarters. The Phillips curve for inflation is of an accelerationist type and relates the inflation rate to the lagged output gap and to four lags of inflation. Denoting the equilibrium real rate of interest by r^*, the federal funds rate by i_t, and indicating four-quarter averages by a bar (i.e. $\bar{\imath}_t = (1/4)\sum_{j=0}^{3} i_{t-j}$ and $\bar{\pi}_t$ accordingly), the model reads,

$$y_t = \beta_{y1} y_{t-1} + \beta_{y2} y_{t-2} - \beta_{yr} (\bar{\imath}_{t-1} - \bar{\pi}_{t-1} - r^*) + \varepsilon_{y,t} \tag{9.1}$$

$$\pi_t = \pi_t^a + \beta_{\pi y}\, y_{t-1} + \varepsilon_{\pi,t} \tag{9.2}$$

$$\pi_t^a = \beta_{\pi 1}\pi_{t-1} + \beta_{\pi 2}\pi_{t-2} + \beta_{\pi 3}\pi_{t-3} + \beta_{\pi 4}\pi_{t-4}, \qquad \sum_k \beta_{\pi k} = 1 \tag{9.3}$$

The random perturbations $\varepsilon_{y,t}$, $\varepsilon_{\pi,t}$ are supposed to be normally distributed (i.i.d.) with variances σ_y^2 and σ_π^2, respectively.

Clearly, the model is based on lags in the manner of a small estimated vector autoregression. The lags in π_t^a are usually said to correspond to autoregressive or adaptive expectations (therefore the superscript 'a'), but this can only be an implicit, or reduced-form, representation. A similar remark, at least from a new-Keynesian perspective, applies to the two lagged output terms in (9.1). Since the model does not discuss an explicit process in which agents form expectations about future inflation and output, it seems appropriate to view eqs (9.1)–(9.3) as semistructural relationships.[5]

A standard objective function serves to evaluate monetary policy in this framework, where the central bank is concerned with the variability in output, inflation around a target π^*, and also the quarterly interest rate changes. The single losses from these variations are treated as symmetric, and total losses L are given by the weighted sum of the unconditional variances of the goal variables,[6]

$$L = \operatorname{var}[\bar{\pi}_t - \pi^*] + \lambda \operatorname{var}[y_t] + \nu \operatorname{var}[i_t - i_{t-1}] \tag{9.4}$$

The weights on output stabilization, $\lambda \geq 0$, and interest rate smoothing, $\nu \geq 0$, are conceived relative to inflation stabilization. Their usual benchmark values in the literature are $\lambda = 1$ and $\nu = 0.5$. Regarding the coefficients in the IS and Phillips curve equation, we take over the estimates from RS (1999, p. 208).[7] Table 9.1 reproduces the numerical values of these parameters.

Optimal monetary policy can be determined analytically in this kind of model. The feedback rule for the interest rate that minimizes the loss function (9.4)

Table 9.1 Numerical coefficients in eqs (9.1)–(9.4)

λ	ν	β_{y1}	β_{y2}	β_{yr}	$\sigma_{\varepsilon,y}$	$\beta_{\pi 1}$	$\beta_{\pi 2}$	$\beta_{\pi 3}$	$\beta_{\pi 4}$	$\beta_{\pi y}$	$\sigma_{\varepsilon,\pi}$
1.00	0.50	1.16	−0.25	0.10	0.819	0.70	−0.10	0.28	0.12	0.14	1.009

5 Indeed, if one dislikes the structural interpretation that Rudebusch and Svensson (1999) attach to the model, they leave it up to the reader to simply consider it a reduced-form VAR (p. 207). Taylor (1999, p. 662) also points out that equations like (9.1)–(9.3) may be viewed as a reduced form that summarizes more complex forward-looking behavior.

6 It is well known that (9.4) is the limit for $\delta \to 1$ of the discounted sums of the (appropriately scaled) expected intertemporal losses $(1-\delta)E_o \sum_{t=0}^{\infty} L_t$, with period losses $L_t = (\bar{\pi}_t - \pi^*)^2 + \lambda y_t^2 + \nu (i_t - i_{t-1})^2$; Rudebusch and Svensson (1999, p. 215).

7 The parameters in later applications of the model are only marginally different; see, e.g., Rudebusch (2001).

involves up to three lags of inflation, the output gap, and the interest rate itself (RS, 1999, p. 232, or Rudebusch, 2001, p. 207). Many studies of the RS model and also forward-looking models, however, have shown that a Taylor rule with a suitable responsiveness to inflation and output comes fairly close to the optimal rule. Since the performance of more sophisticated policy designs is generally also sensitive to their specific modelling framework, much of the literature on monetary policy models concentrates directly on such an elementary feedback mechanism. We follow this strategy with the additional assumption that the central bank does not try to forecast future inflation.

To begin with, let us suppose that the central bank has precise data of current prices and output. The Taylor rule then reads,

$$T_o: \quad i_t = r^* + \pi^* + g_\pi (\bar{\pi}_t - \pi^*) + g_y y_t \tag{9.5}$$

where the letter T stands for Taylor and the index indicates the zero information lag of the data. In this formulation, the classical coefficients put forward by Taylor (1993, p. 202) are $g_\pi = 1.50$ and $g_y = 0.50$. RS (1999, p. 233) refer to slightly higher estimates $g_\pi = 1.76$ and $g_y = 0.74$ for the sample 1985:2–96:2. These values are well within the range of the estimation results from the literature that Rudebusch (2001, p. 204) briefly summarizes as $1.4 \le g_\pi \le 2.0$ and $0.5 \le g_y \le 1.0$ (cf. also the overview in Woodford, 2003, p. 41).

In evaluating the performance of these reference values or of an optimized rule in the RS model, one will relate the induced volatilities of the goal variables to their empirical counterparts. A direct comparison can, however, be somewhat misleading. This, in particular, holds true for inflation. Here the Volcker disinflation policy gave rise to a pronounced decline in the trend rate of inflation over the first half of the 1980s, a decline that causes the historical variability of inflation to be overstated in comparison to the simulation results, which do not incorporate similar disinflationary episodes. A similar reasoning applies to the previously soaring inflation rates in the 1970s. Since the target rate of inflation is always held constant in the model and so the long-run trend rate of inflation is stationary, the simulations should yield an inflation variability that is considerably lower than the historical standard deviation of $\bar{\pi}_t$, which RS (1999, p. 229) report as 2.33 percentage points over the sample period 1961:1–96:2.

A more appropriate benchmark may therefore have these trend episodes removed from the data. Using the prices of nonfinancial corporations, we detrended their quarterly inflation rates by the convenient Hodrick-Prescott filter (HP, with the usual smoothing parameter $\lambda = 1600$) and computed the four-quarter averages. While the two inflation peaks are still standing out in 1975 and 1981, this series exhibits a much lower variability of $\text{Std}[\bar{\pi}_t] = 1.29$ percentage points.

Besides the estimated standard error of the regression, the variability of the output gap is in the first instance determined by the AR(2) coefficients β_{y1} and β_{y2} in the IS equation (9.1). Owing to the small coefficient β_{yr}, the impact of the real interest rate fluctuations on output will be of secondary importance as long as they remain moderate. To refer to a specific benchmark value of $\text{Std}[y_t]$, it could be argued that the underlying estimations of potential GDP (Gross Domestic Product) by the CBO (Congressional Budget Office) concept tends to overemphasize the variability of this variable for the present model.[8] On the other hand, production of the nonfinancial corporations may be considered an equally or even more suitable data source than GDP. Thus, a figure like $\text{Std}[y_t] = 2.35$ for the percentage deviations of this sector from its HP output trend may serve as a reasonable magnitude.

Although the volatility of the level of the nominal interest rate does not feature in the central bank's loss function, the fluctuations of this variable should not be completely neglected. RS (1999, p. 238), for example, divulge that most of the optimized rules in (at least) one of their tables imply about a 20 percent probability of a negative interest rate. As the zero-bound on interest rates has so far not been much of a problem to the Federal Reserve, the model should not exhibit excessively large interest rate fluctuations, either; especially in the absence of upward or downward trending inflation.

Accordingly, also the federal funds rate was detrended by HP, which yields a standard deviation of 1.74 percentage points. Since this figure might be felt to be too low, brought about by a trend line that in one or two episodes nestles too close to the raw series, it was a straightforward device to take the trend series and apply the HP filter a second time. In fact, the new and less flexible trend line increases the variability of the trend deviations to $\text{Std}[i_t] = 1.97$ percentage points.

The loss function's first differences of the interest rate remain almost unaffected by the detrending procedures, the standard deviations ranging between 1.07 and 1.10. The benchmarks that we thus derive for the standard deviations of $\bar{\pi}_t, y_t, \Delta i_t$ and i_t are summarized in the first row of Table 9.3.

9.2.2 The Taylor rule in the basic model

In carrying out the numerical simulations of the RS model, we follow Rudebusch (2001, 206) and compute the variances (or standard deviations) of the variables on a basis of 100,000 quarterly observations. It turns out, however, that the organization of these observations has a certain bearing on the results. We therefore distinguish two cases to evaluate a given pair of policy coefficients g_π, g_y. In the first case, 50 sample runs are performed that extend over 510 years, where an initial transition period of ten years after the start in the steady state is discarded. The summary statistics are computed for each single run and are then averaged, so the total of these 50 simulation runs may be regarded as one evaluation run. In the second case, an evaluation run consists of 500 single runs over 60 years, where again the first ten years are discarded. For short, the recapitulation in Table 9.2 calls

---

8 RS (1999, p. 207, fn6) mention that their output gap series is essentially identical to that obtained
   by the Congressional Budget Office. They measure the variability of this series as $\text{Std}[y_t] = 2.80$
   (p. 229).

Table 9.2 Alternative specifications of an "evaluation run"

	Single runs	Interval evaluated (years)	Observations
Long samples:	50	10–510	100,000
Short samples:	500	10–60	100,000

Table 9.3 Policy coefficients in the Rudebusch-Svensson model

				Standard deviations of			
g_π	g_y	Loss	$\bar{\pi}_t$	y_t	Δi_t	i_t
1. Benchmarks:			1.30	2.35	1.10	2.00
A. Taylor rule without measurement error (T_o)						
2. 1.76	0.74	17.11	3.42	2.27	0.71	4.90
3. 2.71	1.62	11.30	2.17	2.23	1.79	5.14
B. Taylor rule with measurement error (T_{me})						
4. 1.25	0.40	27.02	4.66	2.22	0.83	5.73
5. 2.33	1.12	13.27	2.38	2.40	1.91	5.20

Note: Rows 2 and 4 are estimated policy coefficients from the literature, rows 3 and 5 are optimized rules based on long-sample evaluations runs.

the underlying sample periods of 500 and 50 years (comparatively) long and (comparatively) short, respectively.

To assess the gains of an optimized policy rule, we first simulate the RS model with the aforementioned estimated coefficients $g_\pi = 1.76$, $g_y = 0.74$. Based on a long-sample evaluation run, the standard deviations of $\bar{\pi}_t$, y_t, Δi_t and i_t reported in the second row of Table 9.3 are obtained. It is immediately seen that the variabilities of the output gap and the quarterly interest rate changes conform quite well to the benchmark values in the first row of the table. At the same time, however, the rule generates large fluctuations of inflation and, consequently, the interest rate that can only be regarded as unsatisfactory.

The statistics are mitigated if the 100,000 observations are obtained from a short-sample evaluation run. Std[$\bar{\pi}_t$] is then reduced to 2.53 and Std[i_t] to 4.22, while Std[y_t] = 2.19 and Std[Δi_t] = 0.92. According to the foregoing discussion of the benchmarks, the fluctuations of $\bar{\pi}_t$ and i_t are nevertheless still too wide.[9]

9 To judge the variability of the interest rate of Std[i_t] = 4.22 percent, consider a two percent target rate of inflation and an equilibrium real rate of interest of 2.5 percent, so that the nominal interest rate may fluctuate with an amplitude of ±4.5 percent without seriously violating the zero-bound condition. The standard deviation of a deterministic eight-year sine wave motion with this amplitude would then be no higher than 3.28.

It is nevertheless interesting to ask why, in particular, inflation becomes so much less volatile by this change in the experimental design. The reason for the reduction is that the accelerationist type of Phillips curve (9.2), (9.3) contains a random walk element (since $\sum \beta_{\pi k} = 1$). Though central bank policy puts a curb on it, the effects on inflation are only indirect by counteracting on the output gap, where the two reaction coefficients β_{yr} in the IS curve and $\beta_{\pi y}$ in the Phillips curve are not very large. Hence even in the presence of sharp reactions of the central bank, the random walk will to some extent still be operative. It is furthermore clear that over 500 consecutive years the random walk has greater scope to unfold its temporarily diverging tendencies than over a sample period of 50 years.[10]

Having established the effects of an estimated Taylor rule in the RS model, we can now turn to its improvement. The optimal policy coefficients g_π, g_y with respect to the loss function (9.4) and the standard weights $\lambda = 1$, $\nu = 0.5$ from Table 9.1 are given in the third row of Table 9.3. They are obtained by making use of an iterative search algorithm that at each step constructs a new pair g_π, g_y, performs an evaluation run that, of course, is based on the same sequences of random shocks, and then computes the corresponding value of the loss function.[11] With the long-sample evaluations runs, the solution at which we thus arrive is essentially the same as the values documented in RS (1999, p. 227). It is also close to the values given in Rudebusch (2001, Table 1, Panel B), whose computations are based on slightly different parameters.

In the light of the foregoing discussion on the random walk element in the model and the resulting drift problems the central bank has to tame, for which its reactions must be strong enough, it is now not very surprising that when the simulations employ the small-sample evaluation runs, the optimal coefficient on the inflation gap decreases from 2.71 to $g_\pi = 2.42$. The output gap coefficient g_y, on the other hand, does not practically change. In this way the standard deviations decrease from 2.17 for the inflation rate in Table 9.3 to 2.11, and from 5.14 for the interest rate to 4.70. Nevertheless, the results of the optimized policy rule do not really become satisfactory. Apart from the fact that the optimal coefficients appear fairly high, they are also not capable of sufficiently reducing the variability of inflation as well as of the interest rate and the interest rate changes.

An obvious attempt to overcome these problems is to change the preferences of the central bank and assume a (very) strong interest rate smoothing motive in the form of a higher weight ν in the loss function (9.4). This procedure is only

---

10 To illustrate the diverging potential of the random walk element in the Phillips curve, we treated the output gap as exogenous and let y_t vary as a stochastically disturbed sine wave (with $\sigma_{\varepsilon,y} = 0.819$ as in Table 9.1). Observing the resulting inflation rates and Taylor rule interest rates in 1000 simulations over 500 years, it was found that 830 of them became meaningless in the sense that eventually at least one of the two rates exceeded 50 percent in modulus.

11 The algorithm is the downhill simplex method. Since it does not require the evaluation of any derivatives, it is a convenient method at least if the computational burden of simulating the dynamics is not too large; see Press *et al.* (1986, pp. 289ff).

partially successful. While raising the weight to $v = 5$ yields optimal coefficients $g_\pi = 1.91$ and $g_y = 0.67$ that are more in line with the estimates, the standard deviation of inflation increases up to 2.72. Even more importantly, the approach lacks persuasiveness since such a strong desire for smooth interest rates is difficult to motivate. There is thus general agreement in the literature that not too much emphasis should be laid on a suitable 'calibration' of preferences.

9.2.3 The role of measurement errors

The elementary formulation of the RS model does not yet take the measurements errors into account that typically plague policymakers in real time. We now correct this omission and introduce data uncertainty. Accordingly, in quarter t the central bank does not respond to the actual values of $\bar{\pi}_t$ and y_t, but to the values that are contaminated with errors (or 'noise') $n_{\pi,t}$ for the rate of inflation and $n_{y,t}$ for the output gap. The modelling of these errors is purely empirically based and, in particular, does not assume that the central bank knows the process generating the measurement.[12] With an index *me* alluding to the measurement errors that are here made explicit, the Taylor rule becomes,

$$T_{me}: \quad i_t = r^* + \pi^* + g_\pi (\bar{\pi}_t + n_{\pi,t} - \pi^*) + g_y (y_t + n_{y,t}) \tag{9.6}$$

Private agents are not affected by this problem since at their disaggregated environments they know the values of the variables that are relevant for them. This carries over to the aggregate level, i.e. the IS relationship and the Phillips curve remain unchanged.

We find in the literature that the data revisions for the central bank are empirically well described by a third-order moving average process for the four-quarter rate of inflation, and a first-order autoregression for the output gap. Rudebusch (2001, p. 214) has estimated these time series processes as follows,

$$n_{\pi,t} = \varepsilon^n_{\pi,t} + 0.63\varepsilon^n_{\pi,t-1} + 0.26\varepsilon^n_{\pi,t-2} + 0.18\varepsilon^n_{\pi,t-3}, \quad \sigma^n_\pi = 0.320 \tag{9.7}$$

$$n_{y,t} = 0.75 n_{y,t-1} + \varepsilon^n_{y,t}, \quad \sigma^n_y = 0.838 \tag{9.8}$$

The dynamics of the augmented RS model with measurement errors in the Taylor rule are thus described by eqs (9.1)–(9.3) and (9.6)–(9.8), where all stochastic disturbances are supposed to be normally distributed (i.i.d.).

Before optimizing the Taylor rule in this new framework, we again investigate the performance of an estimated rule. Preferably, the estimation should allow

---

12 The latter assumption is employed by Smets (2002) for the output gap, which allows the central bank to apply the Kalman filter and thus compute an optimal estimate of the current state of the economy. Also, we continue to neglect the central bank's uncertainty about the equilibrium real rate of interest.

for some kind of measurement errors. A straightforward approach is offered by Rudebusch (2002a, Section 6), which does not specify the errors in detail but instead assumes autocorrelated disturbances in general. His maximum likelihood estimation of the federal funds rate over the sample 1987:4–99:4 yields the following coefficients,

$$i_t = 1.24\,\bar{\pi}_t + 0.33\,y_t + \xi_t, \qquad \xi_t = 0.92\,\xi_{t-1} + \varepsilon_{\xi,t} \tag{9.9}$$

Although Rudebusch explains that the terms ξ_t reflect more than just measurement errors, let us take these policy coefficients as a reasonable proxy for the outcome of a more specific estimation of rule T_{me}. Regarding the output gap coefficient in (9.9), which is based on the CBO measure of potential GDP, we recall that this output gap concept implies a higher variability than our benchmark of Std[y_t] = 2.35. We may therefore scale the coefficient upward and, referring to footnote 8, multiply 0.33 by 2.80/2.35.

In sum, with a little rounding, our reference coefficients for T_{me} are $g_\pi = 1.25$ and $g_y = 0.40$. However, simulating the RS model with this rule leads to no gain in realism. On the contrary, row 4 of Table 9.3 shows that inflation and the interest rate become more volatile than before. The assumed responsiveness of the central bank is obviously too weak. In fact, as can be seen in row 5 of the table, the optimized T_{me} rule requires both policy coefficients g_π and g_y to increase. Unfortunately, the corresponding standard deviations of the state variables are even slightly higher than those brought about by the optimized T_o rule in row 3. The introduction of data uncertainty, therefore, does not improve the realism of the model dynamics.

Despite these shortcomings, the model is insofar useful as it allows us to assess the effects of data uncertainty on optimal policy, which might also survive in a modified framework. Comparing row 3 and 5 of Table 9.3, it is seen that the measurement errors lead to a moderate reduction of the inflation gap coefficient g_π and a substantial reduction of the output gap coefficient g_y. Rudebusch (2001, Table 5) has demonstrated that the latter is mainly due to the noise in the output data and much less to the noise in the perceived inflation rates.

More precisely, it is the autocorrelation in the data noise that is essential. It causes the central bank to underestimate the speed at which actual output returns to potential output, so that its reaction in the interest rate, with an unchanged responsiveness g_y, would be inadequately strong.[13] We can check this intuition by taking the optimal coefficients $g_\pi = 2.71$, $g_y = 1.62$ from row 3 in Table 9.3, which were derived in the setting without measurement errors. If here the output noise (9.8) is introduced in (9.6), with the noise in inflation still being absent (i.e. putting $\sigma_\pi^n = 0$ in (9.7)), then Std[Δi_t] increases from 1.79 to 2.37, while the increase in Std[$\bar{\pi}_t$] is much weaker, from 2.17 to 2.24. On this basis it can

---

13 As remarked by Rudebusch (2001, p. 214, fn23), a high frequency measurement error may simply wash out.

be argued that the central bank can avoid the increase in Std[Δi_t] by a lower responsiveness to the perceived output gap. It thus accepts an increase in the variability of inflation, but this effect will be dominated by the first differences in the interest rates. Actually, still with $\sigma_\pi^n = 0$, the optimal policy coefficients are computed as $g_\pi = 2.43$ and $g_y = 1.16$, where Std[$\bar{\pi}_t$] increases only mildly to 2.31, and Std[Δi_t] falls to 1.75.

9.2.4 Small sample variability

Results on optimal coefficients in stochastic models are usually based on the law of large numbers. In the numerical simulations above, the law was approximated by samples of 100,000 observations (which proved to be large enough). Nevertheless, a rule that is optimal in this sense need not be optimal, or not even good, for a small sample. If the policy coefficients obtained so far and the associated variabilities of inflation, etc., deviate so much from their empirical counterparts, then it could at least theoretically be argued that the demand and supply shocks occurring in the real world over the last 20 or 50 years, say, do not yet obey the law of large numbers. Accepting for the sake of the argument that the real world is appropriately described by the private sector of the present model, this could mean the actual shocks were so specific that the central bank was well advised not to adopt the policy coefficients suggested by Table 9.3. In its own way, the central bank may even have been able to achieve lower variabilities of inflation and the interest rate than the table predicts.

Rather than re-estimate the IS and Phillips curves (9.1), (9.2), extract the specific demand and supply shock sequences from there, and substitute them for the disturbances $\varepsilon_{y,t}$ and $\varepsilon_{\pi,t}$ (besides the measurement errors as far as they are available), we wish to study the problem of small sample variability at a more general level. To this end, the following scenario is set up. Limiting our interest to T_{me}-rules and to time intervals of fifty years, a specific set of the four random shock sequences $\varepsilon_{y,t}$, $\varepsilon_{\pi,t}$, $\varepsilon_{y,t}^n$, $\varepsilon_{\pi,t}^n$ defines a sample for which we then compute the values of g_π and g_y that minimize the loss function.[14] Another set of shock sequences will, of course, give rise to another optimal solution. On the whole, the second row in Table 9.4 considers 5000 such samples and computes the mean values of the optimal policy coefficients as well as of the induced variabilities of the economic variables.

These sample averages show that it is not the same whether 100,000 observations are generated from alternative coefficients g_π, g_y and the loss minimizing pair is selected, or if the same is done for a small sample of 200 observations, but repeatedly 500 times (in the present case even 5000 times) and then the average of these 500 (or 5000) optimal pairs is calculated. As a matter of fact, each entry in the second row of Table 9.4 is lower than the corresponding value in the last row of Table 9.3. Incidentally, all of these entries are also

---

14 Actually, the simulations run over 60 years, and the first ten years are again discarded as transitional.

Table 9.4 Policy coefficients in fifty-year samples of the Rudebusch-Svensson model

				Standard deviations of		
g_π	g_y	*Loss*	$\bar\pi_t$	y_t	Δi_t	i_t
1. Benchmarks:			1.30	2.35	1.10	2.00
A. Averages of optimal T_{me} across 5000 samples						
2. 1.66	0.98	10.81	2.19	2.07	1.57	3.95
(0.69)	(0.35)	(3.55)	(0.47)	(0.34)	(0.47)	(1.27)
B. Two locally optimal T_{me} solutions for a selected sample						
3. 0.76	0.30	6.08	1.66	1.79	0.49	1.47
4. 2.17	1.36	9.69	2.08	1.87	1.93	4.68
C. Average performance of one T_{me} rule across 5000 samples						
5. 1.66	0.98	12.96	2.63	2.08	1.53	4.43
–	–	(4.52)	(0.68)	(0.25)	(0.08)	(0.88)

Note: Standard deviations of the entries in parentheses.

lower than the values resulting from the small-sample evaluation runs for the 100,000 observations.

Representing the law of large numbers in the way of part A of Table 9.4 reduces the average policy coefficients on both the output gap and the inflation gap even so strongly that they are now in an largely acceptably range. On the other hand, the variables $\bar\pi_t$, Δi_t and i_t continue to be unsatisfactorily volatile.

With regard to the policy coefficients it has to be taken into account that they are widely dispersed, as it is indicated by the standard deviations which are given in parentheses. Especially for the inflation gap coefficient this has a highly remarkable consequence: in a nonnegligible number of cases g_π is less than one and so violates the Taylor principle, according to which a stable economy requires the central bank to adjust the nominal rate of interest more than proportionately to the changes in inflation. Instability (however specified in detail) will in fact prevail in the (very) long-run, but not necessarily within a fifty-year period. This is exemplified in the third row of Table 9.4. It documents that for a specific set of random disturbances, the model economy not only remains viable for a value $g_\pi < 1$, but this value together with a certain (low) value of g_y is even optimal! The latter is indicated by the unprecedentedly low loss of 6.08 that summarizes the relatively, or even extraordinarily, low variabilities of inflation, the interest rate, and the interest rate changes. But note that nonetheless the variability of inflation is still somewhat higher than desired.

The random shocks underlying row 3 are also interesting in another respect. They provide an example where we have found a second local minimum of the loss function. Toward which of the two minima the search algorithm converges is contingent on its initialization. Actually, most of the initial conditions that we have checked lead it to the configuration given in row 4 of Table 9.4, which looks more familiar again.[15]

To explore the fifty-year economies further, consider a central bank that commits itself to a Taylor rule with fixed coefficients over this span of time. Having no expectations about the shocks the economy is subjected to but only knowing the results of the above simulations, it may be assumed to settle upon the averages of the optimal coefficients in row 2 of Table 9.4. How well the central bank does with the rule depends, of course, on the specific shock sequences over its one-time experiment, where it may have good luck or bad luck. On the basis of 5000 simulation runs, the number in parentheses in the fifth row of the table show that this policy would indeed produce a wide range of results. Which illustrates the necessity for a central bank to be more flexible than just sticking to a rigid rule, however useful it might be in (very) large samples.

It is clear that the average loss reported for the rule in row 5 is higher than the average loss of the specifically optimized rules in row 2.[16] Similarly, the average variabilities of inflation and also the level of the interest rate in row 5 exceed those in the second row. The repeated observation that they are unsatisfactorily large, although the average optimal policy coefficients across the fifty-year samples may be fairly acceptable, brings us now to a reconsideration of the RS model.

9.3 Sophisticatedly simple expectations and their implications

9.3.1 The concept of the adaptive inflation climate

Another problem of the RS model, besides the high volatility of the variables that it typically produces, is the treatment of expectations about future inflation. Though the lags specifying π_t^a in (9.3) are said to represent adaptive expectations of inflation (RS, 1999, p. 207), the estimated positive and negative coefficients $\beta_{\pi k}$ from Table 9.1 appear hard to reconcile with any stylized psychological principle of partial adjustments. While eq. (9.3) could still be interpreted as a reduced-form representation of an adaptive mechanism, a gap remains as long as the extensive form that may possibly be underlying is not made explicit. One may therefore wish to have a clearer structure regarding the expectations of inflation—without immediately changing to rational expectations.

In this section, the four lags of π_t^a in (9.3) are replaced with the concept of a so-called *adaptive inflation climate*, which is borrowed from Franke (2005). It starts

---

15 The selected shock sequences of Part B of the table is among the samples considered in Part A, and there the algorithm happened to converge to the policy coefficients of row 3. As can be inferred from the standard deviation of g_π in row 2, there are many other cases where the algorithm was not fooled by a local minimum like that of row 4, but where it spotted one with $g_\pi < 1$.

16 It might also be mentioned that the frequency distribution of the losses is not normal. Regarding the distributions of $\mathrm{Std}[\tilde{\pi}_t]$, $\mathrm{Std}[y_t]$, etc., some of them are nearly normal and some are definitely not.

out from a reconsideration of the new-Keynesian Phillips curve in the usual Calvo (1983) setting by dropping the assumption that all firms are uniformly blessed with rational expectations. Reasonably, then, the expectation variable on the right-hand side of the Philips curve is not the rate of inflation that all firms expect to prevail in the next period. It rather summarizes in a single number the heterogeneous beliefs of the firms, where the individual beliefs are about inflation over the whole future and the inflation rates are suitably discounted by the probability with which the single firm is allowed to change its price in a given quarter. The resulting aggregate variable is called the inflation climate, denoted as π_t^c. The previous Phillips curve (9.2) is thus reformulated as

$$\pi_t = \pi_t^c + \beta_{\pi y} y_{t-1} + \varepsilon_{\pi,t} \tag{9.10}$$

The formulation of the dynamic process that governs the adjustments of π_t^c on the arrival of new information was motivated by the patterns one can identify in survey measure data on expected inflation. The inflation climate π_{t-1}^c is predetermined in a given quarter $t - 1$ and modified by the firms at the beginning of the next quarter t as the variables of the previous quarter are observed. The updating procedure is grounded on the concept of a general benchmark rate of inflation, toward which the current value of the climate is adjusted in a gradual manner. This benchmark, in turn, is a combination of four single components: (i) The current rate of inflation. (ii) The (constant) target rate of inflation, π^*, which is set by the central bank and publicly known. (iii) An output-adjusted rate of inflation which expresses the idea that the firms see a tendency for higher inflation if economic activity is presently above normal. (iv) A growth-adjusted rate of inflation which expresses the idea that the firms see a tendency for higher inflation if the economy is presently growing faster than potential output.

In total, the updating process can be compactly described on the basis of four nonnegative behavioral parameters α_c, γ, α_y, α_g (with $\alpha_c, \gamma \leq 1$). Δ being the difference operator, it results like

$$\pi_t^c = \pi_{t-1}^c + \alpha_c [\gamma \pi^* + (1 - \gamma)(\pi_{t-1} + \alpha_y y_{t-1} + \alpha_g \Delta y_{t-1}) - \pi_{t-1}^c] \tag{9.11}$$

Equation (9.11) summarizes how the single firms' views about future inflation cause the general inflation climate to change in an adaptive way; where, as usual in the learning literature on heterogeneous agents, the expression 'adaptive' is used in a broader sense than just an 'adaptive expectations' rule. In this sense, the equation can be said to represent the notion of an adaptive inflation climate, which we abbreviate to AIC. Accordingly, the modified core of the RS model, which is now given by eqs (9.1), (9.10), (9.11), may be referred to as the AIC model.[17]

Since the climate variable is unobservable, the structural coefficients in (9.11) cannot be directly estimated. Thus, in Franke (2005) a combination of estimation

---

17 In the present context which invokes no econometrics, there is no risk of confusing this acronym with the Akaike information criterion.

and calibration methods was employed to derive reasonable values from the implications of (9.10) and (9.11) for the inflation dynamics, where in order to stay close to RS at least as far as the driving variable is concerned, the slope parameter $\beta_{\pi y} = 0.14$ in the Phillips curve was maintained. This fitting procedure arrived at the following parameter values,[18]

$$\alpha_c = 0.410 \qquad \gamma = 0.453 \qquad \alpha_y = 0.292 \qquad \alpha_g = 0.000 \qquad (9.12)$$

The coefficient α_c in (9.11) is plainly the general speed of adjustment in the updating of the inflation climate. The economic significance of the parameter γ and its relationship to the literature is less evident. To reveal it, consider an elementary specification of expectations in the Phillips curve which can reflect the faith firms have got in the conduct of monetary policy. Following Freedman (1996, pp. 253f), such a Phillips curve may read

$$\pi_t = \mu \pi^* + (1 - \mu)A(L)\pi_{t-1} + \beta y_{t-1} \qquad (9.13)$$

where $A(L)$ is a normalized polynomial lag function indicating that expected inflation is tied to the past rates of inflation, whose coefficients add up to unity. The weight μ expresses the degree to which inflation expectations are anchored on the target rate of inflation, so that the coefficient can be interpreted as measuring the credibility of the central bank.[19] On the other hand, $1 - \mu$ as the sum of the coefficients on the lagged rates of inflation is commonly viewed as a measure of inflation persistence.

The AIC approach can be compared to (9.13) by repeatedly dating (9.11) one period backward and substituting it in (9.10) (or the equation resulting from the previous step). Using $\sum_{k=0}^{\infty}(1-\alpha_c)^k = 1/\alpha_c$, we finally get

$$\pi_t = \gamma \pi^* + (1-\gamma)\sum_{k=0}^{\infty}\alpha_c(1-\alpha_c)^k \pi_{t-k-1}$$

$$+ \beta_{\pi y} y_{t-1} + \alpha_c(1-\gamma)\sum_{k=0}^{\infty}(1-\alpha_c)^k (\alpha_y y_{t-k-1} + \alpha_g \Delta y_{t-k-1}) \quad (9.14)$$

Since the terms $\alpha_c(1-\alpha_c)^k$ sum up to unity, we can summarize

γ	credibility of the central bank
$1-\gamma$	inflation persistence in the Phillips curve

$$(9.15)$$

---

18 The underlying empirical series for fitting was detrended inflation in the sector of nonfinancial corporations.

19 Note that this concept is inherent in Phillips curve estimations with demeaned or detrended inflation rates where the sum of the coefficients on lagged inflation is significantly less than one. This is easily seen by adding target inflation on both sides of such a regression equation, when it is assumed that π^* approximately equals the trend inflation in the data.

It is apparent in this way that with its accelerationist Phillips curve, the RS model assigns minimal credibility to the central bank. On the other hand, the present AIC model with the calibration of eq. (9.12) exhibits inflation persistence distinctly less than one.

In addition to highlighting the role of the parameter γ, eq. (9.14) shows the main difference of our modelling from the familiar Phillips curves, even if they include a target rate of inflation: when reformulated as a backward-looking Phillips curve, the AIC approach is seen to include not only the (discounted) past rates of inflation, as implied by a textbook adaptive expectations mechanism, but also the entire (discounted) history of output evolution.

9.3.2 A comparison of impulse-response functions

The results of the policy experiments in the AIC model can be better understood if before we compare two selected impulse-response functions in the AIC model with their counterparts in the RS model. We limit ourselves to an inflation shock $\Delta \pi = 1$ percent to the equilibrium (where $\pi = 2$ percent and $i = 4.5$ percent), which occurs at $t = 0$ and, by hypothesis, has no simultaneous impact on the output gap. Suppose, however, that the shock gives rise to an increase in the inflation climate by 0.5 percent. Neglecting the measurement errors, let us first adopt the estimated policy coefficients from Table 9.3, $g_\pi = 1.76$ and $g_y = 0.74$. The bold line in Figure 9.1 shows the response of y_t, π_t and i_t in the AIC model over the next eight years. Convergence back to the equilibrium values is essentially completed after three years for inflation, and after five years for the output gap.[20]

In contrast, the thin solid in Figure 9.1 demonstrates that the adjustments in the RS model are considerably slower. A long convergence time was also noted by RS (1999, pp. 210ff), but they attributed it to the VAR funds rate reaction function that they used for i_t, which has an extremely weak interest rate response to inflation. Here, we see that slow convergence basically persists with stronger reactions of the interest rate, such that a few quarters after the shock the interest rate has risen by more than the inflation shock and the corresponding rise in the real rate induces a (mild) contraction of economic activity.[21] Nevertheless, it takes 15 to 20 years for output to return to its potential level.

Regarding the fluctuations of the economic variables, we can predict from the different convergence speeds in the two models that the same policy coefficients should be associated with less volatility in the AIC model than in the RS model. Or, if the central bank is to lead inflation back to equilibrium in a given (feasible) period, it should have to react more vigorously in the RS model than in the

---

20 Convergence does not take much longer if at $t = 0$ the inflation climate experiences the same shock as π_t.

21 Notice that the interest rate does not rise immediately more than one-to-one with the inflation shock, because it responds to the average of the last four quarters.

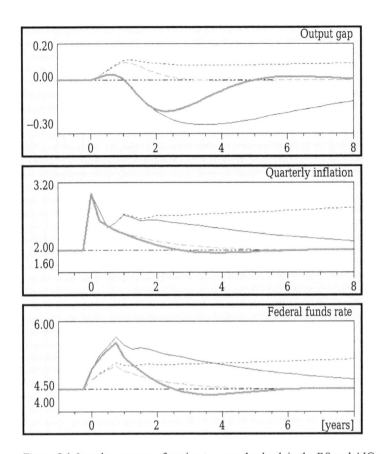

Figure 9.1 Impulse-response function to a supply shock in the RS and AIC model.

Note: Common to all trajectories is rule T_o with $g_y = 0.74$. The solid and bold lines result from $g_\pi = 1.76$ in the RS and the AIC model, respectively. The other lines result from $g_\pi = 0.80$, with divergence in the RS model (dotted line) and convergence in the AIC model (dashed line). The impulse at $t = 0$ is $\pi = 2.0 + 1.0$, where the AIC model assumes a simultaneous rise of $\pi^c = 2.0 + 0.5$.

AIC model. It can thus be expected that the AIC model will also require lower optimal policy coefficients in the full stochastic framework.

In a second scenario, we violate the Taylor principle and decrease the inflation gap coefficient below unity. In Figure 9.1, $g_\pi = 0.80$ is supposed. At least, textbook discussions of monetary policy argue that such a low responsiveness destabilizes the economy. Indeed, this holds true for the RS model, as it is illustrated by the dotted lines in the diagram. It is, however, remarkable that the variables diverge rather slowly. This explains the phenomenon that we observed in Table 9.4 earlier, namely, that favorable sequences of the various random shocks admit reasonable, or even optimal, economic behavior over a medium span of time.

The dashed lines in Figure 9.1 point out that the low inflation persistence in the AIC model allows the coefficient $g_\pi = 0.80$ to be compatible with dynamic stability. Moreover, convergence in output is even faster than under $g_\pi = 1.76$. A qualitative difference from the latter coefficient is only that the output gap remains positive on its convergence path, which of course is due to the initial decline in the real interest rate caused by the weak reactions of the nominal rate of interest.

Stability and faster convergence of the economy under $g_\pi = 0.80$ is a first observation that undermines the general validity of $g_\pi > 1$ as a condition for perhaps stability, but in any case for better monetary policy performance.[22] As will be discussed in greater detail in the following Section, the effects of $g_\pi > 1$ or, possibly, $g_\pi < 1$ depend very much on the implied inflation persistence in the Phillips curve, which in the present model is the direct complement of central bank policy credibility.

Incidentally, stability of the steady state position continues to prevail even if the interest rate does not respond at all, neither to inflation nor output ($g_\pi = g_y = 0$). To understand this, consider eq. (9.14), which shows that, at zero output gaps, π_t would converge to π^* if only $\gamma < 1$ and $\alpha_c < 1$. The IS equation (9.1) is an AR(2) process in y_t which is stable at the estimated values of β_{y1}, β_{y2}. That is, y_t converges to zero if π_t is equal to π^* or converges toward it. As the stability conclusion for (9.14) is maintained if the equation contains an output sequence converging to zero, we have: π_t converges to π^* if y_t converges to zero, which it does if π_t converges to π^*. Of course, this is no compelling argument for the convergence of π_t or y_t, but it clarifies that convergence need by no means be an exotic phenomenon. This insight may here suffice to indicate that the Taylor principle is no longer a necessary condition for stability.

The main results of the experiments with the impulse-response functions can be summed up as follows. (1) As opposed to the RS model, the AIC model implies a reasonable convergence time. (2) The AIC model can be expected to produce similar effects with lower policy coefficients than the RS model; or with the same coefficients the AIC model should produce lower variabilities of the economic variables. (3) In the AIC model, a low responsiveness $g_\pi < 1$ to the inflation gap preserves stability and may even be preferable to coefficients $g_\pi > 1$.

9.3.3 Monetary policy in the AIC model

We are thus ready to carry out the same investigations for the AIC model as in the RS model and check the conclusions from the impulse-response functions in

---

22 For example, Taylor (1999, p. 663) in emphasizing the crucial role of this condition concludes with the recommendation to the European Central Bank, 'I believe that having an [inflation gap] response coefficient greater than one will be the first step to achieving good performance'. The Taylor principle also has its place in the new-Keynesian forward-looking models; see Woodford (2003, Chapters 2 and 4).

Table 9.5 Policy coefficients in the AIC model

			Standard deviations of			
g_π	g_y	*Loss*	$\bar{\pi}_t$	y_t	Δi_t	i_t
1. Benchmarks:			1.30	2.35	1.10	2.00
A. Taylor rule without measurement error (T_o)						
2. 1.76	0.74	5.15	1.08	1.88	0.94	2.67
3. 0.95	1.29	4.73	1.04	1.71	1.20	2.68
B. Taylor rule with measurement error (T_{me})						
4. **1.25**	**0.40**	**5.99**	**1.23**	**2.04**	**0.83**	**2.14**
5. 1.00	0.82	5.57	1.14	1.89	1.17	2.46
6. 0.93	0.62	–	1.19	1.96	0.93	2.13
C. Averages of optimal T_{me} **across 5000 fifty-year samples**						
7. 0.86	0.74	5.20	1.09	1.83	1.07	2.17
(0.46)	(0.22)	(1.06)	(0.13)	(0.19)	(0.28)	(0.65)
D. Average performance of one T_{me} **rule across 5000 fifty-year samples**						
8. 0.86	0.74	5.46	1.13	1.89	1.04	2.18
–	–	(1.12)	(0.16)	(0.22)	(0.05)	(0.27)

Note: Rows 2 and 4 are estimated policy coefficients from the literature, rows 3, 5, 6 are optimized rules based on long-sample evaluations runs (cf. Table 9.2), where in row 6 the weight v in the loss function is changed from 0.50 to 1.00. Standard deviations in parentheses.

the previous subsection. The results of the simulations are collected in Table 9.5. We again begin with the estimated rule in the absence of measurement errors $(g_\pi = 1.76, g_y = 0.74)$. Comparing the second rows of Table 9.3 and 9.5, the differences are striking: the lower inflation persistence in the AIC model reduces the variabilities of inflation and the interest rate in a dramatic way. The standard deviation of inflation now even falls short of its benchmark value. Also Std[y_t] is noticeably lower than in the RS model, while, perhaps somewhat surprisingly, Std[Δi_t] has somewhat increased.

The effects of the estimated rule T_{me} that we use for the employment with measurement errors are documented in row 4 of Table 9.5. Here, the variabilities of the economic variables come quite close to their benchmark values; especially the standard deviations of inflation and the interest rate, which have always been displeasingly high in the RS model. In fact, we take the results of this row as further important support for the AIC approach to expectations about inflation in the Phillips curve. Given that eqs (9.1), (9.10), (9.11) together with (9.6)–(9.8) constitute a small and parsimonious model, its dynamic properties are remarkably realistic. In short, row 4 with its bold face characters highlights the high reliability as a workhorse that these results lend to the model.

On this basis, we can turn to the optimization of the Taylor rule. In the third row where the measurement errors are still neglected, we see another astonishing difference from the RS model. Whereas in the latter the optimized versus the estimated Taylor rule is characterized by a higher policy coefficient on the inflation gap (see row 3 of Table 9.3), it is here the other way round. Furthermore, the optimal g_π is slightly below unity.

The optimal output gap coefficient, on the other hand, shares with the optimal g_y in the RS model the property that it increases relatively to the estimated $g_y = 0.74$, though it does so to a lesser extent.

Allowing for the measurement errors as in T_{me}, the revisions that the optimized rule in the fifth row of Table 9.5 makes to the estimated rule in row 4, and the differences from the same rows in Table 9.3, can be described in much the same way (except that the optimal g_π now exactly equals unity). Again, we point out, an optimized rule requires weaker, rather than stronger, reactions of the central bank to the evolution of the perceived inflation gap.[23] The recommended decrease of g_π is, however, not very large, where it will be noted that the estimated $g_\pi \approx 1.25$ is already fairly low.

Compared with row 4 in Table 9.5, the optimized rule in row 5 moderately reduces the variabilities of inflation and output, which is achieved at the price of a rising standard deviation of the interest rate changes. The latter also imply larger fluctuations of the interest rate itself, with a standard deviation well above the benchmark of 2 percent. We could improve on these negative effects by supposing that the central bank has a higher priority for interest rate smoothing, in the form of an increase of the corresponding weight ν in the loss function from 0.5 to 1. In this case, the optimized rule is given by the configuration of row 6 (the associated loss is not reported since it is not comparable to the other losses), where also the lower output gap coefficient might be a desirable result. As noted at the end of Section 2.2, however, not too much stress should be laid on such a 'reverse engineering' of the central bank's preferences.

After so far evaluating each rule, taken on its own or within the iterative optimization algorithm, on the basis of 100,000 data points, the remainder of Table 9.5 is concerned with the small sample properties. Row 7 is comparable with the second row in Table 9.4 for the RS model, where a sample is given by sequences of the random shocks over 50 years (plus a 10-year transition period) and for each of 5000 such samples the Taylor rule T_{me} is optimized. Row 7 in Table 9.5 reports the resulting mean values together with the standard deviations in parentheses. Similar to what has been observed in the RS model, on average

---

23 While these policy experiments are based on the long-sample evaluations with 500 years per sample, generating the 100,000 data points by the short samples over 50 years reduces g_π in rows 3 and 5 by about 0.10, and g_y by no more than 0.05. The downward modifications of g_π through this organization of the observations have also been mentioned in the Rs model, but owing to its random walk element they were stronger there.

the optimal policy coefficients are lower than their counterparts from the long-sample evaluations, though the reduction of the inflation gap coefficient (from 1.00 to 0.86) is less pronounced here than in the RS model (from 2.33 to 1.66). We also call attention to the fact that the optimized rules are now considerably less dispersed than in the RS model, which concerns the policy coefficients as well as the associated losses and their single components.

Nevertheless, there is still a wide range of coefficients that prove to be optimal with respect to a specific set of random shocks. Regarding g_π with its mean of 0.86, for example, 2.5 percent of the optimal coefficients exceed 1.76. The equal-tailed interval that contains 95 percent of the optimal output gap coefficients extends from 0.27 to 1.13 (the other 5 percent lie outside). Despite the narrower dispersion in the AIC model, these numbers again demonstrate that different exogenous influences, even if they are only captured in their entirety over the full period of fifty years, require an optimizing central bank to choose very different degrees of responsiveness.

While these remarks refer separately to the policy coefficients, it could be suspected that the optimal values are not independent of each other. According to the two optimized rules in row 4 and 5 of Table 9.5, one might perhaps expect that lower values of g_π are associated with lower values of g_y. A scatter plot of the 5000 pairs of optimal coefficients, however, disproves the conjecture of a systematic statistical relationship; see Figure 9.2 (where the cross designates the mean values of the single coefficients).

Besides, the diagram indicates that a lower bound $g_\pi = 0.10$ has been imposed on the inflation gap coefficient.[24] The discussion of the impulse-response functions earlier has revealed that even such extremely weak reactions do not destabilize the economy, and Figure 9.2 shows that under special, but not completely exotic, circumstances they moreover can be optimal.

The last row in Table 9.5 considers the sample variability a central bank faces if it commits itself to the mean values of the optimal policy coefficients. The average loss for this selected rule exceeds, of course, the average loss of the 5000 optimized rules in row 7; but the difference is rather small, which also holds for the single variabilities of inflation, output and the interest rate. Here, too, the standard deviations of all of the summary statistics are substantially lower than their counterparts in the RS model, as in row 5 in Table 9.4.

If with respect to a fifty-year horizon the Taylor rule T_{opt} specified by $g_\pi = 0.86$, $g_y = 0.74$ is the best the model can offer to a central bank with no information on the demand and supply shocks, one may inquire into the relative merits of this recommendation. For example, the estimated rule T_{est} with the (rounded) coefficients $g_\pi = 1.25$, $g_y = 0.40$ yields an average loss of 5.80 across the 5000 samples (which is a bit lower than the 5.99 from the long-sample evaluation in

---

24 Although the search algorithm is designed for unconstrained optimization, lower (or upper) bounds can be easily incorporated by adding a high penalty to the central bank's loss function if the constraint is violated (since we do not have to care about derivatives).

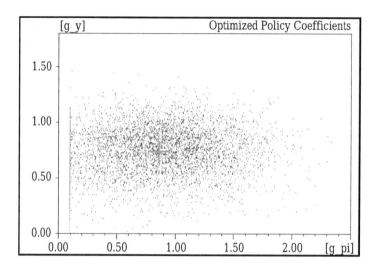

Figure 9.2 Scatter plot of optimal policy coefficients in the AIC model from 5000 fifty-year samples.

row 4). Since its standard deviation is 1.31 (slightly higher than the 1.12 from T_{opt} in row 8) and the average loss of T_{opt} amounts to 5.46, there will be a large overlap of the loss distribution functions of T_{opt} and T_{est}.

More precisely we compute the following. Consider two countries with an identical private sector but exposed to different sequences of the random shocks. Central bank A in the first country exercises rule T_{opt} and central bank B in the other country adopts rule T_{est}. Then, in the present model, bank B turns out to have a chance of 40.6 percent to end up with a lower loss than bank A, and the chances that the two losses are about the same are 2.7 percent. If told in this way, the effects of the two rules do not appear very different. (Two losses are classified as approximately equal if they do not differ by more than 5 percent of the standard deviation of the losses from T_{opt}, i.e. by no more than $0.05 \cdot 1.12 = 0.056$; otherwise, omitting an expression like 'significant', the losses are reported as 'lower' or 'higher'.)

In an extremely stylized manner, such a comparison may mirror a historical evaluation of monetary policy in two countries. However, it unduly oppresses a good policy with unfavorable shocks. An appropriate comparison would invoke the same shock sequences for the two countries. According to this view, we confront each policy rule with the same sequences of the four random shocks over a fifty-year period, compute the resulting losses and record bank A as better than, worse than, or approximately equal to bank B. Repeating this 5000 times with alternative shock series, the pairwise comparisons yield the results given in Table 9.6.

Table 9.6 Pairwise comparison of optimized (T_{opt}) and estimated (T_{est}) rule T_{me} in the AIC model across 5000 samples

		Samples in %
T_{opt} approx. equal T_{est}	:	9.4
T_{opt} better than T_{est}	:	80.9
T_{opt} worse than T_{est}	:	9.7
Total	:	100.0

Note: Pairwise compared are samples that have the same sequences of random shocks underlying. T_{opt} is given by $g_\pi = 0.86$, $g_y = 0.74$ and T_{est} by $g_\pi = 1.25$, $g_y = 0.40$ (cf. Table 9.5). 'Approximately equal' are losses that differ by less than 0.05 times 1.12 (the standard deviation of the losses from T_{opt} in row 8 of Table 9.5).

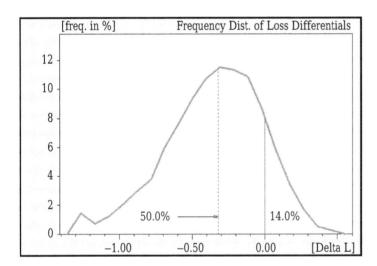

Figure 9.3 Frequency distribution of the loss differentials ΔL between T_{opt} and T_{est}.
Note: The average loss of T_{opt} is $L = 5.46$.

From this perspective, T_{opt} is distinctly superior to T_{est}. Nonetheless, a complete evaluation has to take into account that in one out of ten samples, T_{est} would be associated with a lower loss than T_{opt}, and that in almost another ten percent of the samples, the differences between the two rules are not significant. This is the range of uncertainty that surrounds the success of the optimal pairs of coefficients g_π and g_y.

The finer details of the frequency distribution of the loss differentials ΔL are illustrated in Figure 9.3, where a negative number means that the loss from T_{opt} is lower than the loss from T_{est}. The vertical line at $\Delta L = 0$ expresses the information of Table 9.6 in a slightly different way: in no less than 14.0 percent of all cases the estimated rule is strictly better than T_{opt}. Hence, a null hypothesis saying that

Table 9.7 Optimized Taylor rules (T_{me}) in the combined RS and AIC model

					Standard deviations of			
μ	Persistence	g_π	g_y	Loss	$\bar{\pi}_t$	y_t	Δi_t	i_t
1.00	1.00 :	2.33	1.12	13.27	2.38	2.40	1.91	5.20
0.90	0.95 :	1.85	1.01	10.10	2.12	2.06	1.63	4.24
0.75	0.89 :	1.48	0.93	7.91	1.79	1.92	1.42	3.45
0.50	0.77 :	1.20	0.87	6.49	1.45	1.88	1.28	2.86
0.25	0.66 :	1.07	0.84	5.89	1.26	1.89	1.21	2.60
0.00	0.55 :	1.00	0.82	5.57	1.14	1.89	1.17	2.46

Note: Optimization based on long-sample evaluations runs. $\mu = 1$ recovers the RS model, $\mu = 0$ the AIC model.

the estimated Taylor rule is at least effective as the optimized rule could not be rejected at the standard econometric levels of significance.

Another way of stating that, over fifty years, a central bank does not do so bad after all if it misses T_{opt} and instead works with T_{est}, can refer to the median of ΔL, which is shown as the dotted line in Figure 9.3. While mostly T_{est} produces a loss in excess of the loss that, under the same circumstances, is produced by T_{opt}, at a probability of 50 percent this difference is no larger than 0.32. Since the distribution function is more or less centered around the median, admitting only a little more play for the difference would increase the probability by another 5 or 10 percent.

9.3.4 The role of inflation persistence

On several occasions when discussing the differences of the AIC model from the RS model, we have held the lower inflation persistence in the AIC model responsible for them; in particular, that it is less than unity. The role of inflation persistence can, however, be more systematically studied if the two approaches to modelling inflation expectations are combined in a hybrid model. A straightforward way to do this is to introduce a weighting parameter μ and reformulate the Phillips curve as follows,

$$\pi_t = \mu \pi_t^a + (1 - \mu)\pi_t^c + \beta_{\pi y} y_{t-1} + \varepsilon_{\pi,t} \tag{9.16}$$

where π_t^a is determined by eq. (9.3) and π_t^c is the inflation climate from eq. (9.11). Clearly, everything else remaining unchanged, the two polar cases $\mu = 1$ and $\mu = 0$ reestablish the RS and AIC model, respectively.

We do not necessarily claim that the interior case, $0 < \mu < 1$, represents a meaningful expectation formation process for future inflation. (9.16) is only used as a convenient tool to verify a systematic relationship between inflation persistence in the present framework on the one hand, and the optimal policy coefficients together with the associated variabilities of the economic variables on the other hand. In the light of (9.15), inflation persistence in the hybrid model is given by $\mu + (1 - \mu)(1 - \gamma)$, which linearly decreases from 1 at $\mu = 1$ to 0.547 at $\mu = 0$.

Regarding the minimization of losses, we directly allow for the measurement errors and limit ourselves to the long-sample evaluations. The optimal results for $\mu = 1$ and $\mu = 0$ are thus given by Table 9.3 (row 5) and Table 9.5 (row 5). The two policy coefficients and all the statistics they give rise to were distinctly lower in the AIC model, and we expect that these figures decrease in a gradual and monotonic manner if μ varies from 1 to 0.

Table 9.7 fully confirms this intuition.[25] In the first and last rows, it reproduces the results from Tables 9.3 and 9.5 just mentioned. The changes between the polar cases are, however, not linear. The main effects already manifest themselves at, say $\mu = 0.75$, which means the inflation persistence is only reduced from 1 to 0.89. It may furthermore be added that we have observed similar phenomena to Table 9.7 within a less ambitious model, where π_t^c in (9.16) is simply replaced by target inflation π^*. Table 9.7 and this evidence underline the crucial role of the implied inflation persistence of expectations in a Phillips curve. The decisive step is a reduction of persistence from 1 to 0.90 or 0.80, and we may conjecture that from that order of magnitude on, optimal monetary policy is similarly characterized in other small-scale models of the type considered here, however they specify their inflation expectations.[26]

A more detailed evaluation of the benefits from greater credibility of monetary policy should nevertheless take the following kind of experiment into account. Within the Canadian Policy Analysis Model with a multilayer process of expectation formation, Amano *et al.* (1999, pp. 24f) observe that, in the presence of an unchanged policy rule, an increase in credibility reduces the variability of inflation, but at the cost of more variability in output. Hence, there is also a dark side to a—desirable—increase in credibility, namely, if the central bank does not reoptimize (by which the authors mean that it would have to lean harder against the demand shocks). With respect to the straightforward variations of μ in the present model, however, the central bank seems to escape this phenomenon. For example, lowering μ from 0.5 to 0 and maintaining the optimal coefficients $g_\pi = 1.20$ and $g_y = 0.87$ for the former, the standard deviations of $\bar{\pi}_t$ and i_t fall from 1.45 to 1.12 and from 2.86 to 2.64, respectively, while those of y_t and Δi_t remain essentially unaffected.

9.3.5 A note on interest rate smoothing

So far, Taylor rules have been considered in a narrow sense, whereas Taylor rules in a broad sense are supposed to allow for partial adjustments such that,

---

25 Results from additional checks with intermediate values of μ perfectly fit into the pattern of the table.

26 The conjecture may even hold for forward-looking models if their reduced form gives rise to inflation persistence less than one. At least, this would be worth investigating in greater detail.

in addition to the inflation and output gap, the lagged interest rate itself enters the policy. This specification, which runs under the heading of interest rate smoothing, is also underlying many estimations, when the coefficient on the lagged interest rate (denoted as h) typically comes our rather large, something like $h \geq 0.80$ or $h \geq 0.90$. The econometric problem is that these versions are (near-) observationally equivalent to serially correlated shocks in a regression, which have been assumed in the elementary reference reaction function (9.9). Therefore, a modelling decision that favors (9.9) or a similar version over a partial adjustment formulation has to rely on more indirect arguments.[27]

Even if it is agreed that a Taylor rule in the narrow sense without interest rate smoothing (but being exposed to measurement errors) is more appropriate as a stylized description of central bank behavior than a partial adjustment rule with high inertia, it will be asked if including this mechanism in the interest rate reaction may improve the performance of monetary policy. Within their framework, RS have found that the gains from this generalization are fairly limited. Not only is the reduction in the loss function almost negligible, but also the coefficient h is in an optimized rule much lower than it is usually estimated, unless it is even negative (see Tables 5.3–5.7 in RS, 1999).

We can now examine if this feature carries over to the AIC model. Since similar results have also been obtained by Smets (2002, Table 2 on p. 123), whose model has inflation persistence less than one in a backward-looking Phillips curve (plus measurement errors in the output gap), we have some reason to expect that it does.

In order for the gap coefficients g_π and g_y to be comparable between the rules without and with interest rate smoothing, we formulate the partial adjustments as follows, where the notation T_o and T_{me} for the rules without and with measurement errors is maintained:

$$i_t^o = r^* + \pi^* + g_\pi (\bar{\pi}_t - \pi^*) + g_y y_t$$
$$T_o : \qquad i_t = h i_{t-1} + (1-h) i_t^o \qquad\qquad (9.17)$$

$$i_t^o = r^* + \pi^* + g_\pi (\bar{\pi}_t + n_{\pi,t} - \pi^*) + g_y (y_t + n_{y,t})$$
$$T_{me} : \qquad i_t = h i_{t-1} + (1-h) i_t^o \qquad\qquad (9.18)$$

Let the minimization of the loss function be based on the long-sample evaluations. For better comparison, the first and fifth row of Table 9.8 repeat the optimal results from Table 9.5 (rows 3 and 5) that are obtained if $h = 0$ is imposed on (9.17) and (9.18). The remaining rows in Table 9.8, then, present the solutions of the full problem where the central bank is free to choose g_π, g_y and the smoothing parameter h, the latter under the constraint $h \geq 0$.

On the whole, the similarities with the results in the RS model (1999) are surprisingly far-reaching, regarding the simulations without as well as with

---

27 One important route is to take the implications for the term structure of interest rates into account, as it is done in Rudebusch (2002a) and, with more advanced methods, in Rudebusch and Wu (2003).

Table 9.8 Optimized Taylor rules with interest rate smoothing in the AIC model

				Standard deviations of			
h	g_π	g_y	*Loss*	$\bar{\pi}_t$	y_t	Δi_t	i_t
A. Taylor rule without measurement error (T_o)							
1. —	0.95	1.29	4.73	1.04	1.71	1.20	2.68
2. 0.26	0.81	1.48	4.66	1.03	1.72	1.11	2.80
3. 0.00	0.89	2.19	$v = 0.1$	0.94	1.58	2.06	3.69
4. 0.00	0.64	2.04	$\lambda = 5.0$	0.96	1.59	1.90	3.44
B. Taylor rule with measurement error (T_{me})							
5. —	1.00	0.82	5.57	1.14	1.89	1.17	2.46
6. 0.30	0.94	0.99	5.46	1.13	1.91	1.03	2.62
7. 0.00	1.06	1.38	$v = 0.1$	1.06	1.81	1.87	3.30
8. +0.00	0.91	1.28	$\lambda = 5.0$	1.08	1.82	1.72	3.08

measurement errors. Most importantly, the comparison of rows 1 and 2, and of 5 and 6, makes clear that the central bank's gain from the smoothing option is really minor. It may in this connection also be noted that inflation and the interest rate changes reduce their variances, while that of the output gap slightly rises.[28] Interestingly, even the proportions of these changes are quite the same as in RS (1999, p. 227). The central bank does exercise its option, but the degree of smoothing is only moderate; it is any case of a considerably lower order of magnitude than the estimated coefficients mentioned earlier.

The remaining rows in Table 9.8 show that a positive smoothing coefficient h is dependent on the preferences of the central bank. They consider a *ceteris paribus* change of the weight v in the loss function from 0.5 to 0.1, and of the weight λ from 1.0 to 5.0 (recall that v weights var$[\Delta i_t]$ and λ weights var$[y_t]$.) In both cases, the central bank plays down its interest rate smoothing motive relative to the output variability motive; in the first case smoothing is also downweighted relative to the inflation variability motive (whose weight is fixed at unity). Turning to the consequences, in both cases and regardless of the presence of measurement errors, it proves optimal for the central bank not to smooth interest rates in its reaction function. In rows 3, 4 and 7, the nonnegativity constraint on h becomes binding, in row 8 the optimal coefficient is $h = 0.003$ (therefore the plus sign in this row). These findings conform well to the negative coefficients reported in RS (1999, Tables 5.5 and 5.6) for the same preferences (but no measurement errors).

The feature that the optimal value of h is connected to the relative strength of the interest rate smoothing motive in the loss function also holds in the

---

28 In this case, the decline in Std[Δi_t] goes along with an increase in the standard deviation of the level of the interest rate.

opposite direction. A *ceteris paribus* increase in the weight to $v = 1.0$ raises the smoothing coefficient to $h = 0.39$ for T_o and $h = 0.42$ for T_{me}, which, however, is still quite limited. Even an excessive priority like $v = 5.0$ lets h only increase to 0.64 for T_{me}.

We can thus conclude that, although the RS and AIC model are different in serious respects, both do not provide support for high inertia coefficients in interest rate reaction functions. The results that we have here obtained rather justify the general conception of the model, which has viewed interest rate smoothing as a topic of subordinate importance.

9.4 Conclusion

Abjuring the hypothesis of rational expectations of inflation but also discarding the usual backward-looking specification of an accelerationist Phillips curve, this chapter has employed the concept of a so-called adaptive inflation climate as an alternative way of modelling expectations. As it is simpler than rational expectations and more sophisticated than adaptive expectations, we have characterized this treatment of expectations as sophisticatedly simple. Incorporating the corresponding concept of a so-called adaptive inflation climate (AIC) into the Phillips curve estimated by Rudebusch and Svensson (1999) and combining it with their dynamic IS equation, a model is obtained whose achievements *vis-à-vis* the Rudebusch-Svensson model (and others) are twofold. First, it offers a more palatable story of expectation formation. Second, its numerical simulations generate a more realistic outcome, regarding the size of the optimal policy coefficients in the Taylor rule as well as the variability of the economic variables that they induce. If anything, the optimized response coefficient on the inflation gap may now even be considered to be somewhat low.[29] Apart from that, estimated Taylor rules do not appear to perform too badly in the AIC model, especially if the small sample properties are taken into account.

Rudebusch and Svensson (1999, p. 239) themselves have remarked that the central bank's prospects for inflation control would be improved if there were an expectations channel for monetary policy through the Phillips curve. The present model provides for this idea by the feature that the inflation climate variable is to some extent anchored on the target rate of inflation, which is tantamount to a reduction of the (implied) inflation persistence in the (reduced-form specification of the) Phillips curve. Actually, the stabilization effect turns out to be so strong that an optimized Taylor rule needs no longer to satisfy the Taylor principle, i.e. the coefficient on the inflation gap in the rule may be less than one. We nevertheless do not wish to overemphasize this possibility.

A fruitful aspect of our approach is that it draws attention to the persistence of inflation in structural or reduced-form Phillips curve equations, which could

---

29 This coefficient increases again if the central bank specifies the inflation gap in the Taylor rule as $\pi_t^c - \pi^*$ (instead of $\bar{\pi}_t - \pi^*$).

be a topic for more careful econometric investigations. The treatment of the related concept of central bank credibility in our model was, however, still rather elementary: the corresponding parameter was (1) exogenous and (2) constant and (3) when optimizing the central bank was supposed to know it with certainty. A next stage of research may, in particular, be concerned with successively modifying or dropping these assumptions (in reverse order).

References

Amano, R., D. Coletti, and T. Macklem (1999): Monetary rules when economic behavior changes. *Bank of Canada Working Paper 99–8.*

Calvo, G.A. (1983): Staggered prices in a utility-maximizing framework. *Journal of Monetary Economics*, 12, 383–398.

Franke, R. (2005): Estimation-supported calibration of an unobservable inflation climate in the Phillips curve. *University of Bielefeld,* mimeo.

Freedman, C. (1996): What operating procedures should be adopted to main tain price stability? Practical issues. In: *The Federal Reserve Bank of Kansas City, Achieving Price Stability: A Symposium*; pp. 241–285 (www.kc.frb.org/publicat/sympos/1996/pdf/s96freed.pdf).

Fuhrer, J.C. and G.D. Rudebusch (2004): Estimating the Euler equation for output. *Journal of Monetary Economics*, 51, 1133–1153.

Lansing, K.J. and B. Trehan (2001): Forward-looking behavior and the optimality of the Taylor rule. *Federal Reserve Bank of San Francisco*, Working Paper 01–03.

Lansing, K.J. and B. Trehan (2003): Forward-looking behavior and optimal discretionary monetary policy. *Economics Letters*, 81, 249–256 (abridged version of former paper).

McCallum, B.T. (2001): Should monetary policy respond strongly to output gaps? *NBER Working Paper 8226.*

Orphanides, A. (2003): Monetary policy evaluation with noisy information. *Journal of Monetary Economics*, 50, 605–631.

Orphanides, A. and J.C. Williams (2003): The decline of activist stabilization policy: Natural rate misperceptions, learning, and expectations. *Federal Reserve Bank of San Francisco, FRBSF Working Paper 2003–24.*

Press, W.H. *et al.* (1986): *Numerical Recipes: The Art of Scientific Computing.* Cambridge: Cambridge University Press.

Rudd, J. and K. Whelan (2001): New tests of the new-Keynesian Phillips curve. *Board of Governors of the Federal Reserve System, Finance and Economics Discussion Series 2001– 30*; forthcoming in *Journal of Monetary Economics.*

Rudebusch, G.D. (2001): Is the fed too timid? Monetary policy in an uncertain world. *Review of Economics and Statistics*, 83, 203–217.

Rudebusch, G. (2002a): Term structure evidence on interest rate smoothing and monetary policy inertia. *Journal of Monetary Economics*, 49, 1161–1187.

Rudebusch, G. (2002b): Assessing nominal income rules for monetary policy with model and data uncertainty, *Economic Journal*, 112, 402–432.

Rudebusch, G.D. and L.E.O. Svensson (1999): Policy rules for inflation targeting. In: J.B. Taylor (ed.): *Monetary Policy Rules.* Chicago: University of Chicago Press, 203–246.

Rudebusch, G.D. and T. Wu (2003): A macro-finance model of the term structure, monetary policy, and the economy. *Federal Reserve Bank of San Francisco.*

Smets, F. (2002): Output gap uncertainty: Does it matter for the Taylor rule? *Empirical Economics*, 27, 113–129.

Swanson, E.T. (2000): On signal extraction and non-certainty-equivalence in optimal monetary policy rules. *Board of Governors of the Federal Reserve System.*

Taylor, J.B. (1993): Discretion versus policy rules in practice. *Carnegie-Rochester Conference Series on Public Policy*, 39, 195–214.

Taylor, J.B. (1999): The robustness and efficiency of monetary policy rules as guidelines for interest rate setting by the European Central Bank. *Journal of Monetary Economics,* 43, 655–679.

Woodford, M. (2003): *Interest and Prices: Foundations of a Theory of Monetary Policy.* Princeton: Princeton University Press.

Zellner, A. (1992): Statistics, science and public policy. *Journal of the American Statistical Association*, 87, 1–6.

Zellner, A. (2002): My experience with nonlinear dynamics models in economics. *Studies in Nonlinear Dynamics and Econometrics*, 6(2), 1–18.

Part III

The road ahead

Real-financial market interaction
from a Keynesian perspective

10 The Keynes-Metzler-Goodwin model and Tobinian portfolio choice

In this final chapter, we depart from the semistructural form of the Keynesian D (isequilibrium) AD–D (isequilibrium) AS model that we have so far considered. We extend this empirically oriented disequilibrium model towards a baseline structural model of Keynesian real markets disequilibrium coupled with a Tobinian equilibrium approach to portfolio choice over a complete (though still narrowly defined) range of financial assets. We therefore now go on from a simple LM- (Liquidity preference Money supply) curve or Taylor rule representation of financial markets to a full portfolio approach with both imperfect asset substitution and imperfect capital gains expectations. The intention is to demonstrate to the reader in this outlook on future work that such an enlarged range of financial markets becomes sooner or later a modeling necessity if one wants to do justice to what is in fact the role of financial markets in a modern capitalist economy. Moreover this chapter also demonstrates that such a more balanced, fairly advanced macromodel of the real-financial market interaction can still be treated analytically as far as steady states and their stability are concerned. In the following sections, we will indeed be able to prove advanced stability propositions and we will also consider some instability scenarios that are very plausible from a Keynesian perspective.

10.1 Real disequilibria, portfolio equilibrium and the real-financial markets interaction

The goal of this chapter[1] is to present a Keynesian macrodynamic model of a growing monetary economy, that builds on the analysis of the working KMG (Keynes-Metzler-Goodwin) model[2] of Chiarella and Flaschel (2000a) and

---

1 This chapter is built on Köper and Flaschel (2000), and Köper (2003). It provides in an appendix alternative formulations and proofs of the propositions that were first established by Carsten Köper in Köper and Flaschel (2000), and Köper (2003).
2 Keynes-Metzler-Goodwin model. This model type makes use of labor and goods market disequilibrium adjustment processes in the tradition of Goodwin and Metzler, respectively. It therefore considers explicitly the interaction of income distribution with economic growth, the

Chiarella, Flaschel, Groh and Semmler (2000), and that explains the real-financial interaction in Keynesian dynamics in a more satisfactory way than in the working KMG model from which it has been derived. In this latter model type, asset markets influence the real dynamics only in a very traditional way, by means of an LM- (Liquidity preference Money supply) curve[3] that gave rise there to a stable relationship between the nominal rate of interest, the output-capital ratio and real balances per unit of capital. Furthermore, neither bond dynamics nor the evolution of the stock of equities could influence the real part of the economy due to the lack of wealth and interest income effects on aggregate demand. The present chapter will now introduce a portfolio theory of asset market behavior in place of a single LM curve and will thereby improve the representation of asset market dynamics considerably, though wealth and interest income effects on demand will still be ignored. Nevertheless, bond and equity stock dynamics will now feed back into the real part of the economy, though by a single route namely through Tobin's average q, which will play an important role in the investment behavior of firms.

Our KMG approach to macrodynamics considers the interaction of all important markets of the macroeconomy (for labor, goods, money, bonds and equities), though still in a nonstochastic environment and without explicit utility maximization of households and profit maximization of firms.[4] Households behavioral equations are in the tradition of the Kaldorian approach to differentiated saving habits and are not derived by optimizing a hypothetical utility function of workers or capitalists. On the one hand, this reflects our skepticism about the relevance of representative agent utility maximization for aggregate behavioral relationships in an economy with labor and goods market disequilibria, and on the other hand, it allows us to leave the model sufficiently simple in order to concentrate on the description and analysis of asset market dynamics.[5] Combining a full disequilibrium approach in the real part of the economy with a general equilibrium approach in its financial part gives rise to various interesting propositions on the dynamics which then drive the economy. The model therefore presents an integrated approach to macrodynamics that accounts for all budget constraints of all types of agents in the economy, exhibits a uniquely determined steady state solution surrounded by a variety of interesting propagation and feedback mechanisms. Therefore, it represents a consistently

---

interaction of disappointed sales expectations of firms and resulting unintended inventory changes, and a simple LM theory of the money market which allows the investigation of Keynes as well as Mundell-effects of wage and price inflation or deflation.

3 The alternative case of a Taylor interest rate policy can be easily added to this chapter, by making use of its formulation as in Chapter 2 and will treated in future work on the KMGT (Keynes-Metzler-Goodwin-Taylor) approach.

4 See however Chiarella, Flaschel, Groh, Köper, and Semmler (1999) for improvements of this approach in this latter direction.

5 See Chiarella, Flaschel, Groh, Köper, and Semmler (1999) for improvements of this approach with respect to workers consumption and savings behavior.

formulated integrated dynamical model on the aggregate level that exhibits a rich dynamic structure with a type of high order dynamics that has not previously been investigated from the theoretical perspective in the macroeconomics literature.

As already stated, the core of the model is given by a Keynes–Metzler–Goodwin (KMG) structure to integrated macrodynamics as developed in Chiarella and Flaschel (2000a) and further analyzed in Chiarella, Flaschel, Groh and Semmler (2000).[6] Foundations for such an integrated approach to macrodynamic model building were already laid in Flaschel, Franke, and Semmler (1997). Further work in Asada, Chiarella, Flaschel, and Franke (2003) extended the KMG approach to the treatment of small or interacting open economies, and in Chiarella, Flaschel, and Semmler (2009) to a theoretical as well as numerical analysis of modern macroeconometric model building. The level of the approach to macrodynamic model building that is reached in the present chapter, in its treatment of financial markets, however, goes beyond the works just cited and represents in this respect part of a larger future research agenda that is developed by Chiarella, Flaschel, Proaño and Semmler (2009).

We now briefly describe the main elements of the approach to be developed in this chapter. The economy consists of various private agents: workers, asset holders and firms. The public sector consists of the government and the central bank. Concerning the goods market, there exists a production good exclusively produced by firms, that can be, on the one hand consumed by the workers, asset holders or the government, and on the other hand invested as business fixed capital or used for inventory investment by firms. Firms do not have perfect foresight with respect to the demand for goods and do not adjust their output instantaneously towards the level of aggregate demand. Hence, in order to be able to satisfy actual and future demands, they hold stocks of inventories of produced goods. The adjustment policy for reaching a desired stock of inventories is modeled in a Metzlerian way as originally laid out in Metzler (1941).

The labor market is assumed to operate under a Keynesian regime in the sense that any demand for labor can be satisfied by an always positive excess supply of labor at the actual wage rate, based on the assumption that a NAIRU type employment rate creates the necessary buffer for the smooth working of the labor market.

The study of the dynamic interaction of employment and the real wage rate in this model is inspired by Goodwin's (1967) contribution. Moreover, we seek to model a monetary economy with various financial assets in order to investigate their interaction with the real markets, namely the goods markets and the labor markets. There are various assets: money and short-term bonds issued by the

---

6 See also Chiarella and Flaschel (1996), Chiarella and Flaschel (1998) and Chiarella and Flaschel (1999), Chiarella and Flaschel (2000b), the latter two for the treatment of open economies in the KMG framework.

government and equities issued by firms in order to finance investments. All of these financial assets are exclusively held by the asset holders.

In Section 10.2, we develop the extensive form of the model and give a detailed explanation of its structure. In Section 10.3, the intensive form of the dynamics is derived in order to allow for steady state considerations on the basis of eight autonomous laws of motion that, as will be shown, do indeed exhibit a unique point of rest or steady state. The stability of the full 8D dynamical system is analyzed in Section 10.5 by way of a sequence of dynamical subsystems of increasing dimension. In Section 10.6, we discuss some routes to local instability and global boundedness that allow for period doubling sequences and the emergence of irregular business fluctuations that – though are mathematically complex – are still rather simple from an economic perspective. An appendix provides detailed mathematical proofs for the (there somewhat reformulated) stability propositions of Section 10.5.

10.2 A portfolio approach to KMG growth dynamics

In this section, we will provide the structural form of a growth model of the KMG type, and that will exhibit a portfolio equilibrium block in place of the LM theory of the short-run rate of interest and the dynamic adjustment (flow-oriented) equations for the prices of the other assets as they were used in Chiarella, Flaschel, Groh and Semmler (2000). We split the model into appropriate modules that primarily concern the sectors of the economy, namely households, firms and the government (fiscal and monetary authority), but also represent the wage–price-interaction and the portfolio structure of the asset markets.

10.2.1 Households

As discussed in the introduction, we disaggregate the sector of households into worker households and asset-holder households. We begin with the description of the behavior of workers:

Worker households

$$\omega = w/p, \tag{10.1}$$

$$C_w = (1 - \tau_w)\omega L^d, \tag{10.2}$$

$$S_w = 0, \tag{10.3}$$

$$\hat{L} = n = \text{ const.} \tag{10.4}$$

Equation (10.1) gives the definition of the real wage ω before taxation, where w denotes the nominal wage and p the actual price level. We operate in a Keynesian framework with sluggish wage and price adjustment processes, hence, we take the real wage to be given exogenously at each moment in time. Further, we follow the

Keynesian framework by assuming that the labor demand of firms can always be satisfied out of the given labor supply, so that we do not allow for regime switches as they are discussed in Chiarella, Flaschel, Groh and Semmler (2000, Ch.5). Then, according to (10.2), real income of workers equals the product of real wages times labor demand, which net of taxes $\tau_w \omega L^d$, equals workers' consumption, since we do not allow for savings of the workers as postulated in (10.3).[7] No savings implies that the wealth of workers is zero at every point in time. This in particular means that the workers do not hold any money and that they consume instantaneously their disposable income.[8] As is standard in theories of economic growth, we finally assume in equation (10.4) a constant growth rate n of the labor force L based on the assumption that labor is supplied inelastically at each moment in time. The parameter n can be easily reinterpreted to be the growth rate of the working population plus the growth rate of labor augmenting technical progress.

The income, consumption and wealth of the asset holders are described by the following set of equations:

Asset holder households

$$r^e = (Y^e - \delta K - \omega L^d)/K, \tag{10.5}$$

$$C_c = (1 - s_c)[r_k^e K + iB/p - T_c], \quad 0 < s_c < 1, \tag{10.6}$$

$$S_p = s_c[r^e K + iB/p - T_c] \tag{10.7}$$

$$= (\dot{M} + \dot{B} + p_e \dot{E})/p, \tag{10.8}$$

$$W_c = (M + B + p_e E)/p, \quad W_c^n = p W_c. \tag{10.9}$$

The first equation (10.5) of this module of the model defines the expected rate of return on real capital r_k^e to be the ratio of the currently expected real cash flow and the real stock of business fixed capital K. The expected cash flow is given by expected real revenues from sales Y^e diminished by real depreciation of capital δK and the real wage sum ωL^d. We assume that firms pay out all expected cash flow in the form of dividends to the asset holders. These dividend payments are one source of income for asset holders. The second source is given by real interest payments on short-term bonds (iB/p) where i is the nominal interest rate and B the stock of such bonds. Summing up these types of interest incomes and taking account of lump sum taxes T_c in the case of asset holders (for reasons of simplicity) we obtain the disposable income of asset holder given by the terms in the square brackets of equation (10.6), which together with a postulated fixed propensity to consume $(1 - s_c)$ out of this income gives us the real consumption of asset holders.

---

7 See Chiarella, Flaschel, Groh and Semmler (2000) for the inclusion of workers' savings into a KMG framework.

8 We explain in the mathematical appendix to Chapter 5 that money holdings for transaction purposes is here only considered with respect to firms which is just the opposite assumption of what is usually considered in the macroeconomic literature.

Real savings of pure asset owners is real disposable income minus their consumption as exposed in equation (10.7). The asset owners can allocate the real savings in the form of money $\dot{M}$, or buy other financial assets, namely short-term bonds $\dot{B}$ or equities $\dot{E}$ at the price p_e, the only financial instruments that we allow for in the present reformulation of the KMG growth model. Hence, the savings of asset holders must be distributed to these assets as stated in equation (10.8). Real wealth of pure asset holders is thus defined in equation (10.9) as the sum of the real cash balance, real short-term bond holdings and real equity holdings of asset holders. Note that the short-term bonds are assumed to be fixed price bonds with a price of one, $p_b = 1$, and a flexible interest rate i.

We now describe the demand equations of asset owning households for financial assets following the general equilibrium approach of Tobin (1969):

$$M^d = f_m(i, r_e^e)W_c^n, \tag{10.10}$$

$$B^d = f_b(i, r_e^e)W_c^n, \tag{10.11}$$

$$p_e E^d = f_e(i, r_e^e)W_c^n, \tag{10.12}$$

$$W_c^n = M^d + B^d + p_e E^d. \tag{10.13}$$

The demand for money balances of asset holders M^d is determined by a function $f_m(i, r_e^e)$ which depends on the interest rate on short-run bonds i and the expected rate of return on equities r_e^e. The value of this function times the nominal wealth W^n gives the nominal demand for money M^d, so that f_m describes the portion of nominal wealth that is allocated to pure money holdings. Note that this formulation of money demand is not based on a transaction motive, since the holding of transaction balances is the job of firms in the present chapter. We also do not assume that the financial assets of the economy are perfect substitutes, but rather the assumption that financial assets are imperfect substitutes is implicit in the approach that underlies the foregoing block of equations. Nevertheless, what is the motive for asset holders to hold a fraction of their wealth in form of money, when there is a riskless interest bearing asset? In our view, it is reasonable to employ a speculative motive: Asset holders want to hold money in order to be able to buy other assets or goods with zero or very low transaction costs. This of course assumes that there are (implicitly given) transaction costs when fixed-price bonds are turned into money. Köper (2003), in his Ch.7, modifies this framework by assuming that money holdings equal $M3$ and that bonds are flexprice or long-term bonds which give rise to capital gains or losses just as the equities of the present chapter.

The nominal demand for bonds is determined by $f_b(i, r_e^e)$ and the nominal demand for equities by $f_e(i, r_e^e)$, which again are functions that describe the fractions that are allocated to these forms of financial wealth. From equation (10.9), we know that actual nominal wealth equals the stocks of financial assets held by the asset holders. We assume, as is usual in portfolio approaches, that the asset holders do demand assets of an amount that equals in sum their nominal wealth as stated in equation (10.9). In other words, they just reallocate their wealth in view of new information on the rates of returns on their assets and thus take account of their wealth constraint.

What remains to be modeled in the household sector is the expected rate of return on equities r_e^e which consists of real dividends per unit of equity ($r_k^e pK / p_e E$), and expected capital gains, π_e, the latter being nothing other than the expected growth rate of equity prices. Thus, we can write

$$r_e^e = \frac{r_k^e pK}{p_e E} + \pi_e. \tag{10.14}$$

In order to complete the modeling of asset holders' behavior, we need to describe the evolution of π_e. We assume here that there are two types of asset holders, who differ with respect to their expectation formation of equity prices. There are *chartists* who in principle employ an adaptive expectations mechanism

$$\dot{\pi}_{ec} = \beta_{\pi_{ec}}(\hat{p}_e - \pi_{ec}), \tag{10.15}$$

where $\beta_{\pi_{ec}}$ is the adjustment speed towards the actual growth rate of equity prices. The other asset holders, the *fundamentalists*, employ a forward looking expectation formation mechanism

$$\dot{\pi}_{ef} = \beta_{\pi_{ef}}(\bar{\eta} - \pi_{ef}) \tag{10.16}$$

where $\bar{\eta}$ is the fundamentalists' expected long-run inflation rate of share prices. Assuming that the aggregate expected inflation rate is a weighted average of the two expected inflation rates, where the weights are determined according to the sizes of the groups, we postulate

$$\pi_e = \alpha_{\pi_{ec}} \pi_{ec} + (1 - \alpha_{\pi_{ec}}) \pi_{ef}. \tag{10.17}$$

Here $\alpha_{\pi_{ec}} \in (0, 1)$ is the ratio of chartists to all asset holders.

10.2.2 Firms

We consider the behavior of firms by means of two submodules. The first describes the production framework and their investment in business fixed capital and the second introduces the Metzlerian approach of inventory dynamics concerning expected sales, actual sales and the output of firms.

Firms: production and investment

$$r_k^e = (pY^e - wL^d - p\delta K)/(pK), \tag{10.18}$$
$$Y^p = y^p K, \tag{10.19}$$
$$u = Y/Y^p, \tag{10.20}$$

$$L^d = Y/x, \tag{10.21}$$

$$e = L^d/L = Y/(xL), \tag{10.22}$$

$$q = p_e E/(pK), \tag{10.23}$$

$$I = i_q(q-1)K + i_u(u-\bar{u})K + nK, \tag{10.24}$$

$$\hat{K} = I/K, \tag{10.25}$$

$$p_e \dot{E} = pI + p(\dot{N} - \mathcal{I}) \tag{10.26}$$

Firms are assumed to pay out dividends according to expected profits (expected sales net of depreciation and minus the wage sum), see the aforesaid module of the asset owning households. The rate of expected profits r_k^e is expected real profits per unit of capital as stated in equation (10.18). Firms produce output utilizing a production technology that transforms demanded labor L^d combined with business fixed capital K into output. For convenience, we assume that the production takes place with a fixed proportion technology.[9] According to (10.19) potential output Y^p is given in each moment of time by a fixed coefficient y^p times the existing stock of physical capital. Accordingly, the utilization of productive capacities is given by the ratio u of actual production Y and the potential output Y^p. The fixed proportions in production also give rise to a constant output-labor coefficient x, by means of which we can deduce labor demand from goods market determined output as in equation (10.21). The ratio L^d/L thus defines the rate of employment in the model.

The economic behavior of firms also comprises the investment decision with regard to business fixed capital, which is determined independently of the savings decision of households. We model here investment decisions per unit of capital as a function of the deviation of Tobin's q, see Tobin (1969), from its long-run value 1, and the deviation of actual capacity utilization from a normal rate of capital utilization, and add an exogenously given trend term, here given by the natural growth rate n in order to allow this rate to determine the growth path of the economy in the usual way. We employ here Tobin's average q which is defined in equation (10.23). It is the ratio of the nominal value of equities and the reproduction costs for the existing stock of capital. Investment in business fixed capital is reinforced when q exceeds one, and is reduced when q is smaller then one. This influence is represented by the term $i_q(q-1)$ in equation (10.24). The term $i_u(u-\bar{u})$ models the component of investment which is due to the deviation of utilization rate of physical capital from its non accelerating inflation value $\bar{u}$. The last component, nK, takes account of the natural growth rate n which is necessary for steady state analysis if natural growth is considered as exogenously given.

---

9 See Chiarella, Flaschel, Groh and Semmler (2000) (Chapter 4) for the treatment of neoclassical smooth factor substitution and discussion as to why this assumption is not as restrictive as might be believed by many economists.

Equation (10.26) is the budget constraint of the firms. Investment in business fixed capital and unintended changes in the inventory stock $p(\dot{N} - \mathcal{I})$ must be financed by issuing equities, since equities are the only financial instrument of firms in this chapter. Capital stock growth finally is given by net investment per unit of capital I/K in this demand determined model of the short-run equilibrium position of the economy.

Next, we model the inventory dynamics following Metzler (1941) and Franke (1996). This approach is a very useful concept for describing the goods market disequilibrium dynamics with all of its implications.

Firms output adjustment:

$$N^d = \alpha_{n^d} Y^e, \tag{10.27}$$

$$\mathcal{I} = nN^d + \beta_n(N^d - N), \tag{10.28}$$

$$Y = Y^e + \mathcal{I}, \tag{10.29}$$

$$Y^d = C + I + \delta K + G, \tag{10.30}$$

$$\dot{Y}^e = nY^e + \beta_{y^e}(Y^d - Y^e), \tag{10.31}$$

$$\dot{N} = Y - Y^d, \tag{10.32}$$

$$S_f = Y - Y^e = \mathcal{I}, \tag{10.33}$$

where $\alpha_{n^d}, \beta_n, \beta_{y^e} \geq 0$.

Equation (10.27) states that the desired stock of physical inventories, denoted by N^d, is assumed to be a fixed proportion of the expected sales. The planned investments $\mathcal{I}$ in inventories follow a sluggish adjustment process towards the desired stock N^d according to equation (10.28). Taking account of this additional demand for goods, equation (10.29) writes the production Y as equal to the expected sales of firms plus $\mathcal{I}$. To explain the expectation formation for goods demand, we need the actual total demand for goods which in (10.30) is given by consumption (of private households and the government) and gross investment by firms. From a knowledge of the actual demand Y^d, which is always satisfied, the dynamics of expected sales is given in equation (10.31). It models these expectations to be the outcome of an error correction process, that incorporates also the natural growth rate n in order take account of the fact that this process operates in a growing economy. The adjustment of sales expectations is driven by the prediction error $(Y^d - Y^e)$, with an adjustment speed that is given by β_{y^e}. Actual changes in the stock of inventories are given in (10.32) by the deviation of production from goods demanded. The savings of the firms S_f is as usual defined by income minus consumption. Because firms are assumed to not consume anything, their income equals their savings and is given by the excess of production over expected sales, $Y - Y^e$. According to the production account in Figure 10.1, the gross accounting profit of firms

Uses	Resources

Production Account of Firms:

Depreciation $p\delta K$	Private consumption pC
Wages wL^d	Gross investment $pI + p\delta K$
Gross accounting profits $\Pi = r_k^e pK + p\mathcal{I}$	Inventory investment $p\dot{N}$
	Public consumption pG

Income Account of Firms:

Dividends $r_k^e p_y K$	Gross accounting profits Π
Savings $p\mathcal{I}$	

Accumulation Account of Firms:

Gross investment $pI + p\delta K$	Depreciation $p\delta K$
Inventory investment $p\dot{N}$	Savings $p\mathcal{I}$
	Financial deficit FD

Financial Account of Firms:

Financial deficit FD	Equity financing $p_e \dot{E}$

Figure 10.1 Accounting sheets of the firms' sector.

finally is $r_k^e pK + p\mathcal{I} = pC + pI + p\delta K + p\dot{N} + pG$. Substituting in the definition of r_k^e from equation (10.18), we compute that $pY^e + p\mathcal{I} = pY^d + p\dot{N}$ or equivalently $(Y - Y^e) = \mathcal{I}$ as stated in equation (10.33).

10.2.3 Fiscal and monetary authorities

The role of the government in this chapter is to provide the economy with public (nonproductive) services within the limits of its budget constraint. Public purchases (and interest payments) are financed through taxes, through newly printed money or newly issued fixed-price bonds ($p_b = 1$). The budget constraint gives rise to some repercussion effects between the public and the private sector.[10]

$$T = \tau_w \omega L^d + T_c,$$ (10.34)

$$T_c - iB/p = t_c K, \qquad t_c = \text{const.}$$ (10.35)

$$G = gK, \qquad g = \text{const.}$$ (10.36)

$$S_g = T - iB/p - G,$$ (10.37)

$$\hat{M} = \mu,$$ (10.38)

$$\dot{B} = pG + iB - pT - \dot{M}.$$ (10.39)

We model the tax income consisting of taxes on wage income and lump sum taxes on capital income T_c. With regard to the real purchases of the government for the provision of government services we assume, again as in Sargent (1987), that these are a fixed proportion g of real capital, which taken together allows us to represent fiscal policy by means of simple parameters in the intensive form representation of the model and in the steady state considerations to be discussed later on. The real savings of the government, which is a deficit if it has a negative sign, is defined in equation (10.37) by real taxes minus real interest payments minus real public services. Again for reasons of simplicity the growth rate of money is given by a constant μ. Equation (10.38) is the monetary policy rule of the central bank and shows that money is assumed to enter the economy via open market operations of the central bank, which buys short-term bonds from the asset holders when issuing new money. Then the changes in the short-term bonds supplied by the government are given residually in equation (10.39), which is the budget constraint of the governmental sector. This representation of the behavior of the monetary and the fiscal authority clearly shows that the treatment of policy questions is not yet a central part of the chapter. See Köper (2003) for an explicit treatment of government interest payments.

---

10 See, for example, Sargent (1987, p.18) for the introduction of net of interest taxation rules.

10.2.4 Wage–price interactions

We now turn to a module of our model that can be the source of significant centrifugal forces within the complete model. These are the three laws of motion of the wage–price spiral, picking up again the approach of Rose (1967) (see also Rose (1990)) of two short-run Phillips curves, i) the wage Phillips curve and ii) the price Phillips curve, that we have already extensively employed and estimated as the DAS (Disequilibrium Aggregate Supply) block in the chapters of Part II. The relevant dynamic equations are given by

$$\hat{w} = \beta_w(e - \bar{e}) + \kappa_w \hat{p} + (1 - \kappa_w)\pi^c, \tag{10.40}$$

$$\hat{p} = \beta_p(u - \bar{u}) + \kappa_p \hat{w} + (1 - \kappa_p)\pi^c, \tag{10.41}$$

$$\dot{\pi}^c = \beta_{\pi^c}(\alpha\hat{p} + (1 - \alpha)(\mu - n) - \pi^c). \tag{10.42}$$

where $\beta_w, \beta_p, \beta_{\pi^c} \geq 0$, $0 \leq \alpha \leq 1$, and $0 \leq \kappa_w, \kappa_p \leq 1$. This approach makes use of the assumption that relative changes in money wages are influenced by demand pressure in the market for labor and price inflation (cost-pressure) terms and that price inflation in turn depends on demand pressure in the market for goods and on money wage (cost-pressure) terms. Wage inflation therefore is described in equation (10.40) on the one hand by means of a demand pull term $\beta_w(e - \bar{e})$, which states that relative changes in wages depends positively on the gap between actual employment e and its NAIRU (Non-Accelerating Inflation Rate Unemployment) value $\bar{e}$. On the other hand, the cost push elements in wage inflation is the weighted average of short-run (perfectly anticipated) price inflation $\hat{p}$ and medium-run expected overall inflation π^c, where the weights are given by κ_w and $1 - \kappa_w$. The price Phillips curve is quite similar, it also displays a demand pull and a cost push component. The demand pull term is given by the gap between capital utilization and its NAIRU value, $(u - \bar{u})$, and the cost push element is the κ_p and $1 - \kappa_p$ weighted average of short-run wage inflation $\hat{w}$ and expected medium-run overall inflation π^c.

What is left to model is the expected medium-run inflation rate π^c. We postulate in equation (10.42) that changes in expected medium-run inflation are due to an adjustment process towards a weighted average of the current inflation rate and steady state inflation. Thus, we introduce here a simple kind of forward looking expectations into the economy. This adjustment is driven by an adjustment velocity β_{π^c}.

It is obvious from this description of the model that it is, on the one hand, already a very general description of macroeconomic dynamics. On the other hand, it is still dependent on some very special assumptions, in particular, with respect to financial markets and the government sector. This can be justified at the present stage of analysis by observing that many of its simplifying assumptions are indeed typical for macrodynamic models, which attempt to provide a complete description of a closed monetary economy with labor, goods markets and three markets for financial assets, see in particular the model of Keynesian dynamics of Sargent (1987).

10.2.5 Capital markets: gross substitutes and stability

We have not yet discussed the determination of the nominal rate of interest i and the price of equities p_e and thus have not yet formulated how capital markets are organized. Following Tobin's (1969) portfolio approach, see also Franke and Semmler (1999), we here simply postulate that the following equilibrium conditions

$$M = M^d = f_m(i, r_e^e)W_c^n, \quad W_c^n = M + B + p_e E, \tag{10.43}$$

$$B = B^d = f_b(i, r_e^e)W_c^n, \tag{10.44}$$

$$p_e E = p_e E^d = f_e(i, r_e^e)W_c^n, \quad r_e^e = \frac{pY^e - wL^d - p\delta K}{p_e E} + \pi_e^e, \tag{10.45}$$

always hold and thus determine the above two prices for bonds and equities as statically endogenous variables of the model. Note here that all asset supplies are given magnitudes at each moment in time and recall from (10.14) that r_e^e is given by $\frac{r_e^e pK}{p_e E} + \pi_e$ and thus varies at each point in time solely due to variations in the share price p_e. Our model thus supports the view that the secondary market is the market where the prices or interest rates for the financial assets are determined such that these markets are cleared at all moments in time. This implies that newly issued assets do not impact significantly on these prices.[11]

The trade between the asset holders induces a process that makes asset prices fall or rise in order to equilibrate demands and supplies. In the short-run (in continuous time), the structure of wealth of asset holders, W_c^n is, disregarding changes in the share price p_e, given to them and for the model. This implies that the functions $f_m(\ )$, $f_b(\ )$, and $f_e(\ )$, introduced in equations 10.10 to 10.12 must satisfy the well known conditions

$$f_m(i, r_e^e) + f_b(i, r_e^e) + f_e(i, r_e^e) = 1, \tag{10.46}$$

$$\frac{\partial f_m(i, r_e^e)}{\partial z} + \frac{\partial f_b(i, r_e^e)}{\partial z} + \frac{\partial f_e(i, r_e^e)}{\partial z} = 0, \quad \forall z \in \{i, r_e^e\}. \tag{10.47}$$

---

11 This representation of the secondary markets as markets characterized by stock equilibrium at each moment in time may be turned into flow equilibrium conditions (including then the new issue on primary markets) if it is assumed that desired stocks only give rise to sluggish desired adjustments to such target values, for example in the following way, where these demand flows are and can then to be coordinated with the new issue of money, bonds and equities.

$$\dot{M} = \dot{M}^d = \beta_m(f_m(i, r_e^e)W^n - M)$$

$$\dot{B} = \dot{B}^d = \beta_b(f_b(i, r_e^e)W^n - B)$$

$$p_e \dot{E} = p_e \dot{E}^d = \beta_e(f_e(i, r_e^e)W^n - p_e E)$$

These conditions guarantee that the number of independent equations is equal to the number of statically endogenous variables (i, p_e) that the asset markets are assumed to determine at each moment in time.

We postulate that the financial assets display the gross substitution property

$$\frac{\partial f_b(i, r_e^e)}{\partial i} > 0, \quad \frac{\partial f_m(i, r_e^e)}{\partial i} < 0, \quad \frac{\partial f_e(i, r_e^e)}{\partial i} < 0, \tag{10.48}$$

$$\frac{\partial f_e(i, r_e^e)}{\partial r_e^e} > 0, \quad \frac{\partial f_m(i, r_e^e)}{\partial r_e^e} < 0, \quad \frac{\partial f_b(i, r_e^e)}{\partial r_e^e} < 0, \tag{10.49}$$

which means that the demand for all other assets increases whenever the price of one asset rises. For a formal definition, see for example Mas-Colell, Whinston, and Green (1995, p. 611). The foregoing discussion concentrates on stocks and their impact on asset prices, including the so-called Walras' law of stocks. The following proposition shows in addition that the Walras' law of flows also holds, representing an important consistency check of the model.

Proposition 1   Assume that the issue of new bonds and money of the government are absorbed by the asset holders. Then, every newly issued amount of equities of firms will be met by the demand for equities by the asset holders.

Proof   In proving this proposition, we refer to the definitions of nominal savings of the three considered sectors, namely

$$S_p^n = \dot{M}^d + \dot{B}^d + p_e \dot{E}^d, \tag{10.50}$$

$$S_g^n = -\dot{M} - \dot{B}, \tag{10.51}$$

$$S_f^n = p\mathcal{I}. \tag{10.52}$$

The assumption made means that $\dot{M}^d = \dot{M}$ and $\dot{B}^d = \dot{B}$ holds. By definition, we know that ex-post investments equal savings. Investment is given by the investment in business fixed capital plus actual inventory investment, whilst savings are the sum of the savings of all sectors. Thus,

$$pI + p\dot{N} = S_p^n + S_g^n + S_f^n$$

$$\Leftrightarrow \qquad pI + p\dot{N} = \dot{M}^d + \dot{B}^d + p_e \dot{E}^d - \dot{M} - \dot{B} + p\mathcal{I}$$

$$\Leftrightarrow \qquad pI + p\dot{N} = p_e \dot{E}^d + p\mathcal{I}$$

$$\Leftrightarrow \quad pI + p(\dot{N} - \mathcal{I}) = p_e \dot{E}^d.$$

From equation (10.26) we conclude that $p_e \dot{E}^d = p_e \dot{E}$, which means that the demand for new equities equals its supply. ∎

We add here without proof that the assumption of gross substitution in the asset demand functions implies a stable ultrashortrun adjustment process for the adjustment of the interest rate i and share price p_e in the form of a Walrasian tâtonnement process. Such disequilibrium adjustment processes that are assumed to implicitly underly the considered asset equilibrium determination are, however, not explicitly investigated, but solely assumed to work smoothly behind the equilibrium positions considered here.

10.2.6 Capital gains: fundamentalists' and chartists' expectations

Next, we consider again, as final closure of the KMGT portfolio approach, the potentially stabilizing and destabilizing capital gains expectations of fundamentalists and chartists. The addition of such expectations may be treated in two steps, first, the fairly tranquil fundamentalists' expectations and than that of the chartists' expectations that tend to be destabilizing if they adjust with sufficient strength. This last feature of the model, the by and large adaptive formation of capital gains expectations, is the most demanding aspect (as far as stability analysis is concerned) of the dynamical system that we are considering and is by and large left to future research as far as exact stability propositions are concerned.

The laws of motion governing the expectations about the equity prices are not changed by the transformation to intensive form and thus continue to read as

$$\dot{\pi}_{ef} = \beta_{\pi_{ef}}(\bar{\eta} - \pi_{ef}), \tag{10.53}$$

$$\dot{\pi}_{ec} = \beta_{\pi_{ec}}(\hat{p}_e - \pi_{ec}). \tag{10.54}$$

In the following, only the value of aggregate capital gains expectations is needed, but its computation requires the historical values of the actual appreciation of equity prices $\hat{p}_e$. However, we lack a law of motion for this latter quality, because the general equilibrium portfolio approach only provides us with $\hat{p}_e$ by taking the time derivative of the equilibrium conditions which leads to very complicated, expressions for equity price appreciation that are only defined implicitly.

We therefore follow Sargent (1987, pp. 117), by employing an equivalent integral representation of the expectation about equity price appreciation, which leads us to the following definition of aggregate expectation of equity price appreciation

$$\pi_e(t) = \alpha_{ec}\left[\pi_{ec}(t_0)e^{-\beta_{\pi_{ec}}(t-t_0)} + \beta_{\pi_{ec}}\int_{t_0}^{t} e^{-\beta_{\pi_{ec}}(t-s)}\hat{p}_e(s)ds\right]$$

$$+ (1 - \alpha_{ec})\left[(\pi_{ef}(t_0) - \bar{\eta})e^{-\beta_{\pi_{ef}}t} + \bar{\eta}\right], \tag{10.55}$$

where $\pi_{ec}(t_0)$ and $\pi_{ef}(t_0)$ are the initial values of the expectations about growth in equity prices, performed respectively by the chartists and the fundamentalists at time t_0.

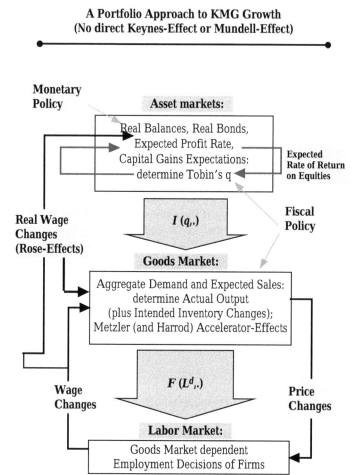

**A Portfolio Approach to KMG Growth
(No direct Keynes-Effect or Mundell-Effect)**

Figure 10.2 Keynes' causal downward nexus, the repercussions of the feedback chains, supply side dynamics and policy rules in the KMG portfolio approach.

Before we come to a consideration of the intensive form of the model, its steady state and its stability properties, as well as among other things the potentially destabilizing role of chartist-type capital gains expectations, we discuss the full structure of the KMGT model by means of what is shown in Figure 10.2. This figure highlights the destabilizing role of the wage–price spiral, where now – due to the assumed investment behavior – we always have a positive impact of real wages on aggregate demand and thus the result that wage flexibility will be destabilizing (if not counteracted by its effects on expected profits and their effect on financial markets and Tobin's q). We have already indicated that financial markets adjust towards their equilibrium in a stable manner as long as expectations do not really enter the scene. Monetary policy, whether money supply oriented and thus of type $i(M, p)$ or of a Taylor type $M(i, \hat{p})$, should – via the gross substitution effects – also contribute to the stability of financial markets. Fiscal policy impacts on the goods and the financial markets and may be of an orthodox type or of a Keynesian countercyclical kind. Due to the very intertwined dynamical structure that we are now facing, it is, however, not clear how fiscal policy contributes to the shaping of the business cycle, a topic that must be left for future research. There remains the discussion of the self-reference within the asset markets (that is the closed loop structure between capital gains expectations and actual capital gains) which must also be the most difficult part of the considered dynamical system and which must also be left for future research.

10.3 The model in intensive form

In this section, we derive the intensive form of the model, that is we will express all stock and flow variables in per unit of capital terms in the laws of motion and also in the associated algebraic equations (that need to be inserted into the laws of motion in order to obtain an autonomous dynamical system). We thus divide nominal stock and flow variables by the nominal value of the capital stock pK and all real ones by K, the real capital stock. This allows the determination of a (unique) economic steady state solution as an interior point of rest of the resulting nine state variables.

We begin with the intensive form of some necessary definitions or identities, which we need in order to represent the dynamical system in a sufficiently comprehensible form. Note here that the function q used in this block of equations will be determined and discussed later on, in Subsection 10.4, where the comparative statics of the portfolio part of the model are investigated. Thus, we set

$$Y/K = y = (1 + \alpha_{n^d}(n + \beta_n))y^e - \beta_n v,$$

$$Y^e/K = y^e,$$

$$N/K = v,$$

$$L^d/K = l^d = y/x,$$

$$L/K = l,$$

$$e = l^d/l,$$

$$u = y/y^p,$$

$$r_k^e = y^e - \delta - \omega l^d,$$

$$C/K = c = (1 - \tau_w)\omega l^d + (1 - s_c)(y^e - \delta - \omega l^d - t_c),$$

$$I/K = i(\cdot) = i_q(q - 1) + i_u(u - \bar{u}) + n,$$

$$Y^d/K = y^d = c + i(\cdot) + \delta + g,$$

$$p_e E/(pK) = q = q(m, b, r_k^e, \pi_e),$$

$$r_e^e = r_k^e/q + \pi_e,$$

$$\pi_e = \alpha_{\pi_e}\pi_{ec} + (1 - \alpha_{\pi_e})\pi_{ef}.$$

The foregoing equations describe output and employment per unit of capital, the rate of utilization of the existing stock of labor and capital, the expected rate of profit, consumption, investment and aggregate demand per unit of capital, Tobin's average q, and the expected rate of return on equities (including expected capital gains π_e).

Now, we translate the laws of motion of the dynamically endogenous variables into capital intensive form. The law of motions for the nominal wages and price level stated in equations (10.40) and (10.41) interact instantaneously and thus depend on each other. Solving these two linear equations for $\hat{w}$ and $\hat{p}$ gives[12]

$$\hat{w} = \kappa\left(\beta_w(e - \bar{e}) + \kappa_w \beta_p(u - \bar{u})\right) + \pi^c, \tag{10.56}$$

$$\hat{p} = \kappa\left(\beta_p(u - \bar{u}) + \kappa_p \beta_w(e - \bar{e})\right) + \pi^c, \tag{10.57}$$

with $\kappa = (1 - \kappa_w \kappa_p)^{-1}$. From these two inflation rates one can compute the growth law of real wages $\omega = w/p$ by means of the definitional relationship $\hat{\omega} = \hat{w} - \hat{p}$, from which

$$\hat{\omega} = \kappa[(1 - \kappa_p)\beta_w(e - \bar{e}) + (\kappa_w - 1)\beta_p(u - \bar{u})]. \tag{10.58}$$

Next, we obtain the set of equations that explains the dynamical laws of the expected rate of inflation, the labor capital ratio, the expected sales, and the stock of inventories in intensive form, which are

$$\dot{\pi}^c = \alpha \beta_{\pi^c}\kappa[\beta_p(u - \bar{u}) + \kappa_p \beta_w(e - \bar{e})] + (1 - \alpha)\beta_{\pi^c}(\mu - n - \pi^c), \tag{10.59}$$

$$\hat{l} = n - i(\cdot) = -i_q(q - 1) - i_u(u - \bar{u}), \tag{10.60}$$

$$\dot{y}^e = \beta_{y^e}(y^d - y^e) + (n - i(\cdot))y^e, \tag{10.61}$$

$$\dot{v} = y - y^d - i(\cdot)v. \tag{10.62}$$

Equation (10.59) is almost the same as in the extensive form model, but here the term $\hat{p} - \pi^c$ is substituted by use of equation (10.57). Equation (10.60), the law of motion of relative factor endowment, follows from (10.4) and (10.25) and is given by the (negative) of the investment function as far as its dependence on

---

12 For details of the calculations involved see Chiarella and Flaschel (2000a) and Köper (2003).

asset markets and the state of the business cycle are concerned. Equation (10.61) is obtained by taking the time derivative of y^e, so that

$$\dot{y}^e = \frac{d(Y^e/K)}{dt} = \frac{\dot{Y}^e K - Y^e \dot{K}}{K^2} = \frac{\dot{Y}^e}{K} - y^e i(\cdot) = \beta_{y^e}(y^d - y^e) + y^e(n - i(\cdot)).$$

In essentially the same way one obtains equation (10.62).

The laws of motion governing the expectations about the equity prices are not changed in the intensive form model and thus again read

$$\dot{\pi}_{ef} = \beta_{\pi_{ef}}(\bar{\eta} - \pi_{ef}),\tag{10.63}$$

$$\dot{\pi}_{ec} = \beta_{\pi_{ec}}(\hat{p}_e - \pi_{ec}).\tag{10.64}$$

The aggregate expectation of equity price inflation continues to be given by (10.55), that is

$$\pi_e(t) = \alpha_{ec}\left[\pi_{ec}(t_0)e^{-\beta_{\pi_{ec}}(t-t_0)} + \beta_{\pi_{ec}}\int_{t_0}^t e^{-\beta_{\pi_{ec}}(t-s)}\hat{p}_e(s)ds\right]$$

$$+ (1-\alpha_{ec})\left[(\pi_{ef}(t_0) - \bar{\eta})e^{-\beta_{\pi_{ef}}t} + \bar{\eta}\right].\tag{10.65}$$

where $\pi_{ec}(t_0)$ and $\pi_{ef}(t_0)$ are the initial values of the expectations about growth in equity prices.

Finally, the laws of motion for real balances and real bonds per unit of capital have to be derived. Based on the knowledge of the laws for inflation $\hat{p}$ and investment $i(\cdot)$, we can derive the differential equation for bonds per unit of capital shown in equation (10.66) from

$$\dot{b} = \frac{d(B/pK)}{dt} = \frac{\dot{B}}{pK} - b(\hat{p} + i(\cdot))$$

where $\dot{B}$ is given by equation (10.39). The same idea is used for the changes in the money supply. We thus finally obtain the two differential equations

$$\dot{b} = g - t_c - \tau_w \omega l^d - \mu m$$

$$- b\left(\kappa[\beta_p(u - \bar{u}) + \kappa_p \beta_w(e - \bar{e})] + \pi^c + i(\cdot)\right),\tag{10.66}$$

$$\dot{m} = m\mu - m(\kappa[\beta_p(u - \bar{u}) + \kappa_p \beta_w(e - \bar{e})] + \pi^c + i(\cdot)).\tag{10.67}$$

According to the forgoing, the dynamics in extensive form can therefore be reduced to nine differential equations, where, however, the law of motion for share prices has not yet been determined, or to seven differential and one integral equation which is easier to handle than the alternative representation, since there is then no law of motion for the development of future share prices to be calculated.

Note with respect to these dynamics that economic policy (fiscal and monetary) is still represented in very simple terms here, since money supply is growing at a given rate and since government expenditures and taxes on capital income net of interest payments per unit of capital are given parameters. This makes the dynamics of the government budget constraint (see (10.66) the law of motion for bonds per unit of capital b) a very trivial one as in Sargent (1987, ch. 5), and thus leaves the problems associated with these dynamics a matter for future research. The advantage is that fiscal policy can be discussed in a very simple way here by means of just three parameters.

A comparison of the present dynamics with those of the working KMG model of Chiarella and Flaschel (2000a) and Chiarella, Flaschel, Groh and Semmler (2000) reveals that there are now two variables from the financial sector that feed back to the real dynamics in this extended system, the bond to capital ratio b representing the evolution of government debt and Tobin's average q. The first (dynamic) variable, however, only influences the real dynamics, since it is one of the factors that influences the statically endogenous variable q which in turn enters the investment function as a measure of the firms' performance. Government bonds do not influence the economy in other ways, since there are not yet wealth effects in consumption and since the interest income channel to consumption has been suppressed by the particular assumption about tax collection concerning capital income. In addition, the interest rate channel of the earlier KMG approaches, where the real rate of interest as compared with the real profit rate entering the investment function, is now absent from this function. The nominal interest rate as determined by portfolio equilibrium thus does not matter in the present formulation of the model, where Tobin's q in the place of this interest rate now provides the channel by which investment behavior is reacting to the results brought about by the financial markets.

A feature of the present dynamics is that there are no laws of motion left implicit in its discussion (as was the case for the bond and the share price dynamics of the working KMG models cited earlier, and is thus now a completely formulated dynamics, yet one where the real financial interaction is represented in very basic terms. Price inflation (via real balances and real bonds) and the expected rate of profit (via the dividend rate of return) influence the behavior of asset markets via their laws of motion, while the reaction of asset markets feeds back into the real part of the economy instantaneously through the change in Tobin's q that they (and the dynamics of expected capital gains) bring about.

In this subsection, we show the existence of a steady state in the economy under consideration. We stress here that this can be done independently of the analysis given in the next section on the comparative statics of the asset market equilibrium system, since Tobin's q is given by 1 in the steady state via the real part of the model and since the portfolio equations can be uniquely solved in conjunction with the government budget constraint for the three variables i, m, b which they then determine. Note that m and b are data in the short-run analysis of the behavior of asset markets of the next subsection (where q and i are determined through them as the variables that bring the asset markets into equilibrium), while m and b are variables in the long-run that are derived from asset market equilibrium conditions and the government budget constraint.

Proposition 2   Assume $s_c > \tau_w$ and $s_c r^{e0} > n + g - t_c$. Assume furthermore that the parameter $\bar{\phi}$ used below has a positive numerator, so that the government runs a primary deficit in the steady state, (and thus between zero and one if the money supply is growing). The dynamical system given by equations (10.58) to (10.67) possesses a unique interior steady state solution $(\omega^o, l^o, m^o > 0)$ with equilibrium on the asset markets, if the fundamentalists long-run reference inflation rate of equity prices equals the steady state inflation rate of goods prices $\bar{\eta} = \hat{p}^o$, and

$$\lim_{i \to 0}(f_m(i, r^{e0} + \pi_e^o) + f_b(i, r^{e0} + \pi_e^o)) < \bar{\phi}, \text{ and}$$

$$\lim_{i \to \infty}(f_m(i, r^{e0} + \pi_e^o) + f_b(i, r^{e0} + \pi_e^o)) > \bar{\phi},$$

holds true with $\bar{\phi} = \dfrac{g - t_c - \tau_w \omega l^{do}}{g - t_c - \tau_w \omega l^{do} + \mu}$. [13]

Proof   If the economy rests in a steady state, then all intensive variables stay constant and all time derivatives of the system become zero. Thus, by setting the left-hand side of the system of equations (10.58) to (10.67) equal to zero, we can deduce the steady state values of the variables.

From equation (10.60) we can derive that $i(\cdot)^o = n$ holds, from (10.61) we get $y^{eo} = y^{do}$, and from (10.67) that $\mu = (\kappa[\beta_p(u - \bar{u}) + \kappa_p\beta_w(e - \bar{e})] + \pi^c + i(\cdot))$. Substituting the last relation into equation (10.42) and using $i(\cdot)^o = n$ we obtain with $\alpha\beta_\pi \neq -(1 - \alpha)\beta_\pi^c$ that $\mu - n - \pi^c = 0$ and $\kappa[\beta_p(u - \bar{u}) + \kappa_p\beta_w(e - \bar{e})] = 0$. Thus, we have for $u - \bar{u}$ and $e - \bar{e}$ the two equations

$$u - \bar{u} = -\kappa_p\beta_w(e - \bar{e})/\beta_p,$$

$$u - \bar{u} = (1 - \kappa_p)\beta_w(e - \bar{e})/[(1 - \kappa_w)\beta_p].$$

By assumption we have $\beta_p, \beta_w > 0$ and $0 \leq \kappa_p, \kappa_w \leq 1$, so $e - \bar{e}$ must equal zero in order that the last two equations be fulfilled. When $e = \bar{e}$, then according to (10.58) we know that $u = \bar{u}$. Then equation (10.60) leads to $q^o = 1$.

With these relations one can easily compute the unique steady state values of the variables y^e, l, π^c, v, ω as

$$y^{eo} = \frac{y^o}{1 + n\alpha_{nd}}, \quad \text{with } y^o = \bar{u}y^p, \tag{10.68}$$

---

13 Note with respect to this part of the proposition that the steady state values used in the aforementioned assumption are calculated before this assumption is applied to a determination of the steady state value of the nominal rate of interest.

$$l^o = y^o/(\bar{e}x),$$ (10.69)

$$\pi^{co} = \mu - n,$$ (10.70)

$$v^o = \alpha_{nd} y^{eo},$$ (10.71)

$$\omega^o = \frac{y^{eo} - n - \delta - g - (1 - s_c)(y^{eo} - \delta - t_c)}{(s_c - \tau_w) l^{do}},$$ (10.72)

$$r^{e0} = y^{eo} - \delta - \omega^o l^{do}.$$ (10.73)

All these values are determined on the goods and labor markets. The steady state value of the real wage has in particular been derived from the goods market equilibrium condition that must hold in the steady state and it is positive under the assumptions made in Proposition 2.

We next take account of the asset markets, which determine the values of the short-term interest rate i (which now bears the burden of clearing the asset markets), but now in conjunction with the determination of the steady state for m and b, where $m + b$ is determined through the government budget constraint. This is the case, because the steady state rate of return on equities relies, on the one hand, solely on r^{e0} (since q has been determined through the condition $i(\cdot) = n$ and shown to equal one in steady state) and, on the other hand, on the expected inflation rate of share prices

$$r_e^{e0} = r^{e0} + \pi_e^o,$$

which equals the goods price inflation rate in the steady state as will be shown in the following.

The steady state values of the two kinds of expectations about the inflation rate of equity prices (of chartists and fundamentalists) are

$$\pi_{ef}^o = \bar{\eta}, \qquad \pi_{ec}^o = \bar{\eta}$$ (10.74)

from which one can derive that $\pi_e^o = \bar{\eta} = \hat{p}^o = \pi^{co} = \mu - n$ must hold. We have seen that, in the steady state, Tobin's q equals one and its time derivative equals zero, so that we can derive

$$\dot{q} = 0$$

$$\Rightarrow \qquad \frac{(\dot{p}_e E + p_e \dot{E}) pK - p_e E(\dot{p}K + p\dot{K})}{p^2 K^2} = 0$$

$$\Rightarrow \qquad \frac{\dot{p}_e E + p_e \dot{E}}{pK} = \hat{p} + n.$$

According to equation (10.26) we have $p_e \dot{E} = pI + p(\dot{N} - \mathcal{I})$ we thus get in the steady state that $p_e \dot{E} = pI$. Inserting this into the last implication shown we get

$\hat{p}_e = \hat{p}$ and thus as an important finding that $\bar{\eta} = \mu - n$ must hold in order to allow for a steady state.

Now, we determine the steady state values of the stocks of real cash balances and the stock of bonds. These values have to be determined in conjunction with the steady state interest rate i^o which is now solely responsible for clearing the asset markets, because the result that Tobin's $q = 1$ has already been determined on the real markets.

The budget constraint of the government is given in intensive form by

$$\dot{b} + \dot{m} = g - t_c - \tau_w \omega l^d - (b+m)(\hat{p} + i(\cdot)). \tag{10.75}$$

One therefore obtains in the steady state that

$$b^o + m^o = (g - t_c - \tau_w \omega l^d)/\mu. \tag{10.76}$$

Furthermore, consider the asset demand functions (10.10) and (10.11), namely

$$m = f_m(i, r_e^e)(m+b+q), \quad q = 1, \tag{10.77}$$

$$b = f_b(i, r_e^e)(m+b+q), \quad q = 1. \tag{10.78}$$

The left side of the last two equations are the supplied amounts and the right sides represent the demand for the assets m, b.

Using now equation (10.76) in the form

$$\mu(m^o + b^o) = g - t_c - \tau_w \omega l^d, \tag{10.79}$$

the system of three linear independent equations (10.77) to (10.79) can be used to deduce the three unique steady state values i^o, b^o, and m^o which we will show below.

Beginning with the steady state interest rate, we sum equations (10.77) and (10.78) and multiplying by μ obtain

$$\mu(m^o + b^o) = (f_m^o + f_b^o)\mu(m^o + b^o + 1),$$

where f_m^o and f_b^o denote the values of $f_m(i^o, r^{e0} + \pi_e^o)$ and $f_b(i^o, r^{e0} + \pi_e^o)$ respectively. Substituting in the budget constraint in the form of equation (10.79) we get

$$f_m^o + f_b^o = \bar{\phi},$$

with $\bar{\phi} = \dfrac{g - t_c - \tau_w \omega^o l^{do}}{g - t_c - \tau_w \omega^o l^{do} + \mu}$. From property (10.47) and (10.49) we can conclude that

$$\frac{\partial(f_m + f_b)}{\partial i} > 0, \tag{10.80}$$

which implies that the cumulated demand for money and bonds is a strictly increasing function in the variable i.

If $\lim_{i \to 0}(f_m(i, r^{eo} + \pi_e^o) + f_b(i, r^{eo} + \pi_e^o)) < \bar{\phi}$ and $\lim_{i \to \infty}(f_m(i, r^{eo} + \pi_e^o) + f_b(i, r^{eo} + \pi_e^o)) > \bar{\phi}$ then by monotonicity and continuity there must be a value of i, which equilibrates the asset markets in the above aggregated form. Then, steady-state supplies of m and b can be calculated by equations (10.77) and (10.78) in a unique way, based on the steady state interest rates $i = i^o$ and $r_e^{e0} = r^{e0} + \pi_e$. This concludes the derivation of the uniquely determined steady-state values for our dynamical system (10.58) to (10.67) which in turn when inserted into this system indeed imply that the dynamics is at a point of rest in this situation.   ∎

We observe finally that the calculation of the steady state value of the rate of wage and the rate of profit can be simplified when it is assumed that government expenditures are given by $g + \tau_w \omega l^d$ in place of only g.

10.4 The comparative statics of the asset markets

After having specified both the extensive and intensive forms of the model and having shown the existence and uniqueness of an interior economic steady state solution of the intensive form, we now focus on the short-run comparative statics of the financial markets module of the system. We derive in particular the function $q = q(m, b, r_k^e, \pi_e)$ of which we have already made use in the intensive form presentation of the model, and which will be needed to investigate the stability properties of the model around its steady state position in the next section.

We assume that the asset demand functions display the properties which guarantee a unique interior steady state solution; see Proposition 2 in the preceding subsection. We now approximate these demand functions by linear functions in a neighborhood of the steady state in order to derive the local stability properties of the next subsection. These *linearized versions of the asset demand functions* can be written as (with $r_e^e = r_k^e/q + \pi_e$):

$$f_m^l(i, r_e^e) = \alpha_{m0} - \alpha_{m1}i - \alpha_{m2}(r_k^e/q + \pi_e),$$

$$f_b^l(i, r_e^e) = \alpha_{b0} + \alpha_{b1}i - \alpha_{b2}r_e^e,$$

$$f_e^l(i, r_e^e) = \alpha_{e0} - \alpha_{e1}i + \alpha_{e2}r_e^e,$$

where the superscript l denotes the linearized form and where

$$\alpha_{ij} \geq 0 \quad \forall \quad i \in \{b, m, e\}, j \in \{0, 1, 2\}.$$

Because of Walrus Law of Stocks it is sufficient to focus on the first two asset market equilibrium conditions in all subsequent equilibrium considerations. For money and bonds these two equilibrium conditions now read

$$m = (\alpha_{m0} - \alpha_{m1}i - \alpha_{m2}(r_k^e/q + \pi_e))(m + b + q), \tag{10.81}$$

$$b = (\alpha_{b0} + \alpha_{b1}i - \alpha_{b2}(r_k^e/q + \pi_e))(m + b + q). \tag{10.82}$$

Solving (10.81) and (10.82) for the interest rate i we obtain, respectively

$$i_{LM} = \frac{\alpha_{m0} - \alpha_{m2}(r_k^e/q + \pi_e) - m/(m+b+q)}{\alpha_{m1}}, \tag{10.83}$$

$$i_{BB} = \frac{-\alpha_{b0} + \alpha_{b2}(r_k^e/q + \pi_e) + b/(m+b+q)}{\alpha_{b1}}. \tag{10.84}$$

The LM-subscript denotes the interest rate that equates demand for real balances and real money supply and the BB-subscript denotes the interest rate that equates real bond demand and supply. Figure 10.3 displays examples of these two functions as a function of q. The intersection of the LM-curve and the BB-curve then provides the equilibrium values for the short-term interest rate i and Tobin's q. The figure only shows examples of such functions and as we know that the functions are not linear in q we do not know yet whether the equilibrium exists and is unique. Note, however, that we are only considering a neighborhood of the steady state solution for the variables i, q, m, b, r_k^e, π_e. In order to show that i and q exist and are uniquely determined for all m, b, r_k^e, π_e sufficiently close to the steady state solution we have to show that the assumptions of the implicit function theorem are valid at the steady state.

Proposition 3   The assumptions of Proposition 2 still hold. There is a unique solution (i, q) to the equations (10.77) and (10.78), which thus clears the asset markets, for all values of m, b, r_k^e, π_e in an appropriately chosen neighborhood of the interior steady state solution of the dynamics (10.58) to (10.67).

Proof   We have to show that the Jacobian of the system

$$f_m(i, r_k^e/q + \pi_e)(m+b+q) - m = 0,$$
$$f_b(i, r_k^e/q + \pi_e)(m+b+q) - b = 0,$$

is regular with respect to the variables i and q, which means that

$$\left| \begin{array}{cc} \frac{\partial}{\partial i}(f_m(i, r_k^e/q + \pi_e)(m+b+q) - m) & \frac{\partial}{\partial q}(f_m(i, r_k^e/q + \pi_e)(m+b+q) - m) \\ \frac{\partial}{\partial i}(f_b(i, r_k^e/q + \pi_e)(m+b+q) - b) & \frac{\partial}{\partial q}(f_b(i, r_k^e/q + \pi_e)(m+b+q) - b) \end{array} \right| \neq 0$$

must hold true. We can readily calculate that the sign configuration of the entries in this Jacobian is

$$\begin{pmatrix} - & + \\ + & + \end{pmatrix}$$

which immediately implies the regularity of this Jacobian.   ∎

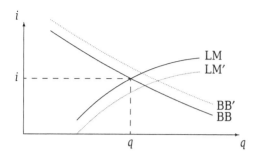

Figure 10.3 The LM and BB Curves: The dashed lines show how these curves
simultaneously shift when one of the statically exogenous variables
r_k^e, π_e, q, m rises or b falls.

We have thus shown that the financial markets can always be cleared through
adjustments of the short-term interest rate and Tobin's q. However, how do these
two variables react in the short-run as the foregoing statically exogenous variables
change over time? We consider this question first on the level of the partial
equilibrium curves shown in Figure 10.3. We can derive for the dependence of the
two interest functions i_{LM} and i_{BB} on the variables r_k^e, π_e, q and m the following:

$$i_{LM}(r_k^e, \pi_e, m, b, q) \qquad i_{BB}(r_k^e, \pi_e, m, b, q).$$
$$\text{and}$$
$$- \;\; - \;\; - \;+ \;+ \qquad\qquad + \;\; + \;\; - \;+ \;-$$

(10.85)

These results follow directly by taking the respective partial derivatives of the
functions in equations (10.83) and (10.84).

Equations (10.83) and (10.84) together through the equilibrium condition by
$i_{LM} = i_{BB}$ yield

$$\frac{\alpha_{m0} - \alpha_{m2}(r_k^e/q + \pi_e) - m/(m+b+q)}{\alpha_{m1}}$$
$$- \frac{-\alpha_{b0} + \alpha_{b2}(r_k^e/q + \pi_e) + b/(m+b+q)}{\alpha_{b1}} = 0.$$

(10.86)

Application of the implicit function theorem then gives the following qualitative
dependencies of Tobin's average q:

$$q(r_k^e, \pi_e, m, b) \qquad \forall \;\; q > \left(\frac{\alpha_{b1}}{\alpha_{m1}} - 1\right)m,$$
$$+ \;\; + \;\; + \;+$$

(10.87)

$$q(r_k^e, \pi_e, m, b) \qquad \forall \;\; q < \left(\frac{\alpha_{b1}}{\alpha_{m1}} - 1\right)m.$$
$$+ \;\; + \;\; + \;-$$

The first situation in (10.87) must apply locally around the steady state if $(\frac{\alpha_{b1}}{\alpha_{m1}} - 1)m^o < 1$ holds true while the other one holds in the opposite case.[14] We thus get the result that an increase in r_k^e, the basis for the dividend rate of return, unambiguously increases Tobin's q, as does an increase in the expected capital gains π_e. Furthermore, an increase in m also pushes q upwards and thus increases investment, just as an increase in m would do in the presence of a negative dependence of the rate of investment on the rate of interest, the Keynes effect in traditional models of the AS–AD variety. The positive influence of m on q thus mirrors the Keynes effect of traditional Keynesian short-run equilibrium analysis. The nominal rate of interest is, however, no longer involved in the real part of the model as it is here formulated which allows us to ignore the comparative statics of this interest rate in the current analysis.

Results with respect to the influence of bonds b on a change in Tobin's q are, however, ambiguous and depend on the steady state value of real balances m as well as on the parameters that determine the interest rate sensitivity of money and bonds demand. We can get more insights into the formation of Tobin's q by means of the following lemma:

Lemma 1 In a neighborhood around the steady state, the partial derivative of Tobin's q with respect to cash balances exceeds the partial derivative of q with respect to bond holdings:

$$\frac{\partial q}{\partial m} > \frac{\partial q}{\partial b}$$

Proof We can rewrite the inequality of the proposition as[15]

$$-\frac{\det \dfrac{\partial(F_1,F_2)}{\partial(i,m)}}{\det \dfrac{\partial(F_1,F_2)}{\partial(i,q)}} > -\frac{\det \dfrac{\partial(F_1,F_2)}{\partial(i,b)}}{\det \dfrac{\partial(F_1,F_2)}{\partial(i,q)}},$$

the denominator of which we know that is negative, so we get equivalently the condition

$$\det \frac{\partial(F_1,F_2)}{\partial(i,m)} > \det \frac{\partial(F_1,F_2)}{\partial(i,b)}$$

$$\Leftrightarrow \quad -\alpha_{m1}b + \alpha_{b1}(b+q) > \alpha_{m1}(m+q) - \alpha_{b1}m$$

---

14 We do not pay attention here to the border case where $(\frac{\alpha_{b1}}{\alpha_{m1}} - 1)m^o = 1$ holds true. Note here also that the α_{ij} sum to one for $j = 0$ and to zero for $j = 1, 2$ which implies that $\frac{\alpha_{b1}}{\alpha_{m1}} - 1$ is always non-negative.

15 Note we use the notation $\det \frac{\partial(F_1,F_2)}{\partial(i,x)}$ to denote the determinant with elements $\frac{\partial F_1}{\partial i}, \frac{\partial F_1}{\partial x}, \frac{\partial F_2}{\partial i}, \frac{\partial F_2}{\partial x}$ for $x \in (m, b, q)$.

$$\Leftrightarrow \qquad \alpha_{b1}(m+b+q) > \alpha_{m1}(m+b+q)$$

$$\Leftrightarrow \qquad \alpha_{b1} > \alpha_{m1}.$$

which is true, because this inequality is an implication of equation (10.80). ∎

This lemma tells us that an open market policy of the government, which means that the central bank buys bonds by means of issuing money ($dm = -db$), indeed has an expansionary effect on Tobin's q since

$$\frac{\partial q}{\partial m}dm + \frac{\partial q}{\partial b}(-dm) > 0. \tag{10.88}$$

Note finally that the effect of r_k^e on q can be related to the Rose effect in the working KMG model of Chiarella and Flaschel (2000a), while there is no longer a Mundell effect in the model as there is no influence of the real rate of interest on aggregate demand.

10.5 Stability

In the following analysis, we suppose that all assumptions stated in Proposition 2 hold. What is left to analyze is the dynamical behavior of the system, when it is displaced from its steady state position, but still remains in a neighborhood of the steady state. In the following, we provide propositions, which in sum imply that there must be a locally stable steady state, if some sufficient conditions that are very plausible from a Keynesian perspective are met.

We begin with an appropriate subsystem of the full dynamics for which the Routh–Hurwitz conditions can be shown to hold. Setting $\beta_p = \beta_w = \beta_{\pi_{ef}} = \beta_{\pi_{ec}} = \beta_n = \beta_{\pi^c} = 0, \beta_{y^e} > 0$, and keeping $\pi^c, \pi_e, \omega, \nu$ thereby at their steady state values we get the following subdynamics of state variables m, b and y^e which are then independent of the rest of the system:[16]

$$\dot{m} = m(\mu - (\pi^c + i(\cdot))),$$

$$\dot{b} = g - t_c - \tau_w \omega \frac{y}{x} - \mu m - b(\pi^c + i(\cdot)), \tag{10.89}$$

$$\dot{y}^e = \beta_{y^e}\left[c + i(\cdot) + \delta + g - y^e\right] + y^e(i(\cdot) - n).$$

Proposition 4[17]　The steady state of the system of differential equations (10.89) is locally asymptotically stable if β_{y^e} is sufficiently large, the investment adjustment speed i_u concerning deviations of capital utilization from the normal capital utilization is sufficiently small and the partial derivatives of desired cash balances with respect to the interest rate $\partial f_m/\partial i$ and the rate of return on equities $\partial f_m/\partial r_e^e$ are sufficiently small.

16　Note that l may vary, but does not feed back into the presently considered subdynamics.
17　The mathematical appendix to this chapter gives alternative formulations of the Propositions 4–9 and their proofs.

Proof See Köper (2003), also with respect to all other following propositions of this section. ∎

The proposition asserts that local asymptotic stability at the steady state of the considered subdynamics holds when, the demand for cash is not very much influenced by the rates of return on the financial asset markets,[18] the accelerating effect of capacity utilization on the investment behavior is sufficiently small, and the adjustment speed of expected sales towards actual demand is fast enough.

Next, we consider the same system but allow β_p to become positive, though only small in amount. This means that ω which had previously entered the m, b, y^e-subsystem only through its steady state value now becomes a dynamic variable, giving rise to the 4D dynamical system

$$\dot{m} = m\left(\mu - \left(\kappa\beta_p\left(\frac{y}{y^p} - \bar{u}\right) + \pi^c + i(\cdot)\right)\right),$$

$$\dot{b} = g - t_c - \tau_w\omega\frac{y}{x} - \mu m - b\left(\kappa\beta_p\left(\frac{y}{y^p} - \bar{u}\right) + \pi^c + i(\cdot)\right),$$

$$\dot{y}^e = \beta_{y^e}\left[c + i(\cdot) + \delta + g - y^e\right] + y^e(i(\cdot) - n),$$ (10.90)

$$\dot{\omega} = \omega\kappa(\kappa_w - 1)\beta_p\left(\frac{y}{y^p} - \bar{u}\right).$$

Proposition 5 The interior steady state of the dynamical system (10.90) is locally asymptotically stable if the conditions in Proposition 4 are met and β_p is sufficiently small.

Enlarging the system (10.90) by letting β_w become positive we get the subsystem

$$\dot{m} = m\left(\mu - \left(\kappa\left[\beta_p\left(\frac{y}{y^p} - \bar{u}\right) + \kappa_p\beta_w\left(\frac{y}{xl} - \bar{e}\right)\right] + \pi^c + i(\cdot)\right)\right),$$

$$\dot{b} = g - t_c - \tau_w\omega\frac{y}{x} - \mu m - b\left(\kappa\left[\beta_p\left(\frac{y}{y^p} - \bar{u}\right) + \kappa_p\beta_w\left(\frac{y}{xl} - \bar{e}\right)\right] + \pi^c + i(\cdot)\right),$$

$$\dot{y}^e = \beta_{y^e}[c + i(\cdot) + \delta + g - y^e] + y^e(i(\cdot) - n),$$ (10.91)

$$\dot{\omega} = \omega\kappa\left[(1 - \kappa_p)\beta_w\left(\frac{y}{xl} - \bar{e}\right) + (\kappa_w - 1)\beta_p\left(\frac{y}{y^p} - \bar{u}\right)\right],$$

$$\dot{l} = l\left[-i_q(q - 1) - i_u\left(\frac{y}{y^p} - \bar{u}\right)\right].$$

---

18 This would correspond to a strong Keynes effect in the corresponding working model of Chiarella and Flaschel (2000a, ch. 6).

Proposition 6   The steady state of the dynamical system (10.91) is locally asymptotically stable if the conditions in Proposition 5 are met and β_w is sufficiently small.

We enlarge the system further by letting β_n become positive to obtain

$$\dot{m}=m\left(\mu-\left(\kappa\left[\beta_p\left(\frac{y}{y^p}-\bar{u}\right)+\kappa_p\beta_w\left(\frac{y}{xl}-\bar{e}\right)\right]+\pi^c+i(\cdot)\right)\right),$$

$$\dot{b}=g-t_c-\tau_w\omega\frac{y}{x}-\mu m-b\left(\kappa\left[\beta_p\left(\frac{y}{y^p}-\bar{u}\right)+\kappa_p\beta_w\left(\frac{y}{xl}-\bar{e}\right)\right]+\pi^c+i(\cdot)\right),$$

$$\dot{y}^e=\beta_{y^e}\left[c+i(\cdot)+\delta+g-y^e\right]+y^e(i(\cdot)-n),\qquad\qquad(10.92)$$

$$\dot{\omega}=\omega\kappa\left[\left(1-\kappa_p\right)\beta_w\left(\frac{y}{xl}-\bar{e}\right)+\left(\kappa_w-1\right)\beta_p\left(\frac{y}{y^p}-\bar{u}\right)\right],$$

$$\dot{l}=l\left[-i_q(q-1)-i_u\left(\frac{y}{y^p}-\bar{u}\right)\right],$$

$$\dot{v}=y-(c+i(\cdot)+\delta+g)-vi(\cdot).$$

Proposition 7   The steady state of the dynamical system (10.92) is locally asymptotically stable if the conditions in Proposition 6 are met and β_n is sufficiently small.

Finally, we let β_{π^c} become positive so that we then are back to the full differential equation system

$$\dot{m}=m\mu-m(\kappa[\beta_p(u-\bar{u})+\kappa_p\beta_w(e-\bar{e})]+\pi^c+i(\cdot)),$$

$$\dot{b}=g-t_c-\tau_w\omega l^d-\mu m-b\left(\kappa[\beta_p(u-\bar{u})+\kappa_p\beta_w(e-\bar{e})]+\pi^c+i(\cdot)\right),$$

$$\dot{y}^e=\beta_{y^e}(y^d-y^e)+(i(\cdot)-n)y^e,$$

$$\dot{\omega}=\omega\kappa[(1-\kappa_p)\beta_w(e-\bar{e})+(\kappa_w-1)\beta_p(u-\bar{u})],\qquad\qquad(10.93)$$

$$\hat{l}=n-i(\cdot)=-i_q(q-1)-i_u(u-\bar{u}),$$

$$\dot{v}=y-y^d-i(\cdot)v,$$

$$\dot{\pi}^c=\alpha\beta_{\pi^c}\kappa[\beta_p(u-\bar{u})+\kappa_p\beta_w(e-\bar{e})]+(1-\alpha)\beta_{\pi^c}(\mu-n-\pi^c).$$

Note, however, that we are still neglecting the integral equation (10.65) and thus the dynamics of capital gains expectations.

Proposition 8   The steady state of the dynamic system (10.93) is locally asymptotically stable if the conditions in Proposition 7 are met and β_{π^c} is sufficiently small.

In sum, we thus have (for given capital gains expectations) that fast sales expectations coupled with sluggish adjustments of wages, prices, inventories and inflationary expectations gives rise to local asymptotic stability if it is furthermore assumed that the investment accelerator term is weak and the real balance effect in the investment equation (transmitted via Tobin's q) is sufficiently strong. We conjecture that slow adjustment of capital gains expectations will also preserve the stability of the interior steady state solution of the then fully interacting dynamical system.

10.6 The quantitative study of persistent business fluctuations

We have already described situations where the steady state of the dynamics can be expected to be attracting (see also the mathematical appendix). Such local stability can be proved despite the high dimensional nature of the considered KMG portfolio dynamics, as shown in Köper (2003) and – for somewhat different parameter constellations – in the appendix to this chapter, namely, if the wage–price spiral is operating in a sufficiently sluggish way (i.e. the parameters β_p, β_w, β_{π^c} are chosen sufficiently small), if the Metzlerian inventory adjustment process is sufficiently slow (the parameter β_n is sufficiently small), but the dynamic multiplier parameter β_{y^e} sufficiently large, if the Harrodian capacity effect, as measured by the parameter i_u, is weak and if money demand is responding to interest rate changes and the rate of return on equities in a way that is also sufficiently weak.

We expect that the aforementioned proposition also holds when capital gain expectations of chartists and fundamentalists are made endogenous and that in particular, loss of stability can be obtained by increasing the adjustment speed of the backward looking part of the expectations mechanism of the two groups of economic agents that we have assumed to exist on the financial markets. Due to the technical difficulties of treating analytically the 9D integro-differential system that represents the full dynamics of the present chapter we do not go into a proof of this assertion here as far as chartist expectation formation is concerned.

The stability result is intuitively very appealing in view of what we already know about Keynesian feedback structures and from what has been discussed in the preceding Sections and other chapters of the book, since it basically states that the wage-spiral must be fairly damped, the Keynesian dynamic multiplier be stable and not too much distorted by the emergence of Metzlerian inventory cycles, and if the Harrodian knife-edge growth accelerator is weak and capital gains expectations and money demand fairly unresponsive to rate of return changes on financial assets (that is money demand is not close to a liquidity trap). Such assumptions represent indeed fairly natural conditions from a Keynesian perspective.

Proposition 9 The steady state of the dynamic system (10.93) always loses its stability by way of a Hopf bifurcation. Such Hopf bifurcations, in particular, are likely to occur if the parameters we have assumed in the preceding Section as being sufficiently small are made sufficiently large.

Proof The proof basically rests on the fact that the determinant of the Jacobian of steady state of the dynamic system (10.93) is always negative, see the proof of Proposition 8, so that eigenvalues have to cross the imaginary axis (excluding zero) when stability gets lost. With respect to the actual loss of stability one has to study, however, the minors of order 1, 2 and more of the Jacobian of the dynamics at the steady state or use numerical methods (such as eigenvalue diagrams, see below) in order to get the result that significant flexibilities in the wage–price spiral or in the financial markets (including high money demand elasticities) will indeed lead to loss of stability by way of persistent or explosive business fluctuations. ∎

Note that as far as the generation of persistent business cycles is concerned, there are further conditions involved to show the existence of supercritical (or subcritical) Hopf bifurcations. There is first the positive speed condition when eigenvalues cross the imaginary axes and secondly the condition that the Liapunov coefficient of the system must be nonzero. Both conditions are, however, purely technical in nature and will nearly always hold in a system with nonlinear functional relationships such as they are present in the dynamical system that we consider. Moreover, as numerical simulations have shown, the range where such local Hopf-bifurcation matter is a very limited one. This implies the need for global changes (regime switches) in behavior if the economy is locally explosive and departs too much from its steady state. There is indeed at least one important example for such a behavioral switch that in many situations (as far as the real markets are concerned) is sufficient to restrict the trajectories of the dynamics to an economically meaningful domain of their whole phase space. This nonlinearity concerns the fact, already observed by Keynes (1936), see here also Ch.2, that money wages may be flexible in an upward direction, but are rigid (or at least considerably less flexible) into the downward direction.

Let us finally assert without proof that the normal or adverse Rose effect of changing real wages leading to changing aggregate demand and thereby to further changes in money wages, the price level and the real wage, see Chiarella and Flaschel (2000a) and Chiarella, Flaschel, Groh and Semmler (2000) in the case of the baseline KMG model, will also be present in the currently considered KMGT dynamics, with their portfolio description of asset market behavior. Either wage or price flexibility will, through their effects on the expected rate of profit and from there on asset markets, be destabilizing and lead to Hopf-bifurcations, limit cycles or (locally) purely explosive behavior eventually. The Mundell or real rate of interest effect is not so obviously present in the considered dynamics as there is no longer a real rate of interest involved in investment (or consumption) behavior. Increasing expected price inflation does not directly increase aggregate demand, economic activity and thus the actual rate of price inflation. This surely implies that the model needs to be extended in order to take account of the role that is generally played by the real rate of interest in macrodynamic models. There are finally two accelerator effects involved in the dynamics, the Metzlerian inventory accelerator mechanism and the Harrodian fixed business investment accelerator.

We therefore expect that increasing the parameters β_n and i_u will also be destabilizing and also lead to Hopf bifurcations and other complex dynamic behavior.

We finally provide some numerical examples, concerning damped oscillations, loss of stability via Hopf-bifurcation, the generation of limit cycles as business fluctuations from the global perspective by the addition of downward money wage rigidity to the money wage Phillips curve and finally – through this kinked wage Phillips curve – the generation of complex dynamics if increases in certain adjustment speeds make the steady state strongly repelling. We refer the reader to Chiarella, Flaschel, Proaño and Semmler (2009) for more detailed numerical studies of the implications of kinked money wage Phillips curves.

The simulations in the top-left of Figure 10.4 show damped oscillations when the parameter choices of our stability propositions are applied. The other three figures show eigenvalue diagrams that plot the maximum real part of eigenvalues against crucial parameters of the dynamical system under consideration namely β_{π^c}, $\beta_{\pi_{ec}}$ and β_p. These show the expected results that increasing speeds of adjustments in the movements of the inflationary climate and the capital gain expectations of chartists will be destabilizing, while price flexibility is stabilizing (and correspondingly: wage flexibility is destabilizing, but tamed in the Figure 10.5

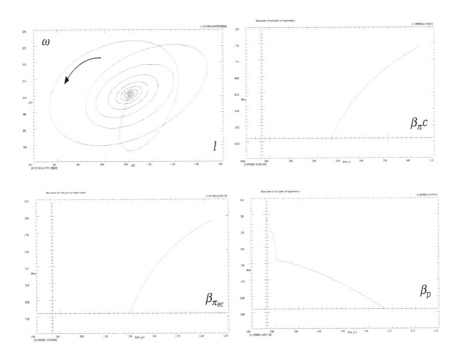

Figure 10.4 Damped oscillations (top left) and the loss of local stability via Hopf-bifurcations with respect to β_{π^c}, $\beta_{\pi_{ec}}$ and β_p.

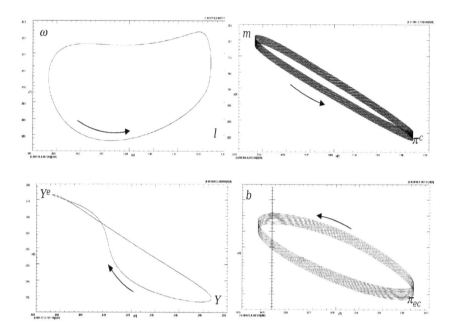

Figure 10.5 Kinked money wage PC's and the generation of persistent business fluctuations.

through the exclusion of wage deflation). However, the graphs in Figure 10.5 top- and bottom-right show that there is a weak, but persistent negative trend in real balances per unit of capital and thus on an average a persistent dominance of inflation over real and money growth. We conjecture that this is caused by the asymmetry in the wage Phillips curve the existence of which affects nominal inflation, but not the real cycle (shown in two projections on the left hand side of Figure 10.5).

Figure 10.6 exemplifies that the KMGT system can generate complex dynamics if the destabilizing feedback channels (here the degree of wage flexibility or a fast adjustment of chartists' expectations) make the steady state strongly repelling. Here, as well as in many other simulations that were performed for various types of models of KMG growth, the kinked wage Phillips curve with its downwardly rigid money wage assumption appears to be a powerful tool that stops the explosiveness existing around the steady state and thus turns the economy in a viable one, exhibiting bounded fluctuations even over very long time horizons.

Yet, here too, there is a weak tendency towards excessive inflation as a downward trend in real money balance per unit of capital as shown in the phase plots in the middle of Figure 10.6 and in the time series presentations of the variable m bottom-right. These time series representations also show that there is decreasing volatility (damped oscillations as time evolves and thus a tendency

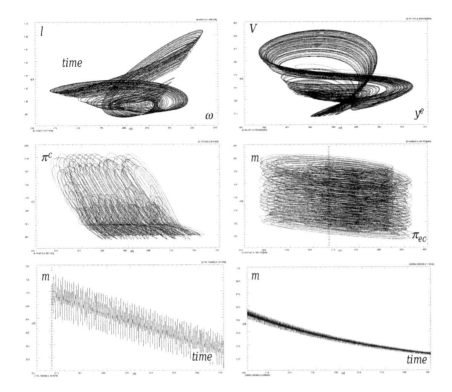

Figure 10.6 Complex real attractors and asymmetric inflation dynamics.

to converge towards an inflationary trend term in the very long-run (from the mathematical perspective = 60,000, years in the plot shown bottom-right).

In Figure 10.7, finally, we show an example of a period (cycle) doubling route to complex dynamics (but not chaos) from the economic point of view, since the cycles that are generated are fairly similar to each other. We increase the speed of adjustment of money wages from $\beta_w = 1.4$ to $\beta_w = 2.0$ and from there to $\beta_w = 2.82$ and then to $\beta_w = 3.0$. The first thing to note is that the dynamics remain viable over such a broad range of adjustment speeds for money wages, due to the kink in the money wage Phillips curve and despite a strong local instability around the steady state described above. To the right of the shown attractors, the trajectories are of a fairly smooth type, yet, top left they are going through some turbulence which makes the attractor more and more complex with the increasing adjustment speed of money wages.

We do not go into the details of such simulations any further here, but only present them as evidence that the considered model type is capable of producing various dynamic outcomes and is thus a very open one with respect to possible implications (and thus needs empirical estimation of its parameter values in order to get more specific results). The reader is again referred to Chiarella, Flaschel,

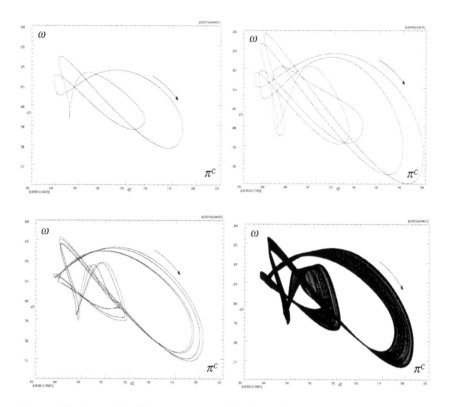

Figure 10.7 A period doubling route to complex dynamics.

Proaño and Semmler (2009) for detailed numerical studies of the KMGT approach of this chapter.

10.7 Outlook

We have reached a stage in the development of the Keynes-Metzler-Goodwin approach to monetary macrodynamics that exhibits a balanced representation of the real as well as the financial markets. Explicit portfolio considerations are normally bypassed in the literature on monetary macrodynamics which uses simple rate of return parity conditions instead or which even ignores these conditions, by reducing everything to a simple LM curve or (in its inverted format) to a Taylor interest rate policy rule as the only representation of the return structure of financial assets (as we have discussed in various chapters of the book). Such a Taylor rule, if it replaces the LM curve by making money supply endogenously adjusting to money demand, now has to work it effect through the assumed portfolio structure (the effects on Tobin's q) and thus no longer impacts on aggregate demand and the goods market directly.

This situation becomes even more difficult (see Chiarella, Flaschel, Proaño and Semmler (2009) for details), if there are two risk-bearing financial assets (equities and long-term bonds) and if the working of the Taylor rule is buried within an $M3$ representation of the money supply (including saving deposits) which is adjusting to the corresponding money demand, while the rate of interest only influences the composition of $M3$, that is only acting within the $M3$ structure through the cash management actions of asset holding households. In the worst case, this can mean that short-term interest rate manipulations of the Central Bank do not reach the essential portfolio decisions of asset holding households at all and thus totally lose their influence on the real sector of the economy. Chiarella, Flaschel, Proaño and Semmler (2009) study details of such a situation, by extending this equity and corporate bonds approach even further, in particular, by allowing that part of the investment projects of firms be financed through credit by commercial banks among others.

The foregoing discussion indicates the route along which the KMG approach to monetary macrodynamics has to be developed further. The KMG model as such is already a significant step forward from the perspective of the DAS–(D)AD models we have primarily discussed in this book as the matured Keynesian monetary macrodynamics equivalent to the New Keynesian equilibrium approach to such macrodynamics. In this book, we wanted to stay by and large in a one to one relationship to the New Keynesian approach with its staggered wage and price setting rules, as the alternative to our wage–price spiral mechanism (the DAS part of our models). In place of the New Keynesian consumption-driven IS curve, we used a traditional AD relationship or later on an empirically motivated disequilibrium version of it (the DAD) part of the model. The theoretical KMG approach of the present chapter differs from the DAD approach in that it allows for consistently formulated disequilibrium dynamics on the market for goods (relating disappointed sales expectations to involuntary inventory changes in a Metzlerian way). In addition, the theory of aggregate demand was made dependent on real interest as well as the real wage, the latter via consumption and investment behavior.

This final chapter has not only provided ways to progress to such a situation, but also made the model much more advanced in its treatment of the markets for financial assets. There is, however, another important extension that has been completely bypassed in the structural model of this chapter and concerns the consideration of open economies.

In an open economy, the portfolio approach of the present chapter in fact needs significant modification in order to allow a discussion of international trade in financial assets and the implications this has for the balance of payments. The balance of payments gives a flow representation of the external relationships of an economy. It therefore shows in its capital account the flow of asset trade between the domestic economy and the rest of the world. Tobin's portfolio (stock) approach must therefore be reformulated in terms of flows in order to allow for the investigation of international trade in financial assets.

A possible way to do this is to assume that there are stock disequilibria at each moment in time (since desired stocks depart from the actually given ones) and that these stock disequilibria lead only to partial adjustment processes whereby these stock disequilibria are reduced in time with a certain speed. These processes lead to a flow demand and supply structure which can be brought into equilibrium by infinitely fast adjustment of asset prices or somewhat sluggishly adjusting asset prices, depending on the extent of these disequilibria.

The end result of such a reformulation of Tobin's portfolio approach is that we would now have a full disequilibrium approach to real as well as financial markets, in striking contrast to the modeling philosophy of the applied Dynamic Stochastic General Equilibrium (DSGE) models that dominate monetary macrodynamics at the moment. Our general view here, however, is that Keynesian monetary macrodynamics puts the focus on the study of nonclearing markets (nearly a must in a continuous time approach) and thus should be carefully distinguished from those approaches that integrate Walrasian components into a Keynesian framework. The drastic consequences of the latter procedure were discussed with respect to conventional AS–AD analysis in Chapter 3.

This book therefore ends with the conclusion that imperfect adjustment processes and imperfect knowledge are basic ingredients of a descriptively oriented Keynesian monetary macrodynamics, a perspective where relatively little work has been done so far due to the methodological prevalence of microfounded rational expectations approaches, that depend on the assumption of macroeconomic equilibrium and that have dominated the literature on monetary macrodynamics for the last three decades.

References

Asada, T., C. Chiarella, P. Flaschel, and R. Franke (2003): *Open Economy Macrodynamics. An Integrated Disequilibrium Approach*. Springer, Heidelberg.

Chiarella, C., and P. Flaschel (1996): "An Integrative Approach to Prototype 2D-Macromodels of Growth, Price and Inventory Dynamics," *Chaos, Solitons & Fractals*, 7, 2105–2133.

——— (1998): "The Dynamics of 'Natural' Rates of Growth and Employment," *Macroeconomic Dynamics*, 2, 345–368.

——— (1999): "Keynesian monetary growth in open economies," *Annals of Operations Research*, 89, 35–59.

——— (2000a): *The Dynamics of Keynesian Monetary Growth. Macro Foundations*. Cambridge University Press, Cambridge, UK.

——— (2000b): "'High Order' Disequilibrium Growth Dynamics: Theoretical Aspects and Numerical Features," *Journal of Economic Dynamics and Control*, 24, 935–963.

Chiarella, C., P. Flaschel, C. Proaño and W. Semmler (2009): "Portfolio Choice, Asset Accumulation and the Business Cycle. Tobin's Legacy Continued," Bielefeld University: Book manuscript.

Chiarella, C., P. Flaschel, G. Groh, C. Köper, and W. Semmler (1999): "Towards Applied Disequilibrium Growth Theory: VI. Substitution, Money Holdings, Wealth-Effects and Further Extensions," School of Finance and Economics, The University of Technology, Sydney, Working paper No. 98.

Flaschel, P., R. Franke, and W. Semmler (1997): *Dynamic Macroeconomics: Instability, Fluctuations and Growth in Monetary Economies*. MIT Press, Cambridge, MA.

Franke, R. (1996): "A Metzlerian Model of Inventory Growth Cycles," *Structural Change and Economic Dynamics.*

Franke, R., and W. Semmler (1999): "Bond Rate, Loan Rate and Tobin's q in a Temporary Equilibrium Model of the Financial Sector," *Metroeconomica*, 50(3), 351–385.

Köper, C. (2003): *Real-Financial Interaction in Contemporary Models of AS–AD Growth.* Peter Lang, Bern.

Köper, C., and P. Flaschel (2000): "Real-Financial Interaction: A Keynes-Metzler-Goodwin Portfolio Approach," Discussion Paper of the Faculty of Economics, University of Bielefeld, No. 442.

Mas-Colell, A., M. D. Whinston, and J. R. Green (1995): *Microeconomic Theory.* Oxford Univ. Press, New York.

Metzler, L. A. (1941): "The Nature and Stability of Inventory Cycles," *Review of Economic Statistics*, 23, 113 – 129.

Rose, H. (1990): *Macroeconomic Dynamics: A Marshallian Synthesis.* Blackwell, Cambridge.

Sargent, T. J. (1987): *Macroeconomic Theory.* Academic Press, New York, 2nd edn.

Tobin, J. (1969): "A General Equilibrium Approach to Monetary Theory," *Journal of Money, Credit, and Banking*, 1, 15–29.

Appendix: Propositions 4–9 (alternative formulations and proofs)

Proposition 4A The steady state of the system of differential equations (10.89) is locally asymptotically stable if the investment adjustment speeds with respect to Tobin's q and the deviations from the capital utilization from the normal capital utilization (i_q and i_u) are sufficiently small, the absolute value of the partial derivative of desired cash balances with respect to the interest rate $|\partial f_m/\partial i|$ is sufficiently small, $0 \leq \tau_w < s_c < 1$, and $r_k^e > 0$ at the steady state.

Proof of Proposition 4A Let us assume that $\beta_p = \beta_w = \beta_{\pi_{ef}} = \beta_{\pi_{ec}} = \beta_n = \beta_{\pi^c} = 0$, $\beta_{y^e} > 0$, and $(\pi^c, \pi_e, \omega, \nu)$ are kept at their steady state values $(\pi^{c0}, \pi_e^0, \omega^0, \nu^0)$. Then, we have the following system of differential equations.

$$\dot{m} = m\{\mu - (\pi^{c0} + i(\cdot)\} \tag{A1}$$

$$\dot{b} = g - t_c - \tau_w \omega^0 \frac{y}{x} - \mu m - b\{\pi^{c0} + i(\cdot)\} \tag{A2}$$

$$\dot{y}^e = \beta_{y^e}[c + i(\cdot) + \delta + g - y^e] + y^e\{i(\cdot) - n\} \tag{A3}$$

where the following relationships are satisfied.

$$i(\cdot) = i_q(q - 1) + i_u(u - \bar{u}) + n = i_q(q - 1) + i_u\left(\frac{y}{y^p} - \bar{u}\right) + n \tag{A4}$$

$$q = q(\underset{+}{r_k^e}, \underset{+}{\pi_e^0}, \underset{+}{m}, b); \quad q_b = \frac{\partial q}{\partial b} < 0 \tag{A5}$$

if $\left|\dfrac{\partial f_m}{\partial i}\right|$ is sufficiently small (cf. equations (10.81) and (10.86)).

$$y = (1 + \alpha_{nd} n) y^e \qquad (A6)$$

$$r_k^e = y^e - \delta - \omega^0 l^d = y^e - \delta - \omega^0 \frac{y}{x} = y^e - \delta - \omega^0 (1 + \alpha_{nd} n) \frac{1}{x} y^e$$

$$= r_k^e(y^e); \quad r_{y^e}^e = \frac{dr_k^e}{dy^e} = 1 - \omega^0 (1 + \alpha_{nd} n) \frac{1}{x} > 0 \qquad (A7)$$

if $r_k^e > 0$ at the steady state.

$$c = (1 - \tau_w) \omega^0 l^d + (1 - s_c)(y^e - \delta - \omega^0 l^d - t_c)$$

$$= (1 - \tau_w) \omega^0 \frac{y}{x} + (1 - s_c)(y^e - \delta - \omega^0 \frac{y}{x} - t_c)$$

$$= (1 - \tau_w) \omega^0 (1 + \alpha_{nd} n) \frac{1}{x} y^e + (1 - s_c) \times$$

$$\{y^e - \delta - \omega^0 (1 + \alpha_{nd} n) \frac{1}{x} y^e - t_c\} = c(y^e);$$

$$c_{y^e} = \frac{dc}{dy^e} = (1 - s_c) + (s_c - \tau_w) \omega^0 (1 + \alpha_{nd} n) \frac{1}{x}$$

$$= 1 - \tau_w \omega^0 (1 + \alpha_{nd} n) \frac{1}{x} - s_c \{1 - \omega^0 (1 + \alpha_{nd} n) \frac{1}{x}\} \qquad (A8)$$

We have $0 < c_{y^e} < 1$ if $0 \leqq \tau_w < s_c < 1$ and $r_k^e > 0$ at the steady state. Substituting Eq. (A7) into Eq. (A5), we have

$$q = q(y^e, m, b); \quad q_{y^e} = \frac{\partial q}{\partial y^e} > 0, \quad q_m = \frac{\partial q}{\partial m} > 0, \quad q_b < 0. \qquad (A9)$$

Substituting equations (A5) and (A9) into Eq. (A4), we obtain

$$i(\cdot) = i_q \{q(y^e, m, b) - 1\} + i_u \{(1 + \alpha_{nd} n) \frac{1}{y^p} y^e - \bar{u}\} + n$$

$$= i(m, b, y^e); \quad i_m = \frac{\partial i}{\partial m} = i_q q_m > 0, \quad i_b = \frac{\partial i}{\partial b} = i_q q_b < 0,$$

$$i_{y^e} = \frac{\partial i}{\partial y^e} = i_q q_{y^e} + i_u (1 + \alpha_{nd} n) \frac{1}{y^p} > 0. \qquad (A10)$$

Substituting equations (A6), (A7) and (A10) into equations (A1)–(A3), we obtain the following complete three dimensional system of differential equations.

(i) $\dot{m} = m\{\mu - \pi^{c0} - i(m,b,y^e)\} = f_1(m,b,y^e)$

(ii) $\dot{b} = g - t_c - \tau_w \omega^0 (1 + \alpha_{nd} n)\dfrac{1}{x} y^e - \mu m - b\{\pi^{c0} + i(m,b,y^e)\} = f_2(m,b,y^e)$

(iii) $\dot{y}^e = \beta_{y^e}[c(y^e) + i(m,b,y^e) + \delta + g - y^e] + y^e\{i(m,b,y^e) - n\} = f_3(m.b,y^e)$

$$\hspace{10cm}\text{(A11)}$$

We assume that at the equilibrium point $(m^0, b^0, y^{e0}) > (0,0,0)$. The Jacobian matrix *at that equilibrium point* becomes as follows.

$$
J_3 = \begin{bmatrix}
f_{11} & f_{12} & f_{13} \\
f_{21} & f_{22} & f_{23} \\
f_{31} & f_{32} & f_{33}
\end{bmatrix}
\tag{A12}
$$

where $f_{11} = \underset{+}{-m^0 i_m} < 0, \quad f_{12} = \underset{-}{-m^0 i_b} > 0, \quad f_{13} = \underset{+}{-m^0 i_{y^e}} < 0, \quad f_{21} = -\mu -$

$\underset{+}{b^0 i_m} < 0, \quad f_{22} = -(\pi^{c0} + n) - b^0 i_b < 0$ if i_q is sufficiently small,

$f_{23} = -\tau_w \omega^0 (1 + \alpha_{nd} n)\dfrac{1}{x} - \underset{-}{b^0 i_{y^e}} < 0, \quad f_{31} = \underset{+}{\beta_{y^e} i_m} > 0, \quad f_{32} = \underset{-}{\beta_{y^e} i_b} < 0,$

and $f_{33} = \beta_{y^e}\{\underset{+}{-(1 - c_{y^e})} + \underset{+}{i_{y^e}}\} < 0$ if i_q and i_u are sufficiently small.

The characteristic equation of this system *at the equilibrium point* becomes as follows.

$$
\Delta_3(\lambda) = |\lambda I - J_3| = \lambda^3 + a_1\lambda^2 + a_2\lambda + a_3 = 0
\tag{A13}
$$

where

$$
a_1 = -\text{trace } J_3 = \underset{-}{-f_{11}} \underset{-}{-f_{22}} \underset{-}{-f_{33}} > 0,
\tag{A14}
$$

$a_2 = $ sum of all principal second-order minors of J_3

$$
= \begin{vmatrix} f_{22} & f_{23} \\ f_{32} & f_{33} \end{vmatrix} + \begin{vmatrix} f_{11} & f_{13} \\ f_{31} & f_{33} \end{vmatrix} + \begin{vmatrix} f_{11} & f_{12} \\ f_{21} & f_{22} \end{vmatrix},
\tag{A15}
$$

$$
\lim_{i_q \to 0} a_2 = \begin{vmatrix} f_{22} & f_{23} \\ 0 & f_{33} \end{vmatrix} + \begin{vmatrix} 0 & f_{13} \\ 0 & f_{33} \end{vmatrix} + \begin{vmatrix} 0 & 0 \\ -\mu & f_{22} \end{vmatrix} = \underset{-}{f_{22}}\,\underset{-}{f_{33}} > 0
\tag{A16}
$$

since $\lim_{i_q \to 0} i_m = \lim_{i_q \to 0} i_b = 0$, and

$$a_3 = -\det J_3 = - \begin{vmatrix} f_{11} & f_{12} & f_{13} \\ f_{21} & f_{22} & f_{23} \\ f_{31} & f_{32} & f_{33} \end{vmatrix}$$

$$= \underset{-\ \ -\ \ -}{-f_{11}f_{22}f_{33}} \underset{+\ \ -\ \ +}{-f_{12}f_{23}f_{31}} \underset{-\ \ -\ \ -}{-f_{13}f_{32}f_{21}} + \underset{-\ \ -\ \ +}{f_{13}f_{22}f_{31}} + \underset{+\ \ -\ \ -}{f_{12}f_{21}f_{33}}$$

$$\underset{-\ \ -\ \ -}{+f_{11}f_{32}f_{23}}$$

$$= \underset{-\ \ -\ \ -}{-f_{11}f_{22}f_{33}} \underset{-\ \ -\ \ -}{-f_{13}f_{32}f_{21}} + \underset{-\ \ -\ \ +}{f_{13}f_{22}f_{31}} + \underset{+\ \ -\ \ -}{f_{12}f_{21}f_{33}} > 0 \qquad \text{(A17)}$$

for all positive values of i_q because we have

$$-f_{12}f_{23}f_{31} + f_{11}f_{32}f_{23} = f_{23}(-f_{12}f_{31} + f_{11}f_{32}) = 0. \qquad \text{(A18)}$$

Furthermore, from the fact that $\lim_{i_q \to 0} f_{11} = \lim_{i_q \to 0} f_{12} = \lim_{i_q \to 0} f_{31} = \lim_{i_q \to 0} f_{32} = 0$ and Eq. (A17), we have $\lim_{i_q \to 0} a_3 = 0$. Therefore, we obtain

$$\lim_{i_q \to 0}(a_1 a_2 - a_3) = \lim_{i_q \to 0}(a_1 a_2) = \underset{-}{(-f_{22}} \underset{-}{-f_{33})} \underset{-\ \ -}{f_{22}f_{33}} > 0. \qquad \text{(A19)}$$

A set of inequalities (A14), (A17), and (A19) means that all of the Routh-Hurwitz conditions for local asymptotic stability of the equilibrium point of the system (A11) ($a_1 > 0, a_3 > 0, a_1 a_2 - a_3 > 0$) are in fact satisfied if the conditions in **Proposition 4A** are met.

Proposition 5A   The interior steady state of dynamic system (10.90) is locally asymptotically stable if the conditions in Proposition 4A are met and β_p is sufficiently small.

Proof of Proposition 5A   Let us assume that $\beta_{y^e} > 0$, $\beta_p > 0$, $\beta_w = \beta_{\pi_{ef}} = \beta_{\pi_{ec}} = \beta_n = \beta_{\pi^c} = 0$, and (π^c, π_e, ν) are kept at their steady state values $(\pi^{c0}, \pi_e^0, \nu^0)$. Then, we have the following four dimensional system of differential equations.

(i) $\dot{m} = m\left[\mu - \kappa\beta_p \left(\dfrac{y(y^e)}{y^p} - \bar{u} \right) - \pi^{c0} - i(m.b, y^e, \omega) \right] = f_1(m, b, y^e, \omega)$

(ii) $\dot{b} = g - t_c - \tau_w \omega \dfrac{y(y^e)}{x} - \mu m - b\left\{ \kappa\beta_p \left(\dfrac{y(y^e)}{y^p} - \bar{u} \right) + \pi^{c0} + i(m, b, y^e, \omega) \right\}$

$= f_2(m, b, y^e, \omega)$

(iii) $\dot{y}^e = \beta_{y^e}[c(y^e,\omega)+i(m,b,y^e,\omega)+\delta+g-y^e]+y^e\{i(m,b,y^e,\omega)-n\}$

$\qquad = f_3(m,b,y^e,\omega)$

(iv) $\dot{\omega}=\omega\kappa(\kappa_w-1)\beta_p\left(\dfrac{y(y^e)}{y^p}-\bar{u}\right)=f_4(y^e,\omega)$ (A21)

where

$$y=y(y^e)=(1+\alpha_{nd}n)y^e; \quad y_{y^e}=\frac{dy}{dy^e}=1+\alpha_{nd}n>1,$$ (A22)

$$c=c(y^e,\omega); \quad 0<c_{y^e}=\frac{\partial c}{\partial y^e}<1, \quad c_\omega=\frac{\partial c}{\partial\omega}=(s_c-\tau_w)(1+\alpha_{nd}n)\frac{1}{x}y^e>0$$ (A23)

if $0\leq\tau_w<s_c<1$ and $r_k^e>0$ at the steady state, and

$$i=i(m,b,y^e,\omega); \quad i_m=\frac{\partial i}{\partial m}=i_q\,q_m\underset{+\ +}{>}0, \quad i_b=\frac{\partial i}{\partial b}=i_q\,q_b\underset{+\ -}{<}0,$$

$$i_{y^e}=\frac{\partial i}{\partial y^e}=i_q\,q_{y^e}+i_u(1+\alpha_{nd}n)\frac{1}{y_p}\underset{+\ +\quad +}{>}0, \quad i_\omega=\frac{\partial i}{\partial\omega}=i_q\,q_{r_k^e}\,r_\omega^e\underset{+\ +\ -}{<}0. \quad \text{(A24)}$$

The Jacobian matrix of this system *at the equilibrium point* becomes as follows.

$$J_4(\beta_p)=\begin{bmatrix} f_{11} & f_{12} & f_{13}(\beta_p) & f_{14} \\ f_{21} & f_{22} & f_{23}(\beta_p) & f_{24} \\ f_{31} & f_{32} & f_{33} & f_{34} \\ 0 & 0 & f_{43}(\beta_p) & 0 \end{bmatrix}$$ (A25)

where

$f_{13}(\beta_p)=-m^0[\kappa\beta_p y_{y^e}/y^p+i_{y^e}]\underset{+\quad\ +}{<}0,\ f_{14}=-m^0 i_\omega\underset{-}{>}0,\ f_{23}(\beta_p)=-(\tau_w\omega^0\frac{1}{x}+$

$b^0\kappa\beta_p\frac{1}{y^p})y_{y^e}-b^0 i_{y^e}\underset{+\qquad\quad +}{<}0,\ f_{24}=-\tau_w\frac{y(y^{e0})}{x}-b^0 i_\omega,\ f_{34}=c_\omega+(\beta_{y^e}+y^{e0})i_\omega,$

$\underset{-}{\qquad\qquad\qquad\qquad\qquad\qquad\qquad\qquad\qquad\qquad\ +}$

$f_{43}(\beta_p)=\omega^0\kappa(\kappa_p-1)\beta_p y_{y^e}/y^p\underset{-\qquad\quad +}{<}0$, and other elements of this matrix are the

same as those of the matrix J_3 in Eq. (A12).

Now, let us consider the following characteristic equation.

$$\Delta_4(\lambda;\beta_p)=|\lambda I-J_4(\beta_p)|=0$$ (A26)

Then, we obtain the following result.

$$\det J_4(\beta_p) = \prod_{j=1}^{4} \lambda_j = -f_{43}(\beta_p) \begin{vmatrix} f_{11} & f_{12} & f_{14} \\ f_{21} & f_{22} & f_{24} \\ f_{31} & f_{32} & f_{34} \end{vmatrix}$$

$$= -f_{43}(\beta_p)\,(f_{11}\,f_{22}\,f_{34} + f_{12}\,f_{24}\,f_{31} + f_{14}\,f_{32}\,f_{21} - f_{14}\,f_{22}\,f_{31}$$

$$- f_{12}\,f_{21}\,f_{34} - f_{11}\,f_{32}\,f_{24})$$

$$= -f_{43}(\beta_p)(f_{11}\,f_{22}\,f_{34} + f_{14}\,f_{32}\,f_{21} - f_{14}\,f_{22}\,f_{31} - f_{12}\,f_{21}\,f_{34}) \qquad (A27)$$

because

$$f_{12}\,f_{24}\,f_{31} - f_{11}\,f_{32}\,f_{24} = f_{24}\,(f_{12}\,f_{31} - f_{11}\,f_{32}) = 0. \qquad (A28)$$

Furthermore, we have

$$f_{11}\,f_{22}\,f_{34} - f_{14}\,f_{22}\,f_{31} = f_{22}\,(f_{11}\,f_{34} - f_{14}\,f_{31}) = -f_{22}\,m^0\,i_m(c_\omega + y^{e0}\,i_\omega), \qquad (A29)$$

which is positive for all sufficient small values of $i_q > 0$ because $\lim_{i_q \to 0} i_\omega = 0$.

Therefore, we obtain from equations (A27) and (A29) the following result for all $\beta_p > 0$ as long as $i_q > 0$ is sufficiently small.

$$\det J_4(\beta_p) = \prod_{j=1}^{4} \lambda_j > 0 \qquad (A30)$$

On the other hand, it follows from equations (A13), (A25) and (A26) that

$$\Delta_4(\lambda; 0) = |\lambda I - J_4(0)| = |\lambda I - J_3|\lambda = \Delta_3(\lambda)\lambda = 0. \qquad (A31)$$

This means that the characteristic equation (A26) has a root $\lambda_4 = 0$ and other three roots are determined by Eq. (A13) in case of $\beta_p = 0$. All roots of Eq. (A13) have negative real parts if the conditions in **Proposition 4A** are met. This means, by continuity, that the characteristic equation (A26) has at least three roots with negative real parts even if $\beta_p > 0$, as long as β_p is sufficiently small. In this case, another root also becomes negative real root because of the inequality (A30). This completes the proof of **Proposition 5A**.

Proposition 6A   The steady state of the dynamic system (10.91) is locally asymptotically stable if the conditions in **Proposition 5A** are met, β_w is sufficiently small, and $0 < \kappa_p \leqq 1/2$.

Proof of Proposition 6A Let us assume that $\beta_{y^e} > 0$, $\beta_p > 0$, $\beta_w > 0$, $\beta_{\pi_{ef}} = \beta_{\pi_{ec}} = \beta_n = \beta_{\pi^c} = 0$, and (π^c, π_e, ν) are kept at their steady state values $(\pi^{c0}, \pi_e^0, \nu^0)$. Then, we have the following five dimensional system of differential equations.

(i) $\displaystyle \dot{m} = m\left[\mu - \kappa\left\{\beta_p\left(\frac{y(y^e)}{y^p} - \bar{u}\right) + \kappa_p\beta_w\left(\frac{y(y^e)}{xl} - \bar{e}\right)\right\} - \pi^{c0} - i(m,b,y^e,\omega)\right]$

$= f_1(m,b,y^e,\omega,l)$

(ii) $\displaystyle \dot{b} = g - t_c - \tau_w\omega\frac{y(y^e)}{x} - \mu m - b\left[\kappa\left\{\beta_p\left(\frac{y(y^e)}{y^p} - \bar{u}\right) + \kappa_p\beta_w\left(\frac{y(y^e)}{xl} - \bar{e}\right)\right\}\right.$

$\left. + \pi^{c0} + i(m,b,y^e,\omega)\right] = f_2(m,b,y^e,\omega,l)$

(iii) $\displaystyle \dot{y}^e = \beta_{y^e}[c(y^e,\omega) + i(m,b,y^e,\omega) + \delta + g - y^e] + y^e\{i(m,b,y^e,\omega) - n\}$

$= f_3(m,b,y^e,\omega)$

(iv) $\displaystyle \dot{\omega} = \omega\kappa\left[(1-\kappa_p)\beta_w\left(\frac{y(y^e)}{xl} - \bar{e}\right) + (\kappa_w - 1)\beta_p\left(\frac{y(y^e)}{y^p} - \bar{u}\right)\right] = f_4(y^e,\omega,l)$

(v) $\displaystyle \dot{l} = -l\left[i_q\left\{q(y^e,m,b,\omega) - 1\right\} + i_u\left\{\frac{y(y^e)}{y^p} - \bar{u}\right\}\right] = f_5(m,b,y^e,\omega,l)$ (A32)

where

$$q = q(y^e,m,b,\omega); \quad q_{y^e} = \frac{\partial q}{\partial y^e} > 0, \quad q_m = \frac{\partial q}{\partial m} > 0, \quad q_b = \frac{\partial q}{\partial b} < 0,$$

$$q_\omega = \frac{\partial q}{\partial \omega} < 0. \tag{10.94}$$

The Jacobian matrix of this system *at the equilibrium point* becomes as follows.

$$J_5(\beta_w,\beta_p) = \begin{bmatrix} f_{11} & f_{12} & f_{13}(\beta_w,\beta_p) & f_{14} & f_{15}(\beta_w) \\ f_{21} & f_{22} & f_{23}(\beta_w,\beta_p) & f_{24} & f_{25}(\beta_w) \\ f_{31} & f_{32} & f_{33} & f_{34} & 0 \\ 0 & 0 & f_{43}(\beta_w,\beta_p) & 0 & f_{45}(\beta_w) \\ f_{51} & f_{52} & f_{53} & f_{54} & 0 \end{bmatrix} \tag{A34}$$

where

$f_{13}(\beta_w,\beta_p) = m^0\left[\kappa\left\{\underset{+}{\kappa_p\beta_w\frac{1}{xl^0}} - \beta_p\frac{1}{y^p}\right\}y_{y^e} - \underset{+}{i_{y^e}}\right]$, $\quad f_{15}(\beta_w) = -m^0\kappa_p\beta_w\frac{y(y^{e0})}{xl^{02}}$

$< 0, \quad f_{23}(\beta_w,\beta_p) = -\left(\tau_w\omega^0\frac{1}{x} + b^0\kappa\beta_p\frac{1}{y^p} + b^0\kappa_p\beta_w\frac{1}{xl^0}\right)\underset{+}{y_{y^e}} - \underset{+}{b^0 i_{y^e}} < 0$,

$$f_{25}(\beta_w) = b^0 \kappa_p \beta_w \frac{y(y^{e0})}{xl^{02}} > 0, \ f_{43}(\beta_w, \beta_p) = \omega^0 \kappa \left[(1 - \kappa_p) \beta_w \frac{1}{xl^0} - (1 - \kappa_w) \beta_p \frac{1}{y^p} \right] y_{y^e},$$

$$f_{45}(\beta_w) = -\omega^0 \kappa (1 - \kappa_p) \beta_w \frac{y(y^{e0})}{xl^{02}} < 0, \quad f_{51} = -l^0 i_q q_m < 0, \quad f_{52} = -l^0 i_q q_b > 0,$$

$$f_{53} = -l^0 \left[i_q q_{y^e} + i_u \frac{1}{y^p} y_{y^e} \right] < 0, \quad f_{54} = -l^0 i_q q_\omega > 0, \text{ and other elements}$$

of this matrix are the same as those of the matrix $J_4(\beta_p)$ in Eq. (A25). Furthermore, we have $f_{13}(0, \beta_p) = f_{13}(\beta_p) < 0$, $f_{23}(0, \beta_p) = f_{23}(\beta_p) < 0$, and $f_{43}(0, \beta_p) = f_{43}(\beta_p) < 0$.

Now, let us consider the following characteristic equation.

$$\Delta_5(\lambda; \beta_w, \beta_p) = |\lambda I - J_5(\beta_w, \beta_p)| = 0 \tag{A35}$$

Then, we obtain the following result.

$$\det J_5(\beta_w, \beta_p) = \prod_{j=1}^{5} \lambda_j = -\beta_w \frac{y(y^{e0})}{xl^{02}} A(\beta_w, \beta_p) \tag{A36}$$

where

$$A(\beta_w, \beta_p) = \begin{vmatrix} f_{11} & f_{12} & f_{13}(\beta_w, \beta_p) & f_{14} & m^0 \kappa_p \\ f_{21} & f_{22} & f_{23}(\beta_w, \beta_p) & f_{24} & -b^0 \kappa_p \\ f_{31} & f_{32} & f_{33} & f_{34} & 0 \\ 0 & 0 & f_{43}(\beta_w, \beta_p) & 0 & \omega^0 \kappa (1 - \kappa_p) \\ f_{51} & f_{52} & f_{53} & f_{54} & 0 \end{vmatrix}. \tag{A37}$$

Therefore, we have the following expressions.

$$A(0, \beta_p) = \begin{vmatrix} f_{11} & f_{12} & f_{13}(\beta_p) & f_{14} & m^0 \kappa_p \\ f_{21} & f_{22} & f_{23}(\beta_p) & f_{24} & -b^0 \kappa_p \\ f_{31} & f_{32} & f_{33} & f_{34} & 0 \\ 0 & 0 & f_{43}(\beta_p) & 0 & \omega^0 \kappa (1 - \kappa_p) \\ f_{51} & f_{52} & f_{53} & f_{54} & 0 \end{vmatrix}$$

$$= -f_{43}(\beta_p) \kappa_p \begin{vmatrix} f_{11} & f_{12} & f_{14} & m^0 \\ f_{21} & f_{22} & f_{24} & -b^0 \\ f_{31} & f_{32} & f_{34} & 0 \\ f_{51} & f_{52} & f_{54} & 0 \end{vmatrix} - \omega^0 \kappa (1 - \kappa_p) \begin{vmatrix} f_{11} & f_{12} & f_{13}(\beta_p) & f_{14} \\ f_{21} & f_{22} & f_{23}(\beta_p) & f_{24} \\ f_{31} & f_{32} & f_{33} & f_{34} \\ f_{51} & f_{52} & f_{53} & f_{54} \end{vmatrix}$$

$$\tag{10.95}$$

$$A_{00}(0,\beta_p) = \lim_{i_q,i_u \to 0} A(0,\beta_p) = \underbrace{-f_{43}(\beta_p)\kappa_p}_{-} \begin{vmatrix} 0 & 0 & 0 & m^0 \\ -\mu & f_{22} & f_{24} & -b^0 \\ 0 & 0 & c_\omega & 0 \\ 0 & 0 & 0 & 0 \end{vmatrix}$$

$$-\omega^0\kappa(1-\kappa_p) \begin{vmatrix} 0 & 0 & f_{13}(\beta_p) & 0 \\ -\mu & f_{22} & f_{23}(\beta_p) & f_{24} \\ 0 & 0 & f_{33} & c_\omega \\ 0 & 0 & 0 & 0 \end{vmatrix} = 0 \qquad (A39)$$

$$\frac{\partial A_{00}(0,\beta_p)}{\partial i_q} = \underbrace{-f_{43}(\beta_p)\kappa_p}_{-} \left(\begin{vmatrix} f'_{11} & 0 & 0 & m^0 \\ f'_{21} & f_{22} & f_{24} & -b^0 \\ f'_{31} & 0 & c_\omega & 0 \\ f'_{51} & 0 & 0 & 0 \end{vmatrix} + \begin{vmatrix} 0 & f'_{12} & 0 & m^0 \\ -\mu & f'_{22} & f_{24} & -b^0 \\ 0 & f'_{32} & c_\omega & 0 \\ 0 & f'_{52} & 0 & 0 \end{vmatrix} \right.$$

$$+ \begin{vmatrix} 0 & 0 & f'_{14} & m^0 \\ -\mu & f_{22} & f'_{24} & -b^0 \\ 0 & 0 & f'_{34} & 0 \\ 0 & 0 & f'_{54} & 0 \end{vmatrix} \left. \right) - \omega^0\kappa(1-\kappa_p) \left(\begin{vmatrix} f'_{11} & 0 & f_{13}(\beta_p) & 0 \\ f'_{21} & f_{22} & f_{23}(\beta_p) & f_{24} \\ f'_{31} & 0 & f_{33} & c_\omega \\ f'_{51} & 0 & 0 & 0 \end{vmatrix} \right.$$

$$+ \begin{vmatrix} 0 & f'_{12} & f_{13}(\beta_p) & 0 \\ -\mu & f'_{22} & f_{23}(\beta_p) & f_{24} \\ 0 & f'_{32} & f_{33} & c_\omega \\ 0 & f'_{52} & 0 & 0 \end{vmatrix} + \begin{vmatrix} 0 & 0 & f'_{13} & 0 \\ -\mu & f_{22} & f'_{23} & f_{24} \\ 0 & 0 & f'_{33} & c_\omega \\ 0 & 0 & f'_{53} & 0 \end{vmatrix} + \begin{vmatrix} 0 & 0 & f_{13}(\beta_p) & f'_{14} \\ -\mu & f_{22} & f_{23}(\beta_p) & f'_{24} \\ 0 & 0 & f_{33} & f'_{34} \\ 0 & 0 & 0 & f'_{54} \end{vmatrix} \left. \right)$$

$$= \underbrace{-f_{43}(\beta_p)\kappa_p}_{-} \left(\underbrace{-f'_{51}}_{-} \begin{vmatrix} 0 & 0 & m^0 \\ f_{22} & f_{24} & -b^0 \\ 0 & c_\omega & 0 \end{vmatrix} + f'_{52} \begin{vmatrix} 0 & 0 & m^0 \\ -\mu & f_{24} & -b^0 \\ 0 & c_\omega & 0 \end{vmatrix} \right)$$

$$-\omega^0\kappa(1-\kappa_p) \left(\underbrace{-f'_{51}}_{-} \begin{vmatrix} 0 & f_{13}(\beta_p) & 0 \\ f_{22} & f_{23}(\beta_p) & f_{24} \\ 0 & f_{33} & c_\omega \end{vmatrix} + f'_{52} \begin{vmatrix} 0 & f_{13}(\beta_p) & 0 \\ -\mu & f_{23}(\beta_p) & f_{24} \\ 0 & f_{33} & c_\omega \end{vmatrix} \right)$$

$$= \underbrace{f_{43}(\beta_p)}_{-}\underbrace{\kappa_p}_{+}\underbrace{m^0}_{+}\underbrace{c_\omega}_{+}(\underbrace{f'_{51}}_{-}\underbrace{f_{22}}_{-}+\underbrace{f'_{52}}_{+}\underbrace{\mu}_{+}) - \underbrace{\omega^0}_{+}\underbrace{\kappa}_{+}(1-\kappa_p)\underbrace{f_{13}(\beta_p)}_{-}\underbrace{c_\omega}_{+}(\underbrace{f'_{51}}_{-}\underbrace{f_{22}}_{-}+\underbrace{f'_{52}}_{+}\underbrace{\mu}_{+})$$

$$= \underbrace{c_\omega}_{+}(\underbrace{f'_{51}}_{-}\underbrace{f_{22}}_{-}+\underbrace{f'_{52}}_{+}\underbrace{\mu}_{+})\{f_{43}(\beta_p)\kappa_p m^0 - \omega^0\kappa(1-\kappa_p)f_{13}(\beta_p)\}$$

$$= \underbrace{c_\omega}_{+}(\underbrace{f'_{51}}_{-}\underbrace{f_{22}}_{-}+\underbrace{f'_{52}}_{+}\underbrace{\mu}_{+})\omega^0 m^0\kappa\beta_p\frac{1}{y_p}\underbrace{y_{y^e}}_{+}\{(1-\kappa_p)\kappa-(1-\kappa_w)\} \qquad (A40)$$

where $f'_{ij} = \partial f_{ij}/\partial i_q$.

On the other hand, we have the following expression.

$$(1-\kappa_p)\kappa - (1-\kappa_w) = (1-\kappa_p)\frac{1}{1-\kappa_w\kappa_p} - (1-\kappa_w)$$

$$= \frac{1-2\kappa_p+\kappa_w\kappa_p\{1+\kappa_p(1-\kappa_w)\}}{1-\kappa_w\kappa_p}, \qquad (A41)$$

which is positive if $\kappa_p \leqq 1/2$. In this case, we have

$$\frac{\partial A_{00}(0,\beta_p)}{\partial i_q} > 0. \qquad (A42)$$

Incidentally, it is worth to note that the condition $\kappa_p \leqq 1/2$ is not a necessary condition but only a sufficient condition that the right hand side of Eq. (A41) becomes positive. In other words, it can be positive even if $1/2 < \kappa_p \leqq 1$.

Equations (A36) and (A39) together with the inequality (A42) implies that we have

$$\det J_5(\beta_w,\beta_p) = \prod_{j=1}^{5} \lambda_j < 0 \qquad (A43)$$

if $\beta_w > 0$, $i_q > 0$, and $i_u > 0$ are sufficiently small.

On the other hand, it follows from equations (A25), (A34), and (A35) that

$$\Delta_5(\lambda; 0, \beta_p) = |\lambda I - J_5(0,\beta_p)| = |\lambda I - J_4(\beta_p)| \lambda = 0. \qquad (A44)$$

This means that the characteristic equation (A35) has a root $\lambda_5 = 0$ and other four roots are determined by Eq. (A26) in case of $\beta_w = 0$. All roots of Eq. (A26) have negative real parts if the conditions in **Proposition 5A** are met. This means, by continuity, that the characteristic equation (A35) has at least four roots with negative real parts even if $\beta_w > 0$, as long as β_w is sufficiently small. In this case, another root also becomes negative real root because of the inequality (A43). This completes the proof of **Proposition 6A**.

Proposition 7A   The steady state of the dynamic system (10.92) is locally asymptotically stable if the conditions in **Proposition 6A** are met and β_n is sufficiently small.

Proof of Proposition 7A   Let us assume that $\beta_{y^e} > 0$, $\beta_p > 0$, $\beta_w > 0$, $\beta_n > 0$, $\beta_{\pi_{ef}} = \beta_{\pi_{ec}} = \beta_{\pi^c} = 0$, and (π^c, π_e) are kept at their steady state values (π^{c0}, π_e^0). Then, we have the following six dimensional system of differential equations.

(i) $\dot{m} = m\left[\mu - \kappa\left\{\beta_p\left(\dfrac{y(y^e, v)}{y^p} - \bar{u}\right) + \kappa_p\beta_w\left(\dfrac{y(y^e, v)}{xl} - \bar{e}\right)\right\} - \pi^{c0}\right.$

$\left. - i(m, b, y^e, \omega, v)\right] = f_1(m, b, y^e, \omega, l, v)$

(ii) $\dot{b} = g - t_c - \tau_w \omega\dfrac{y(y^e, v)}{x} - \mu m - b\left[\kappa\left\{\beta_p\left(\dfrac{y(y^e, v)}{y^p} - \bar{u}\right)\right.\right.$

$\left.\left. + \kappa_p\beta_w\left(\dfrac{y(y^e, v)}{xl} - \bar{e}\right)\right\} + \pi^{c0} + i(m, b, y^e, \omega, v)\right] = f_2(m, b, y^e, \omega, l, v)$

(iii) $\dot{y}^e = \beta_{y^e}[c(y^e, \omega, v) + i(m, b, y^e, \omega, v) + \delta + g - y^e]$

$\qquad + y^e\{i(m, b, y^e, \omega, v) - n\} = f_3(m, b, y^e, \omega, l, v)$

(iv) $\dot{\omega} = \omega\kappa\left[(1 - \kappa_p)\beta_w\left(\dfrac{y(y^e, v)}{xl} - \bar{e}\right) + (\kappa_w - 1)\beta_p\left(\dfrac{y(y^e, v)}{y^p} - \bar{u}\right)\right]$

$\qquad = f_4(y^e, \omega, l, v)$

(v) $\dot{l} = -l\left[i_q(q(y^e, m, b, \omega, v) - 1) + i_u\left(\dfrac{y(y^e, v)}{y^p} - \bar{u}\right)\right] = f_5(m, b, y^e, \omega, l, v)$

(vi) $\dot{v} = y(y^e, v) - \{c(y^e, \omega, v) + i(m, b, y^e, \omega, v) + \delta + g\} - vi(m, b, y^e, \omega, v)$

$\qquad = f_6(m, b, y^e, \omega, v)$ $\hfill$ (A45)

where

$$y = y(y^e, v) = \{1 + \alpha_{nd}(n + \beta_n)\}y^e - \beta_n v \,;\, y_{y^e} = \dfrac{\partial y}{\partial y^e} = 1 + \alpha_{nd}(n + \beta_n) > 1,$$

$$y_v = \dfrac{\partial y}{\partial v} = -\beta_n < 0. \hfill \text{(A46)}$$

The Jacobian matrix of this system *at the equilibrium point* becomes as follows.

$$J_6(\beta_n, \beta_w, \beta_p) = \begin{bmatrix} f_{11} & f_{12} & f_{13}(\beta_w, \beta_p) & f_{14} & f_{15}(\beta_w) & f_{16}(\beta_n, \beta_w, \beta_p) \\ f_{21} & f_{22} & f_{23}(\beta_w, \beta_p) & f_{24} & f_{25}(\beta_w) & f_{26}(\beta_n, \beta_w, \beta_p) \\ f_{31} & f_{32} & f_{33} & f_{34} & 0 & f_{36}(\beta_n) \\ 0 & 0 & f_{43}(\beta_w, \beta_p) & 0 & f_{45}(\beta_w) & f_{46}(\beta_n, \beta_w, \beta_p) \\ f_{51} & f_{52} & f_{53} & f_{54} & 0 & f_{56}(\beta_n) \\ f_{61} & f_{62} & f_{63} & f_{64} & 0 & f_{66}(\beta_n) \end{bmatrix}$$

$\hfill$ (A47)

where

$$f_{16}(0, \beta_w, \beta_p) = f_{26}(0, \beta_w, \beta_p) = f_{36}(0) = f_{46}(0, \beta_w, \beta_p) = f_{56}(0) = 0, \quad \text{(A48)}$$

$$f_{66}(0) = -n < 0. \hfill \text{(A49)}$$

Now, let us consider the following characteristic equation.

$$\Delta_6(\lambda; \beta_n, \beta_w, \beta_p) = |\lambda I - J_6(\beta_n, \beta_w, \beta_n)| = 0 \tag{A50}$$

It follows from equations (A34), (A47), (A48) and (A49) that

$$\Delta_6(\lambda; 0, \beta_w, \beta_p) = |\lambda I - J_5(\beta_w, \beta_p)|(\lambda + n) = 0. \tag{A51}$$

This means that the characteristic equation (A50) has a negative real root $\lambda_6 = -n$ and other five roots are determined by Eq. (A35) in case of $\beta_n = 0$. All roots of Eq. (A35) have negative real parts if the conditions in **Proposition 6A** are met. This means, by continuity, that all roots of the characteristic equation (A50) have negative real parts even if $\beta_n > 0$, as long as β_n is sufficiently small. This completes the proof of **Proposition 7A**.

Proposition 8A   The steady state of the dynamic system (10.93) is locally asymptotically stable if the conditions in **Proposition 7A** are met, $0 \le \alpha < 1$, and either of the following condition (1) or (2) is satisfied.

(1) β_{π^c} is positive, and α is sufficiently close to zero.
(2) β_{π^e} is positive, but it is sufficiently small, and κ_p is sufficiently small.

Proof of Proposition 8A   Let us assume that $\beta_{y^e} > 0$, $\beta_p > 0$, $\beta_w > 0$, $\beta_n > 0$, $\beta_{\pi^c} > 0$, $\beta_{\pi_{ef}} = \beta_{\pi_{ec}} = 0$, and π_e is kept at its steady state value π_e^0. Then, we have the following seven dimensional system of differential equation.

(i) $\dot{m} = m\left[\mu - \kappa\left\{\beta_p\left(\dfrac{y(y^e,v)}{y^p} - \bar{u}\right) + \kappa_p\beta_w\left(\dfrac{y(y^e,v)}{xl} - \bar{e}\right) - \pi^c\right.\right.$

$$\left.\left. - i(m,b,y^e,\omega,v)\right] = f_1(m,b,y^e,\omega,l,v,\pi^c)$$

(ii) $\dot{b} = g - t_c - \tau_w\omega\dfrac{y(y^e,v)}{x} - \mu m - b\left[\kappa\left\{\beta_p\left(\dfrac{y(y^e,v)}{y^p} - \bar{u}\right)\right.\right.$

$$\left.\left. + \kappa_p\beta_w\left(\dfrac{y(y^e,v)}{xl} - \bar{e}\right)\right\} + \pi^c + i(m,b,y^e,\omega,v)\right]$$

$$= f_2(m,b,y^e,\omega,l,v,\pi^c)$$

(iii) $\dot{y}^e = \beta_{y^e}[c(y^e,\omega,v) + i(m,b,y^e,\omega,v) + \delta + g - y^e]$

$$+ y^e\{i(m,b,y^e,\omega,v) - n\} = f_3(m,b,y^e,\omega,l,v)$$

(iv) $\dot{\omega} = \omega\kappa\left[(1 - \kappa_p)\beta_w\left(\dfrac{y(y^e,v)}{xl} - \bar{e}\right) + (\kappa_w - 1)\beta_p\left(\dfrac{y(y^e,v)}{y^p} - \bar{u}\right)\right]$

$$= f_4(y^e,\omega,l,v)$$

(v) $\dot{l} = -l\left[i_q(q(y^e, m, b, \omega, v) - 1) + i_u\left(\dfrac{y(y^e, v)}{y^e} - \bar{u}\right)\right]$

$\quad = f_5(m, b, y^e, \omega, l, v)$

(vi) $\dot{v} = y(y^e, v) - \{c(y^e, \omega, v) + i(m, b, y^e, \omega, v) + \delta + g\}$

$\quad - vi(m, b, y^e, \omega, v) = f_6(m, b, y^e, \omega, v)$

(vii) $\dot{\pi}^c = \beta_{\pi^c}\left[\alpha\kappa\left\{\beta_p\left(\dfrac{y(y^e, v)}{y^p} - \bar{u}\right) + \kappa_p\beta_w\left(\dfrac{y(y^e, v)}{xl} - \bar{e}\right)\right\}\right.$

$\quad\quad \left. + (1 - \alpha)(\mu - n - \pi^c)\right] = f_7(y^e, l, v, \pi^c)$ \hfill (A52)

where $0 \leq \alpha < 1$.

The Jacobian matrix of this system *at the equilibrium point* becomes as follows.

$J_7(\alpha, \beta_{\pi^c}, \beta_n, \beta_w, \beta_p) =$

$$
\begin{bmatrix}
f_{11} & f_{12} & f_{13}(\beta_w, \beta_p) & f_{14} & f_{15}(\beta_w) & f_{16}(\beta_n, \beta_w, \beta_p) & -m^0 \\
f_{21} & f_{22} & f_{23}(\beta_w, \beta_p) & f_{24} & f_{25}(\beta_w) & f_{26}(\beta_n, \beta_w, \beta_n) & -b^0 \\
f_{31} & f_{32} & f_{33} & f_{34} & 0 & f_{36}(\beta_n) & 0 \\
0 & 0 & f_{43}(\beta_w, \beta_p) & 0 & f_{45}(\beta_w) & f_{46}(\beta_n, \beta_w, \beta_p) & 0 \\
f_{51} & f_{52} & f_{53} & f_{54} & 0 & f_{56}(\beta_n) & 0 \\
f_{61} & f_{62} & f_{63} & f_{64} & 0 & f_{66}(\beta_n) & 0 \\
0 & 0 & f_{73}(\alpha, \beta_{\pi^c}, \beta_w, \beta_p) & 0 & f_{75}(\alpha, \beta_{\pi^c}, \beta_w) & f_{76}(\alpha, \beta_{\pi^c}, \beta_n, \beta_w, \beta_p) & -\beta_{\pi^c}(1-\alpha)
\end{bmatrix}
$$
\hfill (A53)

where

$$f_{73}(\alpha, \beta_{\pi^c}, \beta_w, \beta_p) = \beta_{\pi^c}\alpha\kappa\left(\beta_p\dfrac{1}{y^p} + \kappa_p\beta_w\dfrac{1}{xl^0}\right)y_{y^e} \leq 0,$$
\hfill (A54)

$$f_{75}(\alpha, \beta_{\pi^c}, \beta_w) = -\beta_{\pi^c}\alpha\kappa_p\beta_w\dfrac{y(y^{e0})}{xl^{02}} \leq 0,$$
\hfill (A55)

$$f_{76}(\alpha, \beta_{\pi^c}, \beta_n, \beta_w, \beta_p) = -\beta_{\pi^c}\alpha\kappa\left(\beta_p\dfrac{1}{y^p} + \kappa_p\beta_w\dfrac{1}{xl^0}\right)\beta_n \leq 0.$$
\hfill (A56)

First, let us consider the case of $\alpha = 0$. In this case, we have

$$f_{73}(0, \beta_{\pi^c}, \beta_w, \beta_p) = f_{75}(0, \beta_{\pi^c}, \beta_w) = f_{76}(0, \beta_{\pi^c}, \beta_n, \beta_w, \beta_p) = 0,$$
\hfill (A57)

and the characteristic equation

$$\Delta_7(\lambda; \alpha, \beta_{\pi^c}, \beta_n, \beta_w, \beta_p) = |\lambda I - J_7(\alpha, \beta_{\pi^c}, \beta_n, \beta_w, \beta_p)| = 0$$
\hfill (A58)

becomes as follows.

$$\Delta_7(\lambda; 0, \beta_{\pi^c}, \beta_n, \beta_w, \beta_p) = |\lambda I - J_7(0, \beta_{\pi^c}, \beta_n, \beta_w, \beta_p)|$$

$$= |\lambda I - J_6(\beta_n, \beta_w, \beta_p)|(\lambda + \beta_{\pi^c}) = 0$$
\hfill (A59)

where $J_6(\beta_n, \beta_w, \beta_p)$ is defined by Eq. (A47). This means that the characteristic equation (A58) has a negative real root $\lambda_7 = -\beta_{\pi^c}$ and other six roots are determined by Eq. (A50). All roots of Eq. (A50) have negative real parts if the conditions in **Proposition 7A** are met. This means, by continuity, that all roots of the characteristic equation (A58) have negative real parts even if $0 < \alpha < 1$, as long as α is sufficiently close to zero. This completes the proof of **Proposition 8A** under the condition (1).

Next, let us consider the case of $0 < \alpha < 1$ and $\beta_{\pi^c} = 0$. In this case, the characteristic equation (A58) becomes as follows.

$$\Delta_7(\lambda; \alpha, 0, \beta_n, \beta_w, \beta_p) = |\lambda I - J_7(\alpha, 0, \beta_n, \beta_w, \beta_p)|$$
$$= |\lambda I - J_6(\beta_n, \beta_w, \beta_p)|\lambda = 0 \qquad (A60)$$

This means that the characteristic equation (A58) has a root $\lambda_7 = 0$ and other six roots have negative real parts in case of $\beta_{\pi^c} = 0$. Therefore, by continuity, the characteristic equation (A58) has at least six roots with negative real parts. We can prove, however, that another root is a negative real root as follows.

We can easily show that

$$\det J_7(\alpha, \beta_{\pi^c}, \beta_n, \beta_w, \beta_p) = \prod_{j=1}^{7} \lambda_j = \beta_{\pi^c}\beta_w D(\alpha, \beta_n, \beta_w, \beta_p) \qquad (A61)$$

where

$$D(\alpha, \beta_n, \beta_w, \beta_p) =$$

$$\begin{vmatrix} f_{11} & f_{12} & f_{13}(\beta_w, \beta_p) & f_{14} & g_{15} & f_{16}(\beta_n, \beta_w, \beta_p) & -m^0 \\ f_{21} & f_{22} & f_{23}(\beta_w, \beta_p) & f_{24} & g_{25} & f_{26}(\beta_n, \beta_w, \beta_n) & -b^0 \\ f_{31} & f_{32} & f_{33} & f_{34} & 0 & f_{36}(\beta_n) & 0 \\ 0 & 0 & f_{43}(\beta_w, \beta_p) & 0 & g_{45} & f_{46}(\beta_n, \beta_w, \beta_p) & 0 \\ f_{51} & f_{52} & f_{53} & f_{54} & 0 & f_{56}(\beta_n) & 0 \\ f_{61} & f_{62} & f_{63} & f_{64} & 0 & f_{66}(\beta_n) & 0 \\ 0 & 0 & g_{73}(\alpha, \beta_w, \beta_p) & 0 & g_{75}(\alpha) & g_{76}(\alpha, \beta_n, \beta_w, \beta_p) & -(1-\alpha) \end{vmatrix},$$
$$(10.96)$$

$$g_{15} = -m^0 \kappa_p \frac{y(y^{e0})}{xl^{02}} < 0, \quad g_{25} = b^0 \kappa_p \frac{y(y^{e0})}{xl^{02}} > 0, \quad g_{45} = -\omega^0 \kappa (1-\kappa_w) \frac{y(y^{e0})}{xl^{02}} < 0,$$

$$g_{73}(\alpha, \beta_w, \beta_p) = \alpha\kappa \left(\beta_p \frac{1}{y^p} + \kappa_p\beta_w \frac{1}{xl^0} \right) y_{ye} > 0, \quad g_{75}(\alpha) = -\alpha\kappa_p \frac{y(y^{e0})}{xl^{02}} < 0,$$

$$g_{76}(\alpha, \beta_n, \beta_w, \beta_p) = -\alpha\kappa \left(\beta_p \frac{1}{y^p} + \kappa_p\beta_w \frac{1}{xl^0} \right) \beta_n < 0 \text{ in case of } 0 < \alpha < 1.$$

Therefore, we have the following expression in case of $\kappa_p = 0$.

$$D(\alpha, 0, 0, \beta_p) = \begin{vmatrix} f_{11} & f_{12} & f_{13}(\beta_p) & f_{14} & 0 & 0 & -m^0 \\ f_{21} & f_{22} & f_{23}(\beta_p) & f_{24} & 0 & 0 & -b^0 \\ f_{31} & f_{32} & f_{33} & f_{34} & 0 & 0 & 0 \\ 0 & 0 & f_{43}(\beta_p) & 0 & g_{45} & 0 & 0 \\ f_{51} & f_{52} & f_{53} & f_{54} & 0 & 0 & 0 \\ f_{61} & f_{62} & f_{63} & f_{64} & 0 & -n & 0 \\ 0 & 0 & g_{73}(\alpha, \beta_p) & 0 & 0 & 0 & -(1-\alpha) \end{vmatrix}$$

$$= n \begin{vmatrix} f_{11} & f_{12} & f_{13}(\beta_p) & f_{14} & 0 & m^0 \\ f_{21} & f_{22} & f_{23}(\beta_p) & f_{24} & 0 & b^0 \\ f_{31} & f_{32} & f_{33} & f_{34} & 0 & 0 \\ 0 & 0 & f_{43}(\beta_p) & 0 & g_{45} & 0 \\ f_{51} & f_{52} & f_{53} & f_{54} & 0 & 0 \\ 0 & 0 & g_{73}(\alpha, \beta_p) & 0 & 0 & 1-\alpha \end{vmatrix}$$

$$= -n g_{45} \begin{vmatrix} f_{11} & f_{12} & f_{13}(\beta_p) & f_{14} & m^0 \\ f_{21} & f_{22} & f_{23}(\beta_p) & f_{24} & b^0 \\ f_{31} & f_{32} & f_{33} & f_{34} & 0 \\ f_{51} & f_{52} & f_{53} & f_{54} & 0 \\ 0 & 0 & g_{73}(\alpha, \beta_p) & 0 & 1-\alpha \end{vmatrix}$$

$$= - \underset{+}{n} \, g_{45} \{ \underset{-}{g_{73}(\alpha, \beta_p)} \} E + \underset{+}{(1-\alpha) F} \} \tag{A63}$$

where $f_{i3}(\beta_p) = f_{i3}(0, \beta_p)(i = 1, 2, 4)$, $g_{73}(\alpha, \beta_p) = g_{73}(\alpha, 0, \beta_p) > 0$, and E, F are defined as follows.

$$E = \begin{vmatrix} f_{11} & f_{12} & f_{14} & m^0 \\ f_{21} & f_{22} & f_{24} & b^0 \\ f_{31} & f_{32} & f_{34} & 0 \\ f_{51} & f_{52} & f_{54} & 0 \end{vmatrix} \tag{A64}$$

$$F = \begin{vmatrix} f_{11} & f_{12} & f_{13}(\beta_p) & f_{14} \\ f_{21} & f_{22} & f_{23}(\beta_p) & f_{24} \\ f_{31} & f_{32} & f_{33} & f_{34} \\ f_{51} & f_{52} & f_{53} & f_{54} \end{vmatrix} \tag{A65}$$

On the other hand, we have the following results.

$$E_{00} = \lim_{i_q, i_u \to 0} E = \begin{vmatrix} 0 & 0 & 0 & m^0 \\ -\mu & f_{22} & f_{24} & b^0 \\ 0 & 0 & c_\omega & 0 \\ 0 & 0 & 0 & 0 \end{vmatrix} = 0 \tag{A66}$$

$$F_{00} = \lim_{i_q, i_u \to 0} F = \begin{vmatrix} 0 & 0 & f_{13}(\beta_p) & 0 \\ -\mu & f_{22} & f_{23}(\beta_p) & f_{24} \\ 0 & 0 & f_{33} & c_\omega \\ 0 & 0 & 0 & 0 \end{vmatrix} = 0 \tag{A67}$$

$$\frac{\partial E_{00}}{\partial i_q} = \begin{vmatrix} f'_{11} & 0 & 0 & m^0 \\ f'_{21} & f_{22} & f_{24} & b^0 \\ f'_{31} & 0 & c_\omega & 0 \\ f'_{51} & 0 & 0 & 0 \end{vmatrix} + \begin{vmatrix} 0 & f'_{12} & 0 & m^0 \\ -\mu & f'_{22} & f_{24} & b^0 \\ 0 & f'_{32} & c_\omega & 0 \\ 0 & f'_{52} & 0 & 0 \end{vmatrix} + \begin{vmatrix} 0 & 0 & f'_{14} & m^0 \\ -\mu & f_{22} & f'_{24} & b^0 \\ 0 & 0 & f'_{34} & 0 \\ 0 & 0 & f'_{54} & 0 \end{vmatrix}$$

$$= -f'_{51} \underset{-}{m^0} \underset{+}{c_\omega} \underset{+}{f_{22}} - f'_{52} \underset{-}{\mu} \underset{+}{m^0} \underset{+}{c_\omega} < 0 \tag{A68}$$

$$\frac{\partial F_{00}}{\partial i_q} = \begin{vmatrix} f'_{11} & 0 & f_{13}(\beta_p) & 0 \\ f'_{21} & f_{22} & f_{23}(\beta_p) & f_{24} \\ f'_{31} & 0 & f_{33} & c_\omega \\ f'_{51} & 0 & 0 & 0 \end{vmatrix} + \begin{vmatrix} 0 & f'_{12} & f_{13}(\beta_p) & 0 \\ -\mu & f'_{22} & f_{23}(\beta_p) & f_{24} \\ 0 & f'_{32} & f_{33} & c_\omega \\ 0 & f'_{52} & 0 & 0 \end{vmatrix}$$

$$+ \begin{vmatrix} 0 & 0 & f'_{13} & 0 \\ -\mu & f_{22} & f'_{23} & f_{24} \\ 0 & 0 & f'_{33} & c_\omega \\ 0 & 0 & f'_{53} & 0 \end{vmatrix} + \begin{vmatrix} 0 & 0 & f_{13}(\beta_p) & f'_{14} \\ -\mu & f_{22} & f_{23}(\beta_p) & f'_{24} \\ 0 & 0 & f_{33} & f'_{34} \\ 0 & 0 & 0 & f'_{54} \end{vmatrix}$$

$$= f'_{11} \underset{-}{f_{13}(\beta_p)} \underset{-}{f_{22}} \underset{+}{c_\omega} + f'_{52} \underset{+}{f_{13}(\beta_p)} \underset{-}{\mu} \underset{+}{c_\omega} < 0 \tag{A69}$$

where $f'_{ij} = \partial f_{ij} / \partial i_q$.

It follows from equations (A63)–(A69) that

$$D(\alpha, 0, 0, \beta_p) < 0 \tag{A70}$$

if $\kappa_p = i_u = 0$ and $i_q > 0$ is sufficiently small. Eq. (A61) and inequality (A70) mean that we have

$$\det J_7(\alpha, \beta_{\pi^c}, \beta_n, \beta_w, \beta_p) \prod_{j=1}^{7} \lambda_j < 0 \qquad (A71)$$

even if all of $\beta_n, \beta_w, \kappa_p, i_u$, and i_q are positive, as long as all of them are sufficiently small, by continuity, in case of $\beta_{\pi^c} > 0$ and $0 < \alpha < 1$.

In this case, another root of the characteristic equation (A58) must be a negative real root if Eq. (A58) has at least six roots with negative real parts. This completes the proof of **Proposition 8A** under the condition (2).

Proposition 9A Suppose that the conditions in **Proposition 7A** are met and κ_p is sufficiently small. Then, we have the following properties (1)–(5).

1. Suppose that α is sufficiently close to 1 and β_{π^c} is sufficiently large. Then, the steady state of the dynamic system (10.93) becomes unstable.
2. Suppose that β_{π^c} is sufficiently large. Then, the steady state of the dynamic system (10.93) is locally asymptotically stable if α is sufficiently small, and it is unstable if α is sufficiently close to 1.
3. Suppose that α is sufficiently close to 1. Then, the steady state of the dynamic system (10.93) is locally asymptotically stable if β_{π^c} is sufficiently small, and it is unstable if β_{π^c} is sufficiently large.
4. Suppose that β_{π^c} is sufficiently large. Then, at some intermediate value $\alpha^0 \in (0, 1)$, the Hopf bifurcation occurs in the dynamic system (10.93). In other words, there exist a family of non-constant closed orbits at some intermediate range of the parameter value $\alpha \in (0, 1)$.
5. Suppose that α is sufficiently close to 1. Then, at some intermediate value $\beta_{\pi^c}^0 > 0$, the Hopf bifurcation occurs in the dynamic system (10.93). In other words, there exist a family of non-constant closed orbits at some intermediate range of the parameter value $\beta_{\pi^c} > 0$.

Proof of Proposition 9A
1. The characteristic equation of the seven dimensional system of differential equations (A52) *at the equilibrium point* becomes as follows.

$$\Delta_7(\lambda; \alpha, \beta_{\pi^c}, \beta_n, \beta_w, \beta_p) = |\lambda I = J_7(\alpha, \beta_{\pi^c}, \beta_n, \beta_w, \beta_p)| = \sum_{j=0}^{7} b_j \lambda^{7-j} = 0 \qquad (A72)$$

where $b_0 = 1$, and

$$b_j = (-1)^j \text{ (sum of all principal j'th-order minors of } J_7(\alpha, \beta_{\pi^c}, \beta_n, \beta_w, \beta_p)) \qquad (A73)$$

for $j \in \{1, 2, \cdots, 7\}$.

Liénard-Chipart expression of the Routh-Hurwitz conditions for stable roots implies that a set of conditions $b_j > 0$ for all $j \in \{1, 2, \cdots, 7\}$ is a set of necessary (but not sufficient) conditions for the local stability of the equilibrium point of the dynamic system (10.93) (cf. Gandolfo 1996, Chap. 16). Therefore, the equilibrium point of this system is unstable if we have $b_j < 0$ for at least one of $j \in \{1, 2, \cdots, 7\}$.

Incidentally, we have the following expression in case of $\kappa_p = 0$ from Eq. (A53).

$$J_7(1, \beta_{\pi^c}, 0, \beta_w, \beta_p) = \begin{bmatrix} f_{11} & f_{12} & f_{13}(\beta_p) & f_{14} & 0 & 0 & -m^0 \\ f_{21} & f_{22} & f_{23}(\beta_p) & f_{24} & 0 & 0 & -b^0 \\ f_{31} & f_{32} & f_{33} & f_{34} & 0 & 0 & 0 \\ 0 & 0 & f_{43}(\beta_w, \beta_p) & 0 & f_{45}(\beta_w) & 0 & 0 \\ f_{51} & f_{52} & f_{53} & f_{54} & 0 & 0 & 0 \\ f_{61} & f_{62} & f_{63} & f_{64} & 0 & -n & 0 \\ 0 & 0 & \beta_{\pi^c} g_{73}(\beta_p) & 0 & 0 & 0 & 0 \end{bmatrix}$$

$$(A74)$$

where $g_{73}(\beta_p) = \kappa \beta_p \frac{1}{y^p} y_{y^e} > 0$. Therefore, we obtain the following result in case of $\alpha = 1$ and $\beta_n = \kappa_p = 0$.

$b_3 = -($sum of all principal third-order minors of $J_7)$

$$= - \begin{vmatrix} f_{22} & f_{23}(\beta_p) & -b^0 \\ f_{32} & f_{33} & 0 \\ 0 & \beta_{\pi^c} g_{73}(\beta_p) & 0 \end{vmatrix} - \begin{vmatrix} f_{33} & f_{34} & 0 \\ f_{43}(\beta_w, \beta_p) & 0 & 0 \\ \beta_{\pi^c} g_{73}(\beta_p) & 0 & 0 \end{vmatrix} + G$$

$$= \underset{+}{\beta_{\pi^c} g_{73}(\beta_p)} \, \underset{+}{b^0} \, \underset{-}{f_{32}} + G \qquad\qquad (A75)$$

where G is independent of the value of the parameter β_{π^c}.

Eq. (75) means that we have $b_3 < 0$ so that the equilibrium point of the dynamic system (10.93) becomes unstable for all sufficiently large values of $\beta_{\pi^c} > 0$ in case of $\alpha = 1$ and $\beta_n = \kappa_p = 0$. By continuity, we have the inequality $b_3 < 0$ for all sufficiently large values of $\beta_{\pi^c} > 0$ even if $0 < \alpha < 1$, $\beta_n > 0$ and $\kappa_p > 0$, as long as α is sufficiently close to 1 and β_n, κ_p are sufficiently small. This completes the proof of **Proposition 9A(1)**.

1. **Proposition 9A** (2) directly follows from **Proposition 8A** and **Proposition 9A** (1).
2. **Proposition 9A** (3) also directly follows from **Proposition 8A** and **Proposition 9A** (1).
3. **Proposition 9A** (2) implies that there exists at least one bifurcation point $\alpha^0 \in (0, 1)$, at which the real part of at least one root of the characteristic equation (A72) becomes zero. However, we cannot have the real root such that $\lambda = 0$ because we already showed in the proof of **Proposition 8A** that we

have the inequality det $J_7 = \prod\limits_{j=1}^{7} \lambda_j < 0$ irrespective of the value of $\alpha \in (0, 1)$.

This means that the point α^0 is in fact the Hopf bifurcation point, because we have a pair of pure imaginary roots at such a point (cf. Gandolfo 1996, Chap. 25).

4. The method of the proof of **Proposition 9A** (5) is almost the same as that of **Proposition 9A** (4).

Notation

Steady state or trend values are indicated by a superscript 'o' (sometimes a subscript). When no confusion arises, letters F, G, H may also define certain functional expressions in a specific context. A dot over a variable $x = x(t)$ denotes the time derivative, a caret its growth rate; $\dot{x} = dx/dt$, $\hat{x} = \dot{x}/x$. In the numerical simulations, flow variables are measured at annual rates.

As far as possible, the notation tries to follow the logic of using capital letters for level variables and lower case letters for variables in intensive form, or for constant (steady state) ratios. Greek letters are most often constant coefficients in behavioral equations (with, however, the notable exceptions being π^c, ω). We use the abreviation 'NAIRU' for the Non-Accelerating-Inflation Rate of Unemployment, but use this acronym also in the case 'Utilization' (of labor or capital) in the place of 'Unemployment'. And the acronym 'RE(S)' stands for the 'Rational Expectations (School)'. Further acronyms are of a local nature only and will be explained in the sections where they are used.

Non-Accelerating-Inflation Rate of Utilization (NAIRU)

B	outstanding government fixed-price bonds (priced at $p_b = 1$)
C	real private consumption (demand is generally realized)
E	number of equities
F	neoclassical production function
	otherwise generic symbol for functions defined in a local context
G	real government expenditure (demand is always realized)
I	real net investment of fixed capital (demand is always realized)
$\mathcal{I}$	desired real inventory investment
J	Jacobian matrix in the mathematical analysis
K	stock of fixed capital
L^d	employment, i.e., total working hours per year (labor demand is always realized)
L^w	Employed workforce, i.e., number of employed people
L	labor supply, i.e., supply of total working hours per year
M	stock of money supply
N	inventories of finished goods
N^d	desired stock of inventories
S_f	real saving of firms
S_g	real government saving
S_p	real saving of private households

S	total real saving; $S = S_f + S_g + S_h$
T	total real tax collections
$T_w(t_w)$	real taxes of workers (per unit of capital)
$T_c(t_c)$	real taxes of asset holders (per unit of capital)
W	real wealth of private households
Y	real output
Y^p	potential real output
Y^f	full-employment real output
Y^d	real aggregate demand
Y^e	expected real aggregate demand
Y^n	output at normal use of capacity; $Y^n = y^n/K$
c	marginal propensity to consume
e	employment rate
$U = 1 - e$	unemployment rate
$f_x = f_1$, etc.	partial derivative
g^o	steady state growth rate of real variables
i	nominal rate of interest on government bonds;
	federal funds rate in Chapters 8 and 9
k	capital intensity K/L (sometimes also parameter in money demand
	function)
$\sigma = 1/y$	capital coefficient K/Y
l	labor intensity (in efficiency units)
m	real balances relative to the capital stock; $m = M/pK$
v	inventory-capital ratio; $n = N/K$
p	price level
p_e	price of equities
q	return differential; $q = r - (i - \pi)$ or Tobin's q
r	rate of return on fixed capital, specified as $r = (pY - wL - \delta pK)/pK$
s_c	propensity to save out of capital income on the part of asset owners
$s = s_h$	households' propensity to save out of total income (in Chapters 2 and 3)
u	rate of capacity utilization; $u = Y/Y^n = y/y^n$
v	wage share (in gross product); $v = wL/pY$
w	nominal wage rate per hour
y	output-capital ratio; $y = Y/K$;
	except in Chapter 1.3, where y denotes the output gap
y^d	ratio of aggregate demand to capital stock; $y^d = Y^d/K$
y^e	ratio of expected demand to capital stock; $y^e = Y^e/K$
y^n	normal output-capital ratio (a constant;
	no recourse to a neoclassical production function)
z or x	labor productivity, i.e., output per worker; $z = Y/L^d$
α	symbol for policy parameters in Taylor rule
α_i	coefficient measuring interest rate smoothing in the Taylor rule
α_p	coefficient on inflation gap in the Taylor rule
α_u	coefficient on output gap in the Taylor rule
β_x	generically, reaction coefficient in an equation determining x, $\dot{x}$ or $\hat{x}$
β_y	adjustment speed in adaptive sales expectations
β_π	general adjustment speed in revisions of the inflation climate
β_{xy}	generically, reaction coefficient related to the determination of variable
	x, $\dot{x}$ or $\hat{x}$ with respect to changes in the exogenous variable y
α_q	responsiveness of investment (capital growth rate) to changes in q
α_u	responsiveness of investment to changes in u
β_n	stock adjustment speed

α_{n^d}	desired ratio of inventories over expected sales
β_{pu}	reaction coefficient of u in price Phillips curve
β_{pv}	reaction coefficient of $(1+\mu)v-1$ in price Phillips curve
β_{we}	reaction coefficient of e in wage Phillips curve
β_{wv}	reaction coefficient of $(v-v^o)/v^o$ in wage Phillips curve
γ	government expenditures per unit of fixed capital; $\gamma = G/K$ (a constant)
τ	lump sum taxes per unit of fixed capital; $\tau = T/K$ (a constant)
δ	rate of depreciation of fixed capital (a constant)
$\eta_{m,i}$	interest elasticity of money demand (expressed as a positive number)
κ	coefficient in reduced-form wage–price equations; $\kappa = 1/(1-\kappa_p\kappa_w)$
κ_p	parameter weighting $\hat{w}$ vs. π in price Phillips curve
κ_w	parameter weighting $\hat{p}$ vs. π in wage Phillips curve
κ_{wp}	same as κ_w
κ_{wz}	parameter weighting $\hat{z}$ vs. $\hat{z}^o$ in wage Phillips curve (only Chapter 5)
κ_π	parameter weighting adaptive expectations vs. regressive expectations in revisions of the inflation climate
ξ	relative excess demand; $\xi = (Y^d - Y)/Y$
π^c	general inflation climate;
θ	log of real wages
$\tau_c = T_c/K$	tax parameter for T^c (net of interest and per unit of capital); $T^c - iB/p$
τ_w	tax rate on wages
ω	real wage rate w/p

Mathematical appendix
Some stability theorems

1. The concepts of local stability and global stability in a system of differential equations

Let $\dot{x} \equiv \frac{dx}{dt} = f(x)$, $x \in R^n$ be a system of n-dimensional differential equations that has an equilibrium point x^* such that $f(x^*) = 0$, where t is interpreted as 'time'. The equilibrium point of this system is said to be *locally asymptotically stable*, if every trajectory starting sufficiently near the equilibrium point converges to it as $t \rightarrow +\infty$. If stability is independent of the distance of the initial state from the equilibrium point, the equilibrium point is said to be *globally asymptotically stable*, or *asymptotically stable in the large*, see Gandolfo (1996, p. 333)

2. Theorems that are useful for the stability analysis of a system of linear differential equations or the local stability analysis of a system of nonlinear differential equations

Theorem A.1 (Local stability/instability theorem, see Gandolfo (1996, pp. 360–362).)

Let $\dot{x}_i = f_i(x)$, $x = [x_1, x_2, \cdots, x_n] \in R^n \mid (i = 1, 2, \cdots, n)$ be an n-dimensional system of differential equations that has an equilibrium point $x^* = [x_1^*, x_2^*, \cdots, x_n^*]$ such that $f(x^*) = 0$. Suppose that the functions f_i have continuous first-order partial derivatives, and consider the Jacobian matrix evaluated *at the equilibrium point* x^*

$$
J = \begin{bmatrix} f_{11} & f_{12} & \cdots & f_{1n} \\ f_{21} & f_{22} & \cdots & f_{2n} \\ \vdots & \vdots & \ddots & \vdots \\ f_{n1} & f_{n2} & \cdots & f_{nn} \end{bmatrix},
$$

where $f_{ij} = \partial f_i / \partial x_j$ $(i, j = 1, 2, \cdots, n)$ are evaluated at the equilibrium point.

(i) The equilibrium point of this system is locally asymptotically stable if all the roots of the characteristic equation $|\lambda I - J| = 0$ have negative real parts.

(ii) The equilibrium point of this system is unstable if at least one root of the characteristic equation $|\lambda I - J| = 0$ has positive real part.

(iii) The stability of the equilibrium point cannot be determined from the properties of the Jacobian matrix if all the roots of the characteristic equation $|\lambda I - J| = 0$ have nonpositive real parts but at least one root has zero real part.

Theorem A.2 (See Murata (1977, pp. 14–16)

Let A be an $(n \times n)$ matrix such that

$$A = \begin{bmatrix} a_{11} & a_{12} & \cdots & a_{1n} \\ a_{21} & a_{22} & \cdots & a_{2n} \\ \vdots & \vdots & \ddots & \vdots \\ a_{n1} & a_{n2} & \cdots & a_{nn} \end{bmatrix}.$$

(i) We can express the characteristic equation $|\lambda I - A| = 0$ as

$$|\lambda I - A| = \lambda^n + a_1 \lambda^{n-1} + a_2 \lambda^{n-2} + \cdots + a_r \lambda^{n-r}$$
$$+ \cdots + a_{n-1}\lambda + a_n = 0, \tag{10.1}$$

where

$$a_1 = -(traceA) = -\sum_{i=1}^{n} a_{ii}, \quad a_2 = (-1)^2 \sum_{i<j} \begin{vmatrix} a_{ii} & a_{ij} \\ a_{ji} & a_{jj} \end{vmatrix}, \cdots,$$

$$a_r = (-1)^r \sum_{i<j<\cdots<k} \underbrace{\begin{vmatrix} a_{ii} & a_{ij} & \cdots & a_{ik} \\ a_{ji} & a_{jj} & \cdots & a_{jk} \\ \vdots & \vdots & \ddots & \vdots \\ a_{ki} & a_{kj} & \cdots & a_{kk} \end{vmatrix}}_{(r)}, \cdots, \quad a_n = (-1)^n \det A.$$

(ii) Let λ_i $(i = 1, 2, \cdots, n)$ be the roots of the characteristic equation (10.1). Then, we have

$$trace J = \sum_{i=1}^{n} a_{ii} = \sum_{i=1}^{n} \lambda_i, \quad \det A = \prod_{i=1}^{n} \lambda_i.$$

Theorem A.3 (Routh-Hurwitz conditions for stable roots in an n-dimensional system, cf. Murata (1977, p. 92), Gandolfo (1996, pp. 221–222))[1]

---

1 See also Gantmacher (1954) for many associated details and Brock and Malliaris (1989) for a compact representation of these conditions.

All of the roots of the characteristic equation (10.1) have negative real parts *if and only if* the following set of inequalities is satisfied:

$$\Delta_1 = a_1 > 0, \quad \Delta_2 = \begin{vmatrix} a_1 & a_3 \\ 1 & a_2 \end{vmatrix} > 0, \quad \Delta_3 = \begin{vmatrix} a_1 & a_3 & a_5 \\ 1 & a_2 & a_4 \\ 0 & a_1 & a_3 \end{vmatrix} > 0, \cdots,$$

$$\Delta_n = \begin{vmatrix} a_1 & a_3 & a_5 & a_7 & \cdots & 0 \\ 1 & a_2 & a_4 & a_6 & \cdots & 0 \\ 0 & a_1 & a_3 & a_5 & \cdots & 0 \\ 0 & 1 & a_2 & a_4 & \cdots & 0 \\ 0 & 0 & a_1 & a_3 & \cdots & 0 \\ \vdots & \vdots & \vdots & \vdots & \ddots & \vdots \\ 0 & 0 & 0 & 0 & \cdots & a_n \end{vmatrix} > 0.$$

The following theorems A.4–A.6 are corollaries of theorem A.3.

Theorem A.4 (Routh-Hurwitz conditions for a two-dimensional system)

All of the roots of the characteristic equation

$$\lambda^2 + a_1\lambda + a_2 = 0$$

have negative real parts *if and only if* the set of inequalities

$$a_1 > 0, \quad a_2 > 0$$

is satisfied.

Theorem A.5. (Routh-Hurwitz conditions for a three-dimensional system)

All of the roots of the characteristic equation

$$\lambda^3 + a_1\lambda^2 + a_2\lambda + a_3 = 0$$

have negative real parts *if and only if* the set of inequalities

$$a_1 > 0, \quad a_3 > 0, \quad a_1 a_2 - a_3 > 0 \tag{10.2}$$

is satisfied.

Remark on theorem A.5:
The inequality $a_2 > 0$ is always satisfied if the set of inequalities (10.2) is satisfied.

Theorem A.6 (Routh-Hurwitz conditions for a four-dimensional system)

All roots of the characteristic equation

$$\lambda^4 + a_1\lambda^3 + a_2\lambda^2 + a_3\lambda + a_4 = 0,$$

have negative real parts *if and only if* the set of inequalities

$$a_1 > 0, \quad a_3 > 0, \quad a_4 > 0, \quad \Phi \equiv a_1 a_2 a_3 - a_1^2 a_4 - a_3^2 > 0, \qquad (10.3)$$

is satisfied.

Remark on theorem A.6:
The inequality $a_2 > 0$ is always satisfied if the set of inequalities (10.3) is satisfied.

3. Theorems that are useful for the global stability analysis of a system of nonlinear differential equations

Theorem A.7 (Liapunov's theorem, cf. Gandolfo (1996, p. 410))

Let $\dot{x} = f(x), x = [x_1, x_2, \cdots, x_n] \in R^n$ be an n-dimensional system of differential equations that has the unique equilibrium point $x^* = [x_1^*, x_2^*, \cdots, x_n^*]$ such that $f(x^*) = 0$. Suppose that there exists a scalar function $L = L(x - x^*)$ with continuous first derivatives and with the following properties (1)–(5):

(1) $L \geq 0$,
(2) $L = 0$ if and only if $x_i - x_i^* = 0$ for all $i \in \{1, 2, \cdots n\}$,
(3) $L \to +\infty$ as $\|x - x^*\| \to +\infty$,
(4) $\dot{L} = \sum_{i=1}^{n} \dfrac{\partial L}{\partial(x_i - x_i^*)} \dot{x}_i \leq 0$,
(5) $\dot{L} = 0$ if and only if $x_i - x_i* = 0$ for all $i \in \{1, 2, \cdots, n\}$.
    Then, the equilibrium point x^* of the above system is globally asymptotically stable.

Remark on theorem A.7:
The function $L = L(x - x^*)$ is called the 'Liapunov function'.

Theorem A.8 (Olech's theorem, cf. Olech (1963), Gandolfo (1996, pp. 354–355))

Let $\dot{x}_i = f_i(x_1, x_2)(i = 1, 2)$ be a two-dimensional system of differential equations that has the unique equilibrium point (x_1^*, x_2^*) such that $f_i(x_1^*, x_2^*) = 0$ $(i = 1, 2)$. Suppose that the functions f_i have continuous first-order partial derivatives. Furthermore, suppose that the following properties (1)–(3) are satisfied:

(1) $\dfrac{\partial f_1}{\partial x_1} + \dfrac{\partial f_2}{\partial x_2} < 0$ everywhere,

(2) $\left(\dfrac{\partial f_1}{\partial x_1}\right)\left(\dfrac{\partial f_2}{\partial x_2}\right) - \left(\dfrac{\partial f_1}{\partial x_2}\right)\left(\dfrac{\partial f_2}{\partial x_1}\right) > 0$ everywhere,

(3) $\left(\dfrac{\partial f_1}{\partial x_1}\right)\left(\dfrac{\partial f_2}{\partial x_2}\right) \neq 0$ everywhere, or alternatively, $\left(\dfrac{\partial f_1}{\partial x_2}\right)\left(\dfrac{\partial f_2}{\partial x_1}\right) \neq 0$ everywhere.

Then, the equilibrium point of the above system is globally asymptotically stable.

4. Theorems that are useful to establish the existence of closed orbits in a system of nonlinear differential equations

Theorem A.9 (Poincaré-Bendixson theorem, cf. Hirsch and Smale (1974, Ch.11))

Let $\dot{x}_i = f_i(x_1, x_2)(i = 1, 2)$ be a two-dimensional system of differential equations with the functions f_i continuous. A nonempty compact limit set of the trajectory of this system, which contains no equilibrium point, is a closed orbit.

Theorem A.10 (Hopf bifurcation theorem for an n-dimensional system, cf. Guckenheimer and Holmes (1983, pp. 151–152), Lorenz (1993, p. 96) and Gandolfo (1996, p. 477))[2]

Let $\dot{x} = f(x; \varepsilon), x \in R^n, \varepsilon \in R$ be an n-dimensional system of differential equations depending upon a parameter ε. Suppose that the following conditions (1)–(3) are satisfied:

(1) The system has a smooth curve of equilibria given by $f(x^*(\varepsilon); \varepsilon) = 0$,
(2) The characteristic equation $|\lambda I - Df(x^*(\varepsilon_0); \varepsilon_0)| = 0$ has a pair of pure imaginary roots $\lambda(\varepsilon_0), \bar{\lambda}(\varepsilon_0)$ and no other roots with zero real parts, where $Df(x^*(\varepsilon_0); \varepsilon_0)$ is the Jacobian matrix of the above system at $(x^*(\varepsilon_0), \varepsilon_0)$ with the parameter value ε_0,
(3) $\dfrac{d\{Re\lambda(\varepsilon)\}}{d\varepsilon}\bigg|_{\varepsilon=\varepsilon_0} \neq 0$, where $Re\lambda(\varepsilon)$ is the real part of $\lambda(\varepsilon)$.

Then, there exists a continuous function $\varepsilon(\gamma)$ with $\varepsilon(0) = \varepsilon_0$, and for all sufficiently small values of $\gamma \neq 0$ there exists a continuous family of nonconstant periodic solution $x(t, \gamma)$ for the above dynamical system,

---

2 See also Strogatz (1994), Wiggins (1990) in this regard.

which collapses to the equilibrium point $x^*(\varepsilon_0)$ as $\gamma \to 0$. The period of the cycle is close to $2\pi/Im\lambda(\varepsilon_0)$, where $Im\lambda(\varepsilon_0)$ is the imaginary part of $\lambda(\varepsilon_0)$.

Remark on theorem A.10:

We can replace the condition (3) in theorem A.10 by the following weaker condition (3a) (cf. Alexander and York (1978)).

(3a) For all ε which are near but not equal to ε_0, no characteristic root has zero real part.

The following theorem by Liu (1994) provides a convenient criterion for the occurrence of the so called 'simple' Hopf bifurcation in an n-dimensional system. The 'simple' Hopf bifurcation is defined as the Hopf bifurcation in which all the characteristic roots *except* a pair of purely imaginary ones have negative real parts.

Theorem A.11 (Liu's theorem, see Liu (1994))

Consider the following characteristic equation with $n \geq 3$:

$$\lambda^n + a_1\lambda^{n-1} + a_2\lambda_{n-2} + \cdots + a_{n-1}\lambda + a_n = 0.$$

This characteristic equation has a pair of pure imaginary roots and $(n-2)$ roots with negative real parts *if and only if* the following set of conditions is satisfied:

$$\Delta_i > 0 \quad \text{for all } i \in \{1, 2, \cdots, n-2\}, \quad \Delta_{n-1} = 0, \quad a_n > 0,$$

where $\Delta_i(i = 1, 2, \cdots, n-1)$ are Routh-Hurwitz terms defined as

$$\Delta_1 = a_1, \quad \Delta_2 = \begin{vmatrix} a_1 & a_3 \\ 1 & a_2 \end{vmatrix}, \quad \Delta_3 = \begin{vmatrix} a_1 & a_3 & a_5 \\ 1 & a_2 & a_4 \\ 0 & a_1 & a_3 \end{vmatrix}, \cdots,$$

$$\Delta_{n-1} = \begin{vmatrix} a_1 & a_3 & a_5 & a_7 & \cdots & 0 & 0 \\ 1 & a_2 & a_4 & a_6 & \cdots & 0 & 0 \\ 0 & a_1 & a_3 & a_5 & \cdots & 0 & 0 \\ 0 & 1 & a_2 & a_4 & \cdots & 0 & 0 \\ 0 & 0 & a_1 & a_3 & \cdots & 0 & 0 \\ \vdots & \vdots & \vdots & \vdots & \ddots & \vdots & \vdots \\ 0 & 0 & 0 & 0 & \cdots & a_n & 0 \\ 0 & 0 & 0 & 0 & \cdots & a_{n-1} & 0 \\ 0 & 0 & 0 & 0 & \cdots & a_{n-2} & a_n \\ 0 & 0 & 0 & 0 & \cdots & a_{n-3} & a_{n-1} \end{vmatrix}.$$

The following theorems A.12–A.14 provide us with some convenient criteria for two-dimensional, three-dimensional, and four-dimensional Hopf bifurcations respectively. It is worth noting that these criteria provide us with useful information on the 'non-simple' as well as the 'simple' Hopf bifurcations.

Theorem A.12.

The characteristic equation

$$\lambda^2 + a_1\lambda + a_2 = 0,$$

has a pair of pure imaginary roots *if and only if* the set of conditions

$$a_1 = 0, \quad a_2 > 0$$

is satisfied. In this case, we have the explicit solution $\lambda = \pm i\sqrt{a_2}$, where $i = \sqrt{-1}$.

Proof. Obvious because we have the solution $\lambda = (-a_1 \pm \sqrt{a_1^2 - 4a_2})/2$.

Theorem A.13 (cf. Asada (1995), Asada and Semmler (1995))

The characteristic equation

$$\lambda^3 + a_1\lambda^2 + a_2\lambda + a_3 = 0$$

has a pair of pure imaginary roots *if and only if* the set of conditions

$$a_2 > 0, \quad a_1a_2 - a_3 = 0,$$

is satisfied. In this case, we have the explicit solution $\lambda = -a_1, \pm i\sqrt{a_2}$, where $i = \sqrt{-1}$.

Theorem A.14 (cf. Yoshida and Asada (2001), Asada and Yoshida (2003))

Consider the characteristic equation

$$\lambda^4 + a_1\lambda^3 + a_2\lambda^2 + a_3\lambda + a_4 = 0. \tag{10.4}$$

(i) The characteristic equation (10.4) has a pair of pure imaginary roots and two roots with non-zero real parts *if and only if* either of the following set of conditions (A) or (B) is satisfied:

(A) $a_1a_3 > 0, \quad a_4 \neq 0, \quad \Phi \equiv a_1a_2a_3 - a_1^2a_4 - a_3^2 = 0.$
(B) $a_1 = a_3 = 0, \quad a_4 < 0.$

(ii) The characteristic equation (10.4) has a pair of pure imaginary roots and two roots with negative real parts *if and only if* the following set of conditions (C) is satisfied:

(C) $a_1 > 0, \quad a_3 > 0, \quad a_4 > 0, \quad \Phi \equiv a_1a_2a_3 - a_1^2a_4 - a_3^2 = 0.$

Remarks on theorem A.14:

(1)   The condition $\Phi = 0$ is always satisfied if the set of conditions (B) is satisfied.
(2)   The inequality $a_2 > 0$ is always satisfied if the set of conditions (C) is satisfied.
(3)   We can derive theorem A.14 (ii) from theorem A.11 as a special case with $n = 4$, although we cannot derive theorem A.14 (i) from theorem A.11.

References

Alexander, J.C. and J.A. York (1978): Global bifurcation of periodic orbits. *American Journal of Mathematics*, 100, 263–292.

Asada, T. (1995): Kaldorian dynamics in an open economy. *Journal of Economics*, 62, 239–269.

Asada, T. and W. Semmler (1995): Growth and finance: An intertemporal model. *Journal of Macroeconomics*, 17, 623–649.

Asada, T. and H. Yoshida (2003): *Coefficient criterion for four-dimensional Hopf-bifurcations: A complete mathematical characterization and applications to economic dynamics. Chaos, Solitons & Fractals*, 18, 525–536.

Brock, W.A. and A.G. Malliaris (1989): *Differential Equations, Stability and Chaos in Dynamic Economics*. Amsterdam: North Holland.

Gandolfo, G. (1996): *Economic Dynamics*. Berlin: Springer Verlag.

Gantmacher, F.R. (1954): *Theory of Matrices*. New York: Interscience Publishers.

Guckenheimer, J. and P. Holmes (1983): *Nonlinear Oscillations, Dynamical Systems, and Bifurcations of Vector Fields*. Berlin: Springer Verlag.

Hirsch, M.W. and S. Smale (1974): *Differential Equations, Dynamical Systems, and Linear Algebra*. New York: Academic Press.

Liu, W.M. (1994): Criterion of Hopf-bifurcations without using eigenvalues. *Journal of Mathematical Analysis and Applications*, 182, 250–256.

Lorenz, H.-W. (1993): *Nonlinear Dynamical Economics and Chaotic Motion*. Berlin: Springer.

Murata, Y. (1977): *Mathematics for Stability and Optimization of Economic Systems*. New York: Academic Press.

Olech, C. (1963): On the global stability of an autonomous system in the plane. In: P. Lasalle and P. Diaz (eds.): *Contributions to Differential Equations*, 1, 389–400.

Strogatz, S.H. (1994): *Nonlinear Dynamics and Chaos*. New York: Addison-Wesley.

Wiggins, S. (1990): *Introduction to Applied Nonlinear Dynamical Systems and Chaos*. Berlin: Springer Verlag.

Yoshida, H. and T. Asada (2001): Dynamic analysis of policy Lagina Keynes-Goodwin Model: Stability, instability, cycles and chaos. *Center for Empirical Macroeconomics, Working paper*: Bielefeld University, Center for Empirical Macroeconomics.

Index

For Product Safety Concerns and Information please contact our EU
representative GPSR@taylorandfrancis.com
Taylor & Francis Verlag GmbH, Kaufingerstraße 24, 80331 München, Germany

www.ingramcontent.com/pod-product-compliance
Ingram Content Group UK Ltd.
Pitfield, Milton Keynes, MK11 3LW, UK
UKHW021836240425
457818UK00006B/209